SOLUTIONS MANUAL

Prepared by

SÜLEYMAN TÜFEKÇİ

School of Industrial & Systems Engineering
Georgia Institute of Technology
Atlanta, Georgia 30332

for

LINEAR PROGRAMMING AND NETWORK FLOWS

by

Mokhtar S. Bazaraa
John J. Jarvis

John Wiley & Sons, Inc.

New York · Santa Barbara · London · Sydney · Toronto

ISBN 0 471 02747 2
Printed in the United States of America

10 9 8 7 6 5 4 3 2 1

PREFACE

The exercises at the end of each chapter represent an integrated part of the textbook. A thorough understanding of the subjects of linear programming and network flows would not be fully achieved without a serious attempt at solving many of the problems in the text.

A variety of problem types are presented throughout the text. These problems fall under one of the following four major categories:

(1) Computational exercises illustrating algorithms and concepts presented in the text.

(2) Proofs, derivations and minor extensions of methods and concepts developed in the text.

(3) Development of important procedures not covered in the text material.

(4) Introduction of advanced topics of linear programming and network flows.

Depending on student interest and course orientation and objectives, the instructor will be able to provide an adequate mix of challenging exercises from one or more of the above categories.

While detailed answers for most exercises are given in the manual, in order to reduce its length only partial solutions to some of the exercises are given. In such cases the iteration numbers are presented so that the reader will know that there are a few intermediate steps that have been skipped. In a few problems we have given references presenting detailed discussions.

Less than 30 out of a total of 521 exercises are left unsolved. These exercises (1) are straightforward but lengthy, (2) involve the development of a flow chart of a procedure in the text, (3) contain a detailed hint, or (4) are of a research nature. The specific unsolved problems are: 3.15, 3.48, 4.33, 4.45, 4.46, 4.47, 4.48, 4.49, 4.50, 5.8, 5.12, 5.14, 5.29, 6.32, 6.39, 7.15, 7.21, 7.22, 7.33, 7.36, 10.13, 10.22, 10.24, 10.25, 10.27, 11.7, 11.8, 11.11, 11.46.

The author welcomes any comments or corrections to the manual. It is strongly recommended that the instructor assign exercises to the students. This will help especially those research-oriented and creative students to demonstrate and expand their abilities.

Süleyman Tüfekçi

School of Industrial & Systems
Engineering
Georgia Institute of Technology
Atlanta, Georgia 30332

TABLE OF CONTENTS

CHAPTER 1 INTRODUCTION

PROBLEM 1.1

Let x_{ij}: amount of ingredient i for product j.

$i = 1,2,3,4$ corn, limestone, soybean, fish-meal

$j = 1,2,3$ cattle, sheep, chicken

$$\min\ 0.2\left(\sum_{j=1}^{3} x_{1j}\right) + 0.12\left(\sum_{j=1}^{3} x_{2j}\right) + .24\left(\sum_{j=1}^{3} x_{3j}\right) + .12\left(\sum_{j=1}^{3} x_{4j}\right)$$

S.T.

$$\sum_{i=1}^{4} x_{i1} \geq 10$$

$$\sum_{i=1}^{4} x_{i2} \geq 6$$

$$\sum_{i=1}^{4} x_{i3} \geq 8$$

$$\sum_{j=1}^{3} x_{1j} \leq 6$$

$$\sum_{j=1}^{3} x_{2j} \leq 10$$

$$\sum_{j=1}^{3} x_{3j} \leq 4$$

$$\sum_{j=1}^{3} x_{4j} \leq 5$$

$$8x_{11} + 6x_{21} + 10x_{31} + 4x_{41} \geq 6(x_{11} + x_{21} + x_{31} + x_{41})$$

$$10x_{11} + 5x_{21} + 12x_{31} + 8x_{41} \geq 6(x_{11} + x_{21} + x_{31} + x_{41})$$

$$6x_{11} + 10x_{21} + 6x_{31} + 6x_{41} \geq 7(x_{11} + x_{21} + x_{31} + x_{41})$$

PROBLEM 1.1 (Continued)

$$8(x_{11}+x_{21}+x_{31}+x_{41}) \geq 8x_{11}+6x_{21}+6x_{31}+9x_{41} \geq 4(x_{11}+x_{21}+x_{31}+x_{41})$$

$$8x_{12}+6x_{22}+10x_{32}+4x_{42} \geq 6(x_{12}+x_{22}+x_{32}+x_{42})$$

$$10x_{12}+5x_{22}+12x_{32}+8x_{42} \geq 6(x_{12}+x_{22}+x_{32}+x_{42})$$

$$6x_{12}+10x_{22}+6x_{32}+6x_{42} \geq 6(x_{12}+x_{22}+x_{32}+x_{42})$$

$$6(x_{12}+x_{22}+x_{32}+x_{42}) \geq 8x_{12}+6x_{22}+6x_{32}+6x_{42} \geq 4(x_{12}+x_{22}+x_{32}+x_{42})$$

$$6(x_{13}+x_{23}+x_{33}+x_{43}) \geq 8x_{13}+6x_{23}+10x_{33}+4x_{43} \geq 4(x_{13}+x_{23}+x_{33}+x_{43})$$

$$10x_{13}+5x_{23}+12x_{33}+8x_{43} \geq 6(x_{13}+x_{23}+x_{33}+x_{43})$$

$$6x_{13}+10x_{23}+6x_{33}+6x_{43} \geq 6(x_{13}+x_{23}+x_{33}+x_{43})$$

$$6(x_{13}+x_{23}+x_{33}+x_{43}) \geq 8x_{13}+6x_{23}+6x_{33}+9x_{43} \geq 4(x_{13}+x_{23}+x_{33}+x_{43})$$

$$x_{ij} \geq 0 \qquad i=1,2,3,4, \qquad j=1,2,3.$$

PROBLEM 1.2

a) Let the peas, green beans, okra, ..., jello be represented by $x_1, x_2, \ldots, x_{13}$, respectively.

$$\min \; .1x_1 + .12x_2 + .13x_3 + .09x_4 + .1x_5 + .07x_6 + .7x_7 + 1.2x_8 + .63x_9 + .28x_{10} + .42x_{11} + .15x_{12} + .12x_{13}$$

s.t.

$$x_1+x_2+x_3+x_4+x_5+x_6 \geq 1$$

$$x_7+x_8+x_9 \geq 1$$

$$x_{10}+x_{11}+x_{12}+x_{13} \geq 1$$

$$x_1+x_2+x_3+2x_4+4x_5+5x_6+2x_7+3x_8+3x_9+x_{10}+x_{11}+x_{12}+x_{13} \geq 5$$

PROBLEM 1.2 (Continued)

$$x_1 + 2x_2 + x_3 + x_4 + x_5 + x_6 + 3x_7 + 5x_8 + 6x_9 + x_{10} \geq 10$$

$$2x_4 + x_5 + x_6 + x_7 + 2x_8 + x_9 \geq 2$$

$$3x_1 + 5x_2 + 5x_3 + 6x_4 + 2x_5 + x_6 + x_7 + 8x_8 + 6x_9 + 3x_{10} + 2x_{11} \geq 10$$

$$x_i \geq 0 \qquad i = 1, 2, \ldots, 13$$

PROBLEM 1.3

a)

Minimize $|x_1 - 3| + |x_1 - 0| + |x_1 + 2| + |x_1 - 1| + |x_2 - 0|$

$+ |x_2 + 3| + |x_2 - 1| + |x_2 - 4|$

or

Minimize $z_1 + z_2 + z_3 + z_4 + z_5 + z_6 + z_7 + z_8$

S.T.

$$z_1 \geq x_1 - 3$$
$$z_1 \geq -x_1 + 3$$
$$z_2 \geq -x_1$$
$$z_2 \geq x_1$$
$$z_3 \geq x_1 + 2$$
$$z_3 \geq -x_1 - 2$$
$$z_4 \geq x_1 - 1$$
$$z_4 \geq -x_1 + 1$$
$$z_5 \geq x_2$$
$$z_5 \geq -x_2$$
$$z_6 \geq x_2 + 3$$
$$z_6 \geq -x_2 - 3$$

PROBLEM 1.3 (Continued)

$$z_7 \geq x_2 - 1$$
$$z_7 \geq -x_2 + 1$$
$$z_8 \geq x_2 - 4$$
$$z_8 \geq -x_2 + 4$$

b)

Minimize $5(|x_1 - 3| + |x_2 - 0|) + 7(|x_1 - 0| + |x_2 + 3|)$
$+ 3(|x_1 + 2| + |x_2 - 1|) + |x_1 - 1| + |x_2 - 4|$

S.T. the same constraints as in part a.

c) In addition to the formulation in parts (a) and (b) we will have

$$x_1 \geq -1$$
$$x_1 \leq 2$$
$$x_2 \leq 1$$
$$x_2 \geq 0$$

d) The additional constraint will be

$$|x_1 - 3| + |x_2| \leq 3/2$$

PROBLEM 1.4

Divide $[0, T]$ into n intervals each of length Δ. Denote $y(j\Delta)$ by y_j and $u(j\Delta)$ by u_j. The problem becomes:

PROBLEM 1.4 (Continued)

$$\text{Minimize} \quad \sum_{j=0}^{n-1} z_j$$

S. T.

$$z_j \geq u_j \qquad j = 0, 1, \ldots, n-1$$

$$z_j \geq -u_j$$

$$y_{j+1} + y_{j-1} - 2y_j = u_{j-1} - g \qquad j = 1, 2, \ldots, n-1$$

$$y_n = b$$

$$y_j \geq 0 \qquad j = 1, \ldots, n$$

PROBLEM 1.5

Let

x_{1j} : # of item 1 produced during month j.

x_{2j} : # of item 2 produced during month j.

$j = 1, 2, \ldots, 12$ as oct = 1, .., sept = 12,

y_{ij} : inventory at the end of month j of item i. $(i = 1, 2)$

d_{ij} : demands of items $i = 1, 2$ during month j.

$$\text{Minimize} \quad 0.2\left(\sum_{j=1}^{12} y_{1j}\right) + 5\left(\sum_{j=1}^{8} x_{1j}\right) + 4.5\left(\sum_{j=9}^{12} x_{1j}\right) + .4\left(\sum_{j=1}^{12} y_{2j}\right)$$

$$+ 8\left(\sum_{j=1}^{8} x_{2j}\right) + 7\left(\sum_{j=9}^{12} x_{2j}\right)$$

PROBLEM 1.5 (Continued)

S. T.

$$y_{1,j-1} + x_{1j} - d_{1j} = y_{1j} \qquad j = 1, 2, \ldots, 12$$

$$y_{2,j-1} + x_{2j} - d_{2j} = y_{2j} \qquad j = 1, \ldots, 12$$

$$2y_{1j} + 4y_{2j} \leq 150\,000 \qquad j = 1, \ldots, 12$$

$$x_{1j} + x_{2j} \leq 120000 \qquad j = 1, \ldots, 12$$

$$x_{1j}, x_{2j}, y_{1j}, y_{2j} \geq 0, \qquad j = 1, \ldots, 12$$

and assume that $y_{10} = y_{20} = 0$.

PROBLEM 1.6

Let y_j : money available for investment at the beginning of year j.

x_{ij} : money invested in activity i at the beginning of period j.

maximize y_6

S. T.

$$y_1 = 2200$$

$$x_{11} + x_{21} \leq y_1$$

$$y_1 + 1.08x_{11} - x_{21} = y_2$$

$$x_{12} + x_{22} \leq y_2$$

$$y_2 + 1.08x_{12} + 1.1x_{21} = y_3$$

$$x_{13} + x_{23} + x_{33} \leq y_3$$

PROBLEM 1.6 (Continued)

$$y_3 + 1.08x_{13} + 1.10x_{22} = y_4$$

$$x_{14} + x_{24} \leq y_4$$

$$y_4 + 1.08x_{14} + 1.10x_{23} = y_5$$

$$x_{15} + x_{25} \leq y_5$$

$$y_5 + 1.08x_{15} + 1.10x_{24} + 1.12x_{33} = y_6$$

$$x_{ij}, \; y_j \geq 0 \qquad i = 1,..,3, \quad j = 1,..6$$

PROBLEM 1.7

Let, x_{ij} : hours of machine i on I-beam size j.
$i = 1, 2, 3$ corresponding to M/C's A, B, and C.
$j = 1, .., 4$ corresponding to beam sizes small, medium, large, extra-large.

Minimize $$30\left(\sum_{j=1}^{4} x_{1j}\right) + 50\left(\sum_{j=1}^{4} x_{2j}\right) + 80\left(\sum_{j=1}^{4} x_{3j}\right)$$

S.T.

$$\sum_{j=1}^{4} x_{ij} \leq 50 \qquad i = 1, 2, 3$$

$$300x_{11} + 600x_{21} + 800x_{31} \geq 10{,}000$$
$$250x_{12} + 400x_{22} + 700x_{32} \geq 8000$$
$$200x_{13} + 350x_{23} + 600x_{33} \geq 6000$$
$$100x_{14} + 200x_{24} + 300x_{34} \geq 6000$$

$$x_{ij} \geq 0 \qquad i = 1, 2, 3; \quad j = 1, ..., 4$$

PROBLEM 1.8

Let z_{1j} : # of workers producing swiss cheese during week j.

z_{2j}: # of workers producing sharp cheese during week j.

y_{1j}: inventory of swiss cheese at the end of week j.

y_{2j}: inventory of sharp cheese at the end of week j.

x_j : # of workers hired at the beginning of week j.

y_j : # of workers training the newly hired employees.

1. One worker produces 400 pounds of swiss cheese per week if working solely on swiss cheese.
2. One worker produces 240 lbs. of sharp cheese per week if working solely on sharp cheese.

Minimize $8x_1 + 7x_2 + 6x_3 + 5x_4 + 4x_5 + 3x_6 + 2x_7$

S.T.

$$\left.\begin{aligned}
400z_{11} + y_{10} &= 12{,}000 + y_{11} \\
400z_{12} + y_{11} &= 12{,}000 + y_{12} \\
400z_{13} + y_{12} &= 12{,}000 + y_{13} \\
400z_{14} + y_{13} &= 16{,}000 + y_{14} \\
400z_{15} + y_{14} &= 16{,}000 + y_{15} \\
400z_{16} + y_{15} &= 20{,}000 + y_{16} \\
400z_{17} + y_{16} &= 20{,}000 + y_{17}
\end{aligned}\right\}\ \text{Satisfying demand of swiss cheese}$$

PROBLEM 1.8 (continued)

$$400 z_{18} + y_{17} = 20,000 + y_{18}$$

$y_{11} \leq 12,000$, $y_{13} \leq 16,000$
$y_{12} \leq 12,000$, $y_{14} \leq 16,000$
$y_{16} \leq 20,000$, $y_{15} \leq 20,000$
$y_{17} \leq 20,000$

} no more than one week inventory

$$240 z_{21} + y_{20} = 8000 + y_{21}$$
$$240 z_{22} + y_{21} = 8000 + y_{22}$$
$$240 z_{23} + y_{22} = 10,000 + y_{23}$$
$$240 z_{24} + y_{23} = 10,000 + y_{24}$$
$$240 z_{25} + y_{24} = 12,000 + y_{25}$$
$$240 z_{26} + y_{25} = 12,000 + y_{26}$$
$$240 z_{27} + y_{26} = 12,000 + y_{27}$$
$$240 z_{28} + y_{27} = 12,000 + y_{28}$$

} Satisfying demand of sharp cheese

$y_{21} \leq 8000$, $y_{24} \leq 12,000$
$y_{22} \leq 10,000$, $y_{25} \leq 12,000$
$y_{23} \leq 10,000$, $y_{26} \leq 12,000$
$y_{27} \leq 12,000$

} No more than one week inventory

$$y_j \geq 3x_j \qquad j = 1, 2, \ldots, 7$$

(Note no hires at the beginning of eighth week)

$$z_{1,j-1} + z_{2,j-1} + y_{j-1} + x_{j-1} + x_{j-2} = z_{1j} + z_{2j} + y_j + x_{j-1}, \quad j = 3, \ldots, 8$$

PROBLEM 1.8 (Continued)

$$Z_{11} + Z_{21} + y_1 = Z_{12} + Z_{22} + y_2$$
$$Z_{11} + Z_{21} + y_1 = 60$$

Period 1 & 2 initial conditions

$$Z_{1,8} + Z_{2,8} + y_8 = 90$$

Desired # of employees at the end of week 8.

$$y_{ij},\ z_{ij},\ x_j,\ y_j \geq 0 \qquad i = 1,2 \quad j = 1, \ldots, 8$$

PROBLEM 1.9

Let
x_1: speed rpm
x_2: depth feed
x_3: length feed

$$\max \min (x_2, x_3)$$

S. T.

$$30x_1 + 4000x_2 \leq 150{,}000$$
$$200 + 0.5x_1 + 150x_2 + 150x_3 \leq 800$$
$$600 \leq x_1 \leq 800$$
$$40x_1 + 6000x_2 + 6000x_3 \leq 100{,}000$$

or

$$\max Z$$

S. T.

$$Z \leq x_2$$
$$Z \leq x_3$$
$$30x_1 + 4000x_2 \leq 150{,}000$$
$$0.5x_1 + 150x_2 + 150x_3 \leq 600$$
$$600 \leq x_1 \leq 800$$
$$40x_1 + 6000x_2 + 6000x_3 \leq 100{,}000$$
$$x_1, x_2, x_3 \geq 0$$

PROBLEM 1.10

Let x_1: # barrel of light crude oil

x_2: # barrel of heavy crude oil

$$\begin{aligned}
\min \quad & 11x_1 + 9x_2 \\
\text{S.T.} \quad & 0.4x_1 + 0.32x_2 \geq 1{,}000{,}000 \\
& 0.2x_1 + 0.4x_2 \geq 400{,}000 \\
& 0.35x_1 + 0.2x_2 \geq 250{,}000 \\
& x_1, x_2 \geq 0
\end{aligned}$$

PROBLEM 1.11

We have, $5 \times 2400 = 12{,}000$ lathe hrs,

24,000 grinding hrs,

48,000 forging hrs,

7200 drilling hrs,

14,400 miller hrs.

Let x_1 : # shafts

x_2 : # frames

$$\begin{aligned}
\text{Maximize} \quad & z \\
\text{S.T.} \quad & 0.5x_1 + 0.8x_2 \leq 48{,}000 \\
& 0.2x_1 \leq 12{,}000 \\
& 0.1x_2 \leq 7{,}200 \\
& 0.3x_1 + 0.5x_2 \leq 24{,}000 \\
& 0.3x_2 \leq 14{,}400 \\
& z \leq x_1 \\
& z \leq x_2 \\
& x_1, x_2 \geq 0
\end{aligned}$$

PROBLEM 1.12

Let x_1 : # color TV.
x_2 : # B-W TV.

$$\text{maximize} \quad 60x_1 + 30x_2$$

$$\begin{aligned} \text{S.T.} \quad & 20x_1 + 15x_2 \le 50{,}000 \\ & x_1 \le 1000 \\ & x_2 \le 4000 \\ & x_1, \; x_2 \ge 0 \end{aligned}$$

PROBLEM 1.13

Let x_1, x_2, x_3, x_4 be the amounts of compounds 1, 2, 3 and 4 respectively, used to form one kilogram of total product.

$$\min \quad 20x_1 + 30x_2 + 20x_3 + 15x_4$$

$$\begin{aligned} \text{S.T.} \quad & 0.3x_1 + 0.2x_2 + 0.4x_3 + 0.2x_4 = 0.2 \\ & 0.2x_1 + 0.6x_2 + 0.3x_3 + 0.4x_4 \ge 0.3 \\ & 0.4x_1 + 0.15x_2 + 0.25x_3 + 0.3x_4 \ge 0.2 \\ & x_1 \le 0.3 \\ & x_2 \le 0.4 \\ & x_1, \; x_2, \; x_3, \; x_4 \ge 0 \end{aligned}$$

PROBLEM 1.14

Let x_{ij} : # product i manufactured on machine j.

$$\text{Minimize} \quad (4x_{11} + 4x_{12} + 5x_{13} + 7x_{14}) + (6x_{21} + 7x_{22} + 5x_{23} + 6x_{24}) + (12x_{31} + 10x_{32} + 8x_{33} + 11x_{34})$$

PROBLEM 1.14 (Continued)

S. T.

$$x_{11} + x_{12} + x_{13} \geq 4000$$

$$x_{21} + x_{22} + x_{23} \geq 5000$$

$$x_{31} + x_{32} + x_{33} \geq 3000$$

$$0.3x_{11} + 0.2x_{21} + 0.8x_{31} \leq 1500.$$

$$0.25x_{12} + 0.3x_{22} + 0.6x_{32} \leq 1200$$

$$0.2x_{13} + 0.2x_{23} + 0.6x_{33} \leq 1500$$

$$0.2x_{14} + 0.25x_{24} + 0.5x_{34} \leq 2000$$

$$x_{ij} \geq 0 \quad , \quad i = 1, 2, 3 \quad , \quad j = 1, 2, 3, 4$$

PROBLEM 1.15

Let x_{ij} : tonnage from lumber company i to furniture company j.

minimize $2x_{11} + 3x_{12} + 5x_{13} + 2.5x_{21} + 4x_{22} + 4.8x_{23} + 3x_{31} + 3.6x_{32} + 3.2x_{33}$

S. T.

$$\sum_{i=1}^{3} x_{i1} = 500$$

$$\sum_{i=1}^{3} x_{i2} = 700$$

$$\sum_{i=1}^{3} x_{i3} = 600$$

$$\sum_{j=1}^{3} x_{3j} \leq 500$$

$$x_{ij} \leq 200 \quad , \quad i = 2, 3 \qquad j = 1, 2, 3$$

$$x_{ij} \geq 0 \quad , \quad i = 1, 2, 3 \qquad j = 1, 2, 3$$

PROBLEM 1.16

Let x_j : investment in project j.

$$\text{Max } 0.08x_1 + 0.06x_2 + 0.07x_3 + 0.05x_4 + 0.08x_5 + 0.09x_6 + 0.1x_7 + 0.06x_8$$

S.T.

$$x_1 + x_2 + x_3 \geq 3$$

$$17 \geq x_4 + x_5 + x_6 \geq 5$$

$$x_7 + x_8 \geq 8$$

$$x_1 + x_2 + x_3 + x_4 + x_5 + x_6 + x_7 + x_8 \leq 30 \quad \text{Redundant}$$

$0 \leq x_1 \leq 6$, $0 \leq x_3 \leq 9$, $0 \leq x_5 \leq 10$

$0 \leq x_2 \leq 5$, $0 \leq x_4 \leq 7$, $0 \leq x_6 \leq 4$

$0 \leq x_7 \leq 6$, $0 \leq x_8 \leq 3$.

PROBLEM 1.17

a) Let x_L : # low-income houses

x_M : # middle-income houses.

$$\text{min } 13000x_L + 18000x_M$$

S.T.

$$13000x_L + 18000x_M \leq 2\,000\,000$$

$$\frac{1}{20}x_L + \frac{1}{15}x_M \leq 10$$

$$60 \leq x_L \leq 100$$

$$30 \leq x_M \leq 70$$

PROBLEM 1.17 (Continued)

$$x_L + x_M \leq 150$$

$$x_L - \frac{1}{2} x_M \geq 50$$

b) The objective function will be

$$\max \quad x_L + x_M$$

PROBLEM 1.18

The answer to this problem can be postponed until chapter 11. It can be handled by a proper network flow problem.

PROBLEM 1.19

a) Let x_{ij} be the number of hearings of class i processed at period j.

$$\max \quad \sum_{i,j} x_{ij}$$

s.t.

$$\sum_i a_i x_{ij} \leq b_j \quad , \quad j = 1, \ldots, n$$

$$x_{ij} - \sum_{l=1}^{j-1} (h_{il} - x_{il}) \leq h_{ij}$$

$$i = 1, \ldots, m$$
$$j = 2, 3, \ldots, n$$

$$x_{i1} = h_{i1} \qquad i = 1, 2, \ldots, m$$

$$x_{ij} \geq 0 \qquad i = 1, 2, \ldots, m$$
$$j = 1, 2, \ldots, n$$

PROBLEM 1.19 (Continued)

b) We can change the objective function into

$$\min \sum_{i=1}^{m} \sum_{j=1}^{n} | h_{ij} - x_{ij} |$$

PROBLEM 1.20

Let x_{ikj} : amount of waste transfered to disposal site j by the transfer station k from source i.

$$\min \sum_{k=1}^{K} \sum_{i=1}^{m} \sum_{j=1}^{n} \left(y_k f_k + [c_{ik} + \bar{c}_{kj} + \alpha_k] x_{ikj} \right)$$

S.T.

$$\sum_{k,j} x_{ikj} = a_i \quad , \quad i = 1, --, m$$

$$\sum_{i,k} x_{ikj} \leq b_j \quad , \quad j = 1, 2, --, n$$

$$\sum_{i,j} x_{ikj} \leq y_k q_k \quad , \quad k = 1, 2, --, K$$

$$y_k = 0 \text{ or } 1 \quad , \quad k = 1, 2, .., K$$

$$x_{ikj} \geq 0 \quad , \quad \begin{array}{l} i = 1, 2, --, m \\ j = 1, 2, --, n \\ k = 1, 2, --, K \end{array}$$

PROBLEM 1.21

a)

$$\min \sum_{i,j} c_{ij} x_{ij}$$

s.t.

$$\sum_{i=1}^{m} x_{ij} = b_j \qquad j=1,\dots,n$$

$$\sum_{j=1}^{n} x_{ij} \le a_i \qquad i=1,\dots,m$$

$$x_{ij} \geq 0 \qquad \forall\, i,j$$

b) Let q_i be the discount percentage. The cost of the item from the ith bidder will be

$$c_{ij} \qquad \text{if} \quad \sum_j x_{ij} \le \alpha_i$$

$$q_i c_{ij} \qquad \text{if} \quad \sum_j x_{ij} > \alpha_i$$

$$\min \sum_{i,j} \left(c_{ij} + y_i (q_i c_{ij} - c_{ij}) \right) x_{ij}$$

s.t.

$$\sum_i x_{ij} = b_j$$

$$\sum_j x_{ij} \le \alpha_i + y_i (a_i - \alpha_i)$$

$$y_i = 0 \text{ or } 1, \qquad i=1,\dots,m$$

$$x_{ij} \geq 0, \qquad i=1,\dots,m, \quad j=1,\dots,n.$$

PROBLEM 1.22

a) Let x_{ij} : amount of fuel i the plant j uses for the mix.

$$\min \quad \sum_{j=1}^{n} \sum_{i=1}^{m} x_{ij} c_i$$

$$\text{S.T.} \quad \sum_i \alpha_{ij} x_{ij} \geq b_j \quad , \quad j = 1, 2, \ldots, n$$

$$\sum_j \gamma_j \left(\sum_i c_{ij} x_{ij} \right) \leq b$$

$$x_{ij} \geq 0 \qquad \begin{array}{l} i = 1, \ldots, m \\ j = 1, \ldots, n \end{array}$$

b) If a specific fuel is wanted to be excluded from the mixes of plant j, we can assign an arbitrarily large cost for that fuel for the specific plant.

If we want to be sure on noncoexist-ance of fuel type i and fuel type k at plant j, we can add the constraints

$$x_{ij} \leq M y_{ij}$$

$$x_{kj} \leq M(1 - y_{ij})$$

$$y_{ij} = 0 \text{ or } 1$$

and M being a large positive number

c) We can add the constraint

PROBLEM 1.22 (Continued)

$$\sum_i c_i x_{ij} \leq p$$

where p is a predetermined constant. This will assure us that none of the plants will be spending more than p dollars. One can vary p until an optimal feasible solution can be obtained to the problem.

PROBLEM 1.23

a) $$\min \ (x_1^+ - x_1^-) - 2(x_2^+ - x_2^-) - 3(x_3^+ - x_3^-)$$

S.T.
$$(x_1^+ - x_1^-) + (x_2^+ - x_2^-) + (x_3^+ - x_3^-) + x_4 = 6$$
$$(x_1^+ - x_1^-) + 2(x_2^+ - x_2^-) + 4(x_3^+ - x_3^-) - x_5 = 12$$
$$(x_1^+ - x_1^-) - (x_2^+ - x_2^-) + (x_3^+ - x_3^-) - x_6 = 2$$
$$x_i^+, x_i^-, x_j \geqslant 0, \quad i = 1, 2, 3, \quad j = 4, 5, 6.$$

b) $$\min \ (x_1^+ - x_1^-) - 2(x_2^+ - x_2^-) - 3(x_3^+ - x_3^-)$$

S.T.
$$-(x_1^+ - x_1^-) - (x_2^+ - x_2^-) - (x_3^+ - x_3^-) \geqslant -6$$
$$(x_1^+ - x_1^-) + 2(x_2^+ - x_2^-) + 4(x_3^+ - x_3^-) \geqslant 12$$
$$(x_1^+ - x_1^-) - (x_2^+ - x_2^-) + (x_3^+ - x_3^-) \geqslant 2$$
$$x_1^+, x_1^-, x_2^+, \ldots\ldots, x_3^+, x_3^- \geqslant 0$$

c) Objective
$$-\max \ -x_1 + 2x_2 + 3x_3$$

PROBLEM 1.24

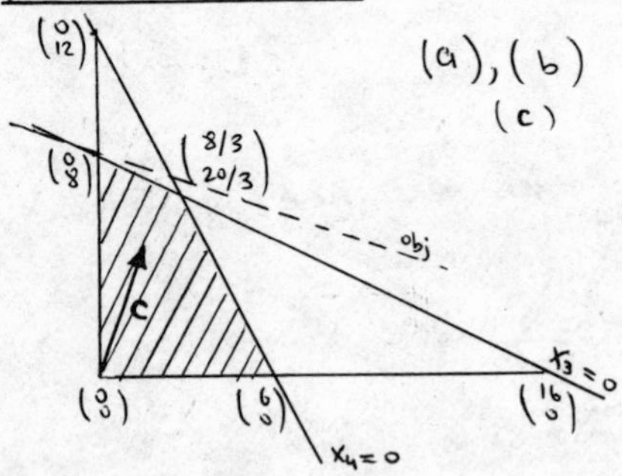

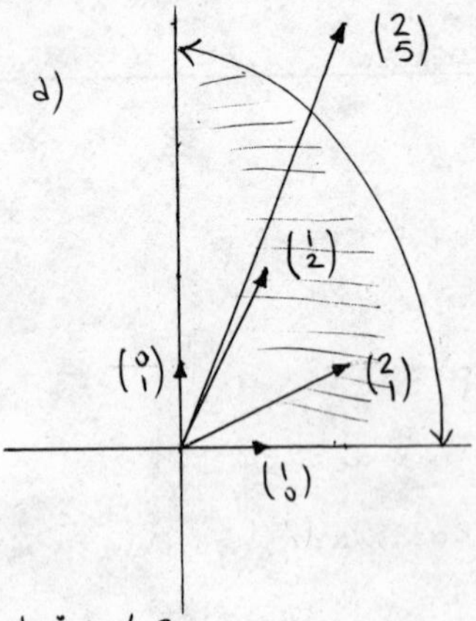

Optimal solution $\binom{0}{8}$, obj = 40.

PROBLEM 1.25

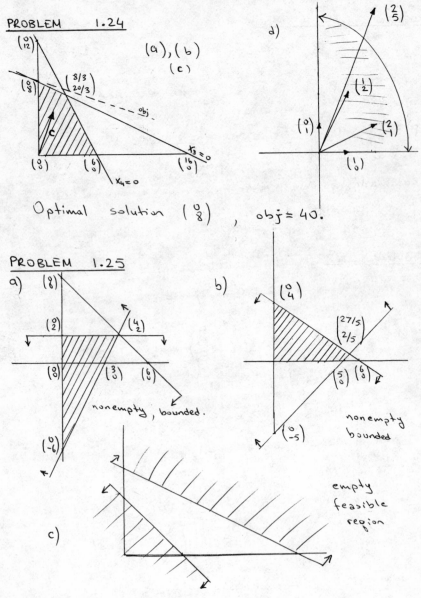

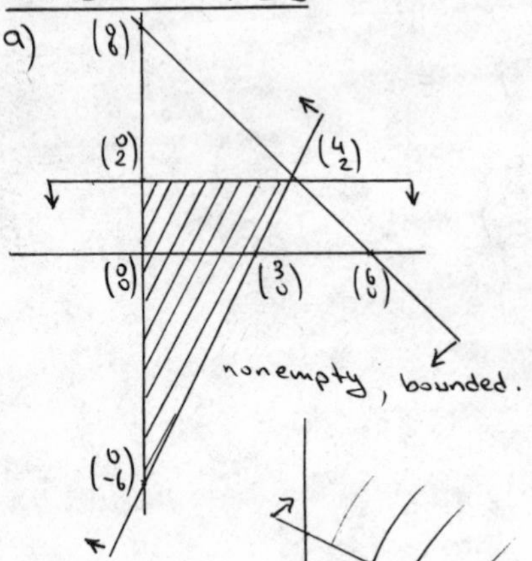

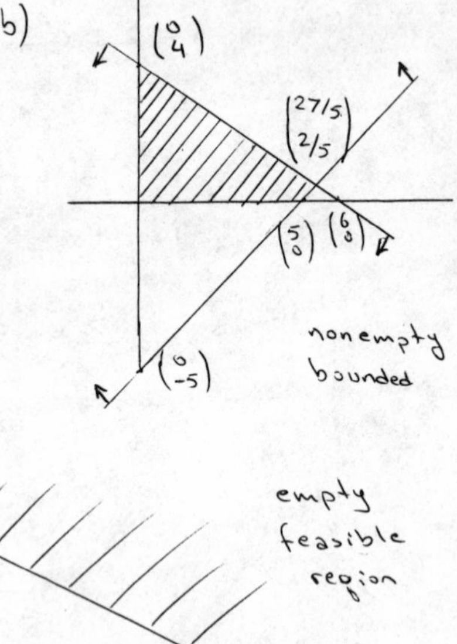

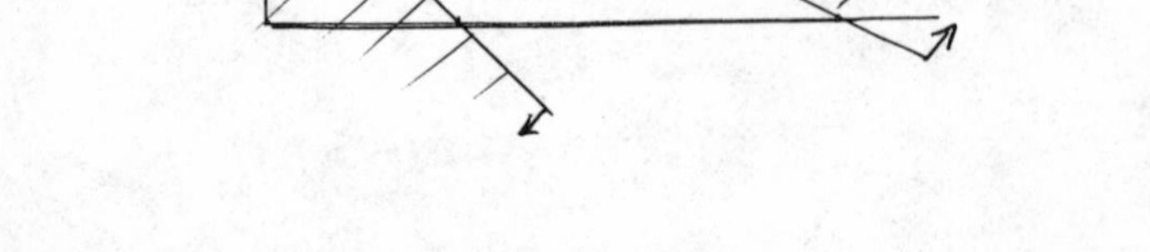

PROBLEM 1.26

a)

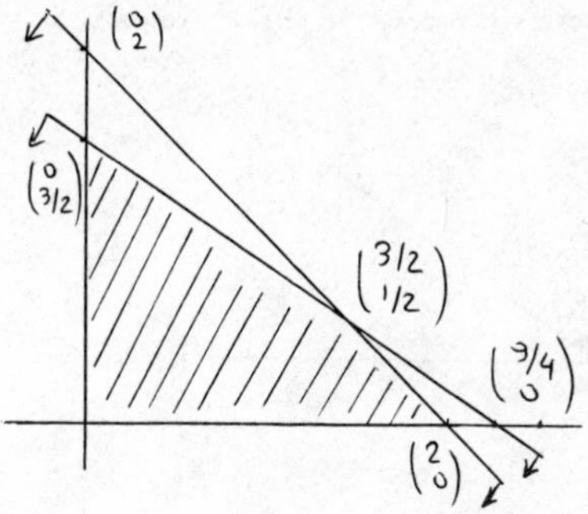

b) Optimal extreme points : $\binom{0}{3/2}$ and $\binom{3/2}{1/2}$.

c) $\lambda \binom{0}{3/2} + (1-\lambda)\binom{3/2}{1/2}$. for $0 \le \lambda \le 1$ is optimal.

PROBLEM 1.27

a)

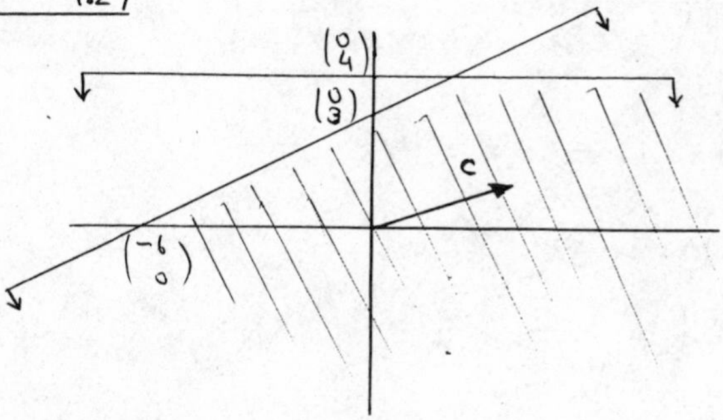

b) We have unbounded feasible region and $\bar{c}$ is in the direction of $x_2 = 4$, $x_1 = \infty$.

PROBLEM 1.28

a) Note that column 1 dominates column 4, so column 4 is deleted.

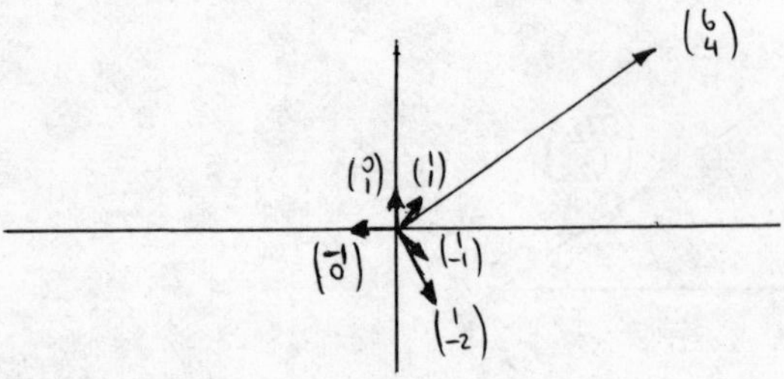

b) Only possibilities are:

$\binom{1}{1}$ and $\binom{1}{-1}$, $\binom{1}{1}$ and $\binom{1}{-2}$, $\binom{0}{1}$ and $\binom{1}{-1}$, and

$\binom{0}{1}$ and $\binom{1}{-2}$.

c) $\binom{1}{1}$ and $\binom{1}{-1}$ $\Rightarrow$ $x_1 = 5$, $x_2 = 1$, obj $= -6$

$\binom{1}{1}$ and $\binom{1}{-2}$ $\Rightarrow$ $x_1 = 16/3$, $x_3 = 2/3$ obj $= -4$

$\binom{0}{1}$ and $\binom{1}{-1}$ $\Rightarrow$ $x_6 = 10$, $x_2 = 6$ obj $= -6$

$\binom{0}{1}$ and $\binom{1}{-2}$ $\Rightarrow$ $x_6 = 16$, $x_3 = 6$ obj $= 12$

Therefore, the optimal solution is

$$x_1 = 5, \; x_2 = 1, \; x_3 = x_4 = 0$$

or

$$x_1 = 0, \; x_2 = 6, \; x_3 = x_4 = 0$$

with obj $= -6$.

PROBLEM 1.29

a) Feasible region may be reduced.
b) Optimal objective may be reduced.

PROBLEM 1.30

$$\partial z^* / \partial b_i \leq 0$$

PROBLEM 1.31

a) Feasible region may be enlarged.
b) Optimal objective may increase
c) $\partial z^* / \partial b_i \geq 0$

PROBLEM 1.32

a) Feasible region may be reduced.
b) Optimal objective may increase.

PROBLEM 1.33

a) We now have a feasible region in an n+1 dimensional space.
b) Optimal objective may decrease

PROBLEM 1.34

a) Feasible region may be enlarged,
b) Optimal objective may be reduced.

PROBLEM 1.35

a) Feasible region in $(n-1)$ dimensional space.

b) Optimal objective may increase.

CHAPTER 2 RESULTS FROM LINEAR ALGEBRA AND CONVEX ANALYSIS

PROBLEM 2.1

a) a_1, a_2, a_3 both span E^3 and form a basis.

b) a_1 and a_2 neither span, nor form a basis of E^3.

c) a_1, a_2, a_3, a_4 span E^3, but do not form a basis.

d) a_1, a_2, a_3 neither span nor form a basis of E^3. (Note that $a_1 + 2a_2 = a_3$).

e) a_1, a_2, a_3 span E^3 and form a basis of E^3.

PROBLEM 2.2

The vectors are linearly independent and span E^3.

PROBLEM 2.3

Suppose that $a_1, a_2, \ldots, a_k$ are not linearly independent. Then there exist scalars $\alpha_1, \ldots, \alpha_k$ not all zero such that

$$\sum_{j=1}^{k} \alpha_j a_j = 0$$

Without loss of generality, suppose that $\alpha_k \neq 0$. Then

$$a_k = \sum_{j=1}^{k-1} - \frac{\alpha_j}{\alpha_k} a_j .$$

From this it can be shown that $a_1, \ldots, a_{k-1}$ span E^n and so, $a_1, \ldots, a_k$ could not

PROBLEM 2.3 (Continued)

have been a basis of E^n. Therefore $a_1, \ldots, a_k$ are linearly independent.
Suppose $k < n$. By contradiction we can find that $k = n$.

PROBLEM 2.4

Those three vectors are in E^3 and are linearly independent, so, they form a basis of E^3.
In particular

$$\begin{bmatrix} 1 & 0 & 1 \\ 0 & 1 & 5 \\ 0 & 0 & 3 \end{bmatrix} \text{ is invertible with inverse } \begin{bmatrix} 1 & 0 & -1/3 \\ 0 & 1 & -5/3 \\ 0 & 0 & 1/3 \end{bmatrix}$$

Note that
$$\begin{bmatrix} 1 & 0 & -1/3 \\ 0 & 1 & -5/3 \\ 0 & 0 & 1/3 \end{bmatrix} \begin{bmatrix} 1 \\ 1 \\ 0 \end{bmatrix} = \begin{bmatrix} 1 \\ 1 \\ 0 \end{bmatrix}.$$

Since the second entry in this column is not zero, then, a_2 can be replaced by $(1,1,0)^T$ and the new set of vectors still form a basis.

PROBLEM 2.5

Note that $y = \sum_{\substack{i=1 \\ i \neq j}}^{n} \lambda_i a_i$. Therefore, $a_1, a_2, \ldots, a_{j-1}, y, a_{j+1}, \ldots a_n$ are not linearly independent and hence do not form a basis.

PROBLEM 2.6

Suppose that B^{-1} and B'^{-1} are inverses of B. Then:

$$BB^{-1} = I \quad , \quad BB'^{-1} = I \quad , \text{ therefore}$$

$$BB^{-1} - BB'^{-1} = B(B^{-1} - B'^{-1}) = \underline{0}$$

multiply by B^{-1} we have

$$B^{-1} - B'^{-1} = \underline{0}$$

so,

$$B^{-1} = B'^{-1}$$

PROBLEM 2.7

Note that

$$\left[\begin{array}{c|c} B & \underline{0} \\ \hline T & I \end{array}\right]\left[\begin{array}{c|c} B^{-1} & \underline{0} \\ \hline -TB^{-1} & I \end{array}\right] = \left[\begin{array}{c|c} I & \underline{0} \\ \hline \underline{0} & I \end{array}\right]$$

Also

$$\left[\begin{array}{c|c} B^{-1} & 0 \\ \hline -TB^{-1} & I \end{array}\right]\left[\begin{array}{c|c} B & 0 \\ \hline T & I \end{array}\right] = \left[\begin{array}{c|c} I & 0 \\ \hline 0 & I \end{array}\right]$$

Therefore A is invertible with the indicated matrix.

PROBLEM 2.8

$$A^{-1} = \begin{bmatrix} 1 & -4/5 & 14/10 & 39/10 \\ 0 & 1/5 & -1/10 & -1/10 \\ 0 & 0 & 1/2 & 5/2 \\ 0 & 0 & 0 & -1 \end{bmatrix}$$

PROBLEM 2.9

$$A^{-1} = \begin{bmatrix} -3/5 & 1/5 & -13/5 & 6/5 \\ 2/5 & 1/5 & 7/5 & -4/5 \\ 1 & 0 & 2 & -1 \\ -4/5 & -2/5 & -9/5 & 8/5 \end{bmatrix}$$

PROBLEM 2.10

Note that $[A^T(A^{-1})^T]^T = A^{-1}A = I \Rightarrow A^T(A^{-1})^T = I$.

Also $[(A^{-1})^T A^T]^T = AA^{-1} = I \Rightarrow (A^{-1})^T A^T = I$.

Therefore, $(A^{-1})^T$ is the inverse of A^T.

PROBLEM 2.11

Note that $(B^{-1}A^{-1})AB = I$, also

$$(AB)B^{-1}A^{-1} = I$$

Therefore, $(AB)^{-1} = B^{-1}A^{-1}$

PROBLEM 2.12

Let e_j be the unit vector with all zeroes except 1 in location j. For any matrix A we can write

$$a_j = Ae_j$$

where a_j is the jth column of A. Therefore

$$A^{-1}a_j = e_j$$

PROBLEM 2.13

Let the new matrix be B' where k th row of B is multiplied by λ.

$$(B')^{-1} = \frac{A'}{\det B'}$$

$$\det B' = \lambda \det B$$

A' is the matrix formed by the cofactors of B'. Note that A' can be obtained by replacing the column of the cofactor of B by λ times that column but leaving the kth column as it is. Then

$(B')^{-1}$ is obtained by $1/\lambda$ times the matrix which is formed from B^{-1} by multiplying each column except the kth column by λ.

PROBLEM 2.14

Suppose the k th column is multiplied by λ. The inverse of the new matrix is $1/\lambda$ times the matrix formed from the old inverse by multiplying each of its rows except the kth row by λ.

PROBLEM 2.15

Consider an arbitrary row of B^{-1}, say, row k. Denote this row by b_k. Let a_j be the jth column of B.

PROBLEM 2.15 (Continued)

If all entries of b_k are nonpositive, then $b_k a_k \leq 0$ since all entries of a_k are nonnegative. This contradicts the fact that $b_k a_k = 1$ (Why?).

PROBLEM 2.16

No. From matrix algebra we know $AB \neq BA$ in most of the cases. Therefore B may not be the inverse of A.

PROBLEM 2.17

a) $\det A = 8$

b) $\det A = -20$

c) $\det A = -17$

PROBLEM 2.18

By utilizing the row operations we can reduce the given matrices into the following forms:

$$\begin{bmatrix} 1 & 0 & 1 & 1 \\ 2 & 2 & 4 & -1 \\ 1 & 0 & 5 & 3 \end{bmatrix} \Rightarrow \begin{bmatrix} 1 & 0 & 0 & 1/2 \\ 0 & 1 & 0 & -2 \\ 0 & 0 & 1 & 1/2 \end{bmatrix}, \quad \operatorname{rank} A = 3$$

$$\begin{bmatrix} -1 & 1 & 0 \\ 1 & 4 & 5 \\ 2 & 3 & 5 \end{bmatrix} \Rightarrow \begin{bmatrix} 1 & 0 & 1 \\ 0 & 1 & 1 \\ 0 & 0 & 0 \end{bmatrix}, \quad \operatorname{rank} A = 2$$

PROBLEM 2.19

Any principal minor that will be obtained from the original triangular matrix will also be triangular. Hence, all the products of the determinant in the cofactors will vanish except the diagonal.

$$\det A = (-1)^{1+1} a_{11} \det A^1 = (-1)^{1+1}(-1)^{2+2} a_{11} a_{22} \det A^2 \cdots$$

$$\det A = a_{11} a_{22} a_{33} \cdots a_{nn}$$

where A^k is the minor of A where first k rows and columns of A are deleted.

PROBLEM 2.20

$$x_1 = \frac{\det\begin{vmatrix} 6 & 1 \\ 4 & -2 \end{vmatrix}}{\det A} = \frac{-12-9}{-9} = \frac{16}{9}$$

$$x_2 = \frac{\det\begin{vmatrix} 2 & 6 \\ 5 & 4 \end{vmatrix}}{\det A} = \frac{22}{9}$$

PROBLEM 2.21

$$A = \begin{bmatrix} 1 & 1 & -1 & 0 & 0 \\ -1 & 0 & 1 & 1 & 0 \\ 0 & 1 & 0 & -1 & 1 \end{bmatrix}$$

(columns labelled a_1, a_2, a_3, a_4, a_5)

PROBLEM 2.21 (continued)

$B_1 = [a_1\ a_2\ a_3]$, $\det B_1 = 0$

$B_2 = [a_1\ a_2\ a_4]$, $\det B_2 = 0$

$B_3 = [a_2\ a_3\ a_4]$, $\det B_3 = 0$

$B_4 = [a_1\ a_3\ a_4]$, $\det B_4 = 0$

$$B_5 = [a_1\ a_2\ a_5] = \begin{bmatrix} 1 & 1 & 0 \\ -1 & 0 & 0 \\ 0 & 1 & 1 \end{bmatrix} \xrightarrow[\text{manipulation}]{\text{row}} \begin{bmatrix} 1 & 0 & 0 \\ 1 & 1 & 0 \\ 0 & -1 & 1 \end{bmatrix}$$

$B_6 = [a_1\ a_3\ a_5]$ — $\det B_6 = 0$

$$B_7 = [a_1\ a_4\ a_5] = \begin{bmatrix} 1 & 0 & 0 \\ -1 & 1 & 0 \\ 0 & -1 & 1 \end{bmatrix} \quad \text{triangular}$$

$$B_8 = [a_2\ a_3\ a_5] = \begin{bmatrix} 1 & -1 & 0 \\ 0 & 1 & 0 \\ -1 & 0 & 1 \end{bmatrix} \xrightarrow[\text{operations}]{\text{row \& col.}} \begin{bmatrix} 1 & 0 & 0 \\ -1 & 1 & 0 \\ 0 & -1 & 1 \end{bmatrix}$$

$$B_9 = [a_2\ a_4\ a_5] = \begin{bmatrix} 1 & 0 & 0 \\ 0 & 1 & 0 \\ -1 & -1 & 0 \end{bmatrix}, \quad \text{triangular.}$$

$$B_{10} = [a_3\ a_4\ a_5] = \begin{bmatrix} -1 & 0 & 0 \\ 1 & 1 & 0 \\ 0 & -1 & 1 \end{bmatrix}, \text{triangular.}$$

PROBLEM 2.22

$$A = \begin{bmatrix} 1 & 2 & 1 \\ -1 & 1 & -1 \\ 2 & 3 & 1 \end{bmatrix}, \quad A^{-1} = \begin{bmatrix} -4/3 & -1/3 & 1 \\ 1/3 & 1/3 & 0 \\ 5/3 & -1/3 & -1 \end{bmatrix}$$

and $x_1 = -7$ $x_2 = 2$ $x_3 = 4$

PROBLEM 2.22 (Continued)

If right hand side of first equation changes to 2, the new solution is

$$\begin{bmatrix} x_1 \\ x_2 \\ x_3 \end{bmatrix} = \begin{bmatrix} -4/3 & -1/3 & 1 \\ 1/3 & 1/3 & 0 \\ 5/3 & -1/3 & -1 \end{bmatrix} \begin{bmatrix} 2 \\ 5 \\ -4 \end{bmatrix} = \begin{bmatrix} -25/3 \\ 7/3 \\ 17/3 \end{bmatrix}$$

PROBLEM 2.23

Let B be an $m \times m$ submatrix of A and let $A = [B, N]$. Then

$$B x_B + N x_N = b$$

$$x_B = B^{-1} b - B^{-1} N x_N$$

$$\text{General solution} = \begin{bmatrix} B^{-1}b - B^{-1}N x_N \\ x_N \end{bmatrix}$$

where x_N is an arbitrary $n-m$ vector.

PROBLEM 2.24

$$x_B = \begin{bmatrix} x_1 \\ x_3 \end{bmatrix} \qquad B = \begin{bmatrix} 1 & 1 \\ -1 & 1 \end{bmatrix}, \quad B^{-1} = \begin{bmatrix} 1/2 & -1/2 \\ 1/2 & 1/2 \end{bmatrix}$$

$$B^{-1}N = \begin{bmatrix} 1/2 & -1/2 \\ 1/2 & 1/2 \end{bmatrix} \begin{bmatrix} 2 \\ 5 \end{bmatrix} = \begin{bmatrix} -3/2 \\ 7/2 \end{bmatrix}$$

$$B^{-1}b = \begin{bmatrix} 1/2 & -1/2 \\ 1/2 & 1/2 \end{bmatrix} \begin{bmatrix} 3 \\ 6 \end{bmatrix} = \begin{bmatrix} -3/2 \\ 9/2 \end{bmatrix}$$

PROBLEM 2.24 (Continued)

General Solution : $\begin{bmatrix} -3/2 - 3/2\, x_2 \\ x_2 \\ 9/2 + 7/2\, x_2 \end{bmatrix}$

PROBLEM 2.25

a) $B = (a_1, a_2)$, $x_1 = -11$, $x_2 = -7$, $x_3 = x_4 = x_5 = 0$

b) $B = (a_1, a_3)$, $x_1 = 3$, $x_3 = 7$, $x_2 = x_4 = x_5 = 0$

c) $B = (a_1, a_4)$, $x_1 = -1/2$, $x_4 = 7/2$, $x_2 = x_3 = x_5 = 0$

d) $B = (a_1, a_5)$, $x_1 = 2/3$, $x_5 = -7/3$, $x_2 = x_3 = x_4 = 0$

e) $B = (a_2, a_3)$, $x_2 = -3/2$, $x_3 = 11/2$, $x_1 = x_4 = x_5 = 0$

f) $B = (a_2, a_4)$, $x_2 = 1/3$, $x_4 = 11/3$, $x_1 = x_3 = x_5 = 0$

g) $B = (a_2, a_5)$, $x_2 = -2/5$, $x_5 = -11/5$, $x_1 = x_3 = x_4 = 0$

h) $B = (a_3, a_4)$, $x_3 = 1$, $x_4 = 3$, $x_1 = x_2 = x_5 = 0$

i) $B = (a_3, a_5)$, $x_3 = -2$, $x_5 = -3$, $x_1 = x_2 = x_4 = 0$

j) $B = (a_4, a_5)$, $x_4 = -7$, $x_5 = 11$, $x_1 = x_2 = x_3 = 0$

PROBLEM 2.26

The system has an infinite number of solutions. The general solution can be given as:

$$x_1 = 1 - \frac{22}{15} x_4$$

$$x_2 = \frac{3}{5} x_4$$

$$x_3 = \frac{2}{3} x_4$$

PROBLEM 2.27

Let $A = [a_1 a_2 \cdots a_n]$. Suppose $x_1, \ldots, x_p \neq 0$ and $x_{p+1} = x_{p+2} = \cdots = x_n = 0$ and $p > m$. We can write

$$a_j = \sum_{i=1}^{p} \lambda_i a_i$$

and therefore $a_1, a_2, \ldots, a_{j-1}, a_{j+1}, a_{j+2} \cdots a_p$ forms a basis for the system. In the new solution with respect to this new basis we have $x_j = 0$ while $x_1, \ldots x_{j-1}, x_{j+1} \cdots x_p \neq 0$ and $x_{p+1}, \ldots, x_n = 0$.

Therefore we have one less nonzero variable. One can continue this procedure until $p = m$ is achieved. This will give us exactly m nonzero variables.

PROBLEM 2.28

a) Convex set

b) Convex set

c) Not convex

d) Convex

e) Convex set

f) Convex

PROBLEM 2.29

Let $x_1, x_2 \in H$, i.e., $px_1 = px_2 = k$. Let $0 < \lambda < 1$. Then $p(\lambda x_1 + (1-\lambda)x_2) = \lambda k + (1-\lambda)k$. Therefore H is a convex set.

Let $x_1, x_2 \in H^+$. Then $px_1 \geq k$ and $px_2 \geq k$. Let $0 < \lambda < 1$. Then

$$p(\lambda x_1 + (1-\lambda)x_2) = \lambda p x_1 + (1-\lambda) p x_2$$
$$\geq \lambda k + (1-\lambda)k = k$$

Therefore, $\lambda x_1 + (1-\lambda)x_2 \in H^+$ and H^+ is convex.

PROBLEM 2.30

The closest point in the set to $\begin{pmatrix}4\\4\end{pmatrix}$ is $\begin{pmatrix}3\\5/2\end{pmatrix}$. The distance is $\frac{1}{2}\sqrt{13}$.

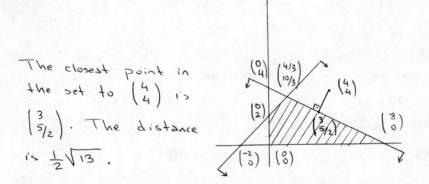

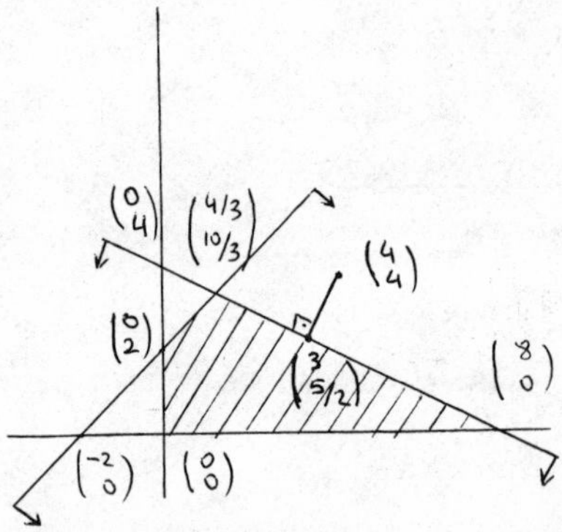

PROBLEM 2.31

The equation of the hyperplane that seperates X and the point $(-2, 1)$ is

$$H = \{(x_1, x_2) : x_1 = -1\}$$

PROBLEM 2.32

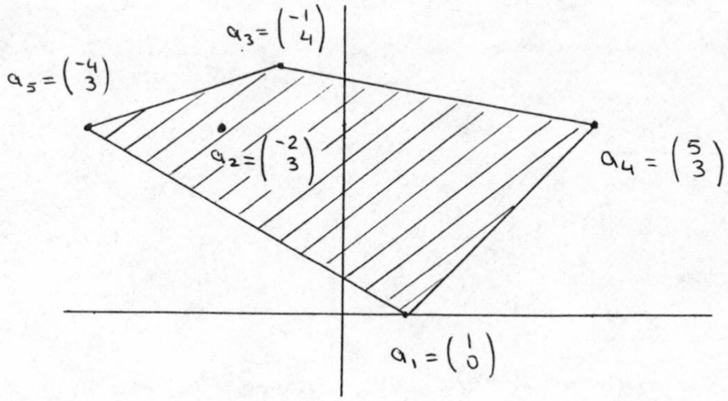

PROBLEM 2.33

Let x_1, x_2 be such that $Ax_1 = b$, $x_1 \geqslant 0$, $Ax_2 = b$, $x_2 \geqslant 0$. Let $0 < \lambda < 1$.

$$A(\lambda x_1 + (1-\lambda)x_2) = \lambda b + (1-\lambda)b = b$$

$$\lambda x_1 + (1-\lambda)x_2 \geqslant 0$$

Therefore, the set of feasible solutions of the linear programming problem is convex.

PROBLEM 2.34

a) Convex

b) Convex

c) Convex

d) Concave

e) Convex

PROBLEM 2.35

The answer to this problem can be found in any standard nonlinear programming text.

PROBLEM 2.36

The solution to this problem can be found in any standard text on NLP.

PROBLEM 2.37

Suppose that x_0 were an optimal solution and let $\epsilon > 0$ be such that

$$\| x - x_0 \| < \epsilon \implies x \in S.$$

Consider

$$x_0 + \frac{c}{\|c\|} \cdot \frac{\epsilon}{2} .$$

Note that this vector belongs to S. Furthermore,

$$c\left(x_0 + \frac{c}{\|c\|} \cdot \frac{\epsilon}{2}\right) = cx_0 + \frac{\epsilon}{2}\|c\| > cx_0$$

contradicting optimality of x_0.

PROBLEM 2.38

Let x be an extreme point of C. Since C is a cone then $1/2\, x$ and $3/2\, x \in C$. But x can be written as a convex combination of $\frac{1}{2}x$ and $\frac{3}{2}x$, e.g.,

$$x = \frac{1}{2}\left(\frac{1}{2}x\right) + \frac{1}{2}\left(\frac{3}{2}x\right) .$$

PROBLEM 2.38 (Continued)

Since x is an extreme point then

$$x = \frac{1}{2}x = \frac{3}{2}x \implies x = 0$$

Therefore, C has at most one extreme point namely the origin.

PROBLEM 2.39

Suppose $\lambda x + \mu y \in C$ for any $x, y \in C$ and any $\lambda, \mu \geq 0$.

Letting $\mu = 0$ it follows that $\lambda x \in C$ for $x \in C$ and $\lambda \geq 0$.

Given $x, y \in C$ and choosing $\lambda, \mu \geq 0$ such that $\lambda + \mu = 1$, it follows that C is a convex cone.

Conversely, suppose that C is a closed convex cone. Let $x, y \in C$ and $\lambda, \mu \geq 0$. Since C is a cone $2\lambda x \in C$ and $2\mu y \in C$. Since C is convex, then

$$\frac{1}{2}(2\lambda x) + \frac{1}{2}(2\mu y) \in C$$

i.e.,

$$\lambda x + \mu y \in C$$

PROBLEM 2.40

$$\begin{aligned} x_1 + x_2 + x_3 + x_4 \quad &= 1 \\ -x_1 + 2x_2 \quad + x_5 &= 1 \\ x_1,\ x_2,\ x_3,\ x_4,\ x_5 &\geq 0 \end{aligned}$$

a) $B = (a_1, a_2)$, $\underline{x} = (1/3, 2/3, 0, 0, 0)$

b) $B = (a_1, a_3)$, $\underline{x} = (-1, 0, 2, 0, 0)$
violates the nonnegativity.

c) $B = (a_1, a_4)$, $\underline{x} = (-1, 0, 0, 2, 0)$
violates the nonnegativity.

d) $B = (a_1, a_5)$, $\underline{x} = (1, 0, 0, 0, 2)$

e) $B = (a_2, a_3)$, $\underline{x} = (0, 1/2, 0, 0, 0)$

f) $B = (a_2, a_4)$, $\underline{x} = (0, 1/2, 0, 0, 0)$

g) $B = (a_2, a_5)$, $\underline{x} = (0, 1, 0, 0, -1)$
violates the nonnegativity.

h) $B = (a_3, a_4)$, violates L.I.

i) $B = (a_3, a_5)$, $\underline{x} = (0, 0, 1, 0, 1)$

j) $B = (a_4, a_5)$, $\underline{x} = (0, 0, 0, 1, 1)$

PROBLEM 2.41

a) $B = (a_1, a_2)$, $x_1 = -\frac{1}{2}$ violates nonnegativity

b) $B = (a_1, a_3)$, $\underline{x} = (4/3, 0, 11/3, 0, 0)$

PROBLEM 2.41 (Continued)

c) $B = (a_1, a_4)$, $x_1 = -6$ violates nonnegativity.

d) $B = (a_1, a_5)$, $\underline{x} = (5, 0, 0, 0, 11)$

e) $B = (a_2, a_3)$, $\underline{x} = (0, 4, 1, 0, 0)$

f) $B = (a_2, a_4)$, $x_4 = -1$ violates nonnegativity.

g) $B = (a_2, a_5)$, $\underline{x} = (0, 5, 0, 0, 1)$

h) $B = (a_3, a_4)$, $\underline{x} = (0, 0, 3, 2, 0)$

i) $B = (a_3, a_5)$, $x_5 = -4$ violates nonnegativity.

j) $B = (a_4, a_5)$, $\underline{x} = (0, 0, 0, 5, 6)$

PROBLEM 2.42

d is a direction if it is nonzero and $A(x + \lambda d) \leq b$ and $x + \lambda d \geq 0$, for all x satisfying $Ax \leq b$, $x \geq 0$ and $\lambda \geq 0$.

This is possible if and only if $Ad \leq 0$ and $d \geq 0$.

$Ax = b$, $x \geq 0$, d is a direction $\Longleftrightarrow$

$d \neq 0$, $d \geq 0$, $Ad = 0$

$Ax \geq b$, $x \geq 0$, d is a direction $\Longleftrightarrow$

$d \neq 0$, $d \geq 0$, $Ad \geq 0$

PROBLEM 2.43

Since $Ax_0 < b$, there is a scalar λ and a nonzero vector y such that: $A(x_0 - \lambda y) < b$ and $A(x_0 + \lambda y) < b$. Thus $x_0 + \lambda y$ and $x_0 - \lambda y$ belong to X. Furthermore,

$$x_0 = \frac{1}{2}(x_0 - \lambda y) + \frac{1}{2}(x_0 + \lambda y)$$

i.e., x_0 can be represented as a convex combination of two distinct points in X. Therefore, x_0 cannot be an extreme point.

PROBLEM 2.44

If X has a direction then obviously X is unbounded in that direction. Now, suppose that X has no directions. In particular it has no extreme directions. By the representation theorem

$$X = \left\{ \sum_{j=1}^{k} \lambda_j x_j : \sum_j \lambda_j = 1, \ \lambda_j \geq 0 \right\},$$

where $x_1, x_2, --, x_k$ are the extreme points of X. Let $x \in X$, we can write

$$\|x\| = \| \sum_{j=1}^{k} \lambda_j x_j \| \leq \sum_{j=1}^{k} \lambda_j \| x_j \| \leq \sum_{j=1}^{k} \| x_j \| = \epsilon .$$

Therefore, X is bounded.

PROBLEM 2.45

The set is bounded. To show this, note that $x_1, x_2 \geq 0$ and $x_1 + x_2 + x_3 \leq 6$. This implies that $x_3 \leq 6$. Since $x_3 \geq 1$ then x_3 lies in the interval $[1, 6]$. Also x_1 and x_2 lie in the interval $[0, 5]$ (Why?). Therefore, X is bounded and hence has no directions.

PROBLEM 2.46

Only if: see appendix.

If: Consider $d = (-y_j^T \; 0 \; 0 \cdots 1 \cdots 0 \; 0)^T$ where $y_j = B^{-1} a_j \leq 0$.

Suppose that $d = \lambda d_1 + \mu d_2$, where d_1 and d_2 are directions of X and $\lambda, \mu > 0$. Note

$$A d_1 = 0, \quad d_1 \geq 0 \qquad \text{let } d_1 = \begin{pmatrix} d_{11} \\ \hdashline d_{12} \end{pmatrix}$$

$$A d_2 = 0, \quad d_2 \geq 0 \qquad \text{let } d_2 = \begin{pmatrix} d_{21} \\ \hdashline d_{22} \end{pmatrix}$$

$$\begin{pmatrix} -y_j \\ \hdashline 0 \\ 0 \\ \vdots \\ 1 \\ \vdots \\ 0 \end{pmatrix} = \lambda \begin{pmatrix} d_{11} \\ \hdashline d_{12} \end{pmatrix} + \mu \begin{pmatrix} d_{21} \\ \hdashline d_{22} \end{pmatrix}$$

Since $d_{12} \geq 0$, $d_{22} \geq 0$, $\lambda > 0$, $\mu > 0$, it follows that d_{12} and d_{22} have zero components

PROBLEM 2.46 (Continued)

except at position j. Moreover, the jth component of each of these vectors is positive (otherwise either d_1 or $d_2 = 0$ which is impossible by definition of a direction). Let the jth component of d_{12} and d_{22} be d_j' and d_j''.

$$\begin{pmatrix} -y_j \\ \hline 0 \\ \vdots \\ 1 \\ \vdots \\ 0 \end{pmatrix} = \lambda \begin{pmatrix} d_{11} \\ \hline 0 \\ \vdots \\ d_j' \\ 0 \\ \vdots \\ 0 \end{pmatrix} + \mu \begin{pmatrix} d_{21} \\ \hline 0 \\ \vdots \\ d_j'' \\ \vdots \\ 0 \end{pmatrix}$$

$$A d_1 = 0 \implies B d_{11} + d_j' a_j = 0$$

$$\implies d_{11} = -B^{-1} a_j d_j' = -d_j' y_j$$

$$\implies \quad d_1 = d_j' \begin{pmatrix} -y_j \\ \hline 0 \\ \vdots \\ 1 \\ \vdots \\ 0 \end{pmatrix}$$

Similarly

$$d_2 = d_j'' \begin{pmatrix} -y_j \\ \hline 0 \\ \vdots \\ 1 \\ \vdots \\ 0 \end{pmatrix}$$

Therefore

$$d = \lambda d_j' d + \mu d_j'' d$$

i.e., d is indeed an extreme direction.

PROBLEM 2.46 (Continued)

$$A = \begin{bmatrix} -1 & 1 & 1 & 0 \\ -1 & 2 & 0 & 1 \end{bmatrix}, \quad b = \begin{bmatrix} 2 \\ 6 \end{bmatrix}$$
$$\quad a_1 \quad a_2 \quad a_3 \quad a_4$$

Let $B = (a_3, a_4) = \begin{bmatrix} 1 & 0 \\ 0 & 1 \end{bmatrix}, \quad B^{-1} = B = I$

$B^{-1}a_1 = a_1 = \begin{bmatrix} -1 \\ -1 \end{bmatrix} \leq 0.$

Therefore, $d^T = (1, 0, 1, 1)$

is an extreme direction.

PROBLEM 2.47

By contradiction, suppose that X has no extreme direction. By the theorem

$$X = \left\{ \sum_{j=1}^{k} \lambda_j x_j : \sum_{j=1}^{k} \lambda_j = 1,\ \lambda_j \geq 0 \quad j = 1, 2, \ldots k \right\}$$

Let $x \in X$. Then $x = \sum_{j=1}^{k} \lambda_j x_j$. By the Schwartz inequality and since $0 \leq \lambda_j \leq 1$ for each j, we have

$$\|x\| = \left\| \sum_{j=1}^{k} \lambda_j x_j \right\| \leq \sum_{j=1}^{k} \lambda_j \|x_j\| \leq \sum_{j=1}^{k} \|x_j\| = \epsilon$$

Therefore $\|x\| \leq \epsilon$ for each $x \in X$, contradicting the assumption that X is unbounded. Therefore X has at least one extreme direction.

PROBLEM 2.48

$$A = \begin{bmatrix} 1 & -1 & 1 & 1 & 0 & 0 \\ 2 & -1 & 2 & 0 & 1 & 0 \\ 3 & -2 & 3 & 0 & 0 & 1 \end{bmatrix}, \quad b = \begin{bmatrix} 10 \\ 40 \\ 50 \end{bmatrix}$$

(columns labelled $a_1, a_2, a_3, a_4, a_5, a_6$)

For finding the extreme points of this set one should try all three-at-a-time combinations of colums of A. As an example let $B = [a_4, a_5, a_6] = I$.

$$B^{-1}b = [10, 40, 50]^T \geq [0,0,0]^T$$

Hence, $(x_1, x_2, x_3, x_4, x_5, x_6) = (0, 0, 0, 10, 40, 50)$ is an extreme point of the region in the six dimensional space {or $(0,0,0)$ is an extreme point of 3-dimensional space (x_1, x_2, x_3)}. For the rest of the extreme points all the possibilities of (a_i, a_j, a_k) $i \neq j \neq k$ should be tried.

For the extreme directions, every time we choose a basis B we should try $B^{-1}a_j$ to see whether $B^{-1}a_j \leq 0$ or not.

Let $B = (a_4, a_5, a_6) = I$

$$B^{-1}a_2 = (-1, -1, -2)^T \leq (0, 0, 0)^T$$

so, $d = (0, 1, 0, 1, 1, 2)^T$ is an extreme direction.

For finding the extreme ray, we need

PROBLEM 2.48 (Continued)

to find a feasible point and an extreme direction. Let x be any feasible point. Then $\{x + \lambda d : \lambda \geq 0\}$ is an extreme ray. Where d is an extreme direction.

Hence

$$(0,0,0,10,40,50) + \lambda(0,1,0,1,1,2) \quad , \lambda \geq 0$$

is an extreme ray.

To find the faces of the polyhedral set, we must check whether the constraints correspond to the faces or not. For example, to check whether the first constraint corresponds to a face, consider the following problem.

$$\min \quad x_4$$

$$\begin{aligned} \text{S.T} \quad & x_1 - x_2 + x_3 + x_4 &&= 10 \\ & 2x_1 - x_2 + 2x_3 \quad + x_5 &&= 40 \\ & 3x_1 - 2x_2 + 3x_3 \quad + x_6 &&= 50 \\ & x_1, x_2, \text{---} , x_6 \geq 0 \end{aligned}$$

If in the optimal solution $x_4 = 0$, then constraint one is a face of the polyhedron.

PROBLEM 2.49

Suppose that x is an extreme point. Let q be any vector which is nonzero and orthogonal to p. Consider the following two points:

$$x_1 = x + q$$
$$x_2 = x - q$$

Note that

$$px_1 = p(x+q) = k + 0 = k$$
$$px_2 = p(x-q) = k - 0 = k$$

So, $x_1 \in X$ and $x_2 \in X$. Furthermore,

$$x = \frac{1}{2}x_1 + \frac{1}{2}x_2$$

Therefore x could not have been an extreme point.

Let d be a direction ($d \neq 0$, $pd = 0$) Again let q be a nonzero vector which is orthogonal to p such that $q \neq d$ and $q \neq -d$. Then $d_1 = d + q$ and $d_2 = d - q$ are directions of X (why?). Furthermore

$$d = \frac{1}{2}d_1 + \frac{1}{2}d_2 \qquad \text{contradiction.}$$

Therefore X has no extreme directions. Note that X is not of the form $\{x : Ax = b, x \geq 0\}$. So, we are not violating the representation theorem.

PROBLEM 2.50

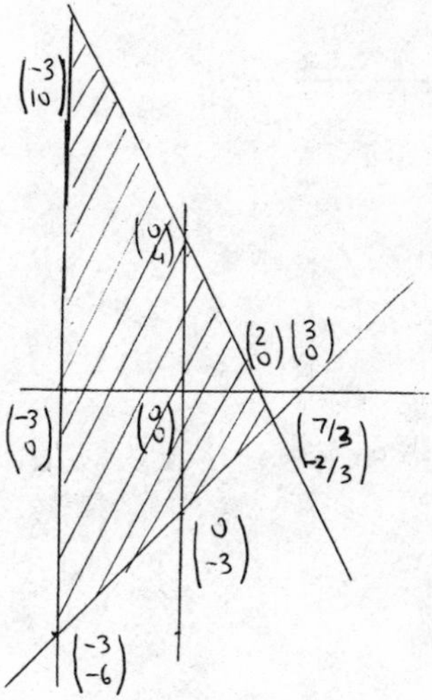

$$\begin{pmatrix}0\\1\end{pmatrix}=\frac{9}{16}\begin{pmatrix}7/3\\-2/3\end{pmatrix}+\frac{4}{16}\begin{pmatrix}-3\\10\end{pmatrix}+\frac{3}{16}\begin{pmatrix}-3\\-6\end{pmatrix}$$

PROBLEM 2.51

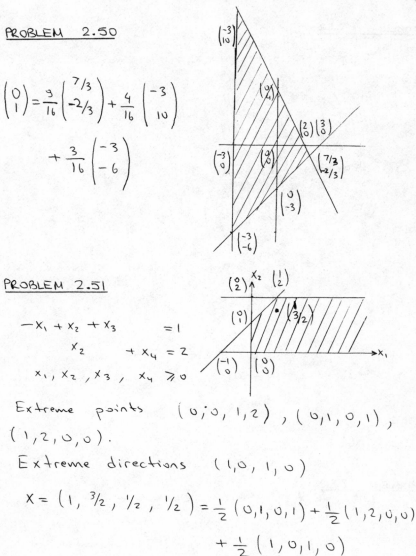

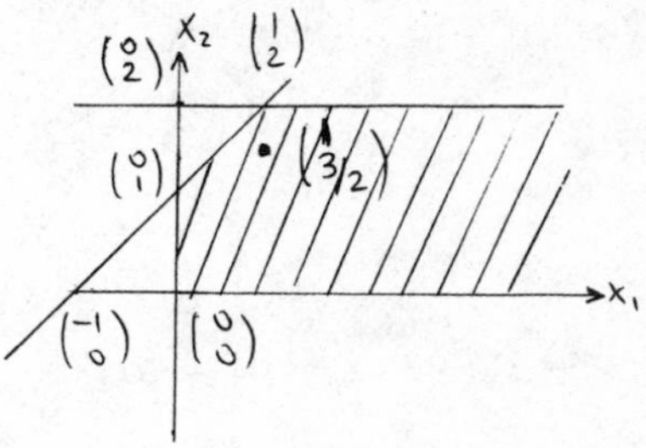

$$\begin{aligned} -x_1 + x_2 + x_3 \quad &= 1 \\ x_2 \quad + x_4 &= 2 \\ x_1, x_2, x_3, x_4 &\geq 0 \end{aligned}$$

Extreme points $(0,0,1,2)$, $(0,1,0,1)$, $(1,2,0,0)$.

Extreme directions $(1,0,1,0)$

$$x = (1, 3/2, 1/2, 1/2) = \frac{1}{2}(0,1,0,1) + \frac{1}{2}(1,2,0,0) + \frac{1}{2}(1,0,1,0)$$

PROBLEM 2.52

$Ax = 0$, $x \geq 0$, $cx > 0$ has no solution

i.e.,

$$\begin{pmatrix} A \\ -A \\ -I \end{pmatrix} x \leq \begin{pmatrix} 0 \\ 0 \\ 0 \end{pmatrix}, \quad cx > 0 \text{ has no solution.}$$

By Farka's Lemma

$$(w_1, w_2, w_3) \begin{pmatrix} A \\ -A \\ -I \end{pmatrix} = c$$

$$w_1, w_2, w_3 \geq 0 \quad \text{has a solution.}$$

i.e.,

$$wA - w_3 = c$$
$$w_3 \geq 0$$
$$w \ \text{U.R.S.}$$

where $w = w_1 - w_2$. In the final form

$$wA \geq 0$$
$$w \ \text{urs}$$

has a solution,

PROBLEM 2.53

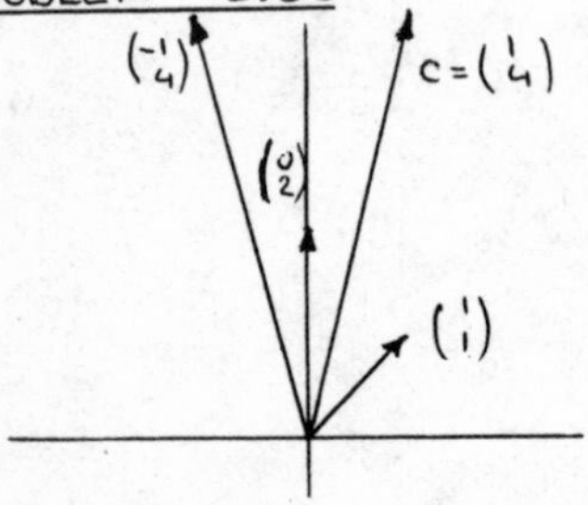

Obviously, from the graph $wA = c$, $w \geq 0$ has a solution. i.e.,

$w = (1, 3/2, 0)$

The system $Ax \leq 0$, $cx > 0$ has no solution.

PROBLEM 2.54

Suppose that $x_1^*, x_2^*, \ldots, x_p^* > 0$
$x_{p+1}^*, \ldots, x_n^* = 0$

The system $Ax = 0$, $-cx > 0$, $x_{p+1}, \ldots, x_n \geq 0$ has no solution, otherwise, $x^* + \lambda x$ for $\lambda > 0$ and sufficiently small would be feasible with objective less than cx^*, violating optimality of x^*. Therefore, the system

$$\begin{bmatrix} A \\ -A \\ \hline 0 \,\vdots\, -I_{n-p} \end{bmatrix} x \leq 0 \quad , \quad -cx > 0$$

has no solution. By farka's lemma the following system has a solution.

$$w_1 A - w_2 A - (0, w_3) = -c$$
$$w_1, w_2, w_3 \geq 0$$

or

$$wA = c - (0, w_3)$$
$$w_3 \geq 0.$$

where $w = w_2 - w_1$, or

$$wA \leq c \quad , \quad w \text{ unrestricted}$$

has a solution.

Furthermore,

$$(wA - c) = -(0, w_3)$$

$$(wA - c)x^* = -(0, w_3)x^*$$

Since the last $n-p$ components of x^* are zero, then obviously $(0, w_3)x^* = 0$. Therefore

$$(wA - c)x^* = 0 \quad , \quad \text{and}$$
$$wA \leq c \quad .$$

CHAPTER 3 THE SIMPLEX METHOD

PROBLEM 3.1

Consider $x_0 - \lambda c$ for $\lambda > 0$ and sufficiently small. $A(x_0 - \lambda c) < b$ and $x_0 - \lambda c > 0$. Therefore $x_0 - \lambda c$ is feasible for $\lambda > 0$ and sufficiently small. But,

$$c(x_0 - \lambda c) = cx_0 - \lambda \|c\|^2 < cx_0$$

so, x_0 cannot be optimal.

PROBLEM 3.2

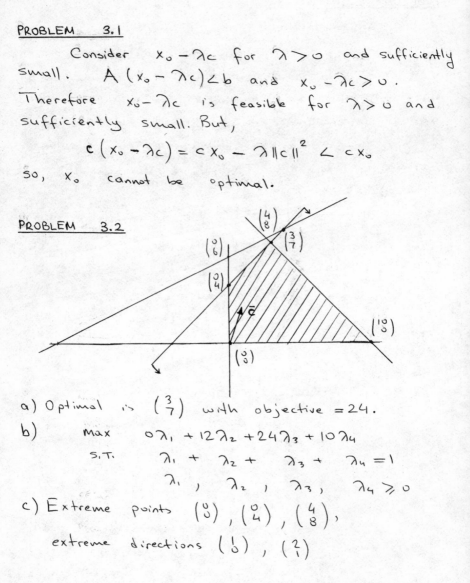

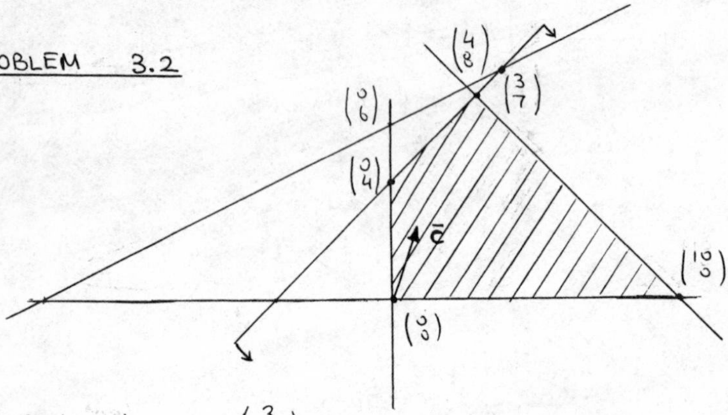

a) Optimal is $\binom{3}{7}$ with objective $= 24$.

b)
$$\begin{aligned} \text{Max} \quad & 0\lambda_1 + 12\lambda_2 + 24\lambda_3 + 10\lambda_4 \\ \text{S.T.} \quad & \lambda_1 + \lambda_2 + \lambda_3 + \lambda_4 = 1 \\ & \lambda_1, \lambda_2, \lambda_3, \lambda_4 \geq 0 \end{aligned}$$

c) Extreme points $\binom{0}{0}$, $\binom{0}{4}$, $\binom{4}{8}$,

extreme directions $\binom{1}{0}$, $\binom{2}{1}$

PROBLEM 3.2 (Continued)

$$\max \quad 0\lambda_1 + 12\lambda_2 + 28\lambda_3 + \mu_1 + 5\mu_2$$
$$\text{s.t.} \quad \lambda_1 + \lambda_2 + \lambda_3 = 1$$
$$\lambda_1, \lambda_2, \lambda_3, \mu_1, \mu_2 \geq 0$$

Optimal is unbounded; i.e., $\lambda_1 = 1$, $\lambda_2 = \lambda_3 = 0$, $\mu_2 = 0$, μ_1 arbitrarily large.

d) No, as the size of the problem gets larger, the number of extreme points become immense.

PROBLEM 3.3

Suppose that rank$(A_1) = n$, $A_1 x_0 = b_1$, $A_2 x_0 \geq b_2$. Let's assume that x_0 is not an extreme point. Let x_1 an x_2 be two feasible points such that $x_0 = \lambda x_1 + (1-\lambda) x_2$ with $0 < \lambda < 1$. Then

$$A_1 x_0 = \lambda A_1 x_1 + (1-\lambda) A_1 x_2$$

Since $A_1 x_1 \geq b_1$, $A_1 x_2 \geq b_1$, $A_1 x_0 = b_1$, then

$$A_1 x_1 = A_1 x_2 = b_1 .$$

Since A_1 is invertible then

$$x_0 = x_1 = x_2 = A_1^{-1} b$$

Therefore, x_0 is an extreme point.

Conversely, suppose that x_0 is an extreme point. Suppose that

PROBLEM 3.3 (Continued)

$$a^i x_0 = b_i \quad \text{for} \quad i = 1, 2, --, k$$
$$a^i x_0 > b_i \quad \text{for} \quad i = k+1, ---, n$$

By contradiction suppose that $k < n$. Then there exists a nonzero vector $y \in E^n$ such that $a^i y = 0$ for $i = 1, 2, --, k$ (why?). Consider $x_0 + \lambda y$ and $x_0 - \lambda y$ for $\lambda > 0$ and sufficiently small.

$$a^i(x_0 + \lambda y) = a^i x_0 + \lambda a^i y = b_i + 0 = b_i \quad , \quad i = 1, .., k.$$

Since $a^i x_0 > b_i$, then $a^i(x_0 + \lambda y) > b_i$, for $\lambda > 0$ and sufficiently small for $i = k+1, ---, n$. Therefore, $x_0 + \lambda y$ is feasible. Similarly $x_0 - \lambda y$ is feasible as well. Furthermore,

$$x_0 = \frac{1}{2}(x_0 + \lambda y) + \frac{1}{2}(x_0 - \lambda y)$$

contradicting the assumption that x_0 is an extreme point. Therefore $k < n$. Thus, the construction of the problem holds (why?).

PROBLEM 3.4

Note by the first constraint and nonnegativity of the variables that the feasible region is bounded.

In order to find the optimal solution,

PROBLEM 3.4 (Continued)

we should try all possible combinations of (a_i, a_j), $i \neq j$ for a potential basis B. The optimal solution can be obtained by letting

$$B = (a_1, a_3) = \begin{bmatrix} 1 & 2 \\ 1 & -1 \end{bmatrix}, \quad B^{-1} = \begin{bmatrix} 1/3 & 2/3 \\ 1/3 & -1/3 \end{bmatrix}.$$

Hence

$$\begin{pmatrix} x_1 \\ x_3 \end{pmatrix} = \begin{bmatrix} \frac{1}{3} & \frac{2}{3} \\ \frac{1}{3} & -\frac{1}{3} \end{bmatrix} \begin{bmatrix} 6 \\ 4 \end{bmatrix} = \begin{bmatrix} 14/3 \\ 2/3 \end{bmatrix}, \quad \begin{pmatrix} x_2 \\ x_4 \\ x_5 \end{pmatrix} = \begin{pmatrix} 0 \\ 0 \\ 0 \end{pmatrix}$$

i.e., $(x_1, x_2, x_3) = (\frac{14}{3}, 0, \frac{2}{3})$, $z = \frac{26}{3}$

is optimal.

If we delete the first constraint, the feasible set becomes unbounded. Therefore, the above approach will be invalid. One has to deal with extreme directions as well as extreme points. In this specific problem, the solution is unbounded.

PROBLEM 3.5

$x_1 = 300$, $x_j = 0$ $j \neq 1$, $z = 300$

$x_2 = 100$, $x_j = 0$ $j \neq 2$, $z = 200$

$x_3 = 200$, $x_j = 0$ $j \neq 3$, $z = 800$

$x_4 = 300$, $x_j = 0$ $j \neq 4$, $z = 0$

$x_5 = 200$, $x_j = 0$ $j \neq 5$, $z = 1000$

$x_6 = 150$, $x_j = 0$ $j \neq 6$, $z = 150$

PROBLEM 3.5 (Continued)

$x_j = 0 \quad , \quad j = 1, 2, \dots, 6 \qquad z = 0$

So, the optimal solution $z = 1000$ is achieved at the extreme point $(0, 0, 0, 0, 200, 0)$.

PROBLEM 3.6

a)

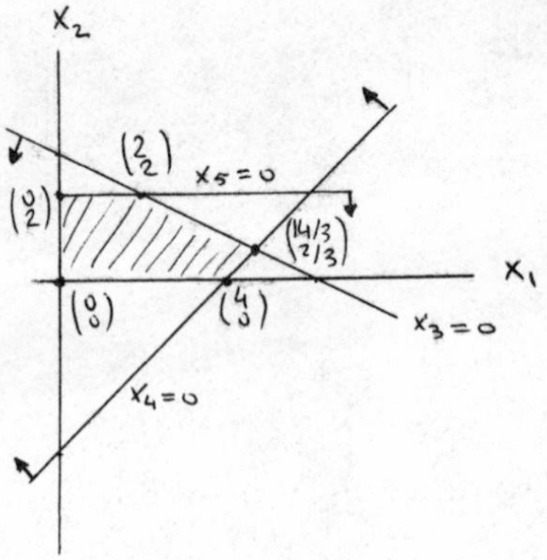

b) Let the slack variables for the three constraints be x_3, x_4, x_5 respectively. Following are the extreme points and the corresponding basic and nonbasic variables:

$\binom{0}{0}$: x_3, x_4, x_5 basics ,

$\binom{0}{2}$: x_2, x_3, x_4 basics,

$\binom{2}{2}$: x_1, x_2, x_4 basics,

$\binom{14/3}{2/3}$: x_1, x_2, x_5 basics,

$\binom{4}{0}$: x_1, x_3, x_5 basics.

c) As one moves from $\binom{4}{0}$ to $\binom{14/3}{2/3}$, x_2 enters the basis and x_3 leaves the basis.

PROBLEM 3.7

Obviously, no extreme points exists.

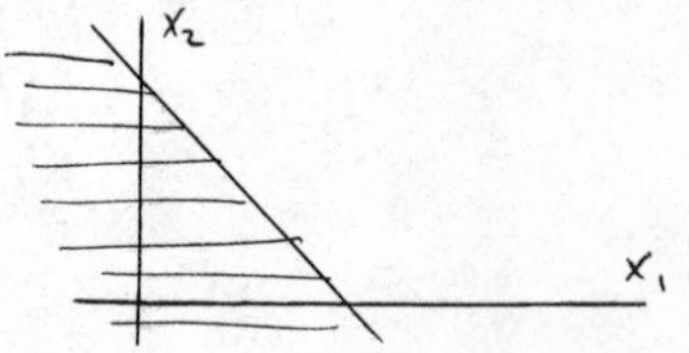

PROBLEM 3.7 (Continued)

To prove mathematically, let $\begin{pmatrix} x_1 \\ x_2 \end{pmatrix}$ be any feasible point such that $x_1 + x_2 \leq 1$.
Consider $\begin{pmatrix} x_1+1 \\ x_2-1 \end{pmatrix}$ and $\begin{pmatrix} x_1-1 \\ x_2+1 \end{pmatrix}$. Obviously, they are also feasible and distinct (Why?)
Furthermore

$$\begin{pmatrix} x_1 \\ x_2 \end{pmatrix} = \frac{1}{2}\begin{pmatrix} x_1+1 \\ x_2-1 \end{pmatrix} + \frac{1}{2}\begin{pmatrix} x_1-1 \\ x_2-1 \end{pmatrix}.$$

Therefore $\begin{pmatrix} x_1 \\ x_2 \end{pmatrix}$ could not have been an extreme point.

Now, consider the following set where x_1 is replaced by $x_1^+ - x_1^-$ and x_2 by $x_2^+ - x_2^-$.

$$\{(x_1^+, x_1^-, x_2^+, x_2^-) : x_1^+ - x_1^- + x_2^+ - x_2^- \leq 1, \; x_1^+, x_2^+, x_1^-, x_2^- \geq 0\}$$

Obviously, $(1, 0, 0, 0)$ is an extreme point of this new set.

PROBLEM 3.8

See discussion on pages 90, 91.

PROBLEM 3.9

Let x_3 and x_4 be the slack variables. $x = (1/2, 1/2, 1, 5/2)$ is obviously not basic because the number of positive variables is 4 whereas the number of constraints is 2. To construct a basic feasible solution starting with the given solution x, we note that

PROBLEM 3.9 (Continued)

a_1, a_2, a_3 and a_4 are linearly dependent. In particular $\gamma_1 a_1 + \gamma_2 a_2 + \gamma_3 a_3 + \gamma_4 a_4 = 0$ where $\gamma_1 = 1$, $\gamma_2 = -1$, $\gamma_3 = 0$ and $\gamma_4 = 3$. Hence, we have

$$\lambda = \min\left[\frac{1/2}{1}, \frac{5/2}{3}\right] = \frac{1}{2}$$

Thus, we get the new feasible solution

$$x'_j = x_j - \lambda\gamma_j \qquad j = 1, 2, 3, 4$$

i.e., $x'_1 = 1/2 - 1/2 = 0$

$x'_2 = 1/2 + 1/2 = 1$

$x'_3 = 1 - 0 = 1$

$x'_4 = 5/2 - 3/2 = 1$

So, we get the new feasible point $(0,1,1,1)$ with one less number of positive numbers. This process can be repeated until we have two nonzero variables.

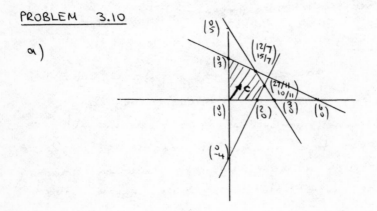

PROBLEM 3.10

a)

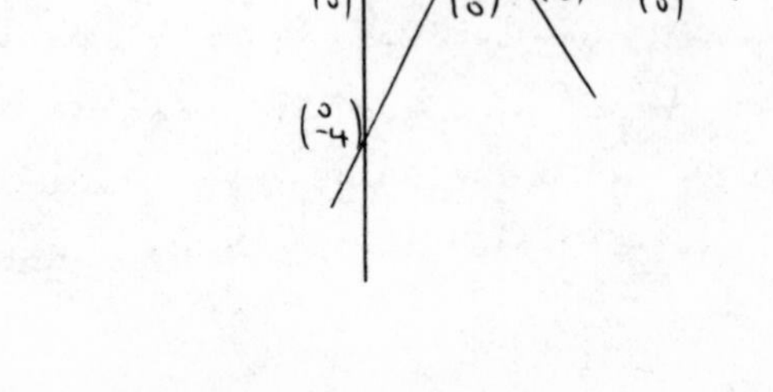

PROBLEM 3.10 (Continued)

b)

	z	x_1	x_2	x_3	x_4	x_5	RHS
	1	-5	-4	0	0	0	0
	0	1	(2)	1	0	0	6
	0	2	-1	0	1	0	4
	0	5	3	0	0	1	15

	z	x_1	x_2	x_3	x_4	x_5	RHS
z	1	-3	0	2	0	0	12
x_2	0	1/2	1	1/2	0	0	3
x_4	0	5/2	0	1/2	1	0	7
x_5	0	(7/2)	0	-3/2	0	1	6

	z	x_1	x_2	x_3	x_4	x_5	RHS
z	1	0	0	5/7	0	6/7	120/7
x_2	0	0	1	5/7	0	-1/7	15/7
x_4	0	0	0	11/7	1	-5/7	19/7
x_5	0	1	0	-3/7	0	2/7	12/7

PROBLEM 3.11

	z	x_1	x_2	x_3	x_4	RHS
z	1	-3	-2	0	0	0
x_3	0	(2)	-3	1	0	3
x_4	0	-1	1	0	1	5

$$B = \begin{bmatrix} 1 & 0 \\ 0 & 1 \end{bmatrix} \ (a_3 \ a_4), \quad B^{-1} = \begin{bmatrix} 1 & 0 \\ 0 & 1 \end{bmatrix}$$

	z	x_1	x_2	x_3	x_4	RHS
z	1	0	-13/2	3/2	0	9/2
x_1	0	1	-3/2	1/2	0	3/2
x_4	0	0	-1/2	1/2	1	13/2

$$B = \begin{bmatrix} 2 & 0 \\ -1 & 1 \end{bmatrix} \ (a_1 \ a_4), \quad B^{-1} = \begin{bmatrix} 1/2 & 0 \\ 1/2 & 1 \end{bmatrix}$$

Optimal is unbounded (note column of x_2).

PROBLEM 3.12

$$\begin{aligned} \max \quad & -x_1 + 2x_2 \\ \text{s.t.} \quad & 3x_1 + 4x_2 = 12 \\ & 2x_1 - x_2 + x_3 = 12 \\ & x_1, x_2, x_3 \geq 0 \end{aligned}$$

PROBLEM 3.12 (Continued)

$$B = \begin{bmatrix} 3 & 0 \\ 2 & 1 \end{bmatrix}, \quad B^{-1} = \begin{bmatrix} 1/3 & 0 \\ -2/3 & 1 \end{bmatrix}, \quad B^{-1}a_2 = \begin{bmatrix} 4/3 \\ -11/3 \end{bmatrix}$$

$$z_2 - c_2 = c_B y_2 - c_2 = (-1, 0)\begin{pmatrix} 4/3 \\ -11/3 \end{pmatrix} - 2 = -\frac{10}{3}$$

	z	x_1	x_2	x_3	RHS
z	1	0	−10/3	0	−4
x_1	0	1	(4/3)	0	4
x_3	0	0	−11/3	1	4

	z	x_1	x_2	x_3	RHS
z	1	5/2	0	0	6
x_2	0	3/4	1	0	3
x_3	0	11/4	0	1	15

PROBLEM 3.13

a)

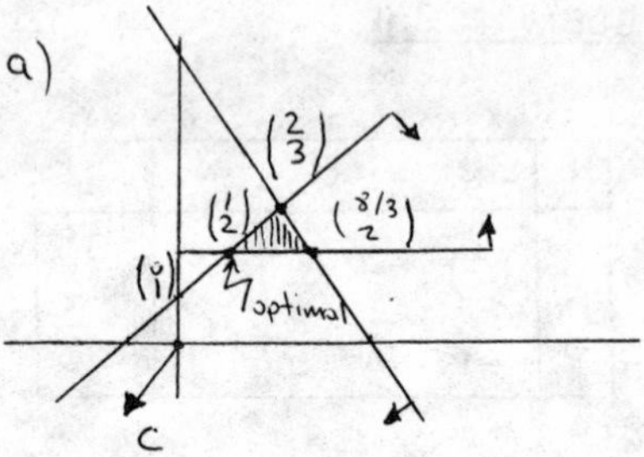

b) max $-3x_1 - 2x_2$

$$\begin{aligned} \text{s.t.} \quad -x_1 + x_2 + x_3 &= 1 \\ 6x_1 + 4x_2 + x_4 &= 24 \\ x_2 - x_5 &= 2 \\ x_1, x_2, \ldots, x_5 &\geq 0 \end{aligned}$$

Basis consists of x_1, x_2 and x_5, where x_5 is the slack variable for $x_2 \geq 2$.

$$B = \begin{bmatrix} -1 & 1 & 0 \\ 6 & 4 & 0 \\ 0 & 1 & -1 \end{bmatrix} \ (\text{columns } a_1, a_2, a_5), \quad B^{-1} = \begin{bmatrix} -0.4 & 0.1 & 0 \\ 0.6 & 0.1 & 0 \\ 0.6 & 0.1 & -1 \end{bmatrix}$$

$$B^{-1}b = \begin{bmatrix} 2 \\ 3 \\ 1 \end{bmatrix}$$

$c_B = (-3, -2, 0)$

	z	x_1	x_2	x_3	x_4	x_5	RHS
z	1	0	0	0	−.5	0	−12
x_1	0	1	0	−.4	.1	0	2
x_2	0	0	1	.6	.1	0	3
x_5	0	0	0	.6	.1	1	1

PROBLEM 3.13 (Continued)

c)

	z	x_1	x_2	x_3	x_4	x_5	RHS
z	1	0	0	3	0	5	−7
x_1	0	1	0	−1	0	−1	1
x_2	0	0	1	0	0	−1	2
x_4	0	0	0	6	1	10	10

i) Basic vectors: a_1, a_2, a_4.

ii) $x_1 = 1$, $x_2 = 2$, $x_3 = x_5 = 0$, $x_4 = 10$.

iii) Yes.

d)

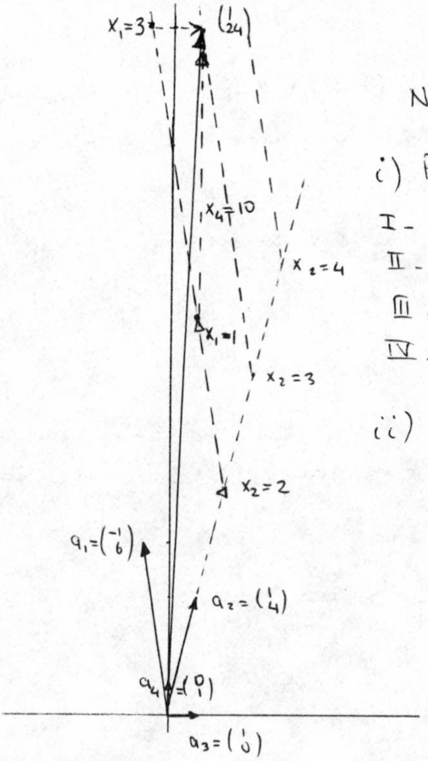

Note that $x_2 \geq 0$.

i) Possible bases:

I – (a_1, a_2, a_4)

II – (a_1, a_2, a_5)

III – (a_1, a_2, a_3)

IV – (a_2, a_3, a_4)

ii) Only I, II and III are the feasible bases.

e)

Feasible point I corresponds to $\binom{8/3}{2}$ in (a)

Feasible point II corresponds to $\binom{2}{3}$ in (a)

Feasible point III corresponds to $\binom{1}{2}$ in (a).

PROBLEM 3.14

Let x' and x'' be the optimal solution of the first and the second problem respectively. Let $0 < \lambda < 1$,

$$A(\lambda x' + (1-\lambda)x'') = \lambda A x' + (1-\lambda) A x''$$
$$= \lambda b + (1-\lambda) b = b$$

Therefore, $\lambda x' + (1-\lambda)x''$ is a feasible point. The nth component of this solution is

$$x_n = \lambda x_n' + (1-\lambda) x_n''$$

i.e., x_n is any number in the interval $[x_n', x_n'']$.

PROBLEM 3.16

Consider the kth column and the r.h.s. of the simplex tableau. $\bar{b}_i >$ for $i = 1, \ldots, m$.

x_k	RHS
y_{1k}	$\bar{b}_1$
y_{2k}	$\bar{b}_2$
$\vdots$	$\vdots$
y_{rk}	$\bar{b}_r$
$\vdots$	$\vdots$
y_{mk}	$\bar{b}_m$

Suppose that $y_{ik} > 0$, then

$$\frac{\bar{b}_i}{y_{ik}} > \frac{\bar{b}_r}{y_{rk}}$$

so that the minimum ratio test occurs at a unique index. The values of the new variables will be: $\frac{\bar{b}_r}{y_{rk}} > 0$, and $\bar{b}_i - \frac{y_{ik}}{y_{rk}} \bar{b}_r$.

If $y_{ik} \le 0$, then $\bar{b}_i - \frac{y_{ik}}{y_{rk}} \bar{b}_r \geq \bar{b}_i > 0$

If $y_{ik} > 0$, then by assumption $\bar{b}_i - \frac{y_{ik}}{y_{rk}} \bar{b}_r > 0$.

Hence the new solution is nondegenerate.

PROBLEM 3.17

	z	x_1	x_2	x_3	x_4	x_5	x_6	RHS
z	1	0	3	0	1	0	0	12
x_3	0	1	1	1	1	0	0	12
x_5	0	3	2	0	1	1	0	18
x_6	0	−1	3	0	0	0	1	9

Optimal Tableau

PROBLEM 3.18

$$B = \begin{bmatrix} 1 & 2 & -1 \\ 2 & 3 & 1 \\ 1 & 0 & 1 \end{bmatrix}, \quad B^{-1} = \begin{bmatrix} 3/4 & -1/2 & 5/4 \\ -1/4 & 1/2 & -3/4 \\ -3/4 & 1/2 & -1/4 \end{bmatrix}$$

$$B^{-1}a_3 = \begin{bmatrix} 13/4 \\ -9/4 \\ -15/4 \end{bmatrix}, \quad B^{-1}b = \begin{bmatrix} 14/4 \\ 6/4 \\ 2/4 \end{bmatrix}$$

Solution is feasible with $(x_1, x_2, x_3, x_4, x_5, x_6, x_7) = (\frac{14}{4}, \frac{6}{4}, 0, \frac{1}{2}, 0, 0, 0)$.

$$w = c_B B^{-1} = (2, 1, 5) B^{-1} = \left(-\frac{10}{4}, \frac{8}{4}, \frac{2}{4}\right)$$

$$z_3 - c_3 = wa_3 - c_3 = \left(\frac{-10}{4}, \frac{8}{4}, \frac{1}{2}\right)\begin{pmatrix} 4 \\ -1 \\ 1 \end{pmatrix} + 3 = -\frac{34}{4}$$

Therefore, the solution is not optimal.

	z	x_1	x_2	x_3	x_4	x_5	x_6	x_7	RHS
z	1	10/3	0	22/3	0	0	25/12	14/3	68/3
x_5	0	4/3	0	13/3	0	1	−2/3	5/3	14/3
x_2	0	1/3	1	−2/3	0	0	1/3	−1/3	8/3
x_4	0	1	0	1	1	0	0	1	4

Optimal tableau

PROBLEM 3.19

After replacing x_i by $x_i^+ - x_i^-$ for $i=1,2$ and adding the slack variables, we have:

$$\min \quad 3x_1^+ - 3x_1^- - x_2^+ + x_2^-$$

$$\begin{aligned} \text{S.T.} \quad -x_1^+ + x_1^- + 3x_2^+ - 3x_2^- + x_3 \qquad\qquad &= 3 \\ -2x_1^+ + 2x_1^- - 3x_2^+ + 3x_2^- \qquad + x_4 \qquad &= 6 \\ 2x_1^+ - 2x_1^- + x_2^+ - x_2^- \qquad\qquad + x_5 \quad &= 8 \\ 4x_1^+ - 4x_1^- - x_2^+ + x_2^- \qquad\qquad\qquad + x_6 &= 16 \end{aligned}$$

The optimal simplex tableau will be

	z	x_1^+	x_1^-	x_2^+	x_2^-	x_3	x_4	x_5	x_6	RHS
z	1	0	0	0	0	$-11/9$	$-8/9$	0	0	-9
x_1^-	0	-1	1	0	0	$1/3$	$1/3$	0	0	3
x_2^-	0	0	0	-1	1	$-2/9$	$1/9$	0	0	0
x_5	0	0	0	0	0	$4/9$	$7/9$	1	0	14
x_6	0	0	0	0	0	$14/9$	$11/9$	0	1	28

Therefore $x_1 = x_1^+ - x_1^- = 0-3 = -3$, $x_2 = x_2^+ - x_2^- = 0-0 = 0$ and $z = -9$.

PROBLEM 3.20

Let x_1, x_2, x_3 be the contents of corn, lime, and fish meal respectively in a pound of cattle feed.

$$\min \quad 0.1x_1 + 0.08x_2 + 0.12x_3$$

$$\begin{aligned} \text{S.T.} \quad 18 \le 25x_1 + 15x_2 + 25x_3 &\le 22 \\ 20 \le 15x_1 + 30x_2 + 20x_3 & \\ 6 \le 5x_1 + 12x_2 + 8x_3 &\le 12 \\ x_1 + x_2 + x_3 &= 1 \\ x_1, \quad x_2, \quad x_3 &\ge 0 \end{aligned}$$

PROBLEM 3.20 (Continued)

	x_1	x_2	x_3	x_4	x_5	x_6	x_7	
min	0.1	0.08	0.12					
s.T	25	15	25	1				= 22
	25	15	25		−1			= 18
	15	30	20			−1		= 20
	~~5~~	~~12~~	~~8~~	Redundant				~~= 12~~
	5	12	8				−1	= 6
	1	1	1					= 1

Consider the basis consisting of x_2, x_3, x_5, x_6, x_7.

$$B = \begin{bmatrix} -I & R \\ 0 & \hat{B} \end{bmatrix}, \quad B^{-1} = \begin{bmatrix} -I & R\hat{B}^{-1} \\ 0 & \hat{B}^{-1} \end{bmatrix}$$

If we have $B = (a_5, a_6, a_7, a_2, a_3)$, then above observation is true. The starting tableau will be

	z	x_5	x_6	x_7	x_2	x_3	x_1	x_4	RHS
z	-1	0	0	0	0	0	.02	.04	0.108
x_5	0	1	0	0	0	0	0	1	4
x_6	0	0	1	0	0	0	5	−1	3
x_7	0	0	0	1	0	0	3	−.4	3.2
x_2	0	0	0	0	1	0	0	−.1	0.3
x_3	0	0	0	0	0	1	1	.1	0.7

The optimal tableau will look like

	z	x_5	x_6	x_7	x_2	x_3	x_1	x_4	RHS
z	1	−.038	0	0	0	−.02	0	0	.086
x_4	0	1	0	0	0	0	0	1	4
x_6	0	1.5	1	0	0	0	0	0	5.5
x_7	0	.7	0	1	0	0	0	0	3.9
x_2	0	.1	0	0	1	0	0	0	0.7
x_1	0	−.1	0	0	0	1	1	0	0.3

PROBLEM 3.20 (Continued)

In the optimal solution, every pound of the cattle feed will consist of 0.7 lbs. of Lime, and 0.3 lb. of corn. The cost per lb. of cattle feed will be 8.6 cents.

PROBLEM 3.21

$$\begin{aligned}
\max \quad & 2x_1 + 4x_2 + 2.5x_3 \\
\text{S.T.} \quad & 3x_1 + 4x_2 + 2x_3 \le 600 \\
& 2x_1 + x_2 + 2x_3 \le 400 \\
& x_1 + 3x_2 + 3x_3 \le 300 \\
& x_1, \; x_2, \; x_3 \ge 0
\end{aligned}$$

	Z	x_1	x_2	x_3	x_4	x_5	x_6	RHS
Z	1	0	0	0.7	2/5	0	4/5	480
x_1	0	1	0	−6/5	3/5	0	−4/5	120
x_5	0	0	0	3	−1	1	1	100
x_2	0	0	1	7/5	−1/5	0	3/5	60

Optimal tableau

PROBLEM 3.22

$$\begin{aligned}
\max \quad & \min(x_2, x_3) \\
\text{S.T.} \quad & 30x_1 + 4000x_2 \le 150{,}000 \\
& 40x_1 + 6000x_2 + 6000x_3 \le 100{,}000 \\
& 0.5x_1 + 150x_2 + 150x_3 \le 600 \\
600 \le \; & x_1 \le 800 \\
& x_1, \; x_2, \; x_3 \ge 0
\end{aligned}$$

PROBLEM 3.22 (Continued)

Obviously, at optimality $x_1 = 600$ (why?). So, x_1 would be totally eliminated from the problem. Denote $\min(x_2, x_3)$ by z.

$$\begin{aligned}
\max\ & z \\
\text{S.T.}\ & z \le x_2 \\
& z \le x_3 \\
& 4000 x_2 \le 150{,}000 - 18{,}000 = 132{,}000 \text{ or} \\
& x_2 \le 33 \quad \text{redundant} \\
& 6000 x_2 + 6000 x_3 \le 100{,}000 - 24{,}000 = 76{,}000 \text{ or} \\
& x_2 + x_3 \le 28/3 \quad \text{redundant} \\
& 150 x_2 + 150 x_3 \le 600 - 300 = 300 \text{ or} \\
& x_2 + x_3 \le 2 \\
& x_2, x_3 \ge 0
\end{aligned}$$

Hence, the problem simply reduces to

$$\begin{aligned}
\max\ & z \\
\text{S.T.}\ & z \le x_2 \\
& z \le x_3 \\
& x_2 + x_3 \le 2 \\
& x_2, x_3 \ge 0
\end{aligned}$$

Obviously, the optimal solution is $x_2 = x_3 = 1$ (why?), with $z = 1$, the optimal objective for $z = 36/x_2x_3$ is 36.

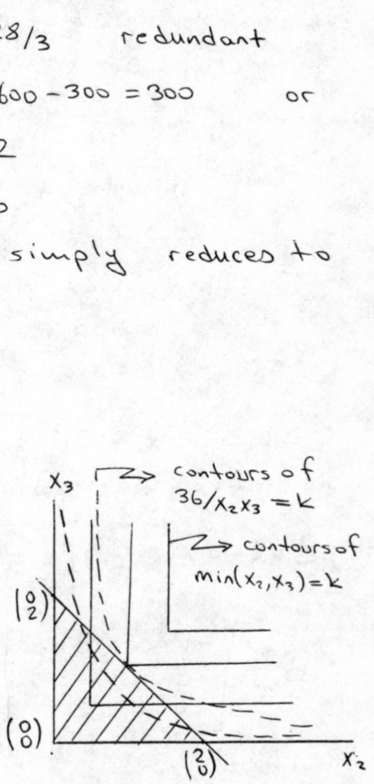

PROBLEM 3.22 (continued)

As we see from the graph, the approximation used in this problem is exact. The optimal is thus $x_1 = 600$, $x_2 = x_3 = 1$ and obj $= 36$.

PROBLEM 3.23

Let x_1 : barrels of light crude

x_2 : barrels of heavy crude.

$$\begin{array}{lllll} \min & 11x_1 & + 9x_2 & & \\ \text{S.T.} & 0.4x_1 & + 0.32x_2 & \geq 1 \\ & 0.2x_1 & + 0.4x_2 & \geq 0.4 \\ & 0.35x_1 & + 0.2x_2 & \geq 0.25 \\ & x_1, & x_2 & \geq 0 \end{array}$$

or

$$\begin{array}{llllllll} \min & 11x_1 & + & 9x_2 & & & & \\ \text{S.T.} & 0.4x_1 & + & 0.32x_2 & - x_3 & & & = 1 \\ & 0.2x_1 & + & 0.4x_2 & & - x_4 & & = 0.4 \\ & 0.35x_1 & + & 0.2x_2 & & & - x_5 & = 0.25 \\ & x_1, & & x_2, & x_3, & x_4, & x_5 & \geq 0 \end{array}$$

$x_1 = 2.5$, $x_4 = 0.1$, $x_5 = 0.625$ gives a starting basic feasible solution (why?). Therefore,

$$B = (a_4, a_5, a_1) = \begin{bmatrix} -1 & 0 & 0.2 \\ 0 & -1 & 0.35 \\ 0 & 0 & 0.4 \end{bmatrix} \quad \text{and}$$

$$B^{-1} = \begin{bmatrix} -1 & 0 & 0.5 \\ 0 & -1 & 0.875 \\ 0 & 0 & 2.5 \end{bmatrix}, \quad B^{-1}a_2 = y_2 = \begin{bmatrix} -0.24 \\ 0.08 \\ 0.8 \end{bmatrix}$$

PROBLEM 3.23 (Continued)

$$B^{-1}a_3 = y_3 = [-.5, -.875, -2.5]^T$$

$$z_2 - c_2 = c_B y_2 - c_2 = (0, 0, 11)(-.24, 0.08, 0.8)^T - 9 = -.2$$

$$z_3 - c_3 = c_B y_3 - c_3 = (0, 0, 11)(-.5, -.875, -2.5)^T - 0 = -27.5$$

The optimal solution is already at hand.

$$x_B = B^{-1}b = (.1, .625, 2.5)^T$$

with cost = 27.5. Hence if we write the optimal solution

$x_1 = 2.5$, $x_2 = 0$ with cost = 27.5 million dollars.

PROBLEM 3.24

The optimal solution has

$x_1 = 155$ cans of cheap-mix

$x_2 = 262$ cans of party-mix

$x_3 = 47.3$ cans of deluxe-mix

with profit = 489.2 dollars.

PROBLEM 3.25

Suppose it is known that x_k will be positive in any optimal solution. Then x_k will be basic in any optimal solution and we don't have to worry about $x_k \geq 0$. Regardless of $z_k - c_k$ perform one pivot to bring x_k into the basis. The system of equations will become

PROBLEM 3.25 (Continued)

$$
\begin{array}{l}
z + (z_1 - c_1)x_1 + \cdots + 0x_k + \cdots + (z_n - c_n)x_n = z_0 \\
\quad a_{11}x_1 + \cdots + 0x_k + \cdots + a_{1n}x_n = \bar{b}_1 \\
\quad \vdots \\
\quad a_{r1}x_1 + \cdots + x_k + \cdots + a_{rn}x_n = \bar{b}_r \\
\quad \vdots \\
\quad a_{m1}x_1 + \cdots + 0x_k + \cdots + a_{mn}x_n = \bar{b}_m
\end{array}
$$

In particular, equation r is

$$\sum_{j \neq k} a_{rj}x_j + x_k = \bar{b}_r$$

or

$$\sum_{j \neq k} a_{rj}x_j \leq \bar{b}_r \iff x_k \geq 0$$

Thus, if we drop equation r from the system, and thereby eliminate variable x_k we will not change the optimal solution since x_k is known to be positive in any optimal solution.

As an example consider

$$
\begin{array}{ll}
\text{Max} & 3x_1 + 2x_2 + x_3 - x_4 \\
\text{s.t.} & 8x_1 + 4x_2 + 2x_3 - 25x_4 \leq 0 \\
 & 2x_1 + 2x_2 + x_3 + 2x_4 \leq 15 \\
 & x_1, x_2, x_3, x_4 \geq 0
\end{array}
$$

Clearly, from constraint 1 and the cost coefficients, x_4 will be positive in any optimal solution (x_4 may represent the capacity of a vehicle, pipeline, etc.). Pivoting on x_4 we get:

PROBLEM 3.25 (Continued)

	z	x_1	x_2	x_3	x_4	x_5	x_6	RHS
z	1	-3	-2	-1	1	0	0	0
x_5	0	8	4	2	-25	1	0	0
x_6	0	2	2	1	(2)	0	1	15

	z	x_1	x_2	x_3	x_4	x_5	x_6	RHS
z	1	-4	-3	-3/2	0	0	-1/2	-15/2
x_5	0	33	29	29/2	0	1	25/2	375/2
~~x_4~~	~~0~~	~~1~~	~~1~~	~~1/2~~	~~1~~	~~0~~	~~1/2~~	~~15/2~~

Crossing out the x_4 row and column we get the following series of tableaus:

	z	x_1	x_2	x_3	x_5	x_6	RHS
z	1	-4	-3	-3/2	0	-1/2	$-\frac{15}{2}$
x_5	0	(33)	29	$\frac{29}{2}$	1	$\frac{25}{2}$	$\frac{375}{2}$

	z	x_1	x_2	x_3	x_5	x_6	RHS
z	1	0	$\frac{17}{33}$	$\frac{17}{66}$	$\frac{4}{33}$	$\frac{67}{66}$	$\frac{335}{22}$
x_1	0	1	$\frac{29}{33}$	$\frac{29}{66}$	$\frac{1}{33}$	$\frac{25}{66}$	$\frac{125}{22}$

Thus, $x_1^* = 125/22$, all other $x_j^* = 0$. Now, from the deleted equation we get

$$x_4^* = 15/2 - x_1^* - x_2^* - 1/2\, x_3^* - 1/2\, x_6^*$$

or $$x_4^* = 15/2 - 125/22 = 20/11$$

which can easily be verified to be the optimal solution.

PROBLEM 3.26

$$\min \; cx$$
$$\text{S.T.} \quad Ax - x_s = b$$
$$x, x_s \geq 0$$

Optimality Condition : $\quad z_j - c_j \leq 0 \quad \forall j$

For slacks we get: $\quad c_B B^{-1}(-I) - 0 \leq 0$

or $$c_B B^{-1} \geq 0 .$$

PROBLEM 3.27

The current basis gives an extreme point. This point is given by: $\begin{pmatrix} B^{-1}b \\ 0 \end{pmatrix}$. The extreme direction is given by:

$$\left\{ \begin{pmatrix} B^{-1}b \\ 0 \end{pmatrix} + \lambda \begin{pmatrix} -B^{-1}a_j \\ \hline e_j \end{pmatrix} :, \lambda \geq 0 \right\}$$

where e_j is a vector of zeros except for 1 at position j, and column j is the column indicating unboundedness (note $a_j \leq 0$).

Example:

	z	x_1	x_2	x_3	x_4	RHS
z	1	0	2	−1	0	5
x_1	0	1	−1	1	0	2
x_4	0	0	−2	3/2	1	1

Current extreme point: $(x_1, x_2, x_3, x_4) = (2, 0, 0, 1)$

Extreme direction : $(d_1, d_2, d_3, d_4) = (1, 1, 0, 2)$

Extreme ray : $\{ (2,0,0,1) + \lambda(1,1,0,2) : \lambda \geq 0 \}$

PROBLEM 3.28

Simplex unboundedness criterion: $B^{-1}a_j \leq 0$ and $z_j - c_j > 0$

Necessary and sufficient conditions for unboundedness : d extreme direction
$cd < 0$

d is an extreme direction $\Longleftrightarrow$ d is of the form $\begin{bmatrix} -B^{-1}a_j \\ \hline e_j \end{bmatrix}$, where e_j is a vector of zeros

PROBLEM 3.28 (Continued)

except for 1 at the jth position, and $B^{-1}a_j \leq 0$.

Note that $cd = (c_B, c_N)\begin{pmatrix} -B^{-1}a_j \\ e_j \end{pmatrix} = -c_B B^{-1} a_j + c_j$

$$= c_j - z_j$$

Therefore, $cd < 0 \iff z_j - c_j > 0$. Hence the two conditions are equivalent.

PROBLEM 3.29

	z	x_1	x_2	x_3	x_4	x_5	x_6	x_7	RHS
	1	0	0	4	−8	0	5/2	1/2	$\frac{53}{2}$
x_5	0	0	0	13	−5	1	1	−3	9
x_2	0	0	1	3	−2	0	1/2	−1/2	7/2
x_1	0	1	0	−1	−1	0	1/2	1/2	13/2

Final tableau

Since $z_4 - c_4 < 0$ and $y_4 \leq 0$ the optimal solution is unbounded. Consider the following feasible point: Let

$$x_4 = \lambda$$
$$x_5 = 9 + 5\lambda$$
$$x_2 = 7/2 + 2\lambda$$
$$x_1 = 13/2 + \lambda$$

The objective is $\frac{53}{2} + 8\lambda$. This can be made arbitrarily large by choosing λ arbitrarily large, e.g. $\lambda = 1000$ gives:

$(x_1, x_2, x_3, x_4, x_5, x_6, x_7) = (1006.5, 2003.5, 0, 1000, 5009, 0, 0)$ with objective 8026.5. Note that $(1, 2, 0, 1, 5, 0, 0)$ is a direction such that $cd = 8 > 0$, which is the unboundedness condition.

PROBLEM 3.30

Consider the following system:

$$\begin{aligned} x_2 + x_3 \quad &= 2 \\ -2x_1 + x_2 \quad + x_4 &= 1 \\ x_1, x_2, x_3, x_4 &\geq 0 \end{aligned}$$

Pivoting at row 2 and column 2 gives:

$$\begin{aligned} 2x_1 \quad + x_3 - x_4 &= 1 \\ -2x_1 + x_2 \quad + x_4 &= 1 \end{aligned}$$

Pivoting at row 1 and column 1 gives:

$$\begin{aligned} x_1 \quad + \tfrac{1}{2}x_3 - \tfrac{1}{2}x_4 &= \tfrac{1}{2} \\ x_2 + x_3 + x_4 &= 2 \end{aligned}$$

Note that x_1 is a basic variable at column 1, but, in the meantime $a_{11} = 0$. Therefore, the assertion of the exercise is false.

PROBLEM 3.31

Let x_j be the rth basic variable, so that $c_j = c_{B_r}$ and $B^{-1}a_j = e_r$, where e_r is a unit vector with a one at position r. Thus:

$$z_j - c_j = c_B B^{-1} a_j - c_j = c_B e_r - c_{B_r} = c_{B_r} - c_{B_r} = 0$$

This simply says that a basic variable can not be modified while maintaining the nonbasic variables at level zero and only modifying the other basic variables.

PROBLEM 3.32

$$\begin{aligned} \min \quad & cx \\ \text{s.t.} \quad & Ax = b + \lambda d \\ & x \geq 0 \end{aligned}$$

B is an optimal basis for all $\lambda \geq 0$ if, and only if, $B^{-1}(b + \lambda d) \geq 0$ for all $\lambda \geq 0$. This can hold only if $B^{-1}d \geq 0$.

PROBLEM 3.33

After pivoting at $y_{jk} > 0$, and since $z_k - c_k > 0$, (for a minimization problem) it follows that $(z_j - c_j)' = -1/y_{jk}(z_k - c_k) < 0$. Hence, x_j cannot enter in the next iteration.

PROBLEM 3.34

Consider the following example

min $-x_1 - 2x_2$

s.t. $x_1 + 4x_2 \le 6$

$x_1, x_2 \ge 0$

	z	x_1	x_2	x_3	RHS
z	1	1	2	0	0
x_3	0	1	4	1	6

x_2 enters the basis and then leaves. We can also find such examples for degenerate cases.

	z	x_1	x_2	x_3	RHS
z	1	1/2	0	−1/2	−3
x_2	0	1/4	1	1/4	3/2

	z	x_1	x_2	x_3	RHS
z	1	0	−2	−1	−6
x_1	0	1	4	1	6

PROBLEM 3.35

	z	x_1	x_2	x_3	x_4	x_5	x_6	x_7	x_8	RHS
	1	0	0	0	2	0	0	1	1	11/2
x_5	0	0	0	−1	0	1	0	−1	−1	13/2
x_6	0	0	0	2	0	0	1	4	2	18
x_2	0	0	1	−5	−3	0	0	6	−4	3
x_1	0	1	0	1	1	0	0	−1	1	1/2

Optimal Tableau

Optimal extreme point:

$$x' = (x_1, x_2, x_3, x_4, x_5, x_6, x_7, x_8) = (1/2, 3, 0, 0, 13/2, 18, 0, 0)$$

Alternate extreme point (x_1 leaves, x_3 enters)

$$x'' = (x_1, x_2, x_3, x_4, x_5, x_6, x_7, x_8) = (0, 11/2, 1/2, 0, 7, 17, 0, 0)$$

Therefore, the optimal nonbasic solution is given by

$$\frac{1}{2}x' + \frac{1}{2}x'' = (1/4, 17/4, 1/4, 0, 27/4, 35/2, 0, 0)$$

PROBLEM 3.36

a) $B = \begin{bmatrix} 1 & 2 & 1 \\ 0 & 3 & 3 \\ 0 & 1 & 2 \end{bmatrix}$, $B^{-1} = \begin{bmatrix} 1 & -1 & 1 \\ 0 & 2/3 & -1 \\ 0 & -1/3 & 1 \end{bmatrix}$

$w = c_B B^{-1} = (0, 5/3, 5)$

$z_3 - c_3 = wa_3 - c_3 = \frac{35}{3} - 5 = \frac{20}{3}$

$z_5 - c_5 = wa_5 - c_5 = 5/3 - 0 = \frac{5}{3}$

$z_6 - c_6 = wa_6 - c_6 = 5 - 0 = 5$

Since $z_j - c_j > 0$ for nonbasic variables then the solution is optimal.

b) $x_B = \bar{b} = B^{-1}b = (1000, 2000, 1000)^T$

$y_3 = B^{-1}a_3 = (1, -4/3, 5/3)^T$

$y_5 = B^{-1}a_5 = (-1, 2/3, -1/3)^T$

$y_6 = B^{-1}a_6 = (1, -1, 1)^T$

	z	x_1	x_2	x_3	x_4	x_5	x_6	RHS
z	1	0	0	20/3	0	5/3	5	35,000
x_4	0	0	0	1	1	−1	1	1000
x_1	0	1	0	−4/3	0	2/3	−1	2000
x_2	0	0	1	5/3	0	−1/3	1	1000

c) $z_7 - c_7 = wa_7 - c_7 = (0, 5/3, 5)(2, 4, 1)^T = -1/3$

Since $z_7 - c_7 < 0$, the new product will increase the profit.

$y_7 = B^{-1}a_7 = (-1, 5/3, -1/3)^T$

After inserting y_7 into the last optimal tableau and performing one pivot operation

PROBLEM 3.36 (Continued)

on x_7, we obtain the following optimal solution:

$(x_1, x_2, x_3, x_4, x_5, x_6, x_7) = (0, 1400, 0, 2200, 0, 0, 1200)$

with $z = 35,400$.

d) The minimal unit profit before a new product can be considered is 35/3.

PROBLEM 3.37

After each pivot of the simplex problem we have:

$$z' = z - \frac{\bar{b}_r}{y_{rk}} (z_k - c_k)$$

Since x_k entered $(z_k - c_k) > 0$. Also $y_{rk} > 0$. Now, if the problem is not degenerate $\bar{b}_r > 0$ and $z' < z$. Thus, in the absence of degeneracy the value of z strictly decreases at each iteration. But

$$z = c_B B^{-1} b$$

Thus z is uniquely defined by each basis.

Now in the absence of degeneracy if we ever cycled

PROBLEM 3.37 (Continued)

(repeated a previous basis) then it must be the case that z increased in an earlier pivot. However, this contradicts the above argument. Hence, we cannot repeat any basis and there are only a finite number of bases.

PROBLEM 3.38

a)

	z	x_1	x_2	x_3	x_4	x_5	RHS
z	1	1	2	−1	0	0	0
x_4	0	2	1	1	1	0	6
x_5	0	0	(2)	−1	0	1	3

$B = \begin{bmatrix} 1 & 0 \\ 0 & 1 \end{bmatrix} = B^{-1}$, $N = \begin{bmatrix} 2 & 1 & 1 \\ 0 & 2 & -1 \end{bmatrix} = B^{-1}N$

$c_B B^{-1} = (0,0)$

$z_j - c_j$'s are the numbers under each variable in zeroth row.

	z	x_1	x_2	x_3	x_4	x_5	RHS
z	1	1	0	0	0	−1	−3
x_4	0	(2)	0	3/2	1	−1/2	9/2
x_2	0	0	1	−1/2	0	1/2	3/2

$B = \begin{bmatrix} 1 & 1 \\ 0 & 2 \end{bmatrix}$, $N = \begin{bmatrix} 2 & 0 & 1 \\ 0 & 1 & -1 \end{bmatrix}$

$B^{-1}N = \begin{bmatrix} 2 & -1/2 & 3/2 \\ 0 & 1/2 & -1/2 \end{bmatrix}$

$c_B B^{-1} = (0, -1)$

	z	x_1	x_2	x_3	x_4	x_5	RHS
z	1	0	0	−3/4	−1/2	−3/4	−21/4
x_1	0	1	0	3/4	1/2	−1/4	9/4
x_2	0	0	1	−1/2	0	1/2	3/2

$B = \begin{bmatrix} 2 & 1 \\ 0 & 2 \end{bmatrix}$, $N = \begin{bmatrix} 1 & 0 & 1 \\ 0 & 1 & -1 \end{bmatrix}$

$B^{-1}N = \begin{bmatrix} 1/2 & -1/4 & 3/4 \\ 0 & 1/2 & -1/2 \end{bmatrix}$

$c_B B^{-1} = (-1/2, -3/4)$

b) $\dfrac{\partial x_1}{\partial x_3} = -\dfrac{3}{4}$, $\dfrac{\partial x_2}{\partial x_4} = 0$, $\dfrac{\partial z}{\partial x_5} = \dfrac{3}{4}$, $\dfrac{\partial x_B}{\partial x_N} = \begin{bmatrix} -1/2 & 1/4 & -3/4 \\ 0 & -1/2 & 1/2 \end{bmatrix}$

PROBLEM 3.38 (Continued)

c) $w = (-1+\Delta_1, -2+\Delta_2)\begin{bmatrix} 1/2 & -1/4 \\ 0 & 1/2 \end{bmatrix} = [-1/2 + 1/2\Delta_1, -3/4 - 1/4\Delta_1 + \frac{1}{2}\Delta_2]$

Solution remains optimal if $z_j - c_j \le 0$ for all nonbasic variables.

$$\left(-\frac{1}{2} + \frac{1}{2}\Delta_1, -\frac{3}{4} - \frac{1}{4}\Delta_1 + \frac{1}{2}\Delta_2\right)\begin{pmatrix} 1 \\ -1 \end{pmatrix} \le 0$$

i.e.,

$$-\frac{1}{2} + \frac{1}{2}\Delta_1 + \frac{3}{4} + \frac{1}{4}\Delta_1 - \frac{1}{2}\Delta_2 \le 0$$

$$\frac{1}{4} + \frac{3}{4}\Delta_1 - \frac{1}{2}\Delta_2 \le 0$$

also

$$-\frac{1}{2} + \frac{1}{2}\Delta_1 \le 0$$

$$-\frac{3}{4} - \frac{1}{4}\Delta_1 + \frac{1}{2}\Delta_2 \le 0$$

or simply

$$3\Delta_1 - 2\Delta_2 \le -1$$
$$\Delta_1 \le 1$$
$$-\Delta_1 + 2\Delta_2 \le 3$$

The shaded area is the region which maintains the optimality of current solution.

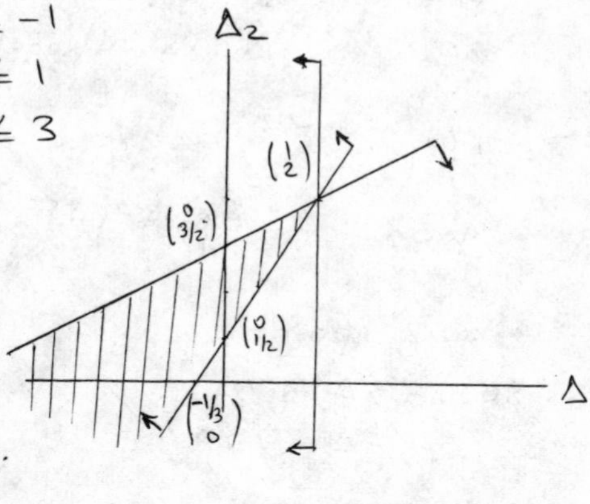

PROBLEM 3.38 (Continued)

d) $\begin{bmatrix} 1/2 & -1/4 \\ 0 & 1/2 \end{bmatrix} \begin{bmatrix} 3 \\ 3 \end{bmatrix} = \begin{bmatrix} 3/4 \\ 3/2 \end{bmatrix}$

$$z_6 - c_6 = c_B y_6 - c_6 = (-1,-2)\begin{pmatrix} 3/4 \\ 3/2 \end{pmatrix} + 3 = -3/4$$

Therefore, x_6 should not be considered.

e) $B^{-1}\begin{pmatrix} 6+\Delta \\ 3 \end{pmatrix} = \begin{bmatrix} 1/2 & -1/4 \\ 0 & 1/2 \end{bmatrix} \begin{bmatrix} 6+\Delta \\ 3 \end{bmatrix} = \begin{pmatrix} 9/4 + \Delta/2 \\ 3/2 \end{pmatrix}$

Therefore $\Delta = [-9/2, \infty)$ will maintain the optimality of the current basis.

f.) $a_3 = \frac{3}{4} a_1 - \frac{1}{2} a_2$

PROBLEM 3.39

a) $\dfrac{\partial z}{\partial b_1} = 0$, $\dfrac{\partial z}{\partial b_2} = 7$

b) $\begin{bmatrix} 1 & -2 \\ 0 & 1 \end{bmatrix} \begin{bmatrix} 10{,}000 \\ 4000+\Delta \end{bmatrix} = \begin{bmatrix} 2000 - 2\Delta \\ 4000 + \Delta \end{bmatrix}$

The range of Δ is, therefore, $[-4000, 1000]$

c) $z = (0,7)\begin{pmatrix} 2000 - 2\Delta \\ 4000 + \Delta \end{pmatrix} = 28{,}000 + 7\Delta$ for the range given in part (b).

d) Breakeven point:

$$3000 + 3\Delta = 7\Delta$$

$$\Delta = 750$$

PROBLEM 3.40

After eliminating the redundant constraints we have:

$$\max \min (x_2, x_3)$$

$$\text{S.T.} \quad 0.3x_1 + 0.5x_2 \le 24{,}000$$

$$x_1 \le 60{,}000$$

$$x_1, \; x_2 \ge 0$$

Optimal solution:

$x_1 = x_2 = 30{,}000$

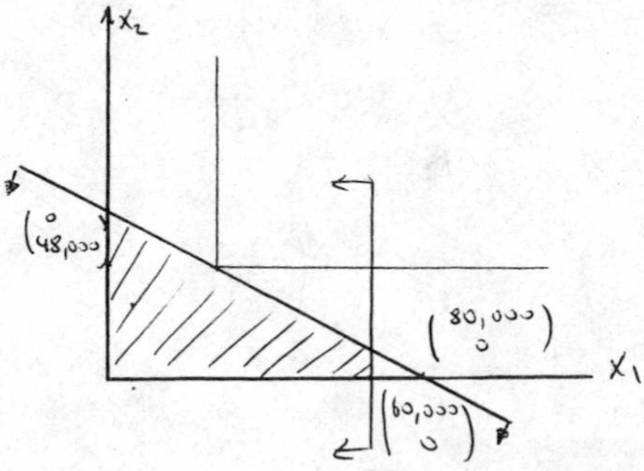

Buy a grinder. Note the grinders constraint is the only binding one. An additional grinder would cause the constraint

$0.3x_1 + 0.5x_2 \le 24{,}000$ to be modified to

$0.3x_1 + 0.5x_2 \le 26{,}400$.

The optimal solution would be $x_1 = x_2 = 33{,}000$. So, the number of assembled components would increase from 30,000 to 33,000.

PROBLEM 3.41

Optimal tableau:

	Z	x_1	x_2	x_3	x_4	x_5	RHS
Z	1	0	0	2	20	0	120,000
x_2	0	0	1	1/15	-20/15	0	2000
x_1	0	1	0	0	1	0	1000
x_5	0	0	0	-1/15	20/15	1	2000

PROBLEM 3.41 (Continued)

The relative worth (contribution to the profit) of each additional man-hour is \$2. Since the cost \$12 > \$2 then it is not profitable to increase the man-hours.

PROBLEM 3.42

$$\begin{pmatrix} f \\ 4 \end{pmatrix} = \begin{pmatrix} 1/2 & 0 \\ 1/2 & 1 \end{pmatrix} \begin{pmatrix} 6 \\ 1 \end{pmatrix} \Rightarrow f = 3$$

$$\begin{pmatrix} 2 \\ i \end{pmatrix} = \begin{pmatrix} 1/2 & 0 \\ 1/2 & 1 \end{pmatrix} \begin{pmatrix} c \\ 3 \end{pmatrix} \Rightarrow c = 4 \qquad i = 5$$

$$\begin{pmatrix} -1 \\ 1 \end{pmatrix} = \begin{pmatrix} 1/2 & 0 \\ 1/2 & 1 \end{pmatrix} \begin{pmatrix} d \\ e \end{pmatrix} \Rightarrow d = -2, \quad e = 2$$

$$g = 1, \quad h = 0$$

$$\begin{pmatrix} 1 \\ 0 \end{pmatrix} = \begin{pmatrix} 1/2 & 0 \\ 1/2 & 1 \end{pmatrix} \begin{pmatrix} b \\ 1 \end{pmatrix} \Rightarrow b = 2$$

$$m = 0$$

$$(1, 0) = (-a, 0) \begin{bmatrix} 1/2 & 0 \\ 1/2 & 1 \end{bmatrix} \Rightarrow a = -2$$

$$j = (1, 0) \begin{pmatrix} -2 \\ 2 \end{pmatrix} - 2 = -4$$

PROBLEM 3.43

$$C_B = [0, 5], \quad C_N = [3, 0]$$

a) $d = 1, \quad b = 0, \quad c = 0, \quad f = 0$

PROBLEM 3.43 (Continued)

$$B^{-1} = \begin{bmatrix} 1 & 1/5 \\ 0 & 1 \end{bmatrix}, \quad w = [0, 5]\begin{bmatrix} 1 & 1/5 \\ 0 & 1 \end{bmatrix} = [0, 5]$$

$$z_2 - c_2 = 1 = c_B y_2 - c_2 = [0, 5]\begin{bmatrix} 0 \\ e \end{bmatrix} - 3 = 1$$

or

$$e = 4/5$$

$$g = z_4 - c_4 = c_B y_4 - c_4 = [0, 5]\begin{bmatrix} 1/5 \\ 1 \end{bmatrix} = 5$$

$$\text{Cost} = 10 = c_B B^{-1} b$$

or

$$10 = [0, 5]\begin{bmatrix} 2 \\ a \end{bmatrix}$$

$$5a = 10$$

$$a = 2$$

b) $$B^{-1} = \begin{bmatrix} 1 & 1/5 \\ 0 & 1 \end{bmatrix}$$

c) $$\frac{\partial x_3}{\partial x_2} = 0, \quad \frac{\partial z}{\partial b_1} = c_B B_1^{-1}$$ where B_k^{-1} is the kth column of B^{-1}.

$$\frac{\partial z}{\partial b_1} = [0, 5]\begin{bmatrix} 1 \\ 0 \end{bmatrix} = 0$$

$$\frac{\partial z}{\partial x_4} = -(z_4 - c_4) = -5$$

d) Since all $z_j - c_j > 0$ for j nonbasic, the solution is optimal.

PROBLEM 3.44

a) $c_B = [-2, 0, -28]$

$g = 0 \longrightarrow x_6$ is basic

$c = e = 0 \longrightarrow x_2$ is basic

$d = 1 \longrightarrow x_2$ is basic

$$w = (b, 0, 0) = c_B B^{-1} = (-6, 0, -28f + \tfrac{28}{3})$$

$$b = -6 \quad , \quad f = \tfrac{1}{3}$$

$$-14 = c_B B^{-1} b = (-6, 0, 0) \begin{bmatrix} a \\ 5 \\ 0 \end{bmatrix}$$

$$-14 = -6a$$

$$a = 7/3$$

b)
$$B^{-1} = \begin{bmatrix} 3 & 0 & -14/3 \\ 6 & 1 & 2 \\ 0 & 0 & 1/3 \end{bmatrix}$$

c) $\partial x_2 / \partial x_1 = -6 \quad , \quad \partial z / \partial x_5 = 1$

$$\partial x_6 / \partial b_3 = -\tfrac{14}{3} + 2 + \tfrac{1}{3} = -\tfrac{7}{3}$$

d) $y_5 = B^{-1} a_5 \Longrightarrow a_5 = B y_5$ or

$$a_5 = y_{51} a_6 + y_{52} a_2 + y_{53} a_4$$

$$= a_6 + \tfrac{5}{2} a_2 + 0 a_4$$

PROBLEM 3.45

For having a bounded optimal solution we must either have

a) Bounded polyhedral set, or

b) with $c \geq 0$ for maximization problem

$$x \leq b > 0$$

or for $c < 0$, $x \geq b < 0$

PROBLEM 3.46

$$\min \quad -2x_1 + x_2$$

$$\text{S.T.} \quad x_1 + x_2 + x_3 = 4$$

$$x_1 - x_2 + x_4 = 6$$

$$x_1 \geq 0$$

$$x_2 \text{ URS}$$

	Z	x_1	x_2	x_3	x_4	RHS
Z	1	2	−1	0	0	0
x_3	0	(1)	1	1	0	4
x_4	0	1	−1	0	1	6

Initial tableau: both x_1 and x_2 are candidate to enter the basis, since $|z_1 - c_1| > |z_2 - c_2|$, x_1 enters.

	Z	x_1	x_2	x_3	x_4	RHS
Z	1	0	−3	−2	0	−8
x_1	0	1	1	1	0	4
x_4	0	0	(−2)	−1	1	2

In this tableau only x_2 is eligible to enter since $|z_2 - c_2| \neq 0$ for x_2 URS. Since $z_2 - c_2 < 0$ we need to let $x_2 < 0$. Therefore x_1 will always

PROBLEM 3.46 (Continued)

stay feasible. In this case we look for y_{zj}'s such that $y_{zj} < 0$.

For our problem we have $y_{22} = -2$

Therefore x_4 leaves, x_2 enters.

	z	x_1	x_2	x_3	x_4	RHS
z	1	0	0	-1/2	-3/2	-11
x_1	0	1	0	1/2	1/2	5
x_2	0	0	1	1/2	-1/2	-1

Optimal tableau.

Since $z_j - c_j \leq 0$ for all $x_j \geq 0$

and $z_j - c_j = 0$ for all x_j URS

the solution is optimal.

PROBLEM 3.47

a) $$B^{-1} = \begin{bmatrix} 0 & 4 & 0 \\ 1 & 5 & 0 \\ 0 & 7 & 1 \end{bmatrix}$$

b) $$B = (B^{-1})^{-1} = \begin{bmatrix} -5/4 & 1 & 0 \\ 1/4 & 0 & 0 \\ -7/4 & 0 & 1 \end{bmatrix}$$

c) Yes, all $z_j - c_j \leq 0$.

d) For the original tableau we need

$$a_2 = -2a_1 - a_2 + 0 \cdot a_3 = [3/2, -1/2, 7/2]^T$$

PROBLEM 3.47 (Continued)

g) Extreme direction = (2, 1, 1, 0, 0)

f) The new tableau is not optimal since $z_2 - c_2 = a > 0$.

h) we have:

$$-200 = c_B B^{-1} b - (z_2 - c_2) x_2 \quad \text{or}$$

$$-200 = -10 - 5 x_2 \quad \text{or}$$

$$x_2 = 38$$

Hence

$$\begin{bmatrix} x_1 \\ x_2 \\ x_3 \\ x_4 \\ x_5 \end{bmatrix} = \begin{bmatrix} c \\ 0 \\ d \\ 0 \\ e \end{bmatrix} + 38 \begin{bmatrix} 2 \\ 1 \\ 1 \\ 0 \\ 0 \end{bmatrix} = \begin{bmatrix} c+76 \\ 38 \\ d+38 \\ 0 \\ e \end{bmatrix}$$

CHAPTER 4 STARTING SOLUTION AND CONVERGENCE

PROBLEM 4.1

	z	x_1	x_2	x_3	x_4	x_5	x_6	x_7	x_8	RHS
z	1	0	0	0	0	0	0	-1	-1	0
x_4	0	1	1	-2	1	0	0	0	0	8
x_7	0	4	-1	1	0	-1	0	1	0	2
x_8	0	2	3	-1	0	0	-1	0	1	4

Phase I

Starting tableau.

	z	x_1	x_2	x_3	x_4	x_5	x_6	x_7	x_8	RHS
z	1	0	0	0	0	0	0	-1	-1	0
x_4	0	0	0	-12/7	1	1/14	5/14	-1/14	-5/14	45/7
x_1	0	1	0	1/7	0	-3/14	-1/14	3/14	1/14	5/7
x_2	0	0	1	-3/7	0	1/7	-2/7	-1/7	2/7	6/7

Last tableau

in phase I.

		x_1	x_2	x_3	x_4	x_5	x_6	x_7	x_8	RHS
z	1	0	4	-2	0	0	-1			4
x_4	0	0	-1/2	-3/2	1	0	1/2			6
x_1	0	1	3/2	-1/2	0	0	-1/2			2
x_5	0	0	7	-3	0	1	-2			6

Phase II

Optimal tableau.

The optimal solution is unbounded along the ray $\{(2,0,0,6,6,0) + \lambda(1/2,0,1,3/2,3,0)\}$, $\lambda \geq 0$.

PROBLEM 4.2

Obviously the optimal is unbounded.

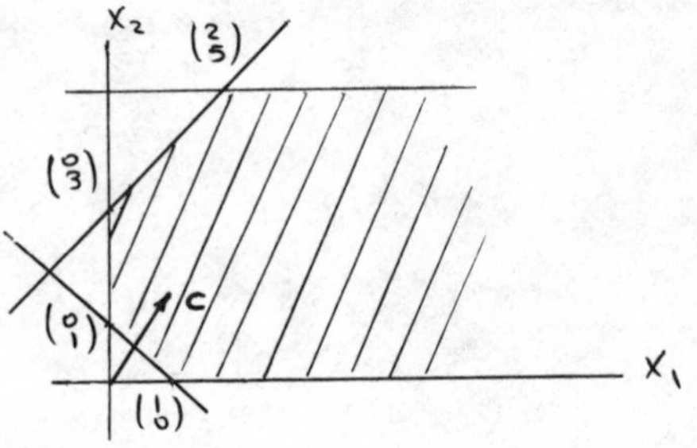

PROBLEM 4.2 (Continued)

	z	x_1	x_2	x_3	x_4	x_5	x_6	RHS
z	1	1	1	-1	0	0	0	1
x_6	0	1	1	-1	0	0	1	1
x_4	0	-1	1	0	1	0	0	3
x_5	0	0	1	0	0	1	0	5

Phase I initial tableau $(x_1, x_2) = (0, 0)$

	z	x_1	x_2	x_3	x_4	x_5	x_6	RHS
z	1	0	0	0	0	0	-1	0
x_2	0	1	1	-1	0	0	1	1
x_4	0	-2	0	1	1	0	-1	2
x_5	0	-1	0	1	0	1	-1	4

Phase I final tableau. $(x_1, x_2) = (0, 1)$

Note that (x_1, x_2) is a basic solution of the system:

$$x_1 + x_2 - x_3 = 1$$
$$-x_1 + x_2 + x_4 = 3$$
$$x_2 + x_5 = 5$$

where $x_3 = -1$, $x_4 = 3$, $x_5 = 5$

PROBLEM 4.3

Phase I can detect redundancy of a system of equations. So, the phase I will not detect redundancy of inequalities. Note, however, that the redundancy in this problem is equivalent to degeneracy which would be detected by the simplex method.

PROBLEM 4.4

	z	x_1	x_2	x_3	x_4 (Slacks)	x_5 (Slacks)	x_6 (Slacks)	x_7 (Art.)	x_8 (Art.)	RHS
z	1	0	0	3	1	−1	−1	0	0	5
x_7	0	1	1	1	−1	0	0	1	0	3
x_8	0	−1	2	0	0	−1	0	0	1	2
x_6	0	−1	5	1	0	0	1	0	0	4

Phase I
First tableau.

	z	x_1	x_2	x_3	x_4	x_5	x_6	x_7	x_8	RHS
z	1	0	0	0	−1/2	−1	−1/2	0	0	3/2
x_3	0	3/2	0	1	−5/4	0	−1/4	1	0	11/4
x_8	0	0	0	0	−1/2	−1	−1/2	0	1	3/2
x_2	0	−1/2	1	0	1/4	0	1/4	0	0	1/4

Phase I
Final tableau

Since the artificial variable x_8 is positive and $z_j - c_j \leq 0$ for all nonbasic variables, the original problem has no feasible solution.

PROBLEM 4.5

Phase I problem:

$$\min \ \underline{1}\, x_a$$
$$\text{S.T.} \quad Ax + x_a = b$$
$$x_a \geq 0$$

Note that x is unrestricted.

If at optimality $x_a = 0$, then the system is consistent. Otherwise, the system is inconsistent. If there is at least one artificial variable in the solution at zero level, then the equations are redundant.

PROBLEM 4.5 (Continued)

If $x_a = 0$, and all artificial variables are out of the basis, then the solution is unique, A^{-1} exists and is stored under the artificial variables.

	z	x_1	x_2	x_3	x_4	x_5	x_6	RHS
z	1	1	0	4	0	0	0	9
x_4	0	1	2	1	1	0	0	4
x_5	0	-1	-1	(2)	0	1	0	3
x_6	0	1	-1	1	0	0	1	2

Phase I

initial tableau.

z	1	3	2	0	0	-2	0	3
x_4	0	3/2	5/2	0	1	-1/2	0	5/2
x_3	0	-1/2	-1/2	1	0	1/2	0	3/2
x_6	0	(3/2)	-1/2	0	0	-1/2	1	1/2

		x_1	x_2	x_3	x_4	x_5	x_6	RHS
z	1	0	3	0	0	-1	-2	2
x_4	0	0	(3)	0	1	0	-1	2
x_3	0	0	-2/3	1	0	1/3	1/3	5/3
x_1	0	1	-1/3	0	0	-1/3	2/3	1/3

	z	x_1	x_2	x_3	x_4	x_5	x_6	RHS
	1	0	0	0	-1	-1	-1	0
x_2	0	0	1	0	1/3	0	-1/3	2/3
x_3	0	0	0	1	2/9	1/3	1/9	19/9
x_1	0	1	0	0	1/9	-1/3	5/9	5/9

Note; while applying the simplex method that x_1, x_2 and x_3 are unrestricted in sign. Therefore x_1, x_2, x_3 are allowed to go negative. Following modification is needed for selection.

a) if $z_j - c_j > 0$ we may increase x_j, $j=1,2,3$

b) if $z_j - c_j < 0$ we may decrease x_j, $j=1,2,3$

c) We have only to pivot at a row in which an artificial variable is basic.

Unique Solution:

$x_2 = 2/3$

$x_3 = 19/9$

$x_1 = 5/9$

PROBLEM 4.6

(Slacks: x_3, x_4; Art.: x_5)

	Z	x_1	x_2	x_3	x_4	x_5	RHS
Z	1	0	0	0	0	−1	0
x_3	0	0	11/2	1	3/2	−3/2	17
x_1	0	1	−1/2	0	−1/2	1/2	1

Phase I Final Tableau

	Z	x_1	x_2	x_3	x_4	RHS
Z	1	0	5/2	0	1/2	−1
x_3	0	0	11/2	1	3/2	17
x_1	0	1	−1/2	0	−1/2	1

Phase II Optimal Tableau.

PROBLEM 4.7

(Slacks: x_4, x_5; Art.: x_6)

	Z	x_1	x_2	x_3	x_4	x_5	x_6	RHS
Z	1	0	0	0	0	0	−1	0
x_4	0	0	7/2	−1/2	1	1/2	−1/2	5
x_1	0	1	1/2	3/2	0	−1/2	1/2	1

Phase I Final Tableau

	Z	x_1	x_2	x_3	x_4	x_5	RHS
Z	1	0	50	0	13	4	70
x_3	0	0	−7	1	−2	−1	−10
x_1	0	1	11	0	3	1	16

Phase II Final Tableau

PROBLEM 4.8

(Slacks: x_4, x_5; Art.: x_6, x_7)

	Z	x_1	x_2	x_3	x_4	x_5	x_6	x_7	RHS
Z	1	0	0	0	0	0	−1	−1	0
x_3	0	0	2	1	1	0	1	−1	9
x_1	0	1	−1	0	−1	0	0	1	1
x_5	0	0	3	0	1	1	−1	−1	9

Phase I

Final Tableau

	Z	x_1	x_2	x_3	x_4	x_5	RHS
Z	1	0	6	0	0	7	40
x_3	0	0	−1	1	0	−1	0
x_1	0	1	2	0	0	1	10
x_4	0	0	3	0	1	1	9

Phase II

Final Tableau

Solution optimal.

PROBLEM 4.9

	z	x_1	x_2	x_3	x_4	x_5	x_6	x_7	x_8	x_9	RHS
z	1	0	$-11/10$	$-19/10$	0	0	$-1/5$	$11/10$	$1/5 - M$	$-11/10 - M$	$-7/5$
x_5	0	0	$13/5$	$2/5$	0	1	$1/5$	($2/5$)	$-1/5$	$-4/10$	$2/5$
x_4	0	0	$-1/10$	$1/10$	1	0	$-1/5$	$1/10$	$1/5$	$-1/10$	$3/5$
x_1	0	1	$-1/2$	$1/2$	0	0	0	$-1/2$	0	$1/2$	1

Tableau #4

	z	x_1	x_2	x_3	x_4	x_5	x_6	x_7	RHS
z	1	0	$-33/4$	-3	0	$-11/4$	$-15/20$	0	$-5/2$
x_7	0	0	$13/2$	1	0	$5/2$	$1/2$	1	1
x_4	0	0	$-3/4$	0	1	$-1/4$	$-1/4$	0	$1/2$
x_1	0	1	$11/4$	1	0	$5/4$	$1/4$	0	$3/2$

Tableau # 5

(Final Tableau)

PROBLEM 4.10

	z	x_1	x_2	x_3	x_4	x_5	x_6	RHS
z	1	$-1/2$	$3/2$	0	$-1/2$	0	$M+1/2$	2
x_3	0	$1/2$	$1/2$	1	$-1/2$	0	$1/2$	2
x_5	0	$1/2$	$-5/2$	0	$1/2$	1	$-1/2$	0

Table # 3

	z	x_1	x_2	x_3	x_4	x_5	RHS
z	1	0	0	$1/3$	$-1/3$	$2/3$	$8/3$
x_2	0	0	1	$1/3$	$-1/3$	$-1/3$	$2/3$
x_1	0	1	0	$5/3$	$-2/3$	$1/3$	$10/3$

Tableau # 5

Optimal is unbounded.

PROBLEM 4.11

If the solution of the big M method is unbounded, then either the original problem has no feasible solution or has an unbounded optimal objective. (See detailed discussion in the text).

PROBLEM 4.12

Consider the region

$$\{ (x, x_a) : Ax + x_a = b \ , \ x, x_a \geq 0 \}$$

Let the extreme points of this region be

$(x^1, x_a^1), (x^2, x_a^2), \ldots\ldots, (x^k, x_a^k)$

and the extreme directions (if any) be

$(d^1, d_a^1), \ldots\ldots, (d^\ell, d_a^\ell)$.

The problem can be restated as

$$\max \sum_{j=1}^{k} \lambda_j \left[(cx^j) - M(\underline{1} x_a^j) \right] + \sum_{j=1}^{\ell} \mu_j \left[(cd^j) - M(\underline{1} d_a^j) \right]$$

$$\text{S.T.} \quad \sum_{j=1}^{k} \lambda_j = 1$$

$$\lambda_j \geq 0 \quad , \quad j = 1, \ldots, k$$

$$\mu_j \geq 0 \quad , \quad j = 1, 2, \ldots, k$$

If for any j $\underline{1} d_a^j < 0$, then regardless of cd^j, $cd^j - M(\underline{1} d_a^j) > 0$ for $M > \dfrac{1 + cd^j}{\| \underline{1} \ d_a^j \|}$

and hence the optimal solution is unbounded along the direction (d^j, d_a^j) for all $M \geq \bar{M} = \dfrac{1 + cd^j}{\| \underline{1} d_a^j \|}$

Now suppose that

$$\underline{1} \ d_a^j \geq 0 \quad \text{for all } j.$$

If $c \cdot d_a^j = 0$ and $cd^j > 0$ for some j, then the problem is unbounded along (d^j, d_a^j) for all $M \geq 0$. Otherwise, the problem is bounded. In this case consider $\min_{1 \leq j \leq k} \underline{1} x_a^j$. If the minimum occurs at a unique index j_0 then the optimal occurs at $(x^{j_0}, x_a^{j_0})$, for M large enough.

PROBLEM 4.12 (Continued)

If the index is not unique, break the ties according to the index j with max cx^j. The corresponding point gives the optimal extreme point for M large enough. (why?). How large is M? can you develope an explicit formula?

PROBLEM 4.13

For M Large enough, by problem 4.12 optimal occurs at a fixed extreme point or along a fixed extreme ray. Since the optimal is finite, there exists $\bar{M}$ such that for $M \geq \bar{M}$ an optimal occurs at (x^j, x_a^j). The optimal objective is thus:

$$cx^j - M(\mathbf{1} x_a^j) \qquad \text{for } M \geq \bar{M}$$

If $x_a^j \neq 0$, then $cx^j - M\mathbf{1}x_a^j$ can be made arbitrarily small by choosing M large enough. But the original problem admits a feasible solution x, so that $(x, 0)$ is a feasible solution of the big-M problem (for any M, in particular $M \geq \bar{M}$) with the objective cx contradicting the assertion that the optimal objective can be made arbitrarily small for M large enough. Therefore, $x_a^j = 0$ and the proof is complete.

PROBLEM 4.14

Yes, the region in E^{n+m} can be unbounded. Take the example

$$\begin{aligned} x_1 + x_2 + x_3 \quad &= 2 \\ -x_1 + x_2 \quad - x_4 &= 1 \end{aligned}$$

Obviously, this region is bounded (Why?). After introducing an artificial variable for the second constraint we get

$$\begin{aligned} x_1 + x_2 + x_3 \quad &= 2 \\ -x_1 + x_2 \quad - x_4 + x_5 &= 1 \end{aligned}$$

This system is obviously unbounded along the ray $\{(1/2, 3/2, 0, 0, 0) + \lambda(0, 0, 0, 1, 1) : \lambda \geq 0\}$. The implications are that the optimal solution of the big-M problem may be unbounded. By the problem 4.11, however, this is only possible if the feasible region of the original problem is empty, or else the original problem has an unbounded optimal solution (and hence an unbounded feasible region).

PROBLEM 4.15

	z	x_1	x_2	x_3	x_4	x_5	x_6	x_7	x_8	RHS
z	1	-2	-4	0	1	0	0	-M	-M	0
x_5	0	1	2	-1	1	1	0	0	0	2
x_7	0	2	1	2	3	0	0	1	0	4
x_8	0	1	0	-1	1	0	-1	0	1	3

initial Starting tableau.

PROBLEM 4.15 (Continued)

	z	x_1	x_2	x_3	x_4	x_5	x_6	x_7	x_8	RHS
z	1	0	$9-2M$	-4	0	$8-M$	0	$-3-M$	0	$4-6M$
x_1	0	1	5	-5	0	3	0	-1	0	2
x_4	0	0	-3	4	1	-2	0	1	0	0
x_8	0	0	-2	0	0	-1	-1	0	1	1

Final tableau

Iteration # 3

Since x_8 is in the final solution with positive level, the original problem has no feasible solution.

PROBLEM 4.16

	z	x_1	x_2	x_3	x_4	x_5	x_6	RHS
z	1	2	0	0	3	$4+M$	M	16
x_3	0	3/4	0	1	-1	1	$-1/4$	2
x_2	0	1/4	1	0	1	0	1/4	2

Optimal tableau

Iteration # 3

Solution is optimal with $x_3 = x_2 = 2$, $x_1 = x_4 = 0$

PROBLEM 4.17

The assertion is true. If M is choosen large enough, the sequences of bases generated by both methods will be the same.

Initial starting basis in both methods consists of artificial variables. For a min problem the criteria to enter the basis will be:

$$z_j - c_j > 0$$

For two phase method at phase I

$$z_j - c_j = c_B B^{-1} a_j - 0 = c_B B^{-1} a_j$$

PROBLEM 4.17 (Continued)

For big-M method

$$z_j - c_j = c_B' B^{-1} a_j - c_j = M c_B B^{-1} a_j - c_j$$

where $c_B' = M c_B$ is the cost vector in big-M method, for basic variables.

Entrance criteria for big-M was

$$z_j - c_j > 0 \implies M c_B B^{-1} a_j - c_j > 0$$

or since $M c_B B^{-1} a_j \gg c_j$ we can delete c_j and have

$$M c_B B^{-1} a_j > 0$$

this criteria is exactly like the criteria used in phase I of two phase method. Therefore both methods are going to choose the same variable. For the variable leaving the basis, the criteria is still the same for both methods. Therefore same variables are going to enter and leave the basis in both methods and, hence, the same bases will be generated.

At any instant of time, in big-M method, the cost vector for basic variables will be like $c_B' = (c_1, \ldots, c_k, \ldots c_\ell, M, M, \ldots, M)$ i.e., combination of c_j's (for original variables in the basis) and M's (for artificial variables

PROBLEM 4.17 (Continued)

in the basis). For two phase method all c_j's will be zero for the original variables that are in the basis and 1's for the artificial variables. $c_B = (0, 1, \ldots 0, \ldots 1)$

Since we started with the same basis we have $B^{-1}a_j$'s same for both problem. call $B^{-1}a_j = [y_{j1}, y_{j2} \ldots y_{jn}]^T$. Hence, for phase I

$$c_B B^{-1} a_j = [0, 1, \ldots 0, \ldots 1][y_{j1}, y_{j2}, \ldots y_{jn}]^T$$

$$= \sum_{\substack{k \ni x_k \text{ is artificial} \\ \text{and } x_k \text{ is basic}}} y_{jk}$$

and

$$z_j - c_j = \sum_{\substack{k \ni x_k \text{ is art.} \\ \text{and basic.}}} y_{jk} - 0$$

for nonbasic, non artificial variable x_j.

For big-M method,

$$c_B' B^{-1} a_j = [c_1, \ldots, M, \ldots, c_\ell, \ldots M][y_{j1}, y_{j2}, \ldots y_{jn}]^T$$

or

$$= \sum_{\substack{k \ni x_k \text{ is artificial} \\ \text{and basic}}} M y_{jk} + \sum_{\substack{k \ni x_k \text{ is not artificial} \\ \text{but basic}}} c_k y_{jk}$$

For a variable x_j to enter the basis

PROBLEM 4.17 (Continued)

$$M \sum_{\substack{k \ni x_k \text{ artificial} \\ \text{and basic}}} y_{jk} + \sum_{\substack{k \ni x_k \text{ is not artificial} \\ \text{and basic}}} c_k y_{jk} > 0$$

In order to have this, first sum must be positive. And observe that

$$M \sum_{\substack{k \ni x_k \text{ artif.} \\ \text{and basic}}} y_{jk} \gg \sum c_k y_{jk}$$

hence the second summation term can be ignored. This leads us to

$$M \sum_{\substack{k \ni x_k \text{ artificial} \\ \text{and basic}}} y_{jk} > 0$$

or since $M > 0$

$$\sum_{\substack{k \ni x_k \text{ artificial} \\ \text{and basic}}} y_{jk} > 0$$

which is exactly the same criteria for two phase method. Therefore they generate the same bases.

PROBLEM 4.18

The two-phase method is usually superior to the big-M method which may suffer numerical roundoff errors plus the difficulties discussed in the text about the interpretation of unboundedness. For a clue of how big-M can be choosen see problem 4.12.

PROBLEM 4.19

Apply the following procedure: At the end of phase I find a nonzero y_{sk} for an s corresponding to an artificial basic variable x_s, replace a_s by a_k. One of the following situation will occur:

1- All artificial vectors could have been eliminated from the basis by this procedure; the (degenerate) basic solution thus obtained would no longer contain artificial variables, and consequently there is no redundancy: $r(A)=m$.

2- p artificial vectors remain in the basis and for each of those a_i we have $y_{ij}=0$ for every j. Therefore, each of the vectors of A may be expressed as a linear combination of the $(m-p)$ vectors of A which remain in the basis. In this case $r(A)=m-p$, and hence there are only $m-p$ independent constraints; $Ax=b$ is inconsistent.

PROBLEM 4.20

Reviewing the proof of subcase B_2 on pages 160 and 161 of the text, it follows that the proof will go through if the requirement that $y_{ik} \leq 0$ for $i = 1, 2, \ldots, m$ is replaced by $y_{ik} \leq 0$ for $i = p+1, \ldots, m$.

PROBLEM 4.21

	z	x_1	x_2	x_3	x_4	x_5	x_6	RHS
z	1	1	1	M	−M	0	0	2M
x_5	0	(1)	−1	−1	0	1	0	1
x_6	0	−1	1	2	−1	0	1	1

	z	x_1	x_2	x_3	x_4	x_5	x_6	RHS
z	1	0	2	M+1	−M	−1	0	2M−1
x_1	0	1	−1	−1	0	1	0	1
x_6	0	0	0	1	−1	1	1	2

Note that $z_2 - c_2 > 0$ and $y_2 \leq 0$. However, the optimal solution of the original problem is <u>not</u> unbounded. Therefore, we have to introduce the variable with most positive $z_j - c_j$.

PROBLEM 4.22

To check geometric redundancy of the ith constraint consider the following problem:

$$\min \; x_{n+i}$$

$$\text{s.t.} \quad \sum_{j=1}^{n} a_{ij} x_j + x_{n+i} = b_i$$

$$x_j \geq 0 \qquad j = 1, 2, \ldots, m+n$$

If the optimal solution is positive then the constraint is geometrically redundant.

PROBLEM 4.23

Examining the ith row we have:

$$x_s = \bar{b}_i - \sum_{j \neq s} y_{ij} x_j$$

Since $\bar{b}_i > 0$, $y_{ij} \leq 0$, $x_{ij} \geq 0$, then $x_s > 0$ and the ith constraint is geometrically redundant by problem 4.22. The constraint can thus be thrown away.

PROBLEM 4.24

	z	x_1	x_2	x_3	x_4	x_5	x_6	RHS
z	1	0	0	0	0	0	−1	0
x_1	0	1	2	1	−1	0	1	5
x_5	0	0	7	2	−3	1	3	19

Last tableau in phase I
Iteration # 1

	z	x_1	x_2	x_3	x_4	x_5	RHS
z	1	3	0	−3	0	−2	−8
x_2	0	−3	1	−1	0	1	4
x_4	0	−7	0	−3	1	2	3

Final tableau in phase II
Iteration # 3

Therefore the optimal is unbounded along the extreme ray $\{(0,4,0) + \lambda(1,3,0) : \lambda \geq 0\}$

	z	x_1	x_2	x_3	x_4	x_5	x_6	
z	1	3	0	−3	0	−2	M	−8
x_2	0	−3	1	−1	0	1	0	4
x_4	0	−7	0	−3	1	2	−1	3

Final tableau in big-M method.
Iteration # 2.

As before, we conclude that the optimal solution is unbounded.

PROBLEM 4.25

	z	x_1	x_2	x_3	x_4	x_5	x_6	x_7	RHS
z	1	-1.23	-1.81	0	0	-1.02	-.372		7.07
x_4	0	.302	-.442	0	1	-6.98	-.116		.209
x_3	0	-.163	.93	1	0	.116	.14		.135

Final Optimal tableau.

Iteration # 4

PROBLEM 4.26

	z	x_1	x_2	x_3	x_4	x_5	RHS
z	1	0	0	1/2	3/2	M-3/2	0
x_1	0	1	0	1/2	1/2	-1/2	1
x_2	0	0	1	1/2	1/2	1/2	2

Final Optimal tableau

Iteration #

PROBLEM 4.27

	z	x_1	x_2	x_3	x_4	x_5	RHS
z	1	0	22	4	5	0	30
x_5	0	0	7	-1	2	1	10
x_1	0	1	4	1	1	0	6

Final tableau in Big-M method.

Iteration # 3.

Note that $\begin{pmatrix} x_5 \\ x_1 \end{pmatrix} = \begin{pmatrix} 10 \\ 6 \end{pmatrix} - \begin{pmatrix} 7 \\ 4 \end{pmatrix} x_2$

and $z = 30 - 22x_2$.

x_2 can be made an arbitrarily large negative number and objective will approach to infinity. Hence, the optimal is unbounded along the extreme ray:

$$\{(6,0,0,0,10) + \lambda(4,-1,0,0,7) : \lambda \geq 0\}$$

PROBLEM 4.28

See page 165 and sections 4.2 and 4.3.

PROBLEM 4.29

z	x_1	x_2	x_3	x_4	x_5 (Slacks)	x_6 (Slacks)	x_7 (Art.)	RHS
1	-4	-5	-7	1	0	0	M	0
0	-1	-1	-2	1	1	0	-1	-1
0	2	-6	3	1	0	1	-1	-3
0	1	4	3	2	0	0	(-1)	-5

x_3 unrestricted.

Initial tableau

	z	x_1	x_2	x_3	x_4	x_5	x_6	x_7	RHS
z	1	$-6/5 - 1/5 M$	$2 - 2M$	0	$12/5 + 7/5 M$	$-7/5 + 3/5 M$	0	0	$-28/5 - 13/5 M$
x_3	0	2/5	1	1	1/5	-1/5	0	0	-4/5
x_6	0	1	-10	0	-1	0	1	0	2
x_7	0	1/5	-1	0	-7/5	-3/5	0	1	13/5

Final tableau

The most negative entry in row 0 is $z_2 - c_2$. Note, however, that x_2 can be increased indefinitely since $y_{i2} < 0$ for x_{Bi} which is restricted to be nonnegative (it doesnot matter that $y_{12} > 0$ since $x_{B_1} = x_3$ is unrestricted). Therefore, the big-M problem is unbounded and the original problem is unbounded.

PROBLEM 4.30

	z	x_1	x_2	x_3	x_4	x_5	x_6	x_7	RHS
z	1	0	1	-2	1	0	0		-4
x_1	0	1	1	1	-1	0	0		4
x_5	0	0	2	3	-2	1	0		5
x_6	0	0	1	1	0	0	1		2

Phase II
Final tableau
Solution is unbounded.

PROBLEM 4.31

Single Artificial variable technique:

Advantages: Only one artificial instead of m artificial variables are used, and the problem is reduced.

Disadvantages: Entries in the tableau are not $B^{-1}A$, so that, B^{-1} is not immediately available. Also, columns in updated tableau are not the y_j's of the original system.

PROBLEM 4.32

Introduce the artificial variable x_a and the constraint $x_a \leq 1$. Introduce the slack variable x_s leading to

$$x_B + B^{-1}Nx_N + \hat{b}\,x_a = \bar{b}$$

$$x_a + x_s = 1$$

Pivoting at the last row and the x_a column gives:

$$x_B + B^{-1}Nx_N - \hat{b}\,x_s = \bar{b} - \hat{b}$$

$$x_a + x_s = 1$$

Thus, we have an immediate basic feasible solution with $x_B = \bar{b} - \hat{b} \geq 0$ and $x_a = 1$. Starting with this solution either the two phase method or the big-M method can be used to drive the artificial variable to zero.

PROBLEM 4.34

$$\max \quad 2x_1 + 2x_2 + 4x_3$$

$$
\begin{aligned}
\text{S.T.} \quad x_1 & & & \geq 100 \\
& x_2 & & \geq 60 \\
& & x_3 & \geq 60 \\
& x_2 + & x_3 & \leq 240 \\
x_1 + & x_2 + & x_3 & \leq 400 \quad \text{Redundant} \\
2x_1 + & x_2 + & x_3 & \leq 360 \\
x_1, & x_2, & x_3 & \geq 0
\end{aligned}
$$

	Z	x_1	x_2	x_3	x_4	x_5	x_6	x_7	x_8	x_9	x_{10}	x_{11}	RHS
Z	1	0	0	0	0	0	0	0	0	−1	−1	−1	0
x_1	0	1	0	0	−1	0	0	0	0	1	0	0	100
x_2	0	0	1	0	0	−1	0	0	0	0	1	0	60
x_3	0	0	0	1	0	0	−1	0	0	0	0	1	60
x_7	0	0	0	0	0	1	2	1	0	0	−1	−2	60
x_8	0	0	0	0	2	1	1	0	1	−2	−1	−1	40

Last tableau of phase I.

	Z	x_1	x_2	x_3	x_4	x_5	x_6	x_7	x_8	RHS
Z	1	0	0	0	0	1/2	0	3/2	1	690
x_1	0	1	0	0	0	1/4	0	−1/4	1/2	105
x_2	0	0	1	0	0	−1	0	0	0	60
x_3	0	0	0	1	0	1/2	0	1/2	0	90
x_6	0	0	0	0	0	1/2	1	1/2	0	30
x_4	0	0	0	0	1	1/4	0	−1/4	1/2	5

Optimal tableau, phase II.

Obj = 690, $x_1 = 105$, $x_2 = 60$, $x_3 = 90$.

PROBLEM 4.35

Let x_1, x_2, x_3, x_4, and x_5 correspond to corn, wheat, okra, tomatos, and green beans respectively.

$$\text{max} \quad 1200x_1 + 600x_2 + 240x_3 + 640x_4 + 330x_5$$

$$\begin{aligned} \text{S.T.} \quad & 120x_1 + 150x_2 + 100x_3 + 80x_4 + 120x_5 \le 18{,}000 \\ & x_1 + x_2 + x_3 + x_4 + x_5 \le 200 \\ & x_1 \ge 25 \\ & x_2 \ge 20 \end{aligned}$$

and all $x \ge 0$

	z	x_1	x_2	x_3	x_4	x_5	x_6 (Slacks)	x_7 (Slacks)	x_8 (Slacks)	x_9 (Slacks)	x_{10} (Art.)	x_{11} (Art.)	RHS
z	1	0	0	0	0	0	0	0	0	0	−1	−1	0
x_6	0	0	0	100	80	120	1	0	120	150	−120	−150	12,000
x_7	0	0	0	1	1	1	0	1	1	1	−1	−1	155
x_1	0	1	0	0	0	0	0	0	−1	0	1	0	25
x_2	0	0	1	0	0	0	0	0	0	−1	0	1	20

Phase I, final tableau.

	z	x_1	x_2	x_3	x_4	x_5	x_6	x_7	x_8	x_9	
z	1	0	0	−760	−160	−870	−10	0	0	−900	162,000
x_8	0	0	0	5/6	2/3	1	1/120	0	1	5/4	100
x_7	0	0	0	1/6	1/3	0	−1/120	1	0	−1/4	55
x_1	0	1	0	5/6	2/3	1	1/120	0	0	5/4	125
x_2	0	0	1	0	0	0	0	0	0	−1	20

Optimal tableau, phase II.

Optimal Solution:

Acres corn : 125

Acres wheat : 20

Acres okra = Acres tomatos = Acres green beans = 0

Return = 43,200

PROBLEM 4.36

Let x_{ij} = # of stoves from warehouse i to store j.

y_{ij} = # of ovens from warehouse i to store j.

$$\min\ 3x_{11} + 5x_{12} + 2x_{21} + 3x_{22} + 6x_{31} + 3x_{32} + 3y_{11} + 5y_{12} + 2y_{21} + 3y_{22} + 6y_{31} + 3y_{32}$$

$$\begin{array}{lr}
\text{S.T.}\quad x_{11} + x_{12} & \leq 60 \\
x_{21} + x_{22} & \leq 80 \\
x_{31} + x_{32} & \leq 50 \\
x_{11} + x_{21} + x_{31} & = 100 \\
x_{12} + x_{22} + x_{32} & = 90 \\
y_{11} + y_{12} & \leq 80 \\
y_{21} + y_{22} & \leq 50 \\
y_{31} + y_{32} & \leq 50 \\
y_{11} + y_{21} + y_{31} & = 60 \\
y_{12} + y_{22} + y_{32} & = 120
\end{array}$$

$$x_{ij},\ y_{ij} \geq 0 \quad \forall i, j$$

Obviously the problem can be decomposed into two independent problems.

	z	x_{11}	x_{12}	x_{21}	x_{22}	x_{31}	x_{32}	x_1 (Slacks)	x_2 (Slacks)	x_3 (Slacks)	x_4 (Art.)	x_5 (Art.)	RHS
	1	0	0	0	0	0	0	0	0	0	−1	−1	0
x_1	0	0	1	0	1	−1	0	1	1	0	−1	0	40
x_2	0	0	0	1	1	0	0	0	1	0	0	0	80
x_3	0	0	0	0	0	0	0	1	1	1	−1	−1	0
x_4	0	1	0	0	−1	1	0	−1	0	0	1	0	20
x_5	0	0	0	0	0	1	1	−1	−1	0	1	1	50

Last tableau in phase I for subproblem 1.

PROBLEM 4.36 (Continued)

	Z	x_{11}	x_{12}	x_{21}	x_{22}	x_{31}	x_{32}	x_1	x_2	x_3	RHS
z	1	0	1	0	0	4	0	0	1	1	530
x_{11}	0	1	1	0	0	0	0	0	−1	−1	60
x_{22}	0	0	1	0	1	−1	0	0	0	−1	40
x_{32}	0	0	0	0	0	1	1	0	0	1	50
x_{21}	0	0	−1	1	0	1	0	0	1	1	40
x_1	0	0	0	0	0	0	0	1	1	1	0

Final tableau (optimal) in phase II for subproblem I.

	z	y_{11}	y_{12}	y_{21}	y_{22}	y_{31}	y_{32}	y_1	y_2	y_3	RHS
z	1	0	0	1	0	5	0	0	2	2	580
y_{12}	0	0	1	−1	0	−1	0	0	−1	−1	20
y_{22}	0	0	0	1	1	0	0	0	1	0	50
y_{32}	0	0	0	0	0	1	1	0	0	1	50
y_{11}	0	1	0	1	0	1	0	0	0	0	60
y_1	0	0	0	0	0	0	0	1	1	1	0

Final tableau (optimal) in phase II for subproblem II.

The overall optimal solution to the original problem is, then

$x_{11} = 60$, $x_{22} = 40$, $x_{32} = 50$, $x_{21} = 40$

$y_{12} = 20$, $y_{22} = 50$, $y_{32} = 50$, $y_{11} = 60$

and $\quad Obj = 530 + 580 = ~~1100~~\ 1110$

and all other vaiables being equal to zero.

PROBLEM 4.37

Let x_i = production of item A at month i

$\hat{x}_i$ = inventory of item A at end of month i.

y_i = production of item B at month i

$\hat{y}_i$ = inventory of item B at end of month i.

PROBLEM 4.37 (Continued)

a) $\hat{x}_j = \hat{x}_{j-1} + x_j - d_j$, d_j being the demand during period $j = 1,2,3,4$ for product A.

where $\hat{x}_0 = 100$

$\hat{y}_j = \hat{y}_{j-1} + x_j - \hat{d}_j$, $\hat{d}_j$: demand for product B.

where $\hat{y}_0 = 150$

$$\hat{y}_j + \hat{x}_j \leq 250 \qquad j = 1,2,3,4$$

$$\left.\begin{array}{l} 0 \leq x_j \leq 500 \\ 0 \leq y_j \leq 650 \end{array}\right\} \quad j = 1,2,3,4$$

$$\hat{x}_j , \hat{y}_j \geq 0 , \quad j = 1,2,3,4$$

$$\min \sum_{j=1}^{4} \hat{x}_j + 0.8 \sum_{j=1}^{4} \hat{y}_j$$

b, c, d) We have 21 constraints (If bounded simplex method of chapter 5 is used we would only have 13 constraints). The starting basis will consist of $x_1, x_2, x_3, x_4, x_5, x_6, x_8$, an artificial for product A at third period, y_1, y_2, y_3, y_4 y_5, y_6, y_8, an artificial for product B at period 3 , $\hat{y}_4$, s_1, s_2, s_3, s_4. The problem can be solved by computer.

PROBLEM 4.38

Let x_1: # trucks of type I

x_2: # trucks of type II

x_3: # trucks of type III

$$\min \quad 400x_1 + 600x_2 + 900x_3$$

$$\begin{aligned} \text{S.T.} \quad x_1 + x_2 + x_3 &\geq 12 \\ x_2 + 2x_3 &\geq 10 \\ 2x_1 + x_2 + x_3 &\geq 16 \\ x_1,\ x_2,\ x_3 &\geq 0 \end{aligned}$$

	z	x_1	x_2	x_3	x_4	x_5	x_6	x_7	x_8	x_9	RHS
z	1	0	0	0	0	0	0	-1	-1	-1	0
x_1	0	1	0	0	1	0	-1	-1	0	1	4
x_2	0	0	1	0	-4	1	2	4	-1	-2	6
x_3	0	0	0	1	2	-1	-1	-2	1	1	2

End of phase I

	z	x_1	x_2	x_3	x_4	x_5	x_6	RHS
z	1	0	0	0	-200	-300	-100	7000
x_1	0	1	0	0	1	0	-1	4
x_2	0	0	1	0	-4	1	2	6
x_3	0	0	0	1	2	-1	-1	2

End of Phase II. Optimal Tableau.

PROBLEM 4.39

Let x_i : production of refrigerators at ith period.

$\hat{x}_i$: inventory of refrigerators at the end of ith period.

y_i : production of stoves at ith period

$\hat{y}_i$: inventory of stoves at the end of ith period.

PROBLEM 4.39 (Continued)

g_i: production of dishwasher at period i.

$\hat{g}_i$: inventory of dishwasher at the end of period i.

$i = 1, 2, 3, 4.$

$$\min \sum_{j=1}^{4} (\hat{x}_j + \hat{y}_j + \hat{g}_j)$$

s.t.

$$\hat{x}_j = \hat{x}_{j-1} + x_j - d_j \quad , \quad j=1,\dots,4$$
$$\hat{x}_0 = 0$$
$$\hat{y}_j = \hat{y}_{j-1} + y_j - d'_j \quad , \quad j=1,\dots,4$$
$$\hat{y}_0 = 0$$
$$\hat{g}_j = \hat{g}_{j-1} + g_j - d''_j \quad , \quad j=1,\dots,4$$
$$\hat{g}_0 = 0$$
$$2x_j + 4y_j + 3g_j \le 18{,}000 \quad , \quad j=1,\dots,4$$
$$x_j, y_j, g_j \ge 150 \quad , \quad j=1,\dots,4$$

where d_j, d'_j, d''_j are the demands at period j for refrigerators, stoves and dishwashers respectively.

PROBLEM 4.40

Let x_1: number of cuts according to pattern 1
x_2: " " " " 2
x_3: " " " " 3
x_4: " " " " 4

PROBLEM 4.40 (Continued)

Note that x_1 and x_3 are practically equivalent. Assume that we will minimize the total length cut.

$$\begin{aligned}
\min \quad & 4x_1 + 4x_2 + 4x_3 + 4x_4 \\
\text{S.T.} \quad & 2x_1 + x_2 + 2x_3 + 6x_4 \geq 2000 \\
& x_1 + x_2 + x_3 \geq 1000 \\
& 4x_2 + 4x_4 \leq 3000 \\
& 4x_1 + 4x_3 \leq 2000 \\
& x_1, x_2, x_3, x_4 \geq 0
\end{aligned}$$

	Z	x_1	x_2	x_3	x_4	x_5	x_6	x_7	x_8	x_9	x_{10}	RHS
Z	1	0	0	0	0	0	0	0	0	−1	−1	0
x_4	0	0	0	0	1	−1/7	2/7	1/28	0	1/7	−2/7	750/7
x_1	0	1	0	1	0	−1/7	−5/7	−3/14	0	1/7	5/7	2500/7
x_2	0	0	1	0	0	1/7	−2/7	3/14	0	−1/7	2/7	4500/7
x_8	0	0	0	0	0	4/7	20/7	6/7	1	−4/7	−20/7	4000/7

End of phase I.

	Z	x_1	x_2	x_3	x_4	x_5	x_6	x_7	x_8	RHS
Z	1	0	0	0	0	−2/3	−10/3	0	−1/6	13,000/3
x_4	0	0	0	0	1	−1/6	1/6	0	−1/24	250/3
x_1	0	1	0	1	0	0	0	0	1/4	500
x_2	0	0	1	0	0	0	−1	0	−1/4	500
x_7	0	0	0	0	0	2/3	10/3	1	7/6	2000/3

End of phase II. Solution is optimal with

$$\begin{aligned}
x_1 \text{ or } x_3 &= 500 \\
x_2 &= 500 \\
x_4 &= 250/3 \\
z &= 13{,}000/3.
\end{aligned}$$

PROBLEM 4.41

	z	x_4	x_5	x_6	x_1	x_2	x_3	RHS
z	1	0	0	0	−1	−2	−1	0
x_4	0	1	0	0	1	4	6	4
x_5	0	0	1	0	−1	(1)	4	1
x_6	0	0	0	1	1	3	1	6

	z	x_4	x_5	x_6	x_1	x_2	x_3	RHS
z	1	0	2	0	−3	0	7	2
x_4	0	1	−4	0	(5)	0	−10	0
x_2	0	0	1	0	−1	1	4	1
x_6	0	0	−3	1	4	0	−11	3

	z	x_4	x_5	x_6	x_1	x_2	x_3	RHS
z	1	1	2/5	0	0	0	1	2
x_1	0	1/5	−4/5	0	1	0	−2	0
x_2	0	1/5	1/5	0	0	1	2	1
x_6	0	−4/5	−1/5	1	0	0	−3	3

Optimal tableau.

PROBLEM 4.42

	z	d_4	d_5	d_6	d_7	d_1	d_2	d_3	RHS
z	1	0	0	0	1	0	0	0	1
d_3	0	1/6	0	−1/9	5/18	0	0	1	5/18
d_5	0	7/6	1	−1/9	5/18	0	0	0	5/18
d_1	0	1/3	0	1/9	2/9	1	0	0	2/9
d_2	0	−1/2	0	0	1/2	0	1	0	1/2

Optimal tableau.

Therefore, we have the direction

$$\left(2/9,\ 1/2,\ 5/18\right) \equiv (4, 9, 5)$$

The procedure may not generate an extreme direction. It will generate an extreme direction if the constraint $d_1+d_2+d_3 \le 1$ is dropped or replaced by the constraint $d_1^2+d_2^2+d_3^2 \le 1$. Note, however, that the simplex method generates extreme optimal point, so that, even with the condition $d_1+d_2+d_3 \le 1$ we obtain extreme direction.

PROBLEM 4.42 (Continued)

We will now solve the problem by dropping $d_1+d_2+d_3 \le 1$.

	z	d_4	d_5	d_6	d_1	d_2	d_3	RHS
	1	0	2	−1	−7	0	0	0
d_4	0	1	4/3	−1/3	−5/3	0	0	0
d_3	0	0	1/3	−1/3	−5/3	0	1	0
d_2	0	0	5/3	−2/3	−13/3	1	0	0

Final tableau, Iteration #2.

By examining either d_6 or d_1 column, we see that the optimal solution is unbounded. The two extreme directions

$$(0, 2/3, 1/3) \equiv (0, 2, 1), \text{ and}$$

$$(1, 13/3, 5/3) \equiv (3, 13, 5)$$

are identified.

PROBLEM 4.43

Review section 4.6 for detailed information.

PROBLEM 4.44

a)

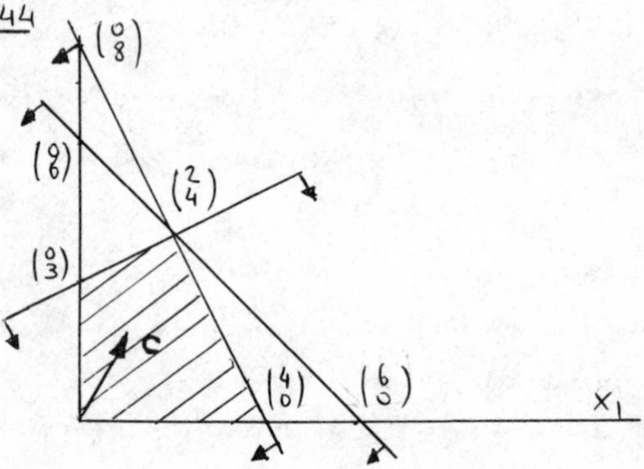

PROBLEM 4.44 (Continued)

Optimal is $\binom{2}{4}$ with obj=22.

b) Left to the reader.

c) The constraint that is causing degeneracy is $x_1 + x_2 \leq 6$ and can be thrown away.

	z	x_1	x_2	x_3	x_4	RHS
z	1	0	0	3	1	22
x_1	0	1	0	2/5	−1/5	2
x_2	0	0	1	1/5	2/5	4

Optimal tableau for the reduced problem.

Obviously, the degeneracy dissapeared after throwing $x_1 + x_2 \leq 6$.

d) If at the optimal extreme point more than m (m the size of the basis) constraints intersect we will have degeneracy. Deleting the proper extra constraint will give us non degenerate optimal solution.

CHAPTER 5 SPECIAL SIMPLEX FORMS

PROBLEM 5.1

						x_2
z	0	0	0	0		2
x_4	1	0	0	4		(2)
x_5	0	1	0	9		1
x_6	0	0	1	5		-1

$w = (0,0,0)$

$z_1 - c_1 = 0$, $z_2 - c_2 = 2$

$z_3 - c_3 = -1$

introduce x_2 ∴ $y_2 = a_2 = \begin{bmatrix} 2 \\ 1 \\ -1 \end{bmatrix}$

						x_1
z	-1	0	0	-4		1
x_2	1/2	0	0	2		-1/2
x_5	-1/2	1	0	7		(3/2)
x_6	1/2	0	1	7		3/2

$c_B = [-2,0,0]$, $w = [-1,0,0]$

$z_1 - c_1 = 1$, $z_3 - c_3 = 0$

$z_4 - c_4 = -1$

Introduce x_1. $y_1 = B^{-1}a_1 = \begin{bmatrix} -1/2 \\ 3/2 \\ 3/2 \end{bmatrix}$

z	-2/3	-2/3	0	-26/3
x_2	1/3	1/3	0	13/3
x_1	-1/3	2/3	0	14/3
x_6	1	-1	1	0

$c_B = [-2,0,0]$, $w = [-2/3, -2/3, 0]$

$z_3 - c_3 = -1$

$z_5 - c_5 = -2/3$

$z_4 - c_4 = -2/3$

Since all $z_j - c_j < 0$, the solution is optimal.

PROBLEM 5.2

Let $B = [a_1, a_5]$, $w = c_B B^{-1} = (1,5)\begin{bmatrix} 1 & 0 \\ 0 & 1 \end{bmatrix} = (1,5)$

					x_3
z	1	5	30		24
x_1	1	0	5		2
x_5	0	1	5		(3)

$z_2 - c_2 = (1, 5)\begin{pmatrix} -3/4 \\ -1/4 \end{pmatrix} - 6 < 0$

$z_3 - c_3 = 24$

introduce x_3, $y_3 = a_3 = (2,3)^T$.

PROBLEM 5.2 (Continued)

				x_4
z	1	-3	-10	1
x_1	1	-2/3	5/3	(1/4)
x_3	0	1/3	5/3	-1/4

$w = (1, -3)$

$z_2 - c_2 = -6$, $z_4 - c_4 = 1$

introduce x_4.

$y_4 = B^{-1}a_4 = [1/4, -1/4]^T$

z	-3	-1/3	-50/3
x_4	4	-8/3	20/3
x_3	1	-1/3	10/3

$w = (-3, -1/3)$

$z_1 - c_1 = -4 < 0$

$z_2 - c_2 = -\frac{1}{3} - 5 < 0$

The solution is optimal.

PROBLEM 5.3

The tableau used in the revised simplex method is $(m+1)\times(m+1)$ matrix. Since the pivot row is subtracted (minus added) from every other row we have $m(m+1)$ additions. In order to get the pivot row we multiply that row by the reciprocal of the pivot entry. This gives $m+1$ multiplications. We then multiply the pivot row by the negative of each entries in the pivot column. This gives us $m(m+1)$ multiplications, or all of them together $(m+1)^2$ multiplications.

PROBLEM 5.3 (Continued)

We have $z_j - c_j = wa_j - c_j$ for $n-m$ nonbasic variables. w is available in the zeroth row. We need $n-m$ vector multiplication of size m each, giving $m(n-m)$ multiplications in total. The amount of additions is $m(n-m)$ of them for wa_j's and $n-m$ additions for $wa_j - c_j$'s. Therefore, the total additions are $(m+1)(n-m)$ in the revised simplex method.

PROBLEM 5.4

Iteration 1:

$$B = (a_1, a_5) \quad , \quad w = (1, 5)$$

$$z_2 - c_2 = -8 \quad , \quad z_3 - c_3 = 24 \quad , \quad z_4 - c_4 = -5$$

Introduce x_3. $\quad y_3 = (2,3)^T \quad , \quad \bar{b} = (5,5)^T$

The minimum ratio is at $r=2$ and $x_{B_2} = x_5$ leaves the basis. The nonidentity column ξ is given by $\xi = (-2/3, 1/3)^T$ at position 2. The new right hand side is given by

$$E_1 \bar{b} = \begin{bmatrix} 1 & -2/3 \\ 0 & 1/3 \end{bmatrix} \begin{bmatrix} 5 \\ 5 \end{bmatrix} = \begin{bmatrix} 5/3 \\ 5/3 \end{bmatrix}$$

Iteration 2:

$$B_2 = (a_1, a_3) \quad , \quad B_2^{-1} = \begin{bmatrix} 1 & -2/3 \\ 0 & 1/3 \end{bmatrix}$$

$$w = c_B B^{-1} = c_B E_1 = [1, -3]$$

PROBLEM 5.4 (Continued)

$z_2 - c_2 = -6$, $z_4 - c_4 = 1$, introduce x_4.

$y_4 = B^{-1} a_4 = E_1 a_4 = (1/4, -1/4)^T$

$\bar{b} = B^{-1} b = E_1 b = (5/3, 5/3)^T$

$x_{B_1} = x_1$ leaves the basis and x_4 enters.

$\xi = (4, 1)^T$, $E_2 = \begin{bmatrix} 4 & 0 \\ 1 & 1 \end{bmatrix}$

$B^{-1}_{new} = E_2 E_1 = \begin{bmatrix} 4 & -8/3 \\ 1 & -1/3 \end{bmatrix}$

$\bar{b} = E_2 E_1 b = (20/3, 10/3)^T$

Iteration 3:

$w = c_B E_2 E_1 = (-3, -1/3)$

$z_1 - c_1 = -4$, $z_2 - c_2 = -35/12$

Since all $z_j - c_j < 0$, the solution is optimal.

PROBLEM 5.5

Iteration 1: $B = [a_5, a_6, a_7]$, $w = [0, 0, 0]$

$z_1 - c_1 = -3$, $z_2 - c_2 = -4$, $z_3 - c_3 = -1$, $z_4 - c_4 = -7$

introduce x_4. $y_4 = (1, 5, 2)^T$, $\bar{b} = (7, 3, 8)^T$

$r = 2$ and $x_{B_2} = x_6$ leaves the basis.

$\xi = (-1/5; 1/5, -2/5)^T$, position $= 2$

$E_1 \bar{b} = [32/5, 3/5, 34/5]^T$

Iteration 2: $B = [a_5, a_4, a_7]$, $w = c_B E_1 = (0, 4/5, 0)$

$z_1 - c_1 = -7/5$, $z_2 - c_2 = 4/5$, $z_3 - c_3 = -1/5$, introduce x_1.

$y_1 = E_1 a_1 = (38/5, 2/5, 1/5)^T$. $r = 1$ and $x_{B_1} = x_5$ leaves the basis, and x_1 enters.

PROBLEM 5.5 (Continued)

$\xi = (5/38, -2/38, -1/38)^T$, position = 1.

$B^{-1} = E_2E_1$. The new right hand side is given by $B^{-1}b = E_2E_1b = (32/38, 10/38, 252/38)^T$

Iteration 3: $B = [a_1, a_4, a_7]$, $w = c_B E_2 E_1$

$w = (1/38, 53/38, 0)$, $z_2 - c_2 = 169/38$,

$z_3 - c_3 = 19/38$, $z_6 - c_6 = 53/38$, $z_5 - c_5 > 0$.

Since all $z_j - c_j > 0$ for nonbasic variables, the optimal solution is at hand.

$x_1 = 32/38$, $x_2 = x_3 = 0$, $x_4 = 10/38$ and $z = 83/19$.

PROBLEM 5.6

				RHS	x_4
z	0	0	0	0	3/4
x_1	1	0	0	0	(1/4)
x_2	0	1	0	0	1/2
x_3	0	0	1	1	0

$w = (0, 0, 0)$

$z_4 - c_4 = 3/4$

$z_5 - c_5 = -20$

$z_6 - c_6 = 1/2$

$z_7 - c_7 = -6$

introduce x_4. $y_4 = a_4 = (1/4, 1/2, 0)^T$

				RHS	x_5
z	-3	0	0	0	4
x_4	4	0	0	0	-32
x_2	-2	1	0	0	(4)
x_3	0	0	1	1	0

$w = (-3, 0, 0)$

$z_1 - c_1 = -3$

$z_5 - c_5 = 4$

$z_6 - c_6 = 7/2$

$z_7 - c_7 = -33$

introduce x_5.

$$y_5 = B^{-1}a_5 = \begin{bmatrix} 4 & 0 & 0 \\ -2 & 1 & 0 \\ 0 & 0 & 1 \end{bmatrix} \begin{bmatrix} -8 \\ -12 \\ 0 \end{bmatrix} = \begin{bmatrix} -32 \\ 4 \\ 0 \end{bmatrix}$$

PROBLEM 5.6 (Continued)

				RHS	x_6
z	-1	-1	0	0	2
x_4	-12	8	0	0	(8)
x_5	-1/2	1/4	0	0	3/8
x_3	0	0	1	1	1

$w = (-1, -1, 0)$
$z_1 - c_1 = -1$
$z_2 - c_2 = -1$
$z_6 - c_6 = 2$
$z_7 - c_7 = -18$

introduce x_6. $B^{-1}a_6 = y_6 = (8, 3/8, 1)^T$

				RHS	x_7
z	2	-3	0	0	3
x_6	-3/2	1	0	0	-21/2
x_5	1/16	-1/8	0	0	(3/16)
x_3	3/2	-1	1	1	21/2

$w = (2, -3, 0)$
$z_1 - c_1 = 2$
$z_2 - c_2 = -3$
$z_4 - c_4 = -1/4$
$z_7 - c_7 = 3$

introduce x_7. $y_7 = B^{-1}a_7 = (-21/2, 3/16, 21/2)^T$

				RHS	x_1
z	1	-1	0	0	1
x_6	2	-6	0	0	(2)
x_7	1/3	-2/3	0	0	1/3
x_3	-2	6	1	1	-2

$w = (1, -1, 0)$
$z_1 - c_1 = 1$
$z_2 - c_2 = -1$
$z_4 - c_4 = 1/2$
$z_5 - c_5 = -16$

introduce x_1. $B^{-1}a_1 = y_1 = (2, 1/3, -2)^T$

				RHS	x_2
	0	2	0	0	2
x_1	1	-3	0	0	-3
x_7	0	1/3	0	0	(1/3)
x_3	0	0	1	1	0

$w = (0, 2, 0)$
$z_2 - c_2 = 2$
$z_4 - c_4 = 7/4$
$z_5 - c_5 = -44$
$z_6 - c_6 = -1/2$

introduce x_2. $y_2 = (-3, \frac{1}{3}, 0)^T$.

If we perform the pivot operation

PROBLEM 5.6 (Continued)

we will obtain the initial tableau. Therefore we had a cycle. The above sequence of pivots generated the bases $B_1, B_2, B_3, B_4, B_5, B_6, B_7$ where $B_7 = B_1 = [a_1, a_2, a_3]$.

If we apply the cycling prevention rule in first tableau, x_4 will enter the basis and x_2 will leave. The new tableau is given as:

				RHS	x_6
z	0	-3/2	0	0	5/4
x_1	1	-1/2	0	0	-3/4
x_4	0	2	0	0	-1
x_3	0	0	1	1	(1)

$w = (0, -3/2, 0)$

$z_2 - c_2 = -3/2$

$z_5 - c_5 = -2$

$z_6 - c_6 = 5/4$

$z_7 - c_7 = -21/2$

introduce x_6. $a_6 = (-3/4, -1, 1)$

				RHS
z	0	-3/2	-5/4	-5/4
x_1	1	-1/2	3/4	3/4
x_4	0	2	1	1
x_6	0	0	1	1

$w = (0, -3/2, -5/4)$

$z_2 - c_2 = -3/2$

$z_3 - c_3 = -5/4$

$z_5 - c_5 = -2$

$z_7 - c_7 = -21/2$

Since all $z_j - c_j < 0$ for nonbasic variables the solution is optimal with

$x_1 = 3/4 \quad x_2 = x_3 = x_7 = 0, \quad x_4 = 1, \quad x_6 = 1$

and $\quad obj = -5/4$.

PROBLEM 5.7

Suppose at some point in the revised simplex method we wish to reinvert B. Select the first column of B and obtain E_1 as follows:

$$E_1 = \begin{bmatrix} \frac{1}{B_{11}} & 0 & \cdots & 0 \\ -\frac{B_{21}}{B_{11}} & 1 & \cdots & 0 \\ \vdots & \vdots & \ddots & \vdots \\ -\frac{B_{m1}}{B_{11}} & 0 & \cdots & 1 \end{bmatrix}$$

Next, let $\hat{B} = E_1 B$. Then E_2 is defined by

$$E_2 = \begin{bmatrix} 1 & -\frac{\hat{B}_{12}}{\hat{B}_{22}} & \cdots & 0 \\ 0 & \frac{1}{\hat{B}_{22}} & \cdots & 0 \\ \vdots & \vdots & \ddots & \vdots \\ 0 & -\frac{\hat{B}_{m2}}{\hat{B}_{22}} & \cdots & 1 \end{bmatrix}$$

Let $\hat{\hat{B}} = E_2 \hat{B}$. Define E_3 in an analogous manner and continue until E_m is defined.

EXAMPLE:

$$B = \begin{bmatrix} 1 & 2 & 1 \\ 2 & 1 & -1 \\ -1 & 3 & 2 \end{bmatrix}, \quad E_1 = \begin{bmatrix} 1/1 & 0 & 0 \\ -2/1 & 1 & 0 \\ 1/1 & 0 & 1 \end{bmatrix}, \quad \hat{B} = \begin{bmatrix} 1 & 2 & 1 \\ 0 & -3 & -3 \\ 0 & 5 & 3 \end{bmatrix}$$

$$E_2 = \begin{bmatrix} 1 & 2/3 & 0 \\ 0 & -1/3 & 0 \\ 0 & 5/3 & 1 \end{bmatrix}, \quad \hat{\hat{B}} = \begin{bmatrix} 1 & 0 & -1 \\ 0 & 1 & 1 \\ 0 & 0 & -2 \end{bmatrix}, \quad E_3 = \begin{bmatrix} 1 & 0 & -1/2 \\ 0 & 1 & 1/2 \\ 0 & 0 & -1/2 \end{bmatrix}$$

$\hat{\hat{\hat{B}}} = I$. Hence, $B^{-1} = E_3 E_2 E_1$.

PROBLEM 5.9

Initial tableau

	Z	x_1 (ℓ)	x_2 (ℓ)	x_3 (ℓ)	x_4	x_5	x_6	RHS
z	1	-1	-1	-3	0	0	0	0
x_4	0	1	1	1	1	0	0	12
x_5	0	-1	1	0	0	1	0	5
x_6	0	0	1	(2)	0	0	1	8

Final Tableau. (Optimal)

	Z	x_1	x_2	x_3	x_4	x_5	x_6	RHS
z	1	1	0	1	0	0	1	15
x_4	0	-1	0	1	1	0	-1	5
x_5	0	1	0	2	0	1	-1	8
x_2	0	0	1	-2	0	0	1	0

PROBLEM 5.10

Let, x_1, x_2, x_3 and x_4 be nonbasic where $x_1^{\ell} = 0$, $x_2^{u} = 4$, $x_3^{\ell} = 0$, $x_4^{\ell} = 2$. The basics are the slack variables x_5, x_6, x_7.

Initial Tableau.

	Z	x_1 (ℓ)	x_2 (u)	x_3 (ℓ)	x_4 (ℓ)	x_5	x_6	x_7	RHS
z	1	-1	-2	-3	1	0	0	0	6
x_5	0	1	-1	1	-2	1	0	0	14
x_6	0	-1	1	-1	(1)	0	1	0	2
x_7	0	2	1	1	0	0	0	1	2

Second Tableau.

	Z	x_1	x_2	x_3	x_4	x_5	x_6	x_7	RHS
z	1	0	-3	-2	0	0	-1	0	4
x_5	0	-1	1	-1	0	1	2	0	18
x_4	0	-1	(1)	-1	1	0	1	0	4
x_7	0	-2	-1	1	0	0	0	1	2

PROBLEM 5.10 (Continued)

	z	x_1	x_2 (ℓ)	x_3 (ℓ)	x_4 (u)	x_5	x_6	x_7 (ℓ)	RHS
z	1	0	$-3/2$	$-7/2$	1	0	0	$-1/2$	$-5/2$
x_5	0	0	$-3/2$	$3/2$	-2	1	0	$1/2$	$33/2$
x_1	0	1	$1/2$	$-1/2$	0	0	0	$-1/2$	$1/2$
x_6	0	0	$3/2$	$-3/2$	1	0	1	$-1/2$	$5/2$

Optimal tableau (Tableau #4)

Optimal solution:

$x_1 = 1/2$, $x_2 = 1$, $x_3 = 0$, $x_4 = 5$ and $z = -5/2$

PROBLEM 5.11

Consider the system $Ax = b$, $\ell \leq x \leq u$ where A is an $m \times n$ matrix of rank m. Let x be a basic feasible solution, i.e.,

$x = (x_B, x_{N_1}, x_{N_2})^T$ where $x_{N_1} = \ell_{N_1}$, $x_{N_2} = u_{N_2}$,

$x_B = B^{-1}b - B^{-1}N_1\ell_{N_1} - B^{-1}N_2u_{N_2}$ and $\ell_B \leq x_B \leq u_B$.

Let x' and x'' be two feasible points such that $x = \lambda x' + (1-\lambda)x''$ and $\lambda \in (0,1)$, then $\ell_{N_1} = \lambda x'_{N_1} + (1-\lambda)x''_{N_1}$. Since $0 < \lambda < 1$ and since x'_{N_1} and $x''_{N_1} \geq \ell_{N_1}$ (by feasibility), then $x'_{N_1} = x''_{N_1} = \ell_{N_1}$. Similarly $x'_{N_2} = x''_{N_2} = u_{N_2}$. This implies that $x'_B = x''_B = B^{-1}b - B^{-1}N_1\ell_{N_1} - B^{-1}N_2u_{N_2}$ and hence $x = x' = x''$. In other words, x is an extreme point of the set $\{x : Ax = b, \ell \leq x \leq u\}$

Now let x be an extreme point of the set.

PROBLEM 5.11 (Continued)

Possibly after rearranging the indices, suppose that $\ell_j < x_j < u_j$ for $j = 1, \ldots, p$, whereas the other x_j's are either at their lower or upper bounds. We will show that $a_1, a_2, \ldots a_p$ are linearly independent. If not, there would exist scalar γ_j's not all zero such that

$$\sum_{j=1}^{p} \gamma_j a_j = 0$$

Consider the two vectors given as follows:

$$x_j' = \begin{cases} x_j + \lambda \gamma_j & , \quad j = 1, \ldots, p \\ x_j & , \quad j = p+1, \ldots, n \end{cases}$$

$$x_j'' = \begin{cases} x_j - \lambda \gamma_j & , \quad j = 1, 2, \ldots, p \\ x_j & , \quad j = p+1, \ldots, n \end{cases}$$

$\lambda > 0$ is chosen small enough such that $\ell_j < x_j + \lambda \gamma_j < u_j$ and $\ell_j < x_j - \lambda \gamma_j < u_j$. Note that x' and x'' are distinct and that $x = \frac{1}{2} x' + \frac{1}{2} x''$. Furthermore, x' and x'' are feasible (why?). This contradicts the assumption that x is an extreme point. Therefore, $a_1, a_2, \ldots, a_p$ are linearly independent (so that $p \leq m$). It then easily follows that x is indeed a basic feasible solution.

PROBLEM 5.13

wrong

Let x_1, x_2, x_3 be the starting nonbasic variables. Let $x_1 = 4$, $x_2 = -2$, and $x_3 = 2$. Let x_4 and x_5 be the initial basic variables. Hence, $x_4 = 4$ and $x_5 = 1$ and $z = -2$.

	z	x_1 (u)	x_2 (ℓ)	x_3 (ℓ)	x_4	x_5	RHS
z	1	-2	-3	2	0	0	-2
x_4	0	1	1	1	1	0	4
x_5	0	-2	-1	(1)	0	1	1

Initial tableau.

	z	x_1 (u)	x_2 (ℓ)	x_3	x_4	x_5 (ℓ)	
z	1	2	-1	0	0	-2	-4
x_4	0	3	2	0	1	-1	3
x_3	0	-2	-1	1	0	1	3

Optimal tableau.

Iteration #1.

The optimal is given by:

$x_1 = 4$, $x_2 = -2$, $x_3 = 3$, $z = -4$.

PROBLEM 5.15

We shall assume that $\ell_j < u_j$, for if this is not the case we can set $x_j = \ell_j = u_j$ and reduce the dimensionality of the problem. Now, if x_k, the entering variable, is blocked by its either limit, then there will be a positive change in z. This leave two other cases.

Let $\beta = B^{-1}$. Utilizing Charnes perturbation technique we let $\underline{b}' = \underline{b} + \sum_{\ell=1}^{m} \epsilon^{\ell} \underline{e}_\ell$ where ϵ is a small positive number. Then

PROBLEM 5.15 (Continued)

$$\frac{\hat{b}_i' - \ell_{Bi}}{y_{ik}} = \frac{\hat{b}_i - \ell_{Bi}}{y_{ik}} + \frac{1}{y_{ik}} \sum_{\ell=1}^{m} \epsilon^\ell \beta_\ell$$

and

$$\frac{u_{Bi} - \hat{b}_i'}{-y_{ik}} = \frac{u_{Bi} - \hat{b}_i}{-y_{ik}} + \frac{1}{y_{ik}} \sum_{\ell=1}^{m} \epsilon^\ell \beta_\ell$$

Thus, the rule is essentially the same as that of Chapter 4. Let I_0 be the set of indices which are tied for minimum θ based on the right-hand side. If $I_0 = \{r\}$, a singleton, pivot on y_{rk}. Otherwise let

$$I_1 = \left\{ \frac{\beta_{r1}}{y_{rk}} = \min \left\{ \frac{\beta_{i\ell}}{y_{ik}} \right\} \right\}$$

if $I_1 = \{r\}$, a singleton, pivot on y_{rk}. Otherwise define I_2 using the second column of B^{-1}. Continue until the tie is broken (as it must be before we run out of colums of B^{-1}).

PROBLEM 5.16

a) $x_1 = \frac{10}{3}$, all other $x = 0$, obj $= \frac{20}{3}$ *

$x_2 = \frac{10}{7}$, all other $x = 0$, obj $= \frac{30}{7}$

$x_3 = \frac{10}{12}$, all other $x = 0$, obj $= \frac{80}{12}$ *

$x_4 = \frac{10}{2}$, all other $x = 0$, obj $= \frac{10}{2}$

$x_5 = \frac{10}{3}$, all other $x = 0$, obj $= \frac{10}{3}$

all $x = 0$, obj $= 0$.

Optimal solutions:

$(\frac{10}{3}, 0, 0, 0, 0)$ and $(0, 0, \frac{5}{6}, 0, 0)$ with obj $= 20/3$.

PROBLEM 5.16 (Continued)

b) Let $c_k/a_k = \max_{1\le j\le n} c_j/a_j$. An optimal solution is thus given by:

$$x_j = \begin{cases} b/a_k, & j=k \\ 0, & j\neq k \end{cases}$$

c) If the a_j's are of any sign, the feasible region may be unbounded, so the optimal solution may be unbounded. Recall that the optimal is unbounded if and only if $cd>0$ for some extreme direction d. But d is an extreme direction if and only if it is of the form $d = [-B^{-1}a_j \mid 0, \ldots, 1, 0, \ldots, 0]^T$ where $B^{-1}a_j \le 0$ and 1 appears at position j. Note that B is a scalar for this problem. Without loss of generality suppose that $b>0$. Therefore, B is given by the positive scalar a_i. Hence d is an extreme direction if and only if it has $-a_j/a_i$ at position i and 1 at position j and is zero elsewhere, and $a_j<0$. Therefore the optimal solution is unbounded if and only if $cd>0$, i.e., if and only if $c_i\left(\frac{-a_j}{a_i}\right)+c_j>0$ where $a_i>0$ and $a_j<0$. To summarize, the optimal solution is unbounded

PROBLEM 5.16 (Continued)

if and only if $c_i/a_i - c_j/a_j > 0$ for some positive a_i and some negative a_j.

As an algorithm to check this, compute

$$\max_{a_i > 0} c_i/a_i \quad \text{and} \quad \min_{a_j < 0} c_j/a_j$$

If $\max_{a_i > 0} c_i/a_i - \min_{a_j < 0} c_j/a_j \leq 0$, then, the optimal is bounded, otherwise it is unbounded along the direction d whose kth component is $-a_k/a_\ell$, and whose ℓth component is 1, where

$$\frac{c_k}{a_k} = \max_{a_i > 0} \frac{c_i}{a_i} \quad \text{and} \quad \frac{c_\ell}{a_\ell} = \min_{a_j < 0} \frac{c_j}{a_j}.$$

If the optimal is bounded, then it occurs at the extreme point x given by:

$$x_j = \begin{cases} b/a_k, & j = k \\ 0 & \text{otherwise} \end{cases}$$

where the index k is computed as follows:

$$\frac{c_k}{a_k} = \max_{a_i > 0} \frac{c_i}{a_i}$$

PROBLEM 5.17

For each P_i pick the most profitable variable (one with the largest c_j). Assign to that variable the minimum of b_i' and u_j. If the value of the variable is equal to its upper bound, choose the next most profitable variable in P and assign to it the minimum of its upper bound and the new value of b_i', after subtracting the previous upper bound. Continue this process until each block P_i has the lower bound b_i satisfied.

Now, choose the most profitable variable in the overall problem and assign to it as much as possible without violating its upper bound, b_0'', and the upper bound b_i'' of its block P_i. Repeat this until no other assignments are possible.

Example:

	x_1	x_2	x_3	x_4	x_5
Satisfying lower Bounds	2	0	10	30	30
Choosing the most profitable variable.	30	0	10	30	30

The last row is the optimal solution.

PROBLEM 5.18

Let x_1, x_2, x_3, x_4, x_5 be nonbasic in their lower bounds and let x_6 and x_7 be the artificial variables.

PROBLEM 5.18 (Continued)

	z	x_1	x_2	x_3	x_4	x_5	x_6 (art.)	x_7 (art.)	RHS
z	1	-2	-6	1	4	-1	0	0	10
x_6	0	2	1	4	(1)	1	1	0	8
x_7	0	-3	-8	3	-1	0	0	1	2

phase I iteration 1

After finishing phase I and eliminating x_6 and x_7 we proceed into phase II. Following is the last tableau of phase II:

	z	x_1	x_2 (ℓ)	x_3	x_4 (ℓ)	x_5	RHS
z	1	5	25/3	0	20/3	0	20/3
x_5	0	6	35/3	0	7/3	1	16/3
x_3	0	-1	-8/3	1	-1/3	0	2/3

Optimal tableau.

Optimal solution:

$x_1 = 0$, $x_2 = x_4 = 1$, $x_3 = 2/3$, $x_5 = 16/3$

obj $= 20/3$.

PROBLEM 5.19

Let x_a be an artificial variable with activity vector $(-15, -8, -25)^T$. Then, we get the following tableau where x_a is not basic at its upper bound of 1.

PROBLEM 5.19 (Continued)

Phase I:

								u	
	z	x_1	x_2	x_3	x_4	x_5	x_6	x_a	RHS
z	1	0	0	0	0	0	0	-1	1
x_4	0	-1	-2	-1	1	0	0	-15	3
x_5	0	-1	-1	2	0	1	0	-8	2
x_6	0	-2	-1	-4	0	0	1	(-25)	1

Initial tableau.

	z	x_1	x_2	x_3	x_4	x_5	x_6	x_a	RHS
z	1	2/25	1/25	4/25	0	0	-1/25	0	24/25
x_4	0	5/25	-35/25	35/25	1	0	-15/25	0	60/25
x_5	0	-9/25	-17/25	32/25	0	1	-8/25	0	42/25
x_a	0	2/25	(1/25)	4/25	0	0	-1/25	1	24/25

Second tableau.

	z	x_1	x_2	x_3	x_4	x_5	x_6	x_a	RHS
z	1	0	0	0	0	0	0	-1	0
x_4	0	3	0	7	1	0	-2	35	36
x_5	0	1	0	6	0	1	-1	17	18
x_2	0	2	1	4	0	0	-1	25	24

Last tableau in phase I (third tableau)

Here we have a basic feasible solution of the original system. Phase II can be started by throwing the x_a column.

PROBLEM 5.20

		ℓ	ℓ	ℓ			
		x_1	x_2	x_3	x_4	x_5	RHS
z	1	-6	-4	-2	0	0	0
x_4	0	(4)	-3	1	1	0	8
x_5	0	1	2	4	0	1	10

Initial tableau

			ℓ	ℓ	ℓ		
	z	x_1	x_2	x_3	x_4	x_5	RHS
z	1	0	-17/2	-1/2	3/2	0	12
x_1	0	1	(-3/4)	1/4	1/4	0	2
x_5	0	0	11/4	15/4	-1/4	1	8

Second tableau

PROBLEM 5.20 (Continued)

		u		l	l		
	z	x_1	x_2	x_3	x_4	x_5	RHS
z	1	$-\frac{34}{3}$	0	$-\frac{10}{3}$	$-\frac{4}{3}$	0	$\frac{70}{3}$
x_2	0	$-\frac{4}{3}$	1	$-\frac{1}{3}$	($-\frac{1}{3}$)	0	$\frac{4}{3}$
x_5	0	$\frac{11}{3}$	0	$\frac{14}{3}$	$\frac{2}{3}$	1	$\frac{13}{3}$

Third tableau

		u	u	l			
	z	x_1	x_2	x_3	x_4	x_5	RHS
z	1	-6	-4	-2	0	0	26
x_4	0	4	-3	1	1	0	2
x_5	0	1	2	(4)	0	1	3

Fourt tableau

Optimal tableau

		u	u			l	
	z	x_1	x_2	x_3	x_4	x_5	RHS
z	1	$-\frac{11}{2}$	-3	0	0	$\frac{1}{2}$	$\frac{55}{2}$
x_4	0	$\frac{15}{4}$	$-\frac{7}{2}$	0	1	$-\frac{1}{4}$	$\frac{5}{4}$
x_3	0	$\frac{1}{4}$	$\frac{1}{2}$	1	0	$\frac{1}{4}$	$\frac{3}{4}$

Fifth tableau.

PROBLEM 5.21

		l	l			
	z	x_1	x_2	x_3	x_4	RHS
z	1	-6	-2	0	0	14
x_3	0	-1	-3	1	0	2
x_4	0	-5	-1	0	1	7

Initial tableau.

		l	l			
	z	x_1	x_2	x_3	x_4	RHS
z	1	-6	-2	0	0	14
x_3	0	-1	-3	1	0	2
x_4	0	-5	-1	0	1	7

Final tableau.

The first tableau is, infact, the optimal tableau. The optimal solution is thus:

$x_1 = 2$, $x_2 = 1$ and obj$= 14$.

PROBLEM 5.22

		l	l			
	z	x_1	x_2	x_3	x_4	RHS
z	1	-6	-4	0	0	0
x_3	0	(3)	2	1	0	4
x_4	0	1	2	0	1	9

			l	l		
	z	x_1	x_2	x_3	x_4	RHS
z	1	0	0	2	0	8
x_1	0	1	$\frac{2}{3}$	$\frac{1}{3}$	0	$\frac{4}{3}$
x_4	0	0	$\frac{4}{3}$	$-\frac{1}{3}$	1	$\frac{23}{3}$

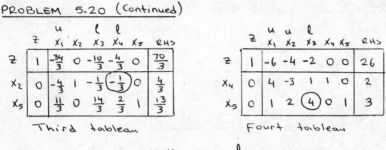

PROBLEM 5.22 (Continued)

The optimal solution is given by
$x_1 = 4/3$, $x_2 = 0$, obj $= 8$.

PROBLEM 5.23

If we prove that the solution space of P_1 is equivalent to the solution space of P_2 then we conclude that P_1 and P_2 are identical.

a- Let x_1 be a solution for P_1. Obviously $Ax_1 \le b_2$. If we add the slack variable s into this inequality we get $Ax_1 + s = b_2$. Since $Ax_1 \geq b_1$ we can write $b_1 + s \le b_2$ or $s \le b_2 - b_1$. Since $Ax_1 \le b_2$, we have $b_2 + s \geq b_2$ or $s \geq 0$. Therefore, any solution for P_1 is also a solution for P_2. The reverse can also be proven in the same manner. i.e., $Ax_1 + s = b_2$ or $Ax_1 \le b_2$ and since $s \le b_2 - b_1$ we can write $Ax_1 + b_2 - b_1 \geq b_2 \Rightarrow Ax_1 \geq b_1$. Therefore any solution to P_2 is also a solution to P_1.

Example:

$$
\begin{aligned}
\min \quad & 3x_1 - 4x_2 \\
\text{S.T.} \quad & x_1 + x_2 + x_3 + x_5 = 5 \\
& 2x_1 - 5x_2 + x_4 + x_6 = 8 \\
& x_3 \le 2 \\
& x_4 \le 6
\end{aligned}
$$

and all $x \geq 0$. Where x_5 and x_6 are

PROBLEM 5.23 (Continued).

artificial variables.

	z	x_1	x_2	x_3	x_4	x_5	x_6	RHS
z	1	0	0	0	0	−1	−1	0
x_2	0	0	1	$\frac{2}{7}$	$-\frac{1}{7}$	$\frac{2}{7}$	$-\frac{1}{7}$	$\frac{2}{7}$
x_1	0	1	0	$\frac{5}{7}$	$\frac{1}{7}$	$\frac{5}{7}$	$\frac{1}{7}$	$\frac{33}{7}$

End of Phase I

	z	x_1	x_2	x_3 (u)	x_4 (u)	RHS
z	1	0	0	1	1	5
x_2	0	0	1	$\frac{2}{7}$	$-\frac{1}{7}$	$\frac{4}{7}$
x_1	0	1	0	$\frac{5}{7}$	$\frac{1}{7}$	$\frac{17}{7}$

End of Phase II

Optimal tableau.

Opt: $x_1 = \frac{17}{7}$, $x_2 = \frac{4}{7}$, $x_3 = 2$, $x_4 = 6$, obj $= 5$.

PROBLEM 5.24

$$\max \quad x_1 + 3x_2 + 2x_3$$

$$\text{s.t.} \quad .6x_1 + 2x_2 + .8x_3 \le 900$$

$$-x_2 + 2x_3 \le 0$$

$$x_2 - 4x_3 \le 0$$

$$200 \le x_1$$

$$200 \le x_2 \le 300$$

$$x_3 \ge 0$$

Phase I: Let x_1, x_2, x_3 be the initial nonbasic variables at their lower bounds. Introduce the artificial variable x_7, with phase I objective min x_7.

	z	x_1 (l)	x_2 (l)	x_3 (l)	x_4	x_5	x_6	x_7	RHS
z	1	0	−1	4	0	0	−1	0	200
x_4	0	.6	2	.8	1	0	0	0	380
x_5	0	0	−1	2	0	1	0	0	200
x_7	0	0	−1	(4)	0	0	−1	1	200

Initial tableau.

PROBLEM 5.24 (Continued)

	z	x_1	x_2	x_3	x_4	x_5	x_6	x_7	RHS
		l	l				l		
z	1	0	0	0	0	0	0	−1	0
x_4	0	.6	2.2	0	1	0	.2	−.2	340
x_5	0	0	−1/2	0	0	1	1/2	−1/2	100
x_3	0	0	−1/4	1	0	0	−1/4	1/4	50

Second tableau. End of phase I.

Phase II.

	z	x_1	x_2	x_3	x_4	x_5	x_6	RHS
		l	l				l	
z	1	−1	−3	−2	0	0	0	0
x_4	0	.6	2.2	0	1	0	.2	340
x_5	0	0	−1/2	0	0	1	1/2	100
x_3	0	0	−1/4	(1)	0	0	−1/4	50

Initial tableau

	z	x_1	x_2	x_3	x_4	x_5	x_6	RHS
		l	l				l	
z	1	−1	−7/2	0	0	0	0	900
x_4	0	.6	2.2	0	1	0	.2	340
x_5	0	0	−1/2	0	0	1	1/2	100
x_3	0	0	−1/4	1	0	0	−1/4	50

Second tableau. x_2 enters and leaves immediately at the upper bound.

	z	x_1	x_2	x_3	x_4	x_5	x_6	RHS
		l	u				l	
z	1	−1	−7/2	0	0	0	−1/2	1250
x_4	0	(.6)	2.2	0	1	0	.2	120
x_5	0	0	−1/2	0	0	1	1/2	150
x_3	0	0	−1/4	1	0	0	−1/4	75

Third tableau.

	z	x_1	x_2	x_3	x_4	x_5	x_6	RHS
			u		l		l	
z	1	0	1/6	0	5/3	0	−1/6	1450
x_1	0	1	11/3	0	5/3	0	1/3	400
x_5	0	0	−1/2	0	0	1	1/2	150
x_3	0	0	−1/4	1	0	0	−1/4	75

Fourth tableau.

	z	x_1	x_2	x_3	x_4	x_5	x_6	RHS
			u		l	l		
z	1	0	0	0	5/3	1/3	0	1500
x_1	0	1	4	0	5/3	−2/3	0	300
x_6	0	0	−1	0	0	2	1	300
x_3	0	0	−1/2	1	0	1/2	0	150

Fifth tableau.

Optimal:

Tanks = 300

Planes = 300

Missiles = 150

PROBLEM 5.25

$$\min \; 20x_1 + 30x_2 + 20x_3 + 15x_4$$

$$\text{S.T.} \quad .3x_1 + .2x_2 + .4x_3 + .2x_4 = 0.2$$
$$.2x_1 + .6x_2 + .3x_3 + .4x_4 \geq 0.3$$
$$.4x_1 + .15x_2 + .25x_3 + .3x_4 \geq 0.2$$
$$x_1 \leq 0.3$$
$$x_2 \leq 0.4$$
$$x_1, x_2, x_3, x_4 \geq 0$$

Phase I initial tableau

						Slacks		Art.			
	z	x_1	x_2	x_3	x_4	x_5	x_6	x_7	x_8	x_9	RHS
z	1	0	0	0	0	0	0	-1	-1	-1	0
x_7	0	.3	.2	.4	.2	0	0	1	0	0	.2
x_8	0	.2	.6	.3	.4	-1	0	0	1	0	.3
x_9	0	.4	.15	.25	.3	0	-1	0	0	1	.2

Phase I optimal tableau

	z	x_1 (u)	x_2 (u)	x_3	x_4	x_5	x_6	x_7	x_8	x_9	RHS
z	1	0	0	0	0	0	0	-1	-1	-1	0
x_5	0	-.33	.41	0	0	1	-1.43	-.143	-1	1.43	.0243
x_3	0	-.143	-.43	1	0	0	2.86	4.29	0	-2.86	.0714
x_4	0	-1.21	-.143	0	1	0	-5.71	-3.57	0	5.71	.0071

Phase II optimal tableau.

	z	x_1	x_2	x_3	x_4	x_5	x_6	RHS
z	1	-5.5	-11	0	0	20	0	13
x_3	0	.8	-.4	1	0	2	0	.2
x_6	0	-.23	.29	0	0	-.7	1	.03
x_4	0	-.1	1.8	0	1	-4	0	.6

$x_1^* = x_2^* = 0$, $x_3 = .2$, $x_4 = .6$ obj = 13

PROBLEM 5.26

$$\min \quad 0.1x_1 + 0.06x_2 + 0.04x_3$$

$$\begin{aligned}
\text{S.T.} \quad & 8x_1 + 4x_2 + 4x_3 \geq 10 \\
& 4x_1 + 2x_2 + 4x_3 \geq 6 \\
& 2x_1 + 3x_2 + 4x_3 \geq 5 \\
& x_1, \quad x_2, \quad x_3 \geq 0
\end{aligned}$$

	z	x_1	x_2	x_3	x_4	x_5	x_6	RHS
z	1	-2	-2	0	-1	0	0	.10
x_6	0	6	1	0	-1	0	1	5
x_3	0	2	1	1	-1/4	0	0	5/2
x_4	0	4	2	0	-1	1	0	4

Optimal tableau

PROBLEM 5.27

$$\min \quad 450x_{11} + 420x_{12} + 420x_{13} + 600x_{22} + 600x_{23}$$

$$\begin{aligned}
\text{S.T.} \quad & x_{11} + x_{12} + x_{13} = 400 \\
& x_{22} + x_{23} = 500 \\
& 12x_{12} + 15x_{22} \leq 4500 \\
& 12x_{13} + 15x_{23} \leq 6000 \\
& x_{11} + x_{12} \geq 250 \\
& x_{11} \leq 200 \\
& x_{22} \geq 200 \\
& x_{ij} \geq 0, \quad \forall\, i, j
\end{aligned}$$

Where x_{ij} : # car type i shipped by ship type j.

PROBLEM 5.27 (Continued)

	Z	x_{11}	x_{12}	x_{13}	x_{22}	x_{23}	S_1	S_2	S_3	S_4	RHS
Z	1	0	0	0	0	0	−5/2	−5/2	0	0	472,000
x_{22}	0	0	0	0	1	0	0	−1/15	4/5	0	220
x_{12}	0	0	1	0	0	0	1/12	1/12	−1	0	100
x_{11}	0	1	0	0	0	0	−1/12	−1/12	0	0	150
x_{13}	0	0	0	1	0	0	0	0	1	0	150
x_{23}	0	0	0	0	0	1	0	1/5	−4/5	1	280
S_4	0	0	0	0	0	0	0	0	0	1	50

Optimal tableau. The solution is optimal with

$x_{11} = 150$, $x_{12} = 100$, $x_{13} = 150$, $x_{22} = 220$, $x_{23} = 280$

$S_4 = 50$ where S_4 is the slack variable for $x_{11} \le 200$. Obj = 472,000.

PROBLEM 5.28

Let x_i: be the production at period i

$\hat{x}_i$: be the net inventory at end of period i

y_4: production in the new facility at period 4.

$$\text{Min } 25x_1 + 25x_2 + 25x_3 + 25x_4 + 30z_4 + 3y_1 + 3y_2 + 3y_3 + 3y_4$$

s.t.

$$x_1 - y_1 = 250$$

$$x_2 + y_1 - y_2 = 600$$

$$x_3 + y_2 - y_3 = 800$$

$$x_4 + z_4 + y_3 - y_4 = 1200$$

$$y_1 \le 400$$

$$y_2 \le 400$$

$$y_3 \le 400$$

$$y_4 = 100$$

and all x_i, y_i and $z_4 \geq 0$, $\forall i$.

PROBLEM 5.30

$$\text{Max } x_1 + 2x_2 + 3x_3$$

$$\begin{aligned} \text{S.T. } 3x_1 + 2x_2 + x_3 &\le 6 \\ -x_1 + 2x_2 + 4x_3 &\le 8 \\ 2x_1 + x_2 - x_3 &\le 2 \\ x_1, x_2, x_3 &\ge 0 \end{aligned}$$

	x_1	x_2	x_3	RHS
z	-1	-2	-3	0
x_4	3	2	1	6
x_5	-1	2	(4)	8
x_6	2	1	-1	2
x_1	-1	0	0	0
x_2	0	-1	0	0
x_3	0	0	-1	0

Initial Column tableau.

	x_1	x_2	x_5	RHS
z	$-\frac{7}{4}$	$-\frac{1}{2}$	$\frac{3}{4}$	6
x_4	($\frac{13}{4}$)	$\frac{3}{2}$	$-\frac{1}{4}$	4
x_5	0	0	-1	0
x_6	$\frac{7}{4}$	$\frac{3}{2}$	$\frac{1}{4}$	4
x_1	-1	0	0	0
x_2	0	-1	0	0
x_3	$-\frac{1}{4}$	$\frac{1}{2}$	$\frac{1}{4}$	2

Second column tableau

	x_4	x_2	x_5	RHS
z	$\frac{7}{13}$	$\frac{4}{13}$	$\frac{8}{13}$	$\frac{106}{13}$
x_4	-1	0	0	0
x_5	0	0	-1	0
x_6	$-\frac{7}{13}$	$\frac{9}{13}$	$\frac{5}{13}$	$\frac{24}{13}$
x_1	$\frac{4}{13}$	$\frac{6}{13}$	$-\frac{1}{13}$	$\frac{16}{13}$
x_2	0	-1	0	0
x_3	$\frac{1}{13}$	$\frac{8}{13}$	$\frac{3}{13}$	$\frac{30}{13}$

Third (optimal) tableau.

Optimal Solution:

$$x_1^* = 16/13, \quad x_2^* = 0, \quad x_3^* = 30/13 \quad \text{with } z^* = \frac{106}{13}$$

PROBLEM 5.31

Assuming the original A matrix contains an identity submatrix I, the basis inverse can be extracted at any iteration. Call the associated

PROBLEM 5.31 (Continued)

variables slacks (even though they may, in fact, represent significant decision variables). If the ith slack is a nonbasic variable in the column simplex tableau, then the partition of $B^{-1}N$ associated with that variable will be $B^{-1}\underline{e}_i = (B^{-1})_i$, which is the ith column of B^{-1}. Now, if the slack i is in the basis, then its column is a unit vector which indicates that the corresponding column of B^{-1} is a unit vector.

Referring to Problem 5.30 we may extract the basis associated with the last tableau as follows: since x_4 and x_5 correspond to unit vectors we may use these nonbasic columns to obtain the inverse columns associated with x_1 and x_3, respectively. Also, since basic variable x_6 is itself a slack variable, then the corresponding column of B^{-1} is a unit column. From pivoting we know that x_1, x_3 and x_6 are basic in row 1, row 2 and row 3, respectively. Immediately, we know that the last column of B^{-1} is $\underline{e}_3$. To obtain the first column of B^{-1} we extract values from the x_4 column of the last tableau, in the order of x_1-row, x_3-row, x_6-row. This gives $(4/13, 1/13, -7/13)^T$. We may repeat the process at the x_5 column to get the second column of B^{-1}. Finally,

$$B = \begin{bmatrix} 4/13 & -1/13 & 0 \\ 1/13 & 3/13 & 0 \\ -7/13 & 5/13 & 1 \end{bmatrix}$$

which the reader may verify as correct. (Try extracting B^{-1} from the next-to-last tableau).

PROBLEM 5.32

a) $Ax \leq b \quad , \quad x \geq 0$

$wA \geq c \quad , \quad w \geq 0$

$w(Ax-b) = 0 \quad , \quad (wA - c)x = 0$

b) $Ax \geq b \quad , \quad x \geq 0$

$wA \geq c \quad , \quad w \leq 0$

$w(Ax-b) = 0 \quad , \quad (wA - c)x = 0$

c) $Ax \leq b \quad , \quad x \geq 0$

$wA \leq c \quad , \quad w \leq 0$

$w(Ax-b) = 0 \quad , \quad (wA - c)x = 0$

d) $A_1 x = b_1 \quad , \quad A_2 x \geqq b_2 \quad , \quad x \geq 0$

$w_1 A_1 + w_2 A_2 \leq c \quad , \quad w_2 \geq 0 \quad , \quad w_1$ unrestricted

$w_2(A_2 x - b_2) = 0 \quad , \quad (w_1 A_1 + w_2 A_2 - c)x = 0$

e) $Ax = b \quad , \quad x \geq \ell \quad , \quad -x \geq -u$

$w_1 A + w_2 - w_3 = c \quad , \quad w_1$ URS $, \quad w_2 , w_3 \geq 0$

$w_2(x - \ell) = 0 , \quad w_3(x - u) = 0$

PROBLEM 5.33

By contradiction suppose that $A_1 d \geq 0$, $d_{p+1}, d_{p+2}, \ldots, d_n \geq 0$ and $cd < 0$ has a solution d. Consider $x + \lambda d$ for $\lambda > 0$.

a) Since $x_1, \ldots, x_p > 0$ and $x_{p+1}, \ldots, x_n = 0$, and $d_{p+1}, \ldots, d_n \geq 0$, then there exists $\delta_1 > 0$ such that $x + \lambda d \geq 0$ for $\lambda \in [0, \delta_1]$.

PROBLEM 5.33 (Continued)

b) Since $A_1x = b_1$ and $A_1d \geq 0$, then $A_1(x+\lambda d) \geq 0$ for all $\lambda \geq 0$. Since $A_2x = b_2$, then there exists δ_2 such that $A_2(x+\lambda d) \geq b_2$ for $\lambda \in [0, \delta_2]$. In other words $A(x+\lambda d) \geq b$ for all $\lambda \in [0, \delta_2]$.

c) From (a) and (b) $x+\lambda d$ is feasible for all λ in the region $[0, \delta]$ where $\delta = \min[\delta_1, \delta_2] > 0$.

d) Since $cd < 0$, then $c(x+\lambda d) = cx + \lambda cd < cx$ for all $\lambda > 0$.

From (c) and the above argument x could not have been an optimal solution of the problem, a contradiction. Therefore the given system has no solution.

PROBLEM 5.34

We give below the Kuhn-Tucker conditions for the two equivalent problems P and P'.

P: max cx s.t. $Ax \leq b$, $x \geq 0$

K-T conditions:

1. $\begin{cases} Ax \leq b \\ x \geq 0 \end{cases}$

2. $\begin{cases} wA - v = c \\ w \geq 0, \quad v \geq 0 \end{cases}$

3. $\begin{cases} w(Ax - b) = 0 \\ vx = 0 \end{cases}$

P': max cx s.t. $Ax + x_s = b$, $x \geq 0$, $x_s \geq 0$

1. $\begin{cases} Ax + x_s = b \\ x \geq 0, \quad x_s \geq 0 \end{cases}$

2. $\begin{cases} \hat{w}A - \hat{v} = c \\ \hat{w} - w' = 0 \\ \hat{v} \geq 0, \ w' \geq 0, \ \hat{w} \text{ urs.} \end{cases}$

PROBLEM 5.34 (Continued)

$$3. \begin{cases} \hat{v}x = 0 \\ w'x_s = 0 \end{cases}$$

Obviously the K-T conditions for problems P and P' are equivalent, where $w = \hat{w}$ and $v = \hat{v}$. Furthermore, for problem P' we have $w' = \hat{w}$, that is the lagrangian multiplier vector w' associated with the nonnegativity constraint $x_s \geq 0$ is equal to the Lagrangian multiplier vector $\hat{w}$ associated with the constraints $Ax + x_s = b$.

PROBLEM 5.35

$$\begin{aligned} \max\ & 2x_1 + x_2 \\ \text{s.t.}\ & x_1 + x_2 \leq 4 \\ & x_2 \leq 3 \\ & x_1, x_2 \geq 0 \end{aligned}$$

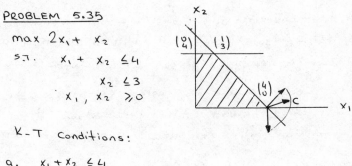

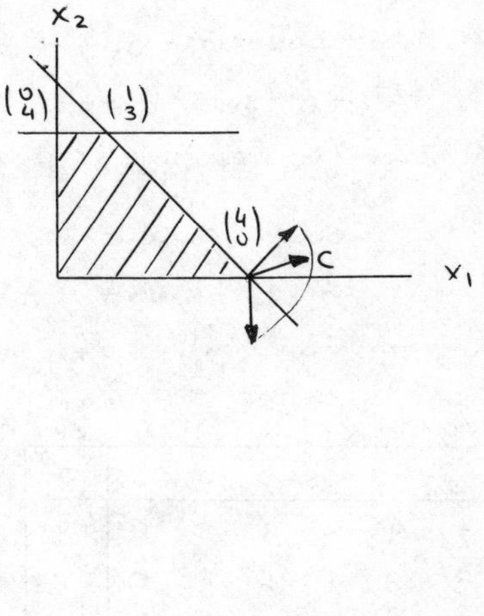

K-T Conditions:

a. $x_1 + x_2 \leq 4$

$x_2 \leq 3$

$x_1, x_2 \geq 0$

b. $w_1 \geq 2$

$w_1 + w_2 \geq 1$

$w_1, w_2 \geq 0$

c. $w_1(x_1 + x_2 - 4) = 0$

$w_2(x_2 - 3) = 0$

$x_1(w_1 - 2) = 0$

$x_2(w_1 + w_2 - 1) = 0$

PROBLEM 5.35 (Continued)

At the point $x_1 = 4$, $x_2 = 0$ the above conditions hold by letting $w_1 = 2$ and $w_2 = 0$. Geometrically, note that the cost vector c belongs to the cone of the gradients of the binding constraints.

PROBLEM 5.36

K-T Conditions:

(1) $2x_1 + x_2 \leq 6000$

(2) $3x_1 + 3x_2 + x_3 \leq 9000$

(3) $x_1 + 2x_2 + 2x_3 \leq 4000$

(4) $x_1, x_2, x_3 \geq 0$

(5) $w_1 + 3w_2 + w_3 \geq 10$

(6) $w_1 + 3w_2 + 2w_3 \geq 15$

(7) $w_2 + 2w_3 \geq 5$

(8) $w_1, w_2, w_3 \geq 0$

(9) $(2x_1 + x_2 - 6000)w_1 = 0$

(10) $(3x_1 + 3x_2 + x_3 - 9000)w_2 = 0$

(11) $(x_1 + 2x_2 + 2x_3 - 4000)w_3 = 0$

(12) $(w_1 + 3w_2 + w_3 - 10)x_1 = 0$

(13) $(w_1 + 3w_2 + 2w_3 - 15)x_2 = 0$

(14) $(w_2 + 2w_3 - 5)x_3 = 0$

All the above conditions hold except possibly (5), (6), (7), and (8). At the termination of the simplex method all of them hold.

	z	x_1	x_2	x_3	x_4	x_5	x_6	RHS
z	1	-10	-15	-5	0	0	0	0
x_4	0	2	1	0	1	0	0	6000
x_5	0	3	3	1	0	1	0	9000
x_6	0	1	(2)	2	0	0	1	4000

$w_1 = w_2 = w_3 = 0$

(6), (5), and (7) are violated.

	z	x_1	x_2	x_3	x_4	x_5	x_6	RHS
z	1	-5/2	0	10	0	0	15/2	30,000
x_4	0	3/2	0	-1	1	0	-1/2	4000
x_5	0	(3/2)	0	-2	0	1	-3/2	3000
x_2	0	1/2	1	1	0	0	1/2	2000

$w_1 = 0$, $w_2 = 0$, $w_3 = 15/2$

(5) is violated

PROBLEM 5.36 (Continued)

	z	x_1	x_2	x_3	x_4	x_5	x_6	RHS
	1	0	0	20/3	0	5/3	5	35,000
x_4	0	0	0	1	1	-1	1	1000
x_1	0	1	0	-4/3	0	2/3	-1	2000
x_2	0	0	1	5/3	0	-1/3	1	1000

(5), (6), (7), and (8) are satisfied. K-T conditions hold. Optimal is at hand.

$w_1 = 0$, $w_2 = 5/3$, $w_3 = 5$

$x_1 = 2000$, $x_2 = 1000$, $x_3 = 0$

PROBLEM 5.37

Suppose we have a degenerate optimal solution. In this case there exists a nonbasic variable x_k with $-z_k + c_k < 0$. But

$$z_k - c_k = wa_k - c_k$$

Therefore in

$$wa_j + v_j = c_j$$

for $j = k$ we have

$$wa_k + v_k = c_k$$

or

$$v_k = c_k - wa_k < 0$$

Therefore in degenerate solution case one of the lagrangian multipliers (shadow prices) of the nonnegativity constraints could be negative.

PROBLEM 5.38

Since x^* is optimal and $A_1x^* = b_1$, $A_2x^* > 0$, then, $w = [w_1, w_2]$ has $w_2 = 0$ by K-T conditions. Consider

$$P_1: \quad \begin{array}{l} \min\ cx \\ \text{s.t. } A_1x \geq b_1 \\ \qquad x \geq 0 \end{array}$$

The K-T conditions for P_1 are:

1) $A_1x \geq b_1$, $x \geq 0$
2) $wA_1 \leq c$, $w \geq 0$
3) $(wA_1 - c)x = 0$
   $w(A_1x - b_1) = 0$

The K-T conditions for the original problem are:

1) $A_1x \geq b_1$, $A_2x \geq b_2$, $x \geq 0$
2) $w_1A_1 + w_2A_2 \leq c$, $w_1, w_2 \geq 0$
   since $w_2 = 0$ we have:
   $w_1A_1 \leq c$, $w_1 \geq 0$
3) $w_1(A_1x - b_1) + w_2(A_2x - b_2) = 0$
   $(w_1A_1 + w_2A_2 - c)x = 0$
   since $w_2 = 0$ we have:
   $w_1(A_1x - b_1) = 0$
   $(w_1A_1 - c)x = 0$

and thus these K-T conditions (ignoring $A_2x > b_2$) reduce to the K-T conditions of P_1. Thus we have found x^* and w satisfying K-T conditions for P_1. The case for the problem with $A_1x = b_1$ is similar.

PROBLEM 5.39

$$\max \ 10x_1 + 15x_2$$
$$\text{s.t.} \quad 4x_1 + 7x_2 \le 300$$
$$3x_1 + 6x_2 \le 500$$
$$x_1, \quad x_2 \ge 0$$

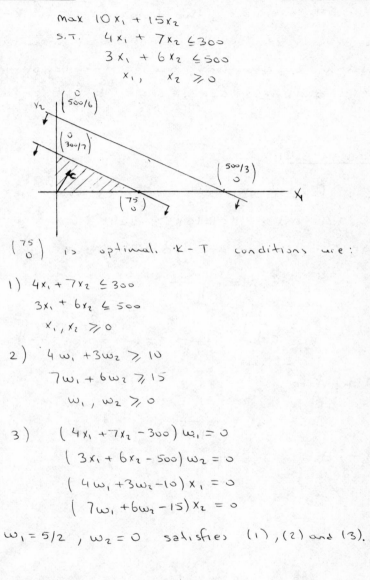

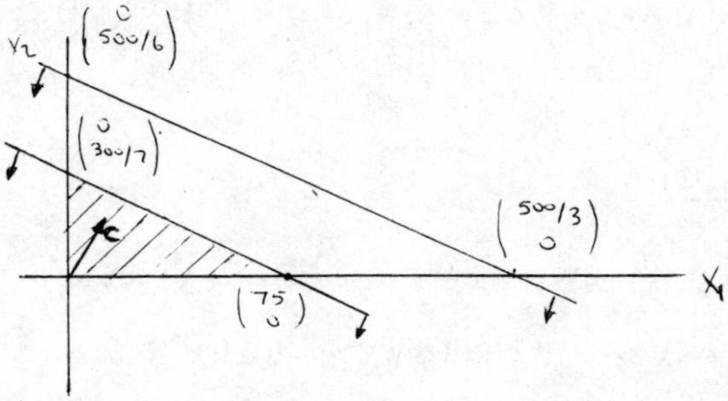

$\begin{pmatrix} 75 \\ 0 \end{pmatrix}$ is optimal. K-T conditions are:

1) $4x_1 + 7x_2 \le 300$
$3x_1 + 6x_2 \le 500$
$x_1, x_2 \ge 0$

2) $4w_1 + 3w_2 \ge 10$
$7w_1 + 6w_2 \ge 15$
$w_1, w_2 \ge 0$

3) $(4x_1 + 7x_2 - 300)w_1 = 0$
$(3x_1 + 6x_2 - 500)w_2 = 0$
$(4w_1 + 3w_2 - 10)x_1 = 0$
$(7w_1 + 6w_2 - 15)x_2 = 0$

$w_1 = 5/2$, $w_2 = 0$ satisfies (1), (2) and (3).

PROBLEM 5.40

Yes. However, the solution of the K-T conditions require the solution of a nonlinear system of equations, due to the complementary slackness conditions.

PROBLEM 5.41

By Schwarts inequality we have:

$$cd \geq -\|c\|\,\|d\| \geq -\|c\|$$

for all d with $\|d\| \leq 1$. Let

$$\bar{d} = -\frac{c}{\|c\|}$$

$$c\bar{d} = -\frac{c \cdot c}{\|c\|} = -\frac{\|c\|^2}{\|c\|} = -\|c\|$$

Therefore,

$$\bar{d} = -\frac{c}{\|c\|}$$

is the optimal direction.

PROBLEM 5.42

The K-T conditions for this problem are:

1) Primal feasibility : $Ax \leq b$, $x \geq 0$

2) Dual feasibility:

$$w_1 + 2w_2 - w_3 \geq 1 \quad \text{----} \quad (1)$$

$$w_1 + w_2 + 2w_3 \geq -2 \quad \text{---} \quad (2)$$

$$w_1 \quad - w_3 \geq 1 \quad \text{---} \quad (3)$$

$$w_1 , w_2 , w_3 \geq 0 \quad \text{---} \quad (4)$$

3) Complementary slackness.

In simplex method primal feasibility and complementary slackness are always satisfied. The procedure works towards the dual feasibility. Therefore the point that satisfies (1), (2), (3) and (4) is the optimal point.

	z	x_1	x_2	x_3	x_4	x_5	x_6	RHS
z	1	-1	2	-1	0	0	0	0
x_4	0	1	1	1	1	0	0	6
x_5	0	(2)	1	0	0	1	0	4
x_6	0	-1	2	-1	0	0	1	4

$w_1 = w_2 = w_3 = 0$

(1) and (3) are violated.

	z	x_1	x_2	x_3	x_4	x_5	x_6	RHS
z	1	0	5/2	-1	0	1/2	0	2
x_4	0	0	1/2	(1)	1	-1/2	0	4
x_1	0	1	1/2	0	0	1/2	0	2
x_6	0	0	5/2	-1	0	1/2	1	6

$w_2 = \frac{1}{2}$, $w_1 = w_3 = 0$

(3) is violated.

PROBLEM 5.42 (Continued)

	z	x_1	x_2	x_3	x_4	x_5	x_6	RHS
z	1	0	3	0	1	0	0	6
x_3	0	0	1/2	1	1	-1/2	0	4
x_1	0	1	1/2	0	0	1/2	0	2
x_6	0	0	3	0	1	0	1	10

$w_1 = 1$, $w_2 = w_3 = 0$,

no violation.

Solution is optimal.

PROBLEM 5.43

a)

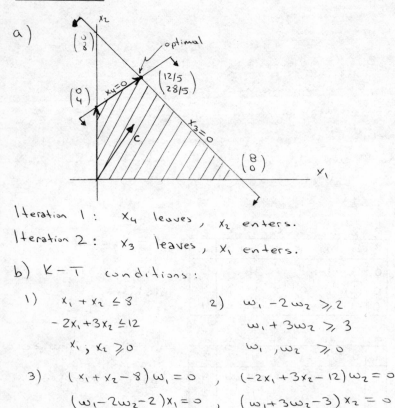

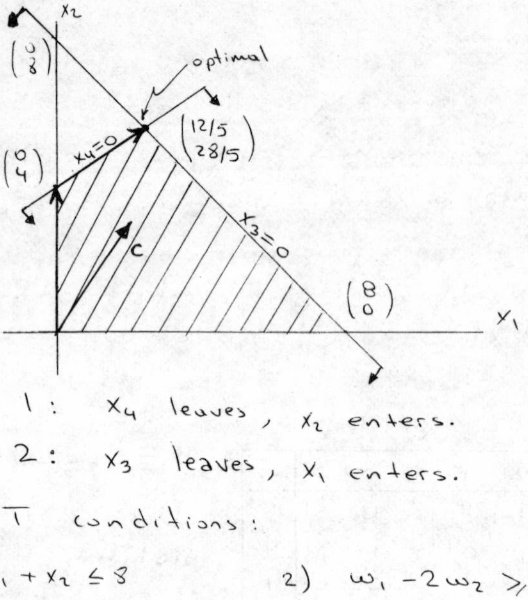

Iteration 1: x_4 leaves, x_2 enters.
Iteration 2: x_3 leaves, x_1 enters.

b) K-T conditions:

1) $x_1 + x_2 \le 8$
$-2x_1 + 3x_2 \le 12$
$x_1, x_2 \ge 0$

2) $w_1 - 2w_2 \ge 2$
$w_1 + 3w_2 \ge 3$
$w_1, w_2 \ge 0$

3) $(x_1 + x_2 - 8)w_1 = 0$, $(-2x_1 + 3x_2 - 12)w_2 = 0$
$(w_1 - 2w_2 - 2)x_1 = 0$, $(w_1 + 3w_2 - 3)x_2 = 0$

all of the above conditions hold at $x = (12/5, 28/5)$ and $w = (12/5, 1/5)$.

PROBLEM 5.44

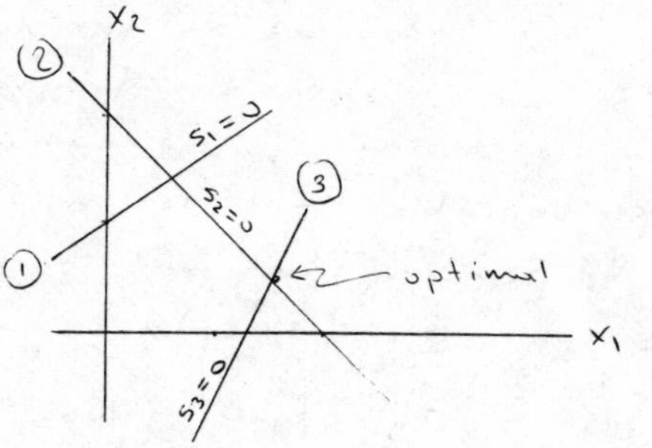

a) Starting basis : s_1, s_2, s_3.
Second basis : x_2, s_2, s_3
Third basis : x_2, x_1, s_3
Fourth basis : x_2, x_1, s_1

b) Since optimal is unique and since gradient of constraint 2 is at 45°, c must be at less than 45°.

PROBLEM 5.45

$$\begin{aligned} \min \quad & cx \\ \text{s.t.} \quad & Ax = b \\ & x \geq 0 \end{aligned}$$

a) Consider a basic feasible solution x with basis B. Consider the following updated tableau:

$$z \qquad + \sum_{j \in R} (z_j - c_j) x_j = c_B \bar{b}$$

$$x_B \; + \sum_{j \in R} y_j x_j \qquad = \bar{b}$$

$$x_B \geq 0, \quad x_j \geq 0 \text{ for } j \in R$$

PROBLEM 5.45 (Continued)

where R is the index set of the nonbasic variables. If $z_j - c_j > 0$, then the function would improve by increasing x_j. One method to modify the nonbasic variables is to let $x_j = \lambda$ for each $j \in R$ with $z_j - c_j > 0$. Then

$$z = c_B \bar{b} - \sum_{j \in R'} (z_j - c_j)\lambda$$

where $R' = \{ j \in R : z_j - c_j > 0 \}$. Now $\lambda \geq 0$ is to be determined. This must be done so that $x_B \geq 0$. The maximum λ which maintains feasibility is given by:

$$\lambda = \underset{1 \leq i \leq m}{\text{minimum}} \left\{ \frac{\bar{b}_i}{\sum_{j \in R'} y_{ij}} : \sum_{j \in R'} y_{ij} > 0 \right\}$$

Obviously if $\sum_{j \in R'} y_{ij} \leq 0$ for $i = 1, \ldots, m$ then the optimal is unbounded.

b) At a general iteration, we may have more than m positive variables. The computations could still be displayed in a simplex tableau. This could be done by identifying m basic columns forming B, say, by selecting the most m positive variables having independent columns. So the nonbasic variables may be positive. A typical tableau may look as follows:

PROBLEM 5.45 (Continued)

	z	x_B	x_j		
z	1	0	$z_j - c_j$	$c_B\bar{b}$	z_0
x_B	0	I	y_j	$\bar{b}$	$\hat{b}$

$$z_0 = c_B\bar{b} - \sum_{j\in R}(z_j - c_j)x_j$$

$$\hat{b} = \bar{b} - \sum_{j\in R} y_j x_j$$

c) If $x_k > 0$ is nonbasic such that $z_k - c_k < 0$ and if x_k is decreased, then the objective function will be reduced. In particular,

$$z = c_B\bar{b} - \sum_{j\in R}(z_j - c_j)x_j$$

If all nonbasic variables are fixed at their values except x_k that is decreased, then:

$$z = z_0 - (z_k - c_k)(-\Delta)$$

where Δ is the positive decrease in x_k. Obviously, since $z_k - c_k < 0$ by assumption, then $z < z_0$, so that the function improves as x_k is decreased.

ALGORITHM

Initialization Step

Choose a starting basic feasible solution of the system $Ax = b$, $x \geq 0$. Let B be the basis.

Main Step

1. For each nonbasic variable examine $z_j - c_j = c_B B^{-1}a_j - c_j$. If $z_j - c_j = 0$ and $x_j > 0$ or else, if $z_j - c_j \leq 0$ and $x_j = 0$ for each

PROBLEM 5.45 (Continued)

nonbasic variable, then stop; the current solution is optimal. Go to step 2, otherwise.

2. Let $R_1 = \{ j : x_j$ is nonbasic, $x_j \geq 0$ and $z_j - c_j > 0 \}$. If $R_1 = \phi$, go to step 3. Otherwise, compute the vector $\hat{y}$ whose ith component is $\hat{y}_i = \Sigma_{j \in R_1} y_{ij}$. If $\hat{y} \leq 0$, then stop, the optimal solution is unbounded. If, on the other hand, $\hat{y} \nleq 0$, then compute λ as follows:

$$\lambda = \underset{1 \leq i \leq m}{\text{minimum}} \left\{ \frac{\hat{b}_i}{\hat{y}_i} : \hat{y}_i > 0 \right\}$$

where $\hat{b}_i$ is the current value of the ith basic variable. Then the new feasible solution is given by:

$$x_j = \lambda \qquad j \in R_1$$

$$x_B = \hat{b} - \Sigma_{j \in R_1} y_j \lambda$$

and all other nonbasic variables are kept the same. Go to step 4.

3. Let $R_2 = \{ x_j : x_j$ nonbasic, $x_j > 0, z_j - c_j < 0 \}$

If $R_2 = \phi$, stop, the current point is optimal. Otherwise, each variable in R_2 is reduced by λ as follows: Let $\hat{y}$ be the vector whose ith component $\hat{y}_i$ is given by $\hat{y}_i = \Sigma_{j \in R_2} y_{ij}$.

If $\hat{y} \geq 0$, then the optimal solution is unbounded. Otherwise, compute λ as follows:

PROBLEM 5.45 (Continued)

$$\lambda = \underset{1 \le i \le m}{\text{minimum}} \left\{ \frac{\hat{b}_i}{-\hat{y}_i} : \hat{y}_i < 0 \right\}$$

where $\hat{b}_i$ is the current value of the ith basic variable. The new feasible solution is given by:

$$x_j = x_j - \lambda \qquad j \in R_2$$

$$x_B = \hat{b} + \sum_{j \in R_2} y_j \lambda$$

and all other nonbasic variables are kept fixed. Go to step 4.

4- Let the new basis consists of the largest m variables whose columns are linearly independent. Compute the new columns y_j's and the new prices $z_j - c_j$'s and go to step 1.

e)

	z	x_1	x_2	x_3	x_4	x_5	x_6	RHS	Solution
z	1	1	2	1	0	0	0	0	0
x_4	0	1	1	3	1	0	0	12	12
x_5	0	1	2	0	0	1	0	6	6
x_6	0	1	0	1	0	0	1	8	8

Increase x_1, x_2, x_3.

$$\lambda = \min\left\{ \frac{12}{5}, \frac{6}{3}, \frac{8}{2} \right\} = 2 \quad . \text{ Thus}$$

$$x_1 = x_2 = x_3 = 2$$

$$x_4 = 12 - 5x_2 = 2$$

$$x_5 = 6 - 3x_2 = 0$$

$$x_6 = 8 - 2x_2 = 4$$

PROBLEM 5.45 (Continued)

New basis consists of x_4, x_6, and x_1 (Thus x_1 enters the basis and x_5 leaves). Note, however, that the nonbasic variables x_2 and x_3 are positive. Hence $z_0 = -8$.

	z	x_1	x_2	x_3	x_4	x_5	x_6	RHS	Solution
z	1	0	0	1	0	-1	0	-6	-8
x_4	0	0	-1	3	1	-1	0	6	2
x_1	0	1	2	0	0	1	0	6	2
x_6	0	0	-2	1	0	-1	1	2	4

x_3 is the only positive nonbasic variable with positive $z_j - c_j$. x_3 is thus increased. The maximum increase is:

$$\min\left\{\frac{2}{3}, \frac{4}{1}\right\} = \frac{2}{3}$$

The new solution is given by:

$$x_4 = 0, \quad x_1 = 2, \quad x_6 = \frac{10}{3}, \quad x_2 = 2, \quad x_3 = \frac{2}{3}, \quad x_5 = 0.$$

The new basis consists of x_1, x_3 and x_6, i.e, x_3 entered the basis and x_4 left. $z_0 = -26/3$.

	z	x_1	x_2	x_3	x_4	x_5	x_6	RHS	Solution
z	1	0	1/3	0	-1/3	-2/3	0	-8	$-\frac{26}{3}$
x_3	0	0	-1/3	1	1/3	-1/3	0	2	8/3
x_1	0	1	2	0	0	1	0	6	2
x_6	0	0	-5/3	0	-1/3	-2/3	1	0	10/3

Now, $z_2 - c_2 > 0$, so x_2 could be further increased. Maximum increase is 1. As x_2 is increased to 3 x_1 drops to zero. The new solution is:

PROBLEM 5.45 (Continued)

$x_1=0,\ x_2=3,\ x_3=3,\ x_4=0,\ x_5=0,\ x_6=5$ and $z_0=-9$

	z	x_1	x_2	x_3	x_4	x_5	x_6	RHS	Solution
z	1	0	0	0	-1/3	-5/6	0	-9	-9
x_3	0	0	0	1	1/3	-1/6	0	3	3
x_2	0	1/2	1	0	0	1/2	0	3	3
x_6	0	5/6	0	0	-1/3	1/6	1	5	5

The optimality criterion hold and the above tableau is an optimal tableau ($R_1=\phi$ and $R_2=\phi$).

f) Rather than adjusting the eligible nonbasic variables by the same amount λ, we can adjust the nonbasic variables in proportion to their z_j-c_j values. This leads to a procedure very similar to that discussed in the exercise in part (d). This procedure is the reduced gradient method developed by Wolfe. The reader may also refer to Bazaraa and Shetty [25] for further details.

PROBLEM 5.46

Note that $a_1x_1+a_2x_2+s=b$. Suppose that (x_1,x_2) satisfies $a_1x_1+a_2x_2=b'$ so that the value of the slack variable for this point is $s=b-b'$. For simplicity suppose that $a_1, a_2>0$. Note that $\frac{b}{a_1}, \frac{b'}{a_1}, \frac{b}{a_2}, \frac{b'}{a_2}$ are displayed in the attached figure. Thus the ℓ_1 shown in the figure is precisely $\frac{b-b'}{a_1}$ and ℓ_2 is $\frac{b-b'}{a_2}$. Thus,

PROBLEM 5.46 (Continued)

the value of the slack is obtained by either multiplying l_1 by a_1 or multiplying l_2 by a_2.

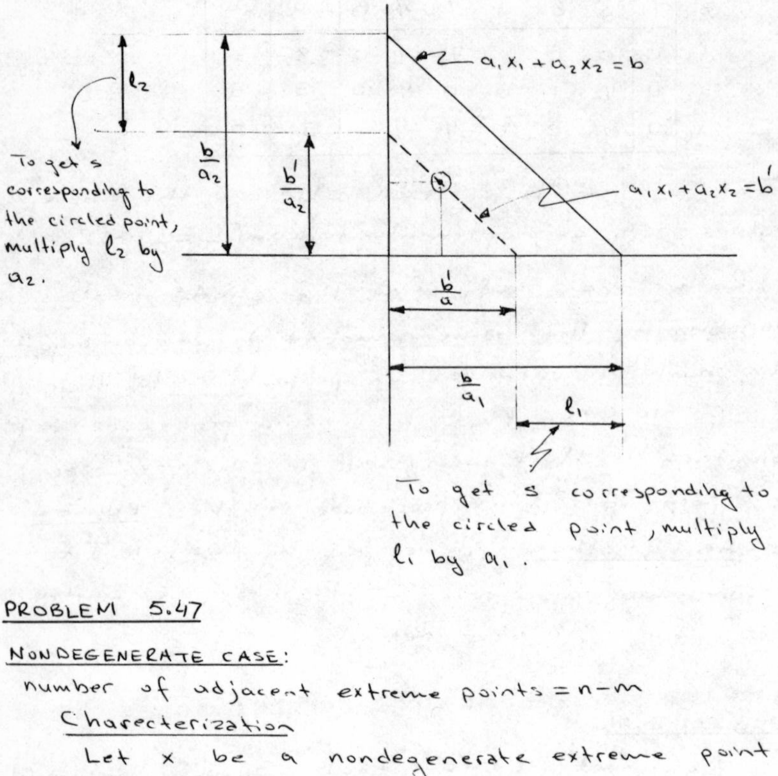

PROBLEM 5.47

NONDEGENERATE CASE:

number of adjacent extreme points $= n-m$

Charecterization

Let x be a nondegenerate extreme point with basis B. $\bar{x}$ is an adjacent extreme point if, and only if, $\bar{x}$ is obtained from x by a single pivot, where one of the nonbasic columns enters the basis and one of the basic columns leaves according to the minimum ratio test.

PROBLEM 5.47 (Continued)

DEGENERATE CASE

In this case $\bar{x}$ is an adjacent extreme point if the basis exchange produces $\bar{x} \neq x$. The number of adjacent extreme points is thus $\leq n-m$ since as a nonbasic variable enters the basis, we may still be at the same point after pivoting (examine iteration 1 of the cycling example on page 167).

Validation of the fact that the number of adjacent extreme points is $\leq n-m$ follows immediately from the charecterization given above. Validation of the charecterization of the adjacent extreme points is given in the solution to Exercise 5.48.

PROBLEM 5.48

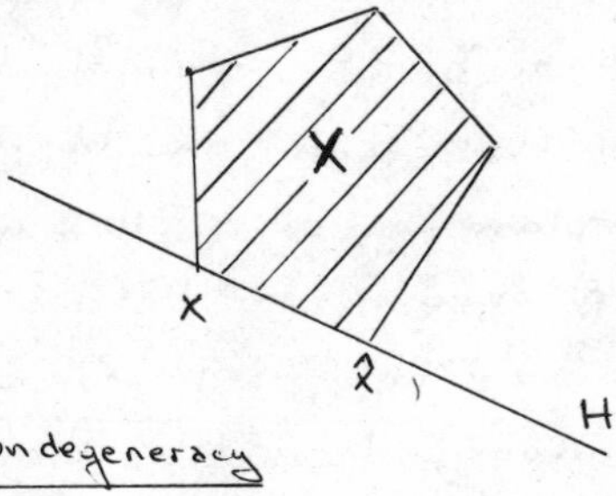

Assuming nondegeneracy

We shall show that the simplex method moves from one extreme point to an adjacent extreme point. Let x be a nondegenerate extreme point with basis B. For simplicity, suppose that the basic columns are $a_1, a_2, \ldots, a_m$.

PROBLEM 5.48 (Continued)

Now, suppose that $\hat{x}$ is obtained by entering the nonbasic variable x_k and removing a basic variable from the basis according to the minimum ratio test. We shall show that $\hat{x}$ is an adjacent extreme point. To prove this, we must construct a hyperplane H that supports the feasible region X at the point x such that $H \cap X$ is the line segment joining x and $\hat{x}$ (see the definition of an adjacent extreme point in Exercise 5.47). Consider the hyperplane

$$H = \left\{ \begin{pmatrix} g_1 \\ \vdots \\ g_n \end{pmatrix} : \sum_{\substack{j=m+1 \\ j \neq k}}^{n} g_j = 0 \right\}$$

Note that the hyperplane passes through x and that for each feasible point $g \in X$ we must have $\sum_{\substack{j=m+1 \\ j\neq k}}^{n} g_j \geq 0$, so that H supports X at x. The reader should note that H is the hyperplane given in the hint to the Exercise with p choosen as the zero vector. Also note that $\hat{x} \in H$. Since $x, \hat{x} \in H \cap X$ and H and X are convex, then the line segment joining x and $\hat{x}$ also belongs to $H \cap X$. It now suffices to show that any point $g \in X$ means that $Ag = b$ and $g \geq 0$. Decomposing g into g_B and g_N it follows that:

PROBLEM 5.48 (Continued)

$$g_B = B^{-1}b - B^{-1}N g_N = \bar{b} - \sum_{j=m+1}^{n} y_j g_j$$

$$g_B \geq 0 \quad , \quad g_j \geq 0 \quad j = m+1, \ldots, n$$

Since $y \in H$ then $\sum_{\substack{j=m+1 \\ j \neq k}}^{n} g_j = 0$. Therefore, $g_j = 0$ for $j = m+1, \ldots, n$ and $j \neq k$. In particular $g_B = \bar{b} - y_k g_k$. Therefore:

$$g = \begin{bmatrix} g_B \\ g_N \end{bmatrix} = \begin{pmatrix} \bar{b} \\ 0 \end{pmatrix} + g_k \begin{bmatrix} -y_k \\ e_k \end{bmatrix}$$

where e_k is a unit vector with 1 at position k. But recall that $\hat{x}$ is obtained from x by entering x_k into the basis and removing a basic variable so that:

$$\hat{x} = x + \lambda_k \begin{pmatrix} -y_k \\ e_k \end{pmatrix} = \begin{pmatrix} \bar{b} \\ 0 \end{pmatrix} + \lambda_k \begin{pmatrix} -y_k \\ e_k \end{pmatrix}$$

where $\lambda_k = \underset{1 \leq i \leq m}{\text{minimum}} \left\{ \frac{\bar{b}_i}{y_{ik}} : y_{ik} > 0 \right\} > 0$.

Recall that λ_k is the maximum possible step size that could be obtained while moving x in the direction $(-y_k, e_k)^T$ and still maintaining feasibility. Since g is feasible and since we showed that it is of the form $(\bar{b}, 0)^T + g_k(-y_k, e_k)^T$ then $g_k \leq \lambda_k$. From this it is obvious that $g = \mu x + (1-\mu)\hat{x}$, where

$$\mu = \frac{\lambda_k - g_k}{\lambda_k} \in [0,1].$$

PROBLEM 5.48 (Continued)

Thus, g is a convex combination of x and $\hat{x}$ and thus $H \cap X$ is the line segment joining x and $\hat{x}$. In particular, $\hat{x}$ is an adjacent extreme point.

The reader can also verify that if $\hat{x}$ is an extreme point of X such that there exists a hyperplane H that supports X at x and that $H \cap X$ is the line segment joining x and $\hat{x}$, then $\hat{x}$ could be obtained from x by a single pivot operation.

In the degenerate case a pivot could give the same extreme point. However, if the pivot gives the distinct point then the same analysis shows that the simplex method would generate an adjacent extreme point.

PROBLEM 5.49

Let $\underline{x}$ be a feasible solution. Then

$\underline{x}_B = B^{-1}\underline{b} - B^{-1}N\underline{x}_N$, $\underline{x}_B \geq 0$; $\underline{x}_N \geq 0$. Since

$\underline{x}_0 = (\underline{0}, B^{-1}\underline{b})^T$, then

$$\underline{x} - \underline{x}_0 = \begin{pmatrix} \underline{x}_N \\ -B^{-1}N\underline{x}_N \end{pmatrix} = \sum_{j=1}^{n-m} \begin{pmatrix} \underline{e}_j \\ -\underline{y}_j \end{pmatrix} x_j \qquad \text{---(1)}$$

where x_j is the jth component of $\underline{x}$. Now, let $\underline{x}_j$ be the jth adjacent extreme point. Then $\underline{x}_j$ is obtained from $\underline{x}_0$ by a single

PROBLEM 5.49 (Continued)

pivot as shown in Exercise 5.48 and mentioned in Exercise 5.47. Thus, since the feasible region is bounded, then:

$$\underline{x}_j = \underline{x}_0 + \lambda_j \begin{pmatrix} \underline{e}_j \\ -\underline{y}_j \end{pmatrix} \qquad j=1,2,\ldots,(n-m) \quad \text{---}(2)$$

where $\lambda_j = \underset{1 \le i \le m}{\text{minimum}} \left\{ \dfrac{\bar{b}_i}{y_{ij}} : y_{ij} > 0 \right\} > 0.$

From (1) and (2), it follows that

$$\underline{x} - \underline{x}_0 = \sum_{j=1}^{n-m} \mu_j \, (\underline{x}_j - \underline{x}_0)$$

where $\mu_j = \dfrac{x_j}{\lambda_j} \geq 0.$

Geometric Interpretation

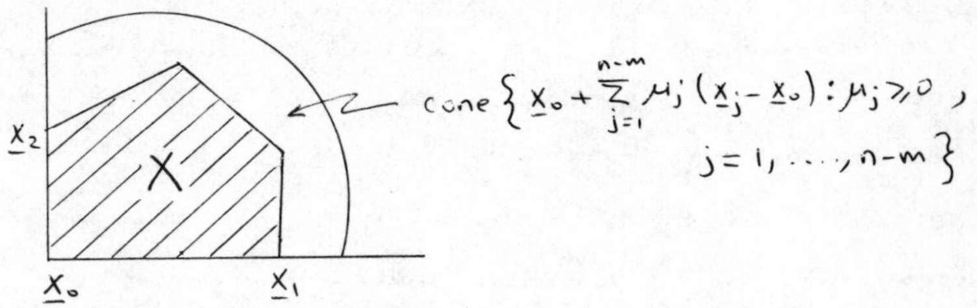

The cone $\left\{ \underline{x}_0 + \sum_{j=1}^{n-m} \mu_j (\underline{x}_j - \underline{x}_0) : \mu_j \geq 0, \ j = 1, \ldots, n-m \right\}$ whose vertex is $\underline{x}_0$ and that is generated by $\underline{x}_j - \underline{x}_0$ for all adjacent extreme points to $\underline{x}_0$ contains the feasible region.

PROBLEM 5.50

If the boundedness assumption of the feasible region X is dropped, then the result does not hold as indicated by the attached figure. Obviously X is not contained in the ray $\{\underline{x}_0 + \mu_j(\underline{x}_j - \underline{x}_0) : \mu_j \geq 0\}$.

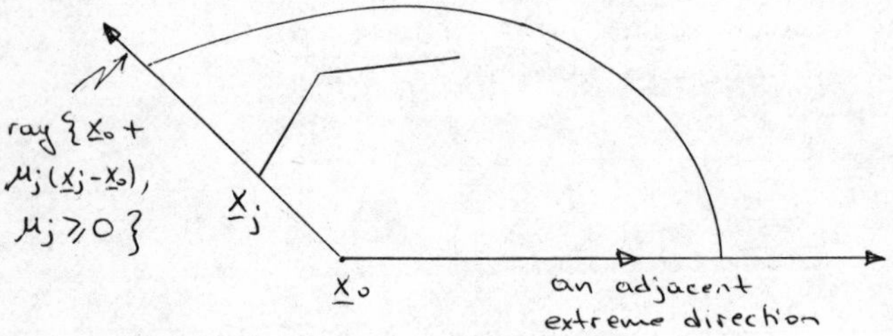

As the figure suggests, however, adjacent extreme directions could be used to generalize the result of Exercise 5.49.

A direction $\underline{d}$ is called adjacent to the extreme point $\underline{x}_0$ whose basis is B, if it is a vector of the form $\underline{d} = (\underline{e}_j, -\underline{y}_j)^T$, where $\underline{y}_j = B^{-1}\underline{a}_j \leq \underline{0}$ and the jth component corresponds to a nonbasic variable x_j.

Now, let $\underline{x}$ be a feasible solution. As shown in Exercise 5.49

$$\underline{x} - \underline{x}_0 = \sum_{j=1}^{n-m} \begin{pmatrix} \underline{e}_j \\ -\underline{y}_j \end{pmatrix} x_j \quad \text{------} \quad (1)$$

Now consider $j \in \{1, \ldots, n-m\}$. If $\underline{y}_j = B^{-1}\underline{a}_j \leq \underline{0}$, then it corresponds to an adjacent extreme direction $\underline{d}_j = (\underline{e}_j, -\underline{y}_j)^T$ .... (2)

PROBLEM 5.50 (Continued)

as defined above. If $\underline{y}_j = B^{-1}\underline{a}_j \nleq 0$, then as proved in Exercise 5.48 $\underline{x}_j$ given below is adjacent to $\underline{x}_o$.

$$\underline{x}_j - \underline{x}_o = \lambda_j \begin{pmatrix} \underline{e}_j \\ -\underline{y}_j \end{pmatrix} \quad \text{- - - - (3)}$$

where $\lambda_j = \underset{1 \leq i \leq m}{\text{minimum}} \left\{ \frac{\bar{b}_i}{y_{ij}} : y_{ij} > 0 \right\}$

From (1), (2) and (3) we get:

$$\underline{x} - \underline{x}_o = \sum_{j \in I} \mu_j (\underline{x}_j - \underline{x}_o) + \sum_{j \in J} \mu_j \underline{d}_j$$

where $\mu_j = \frac{x_j}{\lambda_j}$ for $j \in I$

$\mu_j = x_j$ for $j \in J$

PROBLEM 5.51

Let $\underline{x}_o$ be any extreme point and $\underline{x}_j$ $(j = 1, 2, .., k)$ be adjacent extreme points. Let $\underline{c}\underline{x}_o \leq \underline{c}\,\underline{x}_j$ for $j = 1, ..., k$ where $\underline{x}_j$ are adjacent to $\underline{x}_o$.

From problem 5.49, any $\underline{x} \in X$ can be written as

$$\underline{x} = \underline{x}_o + \sum_{j=1}^{k} \lambda_j (\underline{x}_j - \underline{x}_o), \quad \lambda_j \geq 0$$

and $c\underline{x} = c\underline{x}_o + \sum_{j=1}^{k} \lambda_j (c\underline{x}_j - c\underline{x}_o)$

PROBLEM 5.51 (Continued)

Since $c\underline{x}_j \geq c\underline{x}_0$ and $\lambda_j \geq 0$ we have

$$\sum_{j=1}^{k} \lambda_j (c\underline{x}_j - c\underline{x}_0) \geq 0$$

and thus

$$c\underline{x} \geq c\underline{x}_0 .$$

PROBLEM 5.52

Suppose that the optimal solution x^* to the problem is unique. Suppose that $\bar{x}$ is a second best extreme point. Suppose by contradiction that $\bar{x}$ is not adjacent to x^* and consider the tableau associated with $\bar{x}$. There must exist a nonbasic variable x_j with $z_j - c_j > 0$. Introducing the variable x_j into the basis we get an improved extreme point. This point could not have been x^* since x^* is not adjacent to $\bar{x}$. This violates the definition of $\bar{x}$ being a second best point. If the uniqueness assumption of x^* is dropped, then obviously $\bar{x}$ is not necessarily adjacent to each optimal point but will be adjacent to one of the optimal points.

CHAPTER 6 DUALITY AND SENSITIVITY

PROBLEM 6.1

a) $x_1 = 20/11$

$x_2 = 18/11$

$z = 16/11$

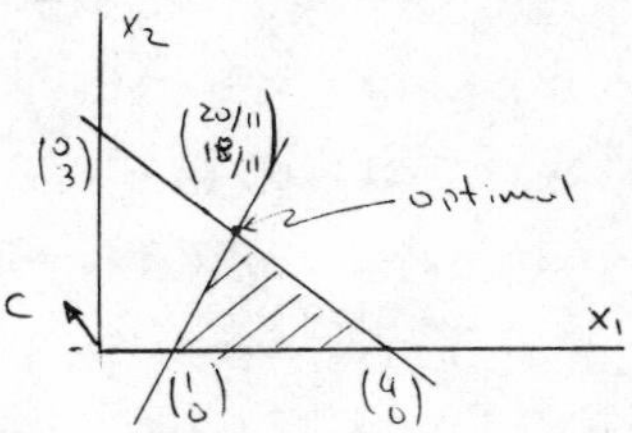

b) $\min\ 12w_1 - 2w_2$

s.t. $3w_1 - 2w_2 \geq -1$

$4w_1 + w_2 \geq 2$

$w_1, w_2 \geq 0$

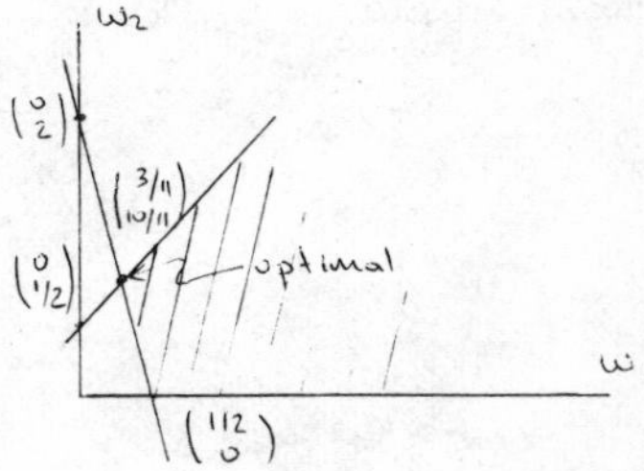

Optimal dual:

$w_1 = 3/11, \quad w_2 = 10/11, \quad obj = 16/11$

$$\left.\begin{array}{l} w_1 > 0 \implies 3x_1 + 4x_2 = 12 \\ w_2 > 0 \implies 2x_1 - x_2 = 2 \end{array}\right\} \implies x_1 = \frac{20}{11}, \quad x_2 = \frac{18}{11}$$

PROBLEM 6.2

a) $\max\ 2w_1 + 3w_2$

s.t. $w_1 + 2w_2 \leq 2$

$2w_1 - w_2 \leq 3$

$3w_1 + w_2 \leq 5$

$w_1 - 3w_2 \leq 6$

$w_1, w_2 \geq 0$

Optimal: $w_1 = 8/5$, $w_2 = 1/5$, $obj = 19/5$

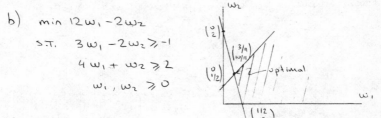

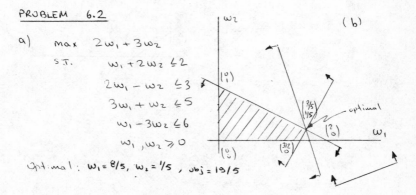

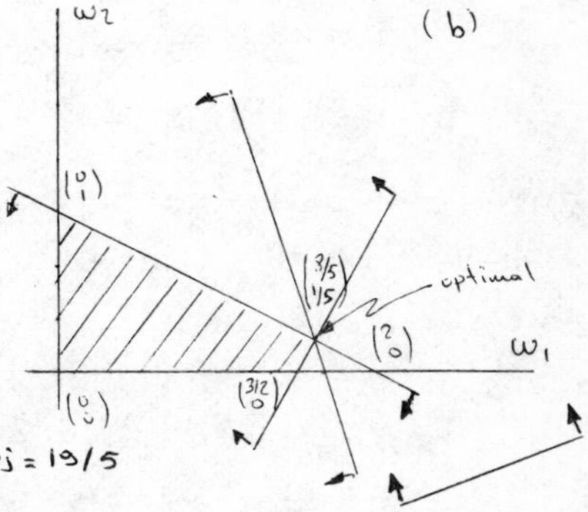

PROBLEM 6.2 (Continued)

c) with dual constraint that is not tight $\Rightarrow x_4 = 0$

$w_1 > 0, w_2 > 0 \Rightarrow$ the two primal constraints are tight. Therefore:

$$x_1 + 2x_2 + 3x_3 = 2$$
$$2x_1 - x_2 + x_3 = 3$$

Note that the third dual constrai can be thrown away without affecting the dual problem. So, $x_3 = 0$ (why). Thus

$$x_1 + 2x_2 = 2$$
$$2x_1 - x_2 = 3$$

The solution to these simultaneous equations is $x_1 = 8/5$ and $x_2 = 1/5$ with obj $= 19/5$.

PROBLEM 6.3

The dual problem is:

$$\min\ 25w_1 + 20w_2$$
$$\text{S.T.}\quad 6w_1 + 3w_2 \geq 3$$
$$3w_1 + 4w_2 \geq 1$$
$$5w_1 + 5w_2 \geq 4$$
$$w_1, w_2 \geq 0$$

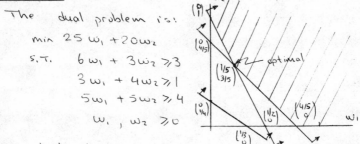

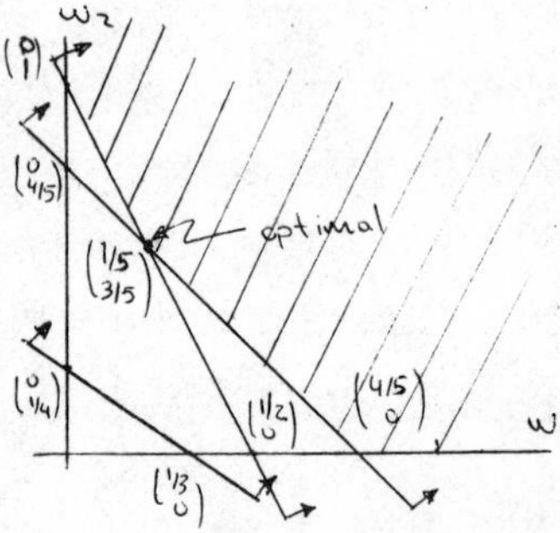

Optimal dual solution:

$w_1 = 1/5$, $w_2 = 3/5$, obj $= 17$.

Since second dual constraint is not tight, then $x_2 = 0$.

$$\left.\begin{array}{l} w_1 > 0 \Rightarrow 6x_1 + 5x_3 = 25 \\ w_2 > 0 \Rightarrow 3x_1 + 5x_3 = 20 \end{array}\right\} \Rightarrow \begin{array}{l} x_1 = 5/3 \\ x_3 = 3 \end{array}$$

primal obj $= 17$.

PROBLEM 6.4

$$\max \; 5w_1 + 4w_2 + 6w_3$$

S.T.
$$w_1 + 2w_2 \geq 2$$
$$w_1 + w_3 \leq 3$$
$$w_1 + w_2 + w_3 \leq -5$$
$$w_1 + w_3 = 0$$

$w_1 \geq 0$, $w_2 \leq 0$, w_3 unrestricted.

PROBLEM 6.5

$$\max \; w_1 b_1 + w_2 b_2 + w_3 b_3$$

S.T.
$$w_1 A_{11} + w_2 A_{21} + w_3 A_{31} \leq c_1$$
$$w_1 A_{12} + w_2 A_{22} + w_3 A_{32} \geq c_2$$
$$w_1 A_{13} + w_2 A_{23} + w_3 A_{33} = c_3$$

$w_1 \geq 0$, $w_2 \leq 0$, w_3 unrestricted.

PROBLEM 6.6

$$\min \; 19w_1 + 57w_2$$

S.T.
$w_1 + 2w_2 \geq 10$ Not tight
$w_1 + 4w_2 \geq 24$ tight
$2w_1 + 3w_2 \geq 20$ not tight
$3w_1 + 2w_2 \geq 20$ not tight
$5w_1 + w_2 \geq 25$ tight
$w_1, w_2 \geq 0$

a) $w_1 = 4$ and $w_2 = 5$ satisfy all the above inequalities.

b) Obtain complementary primal solution. First, third and fourth dual constraints are not tight. Thus $x_1 = x_3 = x_4 = 0$.

PROBLEM 6.6 (Continued)

$w_1, w_2 > 0$, so primal constraints are tight. Thus:

$$\left.\begin{aligned} x_2 + 5x_5 &= 19 \\ 4x_2 + x_5 &= 57 \end{aligned}\right\} \Rightarrow \quad \begin{aligned} x_5 &= 1 \\ x_2 &= 14 \end{aligned}$$

primal objective = dual objective = 361. Therefore the optimal solutions to the primal and dual problems are:

$$(x_1, x_2, x_3, x_4, x_5) = (0, 14, 0, 0, 1)$$

$$(w_1, w_2) = (4, 5)$$

PROBLEM 6.7

a)

$$\begin{aligned} \max \quad & 3w_1 \\ \text{S.T.} \quad & w_1 = 6 \\ & 2w_1 \leq 2 \\ & w_1 \geq 0 \end{aligned}$$

b) Obviously the feasible region of the dual is empty.

c) Equivalent P:

$$\begin{aligned} \min \quad & 6x_1' - 6x_1'' + 2x_2 \\ \text{S.T.} \quad & x_1' - x_1'' + 2x_2 \geq 3 \\ & x_1', x_1'', x_2 \geq 0 \end{aligned}$$

Dual

$$\begin{aligned} \max \quad & 3w_1 \\ \text{S.T.} \quad & w_1 \leq 6 \\ & -w_1 \leq -6 \\ & w_1 \leq 2 \\ & w_1 \geq 0 \end{aligned}$$

PROBLEM 6.7 (Continued)

d) Again, the feasible region is empty.

e) Transformation did not effect the feasible region.

PROBLEM 6.8

Performing the required row operations, the given tableau can be reduced to:

	z	x_1	x_2	x_3	x_4	x_5	RHS
z	1	6	-2	10	0	0	0
x_4	0	0	1	2	1	0	5
x_5	0	3	-1	1	0	1	10

initial tableau

a)

$$\min \; -6x_1 + 2x_2 - 10x_3$$

S.T.

$$x_2 + 2x_3 \leq 5$$

$$3x_1 - x_2 + x_3 \leq 10$$

$$x_1, x_2, x_3 \geq 0$$

b)

$$\max \; 5w_1 + 10w_2$$

S.T.

$$3w_2 \geq -6$$

$$w_1 - w_2 \geq 2$$

$$2w_1 + w_2 \geq -10$$

$$w_1, w_2 \leq 0$$

c) Optimal:

$w_1 = -4$, $w_2 = -2$ which are the $z_j - c_j$ values for slack variables x_4 and x_5.

PROBLEM 6.9

a) min $10w_1 + 6w_2$

s.t.

$$w_1 + w_2 \geq 2 \quad (1)$$

$$2w_1 - w_2 \geq 3 \quad (2)$$

$$w_1 + 3w_2 \geq 6 \quad (3)$$

$$w_1, w_2 \geq 0$$

b)

	z	x_1	x_2	x_3	x_4	x_5	RHS
z	1	-2	-3	-6	0	0	0
x_4	0	1	2	1	1	0	10
x_5	0	1	-1	(3)	0	1	6

$w_1 = w_2 = 0$

(1), (2) and (3) are violated. Violation is indicated in row 0 under x_1, x_2 and x_3 respectively.

	z	x_1	x_2	x_3	x_4	x_5	RHS
z	1	0	-5	0	0	2	12
x_4	0	2/3	(7/3)	0	1	-1/3	8
x_3	0	1/3	-1/3	1	0	1/3	2

$w_1 = 0, \; w_2 = 2$

(2) is violated.

	z	x_1	x_2	x_3	x_4	x_5	RHS
z	1	10/7	0	0	15/7	9/7	204/7
x_2	0	2/7	1	0	3/7	-1/7	24/7
x_3	0	3/7	0	1	1/7	2/7	22/7

$w_1 = 15/7, \; w_2 = 9/7$

All dual constraints are satisfied.

This is the optimal tableau.

c)

$$w_1 + w_2 - w_3 = 2$$

$$2w_1 - w_2 - w_4 = 3$$

$$w_1 + 3w_2 - w_5 = 6$$

$$w_1, w_2, w_3, w_4, w_5 \geq 0$$

PROBLEM 6.9 (Continued)

Iteration	Basics	Nonbasics	Dual Objective
1	w_3, w_4, w_5	w_1, w_2	0
2	w_2, w_3, w_4	w_1, w_5	12
3	w_1, w_2, w_3	w_4, w_5	204 / 7

d) Examining the last column of the above tableau and noting that the dual problem is a minimization problem, it follows that the dual objective worsens from iteration to iteration (but in the mean time we are approaching the dual feasibility).

e) $x_1 = 0$, $x_2 = 24/7$, $x_3 = 22/7$

$w_1 = 15/7$, $w_2 = 9/7$

are feasible to the primal and dual problems respectively. That complementary slackness can be checked to hold immediately. Finally dual objective = primal objective = 204/7.

PROBLEM 6.10

P. $\min \; cx$

s.t. $Ax = b$

$x \geq 0$

D. $\max \; wb$

s.t. $wA \leq c$

PROBLEM 6.10 (Continued)

If we can find an x_0 satisfying P and a w_0 satisfying D such that $cx_0 = w_0 b$, we are optimal.

There exists x_0 such that $Ax_0 = b$, $x_0 \geq 0$.

Consider $w_0 = x_0^t$.

$$w_0 A = x_0^t A = x_0^t A^t = b^t = c$$

so w_0 satisfies D, also

$$w_0 b = x_0^t b = x_0^t c^t = cx_0$$

and thus the objectives are equal. QED.

PROBLEM 6.11

a)

min z		Dual	max wb
S.T. $z - cx = 0$	(α)		S.T. $\alpha = 1$
$Ax = b$	(w)		$wA - \alpha c \leq 0$
$x \geq 0$			$w \geq 0$, α URS.

b) Any feasible solution to the dual problem must have $\alpha = 1$. Eliminating α we get the usual dual problem in standard format.

PROBLEM 6.12

Dantzig [97] suggests one method, which he calls the "self-dual parametric algorithm", for handling such a problem. Add a single parameter, θ, to each right-hand-side value which violates primal feasibility, i.e., $\bar{b}_i < 0$, and subtract

PROBLEM 6.12 (Continued)

it from each objective function value which violates dual feasibility, i.e., $z_j - c_j > 0$. This gives

$$\bar{b}_i = \begin{cases} \bar{b}_i & \text{if } \bar{b}_i \geq 0 \\ \bar{b}_i + \theta & \text{if } \bar{b}_i < 0 \end{cases}$$

$$(z_j - c_j)' = \begin{cases} (z_j - c_j) & \text{if } (z_j - c_j) \leq 0 \\ (z_j - c_j) - \theta & \text{if } (z_j - c_j) > 0 \end{cases}$$

Begin with θ equal to a large positive value. Parametrically reduce θ until the first time the problem becomes either primal or dual infeasible. If the problem first becomes primal infeasible at $\theta = \theta_0$, then perform a dual simplex pivot at $\theta = \theta_0$. If, the problem first becomes dual infeasible at $\theta = \theta_0$, then perform a primal simplex pivot. Continue to reduce θ and performing appropriate pivots. For additional details and verification of the procedure the reader is referred to Dantzig [97].

PROBLEM 6.13

Let B be an optimal basis of an LP problem with a given right-hand-side vector b. If the right-hand-side is replaced by $\hat{b}$ the same basis will be optimal if $B^{-1}\hat{b} \geq 0$. Let $\lambda = B^{-1}\hat{b}$. Then $\hat{b} = B\lambda$.

PROBLEM 6.13 (Continued)

By definition, $\hat{b}$ belongs to the cone generated by the colums of B, if and only if, $\lambda \geq 0$. Thus for any $\hat{b}$ in this cone $B^{-1}\hat{b} \geq 0$ and the current basis remains optimal.

PROBLEM 6.14

Let x_1: # of top-of the line recliner
x_2: # of second line recliner.

$$\max\ 50x_1 + 30x_2$$
$$\text{S.T.}\quad 3/2\,x_1 + 1/2\,x_2 \leq 100$$
$$x_1 + 1/2\,x_2 \leq 80$$
$$x_1,\ x_2 \geq 0$$

	z	x_1	x_2	x_3	x_4	RHS
z	1	10	0	0	60	4800
x_3	0	1/2	0	1	−1	20
x_2	0	2	1	0	2	160

Optimal tableau.

An hour of assembly : worth nothing, \$0.
An hour of finishing : worth \$60.

PROBLEM 6.15

Suppose by contradiction that the problem min cx s.t. $Ax = b'$, $x \geq 0$ is unbounded. Then the region $wA \leq c$ is empty. In particular, the following problem is infeasible

$$\max\ wb$$
$$\text{S.T.}\quad wA \leq c$$
$$w \text{ URS}$$

PROBLEM 6.15 (Continued)

Since the above problem is infeasible, then the problem min cx s.t. $Ax = b$, $x \geq 0$ is either infeasible or unbounded, contradicting the assumption that it has a finite optimal.

PROBLEM 6.16

If the system $Ax \geq b$, $x \geq 0$ has no solution, then by Farkas' lemma the system $wA \leq 0$, $w \geq 0$, $wb > 0$ has a solution $\bar{w}$. If the dual problem

$$\begin{aligned} \max\ & wb \\ \text{s.t.}\ & wA \leq c \\ & w \geq 0 \end{aligned}$$

has a feasible point, say w, then consider $w + \lambda\bar{w}$ for $\lambda \geq 0$. Points of this form are feasible since

$$w \geq 0,\ \bar{w} \geq 0,\ \lambda > 0 \Rightarrow (w + \lambda\bar{w})A \leq c$$

Furthermore $(w + \lambda\bar{w})b = wb + \lambda\bar{w}b$. Since $\bar{w}b > 0$ then the objective can be made arbitrarily large by choosing λ arbitrarily large. So the dual problem has an unbounded solution.

PROBLEM 6.17

		Dual Variables
min	cx	
s.t.	$Ax = b$	(w)
	$x \geq \ell$	(y)
	$-x \geq -u$	(h)

PROBLEM 6.17 (Continued)

Dual Problem:

$$\begin{aligned} \max\ & wb + g\ell - uh \\ \text{S.T.}\ & wA + g - h = c \\ & w \text{ ures} \\ & g \geq 0,\ h \geq 0 \end{aligned}$$

b) The dual problem posesses a feasible solution. For example, let $w = 0$ and $g_j = \max(0, c_j)$ and $h_j = \max(0, -c_j)$ for all j satisfy the dual restrictions.

c) If the primal has a feasible solution, and since the dual has a feasible solution, then both problems have finite optimal solutions with equal objectives.

PROBLEM 6.18

a) True
b) True
c) True
d) False
e) True
f) False
g) True
h) True
i) True
j) False
k) False

PROBLEM 6.19

Note that the dual problem always posesses a feasible solution. If there is a w such that $wA \leq 0$ and $wb > 0$ then the dual problem is unbounded by considering λw

PROBLEM 6.19 (Continued)

for $\lambda > 0$ and arbitrarily large. By the main duality theorem the primal problem must be inconsistent. Thus:

$wA \le 0$, $wb > 0$ has a solution $\Rightarrow$ $Ax = b$, $x \geq 0$ has no solution.

Now suppose that $wA \le 0$, $wb > 0$ has no solution. Then the optimal objective value of the dual problem is finite and equal to zero. By duality, the primal problem must be consistent, i.e.,

$wA \le 0$, $wb > 0$ has no solution $\Rightarrow$ $Ax = b$, $x \geq 0$ has a solution. QED.

PROBLEM 6.20

a) Note the basis remains optimal since $w = c_B B^{-1}$, examine the effect on inverse if one of its rows is multiplied by a nonzero scalar λ.

b) Basis still optimal. Examine the effects on B^{-1}.

PROBLEM 6.21

Note that if a set of constraints is redundant then it can not contain a basis. The basis must contain at least one artificial variable. In this case $w = c_B B^{-1}$ will depend on the cost assigned to the basic artificial variable(s).

PROBLEM 6.22

a) max α or equivalently

$$\begin{aligned} \text{S.T.} \quad & w_1 + w_2 = 1 \\ & \alpha - 2w_1 + 3w_2 \leq 0 \\ & \alpha + w_1 - w_2 \leq 0 \\ & \alpha \quad - w_2 \leq 0 \\ & w_1, w_2 \geq 0 \end{aligned}$$

$$\begin{aligned} \max \quad & \alpha \\ \text{S.T.} \quad & 2w_1 - 3w_2 \geq \alpha \\ & -w_1 + w_2 \geq \alpha \\ & w_1 + w_2 = 1 \\ & w_1, w_2 \geq 0 \end{aligned}$$

b) w_1 and w_2 are the probabilities with which the row player chooses rows 1 and 2. The row player's problem is thus to maximize the minimum expected income from the column player.

c) Note that for $w_1 \geq 0$, $(-w_1 + w_2)$ is always less than or equal to w_2. Thus we are interested in maximizing the min $(2w_1 - 3w_2, -w_1 + w_2)$ over the region $\{(w_1, w_2) : w_1 \geq 0, w_2 \geq 0, w_1 + w_2 = 1\}$. The contours are shown in the figure.

PROBLEM 6.22 (Continued)

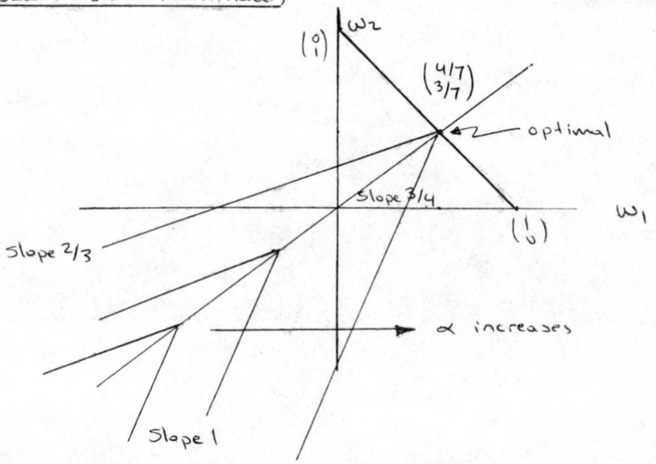

The optimal is $w_1 = 4/7$ and $w_2 = 3/7$ with expected return $= -1/7$.

d) Since $w_1, w_2 \geq 0$ then $z - 2x_1 + x_2 = 0$ and $z + 3x_1 - x_2 - x_3 = 0$.

Since the primal and dual objectives must be equal at optimality, then $z = \alpha = -1/7$. Finally, since $w_2 \geq \alpha$ is not binding ct then $x_3 = 0$. Thus

$$\left.\begin{array}{r} -2x_1 + x_2 = 1/7 \\ 3x_1 - x_2 = 1/7 \end{array}\right\} \Rightarrow x_1 = 2/7, x_2 = 5/7$$

e) Consider the payoff matrix. If a column dominates another column then the probability of playing that dominated column is zero. Same argument is valid for the rows.

PROBLEM 6.23

Consider

$$P: \text{minimize } cx \quad \text{s.t. } Ax = b, \; x \geq 0$$

where $\underline{a}^k = \sum_{i \neq k} \lambda_i \underline{a}^i$.

Assuming P has a feasible solution then

$$\sum_{i \neq k} \lambda_i b_i = b_k .$$

Now the dual of P is:

$$D: \text{Maximize } wb \quad \text{s.t. } wA \leq c$$

Suppose w^* solves D. Then

$$w^* A \leq \underline{c}$$

$$\sum_{i=1}^{m} w_i^* a^i \leq \underline{c}$$

$$\sum_{i \neq k} w_i^* \underline{a}^i + w_k^* \underline{a}^k \leq \underline{c}$$

$$\sum_{i \neq k} w_i^* \underset{\sim}{a}^i + w_k^* \sum_{i \neq k} \lambda_i a^i \leq \underline{c}$$

$$\sum_{i \neq k} (w_i^* + w_k^* \lambda_i) \underline{a}^i \leq \underline{c}$$

$$\sum_{i \neq k} w_i' \underline{a}^i \leq \underline{c}$$

PROBLEM 6.23 (Continued)

$$\sum_{i=1}^{m} w_i' \underline{a}^i \leq \underline{c}$$

where

$$w_i' = \begin{cases} w_i^* + w_k^* \lambda_i & \text{for } i \neq k \\ 0 & \text{for } i = k \end{cases}$$

Also,

$$\begin{aligned} \underline{w}'\underline{b} &= \Sigma_{i \neq k} w_i' b_i + w_k' b_k \\ &= \Sigma_{i \neq k} (w_i^* + w_k^* \lambda_i) b_i \\ &= \Sigma_{i \neq k} w_i^* b_i + w_k^* \Sigma_{i \neq k} \lambda_i b_i \\ &= \Sigma_{i \neq k} w_i^* b_i + w_k^* b_k \\ &= \underline{w}^* \underline{b} \end{aligned}$$

Thus, $\underline{w}'$ is also optimal to D with $w_k' = 0$. Now, if x^* is optimal to P, then x^* is also optimal to P' with row k deleted. Also, $\underline{\bar{w}}'$, $\underline{w}'$ with w_k' deleted, is optimal to D', the dual of P'; and $\underline{\bar{w}}'$ is complementary to x^*.

Summarizing, $\underline{\bar{w}}'$ is the optimal solution to the dual of the reduced primal problem, P, with the redundant constraint deleted. But we have shown that $\underline{\bar{w}}'$ with $w'_k = 0$ added is also optimal to D.

PROBLEM 6.24

x^* solves the problem $\min\ (c + w_k^* a^k)x$ S.T. $a^i x = b_i$ $i = 1, 2, .., m$, $i \neq k$, $x \geq 0$ if there exists a vector w such that:

$$\sum_{\substack{i=1\\ i \neq k}}^{m} w_i a^i \leq c - w_k^* a^k$$

or

$$\left(\sum_{\substack{i=1\\ i \neq k}}^{m} w_i a^i - c + w_k^* a^k \right) x^* = 0$$

(The above conditions are dual feasibility and complementary slackness). Note that the primal feasibility automatically holds since x^* is an optimal solution of the more constrained problem.

Noting that w^* is the optimal dual solution of the original problem, letting $w_i = w_i^*$ for all i, it is clear that the above conditions hold.

PROBLEM 6.25

$$B^{-1} = \begin{bmatrix} -1/7 & 4/7 \\ -5/7 & 13/7 \end{bmatrix} \Rightarrow B = \begin{bmatrix} 13/7 & -4/7 \\ 5/7 & -1/7 \end{bmatrix}$$

$$\begin{bmatrix} -2/7 \\ -3/7 \end{bmatrix} = B^{-1} \begin{bmatrix} b \\ c \end{bmatrix}, \quad \begin{bmatrix} b \\ c \end{bmatrix} = B \begin{bmatrix} -2/7 \\ -3/7 \end{bmatrix} = \begin{bmatrix} -2/7 \\ -1/7 \end{bmatrix}$$

PROBLEM 6.25 (Continued)

$z_4 - c_4 = c_B y_4 - c_4 \Rightarrow 11/7 = (7, 6)\begin{bmatrix} -2/7 \\ -3/7 \end{bmatrix} - c_4$

$c_4 = \frac{4}{7} - \frac{11}{7} = -1 \Rightarrow a = 1$

a) $a = 1$, $b = -2/7$, $c = -1/7$

b) $B^{-1} = \begin{bmatrix} -1/7 & 4/7 \\ -5/7 & 13/7 \end{bmatrix}$

c) $\frac{\partial x_2}{\partial x_5} = -8/7$

d) $\frac{\partial x_3}{\partial b_2} = 4/7$

e) $\frac{\partial z}{\partial x_6} = -23/7$

f) $w_1 = 23/7$, $w_2 = -50/7$

PROBLEM 6.26

a) $x_1 = 2$, $x_2 = 0$, $x_3 = 3/2$

b) $w_1 = 4$, $w_2 = 0$, $w_3 = 9$

c) $\partial z / \partial b_1 = 4$

d) $\partial x_1 / \partial x_3 = -1$

e) Yes. Return = 4 and cost = 5/2.

f) At least \$9.

g) An alternate optimal solution exists since $z_2 - c_2 = 0$ for the nonbasic variable x_2. By introducing x_2 we get the alternative basic optimal solution $x_1 = 0$, $x_2 = 2$, $x_3 = 3/2$.

PROBLEM 6.27

	z	x_1	x_2	x_3	x_4	x_5	RHS
z	1	4	6	18	0	0	0
x_4	0	-1	0	-3	1	0	-3
x_5	0	0	(-1)	-2	0	1	-5

	z	x_1	x_2	x_3	x_4	x_5	RHS
z	1	4	0	6	0	6	-30
x_4	0	-1	0	(-3)	1	0	-3
x_2	0	0	1	2	0	-1	5

	z	x_1	x_2	x_3	x_4	x_5	RHS
z	1	2	0	0	2	6	-30
x_3	0	1/3	0	1	-1/3	0	1
x_2	0	-2/3	1	0	2/3	-1	3

Optimal tableau.

Primal:

$x_1 = 0, x_2 = 3, x_3 = 1$

obj = -36

Dual

$w_1 = -2, \; w_2 = -6$

obj = -36

$w_1(x_1 + 3x_3 - 3) = w_2(x_2 + 2x_3 - 5) = 0$

$x_1(w_1 + 4) = x_2(w_2 + 6) = x_3(3w_1 + 2w_3 + 18) = 0$

holds.

PROBLEM 6.28

Dual:

$$\begin{aligned} \min \quad & -3w_1 + 6w_2 \\ \text{s.t.} \quad & -w_1 + 3w_2 \geq 2 \\ & -w_1 + w_2 \geq -3 \\ & w_1, w_2 \geq 0 \end{aligned}$$

Since $x_1 > 0$, $x_2 > 0$ then

$$\left.\begin{aligned} -w_1 + 3w_2 &= 2 \\ -w_1 + w_2 &= -3 \end{aligned}\right\} \Rightarrow \begin{aligned} w_1 &= 11/2 \\ w_2 &= 5/2 \end{aligned}$$

Since $w_1, w_2 > 0$, any optimal primal must have tight primal constraints. $x = (3/2, 3/2)$ makes the two primal constraints tight, hence it is optimal.

PROBLEM 6.28 (Continued)

To use the dual simplex method, add the artificial constraint $x_1 + x_2 \leq M$ where M is a large number greater than zero.

	Z	x_1	x_2	x_3	x_4	x_5	RHS
Z	1	-2	3	0	0	0	0
x_3	0	-1	-1	1	0	0	-3
x_4	0	3	1	0	1	0	6
x_5	0	(1)	1	0	0	1	M

initial tableau

	Z	x_1	x_2	x_3	x_4	x_5	RHS
z	1	0	0	11/2	5/2	0	-3/2
x_2	0	0	1	-3/2	-1/2	0	3/2
x_5	0	0	0	1	0	1	M-3
x_1	0	1	0	1/2	1/2	0	3/2

Final tableau (optimal)
Iteration # 3

Optimal:

$x_1 = 3/2$, $x_2 = 3/2$, $x_3 = 0$

PROBLEM 6.29

	Z	x_1	x_2	x_3	x_4	x_5	x_6	RHS
z	1	-2	-3	-5	-6	0	0	0
x_5	0	-1	-2	-3	-1	1	0	-2
x_6	0	-2	1	-1	3	0	1	-3

initial tableau

	Z	x_1	x_2	x_3	x_4	x_5	x_6	RHS
z	1	0	0	0	-5	-8/5	-1/5	19/5
x_3	0	0	1	1	1	-2/5	1/5	1/5
x_1	0	1	-1	0	-2	1/5	-3/5	7/5

Final (optimal) tableau

Optimal: $x_1 = 7/5$, $x_3 = 1/5$, $x_2 = x_4 = 0$, obj $= 19/5$

PROBLEM 6.30

a) $\max\ -6w_1 + 3w_2$

S.T.
$-w_1 - w_2 \leq 3$ ← redundant
$-w_1 - w_2 \leq 5$ ← redundant
$-w_1 + 2w_2 \leq -1$
$-3w_1 + w_2 \leq 2$
$-w_1 - w_2 \leq -4$; $w_1, w_2 \geq 0$

PROBLEM 6.30 (Continued)

Add the constraint $w_1 + w_2 \leq M$

	z	w_1	w_2	w_3	w_4	w_5	w_6	RHS
z	1	6	-3	0	0	0	0	0
w_3	0	-1	2	1	0	0	0	-1
w_4	0	-3	1	0	1	0	0	2
w_5	0	-1	-1	0	0	1	0	-4
w_6	0	1	(1)	0	0	0	1	M

Initial tableau

	z	w_1	w_2	w_3	w_4	w_5	w_6	RHS
z	1	0	0	3	0	3	0	-15
w_6	0	0	0	0	0	1	1	M-4
w_4	0	0	0	-4/3	1	-5/3	0	10
w_1	0	1	0	-1/3	0	-2/3	0	3
w_2	0	0	1	1/3	0	-1/3	0	1

Final (optimal) tableau.

Optimal dual:

$w_1 = 3$, $w_2 = 1$

obj = -15

c) The first and second conditions of the dual are not tight, therefore $x_1 = x_2 = 0$, also the fourth constraint is not tight, hence $x_4 = 0$. $w_1, w_2 > 0$ implies that the primal constraints must be tight. Thus;

$$\left.\begin{array}{l} x_3 + x_5 = 6 \\ 2x_3 - x_5 = 3 \end{array}\right\} \Longrightarrow x_3 = 3, \; x_5 = 3$$

PROBLEM 6.31

The dual problem is max wb, s.t. $wA \leq c$, w unrestricted. Suppose that $\bar{b}_r < 0$ and $y_{rj} \geq 0$, for all j. Consider the vector

PROBLEM 6.31 (Continued)

$(0, 0, --, -1, 0, -- 0)B^{-1}$, where -1 appears at the rth position. This vector is precisely the (−)ve rth row of B^{-1}. Let w be any feasible solution of the dual problem, i.e., $wA \leq c$. Then

$$[w + \lambda(0, --, -1, 0, -- 0)B^{-1}]A = wA + \lambda(0, --, -1, 0 -- 0)B^{-1}A$$

but $B^{-1}A$ is the current tableau, and $(0, --, -1, -- 0)B^{-1}A$ is precisely $-(y_{r1}, y_{r2}, ---, y_{rn}) \leq 0$ by assumption. Thus $(0, ---, -1, -- 0)B^{-1}$ is feasible for all $\lambda \geq 0$. Therefore, it is a direction of the feasible dual region. Furthermore $(0, --, -1, 0, --, 0)B^{-1}b = -\bar{b}_r > 0$ since $\bar{b}_r < 0$. Therefore we established a direction $\bar{w}$ of the feasible dual region such that $\bar{w}b > 0$. This is the necessary and sufficient condition for unboundedness of the dual.

PROBLEM 6.33

Implementation of the lexicographic method in the dual simplex method results in a practical rule for avoiding cycling which is analogous to the one presented in chapter 4. Assuming that an initial dual feasible tableau has been obtained in which all columns are lexicographically negative (for a minimization problem) the rule becomes (where r is the exit row): Let

PROBLEM 6.33 (Continued)

$$J_0 = \left\{ s : \frac{y_{0s}}{y_{rs}} = \underset{1 \le j \le n}{\text{minimum}} \left[\frac{y_{0j}}{y_{rj}} : y_{rj} < 0 \right] \right\}$$

If J_0 is a singleton, namely $J_0 = \{s\}$, then x_s enters the basis. Otherwise, form J_1 as follows:

$$J_1 = \left\{ s : \frac{y_{1s}}{y_{rs}} = \underset{j \in J_0}{\text{minimum}} \left[\frac{y_{1j}}{y_{rj}} \right] \right\}$$

If J_1 is singleton, namely $J_1 = \{s\}$, then x_s enters the basis. Otherwise form J_2. In general J_i is formed from J_{i-1} as follows:

$$J_i = \left\{ s : \frac{y_{is}}{y_{rs}} = \underset{j \in J_{i-1}}{\text{minimum}} \left[\frac{y_{ij}}{y_{rj}} \right] \right\}$$

Eventually, for some $i \le m$, J_i will be a singleton and a unique variable will be selected to enter the basis.

Obviously, this discussion leaves questions unanswered concerning starting and converging. We refer the reader to Beale [27] for a more detailed development.

PROBLEM 6.34

a) Starting tableau:

1	b^T	0	0	0
0	B^T	0	I_m	c^T
	N^T	I_{n-m}	0	

b)

$$\begin{bmatrix} B^T & 0 \\ N^T & I_{n-m} \end{bmatrix}^{-1} = \begin{bmatrix} (B^{-1})^T & 0 \\ -N^T(B^{-1})^T & I_{n-m} \end{bmatrix}$$

PROBLEM 6.34 (Continued)

c)

0	0	$-b^T(B^{-1})^T$	$-b^T(B^{-1})^T c_B^T$
I_m	0	$(B^{-1})^T$	$(B^{-1})^T c_B^T$
0	I_{n-m}	$-N^T(B^{-1})^T$	$c_N^T - N^T(B^{-1})^T c_B^T$

Complete current tableau.

PROBLEM 6.35

See [470].

PROBLEM 6.36

a) Primal: min $2x_1 - 3x_2$

s.t. $x_1 + x_2 \geq 2$

$-x_2 \geq -4$

$x_1, x_2 \geq 0$

(b) Dual: max $2w_1 - 4w_2$

s.t. $w_1 \leq 2$

$w_1 - w_2 \leq -3$

$w_1, w_2 \geq 0$

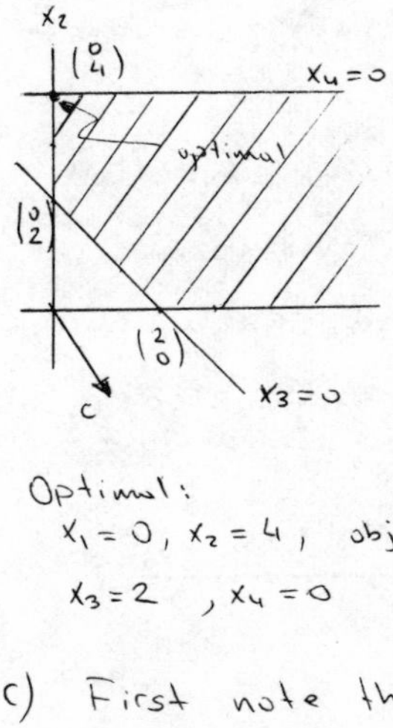

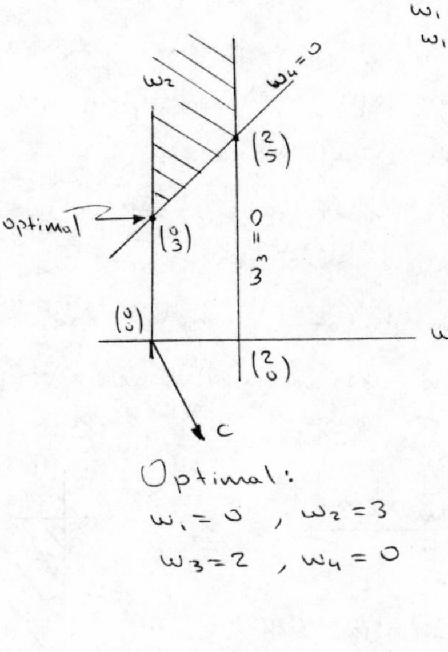

Optimal:

$x_1 = 0$, $x_2 = 4$, obj $= -12$

$x_3 = 2$, $x_4 = 0$

Optimal:

$w_1 = 0$, $w_2 = 3$

$w_3 = 2$, $w_4 = 0$

c) First note that

$$\left\{\begin{matrix} x_3, w_1 \\ x_4, w_2 \\ x_1, w_3 \\ x_2, w_4 \end{matrix}\right\}$$

are complementary pairs.

PROBLEM 6.36 (Continued)

At optimality

$x_1 = 0$, the complementary dual variable $w_3 > 0$.

$x_4 = 0$, the complementary dual variable $w_2 > 0$.

Note that x_1 is unbounded in the feasible primal region. The complementary dual variable w_3 is bounded (between 0 and 2) in the dual feasible region. Similarly x_3 is unbounded in the primal feasible region and the complementary dual variable w_1 is bounded. The two dual variables w_2 and w_4 are unbounded in the dual problem and their complementary primal variables x_4 and x_2 are bounded in the primal region. This illustrates part (b) of the theorem.

In part (c) it follows that since all primal variables are bounded in the primal optimal set (namely one row) and each dual variable assumes values different than zero in the dual space.

PROBLEM 6.37

$$\min \; -x_2$$
$$\text{S.T.} \quad x_1 + x_2 \geq 2$$
$$-x_2 \geq -4$$
$$x_1, x_2 \geq 0$$

many optimum.

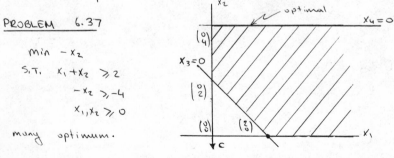

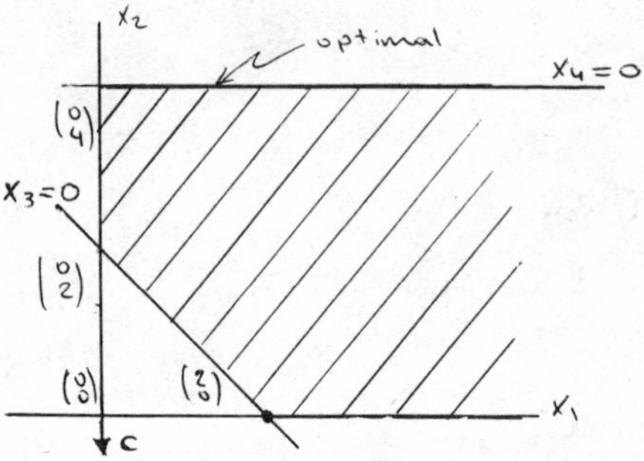

PROBLEM 6.37 (Continued)

b) Dual max $2w_1 - 4w_2$

s.t. $w_1 \leq 0$

$w_1 - w_2 \leq -1$

$w_1, w_2 \geq 0$

or

max $-4w_2$

s.t. $w_2 \geq 1$

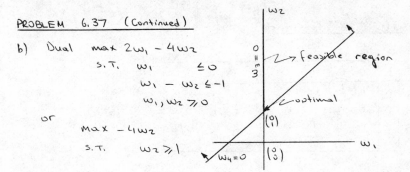

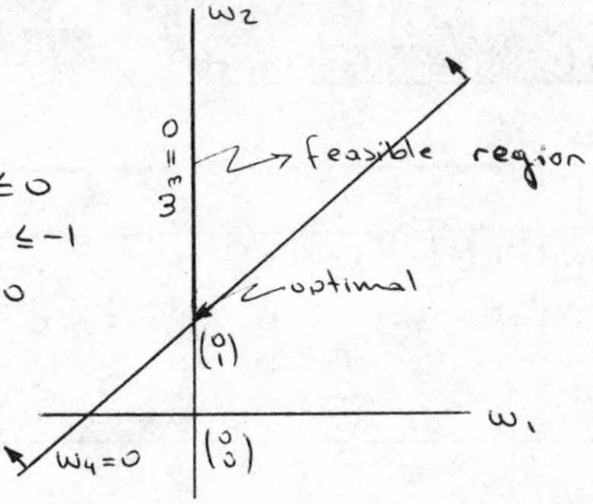

c) (x_3, w_1), (x_4, w_2), (x_1, w_3), (x_2, w_4) are the complementary pairs. At optimality

$x_4 = 0 \Rightarrow w_2 > 0$

$x_3 > 0 \Rightarrow w_1 = 0$

$w_3 = 0 \Rightarrow x_1 > 0$

$w_4 = 0 \Rightarrow x_2 > 0$

Note that x_1 is unbounded in the primal feasible region, the complementary dual variable w_3 is bounded to be zero. Similarly, x_2 is bounded in the primal feasible region and the corresponding complementary dual variable w_4 is unbounded in the feasible dual region. The dual variable w_1 is bounded in the dual feasible region and the complementary primal variable x_1 is unbounded in the primal feasible region. Similarly, w_2 is unbounded, and the corresponding complementary primal variable x_2 is bounded.

PROBLEM 6.38 (Continued)

	z	w_1	w_2	w_3	w_4	w_5	w_6	w_7	RHS
z	1	0	0	-1	0	0	0	0	0
w_4	0	-1/4	(-1/2)	0	1	0	0	0	-3/4
w_5	0	8	12	0	0	1	0	0	20
w_6	0	1	1/2	-1	0	0	1	0	-1/2
w_7	0	9	-3	0	0	0	0	1	6

Initial tableau

	z	w_1	w_2	w_3	w_4	w_5	w_6	w_7	RHS
z	1	-3/4	0	0	-1	0	-1	0	5/4
w_2	0	1/2	1	0	2	0	0	0	3/2
w_5	0	2	0	0	-24	1	0	0	2
w_3	0	-3/4	0	1	-1	0	-1	0	5/4
w_7	0	15/2	0	0	6	0	0	1	21/2

Optimal tableau (Tableau #3)

PROBLEM 6.40

Consider

$$P: \quad \text{minimize} \quad 0\underline{x}_B + (\underline{c}_N - \underline{c}_B B^{-1}N)\underline{x}_N$$

$$\text{S.T.} \qquad \underline{1}\,\underline{x}_N \le M$$

$$\underline{x}_B \qquad + B^{-1}N\underline{x}_N = B^{-1}\underline{b}$$

$$\underline{x}_B, \underline{x}_N \geq \underline{0}$$

which corresponds to the artificial constraint applied to the primal problem when one or more of the elements of $\underline{c}_N - \underline{c}_B B^{-1}N$ is negative. The dual of the above problem is:

$$D: \quad \text{maximize} \quad \underline{w}B^{-1}\underline{b} + w_0 M$$

$$\text{S.T.} \quad \underline{w}B^{-1}N + w_0\underline{1} \le \underline{c}_N - \underline{c}_B B^{-1}N$$

$$\underline{w} \geq \underline{0}$$

$$w_0 \geq 0$$

PROBLEM 6.40 (Continued)

Adding slack variables for a starting basis we get:

$$\text{maximize} \quad \underline{w} B^{-1} \underline{b} + w_0 M$$

$$\text{S.T.} \quad \underline{w} B^{-1} N + I \underline{w}_s + w_0 \underline{1} = \underline{c}_N - \underline{c}_B B^{-1} N$$

$$\underline{w}, \underline{w}_s \geq \underline{0}$$

$$w_0 \geq 0$$

Since one or more of the right-hand-side values is negative we may pivot w_0 into the basis as described in Chapter 4 and continue.

PROBLEM 6.41

P: minimize cx
S.T. $Ax = b$
$x \geq 0$

P_M: minimize cx
S.T. $Ax = b$
$-\underline{1} x \geq -M$
$x \geq 0$

Let x^* be an optimal solution of problem P_M. Let $(w, v)^T$ be an optimal extreme point dual solution of P_M. Further suppose that $v > 0$, so that, $\underline{1} x = M$. Then, the optimal solution to the original problem is unbounded provided that M is large enough. We shall now exhibit how large M should be in order to validate this conclusion.

Let $(w_j, v_j)^T$ for $j \in I$ be the extreme points of the dual feasible region of problem

PROBLEM 6.41 (Continued)

P_M with $v_j > 0$. Let $\bar{x}$ be an extreme point of P with the smallest objective value among all the extreme points. Choose M such that:

$$M > \frac{|w_j b - c\bar{x}|}{v_j} + 1 \quad \text{for each } j \in I.$$

Now, suppose at termination of P_M we have an optimal extreme point x^* and a dual optimal extreme point $(w, v)^T$ with $v > 0$. Since the objectives of primal and dual are equal, then:

$$cx^* = wb - Mv \quad - - - - (1)$$

By choice of M, $M > \frac{|wb - c\bar{x}|}{v} + 1 \geq \frac{wb - c\bar{x}}{v} + 1$

therefore $Mv > wb - c\bar{x} + v$. Substituting into (1) we get:

$$cx^* = wb - Mv < wb - (wb - c\bar{x} + v) = c\bar{x} - v < c\bar{x}$$

Thus we established a feasible solution x^* to P whose objective value is strictly less than that of each extreme points of problem P. Therefore, problem P has an unbounded optimal objective value.

PROBLEM 6.42

Primal: min $-x_1 - 6x_2$

S.T. $x_1 + x_2 - x_3 = 2$

$x_1 + 3x_2 + x_4 = 3$

$x_1, x_2, x_3, x_4 \geq 0$

Dual: max $2w_1 + 3w_2$

S.T. $w_1 + w_2 \leq -1$

$w_1 + 3w_2 \leq -6$

$-w_1 \leq 0$, $w_2 \leq 0$

Let $w_1 = 0$, $w_2 = -2$. Then, dual feasibility holds. $z_1 - c_1 = -1$ $z_2 - c_2 = 0$, $z_3 - c_3 = 0$, $z_4 - c_4 = -2$.

Phase I

Initial tableau

	x_1	$\square$ x_2	$\square$ x_3	x_4	x_5 (Artificials)	x_6	RHS
z	-1	0	0	-2	0	0	0
x_0	0	0	0	0	-1	-1	0
x_5	1	1	-1	0	1	0	2
x_6	1	3	0	1	0	1	3

PROBLEM 6.42 (Continued)

	x_1	x_2	x_3	x_4	x_5	x_6	RHS
z	-1	0	0	-2	0	0	0
x_0	2/3	0	-1	$-1/3$	0	$-4/3$	1
x_5	2/3	0	-1	$-1/3$	1	$-1/3$	1
x_2	1/3	1	0	1/3	0	1/3	1

Optimal tableau of phase I (Tableau # 3)

$$\theta = \min\left\{ -\frac{(z_j - c_j)}{\hat{z}_j - \hat{c}_j} : \hat{z}_j - \hat{c}_j > 0 \right\} = \min\left\{ \frac{1}{2/3} \right\} = 3/2$$

Add 3/2 times the x_0 row to the z row.

	x_1 □	x_2 □	x_3	x_4	x_5	x_6	RHS
z	0	0	$-3/2$	$-5/2$	0	-2	3/2
x_0	2/3	0	-1	$-1/3$	0	$-4/3$	1
x_5	(2/3)	0	-1	$-1/3$	1	$-1/3$	1
x_2	1/3	1	0	1/3	0	1/3	1

	x_1	x_2	x_3	x_4	x_5	x_6	RHS
z	0	0	$-3/2$	$-5/2$	0	-2	3/2
x_0	0	0	0	0	-1	-1	0
x_1	1	0	$-3/2$	$-1/2$	3/2	$-1/2$	3/2
x_2	0	1	1/2	1/2	$-1/2$	1/2	1/2

Since $x_0 = 0$, then the optimal solution is obtained. $x_1 = 3/2$, $x_2 = 1/2$, obj $= 9/2$.

PROBLEM 6.43

Primal:

$$\begin{aligned} \min\ & 9x_1 + 2x_2 + 4x_3 + 2x_4 + 6x_5 + 10x_6 \\ \text{s.t.}\ & x_1 + x_2 + x_3 = 8 \\ & x_4 + x_5 + x_6 = 5 \\ & x_1 + x_4 = 6 \\ & x_2 + x_5 = 4 \\ & x_3 + x_6 = 3 \\ & x_1, x_2, x_3, x_4, x_5, x_6 \geq 0 \end{aligned}$$

PROBLEM 6.43 (Continued)

Dual:

$$\max \; 8w_1 + 5w_2 + 6w_3 + 4w_4 + 3w_5$$

$$\text{S.T.} \quad \begin{aligned} w_1 + w_3 &\le 9 \\ w_1 + w_4 &\le 7 \\ w_1 + w_5 &\le 4 \\ w_2 + w_3 &\le 2 \\ w_2 + w_4 &\le 6 \\ w_2 + w_5 &\le 10 \end{aligned}$$

w_1, w_2, w_3, w_4, w_5 unrestricted.

Let $w_1 = 0$, $w_2 = 0$, $w_3 = 0$, $w_4 = 0$, $w_5 = 0$. This is a feasible solution.

$z_1 - c_1 = -9$, $z_2 - c_2 = -7$, $z_3 - c_3 = -4$, $z_4 - c_4 = -2$, $z_5 - c_5 = -6$, $z_6 - c_6 = -10$

Artificial (x_7 – x_{11})

	x_1	x_2	x_3	x_4	x_5	x_6	x_7	x_8	x_9	x_{10}	x_{11}	RHS
z	-9	-7	-4	-2	-6	-10	0	0	0	0	0	0
x_0	2	2	2	2	2	2	0	0	0	0	0	26
x_7	1	1	1	0	0	0	1	0	0	0	0	8
x_8	0	0	0	1	1	1	0	1	0	0	0	5
x_9	(1)	0	0	1	0	0	0	0	1	0	0	6
x_{10}	0	1	0	0	1	0	0	0	0	1	0	4
x_{11}	0	0	1	0	0	1	0	0	0	0	1	3

First tableau.

Since $z_j - c_j = 0$ for all variables in the restricted primal this tableau is an optimal one for phase I.

$$\theta = \min\left\{\frac{9}{2}, \frac{7}{2}, \frac{4}{2}, \frac{2}{2}, \frac{6}{2}, \frac{10}{2}\right\} = \frac{2}{2} = 1$$

Thus add x_0 row into z row.

PROBLEM 6.43 (Continued)

	x_1	x_2	x_3	□ x_4	x_5	x_6	□ x_7	□ x_8	□ x_9	□ x_{10}	□ x_{11}	RHS
z	-7	-5	-2	0	-4	-8	0	0	0	0	0	26
x_0	2	2	2	2	2	2	0	0	0	0	0	26
x_7	same as previous tableau			0	Same as previous tableau							8
x_8				(1)								5
x_9				1								6
x_{10}				0								3
x_{11}				0								4

	x_1	x_2	x_3	□ x_4	x_5	x_6	□ x_7	□ x_8	□ x_9	□ x_{10}	□ x_{11}	RHS
z	-7	-5	-2	0	-4	-8	0	0	0	0	0	26
x_0	2	2	2	0	0	0	0	-2	0	0	0	16
x_7	1	1	1	0	0	0	1	0	0	0	0	8
x_4	0	0	0	1	1	1	0	1	0	0	0	5
x_9	1	0	0	0	-1	-1	0	-1	1	0	0	1
x_{10}	0	1	0	0	1	0	0	0	0	1	0	4
x_{11}	0	0	1	0	0	1	0	0	0	0	1	3

Optimal tableau for phase I.

$$\theta = \min\left\{\frac{7}{2}, \frac{5}{2}, \frac{2}{2}\right\} = \frac{2}{2} = 1$$

Add x_0 row into z row. After this addition x_3 passes down into the restricted primal. and x_3 enters the basis while x_{11} leaving. Next θ value turns out tobe 3/2. This time x_2 passes down into the restricted primal. Last θ is equal to 1. This lets x_1 pass down into the restricted primal. Following is the final tableau of the overall problem:

PROBLEM 6.43 (Continued)

	x_1 □	x_2 □	x_3 □	x_4 □	x_5	x_6	x_7 □	x_8	x_9 □	x_{10}	x_{11}	RHS
z	0	0	0	0	−6	−13	0	−7	0	−2	−5	59
x_0	0	0	0	0	0	0	0	0	−2	−2	−2	0
x_7	0	0	0	0	0	0	1	1	−1	0	−1	0
x_4	0	0	0	1	1	1	0	1	0	0	0	5
x_1	1	0	0	0	−1	−1	0	−1	1	0	0	1
x_2	0	1	0	0	1	0	0	0	0	1	1	4
x_3	0	0	1	0	0	1	0	0	0	0	1	3

The optimum solution is:

$x_1 = 1$, $x_2 = 4$, $x_3 = 3$, $x_4 = 5$, $x_6 = 0$, $x_5 = 0$

(Note that this is a transportation problem. The primal dual algorithm could be applied in a more efficient way for solving such problems).

PROBLEM 6.44

Primal:

$$\min \; x_1 + 2x_3 - x_4$$

$$\begin{aligned} \text{s.t.} \quad & x_1 + x_2 + x_3 + x_4 + x_5 = 6 \\ & 2x_1 - x_2 + 3x_3 - 3x_4 - x_6 = 5 \\ & x_1, x_2, x_3, x_4, x_5, x_6 \geq 0 \end{aligned}$$

Dual:

$$\max \; 6w_1 + 5w_2$$

$$\begin{aligned} \text{s.t.} \quad & w_1 + 2w_2 \leq 1 \\ & w_1 - w_2 \leq 0 \\ & w_1 + 3w_2 \leq 2 \\ & w_1 - 3w_2 \leq -1 \\ & w_1 \leq 0 \\ & -w_2 \leq 0 \end{aligned}$$

Let $w_1 = 0$ and $w_2 = 1/3$. This is a feasible solution.

$z_1 - c_1 = -1/3$, $z_2 - c_2 = -1/3$, $z_3 - c_3 = -1$, $z_4 - c_4 = z_5 - c_5 = 0$

$z_6 - c_6 = -1/3$.

PROBLEM 6.44 (Continued)

	x_1	x_2	x_3	x_4 □	x_5 □	x_6	x_7 (Art.)	x_8 (Art.)	RHS
z	$-1/3$	$-1/3$	-1	0	0	$-1/3$	0	0	0
x_0	3	0	4	-2	1	-1	0	0	11
x_7	1	1	1	1	(1)	0	1	0	6
x_8	2	-1	3	-3	0	-1	0	1	5

initial tableau.

⋮

	x_1	x_2	x_3	x_4	x_5	x_6	x_7	x_8	RHS
z	0	$-1/2$	$-1/2$	$-1/2$	0	$-1/2$	$-1/6$	0	—
x_0	0	0	0	0	0	0	-1	-1	0
x_5	0	$3/2$	$-1/2$	$5/2$	1	$1/2$	1	$-1/2$	$7/2$
x_1	1	$-1/2$	$3/2$	$-3/2$	0	$-1/2$	0	$1/2$	$5/2$

Final tableau

This is the optimal solution.

$x_1 = 5/2$, $x_2 = x_3 = x_4 = 0$, obj $= 5/2$

PROBLEM 6.45

By assumption the system $vb > 0$, $vA \leq 0$ has a solution. By Farkas' lemma $Ax = b$ and $x \geq 0$ has no solution. Thus the primal problem is not feasible.

PROBLEM 6.46

If a starting dual solution is available but the basic dual feasible solution is not available one prefers primal-dual approach.

PROBLEM 6.47

	z	x_1	x_2	x_3	x_4	x_5	x_6	RHS
z	1	2065/69	0	0	0	650/69	−157/69	7598/69
x_4	0	305/69	0	0	1	94/69	−14/69	892/69
x_2	0	445/69	1	0	0	248/69	−34/69	1427/69
x_3	0	146/23	0	1	0	64/23	−11/23	392/23

Phase II Final tableau. Solution is unbounded.

PROBLEM 6.48

If we apply the perturbation technique of Charnes to the Phase I problem, then at each iteration x_0 will strictly decrease. In this case the discussion on finiteness in the primal-dual section holds. To implement Charnes' method, all we need is $\bar{b}$ and B^{-1}, both of which can be made available.

PROBLEM 6.49

a) Dual:

$$\begin{aligned} \min\ & 8w_1 + 4w_2 \\ \text{s.t.}\ & w_1 - w_2 \geq 2 \\ & 2w_1 + w_2 \geq 1 \\ & w_1 - 2w_2 \geq -1 \\ & w_1, w_2 \geq 0 \end{aligned}$$

Optimal dual variables can be read in zeroth row under the slack variables x_4 and x_5, i.e., $w_1 = 2$, $w_2 = 0$.

b) $z_2 - c_2 = wa_2 - c_2 = (2,0)(2,1)^T - 5 = -1$. Thus, the solution is not optimal anymore.

	z	x_1	x_2	x_3	x_4	x_5	RHS
z	1	0	−1	3	2	0	16
x_1	0	1	2	1	1	0	8
x_5	0	0	(3)	−1	1	1	12

	z	x_1	x_2	x_3	x_4	x_5	RHS
z	1	0	0	8/3	7/3	1/3	20
x_1	0	1	0	4/3	2/3	0	0
x_2	0	0	1	−1/3	1/3	1/3	4

OPTIMAL !

PROBLEM 6.49 (Continued)

c) $y_3' = B^{-1}a_3' = \begin{bmatrix} 1 & 0 \\ 1 & 1 \end{bmatrix}\begin{bmatrix} 1 \\ 1 \end{bmatrix} = \begin{bmatrix} 1 \\ 2 \end{bmatrix}$

$z_3 - c_3 = c_B B^{-1} a_3' - c_3 = 3 > 0$, therefore the solution is still optimal.

d) $x_2 + x_3 \geq 2 \Rightarrow -x_2 - x_3 + x_6 = -2$

	z	x_1	x_2	x_3	x_4	x_5	x_6	RHS
z	1	0	3	3	2	0	0	16
x_1	0	1	2	1	1	0	0	8
x_5	0	0	3	-1	1	1	0	12
x_6	0	0	(-1)	-1	0	0	1	-2

	z	x_1	x_2	x_3	x_4	x_5	x_6	RHS
z	1	0	0	0	2	0	3	10
x_1	0	1	0	-1	1	0	2	4
x_5	0	0	0	-4	1	1	3	6
x_2	0	0	1	1	0	0	1	2

Optimal tableau.

e) There is no sense of increasing the right-hand side of the first constraint since it is not tight. Dual variables gives us the required information. $w_2 > 0 \Rightarrow$ second primal constraint is tight. A unit increase in the right-hand side of the constraint 2 will add 2 units of profit into the objective function.

f) $c_6 = 4$, $a_6 = (1, 2)^T$

$z_6 - c_6 = wa_6 - c_6 = (2, 0)\begin{pmatrix} 1 \\ 2 \end{pmatrix} - 4 = -2$

$y_6 = B^{-1}a_6 = (1, 3)^T.$

PROBLEM 6.49 (Continued)

	z	x_1	x_2	x_3	x_4	x_5	x_6	RHS
z	1	0	3	3	2	0	-2	16
x_1	0	1	2	1	1	0	1	8
x_5	0	0	3	-1	1	1	(3)	12

	z	x_1	x_2	x_3	x_4	x_5	x_6	RHS
z	1	0	5	7/3	8/3	2/3	0	24
x_1	0	1	1	4/3	2/3	-1/3	0	4
x_6	0	0	1	-1/3	1/3	1/3	1	4

Optimal tableau.

PROBLEM 6.50

a) $w = (2, 1/10, 2)$, $z_9 - c_9 = 5 > 0$. Hence the optimal solution will not be altered.

b) We are looking for $\lambda > 0$ such that $b + \lambda b'$ will give us feasible solution, i.e.,

$$\bar{x}'_B = B^{-1}(b + \lambda b') \geq 0, \text{ where } b' = (1, 0, 0)$$

$$B^{-1} b' = (1/2, -1, 5)^T$$

$$\lambda = \min \left\{ \frac{-\bar{b}_i}{\bar{b}'_i}, \; \bar{b}'_i < 0 \right\}$$

$$\lambda = \min \{1/1\} = 1$$

Therefore, b_1 can be increased by one unit before violating the feasibility of the current solution. (Note that for $\lambda > 1$, x_2 becomes negative).

PROBLEM 6.51

$$x_1 - x_2 + 2x_3 + x_9 = 10$$

after adding this constraint into the tableau and eliminating the nonzero entries corresponding to the basis, we get:

	z	x_1	x_2	x_3	x_4	x_5	x_6	x_7	x_8	x_9	RHS
z	1	0	0	0	2	0	2	1/10	2	0	17
x_1	0	1	0	0	−1	0	1/2	1/5	−1	0	3
x_2	0	0	1	0	2	1	−1	0	1/2	0	1
x_3	0	0	0	1	−1	−2	5	−3/10	2	0	7
x_9	0	0	0	0	5	5	**−23/2**	2/5	−5/2	1	−6

	z	x_1	x_2	x_3	x_4	x_5	x_6	x_7	x_8	x_9	RHS
z	1	0	0	0	66/23	20/23	0	39/230	36/23	4/23	367/23
x_1	0	1	0	0	−18/23	5/23	0	25/23	−51/46	1/23	63/23
x_2	0	0	1	0	73/23	13/23	0	−4/115	33/46	−2/23	35/23
x_3	0	0	0	1	27/23	4/23	0	−29/230	56/23	10/23	101/23
x_6	0	0	0	0	−10/23	−10/23	1	−4/115	5/23	−2/23	12/23

Optimal tableau.

PROBLEM 6.52

Let x_i : acreage of the land allocated to crop i, $i = 1, 2, 3$ for wheat, corn, and soybean respectively.

$$\begin{aligned}
\text{Max} \quad & 60x_1 + 100x_2 + 80x_3 \\
\text{s.t.} \quad & 6x_1 + 8x_2 + 10x_3 \le 5000 \\
& 100x_1 + 150x_2 + 120x_3 \le 60{,}000 \\
& x_1 + x_2 + x_3 \le 500 \\
& x_1, x_2, x_3 \ge 0
\end{aligned}$$

PROBLEM 6.52 (Continued)

	Z	x_1	x_2	x_3	x_4	x_5	x_6	RHS
Z	1	20/3	0	0	0	2/3	0	40,000
x_4	0	2/3	0	18/5	1	-4/75	0	1800
x_2	0	2/3	1	4/5	0	1/150	0	400
x_6	0	1/3	0	1/5	0	-1/150	1	100

Optimal tableau

Optimal: $x_1 = x_3 = 0$, x_2 (corn) $= 400$ acres.
Profit $= 40,000$.

b) No. since corresponding primal constraint is not tight, additional man-hours will not alter the optimal solution but will cost extra money.

c) $x_1 \geq 100 \implies -x_1 + x_7 = -100$

	Z	x_1	x_2	x_3	x_4	x_5	x_6	x_7	RHS
Z	1	20/3	0	0	0	2/3	0	0	40,000
x_4	0	2/3	0	18/5	1	-4/75	0	0	1800
x_2	0	2/3	1	4/5	0	1/150	0	0	400
x_6	0	1/3	0	1/5	0	-1/150	1	0	100
x_7	0	(-1)	0	0	0	0	0	1	-100

	Z	x_1	x_2	x_3	x_4	x_5	x_6	x_7	RHS
Z	1	0	0	0	0	2/3	0	20/3	118,000/3
x_4	0	0	0	18/5	1	-4/75	0	2/3	5200/3
x_2	0	0	1	4/5	0	1/150	0	2/3	1000/3
x_6	0	0	0	1/5	0	-1/150	1	1/3	200/3
x_1	0	1	0	0	0	0	0	-1	100

Optimal tableau.

wheat = 100 acres, corn = 1000/3 acres, soybean = 0 acres. Profit = 118,000/3 dollars.

PROBLEM 6.53

a) Let x_i : be the number of part i produced. If we assume 8 hrs/day, then we have 24 available hours on machine A and 40 available hours on machine B.

$$\text{Max } x_1 + x_2 + x_3$$

$$\text{S.T. } 5x_1 + 4x_2 \leq 1440$$

$$100x_1 + 50x_2 + 24x_3 \leq 24000$$

$$x_1 - x_2 = 0$$

$$x_2 - x_3 = 0$$

$$x_1, x_2, x_3 \geq 0$$

	Z	x_1	x_2	x_3	x_4	x_5	RHS
Z	1	0	0	0	0	1/58	12000/29
x_4	0	0	0	0	1	−3/38	5760/29
x_3	0	0	0	1	0	1/174	4000/29
x_1	0	1	0	0	0	1/174	4000/29
x_2	0	0	1	0	0	1/174	4000/29

Phase II
Optimal tableau.

Optimal Solution: 4000/29 pieces are produced from every part hence the total number of assemblies produced are 4000/29 $\cong$ 140.

b) We recommend machine type B since the constraint that belongs to machine B is tight.

c) No, there is no need to introduce machine A. We have excess capacity of machine A.

PROBLEM 6.54

Let $x_1, x_2, \ldots, x_{12}$ correspond to the projects A, B, ..., L respectively.

$$\text{Max } 5x_1 + 6x_2 + 2x_3 + 8x_4 + 11x_5 + x_6 + 7x_7 + 2x_8 + 10x_9 + 9x_{10} + 5x_{11} + 4x_{12}$$

$$\text{S.T. } 5x_1 + 7x_2 + 3x_3 + 15x_4 + 12x_5 + 5x_6 + 7x_7 + 2x_8 + 15x_9 + 22x_{10} + 8x_{11} + 10x_{12} \le 80$$

$$1 \le x_5 + x_6$$

$$1 \le x_4 + x_5 + x_6 + x_7 \le 2$$

$$1 \le x_8 + x_9 + x_{10} + x_{11} + x_{12} \le 3$$

$$1 \le x_1 + x_2 + x_3$$

$$0 \le x_i \le 1 \qquad i = 1, \ldots, 12$$

The optimal solution to the above linear programming problem gives:

$x_1 = 1$, $x_2 = 1$, $x_3 = 1$, $x_4 = 1/8$, $x_5 = 1$, $x_7 = 7/8$

$x_9 = 1$, $x_{10} = 1$, $x_{11} = 1$, $x_6 = x_8 = x_{12} = 0$

with obj $= 441/8$.

If we let $x_7 = 1$ and $x_4 = 0$ we will have the integer solution to the overall problem with the objective value $440/8 = 55$. For $x_4 = 1$, $x_7 = 0$ the solution is not feasible, it violates the first constraint.

PROBLEM 6.55

Since every plane can make 2 daily trips then we have 3x2 = 6 trips available on plane type A and 4x2 = 8 trips available on plane type B for any route.

Let x_{ij} be the number of trips of plane type i assigned to route j, $i=1,2$, $j=1,2,3$.

$$\text{Min } 3000x_{11} + 2500x_{12} + 2000x_{13} + 2400x_{21} + 2000x_{22} + 1800x_{23}$$

$$\text{s.t. } 140x_{11} + 100x_{21} \geq 300$$

$$140x_{12} + 100x_{22} \geq 700$$

$$140x_{13} + 100x_{23} \geq 220$$

$$x_{11} + x_{12} + x_{13} \leq 6$$

$$x_{21} + x_{22} + x_{23} \leq 8$$

$$x_{ij} \geq 0 \quad i=1,2, \quad j=1,2,3$$

The optimum LP solution to this problem is given by:

$x_{11} = 15/7$, $x_{12} = 16/7$, $x_{13} = 11/7$

$x_{21} = 0$, $x_{22} = 19/5$, $x_{23} = 0$

obj = 160200/7

Since every plane can make two trips, the above solution can be interpreted as:

15/14 plane type A to route #1

16/14 plane type A to route #2

⋮

19/10 plane type B to route #2

PROBLEM 6.55 (Continued)

b) As seen, the optimal solution is not integer. One can apply the cutting plane algorithm of section 6.9 to this optimal L.P. solution to obtain the following integer solution:

$x_{11} = 0$, $x_{12} = 5$, $x_{13} = 1$

$x_{21} = 3$, $x_{22} = 0$, $x_{23} = 1$

obj = 23500

The interpretation is: Assign 2 plane-A strictly to route 2 and assign one plane type A to route 2 for one trip and to route 3 for another trip.

Assign one plane type B strictly (i.e., two trips) to route 1 and assign one plane type B for one trip to route 1 and one trip to route 3

PROBLEM 6.56

$$B^{-1} = \begin{bmatrix} 1/2 & 1/5 & -1 \\ -1 & 0 & 1/2 \\ 5 & -3/10 & 2 \end{bmatrix}$$

Let $b' = (1, 0, 0)$. We are looking for the solutions as $b - \lambda b'$ changes with $\lambda \geq 0$. We need to find $\bar{b}$ and $\bar{b}'$ of the current problem. They can be obtained

PROBLEM 6.56 (Continued)

from $\bar{b} = B^{-1}b$ (the right hand side of the tableau) and $\bar{b}' = B^{-1}b'$. The new right hand side with the introduction of $b - \lambda b'$ is $B^{-1}(b - \lambda b') = B^{-1}b - \lambda B^{-1}b' = (3,1,7)^T - \lambda(1/2,-1,5)^T$. Thus for λ in the interval $[0, 7/5]$ the given tableau is optimal. The right hand side is $(3 - \lambda/2, 1+\lambda, 7 - 5\lambda)^T$, and the objective value is $c_B B^{-1}(b - \lambda b') = c_B B^{-1} b - \lambda c_B B^{-1} b' = 17 - \lambda w_1 = 17 - 2\lambda$. The corresponding tableau is shown below:

	z	x_1	x_2	x_3	x_4	x_5	x_6	x_7	x_8	RHS
z	1	0	0	0	2	0	2	$\frac{1}{10}$	2	$17-2\lambda$
x_1	0	1	0	0	-1	0	$\frac{1}{2}$	$\frac{1}{5}$	-1	$3-\frac{1}{2}\lambda$
x_2	0	0	1	0	2	1	-1	0	$\frac{1}{2}$	$1+\lambda$
x_3	0	0	0	1	-1	-2	5	$-\frac{3}{10}$	2	$7-5\lambda$

At $\lambda = 7/5$ x_3 leaves, x_5 enters.

	z	x_1	x_2	x_3	x_4	x_5	x_6	x_7	x_8	RHS
z	1	0	0	0	2	0	2	$\frac{1}{10}$	2	$\frac{71}{5}$
x_1	0	1	0	0	-1	0	$\frac{1}{2}$	$\frac{1}{5}$	-1	$\frac{23}{10}$
x_2	0	0	1	$\frac{1}{2}$	$\frac{3}{2}$	0	$\frac{3}{2}$	$-\frac{3}{20}$	$\frac{3}{2}$	$\frac{12}{5}$
x_5	0	0	0	$-\frac{1}{2}$	$\frac{1}{2}$	1	$-\frac{5}{2}$	$\frac{3}{20}$	-1	0

Current tableau at $\lambda = 7/5$

Let B be the current basis $[a_1, a_2, a_5]$. The new right hand side is given by:

$$B^{-1}(b - \lambda b') = B^{-1}(b - \tfrac{7}{5}b') - (\lambda - \tfrac{7}{5})B^{-1}b'$$

PROBLEM 6.56 (Continued)

$$= (23/10,\ 12/5,\ 0)^T - (\lambda - 7/5)(1/2,\ 3/2,\ -5/2)^T$$

From this,

$$\frac{23}{10} = \left(\lambda - \frac{7}{5}\right)\left(\frac{1}{2}\right) \Rightarrow \lambda = 6$$

$$\frac{12}{5} = \left(\lambda - \frac{7}{5}\right)\left(\frac{3}{2}\right) \Rightarrow \lambda = 3$$

Thus for λ in the interval $[7/5, 3]$ the basis $[a_1, a_2, a_5]$ is optimal. The right hand side is $(3 - \lambda/2,\ 9/2 - 3\lambda/2,\ -7/2 + 5\lambda/2)^T$. The objective value is

$$c_B\left[B^{-1}\left(b - \frac{7}{5}e_1\right) - \left(\lambda - \frac{7}{5}\right)B^{-1}e_1\right] = \frac{71}{5} - \left(\lambda - \frac{7}{5}\right)c_B B^{-1}e_1$$

$$= \frac{71}{5} - (\lambda - 7/5)w_1 = 71/5 - (\lambda - 7/5)2 = 17 - 2\lambda$$

(Note we have the same formula for the obj. as before since we took a degenerate pivot so that the lagrangian multiplier w_1 did not alter from its previous value of 2).

At $\lambda = 3$ x_2 drops out and x_7 enters.

	z	x_1	x_2	x_3	x_4	x_5	x_6	x_7	x_8	RHS
z	1	0	0	0	2	0	2	1/10	2	$17-2\lambda$
x_1	0	1	0	0	-1	0	1/2	1/5	-1	$3-\lambda/2$
x_2	0	0	1	1/2	3/2	0	3/2	(-3/20)	3/2	$9/2-3\lambda/2$
x_5	0	0	0	-1/2	1/2	1	-5/2	3/20	-1	$\frac{-7}{2}+\frac{5\lambda}{2}$

At $\lambda = 3$ x_2 exits and x_7 enters.

PROBLEM 6.56 (Continued)

	z	x_1	x_2	x_3	x_4	x_5	x_6	x_7	x_8	RHS
z	1	0	2/3	1/3	3	0	3	0	3	11
x_1	0	1	4/3	2/3	1	0	5/2	0	1	3/2
x_7	0	0	-20/3	-10/3	-10	0	-10	1	-10	0
x_5	0	0	1	0	2	1	-1	0	1/2	4

Let $B = [a_1, a_7, a_5]$.

right hand side $= B^{-1}(b - \lambda b') = (3/2, 0, 4)^T - (\lambda - 3)(5/2, -10, -1)^T$

from here, $\lambda = 18/5$

Thus for $\lambda \in [3, 18/5]$ the basis $[a_1, a_5, a_7]$ is optimal. The right hand side is

$$\bar{b} = (9 - 5/2\,\lambda,\ -30 + 10\lambda,\ 1 + \lambda)^T.$$

The objective value is

$$c_B B^{-1}[(b - 3e_1) - (\lambda - 3)e_1] = 11 - (\lambda - 3)\, c_B B^{-1} e_1$$
$$= 11 - (\lambda - 3)w_1 = 11 - (\lambda - 3)3 = 20 - 3\lambda$$

Since all entries in row 1 are nonnegative, then for $\lambda > 18/5$ there exists no feasible solution.

Following is the summary.

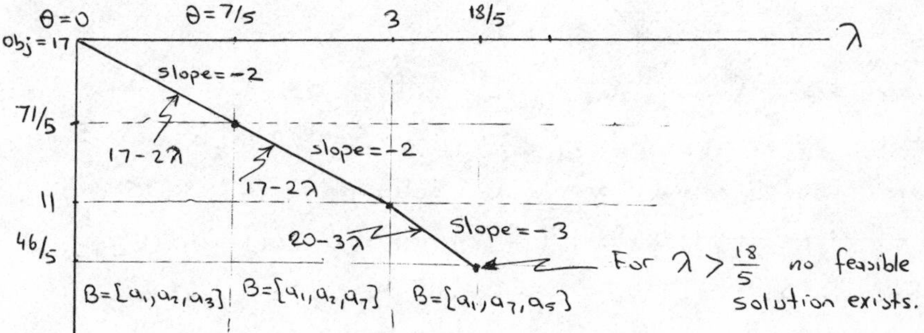

PROBLEM 6.57

$$\max \ -x_1 + 2x_2$$
$$\text{S.T.} \quad 2x_1 + 4x_2 \leq 12$$
$$2x_1 - 2x_2 \geq 2$$
$$x_1, x_2 \geq 0$$

If the cost vector is modified in the direction of $(-1,-1)$ we have

$$\max \left[(-1,2) + \lambda(-1,-1) \right] \begin{bmatrix} x_1 \\ x_2 \end{bmatrix}$$

S.T. The same constraints as above.

Graphically,

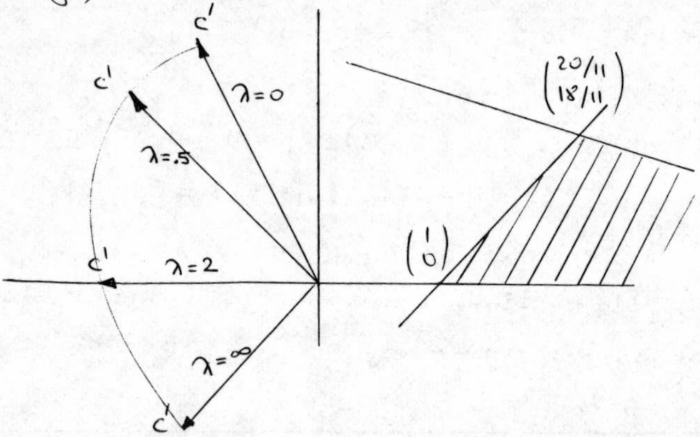

As seen from the graph, for $0 \leq \lambda < .5$ the optimal is $x_1^* = 20/11$, $x_2^* = 18/11$. At $\lambda = .5$ we have many optimal solutions given by $(x_1^*, x_2^*) = \alpha(1,0)^T + (1-\alpha)[20/11, 18/11]^T$, $\alpha \in [0,1]$. For $\lambda > .5$ The optimal is $x_1^* = 1$, $x_2^* = 0$.

PROBLEM 6.58

a)

	z	x_1	x_2	x_3	x_4	x_5	RHS
z	1	0	-11/4	0	-5/4	-1/4	-39/4
x_1	0	1	1/4	0	3/4	-1/4	9/4
x_3	0	0	3/4	1	1/4	1/4	15/4

Optimal tableau.

b) For $\lambda > 0$

$$z_j' - c_j' = c_B' y_j - c_j'$$

$$z_2' - c_2' = -11/4 + \lambda[\,(2,1)\begin{pmatrix}1/4\\3/4\end{pmatrix} - 1\,] = -11/4 + \frac{1}{4}\lambda$$

$$z_4' - c_4' = -5/4 + \lambda[\,(2,1)\begin{pmatrix}3/4\\1/4\end{pmatrix} - 0\,] = -5/4 + \frac{7}{4}\lambda$$

$$z_5 - c_5 = -\frac{1}{4} - \frac{1}{4}\lambda$$

$$\text{Obj} = -\frac{39}{4} + \lambda(2,1)\begin{pmatrix}9/4\\15/4\end{pmatrix} = -\frac{39}{4} + \frac{33}{4}\lambda$$

Thus we get the following tableau (Note that $\{a_1, a_3\}$ is optimal in the interval $[0, 5/7]$).

	z	x_1	x_2	x_3	x_4	x_5	RHS
	1	0	$-11/4 + \lambda/4$	0	$-5/4 + 7\lambda/4$	$-1/4 - \lambda/4$	$-\frac{39}{4} + \frac{33\lambda}{4}$
x_1	0	1	1/4	0	(3/4)	-1/4	9/4
x_3	0	0	3/4	1	1/4	1/4	15/4

At $\lambda = 5/7$ we have the following tableau:

	z	x_1	x_2	x_3	x_4	x_5	RHS
z	1	0	-18/7	0	0	-3/7	-27/7
x_4	0	4/3	1/3	0	1	-1/3	3
x_3	0	-1/3	2/3	1	0	1/3	3

$z_1' - c_1' = 0 - 2 < 0$, $z_2' - c_2' = 0 - 1 < 0$, $z_5' - c_5' = 0$

PROBLEM 6.58 (Continued)

Since $z'_j - c'_j \le 0$ for all nonbasic variables, then the basis $\{a_4, a_3\}$ is optimal for all $\lambda \geq 5/7$ and the $obj = (-2+\lambda)3 = -6+3\lambda$.

For $\lambda < 0$

This is equivalent to replacing the perturbation cost vector from $(2,1,1)$ to $(-2,-1,-1)$ and using the same rules.

$$z'_2 - c'_2 = -11/4 - \frac{1}{4}\lambda$$
$$z'_4 - c'_4 = -5/4 - 5/4\,\lambda$$
$$z'_5 - c'_5 = -1/4 + \frac{1}{4}\lambda$$

Thus the above tableau (initial) is optimal for all λ in the interval $[0,1]$. (or $[-1,0]$ if we talk about the original problem)

$Obj = -39/4 - \frac{33}{4}\lambda$ (or $-39/4 + \frac{33}{4}\lambda$ in the original problem). At $\lambda = 1$ x_5 enters and x_3 leaves

	z	x_1	x_2	x_3	x_4	x_5	RHS
z	1	0	$-11/4 - \lambda/4$	0	$-5/4 - 5/4\lambda$	$-1/4 + \lambda/4$	$-\frac{39}{4} - \frac{33}{4}\lambda$
x_1	0	1	1/4	0	3/4	−1/4	9/4
x_3	0	0	3/4	1	1/4	(1/4)	15/4

	z	x_1	x_2	x_3	x_4	x_5	RHS
z	1	0	−3	0	−5/2	0	−18
x_1	0	1	1	1	1	0	6
x_5	0	0	3	4	1	1	15

PROBLEM 6.58 (Continued)

$$z_2' - c_2' = (-2,0)\begin{pmatrix}1\\3\end{pmatrix} + 1 = -1 < 0$$

$$z_3' - c_3' = (-2,0)\begin{pmatrix}1\\4\end{pmatrix} + 1 = -1 < 0$$

$$z_4' - c_4' = (-2,0)\begin{pmatrix}1\\1\end{pmatrix} - 0 = -2 < 0$$

Since all $z_j' - c_j' < 0$ for nonbasic variables then the basis $[a_1, a_5]$ is optimal for all values of $\lambda \le -1$. The figure below is the summary of the above findings:

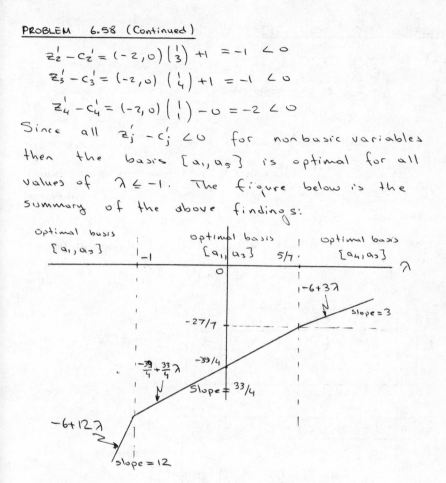

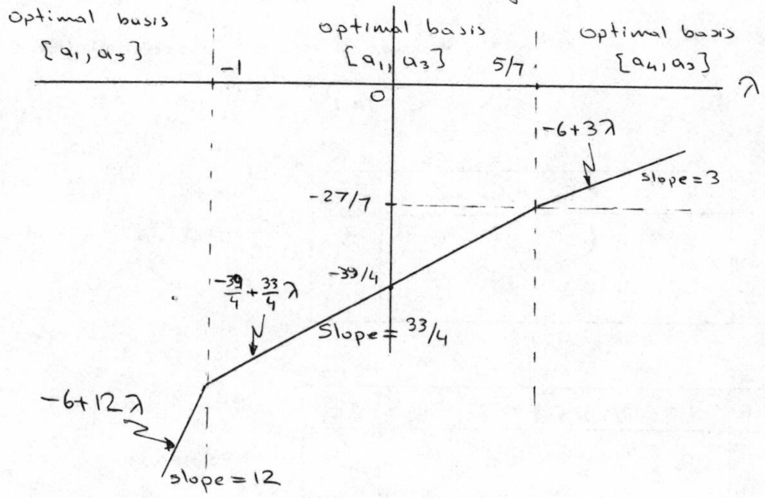

PROBLEM 6.59

	z	x_1	x_2	x_3	x_4	x_5	RHS
z	1	1	0	1	3	0	24
x_2	0	1	1	2	1	0	8
x_5	0	2	0	3	1	1	12

Optimal tableau.

PROBLEM 6.59 (Continued)

b) $z_j' - c_j = (z_j - c_j) + (c_2' - c_2) y_{2j}$ for all j

For $j = 2$, $z_2 - c_2 = 0$ and $y_{22} = 1$ and hence $z_2' - c_2 = c_2' - c_2$ and $z_2' - c_2' = 0$. We can update the cost row by adding the net change in the cost of x_2 times the current x_2 row of the final tableau to the original cost row. Then $z_2' - c_2$ is updated to $z_2' - c_2'$. The new objective value can be obtained from

$$c_B' B^{-1} b = c_B B^{-1} b + (c_2' - c_2) \bar{b}_2$$

Tableau after replacing $c_2 = 3$ by $c_2' = -4$

	z	x_1	x_2	x_3	x_4	x_5	RHS
z	1	−6	0	−13	−4	0	−32
x_2	0	1	1	(2)	1	0	8
x_5	0	2	0	3	1	1	12

New optimal tableau

	z	x_1	x_2	x_3	x_4	x_5	RHS
z	1	1/2	13/2	0	5/2	0	20
x_3	0	1/2	1/2	1	1/2	0	4
x_5	0	1/2	−3/2	0	−3/2	1	0

c) This question can be answered similar to the answer given in Exercise 6.58.

PROBLEM 6.60

$$z(\lambda) = \min \ (c+\lambda c')x$$
$$\text{s.t.} \quad Ax = b$$
$$x \geq 0$$

For simplicity suppose that the region $\{x : Ax = b,\ x \geq 0\}$ is bounded (and not empty). Thus there is a finite number of extreme points $x_1, \ldots, x_k$ and for any given λ there must exist an optimal extreme point. Thus:

$$z(\lambda) = \min_{1 \le j \le k} (c+\lambda c')x_j = \min_{1 \le j \le k} (cx_j + \lambda c' x_j)$$

$$= \min_{1 \le j \le k} r_j + \lambda s_j$$

where $r_j = cx_j$ and $s_j = c'x_j$. This equation shows that indeed z is a piecewise linear function (why?). Now consider λ_1, λ_2 and let μ be a number in the interval $[0,1]$ then

$$z(\mu\lambda_1 + (1-\mu)\lambda_2) = \min_{1 \le j \le k} [r_j + (\mu\lambda_1 + (1-\mu)\lambda_2)s_j]$$

$$= \min_{1 \le j \le k} [\mu(r_j + \lambda_1 s_j) + (1-\mu)(r_j + \lambda_2 s_j)]$$

Since the minimum of the sum is greater than or equal to the sum of the minimum, we have:

$$z(\mu\lambda_1 + (1-\mu)\lambda_2) \le \left\{\mu \min_{1 \le j \le k} (r_j + \lambda_1 s_j)\right\} + \left\{(1-\mu) \min_{1 \le j \le k} (r_j + \lambda_2 s_j)\right\}$$

$$= \mu z(\lambda_1) + (1-\mu) z(\lambda_2)$$

PROBLEM 6.60 (Continued)

The above inequality shows that z is indeed a concave function of λ.

PROBLEM 6.61

$$z(\lambda) = \min \; cx$$
$$\text{s.t.} \quad Ax = b + \lambda b'$$
$$x \geq 0$$

Let $\Lambda = \{\lambda : \text{the set } [x : Ax = b + \lambda b', x \geq 0] \text{ is not empty}\}$.

Note that Λ is convex (why?). By exercise 6.15 if $z(\lambda)$ is finite at any point in Λ, then it is finite everywhere in Λ. Assume that this is the case, (otherwise $z(\lambda) = -\infty$ over Λ, a trivial case). Take the dual of the above family of problems for $\lambda \in \Lambda$. By duality, and since we have a finite solution we must have:

$$z(\lambda) = \max \; w(b + \lambda b')$$
$$\text{s.t.} \quad wA \leq c$$

for each $\lambda \in \Lambda$. Since for each $\lambda \in \Lambda$, the above problem has a finite optimal solution at an extreme point, it could be replaced by

$$z(\lambda) = \max_{1 \leq j \leq k} \; w_j (b + \lambda b')$$

$$= \max_{1 \leq j \leq k} \; r_j + \lambda s_j$$

PROBLEM 6.61 (Continued)

where $w_1, w_2, \ldots, w_k$ are the extreme points of $\{w: wA \leq c\}$, $r_j = wb_j$ and $s_j = w_j b'$. Similar to problem 6.68 z is piecewise linear and convex function.

PROBLEM 6.62

Consider the following two systems:

I. $Kx \geq 0$, $x \geq 0$, $e_j x > 0$

II. $-wK \geq e_j$, $w \geq 0$

Either I or II has a solution. If I has a solution, say $\bar{x}_j$ then $K\bar{x}_j + \bar{x}_j \geq 0$ with the jth component of the vector $K\bar{x}_j + \bar{x}_j$ strictly positive. If II has a solution, then $Kw \geq e_j$ and $w \geq 0$ (recall that $-K^T = K$) and thus again $K\bar{x}_j + \bar{x}_j \geq 0$ with the jth component strictly positive where $\bar{x}_j = w$. Doing this for $j = 1, 2, \ldots, n$ and letting $\bar{x} = \bar{x}_1 + \bar{x}_2 + \cdots + \bar{x}_n$ it follows that there exists an $\bar{x}$ such that

$$K\bar{x} + \bar{x} > 0$$

<u>PROBLEM 6.63</u>

Let
$$K = \begin{array}{c} \begin{matrix} w^t & \;\; x & \;\; r \end{matrix} \\ \begin{bmatrix} 0 & A & -b \\ -A^t & 0 & c^t \\ b^t & -c & 0 \end{bmatrix} \end{array}$$

Note that K is skew-symmetric. Therefore by exercise 6.62 the following system has a solution

$$\begin{aligned} &Ax - rb \geq 0 \;, && x \geq 0 \;, && (Ax - rb) + w^t > 0 \\ &-A^t w^t - rc^t \geq 0 \;, && w \geq 0 \;, && (-A^t w^t - rc^t) + x > 0 \\ &b^t w^t - cx \geq 0 \;, && r \geq 0 \;, && (b^t w^t - cx) + r > 0 \end{aligned}$$

The following two cases are possible:

<u>Case I</u>: $r > 0$.

If $r > 0$, then replacing x by $\frac{x}{r}$ and w by w/r we get

$$\begin{aligned} &Ax \geq b \;, \quad x \geq 0 \\ &wA \leq c \;, \quad w \geq 0 \\ &wb - cx \geq 0 \end{aligned}$$

Thus we have primal feasible and dual feasible solutions which satisfy $wb \geq cx$. Noting the weak duality theorem we conclude that $wb \leq cx$. Thus $wb = cx$, and hence x and w are optimal solutions to the primal and dual problems in canonical format.

PROBLEM 6.63 (Continued)

Case II : $r = 0$

Note in this case we have a solution to the system

$$Ax \geq 0 \ , \ x \geq 0 \qquad Ax + w^t > 0$$
$$wA \leq 0 \ , \ w \geq 0 \qquad -A^t w^t + x > 0$$
$$wb - cx > 0$$

First of all, note that both the primal and the dual problems cannot have feasible solutions. By contradiction suppose that $\bar{x}$ and $\bar{w}$ are feasible points of both problems. Furthermore, consider $\bar{x} + \lambda x$ and $\bar{w} + \lambda w$ for $\lambda > 0$. Feasibility of these points is obvious. We also have,

$$(\bar{w} + \lambda w)b - c(\bar{x} + \lambda x) = (\bar{w}b - c\bar{x}) + \lambda(wb - cx)$$

Since $wb - cx > 0$, then the above difference could be made arbitrarily large by choosing λ sufficiently large, violating the weak duality theorem. Thus not both problems possess feasible solutions. One of the following cases must occur:

a- neither have feasible solutions.
b- primal admits feasible solution but dual does not.
c- dual admits feasible solution but primal does not.

PROBLEM 6.63 (Continued)

In cases b and c it can be shown that the primal and dual problems respectively are unbounded. Thus we concluded the fundamental duality theorem.

b) The result is immediate from part a. case I. In this case (after $x \leftarrow \frac{x}{r}$, and $w \leftarrow \frac{w}{r}$) we have:

$$Ax - b \geq 0 \ , \quad x \geq 0 \ , \quad (Ax-b) + w^t > 0$$
$$wA - c \leq 0 \ , \quad w \geq 0 \ , \quad (-A^t w^t + c) + x > 0$$
$$wb - cx \geq 0$$

Noting that $Ax - b = x_s$, then $(Ax-b) + w^t > 0$ $\Leftrightarrow$ $x_s + w^t > 0$. Thus if a slack variable is zero, the corresponding dual variable is positive, and vice versa, if a dual variable is zero, then the corresponding slack variable is positive. Similarly, $(-A^t w^t + c) + x > 0$ means that if the variable $x_j = 0$ then the corresponding dual slack is positive, and vice versa.

e) Consider the following problem

$$\min \ -x_1 - x_2$$
$$\text{s.t.} \quad x_1 + x_2 + x_3 = 1$$
$$x_1, x_2, x_3 \geq 0$$

PROBLEM 6.63 (Continued)

This problem has alternative optimal. The two extreme point optimals are:

(1, 0, 0) and (0, 1, 0)

The dual problem is

$$\max \quad w$$
$$\text{S.T} \quad w \leq -1, \quad w \leq -1, \quad w \leq 0.$$

The optimal for the dual is $w = -1$. At neither of the optimal extreme points does strong complementary theorem hold. In particular, at (1, 0, 0), $x_2 = 0$ and in the mean time the second dual slack = 0. Similarly at (0, 1, 0) $x_1 = 0$ and the first dual slack = 0.

Note however that, there exists a nonextreme optimal point (1/2, 1/2, 0) satisfying the theorem. Note that for this point either the variable (primal or dual) or its complementary variable is not zero.

PROBLEM 6.64

a) Let x_o and w_o be feasible solutions to the primal and lagrangian dual problems. Then

$$cx_o \geq cx_o - w_o(Ax_o - b)$$

$$= w_o b + (c - wA)x_o$$

$$\geq w_o b + \underset{x \in X}{\text{minimum}}\ (c - w_o A)x$$

$$= f(w_o)$$

b) From part (a),

$$\underset{\substack{Ax \geq b \\ x \in X}}{\text{Minimum}}\ cx \geq \underset{w \geq 0}{\text{minimum}}\ f(w)$$

If we can exhibit a feasible x and a feasible w such that $cx = f(w)$, then they are optimal to their respective problems, and equality holds. Denote the set X by $\{x: Bx \geq d,\ x \geq 0\}$ and let x^* be an optimal solution to the primal problem. Then there must exist vectors v^* and w^* such that:

1. $Ax^* \geq b$
2. $Bx^* \geq d$
3. $x^* \geq 0$

} Primal feasibility

4. $w^* A + v^* B \leq c$
5. $w^*, v^* \geq 0$

} Dual feasibility

PROBLEM 6.64 (Continued)

6. $w^*(Ax^*-b)=0$ } Complementary Slackness
7. $v^*(Bx^*-d)=0$

Now, consider the problem of evaluating $f(w^*)$, that is, to minimize $(c-w^*A)x$ subject to $Bx \geq d$, $x \geq 0$. Note that $\bar{x}$ is an optimal solution if, and only if, there exists a vector $\bar{v}$ such that:

8. $B\bar{x} \geq d$ } Primal feasibility
9. $\bar{x} \geq 0$

10. $\bar{v}B \leq (c-w^*A)$ } Dual feasibility
11. $\bar{v} \geq 0$

12. $\bar{v}(B\bar{x}-d)=0$ Complementary slackness.

Noting 1 → 7 it follows that conditions 8 – 12 hold for $\bar{x}=x^*$ and $\bar{v}=v^*$. Thus, x^* is an optimal solution to the problem

$$\min_{\substack{Bx \geq d \\ x \geq 0}} (c-w^*A)x$$

In particular:

$$f(w^*) = w^*b + \min_{\substack{Bx \geq d \\ x \geq 0}} (c-w^*A)x$$

$$= w^*b + (c-w^*A)x^*$$

by condition (6)

$$= w^*b + cx^* - w^*b$$

$$= cx^*$$

PROBLEM 6.64 (Continued)

Since x^* is feasible to the primal problem and w^* is feasible to the lagrangian dual problem, such that $f(w^*) = cx^*$, then by part (a) of the problem it follows that:

$$\min_{\substack{Ax \geq b \\ x \in X}} cx = \max_{w \geq 0} f(w)$$

PROBLEM 6.65

a) $$\underset{w \geq 0}{\text{maximize}} \; f(w)$$

where $$f(w) = 6w + \underset{\substack{-x_1 + x_2 \leq 2 \\ x_1 + x_2 \leq 8 \\ x_1, x_2 \geq 0}}{\text{minimum}} \{(1-3w)x_1 + (2-w)x_2\}$$

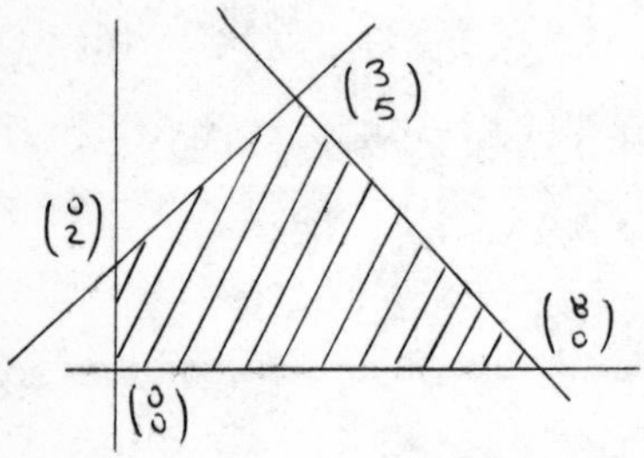

The extreme points of X are $\{(0,0), (0,2), (3,5), (8,0)\}$. The minimum in the definition of f for any given w occurs at one of the extreme points. Thus:

$$f(w) = 6w + \underset{\binom{0}{0},\binom{0}{2},\binom{3}{5},\binom{8}{0}}{\text{minimum}} \{(1-3w)x_1 + (2-w)x_2\}$$

PROBLEM 6.65 (Continued)

$$f(w) = 6w + \min\{0,\ 4-2w,\ 13-14w,\ 8-24w\}$$
$$= \min\{6w,\ 4+4w,\ 13-8w,\ 8-16w\}$$

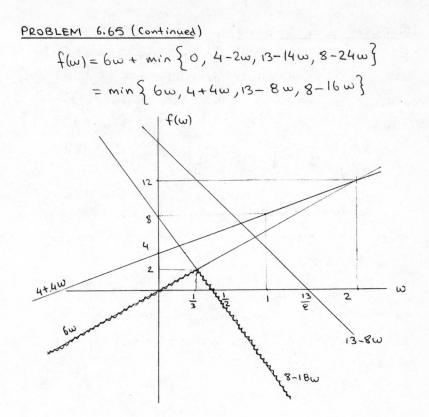

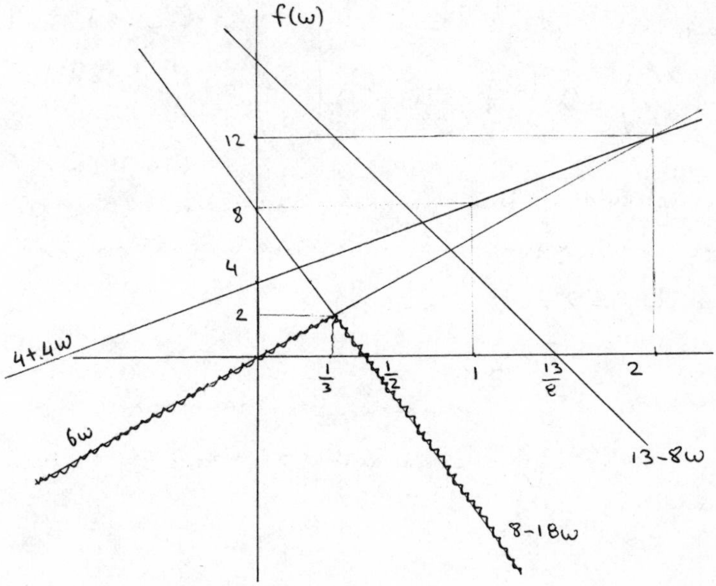

d) $f(w)$ is the zig-zag function. Note that it is piecewise linear. The optimal w^* occurs at $\frac{1}{3}$. i.e., $f(w^*) = 2$ for $w^* = \frac{1}{3}$.

e) The optimal solution to the primal problem is a convex combination of the optimal extreme points of the problem:

$$\text{minimize } (c - w^*A)x$$
$$x \in X$$

PROBLEM 6.65 (Continued)

For $w^* = \frac{1}{3}$ the optimal extreme points of the above problem are $\begin{pmatrix} 0 \\ 0 \end{pmatrix}$ and $\begin{pmatrix} 8 \\ 0 \end{pmatrix}$, (these actually correspond to the two lines defining $f(w)$ at w^* as shown in the figure). Thus,

$$\begin{pmatrix} x_1^* \\ x_2^* \end{pmatrix} = \lambda \begin{pmatrix} 0 \\ 0 \end{pmatrix} + (1-\lambda) \begin{pmatrix} 8 \\ 0 \end{pmatrix} = \begin{pmatrix} 8-8\lambda \\ 0 \end{pmatrix}$$

In particular, the primal and dual objectives must be equal at optimality. Therefore:

$$f(w^*) = 2 = cx^* = 8 - 8\lambda .$$

Hence, $\lambda = \frac{3}{4}$, and $x_1^* = 2$, $x_2^* = 0$. Note that (x_1^*, x_2^*) is not an extreme point of X but the coupling constraint $3x_1 + x_2 \geq 6$ is binding at x^*.

PROBLEM 7.1

$\underline{X}$ is represented by:

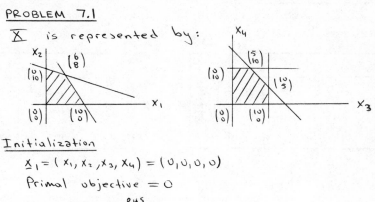

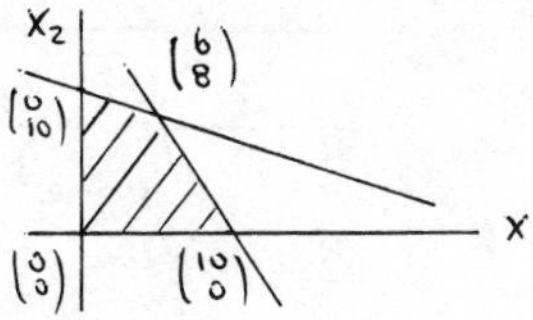

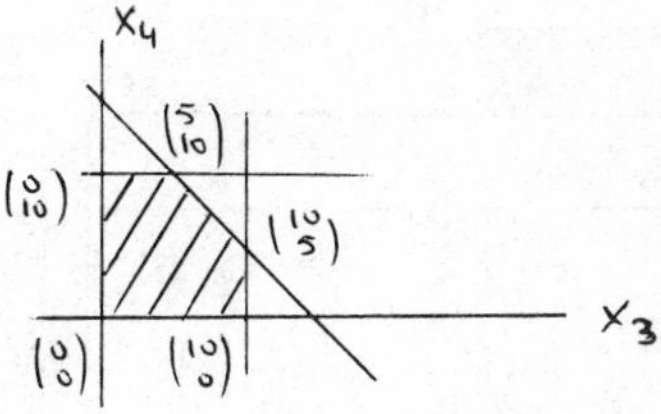

Initialization

$\underline{x}_1 = (x_1, x_2, x_3, x_4) = (0, 0, 0, 0)$

Primal objective $= 0$

				RHS
z	0	0	0	0
s_1	1	0	0	40
s_2	0	1	0	10
λ_1	0	0	1	1

$w_1 = 0$

$w_2 = 0$

$\alpha = 0$

Iteration 1

Subproblem:

$$\max_{\underline{x} \in \underline{X}} (wA - c)\underline{x} + \alpha \quad \equiv \quad \max_{\underline{x} \in \underline{X}} x_1 + x_2 + 2x_3 + x_4$$

The optimum occurs at

$$\underline{x}_2 = (6, 8, 10, 5)$$

$(wA - c)\underline{x}_2 + \alpha = 39 > 0$, λ_2 is introduced.

Lower bound $= wb - (wA - c)\underline{x}_2 = -39$.

$$\begin{bmatrix} A\underline{x}_2 \\ 1 \end{bmatrix} = \begin{bmatrix} 47 \\ 17 \\ 1 \end{bmatrix} = \text{updated column.}$$

PROBLEM 7.1 (Continued)

Master Prob.

				RHS	λ_2
z	0	0	0	0	39
s_1	1	0	0	40	47
s_2	0	1	0	10	(17)
λ_1	0	0	1	1	1

				RHS
z	0	$-39/17$	0	$\frac{-390}{17}$
s_1	1	$-47/17$	0	$210/17$
λ_2	0	$1/17$	0	$10/17$
λ_1	0	$-1/17$	1	$7/17$

$w = (0, -39/17)$, $\alpha = 0$, primal objective $= -390/17$.

ITERATION II

Subproblem:

$$\max_{\underline{x} \in \underline{X}} (wA - c)\underline{x} + \alpha \equiv \max_{\underline{x} \in \underline{X}} \frac{56}{17}x_1 - \frac{22}{17}x_2 - 5/17\, x_3 - \frac{22}{17}x_4$$

$\underline{x}_3 = (10, 0, 0, 0)$, $(wA - c)\underline{x}_3 + \alpha = \frac{560}{17}$ hence introduce λ_3.

$$\text{Lower bound} = 10\left(-\frac{39}{17}\right) - \frac{560}{17} = -\frac{950}{17}$$

$$\begin{bmatrix} A\underline{x}_3 \\ 1 \end{bmatrix} = \begin{bmatrix} 10 \\ -10 \\ 1 \end{bmatrix}, \text{ updated column } B^{-1}\begin{bmatrix} A\underline{x}_3 \\ 1 \end{bmatrix} = \begin{bmatrix} 640/17 \\ -10/17 \\ 27/17 \end{bmatrix}$$

Master

				RHS	λ_3
z	0	$-39/17$	0	$-\frac{390}{17}$	$\frac{560}{17}$
s_1	1	$-47/17$	0	$210/17$	$640/17$
λ_2	0	$1/17$	0	$10/17$	$-10/17$
λ_1	0	$-1/17$	1	$7/17$	(27/17)

				RHS
z	0	$-29/27$	$-\frac{560}{27}$	$-\frac{850}{27}$
s_1	1	$-\frac{37}{27}$	$\frac{-640}{27}$	$70/27$
λ_2	0	$\frac{1}{27}$	$\frac{10}{27}$	$20/27$
λ_3	0	$\frac{-1}{27}$	$\frac{17}{27}$	$7/27$

$w = (0, -29/27)$, $\alpha = -560/27$

primal objective $= -850/27$.

PROBLEM 7.1 (Continued)

ITERATION III

Subproblem

$$\max_{x \in \underline{X}} (wA - c)\underline{x} - \frac{560}{27} \equiv \max_{x \in \underline{X}} \frac{56}{27}x_1 - \frac{2}{27}x_2 + \frac{25}{27}x_3 - \frac{2}{27}x_4 - \frac{560}{27}$$

$\underline{x}_4 = (10, 0, 10, 0)$

$(wA - c)\underline{x}_4 + \alpha = 250/27$ introduce λ_4.

Lower bound $= -290/27 - \frac{810}{27} = -1100/27$

$$\begin{pmatrix} A\underline{x}_4 \\ 1 \end{pmatrix} = \begin{pmatrix} 30 \\ 0 \\ 1 \end{pmatrix} \quad \text{updated column} = \begin{pmatrix} 10 \\ 10/27 \\ 17/27 \end{pmatrix}$$

				RHS	λ_4
z	0	29/27	−560/27	−850/27	250/27
s_2	1	−37/27	−640/27	70/27	(10)
λ_2	0	1/27	10/27	20/27	10/27
λ_3	0	−1/27	17/27	7/27	17/27

After the pivot operation the current primal objective is found to be $-24700/729 \cong -33.9$. The best known lower bound $= -39$, we can either stop at sub optimal solution or keep continuing until $(wA - c)\underline{x}_k + \alpha = 0$. At this step the current suboptimal solution is

$$x_{sub} = \lambda_2 \underline{x}_2 + \lambda_3 \underline{x}_3 + \lambda_4 \underline{x}_4$$

$$= \frac{470}{729}\begin{pmatrix} 6 \\ 8 \\ 10 \\ 5 \end{pmatrix} + \frac{70}{729}\begin{pmatrix} 10 \\ 0 \\ 0 \\ 0 \end{pmatrix} + \frac{189}{729}\begin{pmatrix} 10 \\ 0 \\ 10 \\ 0 \end{pmatrix}$$

PROBLEM 7.2

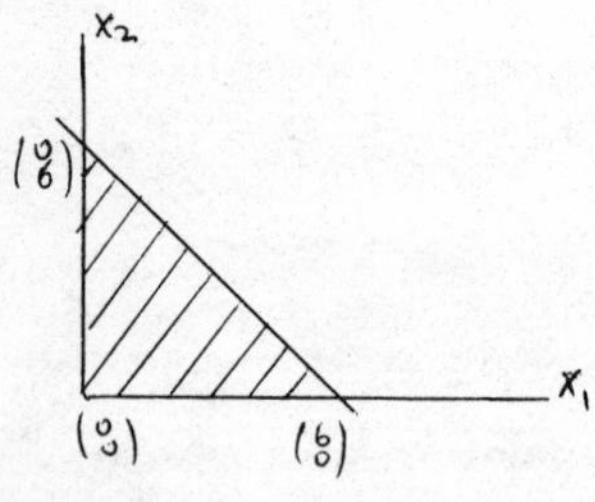

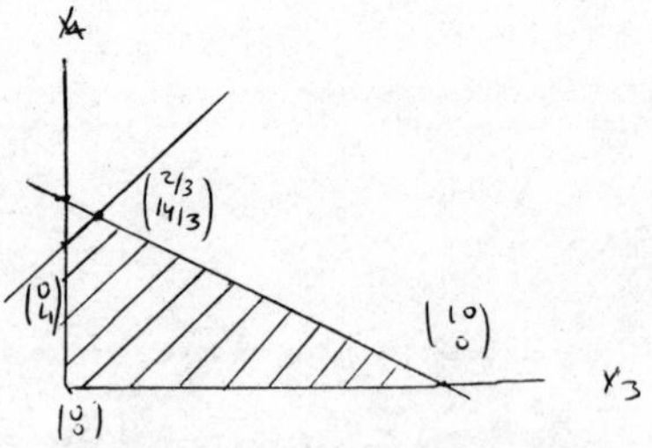

Initialization

$\underline{x}_1 = (0,0,0,0)$, $w = 0$, $\alpha = 0$

primal objective $= 0$

			RHS
z	0	0	0
s	1	0	8
λ_1	0	1	1

Iteration I

Subproblem:

$$\max_{x \in \bar{X}} (wA - c)\underline{x} + \alpha \equiv \max_{x \in \bar{X}} x_1 + 3x_2 - x_3 + x_4$$

The optimum solution is $\underline{x}_2 = (0, 6, 0, 4)$

$(wA - c)\underline{x}_2 + \alpha = 22$, so introduce λ_2.

Current lower bound $= wb - (wA - c)\underline{x}_2 = 0 - 22 = -22$

$\begin{pmatrix} A\underline{x}_2 \\ 1 \end{pmatrix} = \begin{pmatrix} 10 \\ 1 \end{pmatrix}$, updated column $= B^{-1}\begin{pmatrix} A\underline{x}_2 \\ 1 \end{pmatrix} = \begin{pmatrix} 10 \\ 1 \end{pmatrix}$

Master problem

			RHS	λ_2
z	0	0	0	22
s_1	1	0	8	(10)
λ_1	0	1	1	1

			RHS
z	-2.2	0	-17.6
λ_2	.1	0	.8
λ_1	$-.1$	1	.2

$w = -2.2$, $\alpha = 0$, primal objective $= -17.6$.

PROBLEM 7.2 (Continued)

Iteration II

Subproblem:

$$\max_{\underline{x} \in \overline{X}} (wA - c)\underline{x} + \alpha \equiv \max_{\underline{x} \in \overline{X}} -1.2x_1 + 0.8x_2 - 3.2x_3 - 1.2x_4 + 0$$

$\underline{x}_3 = (0, 6, 0, 0)$, $(wA - c)\underline{x}_3 + \alpha = 4.8$, introduce λ_3.

Current lower bound $= wb - (wA - c)\underline{x}_3 = -17.6 - 4.8 = -22.4$

Lower bound from last iteration is better.

$\begin{pmatrix} A\underline{x}_3 \\ 1 \end{pmatrix} = \begin{pmatrix} 6 \\ 1 \end{pmatrix}$, updated column $= \begin{bmatrix} .1 & 0 \\ -.1 & 1 \end{bmatrix} \begin{bmatrix} 6 \\ 1 \end{bmatrix} = \begin{bmatrix} .6 \\ .4 \end{bmatrix}$

Master Problem

			RHS	λ_3
z	-2.2	0	-17.6	4.8
λ_2	0.1	0	.8	0.6
λ_1	-0.1	1	.2	(0.4)

			RHS
z	-1	-12	-20
λ_2	0.25	-1.5	0.5
λ_3	-0.25	2.5	0.5

Primal objective 20 , $w = -1$, $\alpha = -12$

Iteration 3

Subproblem:

$$\max \; 0x_1 + 2x_2 - 2x_3 + 0x_4$$
$$\text{S.T. } \underline{x} \in \overline{X}$$

The optimum is $\underline{x}_4 = (0, 6, 0, 0)$

$(wA - c)\underline{x}_4 + \alpha = 0$, therefore we already have the optimal , $x^* = \lambda_2 \underline{x}_2 + \lambda_3 \underline{x}_3$

$$x^* = 0.5 \begin{pmatrix} 0 \\ 6 \\ 0 \\ 4 \end{pmatrix} + 0.5 \begin{pmatrix} 0 \\ 6 \\ 0 \\ 0 \end{pmatrix} = \begin{pmatrix} 0 \\ 6 \\ 0 \\ 2 \end{pmatrix}$$

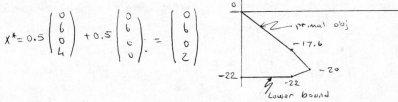

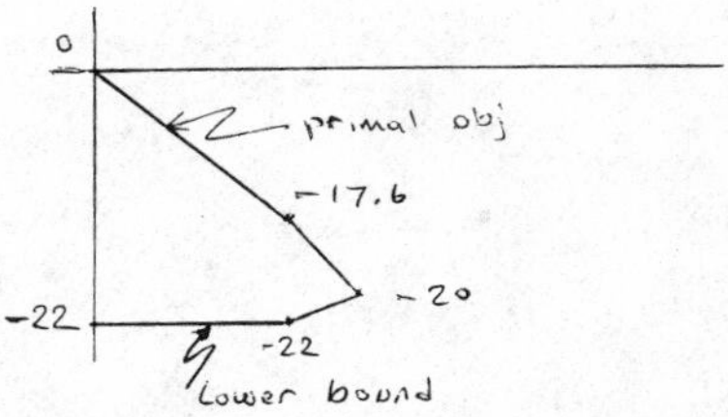

PROBLEM 7.3

First, note that x^* is an optimal solution of the following problem:

$$\min \ (c - wA)x \quad \text{s.t.} \quad x \in \bar{X}$$

where w is an optimal lagrangian multiplier vector. To prove this let $x \in \bar{X}$. Then:

$$(c - wA)x \geq \min_{y \in \bar{X}} (c - wA)y = -\max_{y \in \bar{X}} (wA - c)y \quad \dots (1)$$

Note, however, that cx^* is equal to the lower bound at optimality. Since the lower bound at optimality is precisely $wb - \max_{y \in \bar{X}} (wA - c)y$, then $cx^* = wb - \max_{y \in \bar{X}} (wA - c)y$. Substituting in (1) it follows that:

$$(c - wA)x \geq cx^* - wb \quad \dots (2)$$

Since x^* satisfies $Ax^* = b$, then from (2)

$$(c - wA)x \geq cx^* - wAx^* = (c - wA)x^*$$

Since the above inequality holds for each $x \in \bar{X}$, then x^* is an optimal solution of the problem

$$\min_{x \in \bar{X}} (c - wA)x$$

Since this is a linear program, the optimal cannot be an interior point unless of course the objective function is identically zero, i.e., $c - wA = 0$, thus x^* could be in the interior of $\bar{X}$ only if $c - wA = 0$.

PROBLEM 7.4

First show that w_1^* is an optimal lagrangian multiplier if the decomposition algorithm were used. Letting $\bar{X}$ be the set $\{x: Dx=d, x \geq 0\}$, then by problem 7.3 above (see details of 7.3) x^* is an optimal solution of the problem:

$$\max \ (w_1^* A - c)x$$
$$\text{s.t.} \quad Dx = d$$
$$x \geq 0$$

Thus x^* can be represented as a convex combination of the extreme points $x_1^*, \ldots, x_k^*$ of the above problem.

PROBLEM 7.5

Let $\bar{X} = \{(x_1, x_2, x_3): 0 \leq x_j \leq 3, \ j=1,2,3\}$

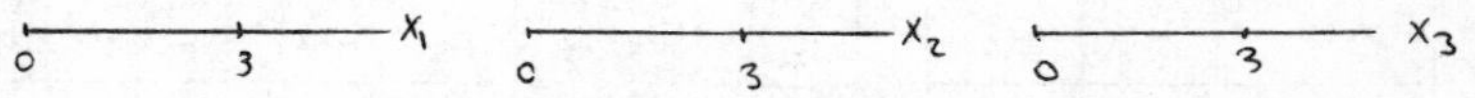

a) $\min \ 2x_1 - 3x_2 - 4x_3$

$$\text{s.t.} \quad x_1 + x_2 + x_3 + s_1 = 6$$
$$-x_1 - x_2 + 2x_3 + s_2 = -2$$
$$x_1, x_2, x_3, s_1, s_2 \geq 0$$

$$\min \sum_{j=1}^{k} \lambda_j (cx_j)$$
$$\text{s.t.} \sum_{j=1}^{k} (Ax_j)\lambda_j + s = b$$
$$\sum_{j=1}^{k} \lambda_j = 1$$

using a single convexity constraint.

b) Let $x_1 = (0,3,0)$, $s_1 = 3$, $s_2 = 1$

$$B = [s_1, s_2, \lambda_1] = \begin{bmatrix} 1 & 0 & 3 \\ 0 & 1 & -3 \\ 0 & 0 & 1 \end{bmatrix}, \quad B^{-1} = \begin{bmatrix} 1 & 0 & -3 \\ 0 & 1 & 3 \\ 0 & 0 & 1 \end{bmatrix}$$

PROBLEM 7.5 (Continued)

$A\underline{x}_1 = \begin{pmatrix} 3 \\ -3 \end{pmatrix}$, right hand side $= B^{-1}\begin{pmatrix} b \\ 1 \end{pmatrix} = \begin{pmatrix} 3 \\ 1 \\ 1 \end{pmatrix}$

$(w, \alpha) = (0, 0, -9)$

				RHS
z	0	0	-9	-9
s_1	1	0	-3	3
s_2	0	1	3	1
λ_1	0	0	1	1

ITERATION I

Subproblem

$\max\ -2x_1 + 3x_2 + 4x_3$
$x \in \overline{X}$

$x_1 = 0$, $x_2 = 3$, $x_3 = 3$ $\Rightarrow$ $\underline{x}_2 = (0, 3, 3)^T$

$(wA - c)\underline{x}_2 - \alpha = 21 - 9 = 12$ introduce λ_2.

$A\underline{x}_2 = \begin{pmatrix} 6 \\ 3 \end{pmatrix}$, $B^{-1}\begin{pmatrix} A\underline{x}_2 \\ 1 \end{pmatrix} = \begin{bmatrix} 6 \\ 3 \\ 1 \end{bmatrix}$

Master STEP

				RHS	λ_2
z	0	0	-9	-9	12
s_1	1	0	-3	3	(6)
s_2	0	1	3	1	3
λ_1	0	0	1	1	1

				RHS
z	0	-4	-21	-13
s_1	1	-2	-9	1
λ_2	0	1/3	1	1/3
λ_1	0	-1/3	0	2/3

$w = (0, -4)$, $\alpha = -21$

ITERATION II

Subproblem:

$\max\ 2x_1 + 7x_2 - 4x_3$ $\Rightarrow$ $\underline{x}_3 = (3, 3, 0)$
$x \in \overline{X}$

$(wA - c)\underline{x}_3 + \alpha = 27 - 21 = 6$

There fore, introduce λ_3

$\begin{bmatrix} A\underline{x}_3 \\ 1 \end{bmatrix} = \begin{bmatrix} 6 \\ -6 \\ 1 \end{bmatrix}$, $B^{-1}\begin{bmatrix} A\underline{x}_3 \\ 1 \end{bmatrix} = \begin{bmatrix} 9 \\ -1 \\ 2 \end{bmatrix}$

PROBLEM 7.5 (Continued)

Master problem

				RHS
z	0	-4	-21	-13
s_1	1	-2	-9	1
λ_2	0	1/3	1	1/3
λ_1	0	-1/3	0	2/3

λ_3
6
(9)
-1
2

				RHS
z	-2/3	-8/3	-15	-41/3
λ_3	1/9	-2/9	-1	1/9
λ_2	1/9	1/9	0	4/9
λ_1	-2/9	1/9	2	4/9

$w_1 = -2/3$, $w_2 = -8/3$, $\alpha = -15$.

ITERATION 3

Subproblem:

$$\max\ (wA-c)x \quad \equiv \quad \max\ 0x_1 + 5x_2 - 2x_3$$
$$\text{st. } x \in \bar{X} \qquad\qquad x \in \bar{X}$$

opt: $\underline{x}_4 = (0, 3, 0)$.

$(wA-c)\underline{x}_4 + \alpha = 15 - 15 = 0$, stop.

Optimal to the overall problem is already at hand.

$$x = \frac{4}{9}\underline{x}_1 + \frac{4}{9}\underline{x}_2 + \frac{1}{9}\underline{x}_3$$

$$= \frac{4}{9}\begin{pmatrix}0\\3\\0\end{pmatrix} + \frac{4}{9}\begin{pmatrix}0\\3\\3\end{pmatrix} + \frac{1}{9}\begin{pmatrix}3\\3\\0\end{pmatrix} = \begin{pmatrix}1/3\\3\\4/3\end{pmatrix}$$

with obj $= -41/3$.

PROBLEM 7.6

a) Let $\underline{X} = \{ (x_{11}, x_{12}, \ldots, x_{24}) : \; x_{11} + x_{21} = 200, \; x_{12} + x_{22} = 300, \; x_{13} + x_{23} = 400, \; x_{14} + x_{24} = 300, \; x_{ij} \geq 0 \}$

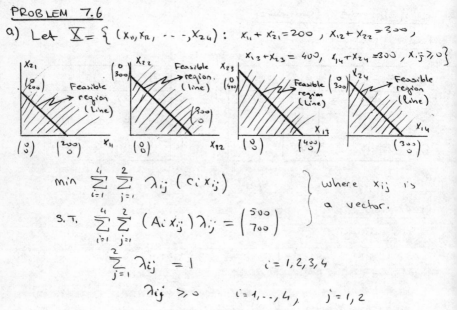

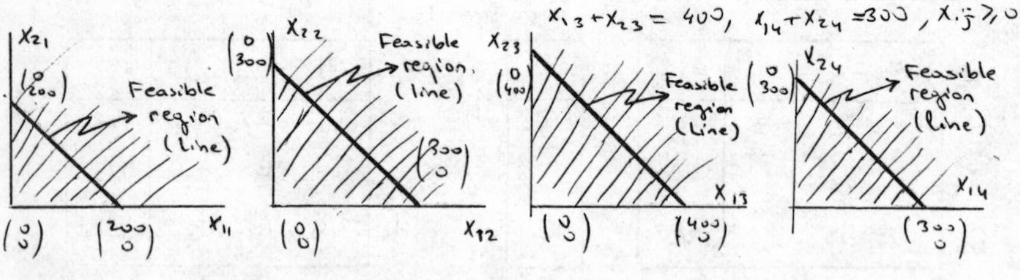

$$\min \sum_{i=1}^{4} \sum_{j=1}^{2} \lambda_{ij} (c_i x_{ij})$$

$$\text{S.T.} \quad \sum_{i=1}^{4} \sum_{j=1}^{2} (A_i x_{ij}) \lambda_{ij} = \begin{pmatrix} 500 \\ 700 \end{pmatrix}$$

where x_{ij} is a vector.

$$\sum_{j=1}^{2} \lambda_{ij} = 1 \qquad i = 1, 2, 3, 4$$

$$\lambda_{ij} \geq 0 \qquad i = 1, \ldots, 4, \quad j = 1, 2$$

We need to use phase I of two phase method to get a basic solution. We will have x_1 and x_2 for two constraints and x_3, x_4, x_5 and x_6 for the convexity constraints as the artificial variables.

$$(w_1, w_2, \alpha_1, \alpha_2, \alpha_3, \alpha_4) = c_B B^{-1} = (1, 1, 1, 1, 1, 1)$$

							RHS
z	1	1	1.	1	1	1	1204
x_1	1						500
x_2		1					700
x_3			1				1
x_4				1			1
x_5					1		1
x_6						1	1

PROBLEM 7.6 (Continued)

ITERATION I c_1, c_2, c_3, c_4 replaced by zero

Subproblem:

$\max (wA_1 - c_1)\underline{x}_1 + \alpha_1, \; \ldots \ldots, \max (wA_4 - c_4)\underline{x}_4 + \alpha_4$

$$\begin{array}{ll} \max & x_{11} + x_{21} \\ \text{s.t.} & x_{11} + x_{21} = 200 \\ & x_{11}, x_{21} \geq 0 \end{array} \Rightarrow \begin{array}{l} x_{11} = 200, \quad x_{21} = 0 \\ \text{Obj} = (wA_1 - c_1)\underline{x} + \alpha_1 = 201 \\ \text{introduce } \lambda_{11}. \end{array}$$

$A_1 \underline{x}_{11} = \begin{bmatrix} 200 \\ 0 \end{bmatrix}$, updated column $= (200, 0, 1, 0, 0, 0)^T$

Master Prob.

							RHS	λ_{11}
z	1	1	1	1	1	1	1204	201
x_1	$I_{6\times 6}$						500	200
x_2							700	0
x_3							1	(1)
x_4							1	0
x_5							1	0
x_6							1	0

							RHS
	1	1	−200	1	1	1	1003
x_1	1	0	−200	0	0	0	300
x_2	0	$I_{5\times 5}$					700
λ_{11}	0						1
x_4	0						1
x_5	0						1
x_6	0						1

$w_1 = w_2 = 1$

$\alpha_1 = -200$

$\alpha_2 = 1$

$\alpha_3 = 1$

$\alpha_4 = 1$

Continue in this fashion until all artificials are driven away from the basis. Then start phase II.

PROBLEM 7.7

Use two convexity constraints. $\bar{X}$ consists of all the constraints except the first one.

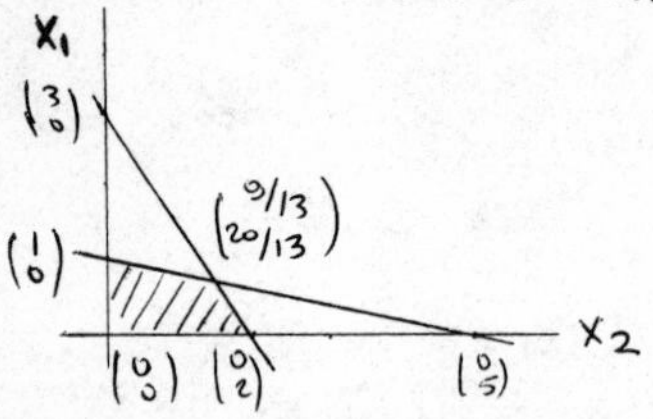

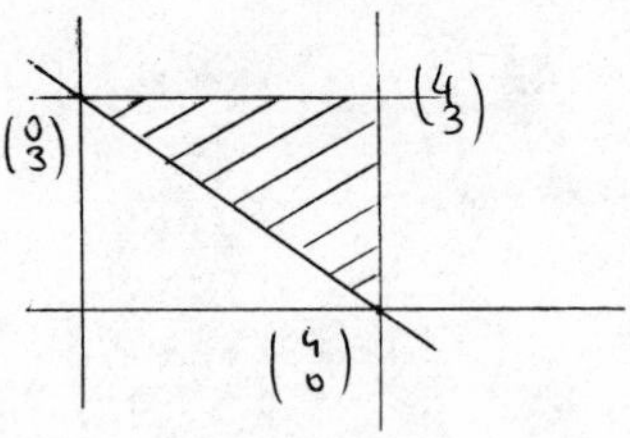

Initialization: Consider $\underline{x}_{11} = \binom{0}{0}$ $\quad \underline{x}_{21} = \binom{0}{3}$

$$B = \begin{bmatrix} 1 & 0 & 6 \\ 0 & 1 & 0 \\ 0 & 0 & 1 \end{bmatrix}_{\begin{matrix} s & \lambda_{11} & \lambda_{21} \end{matrix}}, \quad (w, \alpha_1, \alpha_2) = c_B B^{-1} = [0, 0, -18]$$

Master Prob:

				RHS
z	0	0	−18	−18
s	1	0	−6	1
λ_{11}	0	1	0	1
λ_{21}	0	0	1	1

ITERATION I

Subproblem:

$\max\limits_{\underline{x}_1 \in \bar{X}_1} (wA_1 - c_1)\underline{x}_1$ $\quad$ or $\quad$ $\max\ x_1 + 8x_2$ $\quad$ s.t. $(x_1, x_2) \in \bar{X}_1$

where $\underline{x}_1$ is a vector. Optimal $(0, 2)$, obj $= 16$

$(wA_1 - c_1)\underline{x}_1 + \alpha_1 = 16$ so introduce λ_{12}.

$$\begin{pmatrix} A_1 \underline{x}_{12} \\ 1 \\ 0 \end{pmatrix} = \begin{pmatrix} 8 \\ 1 \\ 0 \end{pmatrix}, \quad \text{updated column} = \begin{pmatrix} 8 \\ 1 \\ 0 \end{pmatrix}$$

				RHS	λ_{12}
z	0	0	−18	−18	16
s	1	0	−6	1	(8)
λ_{11}	0	1	0	1	1
λ_{21}	0	0	1	1	0

				RHS
z	−2	0	−6	−20
λ_{12}	1/8	0	−3/8	1/8
λ_{11}	−1/8	1	0	7/8
λ_{21}	0	0	1	1

PROBLEM 7.7 (Continued)

ITERATION II

Subproblem:

$$\max_{\underline{x}_1 \in \overline{X}_1} (wA_1 - c_1)\underline{x}_1 \equiv \max \; -x_1 + 0x_2 \quad \text{s.t.} \quad (x_1, x_2) \in \overline{X}_1$$

Optimal = (0, 0) i.e., no points from $\overline{X}_1$ is eligible to enter.

$$\max_{\underline{x}_2 \in \overline{X}_2} (wA_2 - c_2)\underline{x}_2 \equiv \max \; -5x_3 + 2x_4 \quad \text{s.t.} \quad (x_3, x_4) \in \overline{X}_2$$

Optimal:

$\underline{x}_2 = (x_3, x_4) = (0, 3)$, obj = 6

$$(wA_2 - c_2)\underline{x}_2 + \alpha_2 = 6 - 6 = 0.$$

Therefore no vector is eligible to enter from the second set, $\overline{X}_2$, either. Thus, we are at the optimal point.

$$\begin{pmatrix} x_1^* \\ x_2^* \end{pmatrix} = \frac{7}{8}\begin{pmatrix} 0 \\ 0 \end{pmatrix} + \frac{1}{8}\begin{pmatrix} 0 \\ 2 \end{pmatrix} = \begin{pmatrix} 0 \\ \frac{1}{4} \end{pmatrix}$$

Optimal objective = −20.

PROBLEM 7.8

If the subproblem for a given $\underline{w}$ has a finite optimal solution, then all of the arguments in section 7.1 hold and the bound is exactly the same as before, i.e.,

$$\hat{c}_B \bar{b} - (z_k - \hat{c}_k).$$

If the subproblem has an unbounded optimal solution for a given $\underline{w}$, then the lower bound at this iteration is $-\infty$.

The reader may wish to derive the above bound using the Lagrangian duality results of Problem 6.64.

PROBLEM 7.9

We will use two convexity constraints.

$X_1 = \{(x_1, x_2) : -x_1 + x_2 \leq 2,\ x_1, x_2 \geq 0\}$

$X_2 = \{(x_3, x_4) : x_3 + x_4 \leq 4,\ -x_3 + x_4 \leq 5,\ x_4, x_3 \geq 0\}$

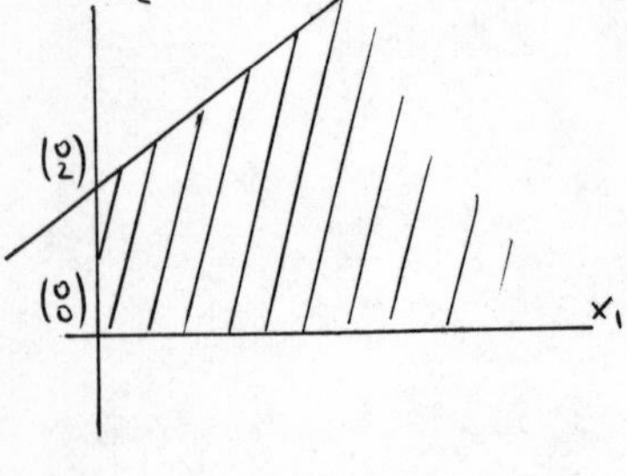

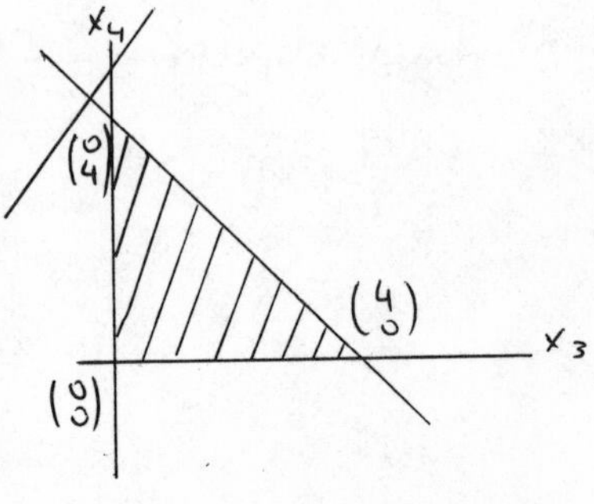

PROBLEM 7.9 (Continued)

Initialization:

$$\underline{x}_{11} = \begin{pmatrix} 0 \\ 0 \end{pmatrix}, \quad \underline{x}_{21} = \begin{pmatrix} 0 \\ 0 \end{pmatrix}$$

$$B = \begin{bmatrix} 1 & 0 & 0 & 0 \\ 0 & 1 & 0 & 0 \\ 0 & 0 & 1 & 0 \\ 0 & 0 & 0 & 1 \end{bmatrix}$$

(columns s_1, s_2, λ_{11}, λ_{21})

$(w_1, w_2, \alpha_1, \alpha_2) = (0, 0, 0, 0)$, $z = 0$.

					RHS
z	0	0	0	0	0
s_1	1	0	0	0	12
s_2	0	1	0	0	5
λ_{11}	0	0	1	0	1
λ_{12}	0	0	0	1	1

Subproblem 1

$\max\ (wA_1 - c_1)\underline{x}_1$

$\underline{x}_1 \in \overline{X}_1$

Optimal unbounded along an extreme direction.

Subproblem 2

$\max\ (wA_2 - c_2)\underline{x}_2$

$\underline{x}_2 \in \overline{X}_2$

Optimal $\underline{x}_{22} = (x_3, x_4) = (4, 0)$

$z_{22} - c_{22} = 12$

Introduce λ_{22}.

$$\begin{bmatrix} A_2 \underline{x}_{22} \\ 0 \\ 1 \end{bmatrix} = \begin{bmatrix} 4 \\ -16 \\ 0 \\ 1 \end{bmatrix}$$

updated column is the same.

					RHS	λ_{22}
z	0	0	0	0	0	12
s_1	1	0	0	0	12	4
s_2	0	1	0	0	5	−16
λ_{11}	0	0	1	0	1	0
λ_{21}	0	0	0	1	1	(1)

					RHS
z	0	0	0	−12	−12
s_1	1	0	0	−4	8
s_2	0	1	0	16	21
λ_{11}	0	0	1	0	1
λ_{22}	0	0	0	1	1

$w_1 = w_2 = 0$, $\alpha_1 = 0$, $\alpha_2 = -12$

Iteration 2

At this iteration subproblem 1 gives an extreme direction $d_{21} = (1, 1)^T$ while subproblem 2 giving $(x_3, x_4) = (4, 0)$. Therefore μ_{21} is introduced with $A_2 d_{21} = (2, 3)^T$ with updated column $(2, 3, 0, 0)^T$. After μ_{21} is introduced, we have the following

PROBLEM 7.9 (Continued)

tableau.

					RHS
z	-1	0	0	-8	-20
μ_{21}	$1/2$	0	0	-2	4
S_2	$-3/2$	1	0	-22	9
λ_{11}	0	0	1	0	1
λ_{22}	0	0	0	1	1

$w_1 = -1, \quad w_2 = 0$

$\alpha_1 = 0, \quad \alpha_2 = -8$

At iteration 3 we have no candidates from the first subproblem. For subproblem 2 we have $(x_3, x_4) = (4, 0)$ with obj $= 8$.

$$\max_{\underline{x}_2 \in \underline{X}_2} (wA_2 - c_2)\underline{x}_2 + \alpha_2 = 8 - 8 = 0$$

Therefore, the optimal is at hand.

$$\begin{pmatrix} x_1^* \\ x_2^* \end{pmatrix} = \lambda_{11}\begin{pmatrix} 0 \\ 0 \end{pmatrix} + \mu_{21}\begin{pmatrix} 1 \\ 1 \end{pmatrix} = \begin{pmatrix} 4 \\ 4 \end{pmatrix}$$

$$\begin{pmatrix} x_3^* \\ x_4^* \end{pmatrix} = \begin{pmatrix} 4 \\ 0 \end{pmatrix}.$$ Hence, $(x_1^*, x_2^*, x_3^*, x_4^*) = (4, 4, 4, 0)$ with obj $= -20$.

PROBLEM 7.10

This problem has no feasible solution. It can be shown by the decomposition algorithm. We start with phase I of two-phase method. with objective function

$$\min 0x_1 + 0x_2 + 0x_3 + 0x_4 + x_a$$

where x_a is the artificial variable. At iteration 2 after introducing λ_{12} we have the following master problem:

PROBLEM 7.10 (Continued)

				RHS	λ_{12}
z	1	0	-12	28	10/3
x_a	1	0	-12	28	10/3
λ_{11}	0	1	0	1	(1)
λ_{22}	0	0	1	1	0

				RHS
z	1	-10/3	-12	74/3
x_a	1	-10/3	-12	74/3
λ_{12}	0	1	0	1
λ_{22}	0	0	1	0

$w = 1$, $\alpha_1 = -10/3$, $\alpha_2 = -12$. But the w obtained in this step is exactly equal to the one we obtained in the previous step. From

Subproblem 1: $\max_{\underline{x}_1 \in \overline{X}_1} (wA_1 - c_1)\underline{x}_1 + \alpha_1 = 10/3 - 10/3 = 0$

Subproblem 2: $\max_{\underline{x}_2 \in \overline{X}_2} (wA_2 - c_2)\underline{x}_2 + \alpha_2 = 12 - 12 = 0$

So, no candidates to enter, but $x_a > 0$. Thus we conclude that there exists no feasible solution to the overall problem.

PROBLEM 7.11

With several convexity constraints, one has more freedom in combining the extreme point solutions of the subproblems. In the single convexity constraint we have to use the same weight for all points from the subproblems at any given iteration. The disadvantage of several convexity constraints is that the master array is of size $(m+T)\times(m+T)$ as opposed to $(m+1)\times(m+1)$. This should cause no alarm

PROBLEM 7.11 (Continued)

though, for moderate values of T. Another advantage of several convexity constraints is that one need not solve all the subproblems to completion, we may go to the master step whenever a subproblem i produces an extreme point x_{ij} with $z_{ij} - \hat{c}_{ij} > 0$. The several convexity constraints is preferred.

PROBLEM 7.12

Let $X = \{(x_1, x_2, x_3) : 0 \le x_1, x_2, x_3 \le 1\}$. We will use 3 convexity constraints.

$x_{11} = x_{21} = x_{31} = 0$. Initial basis is an identity matrix with $s, \lambda_{11}, \lambda_{21}, \lambda_{31}$ being in the basis.
$(w, \alpha_1, \alpha_2, \alpha_3) = (0, 0, 0, 0)$

Iteration 1

Subproblem 1	Subproblem 2	Subproblem 3
max $2x_1$	max $-x_2$	max $5x_3$
s.t. $0 \le x_1 \le 1$	s.t. $0 \le x_2 \le 1$	s.t. $0 \le x_3 \le 1$
Opt: $x_1 = 1$	$x_2 = 0$	$x_3 = 1$

Introduce λ_{32}. $A_3 x_{32} = (3)$. The tableau after introducing λ_{32} will look like:

					RHS
z	0	0	0	-5	-5
s	1	0	0	-3	1
λ_{11}	0	1	0	0	1
λ_{21}	0	0	1	0	1
λ_{32}	0	0	0	1	1

$w = 0$

$\alpha_1 = \alpha_2 = 0$

$\alpha_3 = -5$

PROBLEM 7.12 (Continued)

Iteration 2

Subproblem 1

max $2x_1$

$0 \le x_1 \le 1$

Subproblem 2

max $-x_2$

$1 \le x_2 \le 1$

Subproblem 3

Max $5x_3$

$0 \le x_3 \le 1$

From subproblem 1 $x_{12} = 1$, $z_{12} - c_{12} = 2 + 0 = 2$, introduce λ_{12}. $A_1 x_{12} = (4) =$ updated $A_1 x_{12}$. After introducing λ_{12}, the tableau in the master problem will be:

					RHS
z	$-1/2$	0	0	$-7/2$	$-11/2$
λ_{12}	$1/4$	0	0	$-3/4$	$1/4$
λ_{11}	$-1/4$	1	0	$3/4$	$3/4$
λ_{21}	0	0	1	0	1
λ_{32}	0	0	0	1	1

$w = -1/2$

$\alpha_1 = \alpha_2 = 0$

$\alpha_3 = -7/2$

Iteration 3

Subproblem 1

max $0x_1$

$0 \le x_1 \le 1$

Subproblem 2

max $0x_2$

$0 \le x_2 \le 1$

Subproblem 3

max $7/2\, x_3$

$0 \le x_3 \le 1$

From the above subproblems

$\max (wA_1 - c_1)x_1 + \alpha_1 = 0$

$\max (wA_2 - c_2)x_2 + \alpha_2 = 0$ and

$\max (wA_3 - c_3)x_3 + \alpha_3 = 0$

Thus, there is no candidate. The optimal solution is:

$x_1^* = 1/4$, $x_2^* = 0$, $x_3^* = 1$ with

obj $= -11/2$.

PROBLEM 7.13

Let the dual variables of the master problem be w and α. For the subproblem $\max_{x \in \bar{X}} (wA - c)x$, let x_{p+1} be an optimal solution. If $(wA - c)x_{p+1} + \alpha > 0$, then replace p by $p+1$ and repeat the master step. Otherwise if $(wA-c)x_{p+1} + \alpha = 0$, then stop, $\sum_{j=1}^{p} \lambda_j x_j$ obtained from the master step is optimal for the overall problem.

Note the difference between this scheme and the method of the chapter. Hence a master problem is solved at each iteration (of course utilizing the optimal tableau of the previous step) where a new column is adjoined to the previous master array. This may involve several pivots to update the master problem. In the decomposition algorithm discussed in this chapter, only one pivot is needed at each master step and the master array has size $(m+1) \times (m+1)$.

PROBLEM 7.14

Dual master problem:

$$\begin{aligned} &\text{Maximize} \quad wb + \alpha \\ &\text{S. T.} \quad wAx_j + \alpha \leq cx_j \quad , \quad j = 1, 2, \ldots, p \end{aligned}$$

PROBLEM 7.14 (Continued)

Decomposition algorithm.

Suppose that $x_1, x_2, \ldots, x_p$ in X are available.

Master Step

$$\max \quad wb + \alpha$$
$$\text{s.t.} \quad wAx_j + \alpha \leq cx_j \quad , \quad j = 1, 2, \ldots, p$$

Let (w^*, α^*) be an optimal solution.

Subproblem

$$\max \ (w^*A - c)x$$
$$x \in X$$

Let x_{p+1} be an optimal solution. If

$$(w^*A - c)x_{p+1} + \alpha^* > 0$$

then replace p by $p+1$ and repeat the master step. Note that if $(w^*A - c)x_{p+1} + \alpha^* > 0$, then $w^*Ax_{p+1} + \alpha^* > cx_{p+1}$, i.e., the current optimal (w^*, α^*) of the master problem violates the restriction $wAx_{p+1} + \alpha \leq cx_{p+1}$, and hence if this constraint is added, it will cut away the current optimal. Thus it is the same as the cutting plane algorithm. The master problem could be updated by the dual simplex method. Of course, if $w^*Ax_{p+1} + \alpha^* = cx_{p+1}$, then $\sum_{j=1}^{p} \lambda_j x_j$ is an optimal solution of the primal problem, where λ_j is the dual of the constraint $wAx_j + \alpha_j \leq cx_j$. Convergence is obvious since we apply the decomposition algorithm, except we solve dual master problem.

PROBLEM 7.16

We will use two convexity constraints.

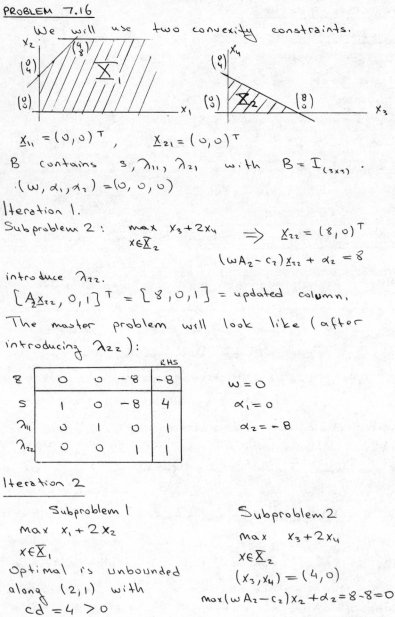

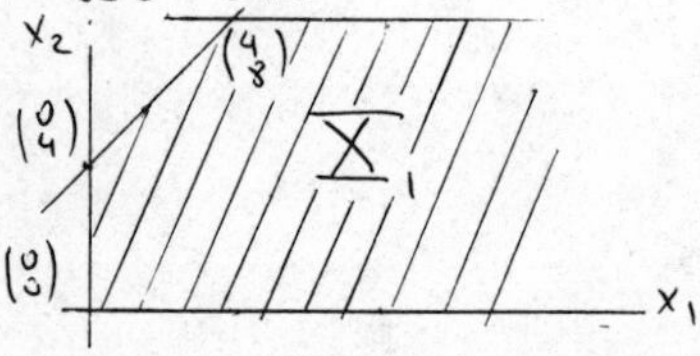

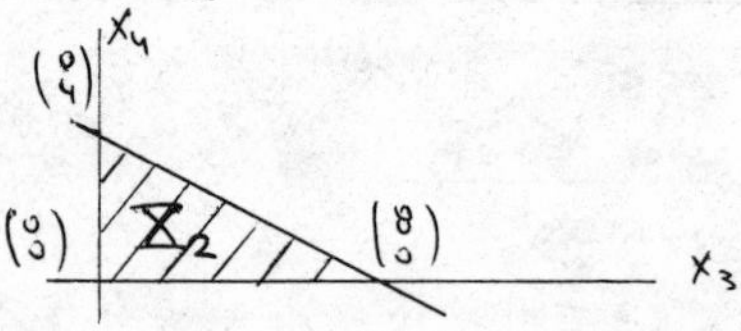

$\underline{x}_{11} = (0,0)^T$, $\underline{x}_{21} = (0,0)^T$

B contains $s, \lambda_{11}, \lambda_{21}$ with $B = I_{(3\times3)}$.

$(w, \alpha_1, \alpha_2) = (0, 0, 0)$

Iteration 1.

Subproblem 2: $\max_{x \in X_2} x_3 + 2x_4 \Rightarrow \underline{x}_{22} = (8,0)^T$

$(wA_2 - c_2)\underline{x}_{22} + \alpha_2 = 8$

introduce λ_{22}.

$[A_2\underline{x}_{22}, 0, 1]^T = [8, 0, 1]$ = updated column.

The master problem will look like (after introducing λ_{22}):

				RHS
z	0	0	−8	−8
s	1	0	−8	4
λ_{11}	0	1	0	1
λ_{22}	0	0	1	1

$w = 0$

$\alpha_1 = 0$

$\alpha_2 = -8$

Iteration 2

Subproblem 1

$\max x_1 + 2x_2$

$x \in X_1$

Optimal is unbounded along (2,1) with

$cd = 4 > 0$

Subproblem 2

$\max x_3 + 2x_4$

$x \in X_2$

$(x_3, x_4) = (4, 0)$

$\max(wA_2 - c_2)x_2 + \alpha_2 = 8 - 8 = 0$

PROBLEM 7.16 (Continued)

Therefore, we have no candidate from subproblem 2. Introduce μ_{11} from subproblem 1.

$[A_1 d_{11}, 0, 0]^T = [3, 0, 0]^T$ = updated column.

After μ_{11} is introduced in the master problem, we will have $(w, \alpha_1, \alpha_2) = (-4/3, 0, 8/3)$. We can continue to the iterations to get $\underline{x}_{12} = (4, 8)$ at iteration 3 with the updated column $(4, 1, 0)^T$. After λ_{12} is introduced in the master problem we have $(w, \alpha_1, \alpha_2) = (-5/3, 0, 16/3)$. The first subproblem will produce $\underline{x}_{13} = (0, 4)$ and the second subproblem will produce $\underline{x}_{23} = (0, 4)$ with later having

$\max_{x \in \underline{X}_2} (wA_2 - c_2)\underline{x}_{23} + \alpha_2 = 20/3$. So we introduce λ_{23}. The updated column will be $(-1/3, 1/3, 1)^T$. The master problem will yield $w = -5/3$ $\alpha_1 = 0$ and $\alpha_2 = 4/3$.

At iteration 4, subproblem 1 yields the same w, hence $\max_{x_1 \in \underline{X}_1} (wA_1 - c_1)\underline{x}_1 + \alpha_1 = 4/3 > 0$.

Introduce λ_{13}. $(A_1 \underline{x}_{13}, 1, 0)^T = (4, 1, 0)^T$. The updated column is $(1/3, 2/3, 0)^T$.

The updated master problem will yield $w = -3/2$, $\alpha_1 = -2$, $\alpha_2 = -2$.

PROBLEM 7.16 (Continued)

Iteration 5

Subproblem 1

max $-1/2\, x_1 + 1/2\, x_2$

s.t. $(x_1, x_2) \in \overline{X}_1$

Optimal: $(x_1, x_2) = (0, 4)$

$\max_{\underline{x}_1 \in \overline{X}_1} (wA_1 - c_1)\underline{x}_1 + \alpha_1 = 2 - 2 = 0$

Subproblem 2

max $-\frac{1}{2} x_3 + \frac{1}{2} x_4$

s.t. $(x_3, x_4) \in \overline{X}_2$

Optimal: $(0, 4)$

$\max_{\underline{x}_2 \in \overline{X}_2} (wA_2 - c_2)\underline{x}_2 + \alpha_2 = 0$

So, no candidates from either problem. Optimal objective = −22. The optimal solution:

$$\begin{pmatrix} x_3^* \\ x_4^* \end{pmatrix} = \begin{pmatrix} 0 \\ 4 \end{pmatrix}, \quad \begin{pmatrix} x_1^* \\ x_2^* \end{pmatrix} = 1/2 \begin{pmatrix} 4 \\ 8 \end{pmatrix} + 1/2 \begin{pmatrix} 0 \\ 4 \end{pmatrix} = \begin{pmatrix} 2 \\ 6 \end{pmatrix}$$

PROBLEM 7.17

Let x_{ij} for $j = 1, 2, \ldots, t_i$ be the extreme points of subproblem i. Then the problem can be reformulated as follows:

$$\begin{aligned} \text{Minimize} \quad & \sum_{i=1}^{T} \sum_{j=1}^{t_i} (c_i x_{ij}) \lambda_{ij} \\ \text{s.t.} \quad & \sum_{i=1}^{T} \sum_{j=1}^{t_i} (A_i x_{ij}) \lambda_{ij} = b \\ & \sum_{j=1}^{t_i} \lambda_{ij} = 1, \quad i = 1, \ldots, T \\ & \lambda_{ij} \geq 0, \quad j = 1, \ldots, t_i \\ & \qquad\qquad i = 1, 2, \ldots, T. \end{aligned}$$

If we display the constraints of the above problem in tableau format we have:

PROBLEM 7.17 (Continued)

$\lambda_{11} \cdots \lambda_{1t_1}$	$\lambda_{21} \cdots \lambda_{2t_2}$	$\cdots$	$\lambda_{T1} \cdots \lambda_{Tt_T}$	
$A_1x_{11} \cdots A_1x_{1t_1}$	$A_2x_{21} \cdots A_2x_{2t_2}$	$\cdots$	$A_Tx_{T1} \cdots A_Tx_{Tt_T}$	$= b$
$1 \cdots 1$				$=1$
	$1 \cdots 1$			$=1$
		$\ddots$		$\vdots$
			$1 \cdots 1$	$=1$

Note that any basis must have $m+T$ rows. If for some i the basis does not contain any λ_{ij}, then the $(m+i)$th row of the basis is identically zero, which is impossible.

PROBLEM 7.18

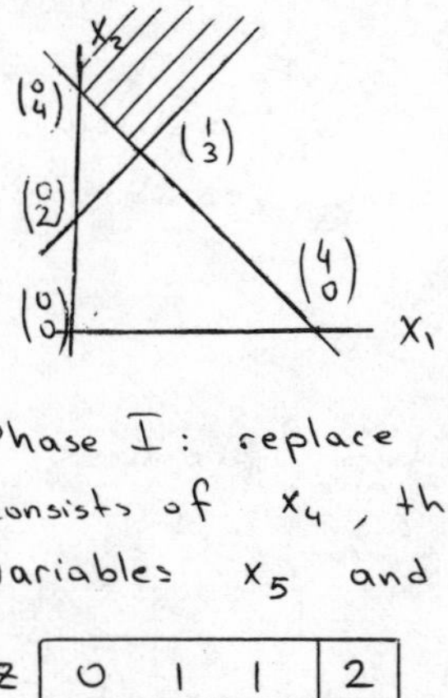

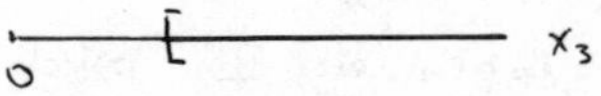

Phase I: replace c by zero. Let the basis consists of x_4, the slack, and the artificial variables x_5 and x_6 respectively.

z	0	1	1	2
x_4	1	0	0	6
x_5	0	1	0	1
x_6	0	0	1	1

$w = 0, \quad \alpha_1 = \alpha_2 = 1$

PROBLEM 7.18 (Continued)

Iteration 1

Subproblem 1:

$\max\ 0x_1 + 0x_2$ $\Rightarrow$ any feasible point is opt.

$x_1 \in \bar{X}_1$ e.g. $(1,3)^T$.

$$\max_{\underline{x}_1 \in \bar{X}_1} (wA_1 - 0)\underline{x}_1 + \alpha_1 = 1$$

So, introduce λ_{11}. $(A_1\underline{x}_{11}, 1, 0)^T = (4, 1, 0)^T$. The updated column being the same. After updating the master problem we have the following tableau:

				RHS
z	0	0	1	1
x_4	1	-4	0	2
λ_{11}	0	1	0	1
x_6	0	0	1	1

$w = 0$

$\alpha_1 = 0$

$\alpha_2 = 1$

At iteration 2 we have the problem for subproblem 2 such that any feasible solution is optimal. For $x_2 = 3$,

$$\max_{x_2 \in \bar{X}_2} (wA_2 - 0)x_2 + \alpha_2 = 0 + 1 > 0$$

We introduce λ_{21}. Master step produces the following dual values:

$$w_1 = -1/3 \ , \quad \alpha_1 = 4/3 \ , \quad \alpha_2 = 1$$

At iteration 3 no candidate exist from both subproblem 1 and subproblem 2. Since the artificial variable x_6 is present in the basis at a positive level, we conclude that the overall problem has no feasible solution.

PROBLEM 7.19

Yes. By construction, the decomposition algorithm finds a convex combination of the extreme points of the subproblem which optimizes the overall problem.

In the presence of alternate optima of the original problem it is thus conceivable that the convex combination of the subproblems does <u>not</u> correspond to an extreme point of the overall problem. To illustrate consider the following problem:

$$\min \; -x_1 - x_2$$

$$\text{S.T.} \quad x_1 + x_2 \le 3/2$$

$$0 \le x_1, x_2 \le 1$$

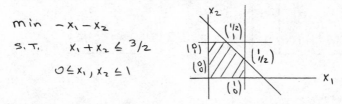

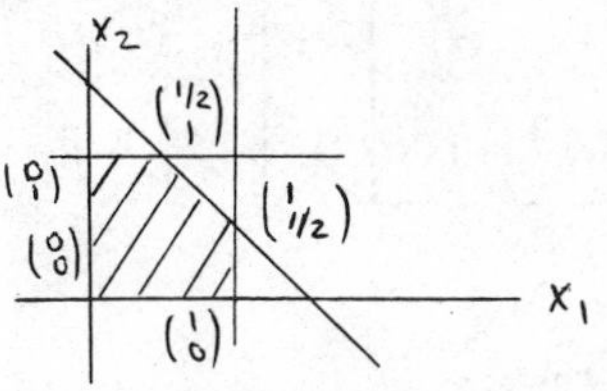

Any convex combination of the extreme points $(1/2, 1)^T$ and $(1, 1/2)^T$ gives an optimal solution of the overall problem. We will now use the decomposition algorithm for solving the problem. We will use one convexity constraint.

<u>Initialization:</u>

$\underline{x}_1 = (0,0)^T$

$$B = \begin{bmatrix} 1 & 0 \\ 0 & 1 \end{bmatrix} \quad (\text{columns } s, \lambda_1)$$

z	0	0	0
s	1	0	3/2
λ_1	0	1	1

$w = 0, \quad \alpha = 0.$

PROBLEM 7.19 (Continued)

Iteration 1

Subproblem:

max $x_1 + x_2$

s.t. $0 \le x_1 \le 1$

$0 \le x_2 \le 1$

Optimal: $(x_1, x_2) = (1, 1)$

$\max_{x \in \bar{X}} (wA - c)x + \alpha = 2 > 0$

introduce λ_2.

$$\begin{bmatrix} Ax_2 \\ 1 \end{bmatrix} = \begin{bmatrix} 2 \\ 1 \end{bmatrix} = \text{updated column}$$

Master Problem

			RHS
z	0	0	0
s	1	0	3/2
λ_1	0	1	1

λ_2
2
(2)
1

			RHS
z	−1	0	−3/2
λ_2	1/2	0	3/4
λ_1	−1/2	1	1/4

$w = -1$

$\alpha = 0$

Iteration 2

Subproblem:

max $0x_1 + 0x_2$

$x \in \bar{X}$

$\Rightarrow$ Any point in $\bar{X}$ is optimal.

$\max_{x \in \bar{X}} (wA - c)x + \alpha = 0 + 0 = 0$

No candidate to enter the master problem. Hence, the optimal point is given by:

$$\begin{pmatrix} x_1^* \\ x_2^* \end{pmatrix} = \lambda_1 x_1 + \lambda_2 x_2 = 1/4 \begin{pmatrix} 0 \\ 0 \end{pmatrix} + 3/4 \begin{pmatrix} 1 \\ 1 \end{pmatrix} = \begin{pmatrix} 3/4 \\ 3/4 \end{pmatrix}$$

Obviously, the decomposition algorithm generated the nonextreme optimal point (3/4, 3/4).

PROBLEM 7.20

a) Whenever an extreme point x_k in the subproblem is found with $z_k - \hat{c}_k > 0$, it would

PROBLEM 7.20 (Continued)

be introduced in the master problem with potential improvement.

Advantage : terminate solution of subproblem before optimality.

Disadvantage : may lead to a small improvement in the master problem.

We may use the rule to stop the subproblem if x_k is found such that $z_k - \hat{c}_k > \epsilon$, where ϵ is a predetermined scalar.

b) In this case the generated columns (satisfying $z_j - \hat{c}_j > 0$) could be adjoined to the master array after updating. The simplex method could be used such that $z_j - \hat{c}_j \leq 0$ for each of these columns. This updates B^{-1}, w, α, and the subproblem step is repeated.

Advantage : master objective improves further if several columns are considered.

Disadvantage : more work at the master problem and no assessment of the overall benefits is available.

c) In this case the size of the master problem increases by one column at each iteration. The master problem becomes that of finding the best convex combination of all the columns generated so far. Of course the master problem is updated at each step.

PROBLEM 7.20 (Continued)

Advantage : objective of the master problem improves at a faster rate since we consider a convex combination of more extreme points.

Disadvantages: more work per master iteration. The size of the master problem grows steadily, also difficulties with storing the extreme points generated so far.

PROBLEM 7.23

Master Constraints	Subproblem constraints
$B_i x_i \le b_i \quad , i=1,..,T$	$\sum_{i=1}^{T} A_i x_i \le b$ $x_i \geq 0$ $i=1,2,\ldots,T$

Master system in λ_{ij} space

$$\sum_{j=1}^{t_i} (B_i x_{ij})\lambda_{ij} \le b_i \quad , \quad i=1,2,\ldots,T$$

$$\sum_{j=1}^{t_i} \lambda_{ij} = 1 \qquad i=1,2,\ldots,T$$

$$\lambda_{ij} \geq 0 \qquad \forall i,j.$$

Let D_i be a basis of the above system.

Initialization

Form the following T arrays:

(w_i, α_i)	$\bar{z}_i$
D_i^{-1}	$D_i^{-1}\begin{pmatrix} b_i \\ 1 \end{pmatrix}$

$i=1,2,\ldots,T$.

PROBLEM 7.23 (Continued)

where $\bar{z}_i = c_{D_i} D_i^{-1} \binom{b_i}{1}$, and the components of c_{D_i} are the costs of the basic variables. In particular, the cost of a basic λ_{ij} is $c_i x_{ij}$ and the cost of a basic slack variable is zero. $(w_i, \alpha_i) = c_{D_i} D_i^{-1}$.

Let $p=1$ and go to the subproblem step.

Subproblem step

$$\max \sum_{i=1}^{T} (w_i B_i - c_i) x_i + \sum_{i=1}^{T} \alpha_i$$

$$\text{s.t.} \quad \sum_{i=1}^{T} A_i x_i \leq b$$

$$x_i \geq 0 \quad , \quad i = 1, 2, \ldots, T.$$

If the optimal objective is zero then stop, the optimal solution is at hand. Otherwise let $x_{1p}, x_{2p}, \ldots, x_{Tp}$ be an optimal solution for the subproblem. Form the columns $\binom{B_i x_{ip}}{1}$. Update the columns multiplying them by D_i^{-1}. Go to the master step.

Master Step

If $(w_i B_i - c_i) x_{ip} + \alpha > 0$, then insert the column

$$\begin{bmatrix} (w_i B_i - c_i) x_{ip} + \alpha_i \\ D_i^{-1} \binom{B_i x_{ip}}{1} \end{bmatrix}$$

in the master array and pivot. Replace p by $p+1$ and go to the subproblem step.

PROBLEM 7.23 (Continued)

(Note that this procedure updates (w_i, α_i), D_i^{-1} and the objective column). One must observe that the master step in this case is quite simple since it decomposes. If the number of constraints $\sum_{i=1}^{T} A_i x_i \leq b$ is small, then the subproblem may not be difficult and could be solved as a general LP.

The advantages of this procedure is that only simple pivots are required to update the master problem and only one LP is solved at the subproblem step.

PROBLEM 7.24

a) This class of problems arises in the context of a discrete control problem, e.g., an inventory production problem.

x_j : state vector

y_j : control vector

b)
$$
\begin{array}{llll}
\min & c_1x_1 + c_2x_2 + \cdots + c_Tx_T + d_1y_1 \cdots\cdots d_Ty_T & & \\
\text{S.T.} & x_0 - x_1 & +A_1y_1 & = b_1 \\
& \quad x_1 - x_2 & \quad +A_2y_2 & = b_2 \\
& \qquad \ddots & \qquad \ddots & \\
& \qquad\quad x_{T-1} - x_T & \qquad\quad +A_Ty_T & = b_T \\
& \qquad\qquad\quad x_T & & = b \\
& 0 \leq x_j \leq u_j & & \\
& 0 \leq y_j \leq u_j' & j = 1, 2, \ldots, T &
\end{array}
$$

PROBLEM 7.24 (Continued)

c)

$$\min \; x_1 + x_2 + x_3 + x_4 + 3y_1 + 5y_2 + 4y_3 + 6y_4$$

$$\begin{array}{lll}
\text{s.t.} \; x_0 - x_1 + y_1 & = 40 & \\
x_2 - x_3 + y_3 & = 60 & \text{master constr.} \\
x_4 & = 30 & \\
x_1 - x_2 + y_2 & = 50 & \\
x_3 - x_4 + y_4 & = 40 & \text{Sub-problem Constr.} \\
0 \le x_1, x_2, x_3, x_4 & \le 40 & \\
0 \le y_1, y_2 & \le 45 & \\
0 \le y_3, y_4 & \le 50 &
\end{array}$$

Assume $x_0 = 0$.

Phase I

Iteration 1

Master: Let the basis consist of $x_{a_1}, x_{a_2}, x_{a_3}$, the artificial variables.

				RHS
z	1	1	1	101
x_{a_1}	1	0	0	40
x_{a_2}	0	1	0	60
x_{a_3}	0	0	1	1

$(w_1, w_2, \alpha) = (1,1,1)$

Subproblem:

$$\max_{x \in \bar{X}} \; (wA - 0)\binom{x}{y}$$

or

$$\max \; -x_1 + x_2 - x_3 + y_1 + y_3$$

$$\begin{array}{ll}
\text{s.t.} \; x_1 - x_2 + y_2 & = 50 \\
x_3 - x_4 + y_4 & = 40
\end{array}$$

Note: Subproblems are knapsack problems.

PROBLEM 7.24 (Continued)

$$0 \le x_1, x_2, x_3, x_4 \le 40$$
$$0 \le y_1, y_2 \le 45$$
$$0 \le y_3, y_4 \le 50$$

or

I.

max $-x_1 + x_2$

S.T. $x_1 - x_2 + y_2 = 50$

$0 \le x_1 \le 40$

$0 \le x_2 \le 40$

$0 \le y_2 \le 45$

II.

max $-x_3$

S.T. $x_3 - x_4 + y_4 = 40$

$0 \le x_3 \le 40$

$0 \le x_4 \le 40$

$0 \le y_4 \le 50$

III.

max $y_1 + y_3$

S.T. $0 \le y_1 \le 45$

$0 \le y_3 \le 50$

Optimal:

I – $x_1 = 5, \quad x_2 = 0, \quad y_2 = 45$

II – $x_3 = 40, \quad x_4 = 30, \quad y_4 = 30$

III – $y_1 = 45, \quad y_3 = 50$

Objective $= -5 - 40 + 45 + 50 = 50$. Introduce

$(x_1, x_2, x_3, x_4, y_1, y_2, y_3, y_4) = (5, 0, 40, 30, 45, 45, 50, 30) = P_1$

Iteration 2

$$x_0 - x_1 + y_1 = 0 - 5 + 45 = 40$$
$$x_2 - x_3 + y_3 = 0 - 40 + 50 = 10$$

updated column $= (40, 10, 1)^T$

Master problem:

				RHS	λ_1
z	1	1	1	101	50
x_{a_1}	1	0	0	40	40
x_{a_2}	0	1	0	60	10
x_{a_3}	0	0	1	1	(1)

				RHS
z	1	1	−50	61
x_{a_1}	1	0	−40	0
x_{a_2}	0	1	−10	50
λ_1	0	0	1	1

PROBLEM 7.24 (Continued)

$w_1 = w_2 = 1$, $\alpha = -50$.

Continue in this fashion until the end of phase I, then start phase II with original cost.

PROBLEM 7.25

Let $a_1, a_2, \ldots, a_p$ be the possible cutting patterns (p is a very large number). Let x_j be the number of rolls cut according to the jth cutting pattern. The problem can be formulated as follows:

$$\min \sum_{j=1}^{p} x_j$$

$$\text{S.T.} \quad \sum_{j=1}^{p} a_{ij} x_j \geq b_i \quad , \quad i = 1, 2, \ldots, m$$

$$\left.\begin{array}{l} x_j \geq 0 \quad , \\ x_j \ \text{integer} \end{array}\right\} j = 1, 2, \ldots, p$$

(Note that a cutting pattern must satisfy $\sum_{i=1}^{m} l_j a_{ij} \leq l$, $j = 1, 2, \ldots, p$).

Suppose that ν cutting patterns have already been generated.

Master Problem

$$\min \sum_{j=1}^{\nu} x_j$$

$$\text{S.T.} \quad \sum_{j=1}^{\nu} a_{ij} x_j \geq b_i \quad , \quad i = 1, 2, \ldots, m$$

$$x_j \geq 0 \quad , \quad j = 1, 2, \ldots, p$$

Let w_i be an optimal dual variable of the ith constraint.

PROBLEM 7.25 (Continued)

Subproblem

If dual feasibility hold for other columns which have not yet been generated, we have an optimal solution. Therefore if $\sum_{i=1}^{m} a_{ij} w_i \leq 1$ for $j = \nu+1, \nu+2, \ldots, p$, then the solution is optimal. In order to check whether this condition holds we solve the following subproblem:

$$\max \sum_{i=1}^{m} a_{ij} w_i$$

$$\text{s.t.} \quad \sum_{i=1}^{m} a_{ij} \ell_i \leq \ell$$

$$a_{ij} \geq 0, \text{ integer}, \quad i = 1, 2, \ldots, m.$$

Let $(a_{1,\nu+1}, a_{2,\nu+1}, \ldots, a_{m,\nu+1})^T$ be an optimal solution. If $\sum_{i=1}^{m} a_{i,\nu+1} w_i - 1 = 0$, then master problem provides an optimal solution. Otherwise replace ν by $\nu+1$ and repeat the master problem (Of course we could always keep the master problem with an m array).

PROBLEM 7.26

Let x_{ij} = pounds of ingredient i used in product j.

$i = 1, 2, 3 \Rightarrow$ corn, lime, fishmeal

$j = 1, 2 \Rightarrow$ cattle feed, chicken feed.

$$\min \; .1x_{11} + .1x_{21} + .08x_{31} + .1x_{12} + .1x_{22} + .08x_{32}$$

$$\begin{aligned}
\text{s.t.} \quad & x_{11} + x_{21} + x_{31} && = 4000 \\
& x_{12} + x_{22} + x_{32} && = 2000 \\
& x_{11} + x_{12} && \leq 3000 \\
& x_{21} + x_{22} && \leq 2500
\end{aligned}$$

PROBLEM 7.26 (Continued)

$$x_{31} \qquad\qquad + x_{32} \le 1000$$

$$18(x_{11}+x_{21}+x_{31}) \le 25x_{11}+15x_{21}+25x_{31} \le 22(x_{11}+x_{21}+x_{31})$$

$$20(x_{11}+x_{21}+x_{31}) \le 15x_{11}+30x_{21}+20x_{31}$$

$$20(x_{12}+x_{22}+x_{32}) \le 25x_{12}+15x_{22}+25x_{32} \le 23(x_{12}+x_{22}+x_{32})$$

$$20(x_{12}+x_{22}+x_{32}) \le 15x_{12}+30x_{22}+20x_{32} \le 25(x_{12}+x_{22}+x_{32})$$

$$x_{ij} \geq 0 \quad \forall i,j.$$

Cattle Subproblem Constr.

$$x_{11}+x_{21}+x_{31} = 4000$$
$$3x_{11}-7x_{21}+3x_{31} \le 0$$
$$7x_{11}-3x_{21}+7x_{31} \geq 0$$
$$-5x_{11}+10x_{21} \geq 0$$
$$x_{11}, x_{21}, x_{31} \geq 0$$

Chicken Subproblem Constr.

$$x_{12}+x_{22}+x_{32} = 2000$$
$$2x_{12}-8x_{22}+2x_{32} \le 0$$
$$5x_{12}-5x_{22}+5x_{32} \geq 0$$
$$-10x_{12}+5x_{22}-5x_{32} \le 0$$
$$-5x_{12}+10x_{22} \geq 0$$
$$x_{12}, x_{22}, x_{32} \geq 0$$

Master Constraints

$$x_{11} \qquad + x_{12} \le 3000$$
$$x_{21} \qquad + x_{22} \le 2500$$
$$x_{31} \qquad + x_{32} \le 1000$$

Initialization

Choose the following solutions of the subproblems which are feasible to the master problem:

$$\underline{X}_{11} = (2000, 1500, 500)$$

$$\underline{X}_{21} = (1000, 1000, 0)$$

The initial basis consists of $\lambda_{11}, \lambda_{21}, s_1, s_2, s_3$.

PROBLEM 7.26 (Continued)

						RHS
z	0	0	0	390	200	590
s_1	1	0	0	0	0	0
s_2	0	1	0	0	0	0
s_3	0	0	1	0	0	500
λ_{11}	0	0	0	1	0	1
λ_{21}	0	0	0	0	1	1

$(w_1, w_2, w_3, \alpha_1, \alpha_2) = (0, 0, 0, 390, 200)$

Iteration 1

Subproblem 1:

$$\max\ (wA_1 - c_1)\underline{x}_1 \quad \Rightarrow \quad \begin{aligned} \max\ & -.1x_{11} - .1x_{21} - .08x_{31} \\ \text{S.T.}\ & x_{11} + x_{21} + x_{31} = 4000 \\ & 3x_{11} - 7x_{21} + 3x_{31} \leq 0 \\ & 7x_{11} - 3x_{21} + 7x_{31} \geq 0 \\ & -5x_{11} + 10x_{21} \geq 0 \\ & x_{11}, x_{21}, x_{31} \geq 0 \end{aligned}$$

$$\underline{x}_1 \in \underline{X}_1$$

This problem can be solved by two phase method. Following is the optimal tableau of phase II:

	z	x_{11}	x_{21}	x_{31}	x_1	x_2	x_3	RHS
z	1	.02	0	0	.002	0	0	−56
x_{31}	0	1	0	1	.1	0	0	2800
x_2	0	0	0	0	1	1	0	16,000
x_{21}	0	0	1	0	−.1	0	0	1200
x_3	0	5	0	0	−1	0	1	12,000

Thus $\max(wA_1 - c_1)\underline{x}_1 + \alpha_1 = -56 + 390 > 0$.

Introduce $(x_{11}, x_{21}, x_{31}) = (0, 1200, 2800)$ in the master array. The updated column will be $(0, 1200, 2800, 1, 0)^T$.

PROBLEM 7.26 (Continued)

						RHS	λ_{12}
z	0	0	0	390	200	590	334
s_1	1					0	0
s_2		1				0	(1200)
s_3			1			500	2800
λ_{11}				1		1	1
λ_{21}					1	1	0

z	0	$-167/600$	0	390	200	590
s_1	1	0	0	0	0	0
λ_{12}	0	$1/1200$	0	0	0	0
s_3	0	$-7/3$	1	0	0	500
λ_{11}	0	$-1/1200$	0	1	0	1
λ_{21}	0	0	0	0	1	1

Proceed the solution procedure in this manner until no candidates exists from both sub-problems and the solution is optimal.

PROBLEM 7.27

Let x_{ijk} be the amount of product k transported from source i to destination j.

$i = 1, 2 \Rightarrow$ Dallas, New York

$j = 1, 2, 3 \Rightarrow$ Kansas City, LA, Detroit

$k = 1, 2, 3 \Rightarrow$ Gasoline, Kerosene, jet fuel.

y_{ij} : amount of crude type i purchased at refinary j.

$i = 1, 2 \Rightarrow$ light crude, heavy crude

$j = 1, 2 \Rightarrow$ Dallas, N.Y.

The problem is formulated in the following page.

PROBLEM 7.27 (Continued)

	Gasoline						Kerosene						Jet fuel				Light Crude		Heavy Crude			
	x_{111}	x_{121}	x_{131}	x_{211}	x_{221}	x_{231}	x_{112}	x_{122}	x_{132}	x_{212}	x_{222}	x_{232}	x_{123}	x_{133}	x_{223}	x_{233}	y_{11}	y_{12}	y_{21}	y_{22}		
minimize	0.6	0.4	0.5	0.35	0.8	0.3	0.6	0.4	0.5	0.35	0.8	0.3	0.4	0.5	0.8	0.3	11	11	9	9		
S. T.	1	1	1														-.4		-.32		≤ 0	Gasoline Transportation
				1	1	1												-.4		-.32	≤ 0	
	1			1																	$\geq$200,000	
		1			1																$\geq$300,000	
			1			1															$\geq$500,000	
							1	1	1								-.2		-.4		≤ 0	
										1	1	1						-.2		-.4	≤ 0	
							1			1											$\geq$400,000	Kerosene Tr.
								1			1										$\geq$200,000	
									1			1									$\geq$100,000	
													1	1			-.35		-.2		≤ 0	Jet Transp.
															1	1		-.35		-.2	≤ 0	
													1		1						$\geq$600,000	
														1		1					$\geq$300,000	
																	1	1			$\le$ 2,000,000	Crude avail.
																			1	1	$\le$ 1,000,000	

$$x_{ijk},\ y_{\ell,m} \geq 0 \quad \forall\, i, j, k, \ell, m$$

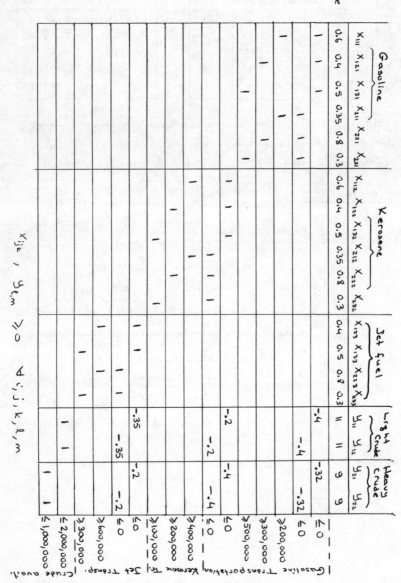

PROBLEM 7.27 (Continued)

b) Take the dual of the problem. The dual has the following structure:

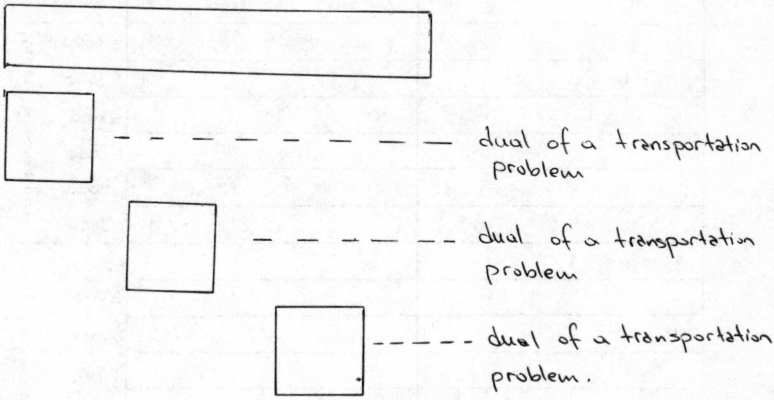

The problem can thus be solved by the decomposition method of this chapter. After the dual problem is solved by decomposition, the primal variables can be obtained as the dual variables of the dual problem solved.

PROBLEM 7.28

Let x_{ijk} be the number of units of product k shipped from source i to destination j.

$i = 1, 2 \Rightarrow$ Atlanta, LA.

$j = 1, 2, 3 \Rightarrow$ N.Y., Seattle, Miami

$k = 1, 2 \Rightarrow$ Refrigerators, Washer/dryers.

The problem can be formulated as follows:

PROBLEM 7.28 (Continued)

	Refrigerators						Washer / Dryers							
	x_{111}	x_{121}	x_{131}	x_{211}	x_{221}	x_{231}	x_{112}	x_{122}	x_{132}	x_{212}	x_{222}	x_{232}		
min	6	14	7	10	8	15	6	14	7	10	8	15		
S.T.	1						1						≤ 6000	Master Constraints
		1						1					≤ 3000	
			1						1				≤ 8000	
				1						1			≤ 3000	
					1						1		≤ 9000	
						1						1	≤ 3000	
	1	1	1										≤ 5000	Subproblem 1 Constr.
				1	1	1							≤ 8000	
	1			1									≥ 4000	
		1			1								≥ 5000	
			1			1							≥ 4000	
							1	1	1				≤ 7000	Subproblem 2 Constr.
										1	1	1	≤ 4000	
							1			1			≥ 3000	
								1			1		≥ 3000	
									1			1	≥ 4000	

$$x_{ijk} \ge 0 \quad \forall\, i, j, k.$$

b) Initialization

Choose a feasible (not necessarily basic) solution to both subproblems satisfying master constraints. We will use transportation algorithm in the subproblems (see chapter 8).

2500	1000	1500	5000
1500	4000	2500	8000
4000	5000	4000	

			Dummy	
3000		4000		7000
	3000		1000	4000
3000	3000	4000	1000	

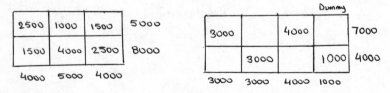

PROBLEM 7.28 (Continued)

$c_1 \underline{x}_{11} = 124{,}000$

$c_2 \underline{x}_{21} = 70{,}000$

Basis consists of $s_1, s_2, s_3, s_4, s_5, s_6, \lambda_{11}, \lambda_{21}$.

$(w_1, w_2, w_3, w_4, w_5, w_6, \alpha_1, \alpha_2) = (0, 0, 0, 0, 0, 0, 124{,}000, 70{,}000)$

Iteration 1

Subproblem:

$$\max_{\underline{x}_1 \in \overline{X}_1} (wA_1 - c_1)\underline{x}_1 \quad \text{or} \quad \min_{\underline{x}_1 \in \overline{X}_1} (c_1 - wA_1)\underline{x}_1$$

					u
	4000	1000	$\langle 14 \rangle$	5000	6
	$\langle -10 \rangle$	4000	4000	8000	0
	4000	5000	4000		
v	0	8	15		

				u
	4000		1000	−8
	$\langle 4 \rangle$	5000	3000	0
v	14	8	15	

				u
	1000	$\langle -4 \rangle$	4000	−4
	3000	5000	$\langle -4 \rangle$	0
v	10	8	11	

Optimal.

$$\max_{\underline{x}_1 \in \overline{X}_1} (wA_1 - c_1)\underline{x}_1 + \alpha_1 = -104{,}000 + 124{,}000 = 20{,}000 > 0$$

so, $\underline{x}_{12}$ enters.

Updated column $= [20{,}000, 10{,}000, 0, 4000, 3000, 5000, 0, 1, 0]^T$

PROBLEM 7.28 (Continued)

									RHS	λ_{12}
Z	0	0	0	0	0	0	124,000	70,000	194,000	20,000
S_1									500	1000
S_2									2000	0
S_3									2500	4000
S_4				$I_{(8\times 8)}$					1500	3000
S_5									2000	(5000)
S_6									500	0
λ_{11}									1	1
λ_{21}									1	0

									RHS
Z	0	0	0	0	-4	0	124,000	70,000	186,000
S_1					$-.2$				100
S_2		$I_{(4\times 4)}$			0		$O_{(5\times 3)}$		2000
S_3					$-.8$				900
S_4					$-.6$				300
λ_{12}					.0002				0.4
S_6		$O_{(4\times 4)}$			0				500
λ_{11}					.0002		$I_{(3\times 3)}$		0.6
λ_{21}					0				1

With the new dual variables proceed to step 2 by solving the subproblems.

PROBLEM 7.29

a)
$$\begin{array}{ll} \min & cx + f(y) \\ \text{s.t.} & Ax + By = b \\ & x \geq 0,\ y \in Y \end{array} \equiv \min_{y \in Y} \left[f(y) + \begin{array}{ll} \min & cx \\ \text{s.t.} & Ax = b - By \\ & x \geq 0 \end{array} \right]$$

PROBLEM 7.29 (Continued)

But
$$\begin{array}{ll} \min & cx \\ \text{S.T.} & Ax = b - By \\ & x \geq 0 \end{array} \quad = \quad \begin{array}{ll} \max & w(b - By) \\ \text{S.T.} & wA \leq c \end{array}$$

Thus the problem is equivalent to:

$$\min_{y \in Y} \left[f(y) + \max_{wA \leq c} w(b - By) \right]$$

Make the substitution $f(y) + \max\limits_{wA \leq c} w(b-By) = z$

Thus $z \geq f(y) + w(b - By)$ for each $wA \leq c$.

The problem thus can be reformulated as follows:

$$\begin{array}{ll} \text{Minimize} & z \\ \text{S.T} & z \geq f(y) + w(b - By) \\ & wA \leq c \\ & y \in Y \\ & w \text{ unrestricted} \end{array}$$

b) Consider $[w : wA \leq c]$ and let $w_1, \ldots, w_t$ be the extreme points and $d_1, d_2, \ldots, d_\ell$ be the extreme directions. Then w is in the set if, and only if,

$$w = \sum_{j=1}^{t} \lambda_j w_j + \sum_{j=1}^{\ell} \mu_j d_j$$
$$\sum_{j=1}^{t} \lambda_j = 1$$
$$\lambda_j \geq 0 \ \forall j, \quad \mu_j \geq 0 \ \forall j.$$

For any given y $z \geq f(y) + w(b - By)$ for each w satisfying $wA \leq c$. In another words,

PROBLEM 7.29 (Continued)

$$z \geq f(y) + \left(\sum_{j=1}^{t} \lambda_j w_j + \sum_{j=1}^{\ell} \mu_j d_j\right)(b - By)$$

$$\sum_{j=1}^{t} \lambda_j = 1 \qquad (1)$$

$$\lambda_j \geq 0 \quad , \quad j = 1, 2, \ldots, t$$

$$\mu_j \geq 0 \quad , \quad j = 1, 2, \ldots, \ell$$

For any given j, let $\lambda_i = 0$ for $i \neq j$ and $\lambda_j = 1$, $\mu_i = 0$. From (1) we get:

$$z \geq f(y) + w_j (b - By)$$

If for any j, we have $d_j(b - By) > 0$, then μ_j could be choosen large enough violating (1). So $d_j(b - By) \leq 0$ must hold for (1) to hold.

c) From (b) the problem in (a) could be reformulated as follows:

$$\begin{aligned} &\text{minimize} && z \\ &\text{S.T.} && z \geq f(y) + w_j(b - By) && j = 1, \ldots, t \\ & && d_j(b - By) \leq 0 && j = 1, \ldots, \ell \\ & && y \in Y \end{aligned}$$

d) Suppose that $w_1, w_2, \ldots, w_{t'}$ and $d_1, d_2, \ldots, d_{\ell'}$ have been generated. Relaxing the rest of the constraints the problem in (c) could be written as:

$$\begin{aligned} &\text{minimize} && z \\ &\text{S.T.} && z \geq f(y) + w_j(b - By) && j = 1, \ldots, t' \\ & && d_j(b - By) \leq 0 && j = 1, \ldots, \ell' \\ & && y \in Y \end{aligned}$$

PROBLEM 7.29 (Continued)

We have an optimal solution of the overall problem if the optimal solution (z^*, y^*) from the above master problem satisfies

$$z^* \geq f(y^*) + w_j(b - By^*)$$

for $j = t'+1, \ldots, t$ and

$$d_j(b - By^*) \leq 0$$

for $j = \ell'+1, \ldots, \ell$. To check this we solve the following linear program (the subproblem):

$$\max \; w(b - By^*)$$

$$\text{s.t.} \quad wA \leq c$$

First, note that a finite optimal exists if, and only if, $d_j(b - By^*) \leq 0$, for $j = 1, \ldots, \ell$. If the optimal is finite we automatically have $d_j(b - By^*) \leq$ for $j = \ell'+1, \ldots, \ell$. Let $w_{t'+1}$ be an optimal extreme point. If

$$z^* = f(y^*) + w_{t'+1}(b - By^*)$$

then $\quad z^* \geq f(y^*) + w_j(b - By^*)$

for all j and (z^*, y^*) is an optimal solution of the overall problem. Otherwise, if $z^* < f(y^*) + w_{t'+1}(b - By^*)$ then t' is replaced by $t'+1$ and the master problem is resolved.

PROBLEM 7.30

$$\begin{array}{ll} \min & -x_1 - x_2 - 3x_3 - x_4 \\ \text{s.t.} & \underbrace{\begin{array}{r} -x_1 - x_2 \\ x_1 - x_2 \\ -2x_1 - x_2 \end{array}}_{A} \;\underbrace{\begin{array}{r} -2x_3 - x_4 \\ \\ \end{array}}_{B} \begin{array}{l} \geq -12 \\ \geq -4 \\ \geq -6 \end{array} \end{array}$$

$$x_1,\ x_2,\ \boxed{\begin{array}{l} x_3 + x_4 \leq 8 \\ x_3,\ x_4 \geq 0 \end{array}}\ Y$$

Initialization

Consider the point $(3/2, 1/2, 0)$ in the feasible region $wA \leq c$, $w \geq 0$ given by

$$\begin{array}{l} -w_1 + w_2 - 2w_3 \leq -1 \\ -w_1 - w_2 - w_3 \leq -2 \\ w_1,\ w_2,\ w_3 \geq 0 \end{array}$$

Iteration 1

Master Step:

$$\begin{array}{ll} \min & z \\ \text{s.t.} & z \geq -3x_3 - x_4 + (3/2, 1/2, 0) \begin{bmatrix} -12 + 2x_3 + x_4 \\ -4 \\ -6 \end{bmatrix} \\ & x_3 + x_4 \leq 8 \\ & x_3,\ x_4 \geq 0 \end{array}$$

Optimal: $(z^*, x_3^*, x_4^*) = (-20, 0, 0)$

Subproblem:

$$\begin{array}{ll} \max & -12w_1 - 4w_2 - 6w_3 \\ \text{s.t.} & -w_1 + w_2 - 2w_3 \leq -1 \\ & -w_1 - w_2 - w_3 \leq -2 \\ & w_1,\ w_2,\ w_3 \geq 0 \end{array} \quad \text{or} \quad \begin{array}{ll} \max & -x_1 - 2x_2 \\ \text{s.t.} & -x_1 - x_2 \geq -12 \\ & x_1 - x_2 \geq -4 \\ & -2x_1 - x_2 \geq -6 \\ & x_1,\ x_2 \geq 0 \end{array}$$

PROBLEM 7.30 (Continued)

Optimal:

$x_1 = 2/3$, $x_2 = 14/3$

Optimal Dual:

$w_1 = 0$

$$\left.\begin{array}{l} w_2 - 2w_3 = -1 \\ -w_2 - w_3 = -2 \end{array}\right\} \Rightarrow \begin{array}{l} w_2 = 1 \\ w_3 = 1 \end{array}$$

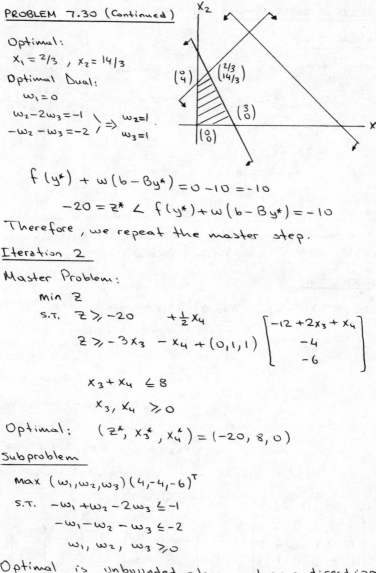

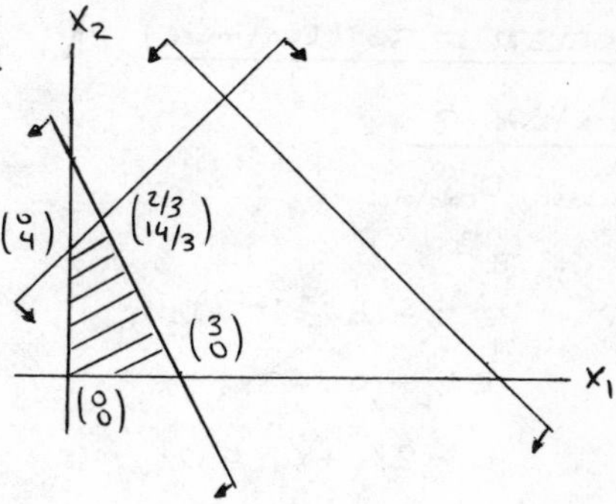

$$f(y^*) + w(b - By^*) = 0 - 10 = -10$$

$$-20 = z^* < f(y^*) + w(b - By^*) = -10$$

Therefore, we repeat the master step.

Iteration 2

Master Problem:

$$\min\ z$$

$$\text{s.t.}\quad z \geq -20 \qquad + \tfrac{1}{2}x_4$$

$$z \geq -3x_3 - x_4 + (0,1,1)\begin{bmatrix} -12 + 2x_3 + x_4 \\ -4 \\ -6 \end{bmatrix}$$

$$x_3 + x_4 \leq 8$$

$$x_3, x_4 \geq 0$$

Optimal: $(z^*, x_3^*, x_4^*) = (-20, 8, 0)$

Subproblem

$$\max\ (w_1, w_2, w_3)(4, -4, -6)^T$$

$$\text{s.t.}\quad -w_1 + w_2 - 2w_3 \leq -1$$

$$-w_1 - w_2 - w_3 \leq -2$$

$$w_1, w_2, w_3 \geq 0$$

Optimal is unbounded along extreme direction (1,0,0).

PROBLEM 7.30 (Continued)

Iteration 3

Master Problem:

$$\min z$$

$$\text{S.T.} \quad z \geq -20 + \tfrac{1}{2}x_4$$

$$z \geq -10 - 3x_3 - x_4$$

$$2x_3 + x_4 \leq 12$$

$$x_3 + x_4 \leq 8$$

$$x_3, x_4 \geq 0$$

Optimal:

$$z^* = -20$$

$$x_3^* = 6$$

$$x_4^* = 0$$

One can proceed to the subproblem and to the master problem (if needed) in this fashion until $z^* \geq f(y^*) + w(b - By^*)$.

PROBLEM 7.31

$$\min \; 1.5x_{11} + 2x_{12} + 2x_{21} + 1.5x_{22} + 2.5x_{31} + 2.25x_{32} + 8000y_1 + 12{,}000y_2 + 7000y_3$$

$$\text{S.T.} \quad x_{11} + x_{12} - 4000y_1 \leq 0$$

$$x_{21} + x_{22} - 5000y_2 \leq 0$$

$$x_{31} + x_{32} - 6000y_3 \leq 0$$

$$x_{11} + x_{21} + x_{31} = 3000$$

$$x_{12} + x_{22} + x_{32} = 5000$$

$$x_{11}, x_{12}, \ldots, x_{32} \geq 0$$

y_1, y_2, y_3 either 0 or 1.

$$A = \begin{bmatrix} 1 & 1 & 0 & 0 & 0 & 0 \\ 0 & 0 & 1 & 1 & 0 & 0 \\ 0 & 0 & 0 & 0 & 1 & 1 \\ 1 & 0 & 1 & 0 & 1 & 0 \\ 0 & 1 & 0 & 0 & 0 & 1 \end{bmatrix}, \quad B = \begin{bmatrix} -4000 & 0 & 0 \\ 0 & -5000 & 0 \\ 0 & 0 & -6000 \end{bmatrix}, \quad b = \begin{bmatrix} 0 \\ 0 \\ 0 \\ 3000 \\ 5000 \end{bmatrix}$$

PROBLEM 7.31 (Continued)

$Y = \{(y_1, y_2, y_3): y_1, y_2, y_3 \text{ either } 0 \text{ or } 1\}$

Consider the region $wA \leq c$, $w \geq 0$:

$$
\begin{aligned}
w_1 \quad\quad\quad + w_4 \quad\quad &\leq 1.5 \\
w_1 \quad\quad\quad\quad\quad + w_5 &\leq 2 \\
w_2 \quad\quad + w_4 \quad\quad &\leq 2 \\
w_2 \quad\quad\quad\quad + w_5 &\leq 1.5 \\
w_3 + w_4 \quad\quad &\leq 2.5 \\
w_3 \quad\quad + w_5 &\leq 2.25
\end{aligned}
$$

$w_1, w_2, w_3 \leq 0$, w_4, w_5 unrestricted.

Consider the direction $(-1,-1,-1,0,0)$ of the above region and the extreme point $(0,0,0,0,0)$.

Iteration 1

Master Problem:

$$\min \; z$$

$$\text{S.T.} \quad z \geq 8000y_1 + 12000y_2 + 7000y_3$$

$$(-1,-1,-1,0,0)(4000y_1, 5000y_2, 6000y_3, 3000, 5000)^T \leq 0$$

y_1, y_2, y_3 either 0 or 1.

or

$$\min \; z$$

$$\text{S.T.} \quad z \geq 8000y_1 + 12{,}000y_2 + 7000y_3$$

$$0 \leq 4000y_1 + 5000y_2 + 6000y_3$$

y_1, y_2, y_3 either 0 or 1.

Optimal: $(y_1^*, y_2^*, y_3^*, z^*) = (0,0,0,0)$

Subproblem

$$\max \; 0w_1 + 0w_2 + 0w_3 + 3000w_4 + 5000w_5$$

$$\text{S.T.} \quad wA \leq c$$

$w_1, w_2, w_3 \leq 0$, w_4, w_5 unrestricted.

PROBLEM 7.31 (Continued)

The solution is unbounded along the direction $d = (-1, -1, -1, 1, 1)$.

Iteration 2

Master Problem:

$$\min z$$

$$\text{s.t.} \quad z \geq 8000y_1 + 12{,}000y_2 + 7000y_3$$

$$8000 \leq 4000y_1 + 5000y_2 + 6000y_3$$

$$y_1, y_2, y_3 \text{ either } 0 \text{ or } 1.$$

Optimal: $y_1^* = 1$, $y_3^* = 1$, $y_2^* = 0$, $z^* = 15{,}000$

Subproblem: By taking the dual

min . . . .

$$\begin{array}{llll} \text{s.t.} & x_{11} + x_{12} & \leq 4000 & \\ & x_{21} + x_{22} & \leq 0 & \longrightarrow x_{21} = x_{22} = 0 \\ & x_{31} + x_{32} & \leq 6000 & \\ & x_{11} + x_{31} & = 3000 & \\ & x_{12} + x_{32} & = 5000 & \\ & x_{ij} \geq 0 & & \end{array}$$

Apply transportation algorithm to the above problem.

3000	1000	⟨-.25⟩	4000	-.25	w_1
⟨-.75⟩	4000	2000	6000	0	w_3
3000	5000	2000			
1.75	2.25	0			
w_4	w_5				

The above tableau is optimal with the optimal dual solution $(w_1, w_2, w_3, w_4, w_5) = (-.25, 0, 0, 1.75, 2.25)$

PROBLEM 7.31 (Continued)

Iteration 3

Master Problem:

$$\min \quad z$$

$$\text{s.t.} \quad z \geq 8000y_1 + 12{,}000y_2 + 7000y_3$$

$$z \geq 16{,}500 + 7000y_1 + 12{,}000y_2 + 7000y_3$$

$$8000 \leq 4000y_1 + 5000y_2 + 6000y_3$$

$$y_1, y_2, y_3 \quad 0 \text{ or } 1$$

Optimal: $(y_1^*, y_2^*, y_3^*, z^*) = (1, 0, 1, 30{,}500)$

Subproblem:

The subproblem has the same vector y^* as the optimal solution as in the last iteration.

Objective of the subproblem $= -1000 + 5250 + 11{,}250 = 15{,}500$

Objective of the subproblem $+ f(y^*) = 15{,}500 + 8000 + 7000$
$= 30{,}500$

From the termination criterion in problem 7.31 we have reached the optimal solution since $z^* =$ objective of the subproblem $+ f(y^*)$. The optimal solution for the warehouse construction and the corresponding shipments depicted below.

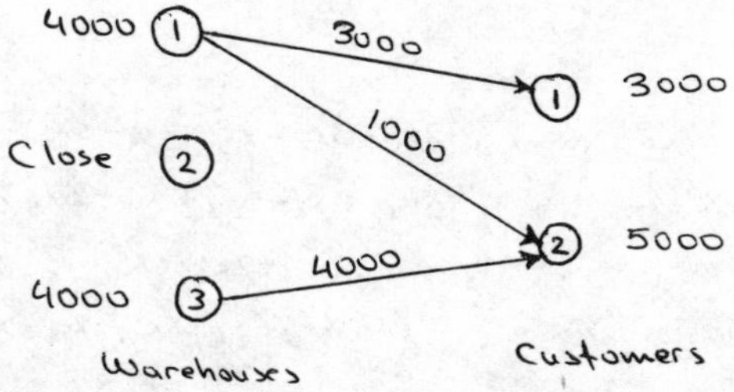

PROBLEM 7.32

Let the first constraint be the constraint corresponding to $Ax \leq b$ and the rest of the constraints be $\underline{X}$.

Initialization

Choose the point $(x_1, x_2, x_3, x_4, x_5) = (0,0,0,5,0) = \underline{X}_1$ in the set $\underline{X}$ which is a feasible solution of the overall problem.

Master Problem:

$$\begin{aligned} \min\ & (c\underline{X}_1)\lambda_1 \\ \text{S.T.}\ & (A\underline{X}_1)\lambda_1 \geq b \\ & \lambda_1 = 1 \\ & \lambda_1 \geq 0 \end{aligned} \equiv \begin{aligned} \min\ & -10\lambda_1 & & \text{Dual Variables} \\ \text{S.T.}\ & 5\lambda_1 \geq 2 & & (w) \\ & \lambda_1 = 1 & & (\alpha) \\ & \lambda_1 \geq 0 \end{aligned}$$

Dual Master problem:

$$\begin{aligned} \max\ & 2w + \alpha \\ \text{S.T.}\ & 5w + \alpha \leq -10 \\ & w \geq 0 \\ & \alpha \text{ unrestr.} \end{aligned}$$

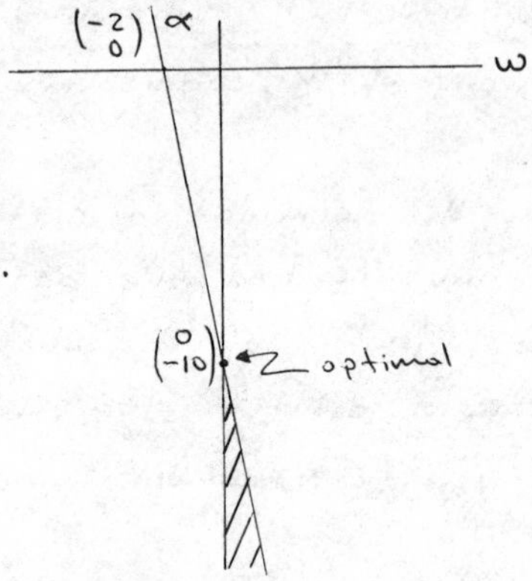

Optimal solution (Dual):

$w = 0 \quad , \alpha = -10$

Optimal solution (Primal):

$\lambda = 1$

Iteration 1

$$\begin{aligned} \max\ & (wA - c)\underline{x} + \alpha \\ & \underline{x} \in \underline{X} \end{aligned} \equiv \begin{aligned} \max\ & (-2x_1 - 5x_2 - x_3 + 2x_4 - 3x_5) - 10 \\ \text{S.T.}\ & 3x_1 + x_2 + 5x_3 + x_4 - 2x_5 \geq 5 \\ & -x_1 + 2x_3 + x_4 \geq 2 \\ & x_1, x_2, x_3, x_4, x_5 \geq 0 \end{aligned}$$

PROBLEM 7.32 (Continued)

Take the dual of this subproblem.

$$
\begin{aligned}
\min\ & 5w_1 + 2w_2 \\
\text{s.t.}\ & 3w_1 - w_2 \leq -2 \quad \text{---}(1) \\
& w_1 \leq -5 \quad \text{---}(2) \\
& 5w_1 + 2w_2 \leq -1 \quad \text{---}(3) \\
& w_1 + w_2 \leq 2 \quad \text{---}(4) \\
& -2w_1 \leq -3 \quad \text{---}(5) \\
& w_1, w_2 \leq 0 \quad \text{---}(6)
\end{aligned}
$$

From (2) and (5) we have $w_1 \geq 3/2$ and $w_1 \leq -5$. So, above problem is not feasible and hence the primal subproblem is unbounded, say, along the direction $(0,0,0,1,0)$.

Master Problem:

$$
\begin{aligned}
\min\ & (cx_1)\lambda_1 + (cd_1)\mu_1 & \Rightarrow \quad & \min\ -10\lambda_1 - 2\mu_1 \\
\text{s.t.}\ & (Ax_1)\lambda_1 + (Ad_1)\mu_1 \geq 2 & & \text{s.t.}\ 5\lambda_1 + \mu_1 \geq 2 \\
& \lambda_1 = 1 & & \lambda_1 = 1 \\
& \lambda_1, \mu_1 \geq 0 & & \lambda_1, \mu_1 \geq 0
\end{aligned}
$$

Obviously the optimal is unbounded, by letting $\lambda_1 = 1$ and μ_1 arbitrarily large. Thus the overall optimal is unbounded;

$(x_1^*, x_2^*, x_3^*, x_4^*, x_5^*) = (0, 0, 0, \lambda, 0)$ where λ is arbitrarily large.

PROBLEM 7.34

Let

$A_1 x = b_1$ m_1 rows for master constraints

$A_2 x = b_2$ m_2 rows for subproblem constraints

PROBLEM 7.34 (Continued)

The extreme cases $m_1 = 0$ and $m_2 = 0$ are interpreted as follows:

$m_1 = 0$ means no decomposition encountered, the problem is solved at once.

$m_2 = 0$ means all the constraints are treated by the master problem . The set $\overline{X} = \{x : x \geq 0\}$ only generates directions.

We will now summarize the effort per iteration.

Master Step

x is generated from the subproblem. Computing $A_1 x$ and updating $(A_1 x, 1)^T$ involves $m_1^2 + (m_1+1)^2$ multiplications and m_1^2 and $(m_1+1)^2$ additions. Pivoting involves $(m_1+2)^2$ additions and $(m_1+2)^2$ multiplications. Thus approximately $3m_1^2$ additions and $3m_1^2$ multiplications are needed per master step.

Subproblem Step

To compute $z_j - c_j$'s for nonbasic variables we need $m_1(n-m_2)$ multiplications and $m_1(n-m_2)$ additions. The iteration of the subproblem involves $(m_2+1)(n-m_2+1)$ additions and the same number of multiplications. Assuming an average of $m_2/2$ iterations per subproblem step, we have

$$m_2/2 \cdot (m_2+1)(n-m_2+1)$$

additions and multiplications.

PROBLEM 7.34 (Continued)

Thus the total number of multiplications and additions per decomposition iteration are:

$$f(m_1, m_2) = 6m_1^2 + 2m_1(n - m_2) + m_2(m_2+1)(n - m_2 + 1)$$

To minimize the total effort above, let $m_1 = m - m_2$ and solve the following problem:

$$\underset{0 \le m_2 \le m}{\text{minimize}} \quad 6(m-m_2)^2 + 2(m-m_2)(n-m_2) + m_2(m_2+1)(n-m_2+1)$$

After the simplification we get:

$$\underset{0 \le m_2 \le m}{\min} \quad -m_2^3 + (8+n)m_2^2 + (-14m - n + 1)m_2 + (2mn + m^2)$$

In order to solve the above problem we take the derivative (ignoring some dominated terms for simplicity)

$$\frac{df(m_2)}{dm_2} = -3m_2^2 + 2m_2 n + (-14m - n)$$

The roots of the equation $df(m_2)/dm_2 = 0$ is given by:

$$\frac{2n \pm \sqrt{4n^2 - 12(14m+n)}}{6} = \frac{n \pm \sqrt{n^2 - 3(14m+n)}}{3}$$

$$[n^2 - (42m + 3n)]^{1/2} = n\left(1 - \frac{42m + 3n}{n^2}\right)^{1/2}$$

If $(42m + 3n)/n^2$ is small (the case for n large) then

$$[n^2 - (42m + 3n)]^{1/2} \cong n\left(1 - \frac{1}{2}\cdot\frac{42m+3n}{n^2}\right) = n - \frac{42m+3n}{2n}$$

PROBLEM 7.34 (Continued)

Thus the roots of $df(m_2)/dm_2 = 0$ occur approximately at

$$\frac{n \pm \left[n - \frac{42m+3n}{2n}\right]}{3} = \begin{cases} 1/2 + 7m/n \\ 2n/3 - \left(\frac{1}{2} + \frac{7m}{n}\right) \end{cases}$$

Hence the derivative and the effort behave in the following general fashion.

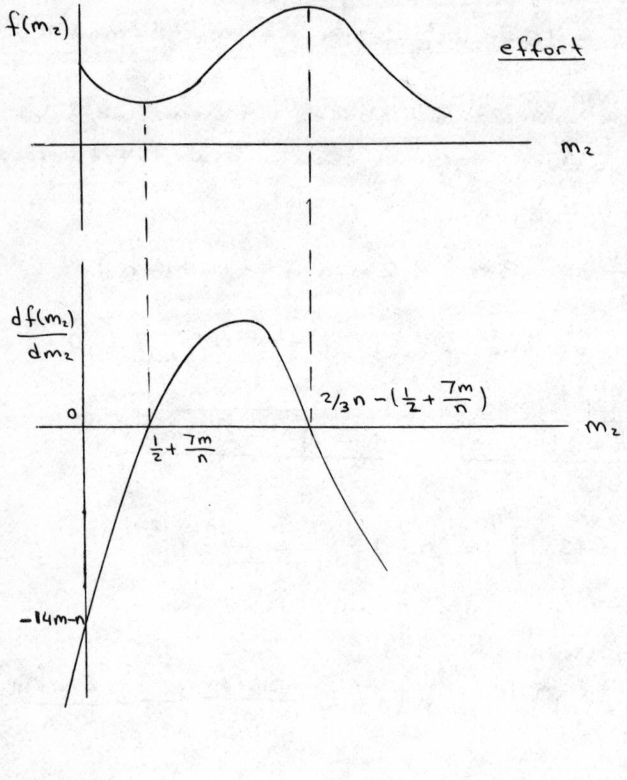

PROBLEM 7.34 (Continued)

From the graphs we see that the effort is minimal for small values of m_2 so that most of the constraints are treated in the master problem and only few of them are treated in the subproblem.

If $m > \frac{2}{3}n$, the effort is a maximum at approximately $m_2 = \frac{2}{3}n$. After that the effort is reduced for large values of m_2. If $m > \frac{2}{3}n$, one must look into the possibility of $m_2 = m$, i.e., all the constraints are treated in the subproblem, i.e., no decomposition.

To summarize, for small values of m/n, the optimal strategy is to place most of the constraints in the master problem with few of the constraints in the subproblem. If m is close to n, then we place all the constraints in the subproblem ($m = m_2$); thus use no decomposition.

PROBLEM 7.35

Now suppose that any subproblem could be solved by approximately 0.05 of the normal effort due to the special structure of the constraints.

PROBLEM 7.35 (Continued)

Total effort per iteration:

Master Step: Approximately $3m_1^2$ multiplications and $3m_1^2$ additions.

Subproblem Step: Approximately $0.05\, m_1(n-m_2) + 0.075\, m_2(m_2+1)(n-m_2+1)$ multiplications and the same number of additions.

Total effort per decomposition iteration:

$$f(m_1, m_2) = 6m_1^2 + 0.1\,(n-m_2) + 0.05\, m_2(m_2+1)(n-m_2+1)$$

To minimize the total effort let $m_1 = m - m_2$ and solve the following problem:

$$\min_{0 \le m_2 \le m} \quad 6(m-m_2)^2 + 0.1(m-m_2)(n-m_2) + 0.05\, m_2(m_2+1)(n-m_2+1)$$

Simplifying we get:

$$\min_{0 \le m_2 \le m} \quad -0.05\, m_2^3 + m_2^2\,(6.1 + 0.05n) + m_2(-12.1m - 0.05n + 0.05) + (6m^2 + 0.1\,mn)$$

Take the derivative and ignore the dominating terms for the purpose of simplification;

$$\frac{df(m_2)}{dm_2} = -0.15\, m_2^2 + [12.2 + 0.1n]\, m_2 + (-1.21m - 0.05n)$$

The roots of the equation $df(m_2)/dm_2 = 0$ occur at

$$\frac{(12.2 + 0.1n) \pm \sqrt{(12.2 + 0.1n)^2 - 0.6\,(12.1\,m + 0.05\,n)}}{0.3}$$

PROBLEM 7.35 (Continued)

The least effort lies at

$$m_2 \cong \frac{(12.2+0.1n) - \sqrt{(12.2+0.1n)^2 - 0.6(12.1m+0.05n)}}{0.3}$$

Trying various values of m and n (or ratios of m/n provided certain approximations could be made) the reader could verify that m_2 is much larger in this case than that of the value obtained in problem 7.34. If m and n are close, it could be verified that the best strategy is to let $m_2 = m$, i.e., no decomposition where the problem is solved at once.

PROBLEM 8.1

In this problem and throughout this chapter the number in the brackets in a cell corresponds to a $z_{ij} - c_{ij}$ of that variable. The cost of the variables are displayed inside of the nested squares in the upper left corner of the cells. The second number in a basic cell corresponds to the value of that basic variable. The illustrative transportation tableau is given below:

				a_i	u_i
	c_{11} x_{11}	c_{12} x_{12}	$\langle z_{13}-c_{13}\rangle$	a_1	u_1
	$\langle z_{21}-c_{21}\rangle$	c_{22} x_{22}	$\langle z_{23}-c_{23}\rangle$	a_2	u_2
	$\langle z_{31}-c_{31}\rangle$	c_{32} x_{32}	c_{33} x_{33}	a_3	u_3
b_j	b_1	b_2	b_3		
v_j	v_1	v_2	v_3		

Returning back to the first problem:

				a_i	u_i
	[3] 1	[4] 1	[1] ⟨6⟩	2	7
	[7] ⟨-6⟩	[2] 2	[5] 3	5	5
b_j	1	3	3		
v_j	-4	-3	0		

				u_i
	1	⟨-6⟩	1	1
	⟨0⟩	3	2	5
v_j	2	-3	0	

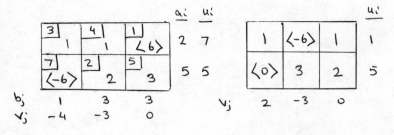

PROBLEM 8.1 (Continued)

The last tableau is the optimal tableau for the transportation problem since $z_{ij} - c_{ij} \leq 0$ for the nonbasic variables.

$Z = 20$

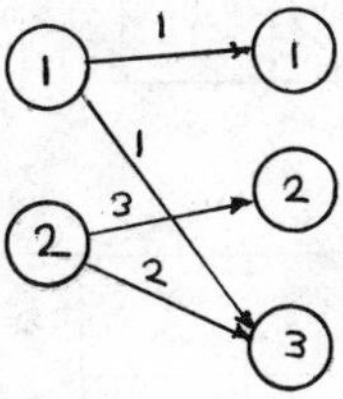

PROBLEM 8.2

	A-St.	Fine Pl.	Goodw.	S.S.	Slack		u_i
IE	[13] 1	[35] 1	[42] 1	[9] 1	[0] ⟨-21⟩	4	-21
Ce.	[6] ⟨28⟩	[61] ⟨5⟩	[18] ⟨45⟩	[30] 0	[0] 1	1	0
Wa.	[15] ⟨19⟩	[10] ⟨46⟩	[5] ⟨58⟩	[9] ⟨21⟩	[0] 2	2	0
	1	1	1	1	3		
v_j	34	56	63	30	0		

						u_i
	1	1	1	1	⟨37⟩	37
					1	0
			0		2	0
v_j	-24	-2	5	-28	0	

Since we found $z_{15} - c_{15} = 37 > 0$ we can stop further calculations and form a cycle around $x_{15}, x_{35}, x_{33}, x_{13}$.

PROBLEM 8.2 (Continued)

					u_i
1	1	<->	1	1	0
<7>	<->	<->	<->	1	0
<->	<25>	1	<0>	1	0
v_j: 13	35	5	9	0	

					u_i
1			1	2	0
<7>				1	0
	1	1		0	0
13	10	5	9	0	

					u_i
<-7>	<-25>	<-37>	1	3	0
1	<-51>	<-13>	<-21>	0	0
<-9>	1	1	<0>	0	0
v_j: 6	10	5	9	0	

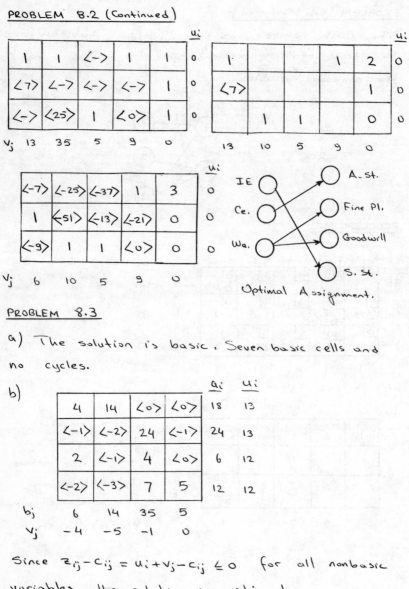

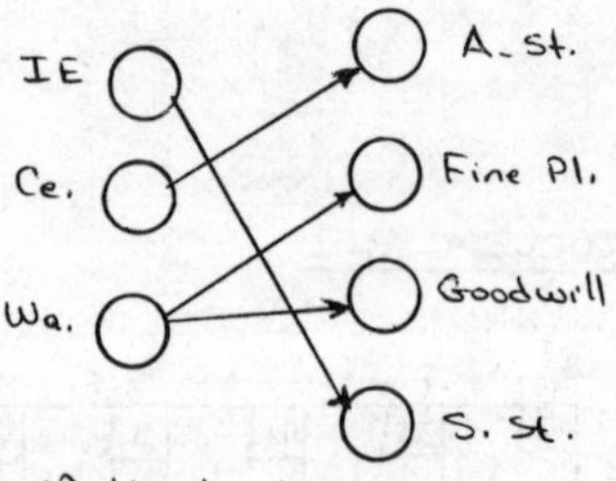

Optimal Assignment.

PROBLEM 8.3

a) The solution is basic. Seven basic cells and no cycles.

b)

				a_i	u_i
4	14	<0>	<0>	18	13
<-1>	<-2>	24	<-1>	24	13
2	<-1>	4	<0>	6	12
<-2>	<-3>	7	5	12	12
b_j: 6	14	35	5		
v_j: -4	-5	-1	0		

Since $z_{ij} - c_{ij} = u_i + v_j - c_{ij} \leq 0$ for all nonbasic variables, the solution is optimal.

PROBLEM 8.3 (Continued)

c) LP problem:

$$\min \; 9x_{11} + 8x_{12} + 12x_{13} + 13x_{14} + 10x_{21} + 10x_{22} + 12x_{23} + 14x_{24}$$
$$+ 8x_{31} + 9x_{32} + 11x_{33} + 12x_{34} + 10x_{41} + 10x_{42} + 11x_{41} + 12x_{44}$$

S.T.

$$x_{11} + x_{12} + x_{13} + x_{14} = 18$$
$$x_{21} + x_{22} + x_{23} + x_{24} = 24$$
$$x_{31} + x_{32} + x_{33} + x_{34} = 6$$
$$x_{41} + x_{42} + x_{43} + x_{44} = 12$$
$$x_{11} + x_{21} + x_{31} + x_{41} = 6$$
$$x_{12} + x_{22} + x_{32} + x_{42} = 14$$
$$x_{13} + x_{23} + x_{33} + x_{43} = 35$$
$$x_{14} + x_{24} + x_{34} + x_{44} = 5$$
$$x_{ij} \geq 0 \quad , \quad i, j = 1, 2, 3, 4.$$

Dual:

$$\text{Max } 18u_1 + 24u_2 + 6u_3 + 12u_4 + 6v_1 + 14v_2 + 35v_3 + 5v_4$$

S.T.

$$u_1 + v_1 \le 9$$
$$u_1 + v_2 \le 8$$
$$u_1 + v_3 \le 12$$
$$u_1 + v_4 \le 13$$
$$u_2 + v_1 \le 10$$
$$u_2 + v_2 \le 10$$
$$u_2 + v_3 \le 12$$
$$u_2 \quad v_4 \le 14$$
$$u_3 + v_1 \le 8$$
$$u_3 + v_2 \le 9$$
$$u_3 + v_3 \le 11$$
$$u_3 + v_4 \le 12$$
$$u_4 + v_1 \le 10$$
$$u_4 + v_2 \le 10$$
$$u_4 + v_3 \le 11$$
$$u_4 + v_4 \le 12$$

PROBLEM 8.3 (Continued)

d) Optimal dual solution:

$u_1 = 13$, $u_2 = 13$, $u_3 = 12$, $u_4 = 12$

$v_1 = -4$, $v_2 = -5$, $v_3 = -1$, $v_4 = 0$

e)

	Z	X_{11}	X_{12}	X_{13}	X_{14}	X_{21}	X_{22}	X_{23}	X_{24}	X_{31}	X_{32}	X_{33}	X_{34}	X_{41}	X_{42}	X_{43}	X_{44}	RHS
Z	1	0	0	0	0	-1	-2	0	-1	0	-1	0	0	-2	-2	0	0	633
X_{11}	0	1		1	1		-1				-1				-1			4
X_{12}	0		1				1				1				1			14
X_{23}	0					1	1	1	1									24
X_{31}	0			-1	-1	1	1			1	1			1	1			2
X_{33}	0			1	1	-1	-1					1	1	-1	-1			4
X_{43}	0				-1				-1				-1	1	1	1		7
X_{44}	0				1				1				1				1	5

f) c_{43} changes from 11 to 16.

				u_i
[9] 4	[8] 14	[12] <0>	[13] <-5>	8
[10] <-1>	[10] <-2>	[12] 24	[14] <-6>	8
[8] 2	[9] <-2>	[11] 4	[12] <-5>	7
[10] <3>	[10] <2>	[16] 7	[12] 5	12
v_j: 1	0	4	0	

introduce x_{41}.

				u_i
4	14	<3>	<-2>	11
<-4>	<-5>	24	<-6>	8
<-3>	<-5>	6	<-5>	7
2	<-1>	5	5	12
v_j: -2	-3	4	0	

introduce x_{13}.

				u_i
<-3>	14	4	<-5>	8
<-4>	<-2>	24	<-6>	8
<-3>	<-2>	6	<-5>	7
6	<2>	1	5	12
v_j: -2	0	4	0	

Introduce x_{42}

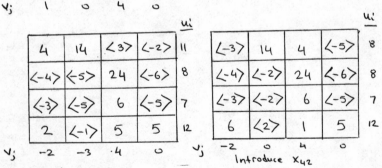

PROBLEM 8.3 (Continued)

				u_i
⟨-1⟩	13	5	⟨-3⟩	10
⟨-2⟩	⟨-2⟩	24	⟨-4⟩	10
⟨-1⟩	⟨-2⟩	6	⟨-3⟩	9
6	1	⟨-2⟩	5	12
v_j: -2	-2	2	0	

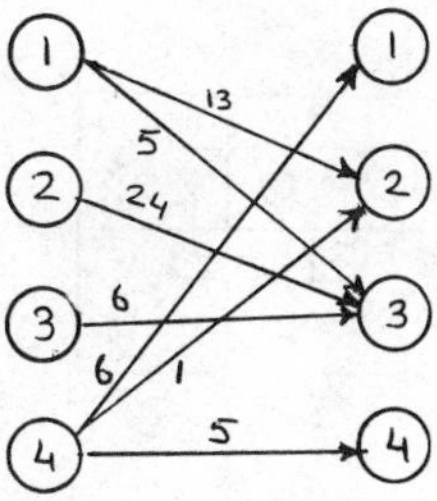

New optimal solution.

PROBLEM 8.4

a) The solution is not basic because the non-zero x_{ij}'s form a cycle.

b) Pick the smallest x_{ij} in the cycle (5 in this problem). Adjust the flows by adding and subtracting the smallest x_{ij} around the cycle.

20			15
	10	17	15
		23	

This tableau depicts a basic feasible solution.

Cost in (a) = 593

Cost in (b) = 593

PROBLEM 8.5

a)

			a_i
1	0		1
	1	1	2
b_j: 1	1	1	

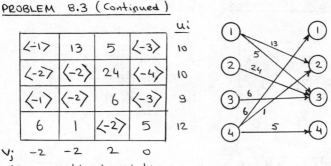

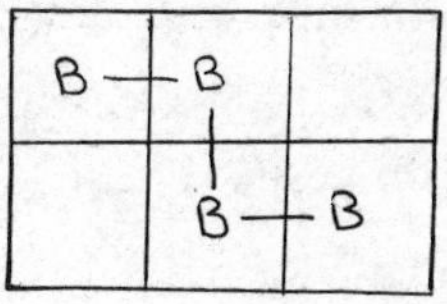

PROBLEM 8.5 (Continued)

b)

				u_i
	[2] 1	[5] 0	[1] ⟨5⟩	6
	[1] ⟨−1⟩	[3] 1	[4] 1	4
v_j	−4	−1	0	

				u_i
	1	⟨−5⟩	0	1
	⟨4⟩	1	1	4
v_j	1	−1	0	

				u_i
	0	⟨−1⟩	1	1
	1	1	⟨−4⟩	0
v_j	1	3	0	

Optimal

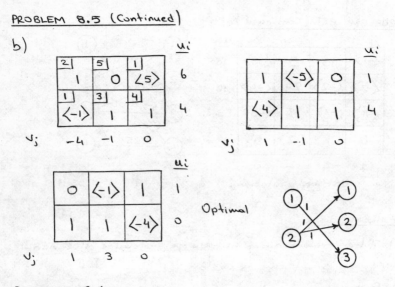

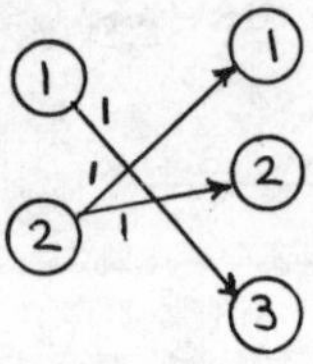

PROBLEM 8.6

a) Let the vector x represent an optimal solution of the transportation problem with cost coefficients c_{ij}. Then there exist $u_1, u_2, \ldots, u_m$ and $v_1, v_2, \ldots, v_m$ such that:

$$u_i + v_j - c_{ij} \leq 0 \quad \text{for each } i, j$$

$$u_i + v_j - c_{ij} = 0 \quad \text{for basic } x_{ij}.$$

Now, suppose that c_{ij} is replaced by $c_{ij}+10$ for every i, j. Construct the dual solution u_i+10, v_j. Then

$$(u_i+10) + v_j - (c_{ij}+10) = u_i + v_j - c_{ij} \leq 0$$

for all i and j. For basic x_{ij}

$$(u_i+10) + v_j - (c_{ij}+10) = u_i + v_j - c_{ij} = 0 .$$

Therefore the original solution is still optimal.

PROBLEM 8.6 (Continued)

b) Suppose that c_{ij} is replaced by $10c_{ij}$ for each i, j. Construct the dual solution $10u_i$ and $10v_j$. Then

$$10u_i + 10v_j - (10c_{ij}) = 10(u_i + v_j - c_{ij}) \leq 0.$$

Thus, the same solution is optimal if each c_{ij} is replaced by $10c_{ij}$.

c) In the case of adding k to each c_{ij} we will have

$$(u_i + k) + v_j - (c_{ij} + k) = u_i + v_j - c_{ij} \leq 0,$$

which implies that the original solution is still optimal.

In the case of multiplying c_{ij} by a constant k, if $k > 0$ we will have

$$(ku_i) + (kv_i) - (kc_{ij}) = k(u_i + v_j - c_{ij}) \leq 0$$

for the dual solution ku_i and kv_i.

If $k < 0$ then the optimal solution will change.

d) We reached the conclusion that if a constant k is added to c_{ij}'s of a transportation problem the solution will not be altered. If a positive constant is multiplied by each c_{ij} the optimal will still be the same. If a negative constant is multiplied by each c_{ij} the optimal solution will change.

PROBLEM 8.7

a) The given solution corresponds to a basic solution. From the complementary slackness

x_{11} basic $\Rightarrow u_1 + v_1 = 4$

x_{12} basic $\Rightarrow u_1 + v_2 = 1$

x_{21} basic $\Rightarrow u_2 + v_1 = 2$

x_{23} basic $\Rightarrow u_2 + v_3 = 1$

Let $v_3 = 0$, then we can obtain the following solution:

$u_2 = 1$, $v_1 = 2$, $u_1 = 2$, $v_2 = -1$

and $u_1 + v_3 - c_{13} = 2 + 0 - 3 = -1 < 0$

$u_2 + v_2 - c_{22} = 1 - 1 - 5 = -5 < 0$

Thus the solution is optimal.

b) u_i: the rate of change of the optimal objective function as a function of the supply a_i.

v_j: the rate of change of the optimal objective value as a function of the demand b_j.

PROBLEM 8.8

a)

					a_i	u_i
	5	⟨7⟩	⟨5⟩	⟨3⟩	5	3
	5	10	10	⟨-4⟩	25	1
	⟨1⟩	⟨6⟩	10	15	25	1
b_j	10	10	20	15		
v_j	3	6	1	0		

PROBLEM 8.8 (Continued)

b) Optimal solution:

				u_i
⟨-5⟩	⟨-3⟩	5	⟨-1⟩	-1
10	⟨-5⟩	15	⟨-3⟩	2
0	10	⟨-1⟩	15	1
2	0	0	0	(v_j)

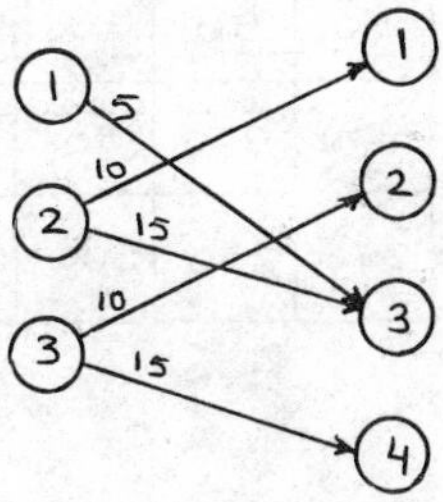

c) c_{11} changes to -4.

$$u_1 + v_1 - c'_{11} = -5 + 6 - (-4) = 5$$

X_{11} enters.

				u_i
5	⟨-8⟩	⟨-5⟩	⟨-6⟩	-6
5	⟨-5⟩	20	⟨-3⟩	2
0	10	⟨-1⟩	15	1
2	0	0	0	(v_j)

New optimal:

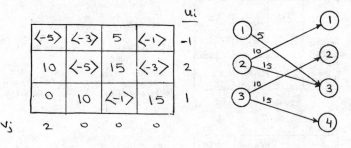

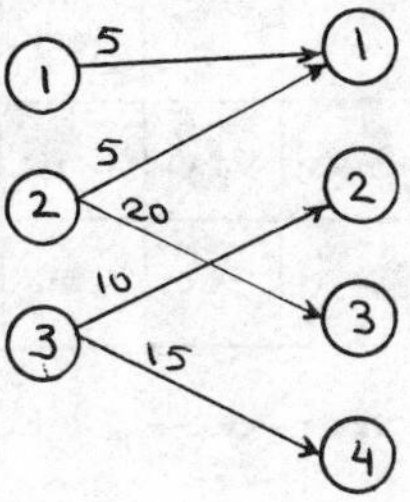

PROBLEM 8.9

$$X_{ij} = \frac{a_i b_j}{d} \quad \text{where} \quad d = \sum_i a_i = \sum_j b_j$$

$$X_{11} = \frac{50}{55}, \quad X_{12} = \frac{50}{55}, \quad X_{13} = \frac{100}{55}, \quad X_{14} = \frac{75}{55}$$

$$X_{21} = \frac{250}{55}, \quad X_{22} = \frac{250}{55}, \quad X_{23} = \frac{500}{55}, \quad X_{24} = \frac{375}{55}$$

$$X_{31} = \frac{250}{55}, \quad X_{32} = \frac{250}{55}, \quad X_{33} = \frac{500}{55}, \quad X_{34} = \frac{375}{55}$$

PROBLEM 8.9 (Continued)

$\frac{1}{55} \times$

50 $-\Delta$	50	100	75 $+\Delta$
250 $+\Delta$	250	500	375 $-\Delta$
250	250	500	375

The minimum of x_{ij}'s is 50/55. Hence construct a circuit with $\Delta = 50/55$ to eliminate the smallest x_{ij}.

$\frac{1}{55} \times$

	50 $-\Delta$	100	125 $+\Delta$
300	250	500 $+\Delta$	325 $-\Delta$
250	250 $+\Delta$	500 $-\Delta$	375

The minimum is 50/55. Set $\Delta = 50/55$. Form a cycle to eliminate that minimum x_{ij}.

$\frac{1}{55} \times$

		100	175
300	250	550	275
250	300	450	375

minimum is 100/55

This procedure continues until there exists six nonzero variables in the transportation tableau and they contain no cycles. Following is the end of these elimination steps:

			5	5
10	10	5		25
		15	10	25
10	10	20	15	

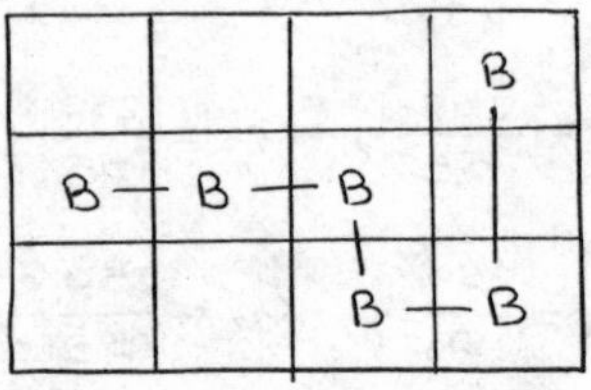

PROBLEM 8.10

Degeneracy (and cycling) can occur in a transportation problem. This happens if a subset of supplies equals a subset of the demands. This is the necessary condition for degeneracy in a transportation problem. This leads, of course, to a degenerate basis. Hence if no such proper subset exists, then the degeneracy (and cycling) will never occur.

PROBLEM 8.11

Use dual simplex algorithm directly on the transportation tableau. We will have a set of u_i and v_j's such that $z_{ij} - c_{ij} \leq 0$, for all i, j, and $z_{ij} - c_{ij} = 0$ for the basic cells.

At every iteration dual simplex method will find a basis (not necessarily feasible) among the cells with $z_{ij} - c_{ij} = 0$. If this basis is primal feasible, then the solution is optimal. Otherwise we proceed with the dual simplex method.

After updating the u_i and v_j's one can realize that every row and every column of the transportation tableau stays lexicographically negative in terms of $z_{ij} - c_{ij}$'s.

PROBLEM 8.11 (Continued)

At the same time the objective value is increased. Since every transportation problem has a finite optimal solution, this increase can not go forever. Objective continiously increases hence we do not repeat the same basis again. Since there is a finite number of basis in a transportation problem, The algorithm will stop at an optimal solution in finite number of iterations.

PROBLEM 8.12

Suppose that the basis structure is not connected. So it has more than one tree.

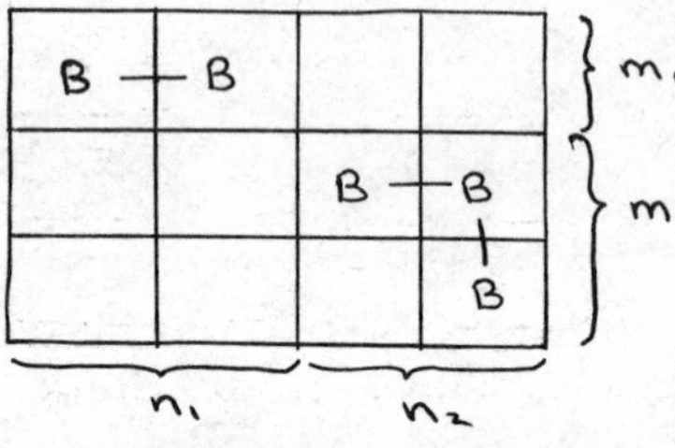

Without loss of generality suppose that the basis structure consists of the two trees T_1 and T_2. Note that T_1 spans m_1 rows while T_2 spans the remaining $m_2 = m - m_1$ rows. Similarly, T_1 spans n_1 columns, whereas, T_2 spans the remaining $n_2 = n - n_1$ columns (otherwise the two trees would be connected).

PROBLEM 8.12 (Continued)

Since a tree is a basis (see section 8.2), then T_1 has m_1+n_1-1 entries and T_2 has m_2+n_2-1 entries. Thus the total number of basic entries is

$$(m_1+n_1-1)+(m_2+n_2-1) = (m_1+m_2)+(n_1+n_2)-2$$
$$= m+n-2$$

a contradiction since the total number of basic cells is $m+n-1$.

PROBLEM 8.13

Initial tableau:

				a_i	u_i
[2] 2	[3] $\langle -3 \rangle$	[1] $\langle 0 \rangle$	[0] $\langle -8 \rangle$	2	-8
[4] 3	[2] 3	[5] $\langle -2 \rangle$	[0] $\langle -6 \rangle$	6	-6
[1] $\langle 0 \rangle$	[8] 0	[9] 2	[0] 4	6	0
b_j: 5	3	2	4		
v_j: 10	8	9	0		

Second Tableau

				u_i
2	$\langle -3 \rangle$	$\langle 9 \rangle$	$\langle 1 \rangle$	1
3	3	$\langle 7 \rangle$	$\langle 3 \rangle$	3
0	$\langle -9 \rangle$	2	4	0
v_j: 1	-1	9	0	

Third tableau

				u_i
0	$\langle -3 \rangle$	2	$\langle 1 \rangle$	1
3	3	$\langle -2 \rangle$	$\langle 3 \rangle$	3
2	$\langle -9 \rangle$	$\langle -9 \rangle$	4	0
v_j: 1	-1	0	0	

Fourth Tableau

				u_i
0	$\langle 0 \rangle$	2	$\langle 1 \rangle$	1
$\langle -3 \rangle$	3	$\langle -5 \rangle$	3	0
5	$\langle -6 \rangle$	$\langle -9 \rangle$	1	0
v_j: 1	2	0	0	

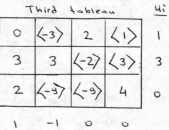

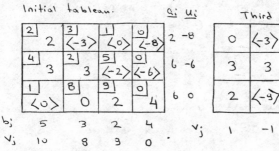

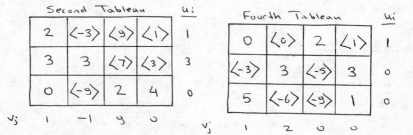

PROBLEM 8.13 (Continued)

Fifth (Optimal) Tableau

				u_i
⟨−1⟩	⟨−1⟩	2	0	0
⟨−3⟩	3	⟨−4⟩	3	0
5	⟨−6⟩	⟨−8⟩	1	0
v_j: 1	2	1	0	

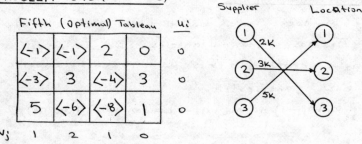

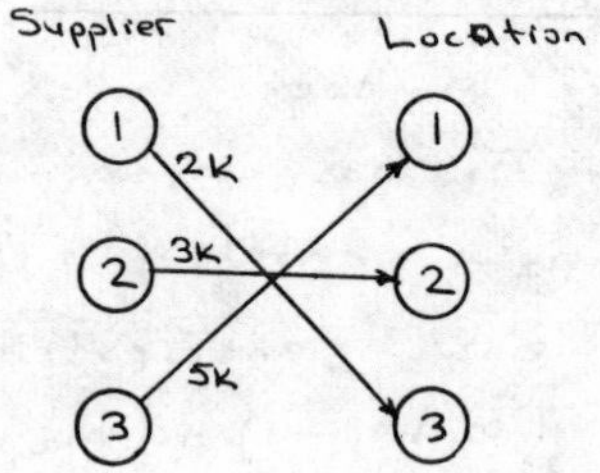

PROBLEM 8.14

Let (u, v) be the dual vector where the cost of the artificial variable is 0. If the cost of the artificial variable is changed to θ, then $\bar{u}_i = u_i - \theta$ and $\bar{v}_i = v_i + \theta$. Thus the new values of $z_{ij} - c_{ij}$ is given by:

$$\bar{u}_i + \bar{v}_j - c_{ij} = (u_i - \theta) + (v_j + \theta) - c_{ij} = u_i + v_j - c_{ij}$$

which are the old values of $z_{ij} - c_{ij}$'s. Thus the value of θ does not effect the entry criterion and could be taken as zero for simplicity.

PROBLEM 8.15

As shown in section 8.6 a necessary condition for degeneracy is that the total supply equals the total demand over a proper subset of the rows and a proper subset of the columns. If no such proper subset exists then there could be no degeneracy, and we may choose $\epsilon = 0$.

PROBLEM 8.15 (Continued)

Suppose that I and J are proper subsets of the rows and columns respectively, such that:

$$\sum_{i \in I} a_i = \sum_{j \in J} b_j$$

Let ϵ be any positive number. Then

$\sum_{i \in I} \hat{a}_i \neq \sum_{j \in J} \hat{b}_j$ because $\sum_{i \in I} \hat{a}_i = \sum_{i \in I} a_i + \nu_1 \epsilon$

whereas $\sum_{j \in J} \hat{b}_j = \sum_{j \in J} b_j + \nu_2 \epsilon$, and $\nu_1 \neq \nu_2$,

where ν_1 is the number of elements in I ($< m$) and ν_2 is zero if $n \notin J$ and $\nu_2 = m$ if $n \in J$.

Thus for any positive ϵ,

$$\sum_{i \in I} \hat{a}_i \neq \sum_{j \in J} \hat{b}_j$$

for any proper subsets I and J, where

$$\sum_i a_i \doteq \sum_j b_j .$$

Now, if $\sum_{i \in I} a_i \neq \sum_{j \in J} b_j$ we must be sure that the modifications of the supply and demand will not cause $\sum_i \hat{a}_i$ to be equal to $\sum_j \hat{b}_j$.

Letting $\delta > 0$ be the smallest absolute difference $\sum_i a_i$ and $\sum_j b_j$ over all proper subsets of the rows and columns, where equality does not hold, by choosing $0 < \epsilon < \delta/m$ we can guarantee that $\sum_i \hat{a}_i \neq \sum_j \hat{b}_j$ will be guaranteed and hence the degeneracy will be prevented.

PROBLEM 8.16

a) When cost is proportional to distance: Every entry in the transportation tableau is multiplied by $k = 0.01$ for simplicity. The supply and demand figures are to be read by the multiplication of 100,000 as well as the values of the basic variables.

				Dummy	a_i	u_i
[10] 10	[80] 10	[18] <82>	[20] <84>	[0] <73>	20	73
[4] <-63>	[7] 5	[9] 8	[14] <11>	[0] <0>	13	0
[8] <-63>	[12] <7>	[9] 4	[11] 7	[0] 5	16	0
b_j: 10	15	12	7	5		
v_j: -63	7	9	11	0		

Initial Tableau

					u_i
10	<-59>	5	<0>	5	9
<-8>	13	<0>	<-3>	<-14>	-5
<-7>	2	7	7	<-9>	0
v_j: 1	12	9	11	-9	

Optimal Tableau.

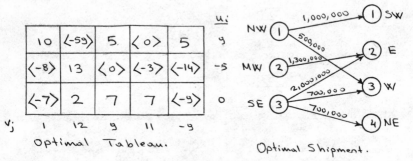

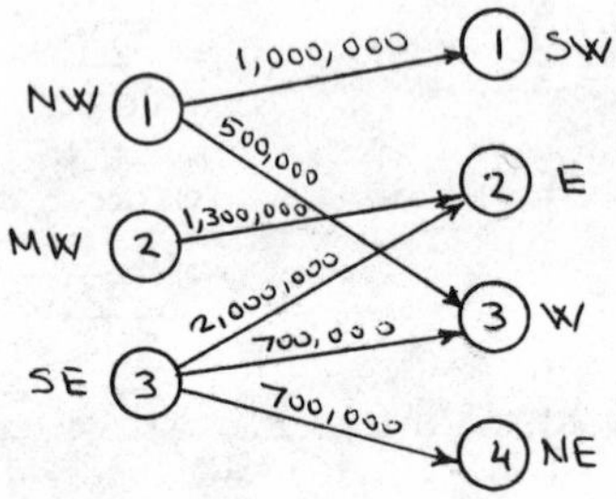

Optimal Shipment.

b) Lets start with the basic solution which was optimal for proportional cost in (a).

					u_i
[100] 10	[6400] <->	[324] 5	[400] <->	[0] 5	243
[16] <->	[49] 13	[81] <->	[196] <->	[0] <->	-95
[64] <->	[144] 2	[81] 7	[121] 7	[0] <->	0
v_j: -143	144	81	121	-243	

Since all $z_{ij} - c_{ij} \leq 0$ for the nonbasic variables, the optimal is the same as in (a).

PROBLEM 8.17

Let's use the least cost method to find a starting basic feasible solution.

			u_i
[2] $\langle -2 \rangle$	[1] 0	[0] 1	0
[1] 1	[3] $\langle -1 \rangle$	[4] $\langle -4 \rangle$	1
[1] 0	[2] 1	[6] $\langle -5 \rangle$	1
v_j: 0	1	0	

The initial tableau is the optimal tableau, as well, since all $z_{ij} - c_{ij} \le 0$ for the nonbasic cells.

PROBLEM 8.18

The algorithm will exactly be the same as the transportation algorithm except:

1- At the starting solution if we assign at cell (i,j), then $x_{ij} = \min(\hat{a}_i, \hat{b}_j / p_{ij})$, where $\hat{a}_i$ and $\hat{b}_j$ are the adjusted values of a_i and b_j.

2- $z_{ij} - c_{ij} = u_i + p_{ij} v_j - c_{ij}$. This will be used both for calculating the dual variables and choosing the entering variable.

3- The value of the entering variable x_{ij} is the maximum value such that neither the supply nor the demand constraints are violated.

PROBLEM 8.19

Let x_{ij} be the number of units of the ith product on the jth machine.

PROBLEM 8.19 (Continued)

Constraints:

$$x_{11} + x_{12} + x_{13} + x_{14} = 4000$$

$$x_{21} + x_{22} + x_{23} + x_{24} = 5000$$

$$x_{31} + x_{32} + x_{33} + x_{34} = 3000$$

$$.3x_{11} + .2x_{21} + .8x_{31} \leq 1500$$

$$.25x_{12} + .3x_{22} + .6x_{32} \leq 1200$$

$$.2x_{13} + .2x_{23} + .6x_{33} \leq 1500$$

$$.2x_{14} + .25x_{24} + .5x_{34} \leq 2000$$

$x_{ij} \geq 0 \quad \forall\ i,j.$

				a_i	u_i
4 | .3 4000	4 | .25 ⟨+⟩	5 | .2 ⟨+⟩	7 | .2 ⟨−⟩	4000	6.25
6 | .2 1500	7 | .3 3500	5 | .2 ⟨+⟩	6 | .25 ⟨+⟩	5000	7.5
12 | .8 ⟨−⟩	10 | .6 250	8 | .6 2500	11 | .5 250	3000	11
b_j: ≤ 1500	≤ 1200	≤ 1500	≤ 2000		
v_j: -7.5	$-5/3$	-5	0		

$u_i + p_{ij} v_j - c_{ij} = 0$ for basic variables.

$11 + 0.6\, v_3 = 8 \Rightarrow v_3 = -5$

$11 + 0.6\, v_2 = 10 \Rightarrow v_2 = -5/3$

$u_2 + 0.3(-5/3) = 7 \Rightarrow u_2 = 7.5$

$7.5 + 0.2\, v_1 = 6 \Rightarrow v_1 = -7.5$

$u_1 + (0.3)(-7.5) = 4 \Rightarrow u_1 = 6.25$

$z_{ij} - c_{ij} = u_i + p_{ij} v_j - c_{ij}.$

PROBLEM 8.19 (Continued)

$$z_{24} - c_{24} = 7.5 + 0 - 6 = 1.5 > 0$$

Introduce x_{24}. Let $x_{24} = \Theta$. Then

$$x_{22} \quad + \Theta \quad = 3500$$

$$x_{32} \quad + \quad x_{34} = 500$$

$$.3x_{22} + .6x_{32} \quad \leq 1200$$

$$.25\Theta + .5x_{34} \leq 2000$$

The maximum value of Θ satisfying these equations and inequalities is 3500. Thus x_{22} reaches zero and drops from the basis.

				u_i
4000	<->	<->	<->	4
1500	<->	<0>	3500	6
<->	250	2500	250	11
v_j: 0	$-5/3$	-5	0	

Since all $z_{ij} - c_{ij} \leq 0$ for the nonbasic cells we reached to an optimal solution.

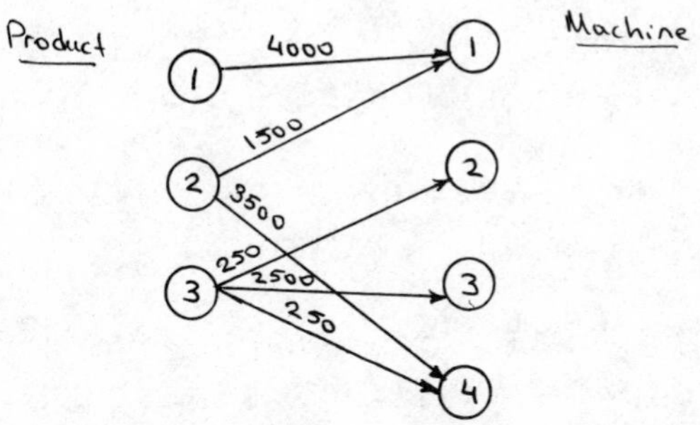

PROBLEM 8.20

The following procedure is suggested to find the unique cycle formed by the basic cells and the nonbasic cell (i,j):

Initialization

Let (i,j) be the entering cell and let (i,k) be a basic cell. If there is at least one more basic cell in column k then label (i,k) by (i,j), otherwise skip cell (i,k). After all the basic cells in row i have been examined go to the main step.

Main Step

1- Let cell (k,ℓ) be a labeled basic cell. If (k,r) is an unlabeled basic cell with at least one more basic cell in column r, then it receives the label (k,ℓ). Similarly, if (s,ℓ) is an unlabeled basic cell with at least one more basic cell in row s, then it receives the label (k,ℓ).

If any cell in column j is labeled go to step 2; otherwise repeat step 1.

2-a. Let $x=1$ and the cell (k,j) be the last labeled cell. Then (i,j), (u,v) is the part of the cycle identified so far, where $(u,v)=(k,j)$. The coefficient of a_{uv} in the representation of a_{ij} is x. Go to (b).

PROBLEM 8.20 (Continued)

b. Replace x by $-x$ and let cell (r, n) be the last cell identified in the cycle so far and let its label be (u, v). Then add (u, v) as the last cell in the cycle and let the coefficient of a_{uv} be x.

If $(u, v) = (i, j)$ then stop; the cycle is completed, otherwise repeat (b).

PROBLEM 8.21

Sensitivity on c_{ij}

a) x_{ij} is not basic: $z_{ij} - c_{ij}$ is replaced by $z_{ij} - c'_{ij} = u_i + v_j - c'_{ij}$ where c'_{ij} is the new cost.

b) x_{ij} is basic: Compute a new set of dual variables based on the new cost. If a non-basic variable is eligible to enter the basis we continue the transportation algorithm; otherwise we stop with the conclusion that the same solution is optimal.

a_i is increased:

Add a new column $n+1$ (dummy demand node $n+1$). Let cell $(i, n+1)$ be a basic with $x_{i,n+1} = \varepsilon$, the increase in the supply of the ith source. Let $v_{n+1} = -u_i$. Compute

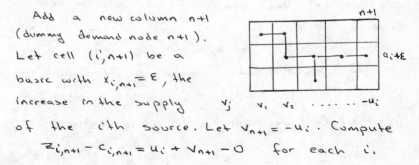

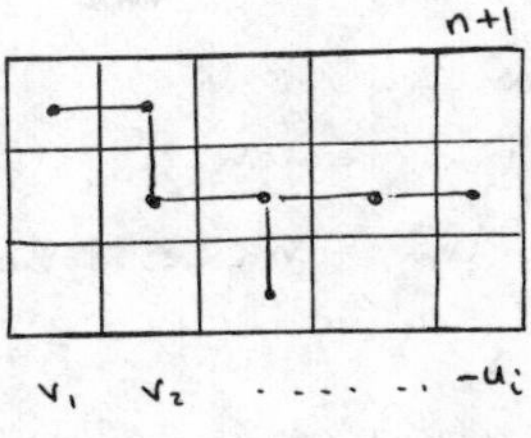

$$z_{i,n+1} - c_{i,n+1} = u_i + v_{n+1} - 0 \quad \text{for each } i.$$

PROBLEM 8.21 (Continued)

If $z_{i,n+1} - c_{i,n+1} \leq 0$ for each i stop, the solution is optimal, Otherwise continue with the transportation algorithm.

b_j is decreased:

In this case supply exceeds the demand. Introduce a dummy destination (column) n+1. Let (i, j) be any basic cell (in column j). Reduce x_{ij} by ϵ and let the basic variable $x_{i,n+1} = \epsilon$. Let $v_{n+1} = -u_i$ and continue with the transportation algorithm.

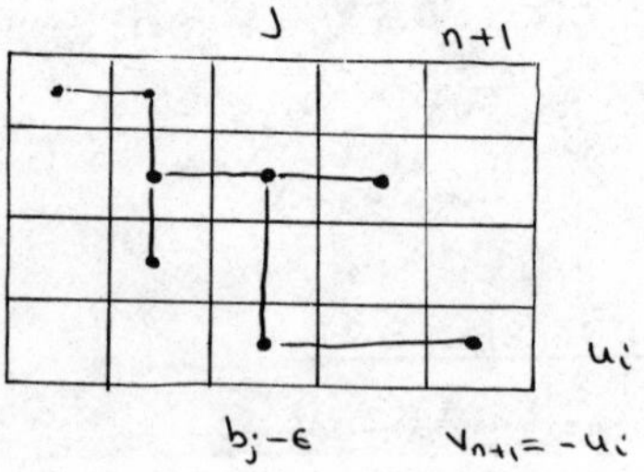

PROBLEM 8.22

Dual:

$$\text{Maximize} \quad \sum_{i=1}^{m} a_i u_i + \sum_{j=1}^{n} b_j v_j$$

$$\text{S.T.} \qquad u_i + v_j \leq c_{ij} \qquad \forall\, i, j.$$

We can get the feasible dual solution as follows:

For each i, let $u_i = \min_j c_{ij}$. After $u_1, u_2, \ldots, u_m$ have been computed, let $v_j = \min (c_{ij} - u_i)$ for each j. Obviously $u_i + v_j \leq c_{ij}$ and hence we have a feasible solution.

PROBLEM 8.22 (Continued)

Also note that for each row i there is at least one j such that $u_i + v_j - c_{ij} = 0$, and for each column j there is at least one row i such that $c_{ij} - u_i - v_j = 0$.

Application of Primal-Dual

Choose the dual variables $u_1, u_2, \ldots, u_m$ and $v_1, v_2, \ldots, v_m$ as described above. The restricted primal problem proceeds as follows: Find a feasible solution of the system:

$$\sum_{j \in J_i} x_{ij} = a_i \qquad i = 1, 2, \ldots, m$$

$$\sum_{i \in I_j} x_{ij} = b_j \qquad j = 1, 2, \ldots, n$$

$$J_i = \{ j : z_{ij} - c_{ij} = 0 \}$$

$$I_j = \{ i : z_{ij} - c_{ij} = 0 \}$$

Note that a feasible solution of the above problem (and hence an optimal solution of the overall problem) is obtained if $\sum_{j \in J_i} x_{ij} + \sum_{i \in I_j} x_{ij}$ is equal to $\sum_{i=1}^{m} a_i + \sum_{j=1}^{n} b_j$.

This could be verified by solving the following maximum flow problem (see chp. 11)

$$\max \; \sum_{j \in J_i} x_{ij} + \sum_{i \in I_j} x_{ij}$$

$$\text{s.t.} \; \sum_{j \in J_i} x_{ij} \le a_i$$

PROBLEM 8.22 (Continued)

$$\sum_{i \in I_j} x_{ij} \leq b_j$$

$$x_{ij} \geq 0 \quad \forall i, j.$$

This problem can be solved by finding the maximum flow from the source s to the sink t. Note that only arcs (i, j) with $z_{ij} - c_{ij} = 0$ are portreyed.

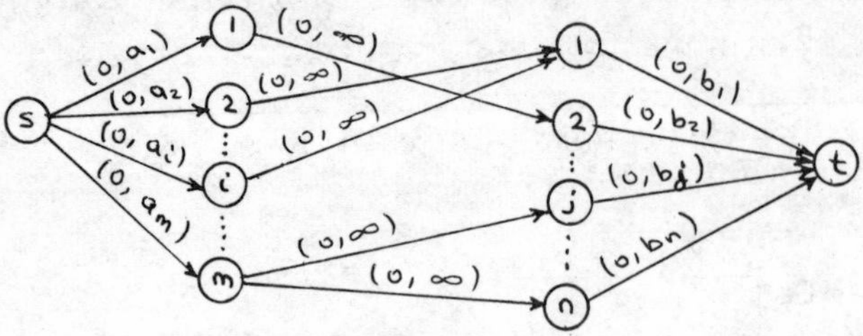

If at the termination flow from s to t is $\sum_{i=1}^{m} a_i + \sum_{j=1}^{n} b_j$, then we have an optimal solution of the overall problem. Otherwise let I be the set of labeled rows and J be the set of labeled columns (see max-flow algorithm in chp. 11). The dual variables are modified as follows:

$$u_i = \begin{cases} u_i & i \in I \\ u_i - \delta & i \notin I \end{cases}$$

$$v_j = \begin{cases} v_j & j \in J \\ v_j + \delta & j \notin J \end{cases}$$

PROBLEM 8.22 (Continued)

where $\delta = \underset{i \in I,\ j \notin J}{\text{minimum}} (c_{ij} - u_i - v_j)$

This provides a new set of dual variables which will admit at least one new arc without deleting any arcs which carried flow at the previous iteration.

Sensitivity analysis is used to determine if the flow will increase as a result.

PROBLEM 8.23

The assertion is false. Consider the given tableau with the basis $a_{11}, a_{13}, a_{22}, a_{23}$.

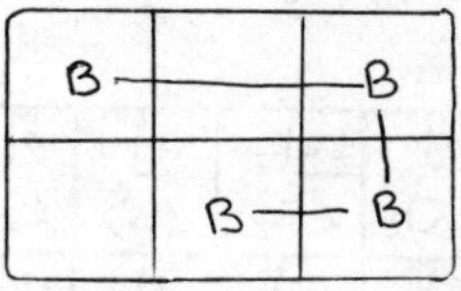

Through a sequence of elementary row operations the following original tableau

x_{11}	x_{12}	x_{13}	x_{21}	x_{22}	x_{23}	x_a
1	1	1	0	0	0	0
0	0	0	1	1	1	0
1	0	0	1	0	0	0
0	1	0	0	1	0	0
0	0	1	0	0	1	1

can be transformed to

	x_{11}	x_{12}	x_{13}	x_{21}	x_{22}	x_{23}	x_a
x_{11}	1	0	0	1	0	0	0
x_{22}	0	1	0	0	1	0	0
x_{13}	0	1	1	-1	0	0	0
x_{23}	0	-1	0	1	0	1	0
x_a	0	0	0	0	0	0	1

PROBLEM 8.23 (Continued)

Note that x_{13} is basic in row 3 whereas it originally had nonzero elements in rows 1 and 5.

PROBLEM 8.24

a-

$$\text{minimize} \sum_{i=1}^{6} \sum_{j=1}^{5} c_{ij} x_{ij}$$

$$\text{S.T.} \quad \sum_{j=1}^{5} x_{ij} \leq 1 \qquad i = 1, 2, \ldots, 6$$

$$\sum_{i=1}^{6} x_{ij} = 1 \qquad j = 1, 2, \ldots, 5$$

$$x_{ij} \geq 0 \qquad (x_{ij} \ 0 \text{ or } 1)$$

where c_{ij} is the cost of assigning job j to plant i.

b)

Plant \ Job	1	2	3	4	5	Dummy	u_i
1	50 / 0	66 / <5>	81 / <5>	40 / <11>	62 / 1	0 / <6>	6
2	55 / <->	70 / <->	78 / <0>	42 / 1	55 / <->	0 / <->	-3
3	42 / 1	X	72 / <6>	38 / <5>	58 / <->	0 / <->	-2
4	57 / <->	68 / <->	80 / 1	15 / 0	60 / <->	0 / 0	0
5	48 / <->	75 / <->	85 / <->	46 / <->	56 / 0	0 / 1	0
6	52 / <->	63 / 1	78 / 0	42 / <1>	65 / <->	0 / <->	-2
v_j	44	65	80	45	56	0	

This is the starting solution by Vogel's approximation method.

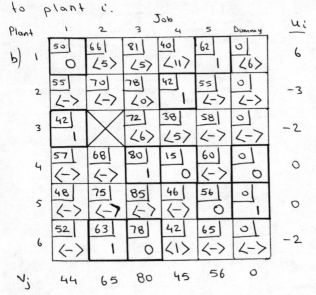

PROBLEM 8.24 (Continued)

After 9 iterations we obtain the following optimal assignment

						u_i
<->	<->	<->	1	<->	<->	-3
<->	<->	<->	0	1	<->	-1
0	<->	1	<->	<->	<->	-6
<->	<->	<->	<->	<->	1	0
1	<->	<->	<->	0	0	0
<->	1	<->	0	<->	<->	-1
v_j 48	64	78	43	56	0	

The optimal assignment is:

Jobs	Plants
1	5
2	6
3	3
4	1
5	2

Plant 4 is idle.

c) This is the optimal tableau of the assignment algorithm. As expected the optimal solution is the same as in part (b).

4	0	5	**0**	8	2
8	3	1	1	**0**	1
0	X	**0**	2	8	6
9	0	2	3	4	**0**
0	7	7	4	0	0
9	**0**	5	5	14	5

PROBLEM 8.24 (Continued)

d.) Utilizing the initial dual solution of part (c) we wish to find the maximal flow in the following network (use max-flow algorithm of Chp. 11).

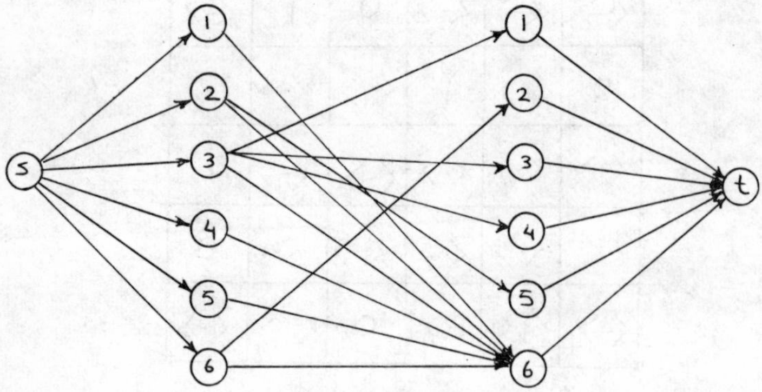

If the maximum flow is equal to 6 then we have an optimal solution. If not then the dual variables are modified according to Exercise 8.22, a new network is formulated admitting the arcs with $z_{ij} - c_{ij} = 0$, and a maximum flow problem is solved.

The reader should attempt to simplify the max-flow algorithm so that it would be executed directly on the transportation tableau.

PROBLEM 8.25

a)

				a_i	u_i
15	5	<-8>	<-12>	20	-7
<4>	30	0	<-6>	30	0
<10>	<8>	20	30	50	7
b_j: 15	35	20	30		
v_j: 11	10	5	0		

initial tableau.

x_{31} will enter.

$(z_{31} - c_{31} = 10 > 0)$

				u_i
<-2>	20	<-6>	<-4>	1
<0>	<-2>	20	10	6
15	15	<-6>	20	7
v_j: 1	2	-1	0	

Optimal tableau

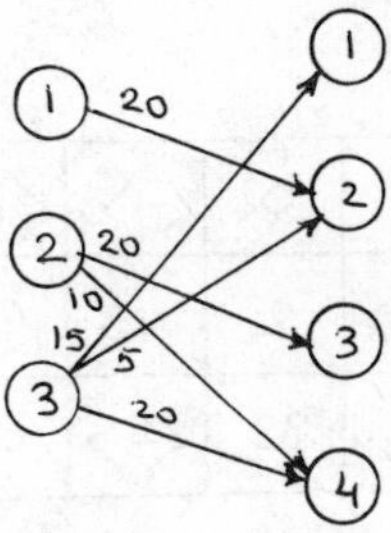

Optimal solution.

b)

				u_i
<-2>	20	<-5>	<-4>	1
<-1>	<-3>	20	10	5
15	15	<-5>	20	7
v_j: 1	2	0	0	

Same solution is optimal. It is unique!

c) If c_{12} is replaced by 5:

$$z_{12} - c_{12} = u_1 + v_2 - c_{12}$$

$$= 1 + 2 - 5 < 0$$

but $x_{12} > 0$, hence the complementary slackness is violated. The same solution is optimal with a new set of u_i and v_j.

PROBLEM 8.26

a)

				u_i
71	0	<->	<7>	34
<->	35	12	<->	13
<->	<54>	33	60	63
v_j: -20	22	8	0	

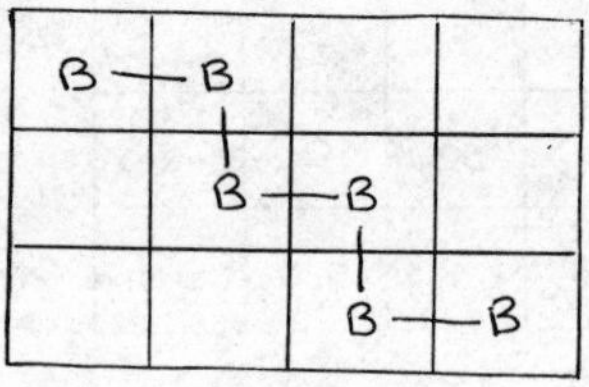

b)

				u_i
71	0	<->	<61>	88
<->	2	45	<->	67
<->	33	<->	60	63
v_j: -74	-32	-46	0	

				u_i
71	<->	<->	0	27
<->	2	45	<->	67
<->	33	<->	60	63
v_j: -13	-32	-46	0	

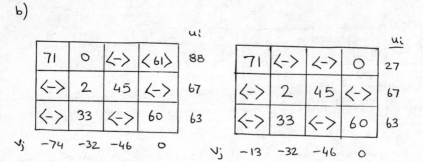

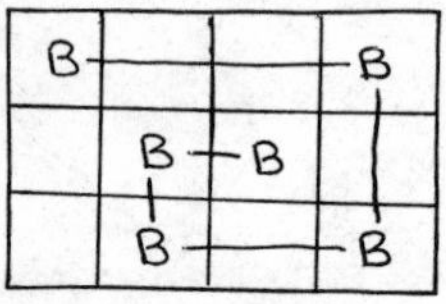

Optimal basis tree.

c) The simplex tableau associated with part (a):

	Z	X_{11}	X_{12}	X_{13}	X_{14}	X_{21}	X_{22}	X_{23}	X_{24}	X_{31}	X_{32}	X_{33}	X_{34}	
Z	1	0	0	-6	7	-89	0	0	-68	-56	54	0	0	8593
X_{11}	0	1	0	0	0	1	0	0	0	1	0	0	0	71
X_{12}	0	0	1	1	1	-1	0	0	0	-1	0	0	0	0
X_{22}	0	0	0	-1	-1	1	1	0	0	1	1	0	0	35
X_{23}	0	0	0	1	1	0	0	1	1	-1	-1	0	0	12
X_{33}	0	0	0	0	-1	0	0	0	-1	1	1	1	0	33
X_{34}	0	0	0	0	1	0	0	0	1	0	0	0	1	60

PROBLEM 8.27

Problem 8.1:

				Row Penalties	
	1		1	2	3
		3	2	3	3
Column Penalties	4	2	4		
		2	5		

Problem 8.8:

					a_i	Row Penalties		
			5		5	1		
	10		15		25	2	2	2
	0	10		15	25	0	1	1
b_j	10	10	20	15				
Column Penalties	1	1	3	1				
	1	6	0	4				

Problem 8.17:

				Row Penalties	
	0		1	1	1
	1			2	2
	0	1		1	1
Column Penalties	0	1	4		
	1	1			

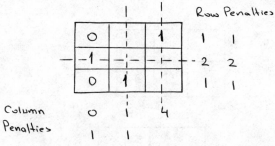

PROBLEM 8.28

After each iteration one allocation is made. After m+n-2 iterations are made there remains only one row and one column not deleted, and hence only one more allocation. Thus, the procedure stops in n+m-1 iterations. with exactly m+n-1 allocations. By construction $\sum_i x_{ij} = b_j$ and $\sum_j x_{ij} = a_i$. To show that the solution is basic it only remains that allocated cells contain no cycle. This would certainly be shown by noting that after each allocation is made either a row or a column is deleted.

PROBLEM 8.29

a) The procedure produces a basic feasible solution in a fashion similar to that of the Vogel's method as indicated in Exercise 8.28 above.

b) Problem 8.1

		2
1	3	3

Problem 8.8

		5	
10		15	
	10	0	15

PROBLEM 8.30

The dual simplex method could be applied directly on the transportation tableau provided that a dual basic feasible solution is at hand. In other words, if there is a set of u_i's and a set of v_j's such that $z_{ij} - c_{ij} \leq 0$ for all i and j and $z_{ij}-c_{ij}=0$ for basic cells.

To illustrate consider problem 8.25. Let the dual solution be $u_1=3$, $u_2=6$, $u_3=7$ $v_1=1$, $v_2=0$, $v_3=-1$, $v_4=0$. This solution is feasible and the $z_{ij}-c_{ij}=u_i+v_j-c_{ij}$ are shown in the tableau below:

0	0	-4	-2
0	-4	0	0
0	-2	-6	0

The dual simplex method finds a basis (not necessarily feasible) among the cells with $z_{ij}-c_{ij}=0$. If the basis is primal feasible we are through, otherwise we proceed with the dual simplex method. Consider the following infeasible basis:

PROBLEM 8.30 (Continued)

	1	2	3	4
1	−15	35		
2			20	10
3	30			20

Note that $x_{11} = -15 < 0$. So we identify the nonbasic variables in the row x_{11} with −1 coefficient. They are x_{22} and x_{32}. The minimum ratio test $\left\{\frac{-4}{-1}, \frac{-2}{-1}\right\}$ leads to x_{32} to enter the basis. This gives the following tableau:

$\langle -2\rangle$	20	$\langle -6\rangle$	$\langle -4\rangle$
$\langle 0\rangle$	$\langle -2\rangle$	20	10
15	15	$\langle -6\rangle$	20

The basis is feasible and hence optimal. It should be noted that it is an easy task to carry the dual simplex method on the transportation tableau once a basic feasible dual solution is at hand.

PROBLEM 8.31

Suppose that a starting basic feasible solution is already available. In other words,

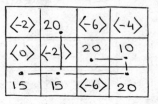

PROBLEM 8.31 (Continued)

suppose that we have a basis tree where $0 \leq x_{ij} \leq u_{ij}$. Furthermore, the nonbasic variables (cells) are either at their lower or upper bounds. The dual variables u_i and v_j are computed in exactly the same manner as before, utilizing the fact that $u_i + v_j - c_{ij} = 0$ for the basic cells. If the computed $z_{ij} - c_{ij}$'s for the nonbasic cells have

$$x_{ij} = u_{ij} \implies z_{ij} - c_{ij} \geq 0 \quad , \text{ and}$$

$$x_{ij} = 0 \implies z_{ij} - c_{ij} \leq 0$$

then the current basis is optimal.

We can introduce a nonbasic variable x_{ij} currently equal to u_{ij} with $z_{ij} - c_{ij} < 0$ or a nonbasic variable x_{ij} currently equal to zero with $z_{ij} - c_{ij} > 0$. These two cases are detailed below:

$x_{ij} = u_{ij}$ and $z_{ij} - c_{ij} < 0$

First identify the cycle formed by the cell (i,j) and the other basic cells. As x_{ij} is reduced, the values of the basic variables in the cycle must be modified. Let Δ_{ij} be the maximum decrease such that $x_{ij} = u_{ij} - \Delta_{ij} \geq 0$ and all the basic variables are between their lower and upper bounds.

PROBLEM 8.31 (Continued)

If a basic variable reaches its lower or upper bound first, then it leaves the basis and x_{ij} enters. Otherwise, if x_{ij} is reduced to zero, the basis remains the same except that the flows are modified. The process is then repeated.

$x_{ij} = 0$ and $z_{ij} - c_{ij} > 0$

Same as above except that x_{ij} is increased. Either a basic variable reaches its lower or upper bound, or else x_{ij} itself reaches its upper bound. In the former case the basis is modified by introducing x_{ij} and in the latter case the basis remains the same but the flows are modified. The process is repeated.

Finding a Starting Basic Feasible Solution

If a starting basic feasible solution is not available we can introduce artificial variables and then drive them out of the basis by phase I. This can be done by utilizing a dummy node and m+n artificial arcs as illustrated. The demand and supply at this (transshipment node is equal to:

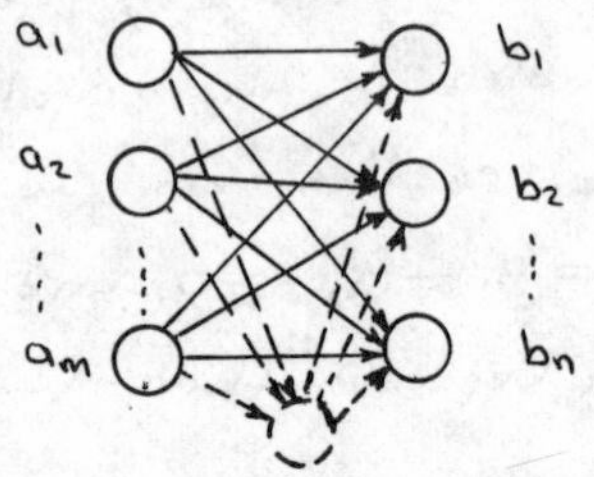

PROBLEM 8.31 (Continued)

$$\sum_{i=1}^{m} a_i = \sum_{j=1}^{n} b_j$$

The transportation tableau becomes:

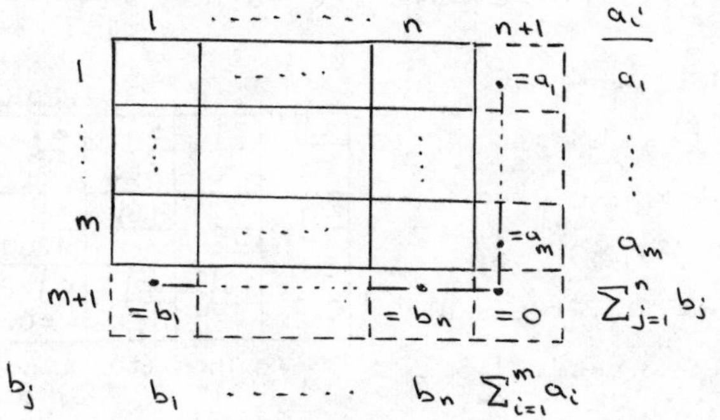

The basis is illustrated above. The cost of the cell $(m+1, n+1)$ is zero, the cost of the cell $(i, n+1)$ for $i = 1, 2, \ldots, m$ is 1 and the cost of the cell $(m+1, j)$ for $j = 1, 2, \ldots, n$ is 1. c_{ij} for each other cell is replaced by 0 during phase I.

PROBLEM 8.32

$$\min\ 2x_{11} + 3x_{12} + 5x_{13} + 2.5x_{21} + 4x_{22} + 4.8x_{23} + 3x_{31} + 3.6x_{32} + 3.2x_{33}$$

S.T.

$$x_{31} + x_{32} + x_{33} \le 500$$

$$x_{11} + x_{21} + x_{31} = 500$$

$$x_{12} + x_{22} + x_{32} = 700$$

$$x_{13} + x_{23} + x_{33} = 600$$

$$x_{ij} \le 200, \quad i = 2, 3, \quad j = 1, 2, 3$$

$$x_{ij} \ge 0 \quad i = 1, 2, 3, \quad j = 1, 2, 3.$$

PROBLEM 8.32 (Continued)

We may add the redundant constraint $\sum_{j=1}^{3} x_{ij} \leq 1800$ for $i = 1,2$ so that the transportation algorithm of this chapter could be applied.

The tableau represents a basic feasible solution. Note that $x_{ij} = 0$ for $i = 2,3$, $j = 1,2,3$ so that the upper bounds on the flow from the second and third lumber companies are observed.

	1	2	3	Dummy	a_i
1	[2] 500	[3] 700	[5] 600	[0]	1800
2	[2.5]	[4]	[4.6]	[0] 1800	1800
3	[3]	[3.6]	[3.2]	[0] 500	500
	500	700	600	2300	

x_{33} is increased (since $z_{33} - c_{33} = 1.8 > 0$). It can be increased up to 500 before x_{34} leaves the basis. But the maximum actual increase is 200 because of the upper bound restriction on x_{33}. Thus x_{33} is nonbasic at its upper bound.

					u_i
	500	700	600	0	0
	⟨-.5⟩	⟨-1⟩	⟨.2⟩	1800	0
	⟨-1⟩	⟨-.6⟩	⟨1.8⟩	500	0
v_j	2	3	5	0	

500	700	400	200
⟨-.5⟩	⟨-1⟩	⟨.2⟩	1800
⟨-1⟩	⟨-.6⟩	⟨1.8⟩	300

From this tableau, x_{23} is increased up to 200 to its upper bound. It remains nonbasic.

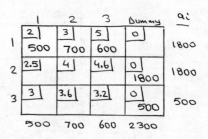

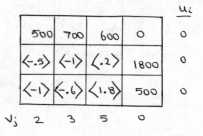

PROBLEM 8.32 (Continued)

	1	2	3	Dummy
1	500	700	200	400
2				1600
3				300

$x_{ij} = u_{ij} \Rightarrow z_{ij} - c_{ij} > 0$

$x_{ij} = 0 \Rightarrow z_{ij} - c_{ij} < 0$

The solution is optimal.

PROBLEM 8.33

This problem can be interpreted as that of maximizing the flow from a source s to a sink t. Only arcs with $\hat{c}_{ij} = 0$ are admitted in the network. The capacity of each arc is one. If the optimal solution is m, then we have an optimal solution to the assignment problem. Following is a typical example of the reduced assignment matrix and corresponding network:

0	0		
		0	
0		0	0
	0		

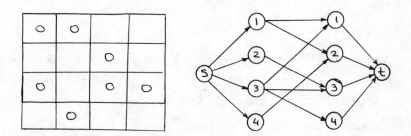

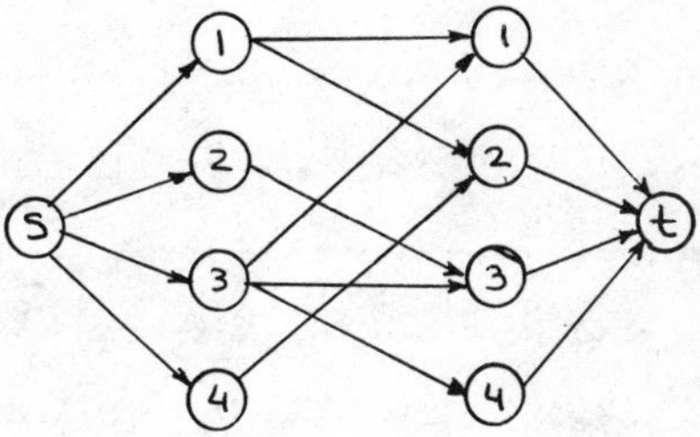

PROBLEM 8.32 (Continued)

Note that the problem can be interpreted as follows: Find the maximum number of assignments that could be made through cells with zero costs without exceeding either the supply of personnel or the demand for the jobs. In particular, the problem attempts to find the maximum number of "independent zero cells".

This problem admits a feasible solution (i.e., all $x_{ij} = 0$) and is bounded (optimal $\leq m$). Thus it has a finite optimal solution. Thus the dual problem is feasible, and has a finite optimal solution whose objective is equal to that of the primal.

Dual Problem:

$$\text{minimize } \sum_{i=1}^{m} u_i + \sum_{j=1}^{n} v_j$$

$$\text{S.T.} \quad u_i + v_j \geq 1, \quad (i,j) \in I$$

$$u_i, v_j \geq 0$$

First note that at optimality each u_i and each v_j is either 0 or 1. Also note that $u_i = 1$ can be interpreted as row i is covered and $u_i = 0$ can be interpreted as row i not covered. Similarly column j is covered if $v_j = 1$, otherwise it is uncovered. Thus the problem can be interpreted as:

PROBLEM 8.33 (Continued)

Find the minimum number of rows and columns which cover all zero cells. By the main duality theorem, the minimum number of rows and columns covering the zero cells is equal to the maximum number of independent zero cells.

PROBLEM 8.34

Let S_r : uncovered rows

S_c : uncovered columns

c_o : minimum uncovered element

$$\bar{u}_i = \hat{u}_i + c_o \quad i \in S_r \qquad \bar{u}_i = \hat{u}_i \quad i \notin S_r$$
$$\bar{v}_j = \hat{v}_j \quad j \in S_c \qquad \bar{v}_j = \hat{v}_j - c_o \quad j \notin S_c$$

a) $i \in S_r$, $j \in S_c$

$$c_{ij} - \bar{u}_i - \bar{v}_j = c_{ij} - \hat{u}_i - c_o - \hat{v}_j = (c_{ij} - \hat{u}_i - \hat{v}_j) - c_o$$

Since c_o is the minimum uncovered element then

$$(c_{ij} - \hat{u}_i - \hat{v}_j) - c_o \geq 0 \Rightarrow c_{ij} - \bar{u}_i - \bar{v}_j \geq 0$$

b) $i \in S_r$, $j \notin S_c$

$$c_{ij} - \bar{u}_i - \bar{v}_j = c_{ij} - \hat{u}_i - c_o - (\hat{v}_j - c_o) = c_{ij} - \hat{u}_i - \hat{v}_j \geq 0$$

because the previous solution was dual feasible.

c) $i \notin S_r$, $j \in S_c$

$$c_{ij} - \bar{u}_i - \bar{v}_j = c_{ij} - \hat{u}_i - \hat{v}_j \geq 0$$

because the old solution was dual feasible.

PROBLEM 8.34 (Continued)

d) $i \notin S_r$, $j \notin S_c$

$$c_{ij} - \bar{u}_i - \bar{v}_j = c_{ij} - \hat{u}_i - \hat{v}_j + c_0 > 0$$

because $c_{ij} - \hat{u}_i - \hat{v}_j \geq 0$ and $c_0 > 0$.

Thus the new dual solution is feasible.

PROBLEM 8.35

Both the Hungarian method and the primal-dual algorithm for the assignment problem are equivalent. They both start with a dual feasible solution which admits at least one cell at each row and column such that $z_{ij} - c_{ij} = 0$. They both attempt to solve a maximal flow problem (not explicitly) only admitting the arcs with $z_{ij} - c_{ij} = 0$. If the flow is m then they both stop; Otherwise, they modify the dual variables such that at least one extra cell is admitted and the maximum flow problem is repeated.

PROBLEM 8.36

3	7	4	0	3	−1
0	4	0	3	4	−1
0	2	4	1	0	0
3	0	1	1	3	1
4	0	1	0	2	2
0	0	1	0	1	

PROBLEM 8.36 (Continued)

2	7	3	[0]	2
[0]	5	0	4	4
0	3	4	2	[0]
2	0	[0]	1	2
3	[0]	0	0	1

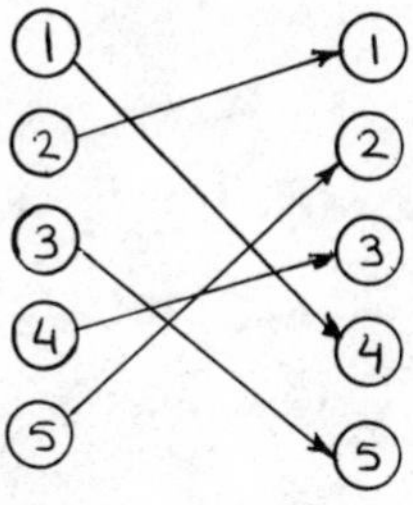

Optimal Assignment.

PROBLEM 8.37

The procedure described here is motivated by the fact that the minimum number of rows needed to cover the zero cells can be found by solving a suitable max-flow problem (see exercise 8.33) and by the max-flow algorithm of section 11.3.

Denote the source node by 0 and the sink node by $2m+1$, the demand nodes by $m+1, m+2, \ldots, 2m$. Introduce the arcs $(0, i)$ for $i = 1, \ldots, m$ and $(j, 2m+1)$ for $j = m+1, \ldots, 2m$. Also include all arcs with $u_i + v_{j-m} - c_{i,j-m} = 0$

Initialization

Set $x_{ij} = 0$, $u_{ij} = 1$ for all i, j.

Main Step

1. Erase any labels and set $L(0) = (-, m)$

PROBLEM 8.37 (Continued)

2- If node i has a label, node j has no label and $x_{ij} < u_{ij}$, then set $L(j) = (i, \Delta_j)$ where $\Delta_j = \min(\Delta_i, u_{ij} - x_{ij})$. If node i has a label and node j has no label, $x_{ji} > 0$ then set $L(j) = (-i, \Delta_j)$ where $\Delta_j = \min(\Delta_i, x_{ji})$. Repeat step 2 until either node $2m+1$ is labeled or else nomore nodes could be labeled.

3- If node $2m+1$ is not labeled, then go to 4. If node $2m+1$ is labeled, then change the flows as follows: begin at node $2m+1$ and consider the first entry of $L(2m+1)$. If the first entry is k then add 1 to $x_{k,2m+1}$. If the first entry is $-k$ then subtract 1 from $x_{k,2m+1}$. Backtrack to node k and repeat the process until the node 0 is reached. Return to step 1.

4- The maximum number of independent cells is given by $\sum_{i=1}^{m} x_{0i}$. Cell (i,j) is an independent cell if $x_{i,j-m} = 1$. The rows to be covered are those with $u_i = 1$ and the columns to be covered are those with $v_j = 1$. The u_i's and v_j's could be computed as follows:

PROBLEM 8.37 (Continued)

$$\sum_i x_{ij} < 1 \Rightarrow v_{j-m} = 0$$

$$\sum_j x_{ij} < 1 \Rightarrow u_i = 0$$

If $x_{ij} = 1$ then $u_i + v_{j-m} = 1$.

PROBLEM 8.38

	Bob	Bill	Ben
Sally	1	0	0 / 1
Susan	2	0 / 1	2
Sandra	0 / 1	0	7

Sally gets Ben

Suzan gets Bill

Sandra gets Bob

If Sally Stays at Home

	Bob	Bill	Ben	u_i
Suzan	3 / 2	1 / 0	5 / 4	1
Sandra	1 / 0	1 / 0	10 / 9	1
Dummy	0 / 0	0 / 0	0 / 0	1
v_j	0	0	0	

Suzan gets Bill

Sandra gets Bob

Ben stays at home.

Total = 2

If Suzan Stays at Home:

Sally → Bill

Sandra → Bob

Ben stays at home.

Total = 2

	Bob	Bill	Ben	
Sally	2 / 1	1 / 0	3 / 2	1
Sandra	1 / 0	1 / 0	10 / 9	1
Dummy	0 / 0	0 / 0	0 / 0	0
	0	0	0	

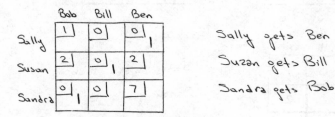

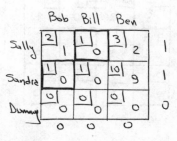

PROBLEM 8.38 (Continued)

Sundra Stays at Home:

				u_i
Sally	[2] 1	[1] 0	[3] 2	1
Suzan	[3] 2	[1] 0	[5] 3	1
Dummy	[0] 0	[0] 0	[0] 0	0
v_j	0	0	0	

1	0	2
2	0	3
0	0	0

	Bob	Bill	Ben
Sally	0	0	1
Suzan	1	0	2
Dummy	0	1	0

Sally gets Bob
Suzan gets Bill
Ben stays at home.

Thus in all cases Ben stays at home, and either Sally or Suzan would stay at home.

PROBLEM 8.39

	Solde.	Fram.	Draft.	Wiring	u_i
Carp.	[11] 2	[2] 0	[5] 3	[3] 1	2
Plum.	[1] 0	[3] 2	[4] 3	[2] 1	1
Eng.	[3] 2	[3] 2	[1] 0	[5] 4	1
Dummy	[0] 0	[0] 0	[0] 0	[0] 0	0
v_j	0	0	0	0	

Optimal Solution immediately available.

Carpenter → Framing
Plumber → Soldering
Engineer → Drafting

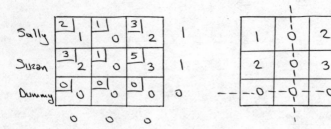

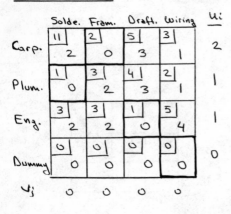

PROBLEM 8.39 (Continued)

	Sold.	Fra.	Draft.	Wire.	Dummy	Dummy	u_i
Carpenter 1	4 / 3	**2 / 0**	5 / 4	3 / 1	0 / 0	0 / 0	0
Carpenter 2	4 / 3	2 / 0	5 / 4	3 / 1	**0 / 0**	0 / 0	0
Plumber 1	**1 / 0**	3 / 1	4 / 3	2 / 0	0 / 0	0 / 0	0
Plumber 2	1 / 0	3 / 1	4 / 3	**2 / 0**	0 / 0	0 / 0	0
Engineer 1	3 / 2	3 / 1	**1 / 0**	5 / 3	0 / 0	0 / 0	0
Engineer 2	3 / 2	3 / 1	1 / 0	5 / 3	0 / 0	**0 / 0**	0
v_j	1	2	1	2	0	0	

The optimal assignment:

Carpenter $\longrightarrow$ Framing

Plumber $\longrightarrow$ Soldering, Wiring

Engineer $\longrightarrow$ Drafting.

PROBLEM 8.40

To form the basis tree on the assignment tableau add a new row and a new column. Start with the basis consisting of all the entries in the new row and new column where $x_{i,m+1} = x_{m+1,j} = 1$ for $i, j = 1, 2, \ldots, m$. and $x_{m+1,m+1} = 0$ (these are the artificial variables). Exactly m of these artificial variables are driven out of the basis by the optimal basis and the remaining m positive artificial variables are driven to zero and remain in the basis. In particular if x_{ij}

PROBLEM 8.40 (Continued)

is basic $(i, j = 1, 2, \ldots, m)$ then either the basic variable $x_{i,m+i}$ or $x_{m+i,j}$ is driven out of the basis and the other variable stays in the basis at zero level. Completing this process provides us with the basis tree.

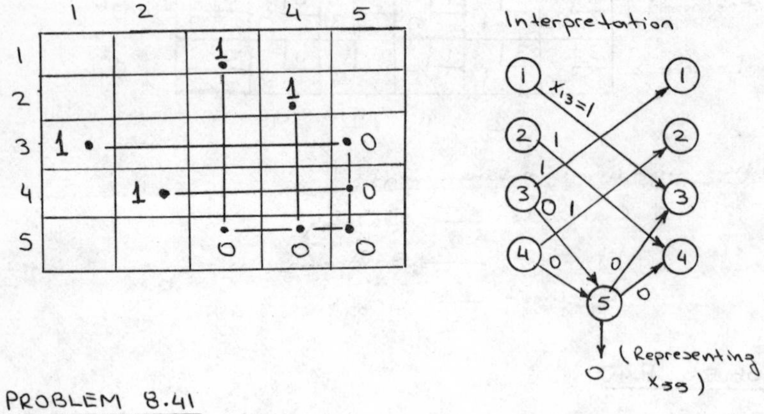

PROBLEM 8.41

Entries in the zeroth row are precisely $z_{ij}-c_{ij}$'s calculated by the assignment algorithm. The $z_{ij}-c_{ij}$ for the artificial variables are taken as zero. The column y_{ij} for a non basic variable is computed by the same method for the transportation problem, i.e., by finding the cycle formed by the basic cells and the nonbasic cell (i, j) and assigning values of $1, 0, -1$ in the corresponding rows.

PROBLEM 8.42

a)

	2	4	5	6	7		Row Penalty
1	[3]	[5]	X	[4] 10	X	10	1
2	[0] 45	[4] 20	[3]	X	X	65	3 4 ∞
3	X	X	[5] 15	X	[12]	15	7
4	X	[0] 20	X	[2] 15	[3] 10	45	2
5	X	[4] 5	[0] 40	X	[6]	45	2 ∞
	45	45	55	25	10		
Column Penalty	3	4	3	2	3		
		5			∞		

b) Initial solution by Vogel's method:

	2	4	5	6	7	u_i
1	<->	<->	X	10	X	5
2	45	20	<->	X	X	7
3	X	X	15	X	<0>	12
4	X	20	X	15	10	3
5	X	5	20	X	<1>	7
v_j	-7	-3	-7	-1	0	

	2	4	5	6	7	u_i
1	<->	<->	X	X	X	5
2	45	20	<->	X	X	7
3	X	X	15	X	<->	11
4	X	25	X	15	5	3
5	X	<->	20	X	5	6
v_j	-7	-3	-6	-1	0	

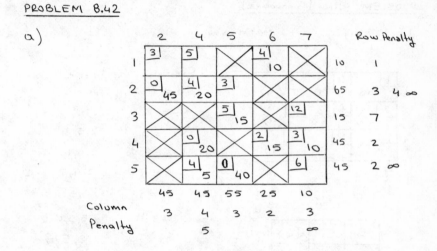

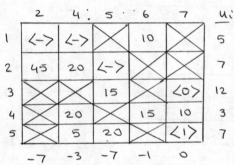

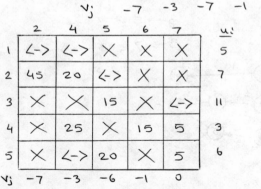

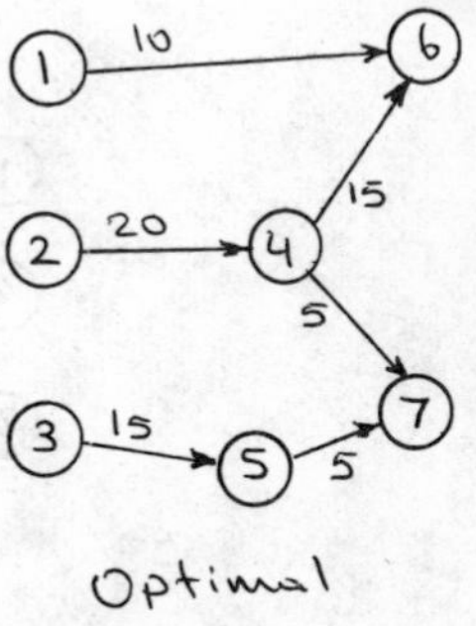

Optimal

PROBLEM 8.42 (Continued)

d) Least cost method:

	5	6	7	u_i
1	[6] 10	[4] 0	[8] <-4>	4
2	[3] <5>	[6] 20	[7] <-1>	6
3	[5] <8>	[11] 5	[11] 10	11
v_j	2	0	0	

			u_i
5	5	<4>	12
<5>	20	<7>	14
5	<-8>	10	11
v_j -6	-8	0	

$c_{15} = 6$ 1, 2, 5
$c_{16} = 4$ 1, 6
$c_{17} = 8$ 1, 4, 7
$c_{25} = 3$ 2, 5
$c_{26} = 6$ 2, 4, 6
$c_{27} = 7$ 2, 4, 7
$c_{35} = 5$ 3, 5
$c_{36} = 11$ 3, 5, 4, 6
$c_{37} = 11$ 3, 5, 7

	5	6	7	u_i
1	<->	10	<->	5
2	<->	15	5	7
3	10	<->	5	11
v_j	-6	-1	0	

Optimal

$1 \to 6 \equiv 1 \xrightarrow{10} 6$

$2 \to 6 \equiv 2 \xrightarrow{15} 4 \xrightarrow{15} 6$

$2 \to 7 \equiv 2 \xrightarrow{5} 4 \xrightarrow{5} 7$

$3 \to 5 \equiv 3 \xrightarrow{10} 5$

$3 \to 7 \equiv 3 \xrightarrow{5} 5 \xrightarrow{5} 7$

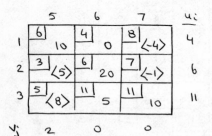

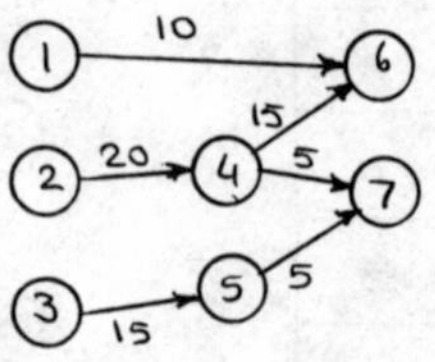

PROBLEM 8.43

If certain variables are known to be positive in the optimal solution, then we always keep them in the basis. We do not need to calculate $z_{ij} - c_{ij}$'s for those variables.

If in the process of forming a cycle one of those variables driven to zero, then we can stop assigning a flow to that $\max(z_{ij} - c_{ij})$ nonbasic cell but choose the next positive one.

This information will reduce the amount of computations required in the transportation algorithm.

CHAPTER 9 MINIMAL COST NETWORK FLOWS

PROBLEM 9.1

a) From the definition of a connected graph we have at least one chain from every node to every other node. This applies to the initial and final nodes as well. Hence there exists a chain from the initial node to the final node such that it contains no cycle (from the definition of a chain).

b) If T has only one end, then it contains a cycle, and hence it is not a tree. Since a tree cannot contain a cycle, it must have at least two ends.

c) This simply can be proven by the lower triangularity of the basis matrix B, corresponding to T. If we delete the column corresponding to the end arc and the row corresponding to the node adjacent to that arc, the remaining matrix B' is again lower triangular, and hence, has an inverse. Thus the remaining figure is a tree.

d) We will prove this by contradiction. Suppose the graph contains a cycle. Let, for example, the arcs (1,1), (1,2), (2,1) form a cycle.

PROBLEM 9.1 (Continued)

Therefore 3 arcs have been used for 2 nodes, namely, for node 1 and node 2. There remains $(m-1)-3 = m-4$ arcs and $m-2$ nodes. We cannot cover $m-2$ nodes with $m-4$ arcs, and hence the assertion in the problem is true, i.e., a connected graph with m nodes and $m-1$ arcs should not have a cycle to be a tree.

PROBLEM 9.2

Let B be any $k \times k$ submatrix of A. We will show by induction that $\det(B) = 0$, 1 or -1, and thus total unimodularity of A will be established. Obviously if $k=1$, then $\det(B) = 0, 1$, or -1. Now suppose that $\det(B) = 1, 0$, or -1 for any square matrix of size $k-1$. Let B be a $k \times k$ submatrix of A. If any column of B is zero then $\det(B) = 0$. If each column of B has a $+1$ and a -1, then $\det(B) = 0$ (rows of B are linearly dependent, by adding them we get the zero vector). Thus, suppose that there is at least one column with a nonzero entry. Then $\det(B) = \pm \det(B')$ where B' is the submatrix of B formed by deleting that column and the row with nonzero entry. By the induction hypothesis $\det(B') = 1, 0$, or -1

PROBLEM 9.2 (Continued)

and hence $\det(B) = 1, 0,$ or -1. Thus the induction argument is complete.

PROBLEM 9.3

Suppose by contradiction that a basis contains two roots at nodes i and j. There is a basis chain between nodes i and j, say (k,i), (k,s), (s,j) as depicted below.

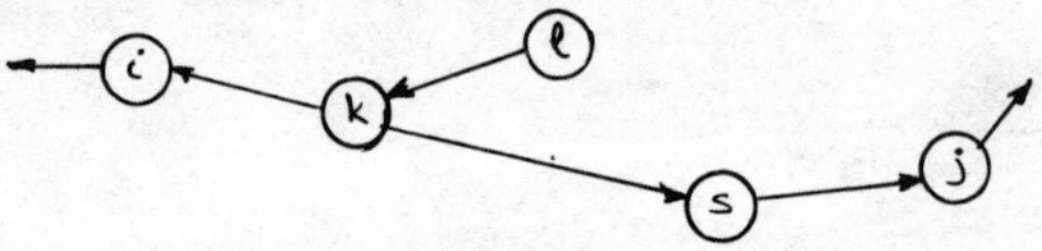

Consider the following linear combination:

$$\begin{matrix} i \\ k \\ s \\ \ell \\ j \end{matrix} \quad -\underset{(k,i)}{\begin{bmatrix} -1 \\ 1 \\ 0 \\ 0 \\ 0 \end{bmatrix}} + \underset{(k,s)}{\begin{bmatrix} 0 \\ 1 \\ -1 \\ 0 \\ 0 \end{bmatrix}} + \underset{(s,j)}{\begin{bmatrix} 0 \\ 0 \\ 1 \\ 0 \\ -1 \end{bmatrix}} - \underset{\text{root at } i}{\begin{bmatrix} 1 \\ 0 \\ 0 \\ 0 \\ 0 \end{bmatrix}} + \underset{\text{root at } j}{\begin{bmatrix} 0 \\ 0 \\ 0 \\ 0 \\ 1 \end{bmatrix}} = \begin{bmatrix} 0 \\ 0 \\ 0 \\ 0 \\ 0 \end{bmatrix}$$

Thus we have a linear combination of the basic vectors adding to zero, contradicting the fact that the basic columns must be linearly independent. Thus a basis cannot contain two roots.

PROBLEM 9.4

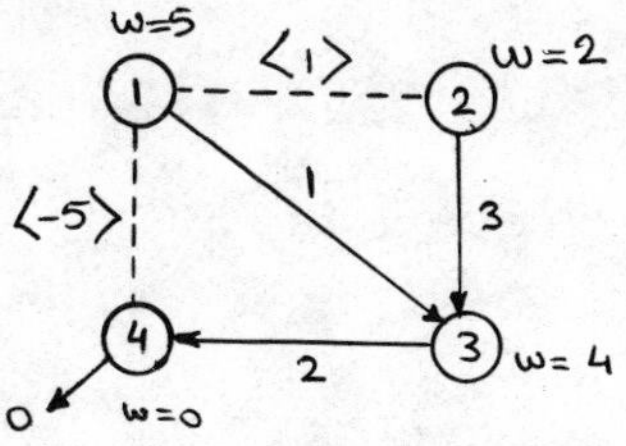

introduce x_{12}.

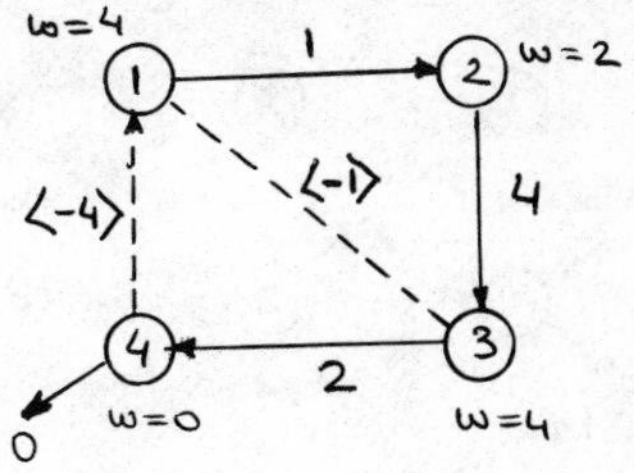

Optimal.

PROBLEM 9.5

Phase I:

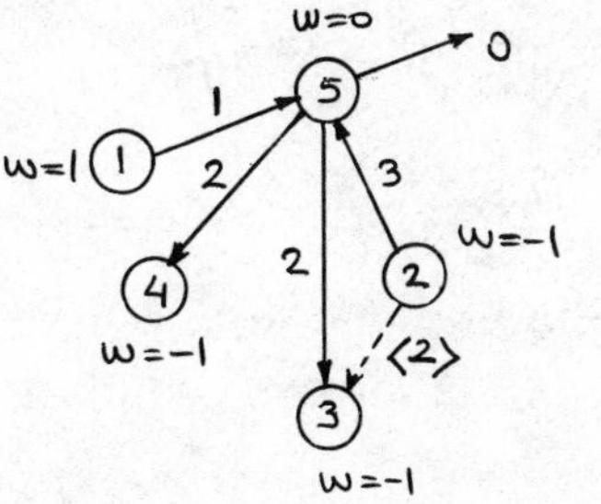

introduce x_{23}.

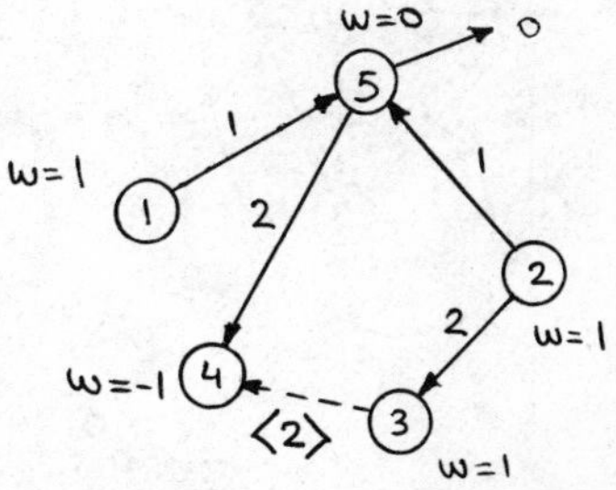

introduce x_{34}

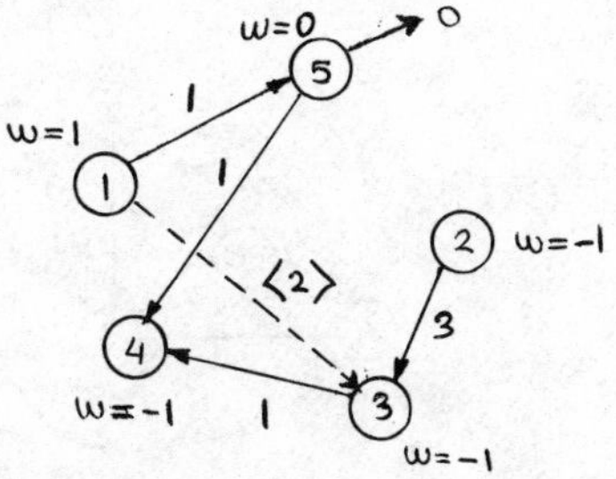

introduce x_{13}

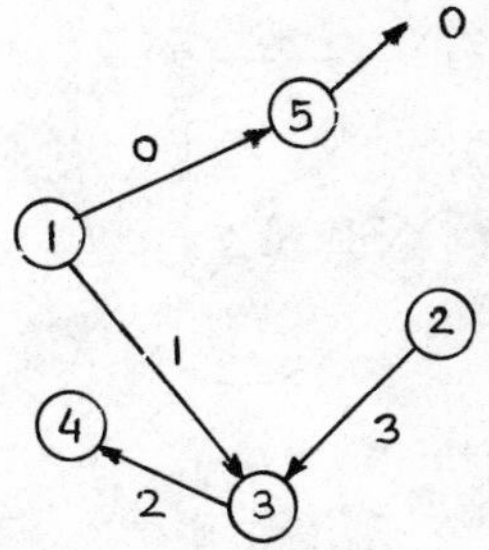

End of phase I.

PROBLEM 9.5 (Continued)

Phase II:

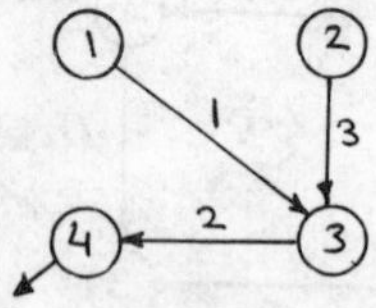

This is the same starting basic solution as that of problem 9.4.

BIG-M METHOD:

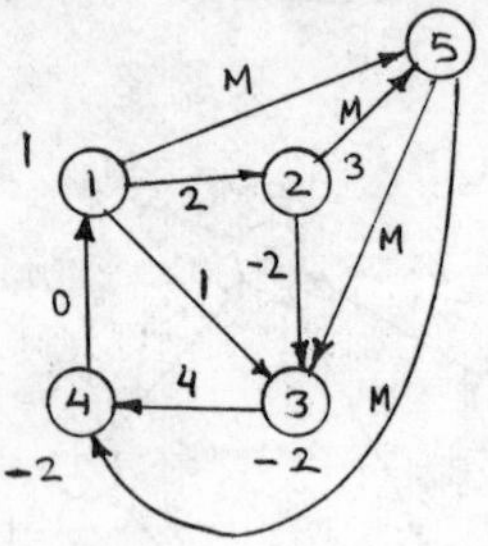

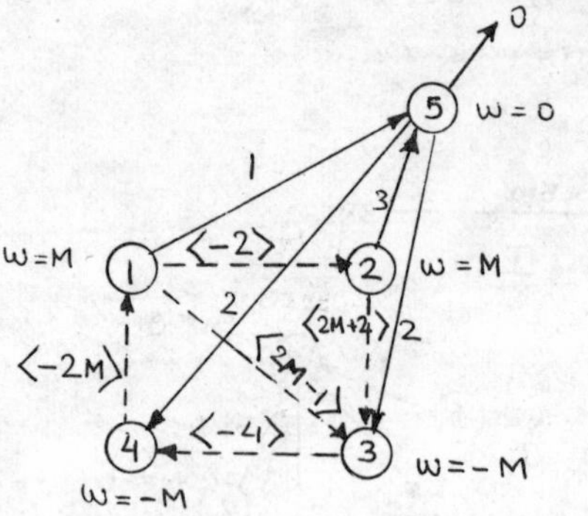

Starting basic solution.

X_{23} enters.

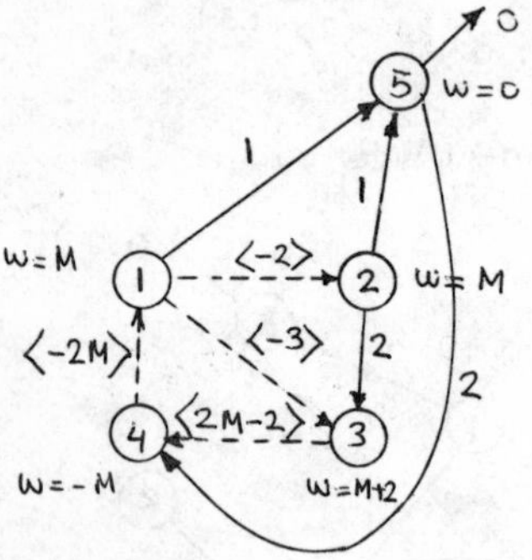

introduce X_{34}.

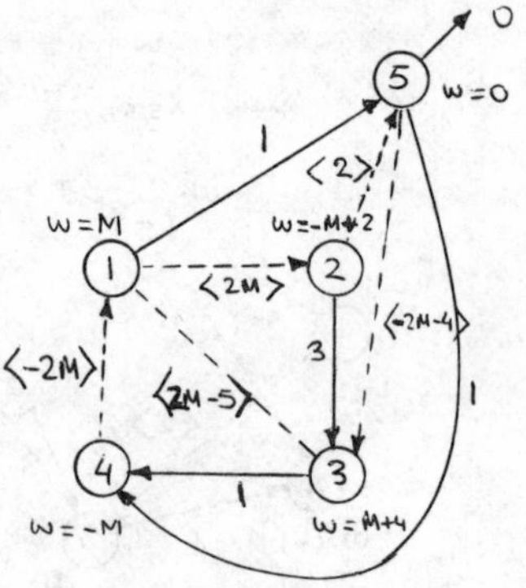

introduce X_{12}

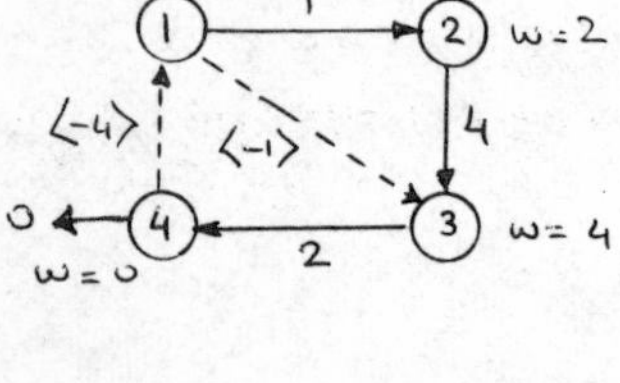

Optimal.

PROBLEM 9.6

Shortest path from node 1 to node 2 is 1→3→6→4→2
Shortest path from node 1 to node 7 is 1→3→6→7
Shortest path from node 3 to node 2 is 3→6→4→2
Shortest path from node 3 to node 7 is 3→6→7
Shortest path from node 6 to node 2 is 6→4→2
Shortest path from node 6 to node 7 is 6→7

with their costs 6, 7, 4, 5, 3, 4 respectively.

	2	7	a_i	u_i
1	[6] 2	[7] <0>	2	7
3	[4] 1	[5] <0>	1	5
6	[3] 2	[4] 4	6	4
b_j	5	4		
v_j	−1	0		

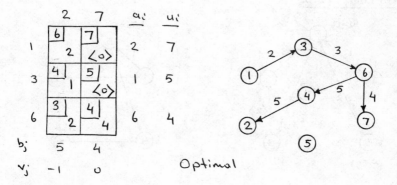

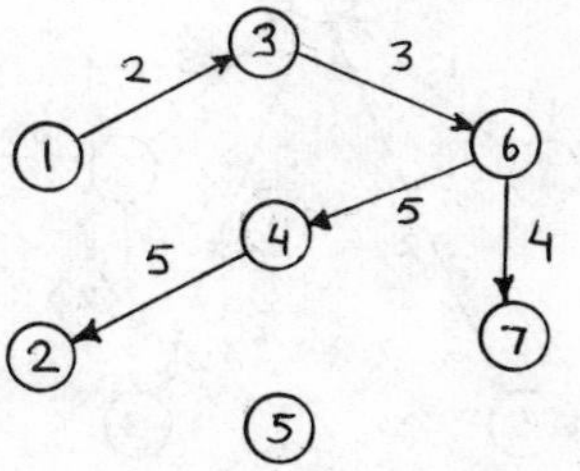

Optimal

PROBLEM 9.7

The solution will not necessarily be basic. If a cycle is identified, flow is modified around the cycle such that a variable drops to zero. This process is repeated until no cycles are present. If the structure is connected, we have a basis tree. Otherwise, arcs are added with zero flow to form a tree.

PROBLEM 9.8

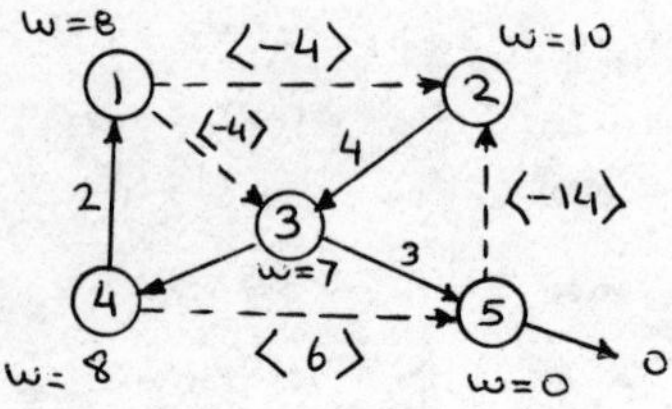

x_{45} enters

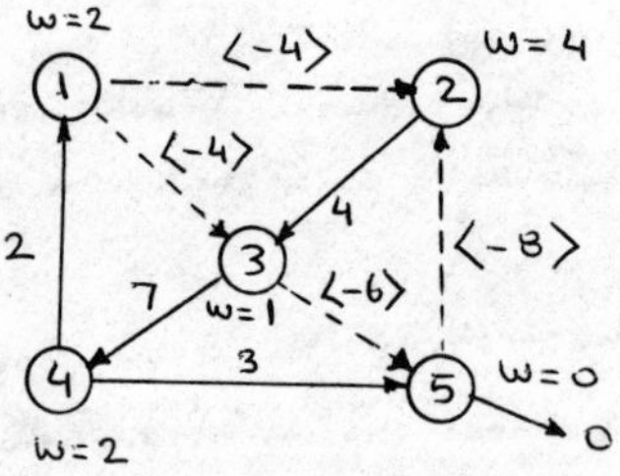

Optimal

PROBLEM 9.9

PHASE I

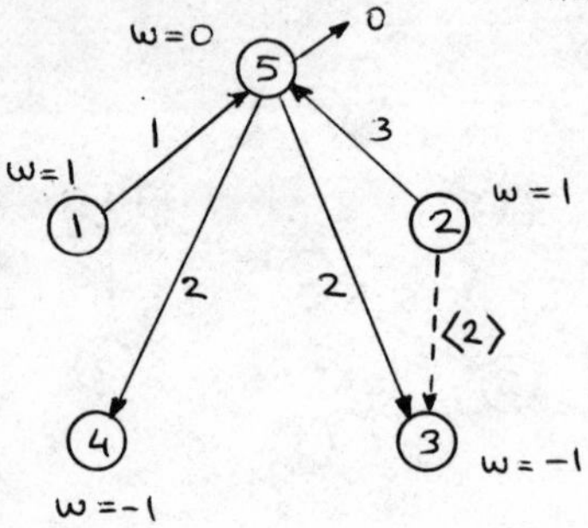

Introduce x_{23}

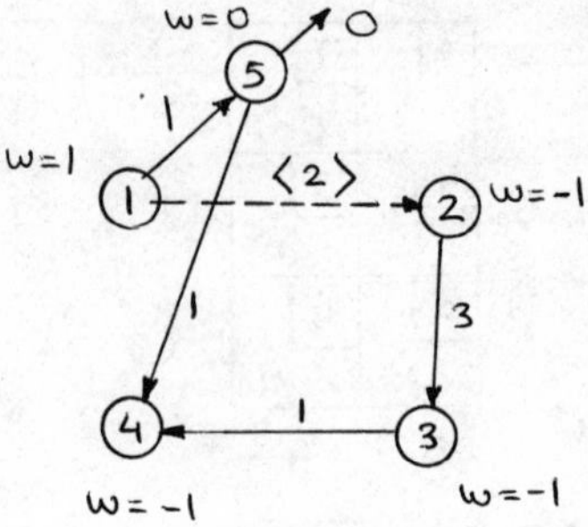

Introduce x_{12}

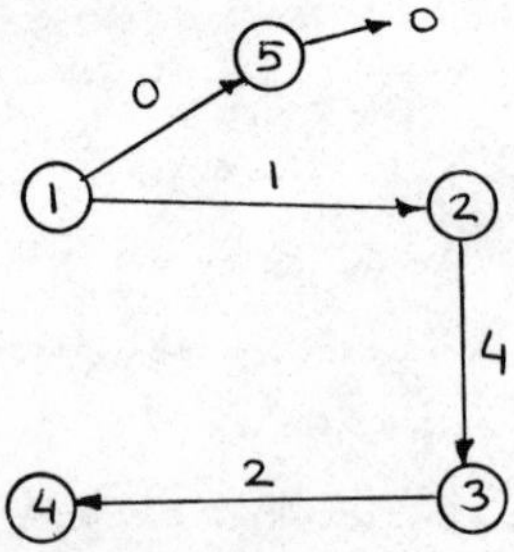

End of phase I.

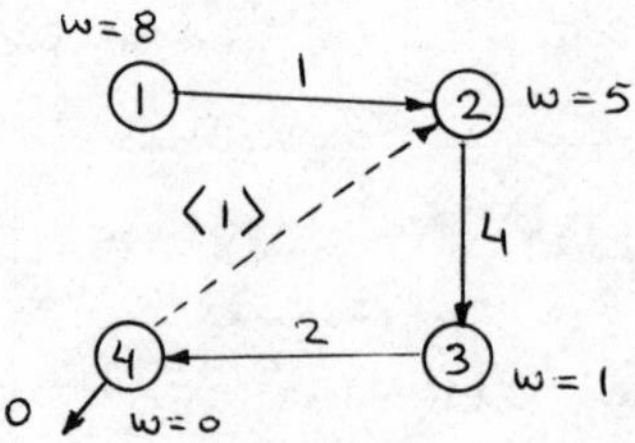

Phase II.

As seen x_{42} can be increased indefinitely. Hence, the optimal is unbounded.

PROBLEM 9.10

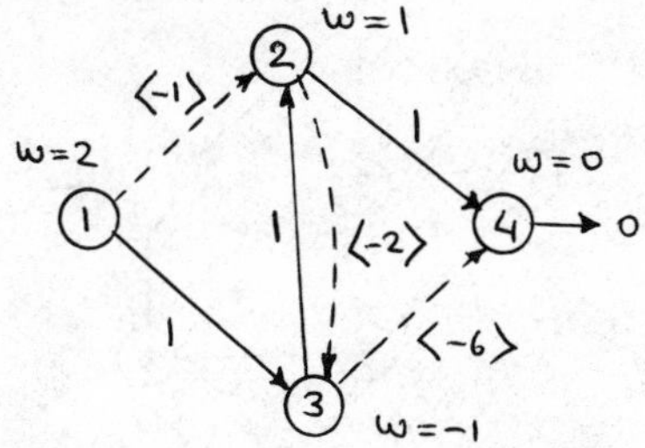

Solution is optimal. The shortest path is: 1 – 3 – 2 – 4.

PROBLEM 9.11

Let the dual variables with the cost of the artificial variable as zero be $w_1, \ldots, w_m$. Now, let the cost of the artificial variable be θ. Let the dual variables be $\bar{w}_1, \bar{w}_2, \ldots, \bar{w}_m$. Obviously $w_m = 0$ and $\bar{w}_m = \theta$. Since the basis tree is connected, there is at least one node i such that (i, m) is basic, or else, (m, i) is basic. In the former case $\bar{w}_i - \bar{w}_m = c_{im} \Rightarrow \bar{w}_i = \bar{w}_m + c_{im} = \theta + c_{im} = \theta + w_i$. In the latter case $\bar{w}_m - \bar{w}_i = c_{mi} \Rightarrow \bar{w}_i = \bar{w}_m - c_{mi} = \theta + w_i$. In either case $\bar{w}_i = w_i + \theta$. Continuing in this fashion it is clear that

$$\bar{w}_j = w_j + \theta \quad \text{for all } j.$$

Thus

$$\bar{w}_i - \bar{w}_j - c_{ij} = (w_i + \theta) - (w_j + \theta) - c_{ij} = z_{ij} - c_{ij}.$$

Hence $z_{ij} - c_{ij}$ does not change regardless of the value assigned to the cost of the artificial variable.

PROBLEM 9.12

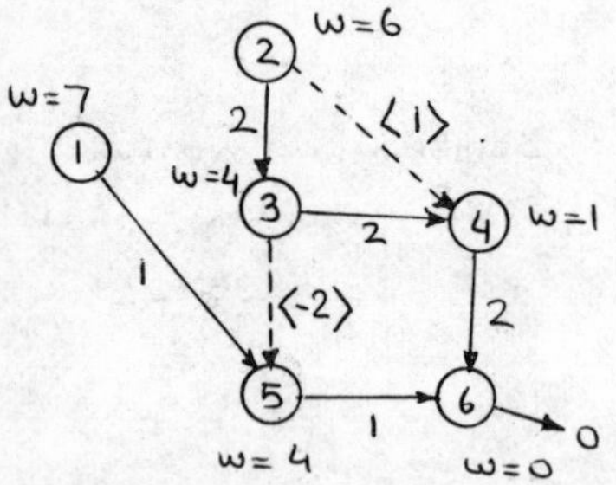

X_{24} enters

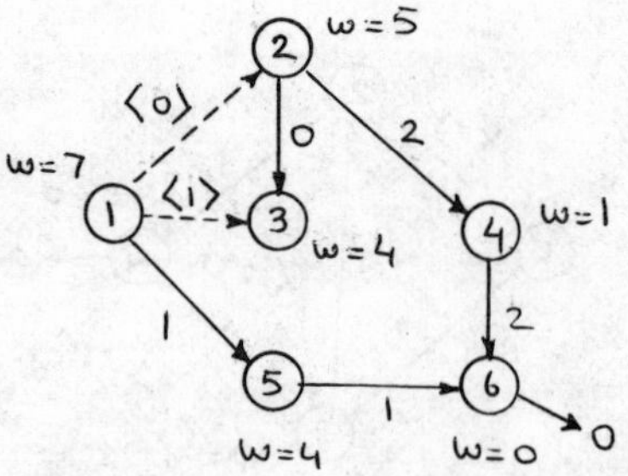

X_{13} enters

Optimal !

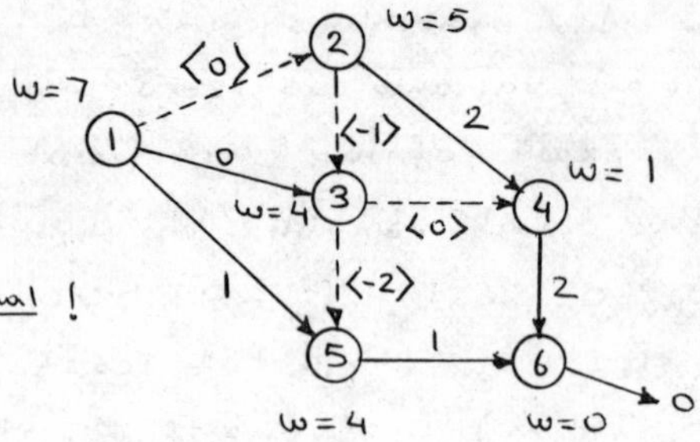

PROBLEM 9.13

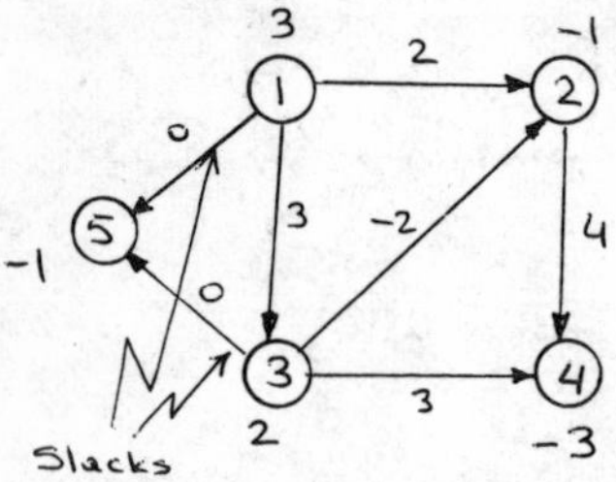

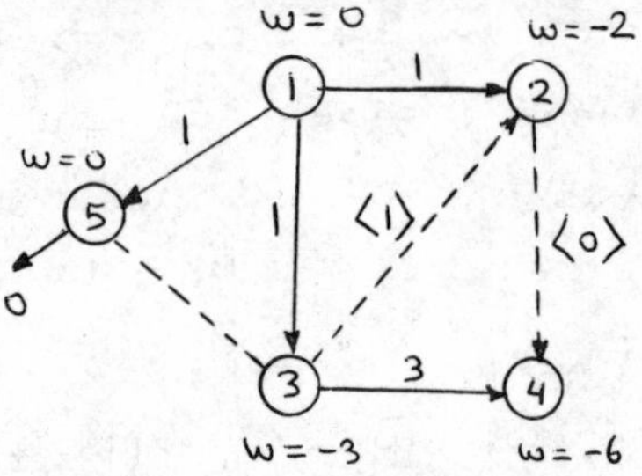

Starting basis, X_{32} enters.

PROBLEM 9.13 (Continued)

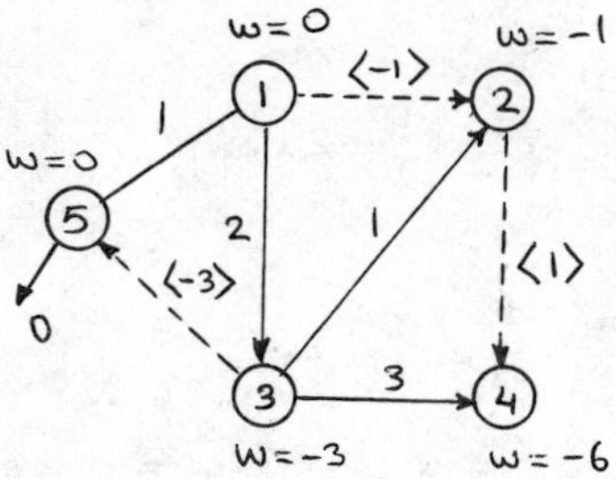

X_{24} enters

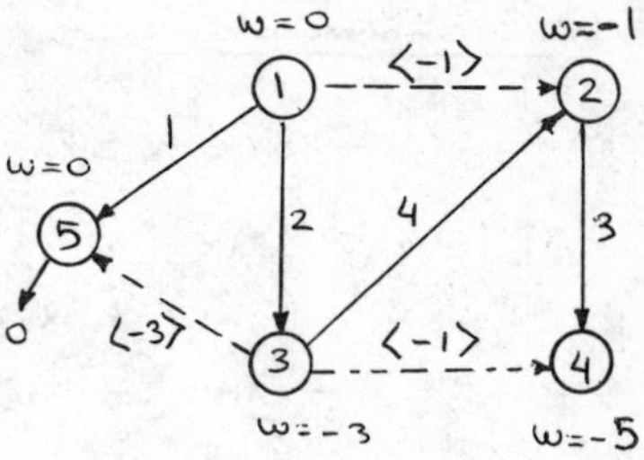

Optimal !

PROBLEM 9.14

Introduce a dummy node (5) and the slack arcs (1,5) and (3,5).

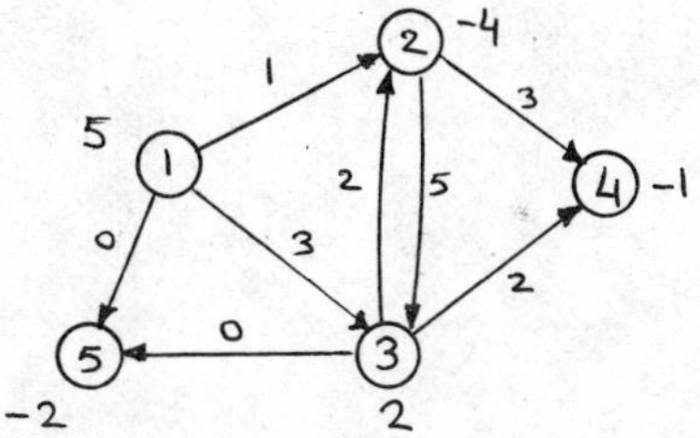

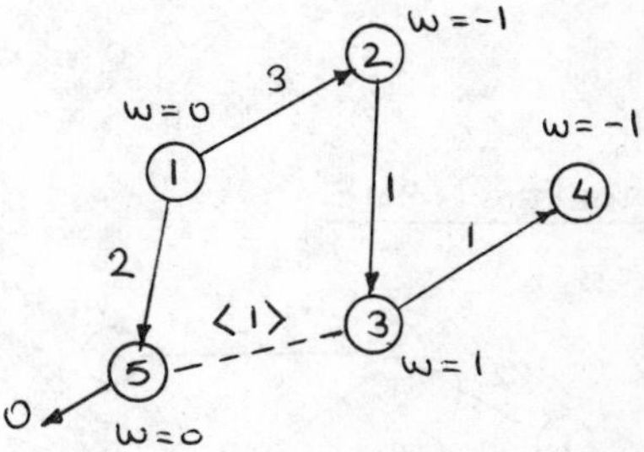

Starting basis. X_{35} enters.

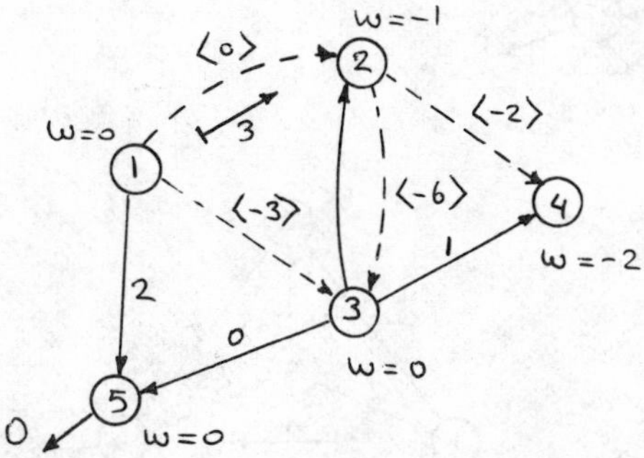

Optimal !

PROBLEM 9.14 (Continued)

LP formulation:

$$\min \quad x_{12} + 3x_{13} + 5x_{23} + 2x_{32} + 3x_{24} + 2x_{34}$$

$$\begin{aligned}
\text{S.T.} \quad & x_{12} + x_{13} && \le 5 \\
& -x_{12} + x_{23} - x_{32} + x_{24} && = -4 \\
& -x_{13} - x_{23} + x_{32} + x_{34} && \le 2 \\
& -x_{24} - x_{34} && = -1
\end{aligned}$$

$$0 \le x_{12} \le 3$$
$$0 \le x_{13} \le 2$$
$$0 \le x_{23} \le 1$$
$$0 \le x_{32} \le 4$$
$$0 \le x_{24} \le 3$$
$$0 \le x_{34} \le 7$$

PROBLEM 9.15

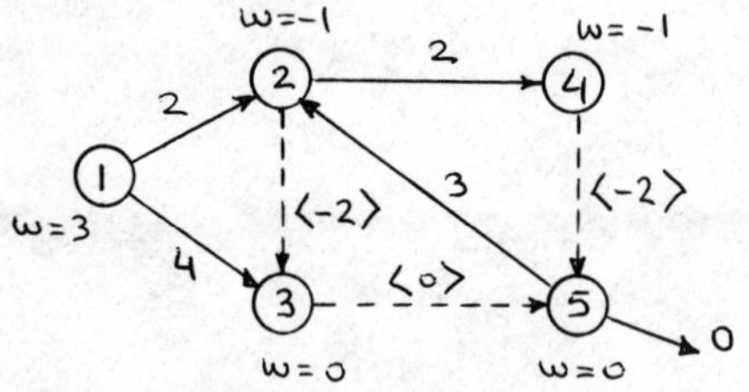

Starting basis

Optimal!

PROBLEM 9.16

Starting basis.
x_{32} enters, Since x_{12} is at its lower limit, x_{12} drops out and $x_{32} = 0$, basic.

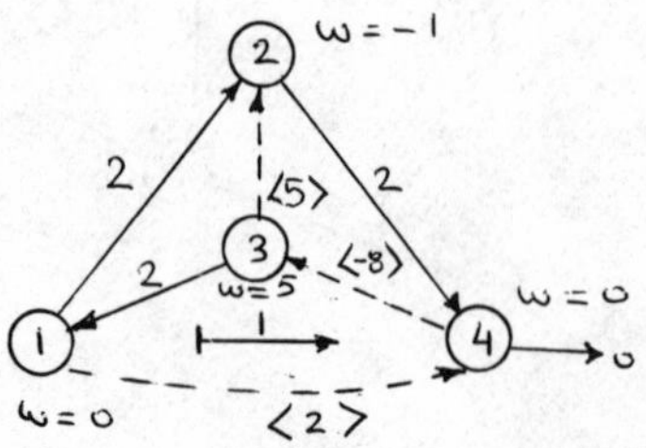

PROBLEM 9.16 (Continued)

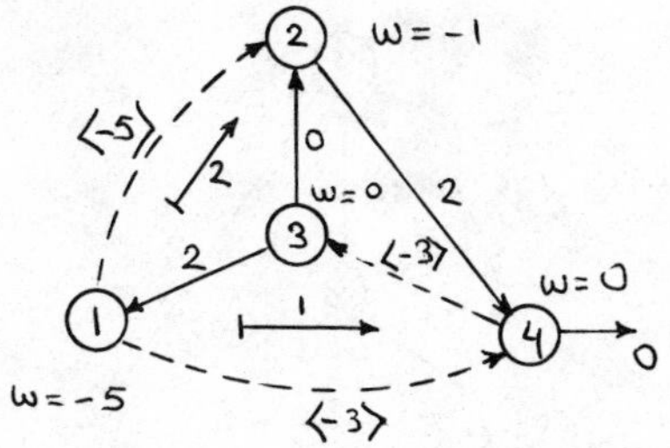

Optimal !

PROBLEM 9.17

PHASE I

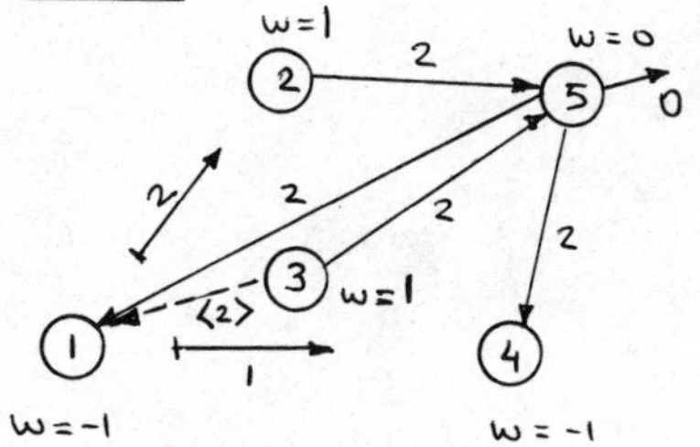

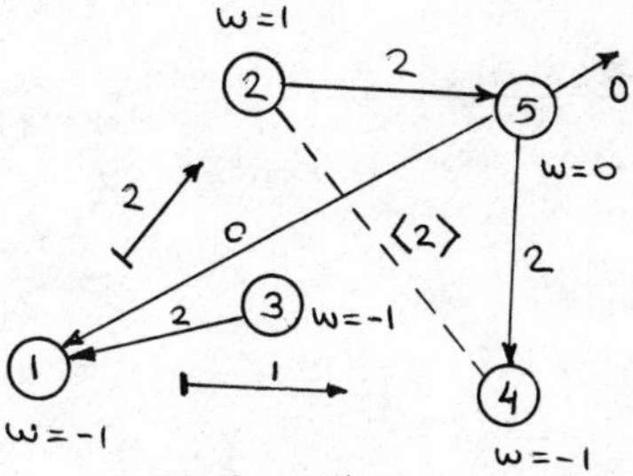

X_{31} enters. X_{24} enters.

(All arcs in or out of node 5 are artificial)

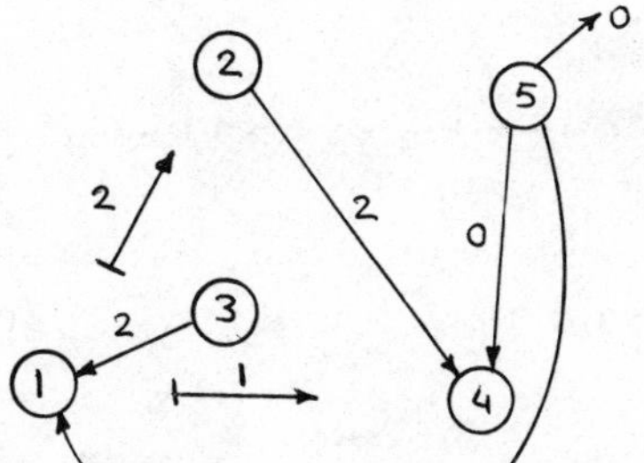

Introduce X_{14} into the basis to drive X_{54} out.

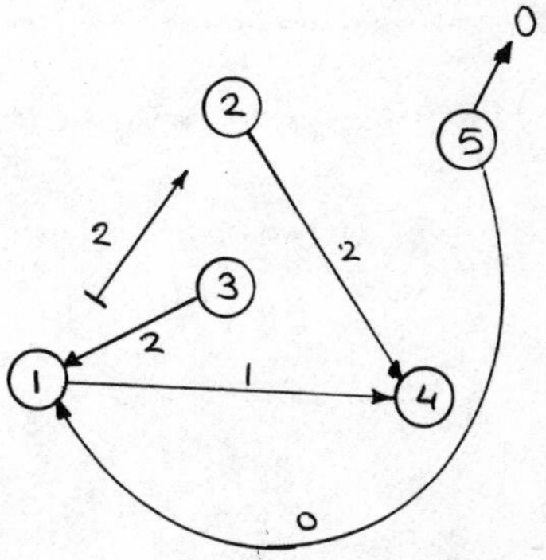

End of phase I

PROBLEM 9.17 (Continued)

PHASE II

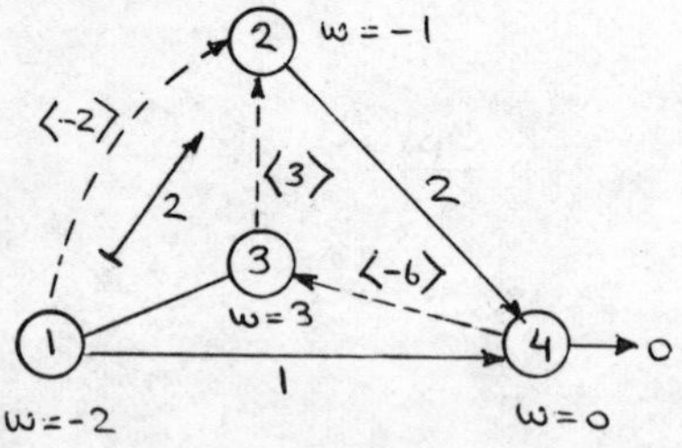

Introduce x_{32}

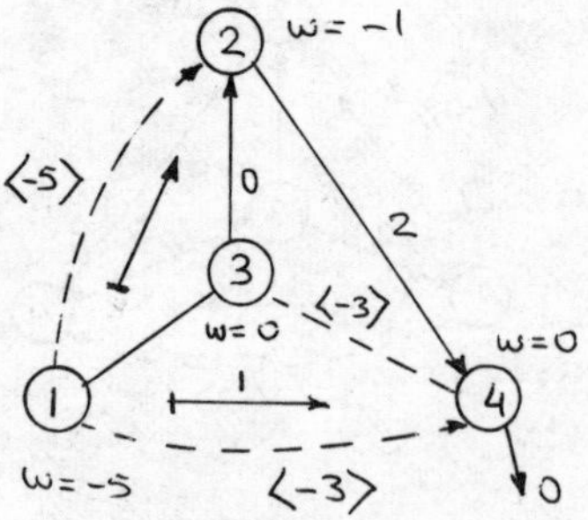

Optimal!

PROBLEM 9.18

a)

$$\text{minimize} \quad \sum_{i=1}^{N} \sum_{k=1}^{M} c_{ik} x_{ik}$$

$$\text{S.T.} \quad \sum_{i \le j} \sum_{i+k > j} x_{ik} \geq D_j \qquad j = 1, 2, \ldots, N$$

$$x_{ik} \geq 0 \qquad i = 1, \ldots, N, \qquad k = 1, \ldots, M$$

$$x_{ik} \text{ integers.}$$

where x_{ik} is the number of machines of life k at the beginning of month i.

b)

$$\min \quad c_{11}x_{11} + c_{12}x_{12} + c_{21}x_{21} + c_{22}x_{22} + c_{31}x_{31} + c_{32}x_{32}$$

$$\begin{array}{llllllll} \text{S.T.} & x_{11} + x_{12} & & & & -y_1 & & = D_1 \\ & -x_{11} & + x_{21} & & - x_{31} & +y_1 - y_2 + y_3 & & = D \\ & - x_{12} & - x_{21} & - x_{22} & & + y_2 & & = -D_2 \\ & & & x_{22} + x_{31} & & & -y_3 & = D_3 \end{array}$$

$$x_{ij} \geq 0, \quad y_j \geq 0$$

where $D = D_2 - D_1 - D_3$.

PROBLEM 9.18 (Continued)

We adopted the following rule for the transformation: originally the linear program was

	X_{11}	X_{12}	X_{21}	X_{22}	X_{31}	X_{32}		
min	C_{11}	C_{12}	C_{21}	C_{22}	C_{31}	C_{32}		
S.T.	1	1					$-y_1$	$\le D_1$
		1	1	1			$-y_2$	$\le D_2$
				1	1	1	$-y_3$	$\le D_3$

$$x_{ik} \geq 0 \ , \quad \text{integer}$$
$$y_j \geq 0 \ , \quad \text{integer}$$

Note that $C_{32} > C_{31}$. Since the colums X_{31} and X_{32} are identical, we can delete column X_{32}. After this deletion subtract the first equation from the second equation. Subtract the third equation from the second equation. Add all the resultant equations together and multiply the resultant equation by (−1). This will give the LP formulation of a network flow problem given above. Following is the graphical representation of the network flow problem:

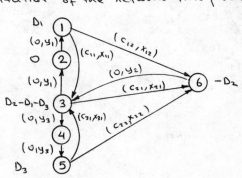

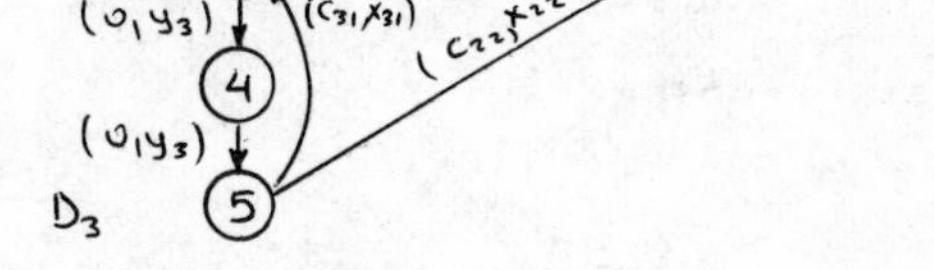

PROBLEM 9.19

In order to differentiate the flow through node 2 (i.e., whether it is comming from node 1 or is it supplied by node 2), let us create a dummy node, say, 5 which is connected to node 2 with an arc with the capacity beiing equal to 3 and cost being equal to 4. We have the following figure:

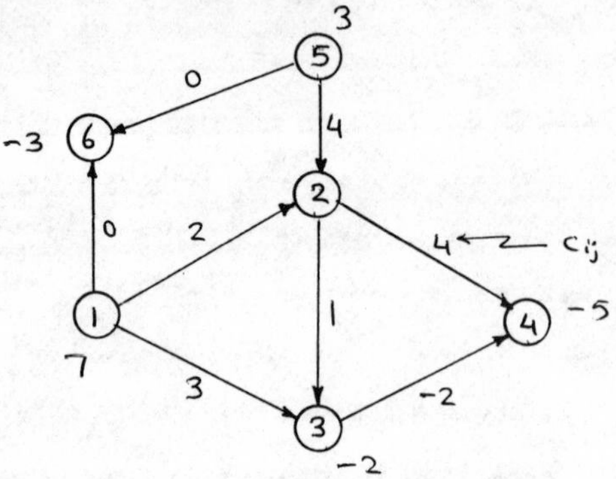

where the node 6 and the arcs (1,6) and (5,6) are for the slack variables.

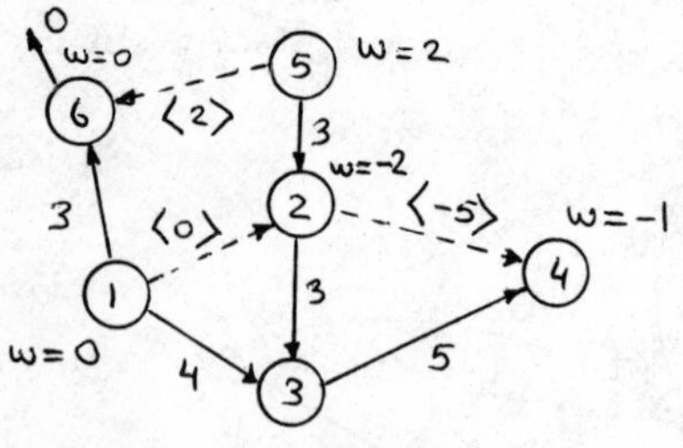

x_{56} enters;

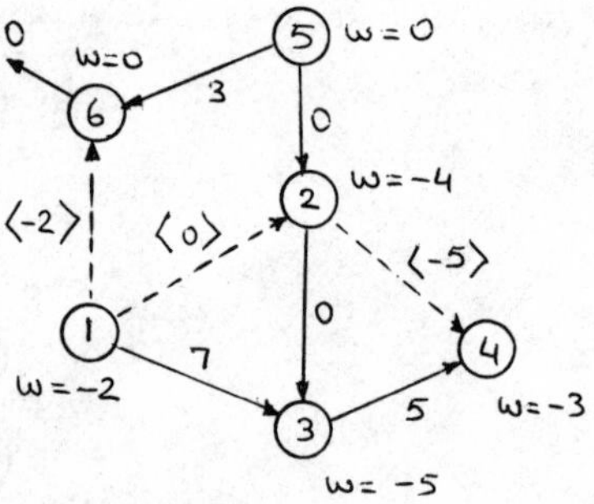

Optimal !

PROBLEM 9.20

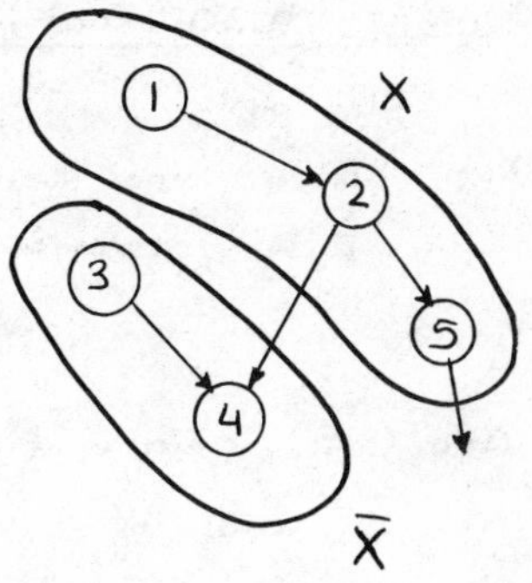

Note that to generate the row corresponding to a basic variable $x_{k\ell}$, we need to find the effect of modifying the nonbasic variables on $x_{k\ell}$.

If the basic column is deleted as shown in the figure, the set of nodes is divided into two mutually exclusive subsets X and $\bar{X}$. A nonbasic variable will have a nonzero coefficient in the (k,ℓ) row if it forms a cycle including $x_{k\ell}$, if introduced. Hence any nonbasic variable whose both ends are either in X or $\bar{X}$ will have zero coefficient in row (k,ℓ). Obviously, if one end of (i,j) is in X and the other end in $\bar{X}$ then (i,j) will be in the cycle formed. Moreover, if $k \in X$ and $\ell \in \bar{X}$ then:

a) If $(i,j) \in (X, \bar{X})$, then as x_{ij} increases $x_{k\ell}$ will decrease, as that the coefficient of x_{ij} in the $x_{k\ell}$ row is 1.

b) If $(i,j) \in (\bar{X}, X)$, then as x_{ij} increases $x_{k\ell}$ increases, so that the coefficient of x_{ij} in the $x_{k\ell}$ row is -1.

PROBLEM 9.20 (Continued)

Obviously all basic variables other than x_{kl} have zero coefficients in the x_{kl} row.

For problem 9.4, deleting arc (1,3) gives the two node sets $X = \{1\}$, $\bar{X} = \{2,3,4\}$.

Arc (1,2) points from X into $\bar{X}$ and thus has the coefficient (+1). Arc(4,1) points from $\bar{X}$ to X and thus has a coefficient of (−1). Thus the row corresponding to the basic variable x_{13} is:

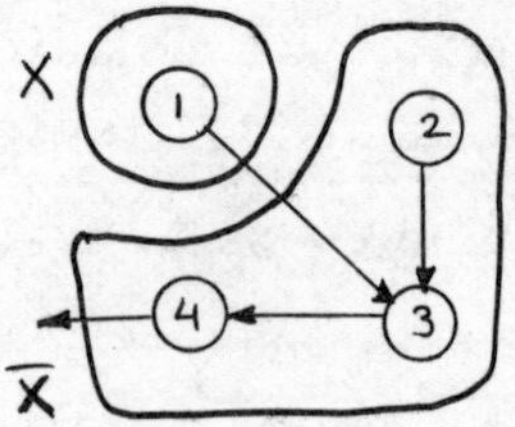

	x_{12}	x_{13}	x_{23}	x_{34}	x_{41}	x_a
x_{13}	1	1	0	0	−1	0

PROBLEM 9.21

See Langley [302] or Johnson [266] for a development of the lexicographic method applied to a network flow problem.

In the chapter we discussed how to generate the updated entering column. In Problem 9.24 we indicate how a column of B^{-1} can be generated. Thus it is straightforward to apply the lexicographic method with all of these quantities available.

PROBLEM 9.22

Johnson [266] discusses the application of the primal dual method to network flows.

Utilizing the results of Problem 9.20 it is also possible to develop a dual simplex procedure for network flows. We begin with an optimal basis which is not necessarily feasible (this may require some effort). From the values of the flow variables it is possible to identify the departing variable. From the $z_{ij} - c_{ij}$ and the row generated in Problem 9.20 we can identify the entering variable. Pivoting is the same as before.

PROBLEM 9.23

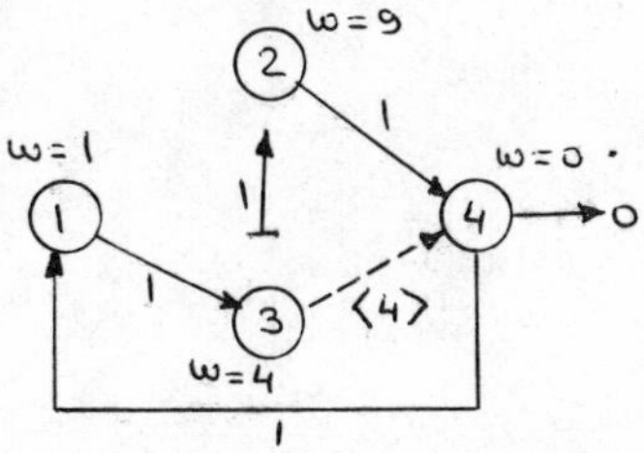

x_{34} enters.

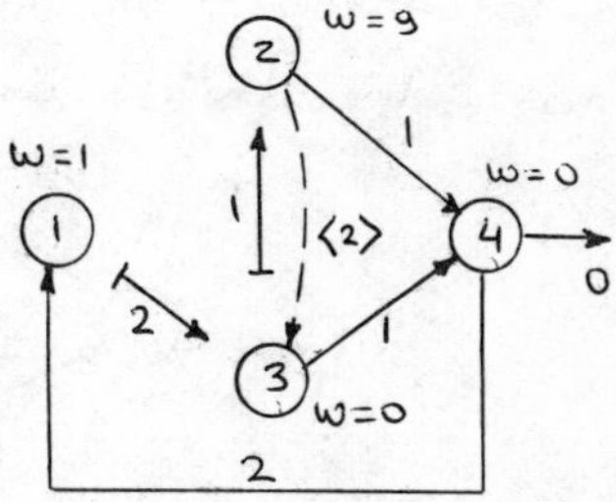

x_{23} enters.

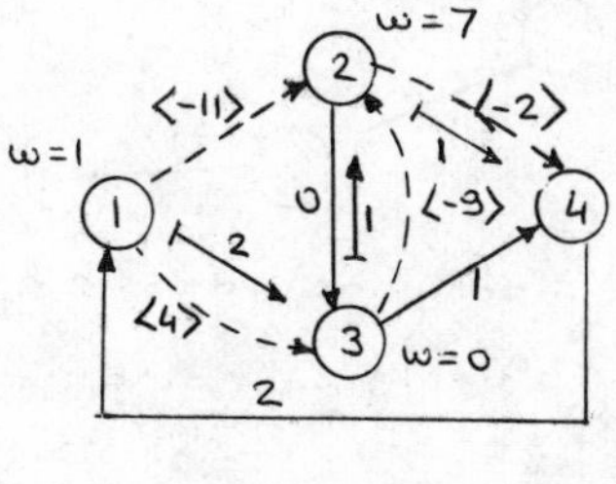

Optimal!

PROBLEM 9.24

In order to generate a column of B^{-1}, we may imagine that we want to generate the updated column of a "slack arc" pointing out of a given node. The original column of such an arc has one +1 and all zeros. The collection of all such columns comprise the identity.

Now, to generate the updated representation of such a slack arc, we find a set of basic arcs which will cancel each other to give the representation of the slack arc. The appropriate set of arcs are given by the chain in the basis tree from the given node to the root. The chain is oriented so that it points toward the root. In this case

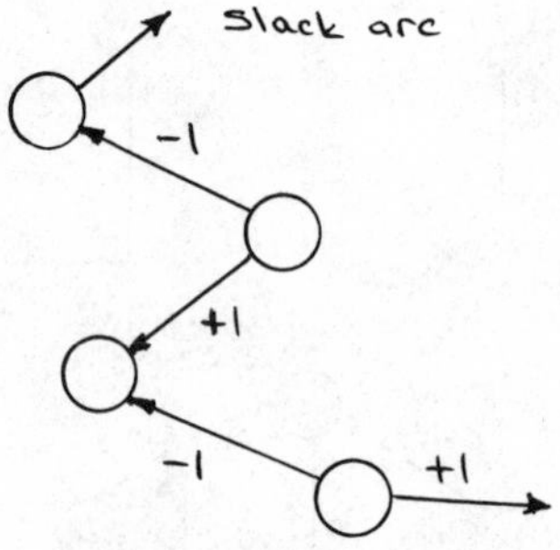

The representation includes the root. It may be easily verified that this gives the

PROBLEM 9.24 (Continued)

proper representation.

Considering the network of Problem 9.4, B is given as follows:

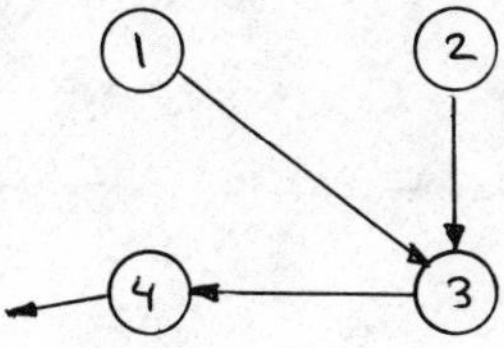

$$B = \begin{bmatrix} 1 & 0 & 0 & 0 \\ 0 & 1 & 0 & 0 \\ -1 & -1 & 1 & 0 \\ 0 & 0 & -1 & 1 \end{bmatrix}$$

To get the first column of B^{-1}, we place a slack arc at node 1 and find its representation.

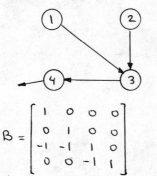

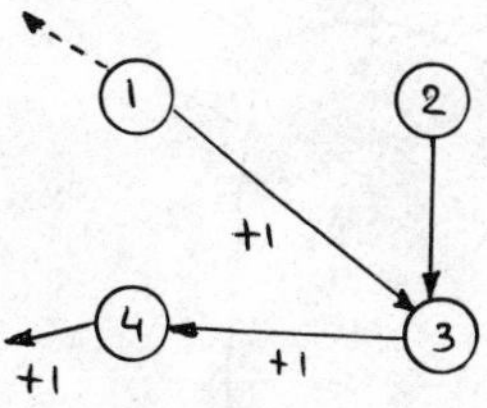

$$B^{-1} = \begin{bmatrix} +1 & & & \\ 0 & & & \\ +1 & & & \\ +1 & & & \end{bmatrix}$$

The other columns of B^{-1} are generated in the same manner giving

$$B^{-1} = \begin{bmatrix} 1 & 0 & 0 & 0 \\ 0 & 1 & 0 & 0 \\ 1 & 1 & 1 & 0 \\ 1 & 1 & 1 & 1 \end{bmatrix}$$

PROBLEM 9.24 (Continued)

Now, to generate a row of B^{-1} we place a slack arc at each node and remove the selected basic arc. Those slack arcs which are no longer connected to the root will have a ± 1 in the corresponding row. If the selected basis arc was pointing toward the root then all nonzero entries in the row will be $+1$; otherwise they will be -1.

Generating the row of B^{-1} associated with x_{13}, we get:

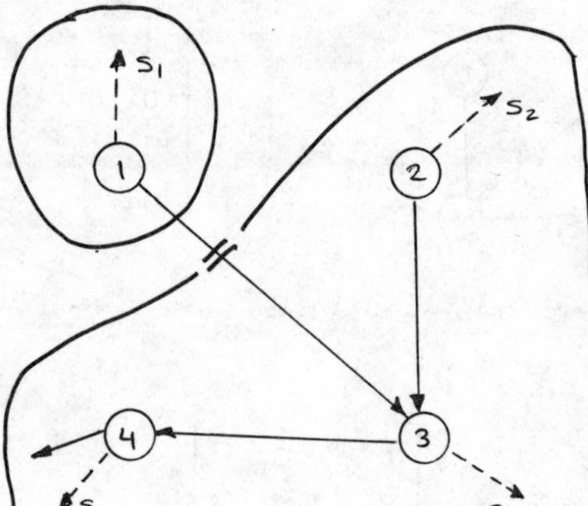

PROBLEM 9.24 (Continued)

	S_1	S_2	S_3	S_4
X_{13}	+1	0	0	0

Since S_1 is the only slack arc disconnected from the root and (1,3) points toward the root.

PROBLEM 9.25

First note that the root will always be in the basis. For the node, say, m the root emits, there has to be an another arc leads into m otherwise the basis tree will be disconnected. Therefore we need to determine the value of that arc previous to determining the value of the root. Same reasoning apply to the arc that is preceeding the root. Let that arc be (k, m). Thus there has to be an another arc, say (ℓ, k) that connects the nodes ℓ and k. If there is no node ℓ, then node k is the end node, and therefore the value of X_{km} must be determined first. Hence, the value of the root will always be determined last.

PROBLEM 9.26

The assertion is false For detail see problem 8.23.

PROBLEM 9.27

We can create two dummy nodes i' and i'' such that the capacity of the arc between i' and i'' has a lower bound ℓ and an upper bound u. Node i' has all the arcs that are entering to node i and node i'' has all the arcs that are emitting from node i. Therefore, the flow between i' and i'' has to stay between ℓ and u which is the requirement for node i. The problem is now a capacitated network flow problem which can be solved by the method described in section 9.7 or the out-of-kilter algorithm described in chapter 10.

PROBLEM 9.28

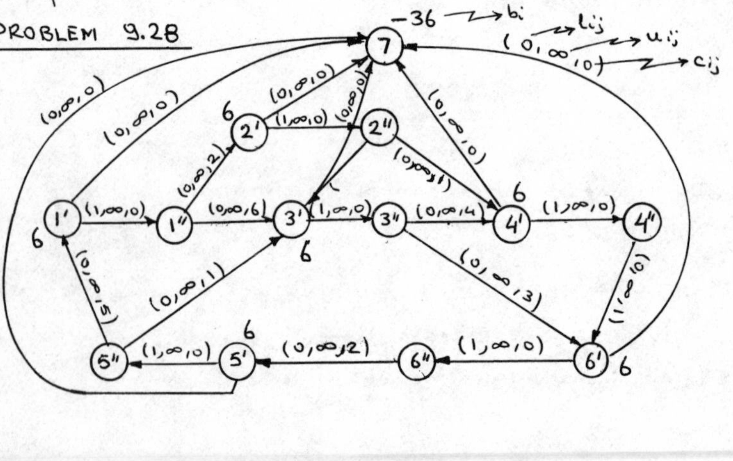

PROBLEM 9.29

Suppose we have the following figure:

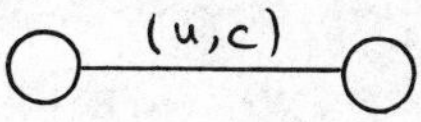

We can replace this arc by two directed arcs

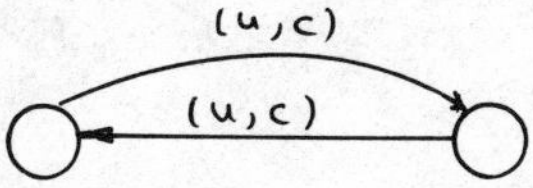

This will enable us to use the methods learned in this chapter to solve the network flow problems. Note that in the final solution will be the absolute difference of the flows on both arcs.

In the case where the undirected arc has a lower bound $l > 0$, we cannot create two arcs with capacities and costs being (l, u, c). If we do this transformation, we can not guarantee that the resultant flow on those two arcs will be greater than the lower bound and it will be lower than the upper bound of the undirected arc. We can say that there is no nice procedure to convert the undirected arcs with lower capacities into two directed arcs.

PROBLEM 9.30

Make the change of variable $x'_{ij} = x_{ij} - l_{ij}$. This modifies the lower and upper bounds. The lower bounds on x'_{ij} are now 0. The upper bounds are $u_{ij} - l_{ij}$. Furthermore;

$$b_i = \sum_j x_{ij} - \sum_j x_{ji} = \sum_j (x'_{ij} - l_{ij}) - \sum_j (x'_{ji} - l_{ji})$$

Thus

$$b'_i = b_i - \sum_j l_{ij} + \sum_j l_{ji} \quad .$$

Thus, we modify the right hand side as indicated above.

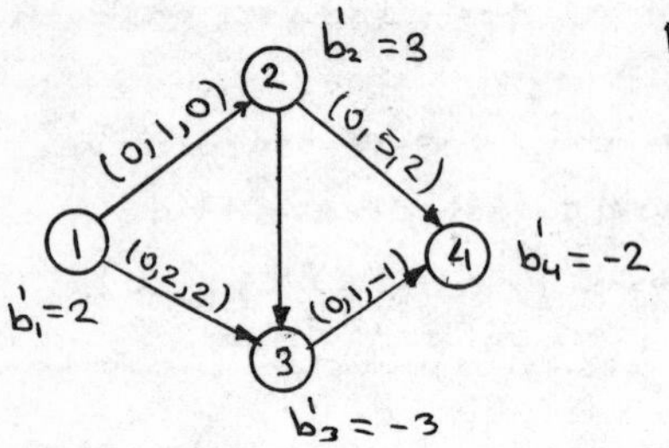

$b'_1 = 2 - (-1) - (1) = 2$

$b'_2 = 1 - (-1 + 0) + 1 = 3$

$b'_3 = -1 - (1) + (-1 + 0) = -3$

$b'_4 = -2 - 1 + 1 = -2$

PROBLEM 9.31

Suppose that the cost function for arc (i,j) is as follows:

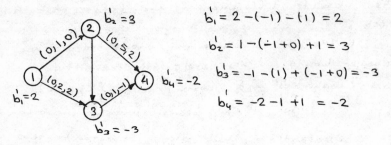

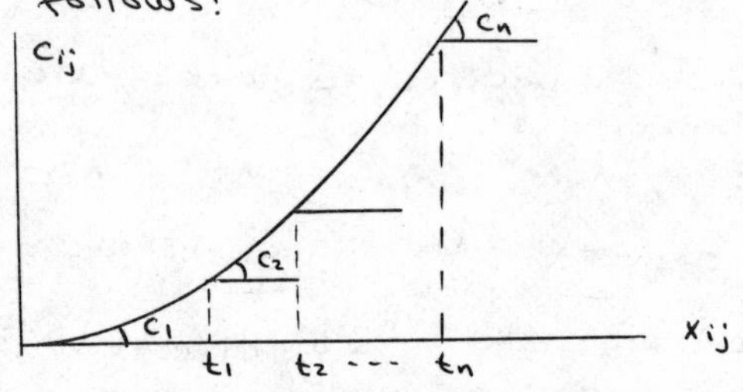

PROBLEM 9.31 (Continued)

We can replace arc (i, j) by the following figure:

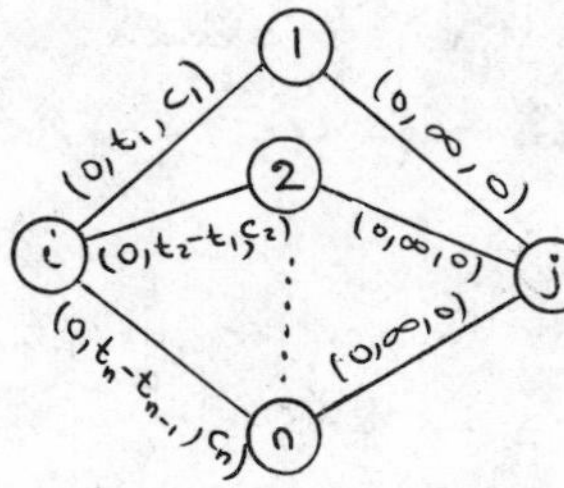

Since $c_k > c_{k-1}$ then the flow on arc (i,k) could be positive only if the flow on arc (i,ℓ) is at the upper bound for $\ell = 1, 2, \ldots, k-1$.

This result can not be generalized for piecewise linear and concave functions. Since x_{ik} may be positive while $x_{i\ell} = 0$ where $\ell < k$.

PROBLEM 9.32

See problem 9.30 for details. The converted network will be:

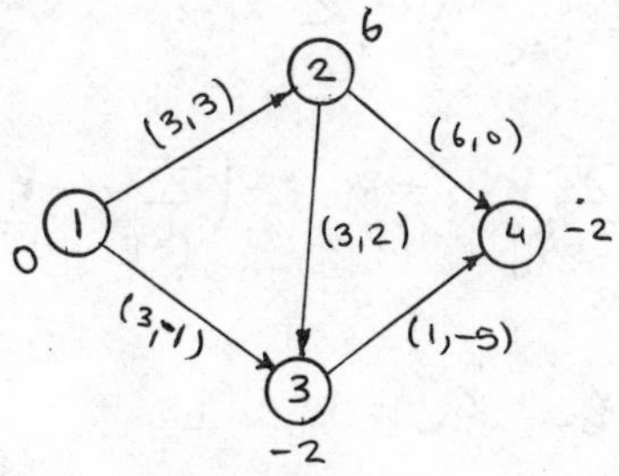

PROBLEM 9.33

Make the following change of variable:

$x_{ij} = x_{ik}$ $\qquad x_{ik} \geq 0 \Rightarrow x_{ij} \geq 0$

$x_{ik} + x_{jk} = u_{ij}$ $\qquad x_{jk} \geq 0 \Rightarrow x_{ij} \leq u_{ij}$

PROBLEM 9.33 (Continued)

Thus we have created a new node k with demand u_{ij}, eliminating arc (i,j) and introduced arcs (i,k) and (j,k) instead. We wish to determine the new supplies and/or demands at nodes i and j.

Let $O_i = \{\ell : (i,\ell) \text{ is an arc in original problem}\}$

$O_i' = \{\ell : (i,\ell) \text{ is an arc in new problem}\}$

$I_i = \{\ell : (\ell,i) \text{ is an arc in original problem}\}$

$I_i' = \{\ell : (\ell,i) \text{ is an arc in the new problem}\}$

$$b_i' = \sum_{\ell\in O_i'} x_{i\ell} - \sum_{\ell\in I_i'} x_{\ell i} = \sum_{\ell\in O_i} x_{i\ell} - \sum_{\ell\in I_i'} x_{\ell i} = b_i$$

$$b_j' = \sum_{\ell\in O_j'} x_{j\ell} - \sum_{\ell\in I_j'} x_{\ell j} = \sum_{\ell\in O_j} x_{j\ell} + x_{jk} - \left(\sum_{\ell\in I_j} x_{\ell j} - x_{ij}\right)$$

$$= \sum_{\ell\in O_j} x_{j\ell} - \sum_{\ell\in I_j} x_{\ell j} + x_{jk} + x_{ik} = b_j + u_{ij}$$

Thus the supplies at nodes i and j and k are replaced by b_i, $b_j + u_{ij}$ and $-u_{ij}$ respectively.

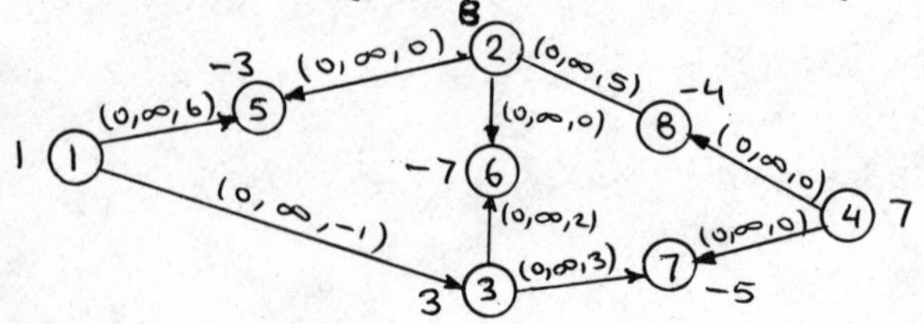

PROBLEM 9.34

Suppose that row m is deleted arcs of the form (i,m) will now have a $+1$ at position i and are considered as one-ended arcs leaving node i. Arcs of the form (m,i) will now have a -1 at position i and are considered one ended arcs entering node i.

Let B be a basis consisting of $m-1$ columns. Obviously the basic arcs do not contain a cycle. So, they form several trees. Each tree has at most one root (see Exercise 9.3). Furthermore, each tree has exactly one root because if a tree has no root then the $m-1$ veetor e_i of zeros except for 1 at the ith position could not be represented as a linear combination of the columns of the basis, where i is an end of the tree. Thus the basis consists of a rooted spanning forest.

The converse is also true.

For represantation of a non basic arc we will have two cases:

Case I: Non basic arc (i,j) has both ends in the same tree: Find the cycle formed by adjoining arc (i,j) to the tree, say, $(i,k), (k,\ell), \ldots, (u,v), (v,w), (w,j)$. Then

PROBLEM 9.34 (Continued)

$$a_{ij} = a_{ik} - a_{kl} + \cdots\cdots + a_{uv} - a_{vw} + a_{wj}$$

Case II: Nonbasic arc (i,j) has both ends at different trees: Let i be in tree T_1 and j be in tree T_2. Let C_1 be the chain in T_1 from the root to node i and C_2 be the chain in T_2 from root to node j. "Imagining" that the roots meet at infinity (initially at the deleted node m), joining nodes i and j together with C_1 and C_2 and the roots form a cycle. Each vector in the cycle is given a -1 or a $+1$ in the representation of a_{ij} depending upon the consistency or unconsistency of the direction of the vector with the orientation of the cycle.

To illustrate consider the following graph:

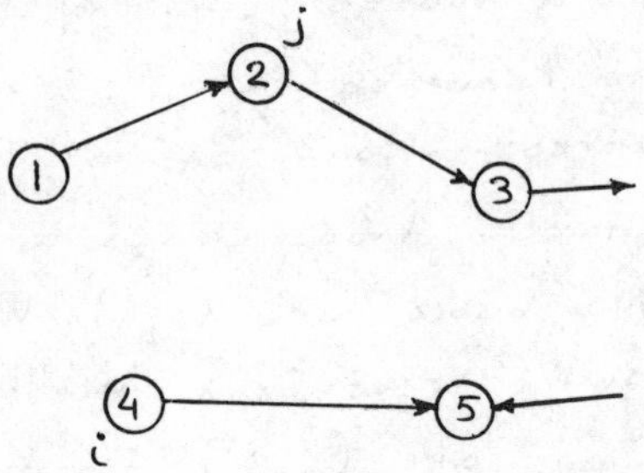

$a_{42} = -a_{23} - a_3 - a_5 + a_{54}$ where a_3 and a_5 are the roots at nodes 3 and 5 respectively.

PROBLEM 9.34 (Continued)

If we delete the last constraint in Exercise 9.4 we have the following configuration:

Row	(1,2)	(1,3)	(2,3)	(3,4)	(4,1)	Dual
1	1	1	0	0	−1	(w_1)
2	−1	0	1	0	0	(w_2)
3	0	−1	−1	1	0	(w_3)
4	0	0	0	−1	1	Delete

Starting basis:

$w_1 - w_3 = 1$

$w_2 - w_3 = -2$

$w_4 = 4$

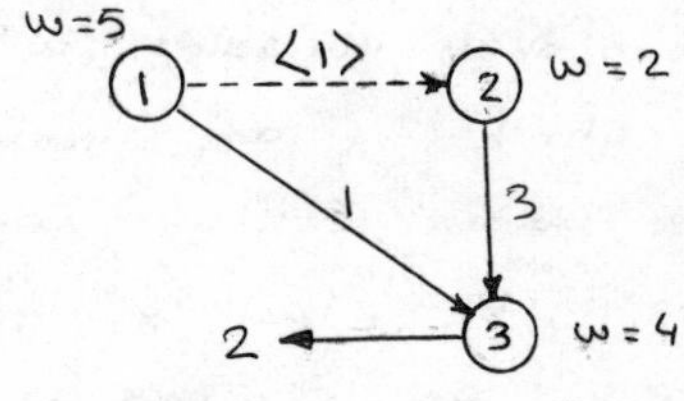

Introduce x_{12}.

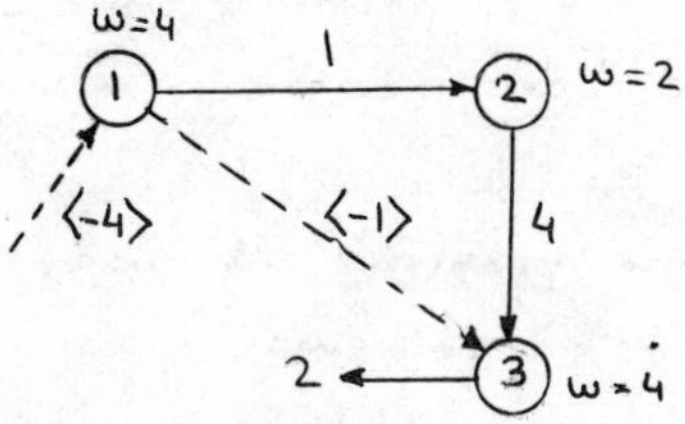

Optimal!

PROBLEM 9.35

See Jewell [261], Johnson [266] or Langley [302].

PROBLEM 9.36

First fix x_{m+1} at value zero, and solve the network flow problem

$$\begin{aligned} \text{Min} \quad & cx \\ \text{s.t.} \quad & Ax = b \\ & x \geq 0 \end{aligned}$$

Let $w_1, w_2, \ldots, w_m$ be the dual variables at optimality. ($w_m = M$ where M is a large positive number).

PROBLEM 9.36 (Continued)

Compute $z_{n+1} - c_{n+1} = wa_{n+1} - c_{n+1}$. If $z_{n+1} - c_{n+1} \le 0$ the current solution with $x_{n+1} = 0$ is optimal for the overall problem. Otherwise, form the array

$$\begin{bmatrix} w & c_B\bar{b} \\ B^{-1} & \bar{b} \end{bmatrix} \quad \begin{array}{|c|} \hline z_{n+1} - c_{n+1} \\ \hline y_{n+1} \\ \hline \end{array}$$

where $y_{n+1} = B^{-1}a_{n+1}$. Pivoting updates B^{-1} and the dual variables. With the new dual variables we check if any nonbasic variable should enter the basis. If there is no $z_{ij} - c_{ij} > 0$, we stop. The last solution is optimal. Otherwise, we proceed with the revised simplex method.

The network of the problem, if we delete a_6 will be as follows:

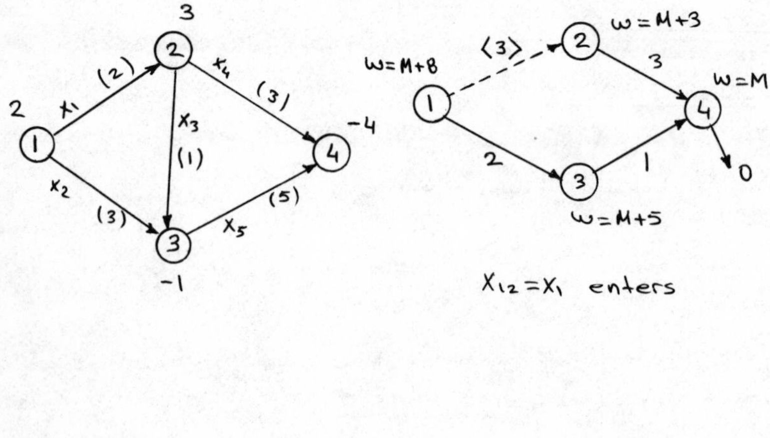

$X_{12} = X_1$ enters

PROBLEM 9.36 (Continued)

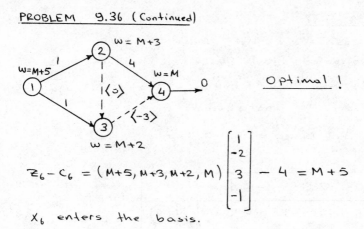

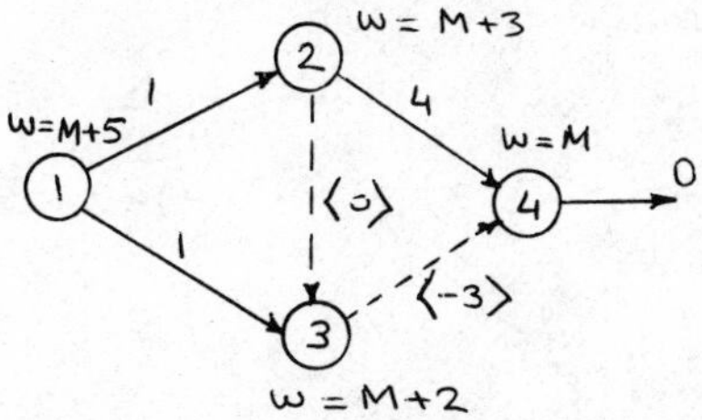

Optimal !

$$z_6 - c_6 = (M+5, M+3, M+2, M)\begin{bmatrix} 1 \\ -2 \\ 3 \\ -1 \end{bmatrix} - 4 = M+5$$

x_6 enters the basis.

						x_6
z	M+5	M+3	M+2	M	17	M+5
$x_{12}=x_1$	1	0	1	0	1	4
$x_{13}=x_2$	0	0	-1	0	1	-3
$x_{24}=x_4$	1	1	1	0	4	2
x_a	1	1	1	1	0	(1)

z	0	-2	-3	-5	17
x_1	-3	-4	-3	-4	1
x_2	3	3	2	3	1
x_4	-1	-1	-1	-2	4
x_6	1	1	1	1	0

Check optimality:

$$z_{23} - c_{23} = w_2 - w_3 - c_{23} = -2 + 3 - 1 = 0$$

$$z_{34} - c_{34} = w_3 - w_4 - c_{34} = -3 + 5 - 5 = -3$$

Thus, we have the overall optimal.

PROBLEM 9.37

Yes. Apply the same procedure for the variables which have a column in D.

$$z_7 - c_7 = wa_7 - c_7 = (0,-2,-3,-5)(2,-3,2,0)^T + 3 = 3$$

So x_7 is introduced.

$$y_7 = B^{-1}a_7 = (8, -5, 1, -1)^T$$

						x_7
z	0	-2	-3	-5	17	3
x_{12}	-3	-4	-3	-4	1	(8)
x_{13}	3	3	2	3	1	-5
x_{24}	-1	-1	-1	-2	4	1
x_6	1	1	1	1	0	-1

						x_{23}
	9/8	-4/8	-15/8	-28/8	133/8	3/8
x_7	-3/8	-4/8	-3/8	-4/8	1/8	-1/8
x_{13}	9/8	4/8	1/8	4/8	13/8	(3/8)
x_{24}	-5/8	-4/8	-5/8	-12/8	31/8	1/8
x_6	5/8	4/8	5/8	4/8	1/8	-1/8

Check optimality:

$$z_{12} - c_{12} = w_1 - w_2 - c_{12} = \frac{9}{8} + \frac{4}{8} - 2 < 0$$

$$z_{23} - c_{23} = w_2 - w_3 - c_{23} = \frac{-4}{8} + \frac{15}{8} - 1 = \frac{3}{8}$$

$$z_{34} - c_{34} = w_3 - w_4 - c_{34} = \frac{-15}{8} + \frac{28}{8} - 5 < 0$$

So, x_{23} enters.

$$y_{23} = B^{-1}a_{23} = \left(-\frac{1}{8}, \frac{3}{8}, \frac{1}{8}, -\frac{1}{8}\right)^T$$

PROBLEM 9.37 (Continued)

					RHS
z	$14/8$	0	$-10/8$	2	15
x_7					$2/3$
x_{23}					$13/3$
x_{24}					$10/3$
x_6					$2/3$

Check optimality:

$$z_{12} - c_{12} = w_1 - w_2 - c_{12} = \frac{14}{8} - 0 - 2 = -\frac{2}{8} < 0$$

$$z_{13} - c_{13} = w_1 - w_3 - c_{13} = \frac{14}{8} + \frac{10}{8} - 3 = 0$$

$$z_{34} - c_{34} = w_3 - w_4 - c_{34} = -\frac{10}{8} - 2 - 5 < 0$$

Thus we have the optimal solution:

$$(x_1, x_2, x_3, x_4, x_5, x_6, x_7) = \left(0, 0, \frac{13}{3}, \frac{10}{3}, 0, \frac{2}{3}, \frac{2}{3}\right)$$

PROBLEM 9.38

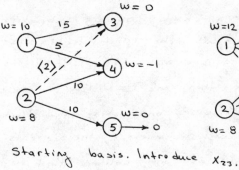

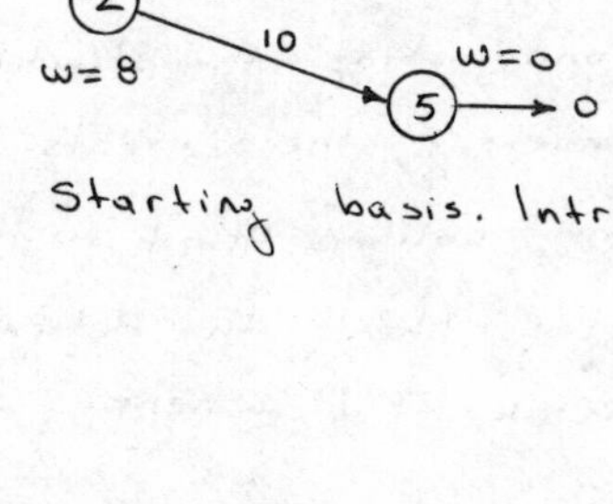

Starting basis. Introduce x_{23}.

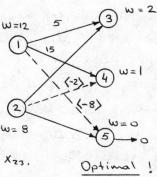

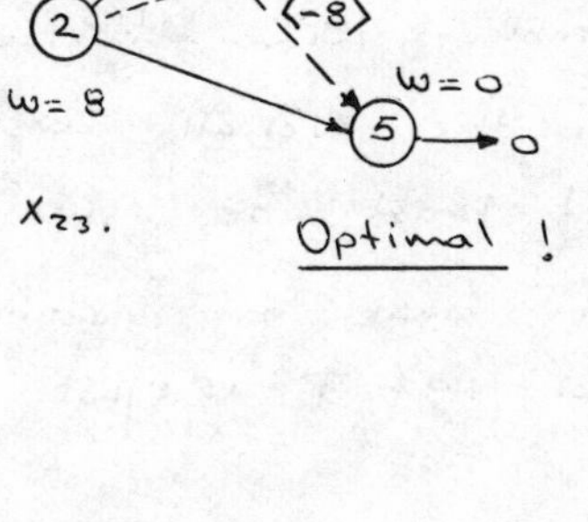

Optimal !

PROBLEM 9.39

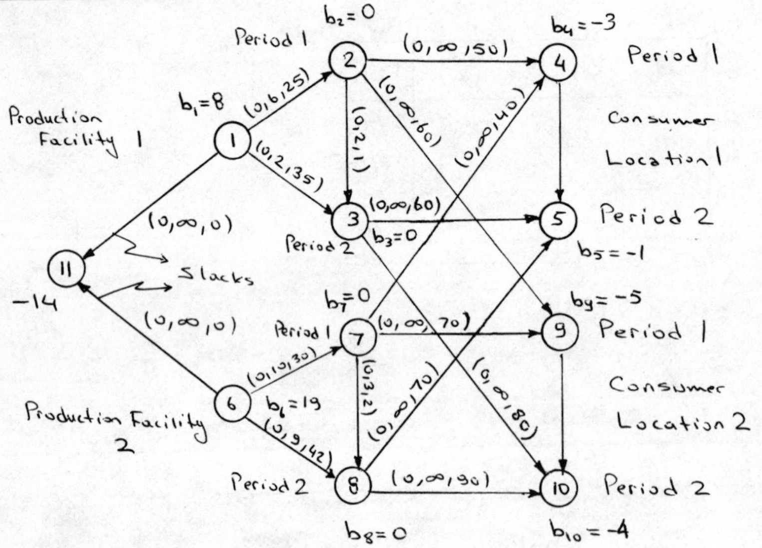

PROBLEM 9.40

Obviously the assertion is true for any 1×1 square submatrix. Suppose that it is also true for any $k \times k$ square submatrix. We will show that the result holds for any $(k+1) \times (k+1)$ square submatrix T. If T is a submatrix of A then rank T = 0, 1, or −1 as in problem 9.2. Otherwise, and noting the structure of the over all constraint matrix, there exists at least one row or one column of T with at most one nonzero entry. Then the determinant of T is equal to $\alpha \cdot \det(T')$, where

PROBLEM 9.40 (Continued)

$\alpha = 0, 1,$ or -1 and T' is a $k \times k$ submatrix of T formed by deleting a certain row and a certain column. By the induction hypothesis $\det(T') = 0, 1,$ or -1; thus $\det(T) = 0, 1$ or -1. This shows that the constraint matrix is totally unimodal.

PROBLEM 9.41

a)

		Dual Variables
min	cx	
S.T.	$Ax = b$	w
	$x \geq l$	v
	$-x \geq -u$	h

where A is a node-arc incidence matrix. The dual of this problem is:

$$\max \quad wb + vl - uh$$

$$\text{S.T.} \quad w_i - w_j + v_{ij} - h_{ij} = c_{ij} \qquad \text{for all } i, j.$$

b)

$w_1 = 10, \quad w_2 = 9, \quad w_3 = 6, \quad w_4 = 0$

$v_{12} = h_{12} = 0$

$v_{13} = h_{13} = 0$

$v_{24} = 0, \quad h_{24} = 7$

$v_{32} = 2, \quad h_{32} = 0$

$v_{34} = h_{34} = 0$

Dual objective $= (50 + 0 + 18 + 0) + (2) - (28) =$ Primal obj. Hence the optimality is verified.

PROBLEM 9.42

a)

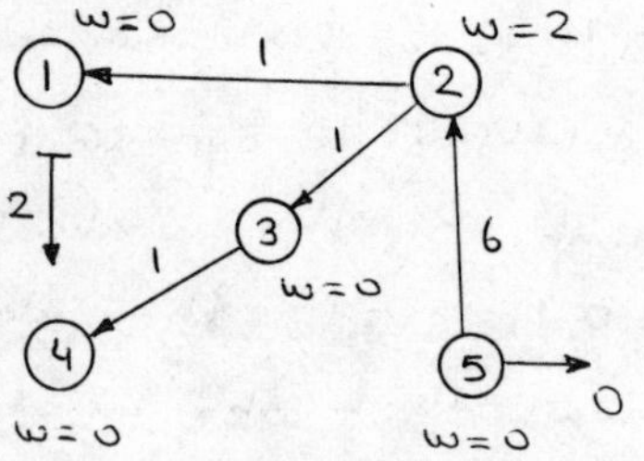

The basic solution is feasible.

b)

	z	x_{14}	x_{21}	x_{23}	x_{31}	x_{34}	x_{35}	x_{45}	x_{52}	x_a	RHS
z	1	-1	0	0	-3	0	-6	-1	0	0	
x_{21}	0	-1	1	0	1	0	0	0	0	0	1
x_{23}	0	1	0	1	-1	0	-1	-1	0	0	1
x_{34}	0	1	0	0	0	1	0	-1	0	0	1
x_{52}	0	0	0	0	0	0	-1	-1	1	0	6
x_a	0	0	0	0	0	0	0	0	0	1	0

c) Dual Program:

$$\max\ w_1 - 4w_2 + 0w_3 - 3w_4 + 6w_5 - 2h_{14} - 5h_{21} - 6h_{23} - h_{31} - 3h_{34} - 4h_{35} - h_{45} - 8h_{52}$$

S.T.

$$\begin{aligned}
w_1 - w_4 - h_{14} &\le 1\\
-w_2 + w_2 - h_{21} &\le 2\\
w_2 - w_3 - h_{23} &\le 2\\
-w_1 + w_3 - h_{31} &\le 3\\
w_3 - w_4 - h_{34} &\le 0\\
w_3 - w_5 - h_{35} &\le 6\\
w_4 - w_5 - h_{45} &\le 1\\
-w_2 + w_5 - h_{52} &\le -2
\end{aligned}$$

w_i unrestricted, $h_{ij} \geq 0$ for all i, j.

PROBLEM 9.42 (Continued)

d) Note that $h_{ij}(u_{ij} - x_{ij}) = 0 \quad \forall i, j$. Thus,

$h_{21} = h_{23} = h_{31} = h_{34} = h_{35} = h_{45} = h_{52} = 0$.

For basic variables, $w_i - w_j - c_{ij} = 0 \Rightarrow$

$w_1 = 0, \quad w_2 = 2, \quad w_3 = w_4 = w_5 = 0$.

Thus, for arc (1,2) we must have

$$w_1 - w_4 - h_{14} - 1 = 0 \Longrightarrow h_{14} = -1.$$

Thus the complementary dual solution is not feasible since $h_{ij} \geq 0$ for all i, j does not hold.

e) 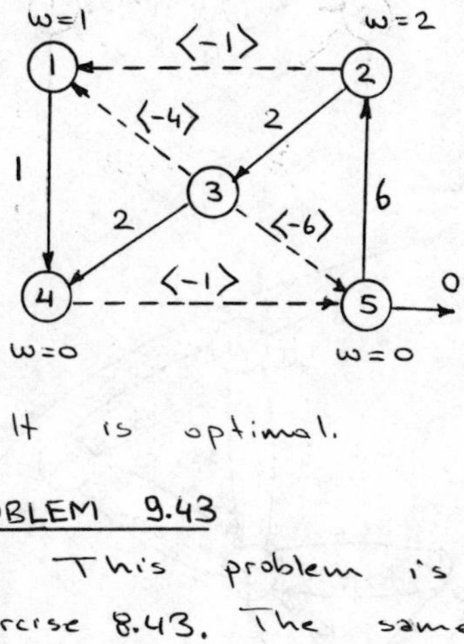

Optimal!

f) It is optimal.

PROBLEM 9.43

This problem is similar to that of Exercise 8.43. The same line of argument apply in this case as well. In this problem we will be dealing with arcs instead of the cells in transportation tableau.

PROBLEM 9.44

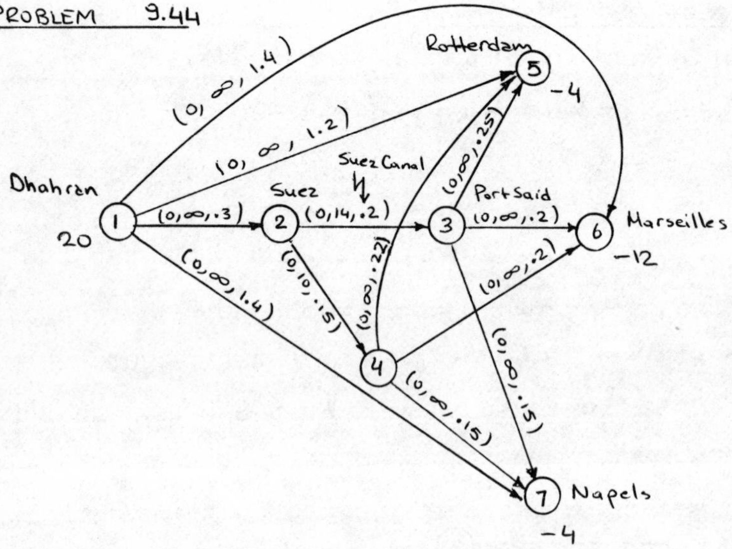

PROBLEM 9.45

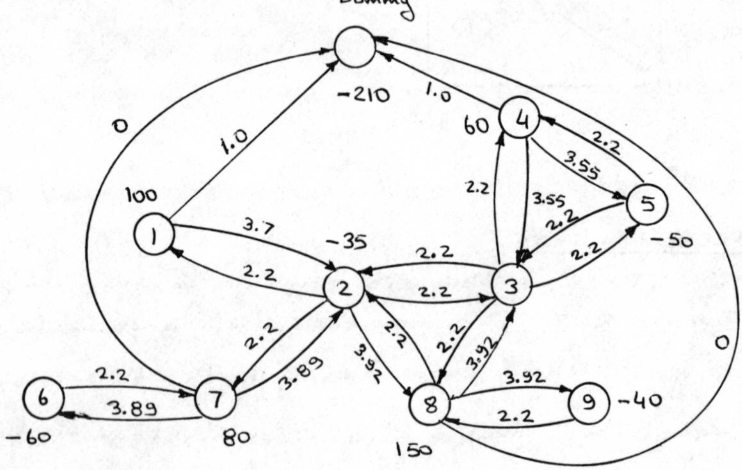

Numbers on the arcs represent unit shipping costs. The network can be simplified by deleting the arcs which will not carry any positive flow.

PROBLEM 9.46

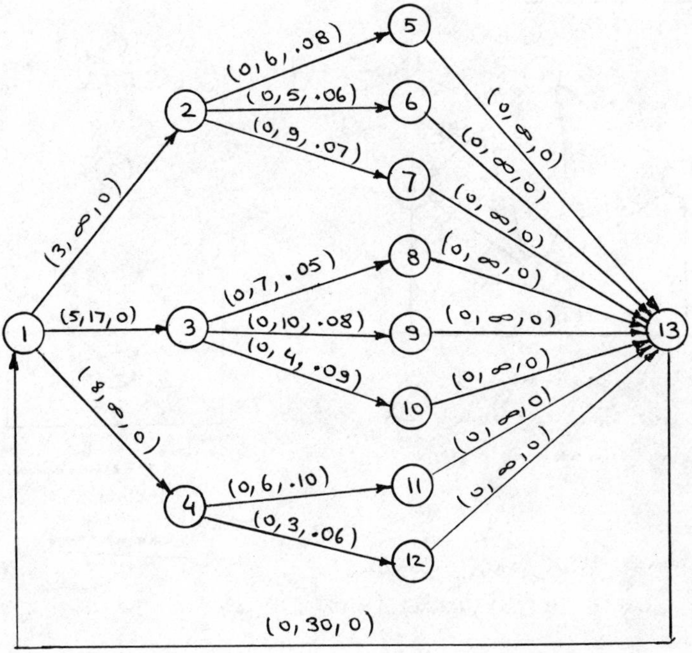

(3, ∞, 0)
(5,17,0)
(8, ∞, 0)
(0, 6, .08)
(0, 5, .06)
(0, 9, .07)
(0, 7, .05)
(0, 10, .08)
(0, 4, .09)
(0, 6, .10)
(0, 3, .06)
(0, ∞, 0)
(0, ∞, 0)
(0, ∞, 0)
(0, ∞, 0)
(0, ∞, 0)
(0, ∞, 0)
(0, ∞, 0)
(0, ∞, 0)
(0, 30, 0)
1
2
3
4
5
6
7
8
9
10
11
12
13

CHAPTER 10 THE OUT-OF-KILTER ALGORITHM

PROBLEM 10.1

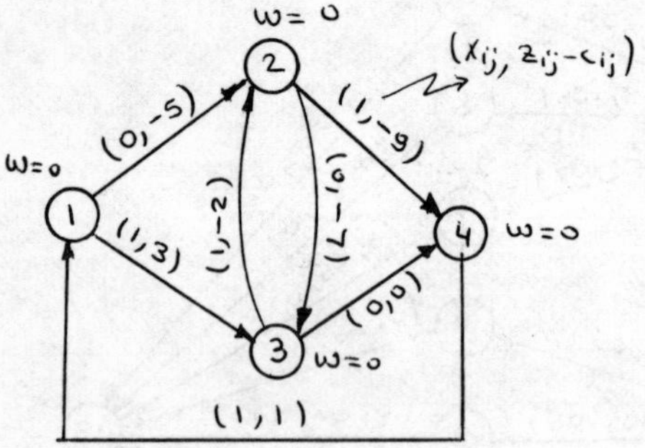

Arc (4,1) is out-of-kilter.

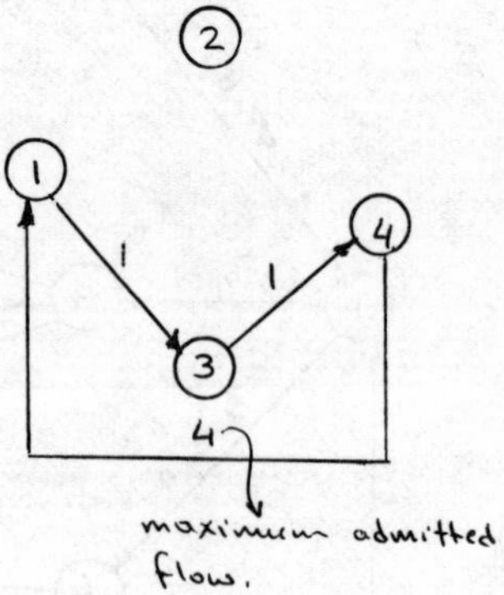

Initial starting flow. Flows are conserved at each node.

Breakthrough!

Change the flow around the cycle (1,3), (3,4), (4,1).

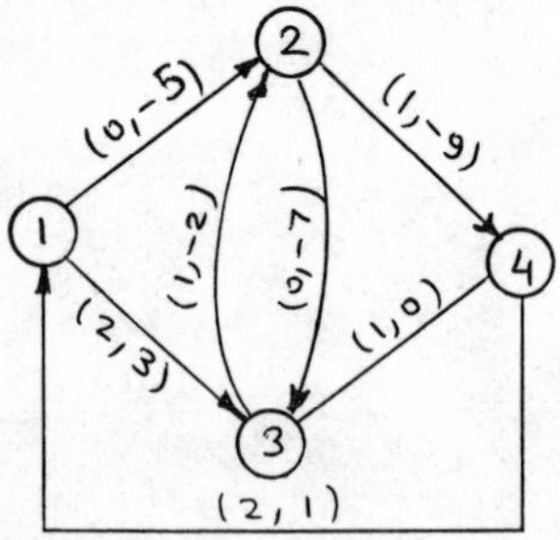

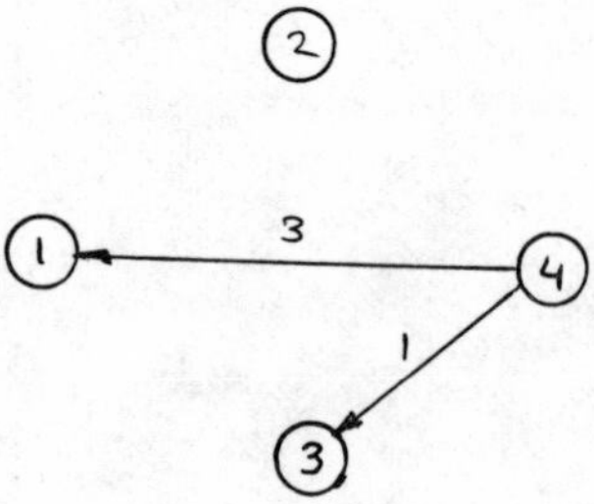

Nonbreakthrough!

PROBLEM 10.1 (Continued)

$$X = \{1\} \quad , \quad \bar{X} = \{2,3,4\}$$

$$S_1 = \{(i,j) : i \in X, \ j \in \bar{X}, \ z_{ij} - c_{ij} < 0, \ x_{ij} \le u_{ij}\}$$

$$S_2 = \{(i,j) : i \in \bar{X}, \ j \in X, \ z_{ij} - c_{ij} > 0, \ x_{ij} \geq \ell_{ij}\}$$

Hence,

$$S_1 = \{(1,2)\} \quad , \quad S_2 = \{(4,1)\}$$

$$\theta_1 = \min_{(i,j) \in S_1} \{|z_{ij} - c_{ij}|\}$$

$$\theta_2 = \min_{(i,j) \in S_2} \{|z_{ij} - c_{ij}|\}$$

$$\theta_1 = \min\{5\} = 5 \quad , \quad \theta_2 = \min\{1\} = 1$$

$$\theta = \min\{\theta_1, \theta_2\}$$

$$\theta = \min\{5, 1\} = 1$$

Modify the dual variables:

$$w_i' = \begin{cases} w_i & \text{if } i \in \bar{X} \\ w_i + \theta & \text{if } i \in X \end{cases}$$

Or, we can directly modify the $z_{ij} - c_{ij}$'s:

$$(z_{ij} - c_{ij})' = \begin{cases} z_{ij} - c_{ij} & \text{if } i \in X, j \in X \\ & \text{or } i \in \bar{X}, j \in \bar{X} \\ (z_{ij} - c_{ij}) + \theta & \text{if } i \in X, \ j \in \bar{X} \\ (z_{ij} - c_{ij}) - \theta & \text{if } i \in \bar{X}, \ j \in X \end{cases}$$

PROBLEM 10.1 (Continued)

Therefore, the new $z_{ij} - c_{ij}$'s are depicted on the graph below.

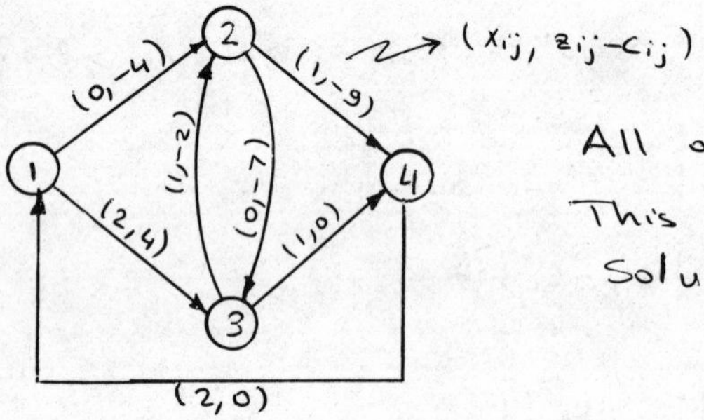

All arcs are in kilter. This is an optimal Solution.

PROBLEM 10.2

a)

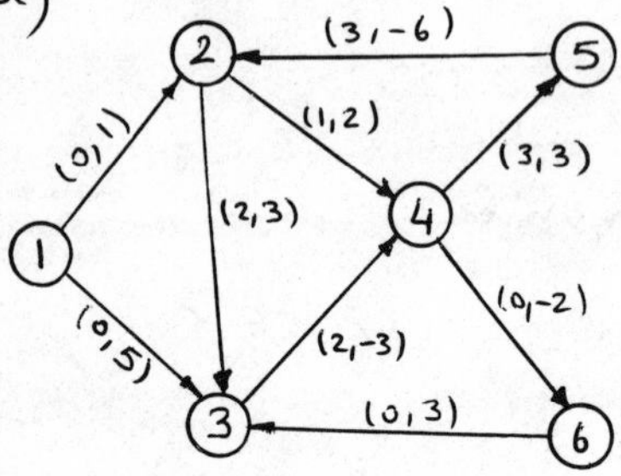

Arcs	Kilter States
(1,2)	out-of-kilter
(1,3)	out of kilter
(2,3)	out of kilter
(2,4)	out of kilter
(3,4)	in kilter
(4,5)	in kilter
(4,6)	out of kilter
(5,2)	in kilter
(6,3)	out of kilter

b) Arc (1,2) is out of kilter.

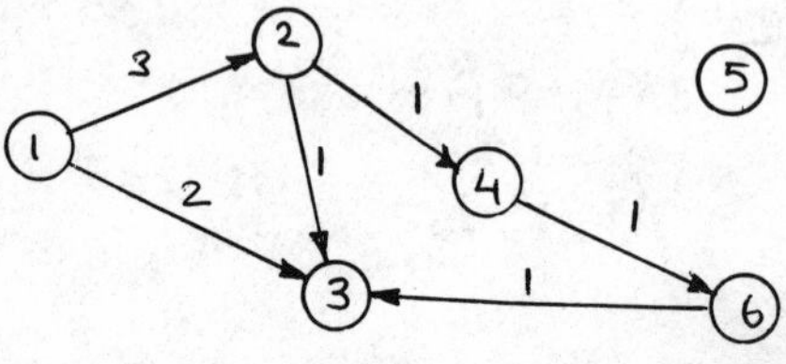

⑤ Nonbreakthrough!

$X = \{2,3,4,6\}$

$\bar{X} = \{1,5\}$

PROBLEM 10.2 (Continued)

$\theta_1 = \infty, \quad \theta_2 = \min\{5\} = 5, \quad \theta = \min\{\infty, 5\} = 5$

Modify the dual variables. The new values of $z_{ij} - c_{ij}$ are depicted on the graph below.

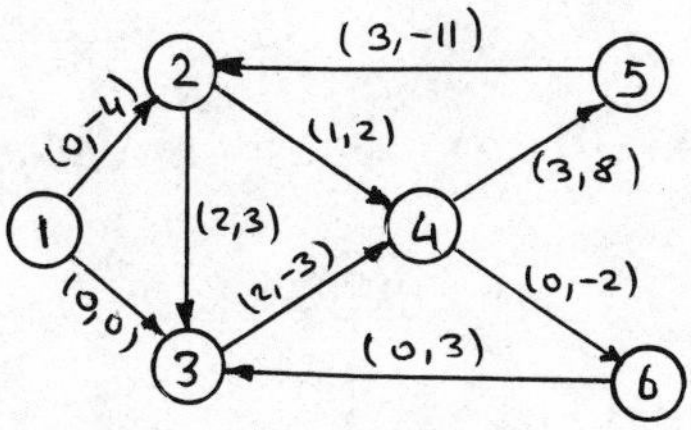

Arc (1,2) is out of kilter.

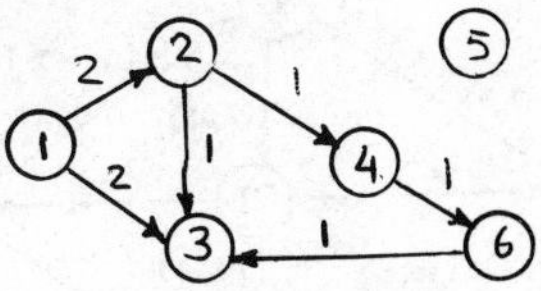

Nonbreakthrough.

$S_1 = \phi \Rightarrow \theta_1 = \infty$

$S_2 = \phi \Rightarrow \theta_2 = \infty$

$\theta = \min\{\infty, \infty\} = \infty$

$X = \{2, 3, 4, 6\}$

$\bar{X} = \{1, 5\}$

Thus there exists no feasible solution. This is also evident by examining node 1.

PROBLEM 10.3

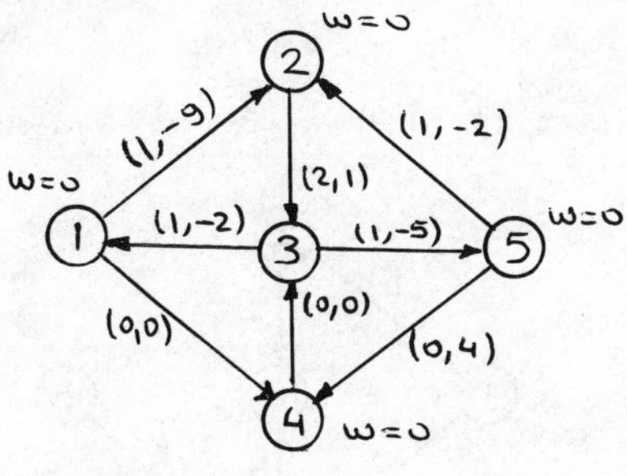

Arc (2,3) is out of kilter.

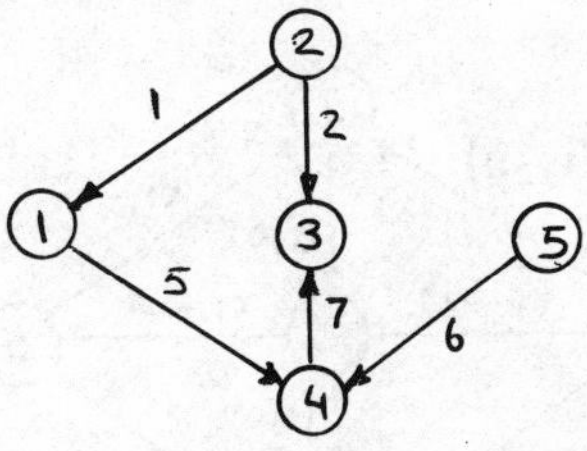

Nonbreakthrough.

$X = \{3\}, \quad \bar{X} = \{1, 2, 4, 5\}$

PROBLEM 10.3 (Continued)

$\theta_1 = \min\{2, 5\} = 2 \qquad \theta_2 = \min\{1\} = 1$

$\theta = \min\{\theta_1, \theta_2\} = 1$

Modify the dual variables. New values of $z_{ij} - c_{ij}$ are depicted below.

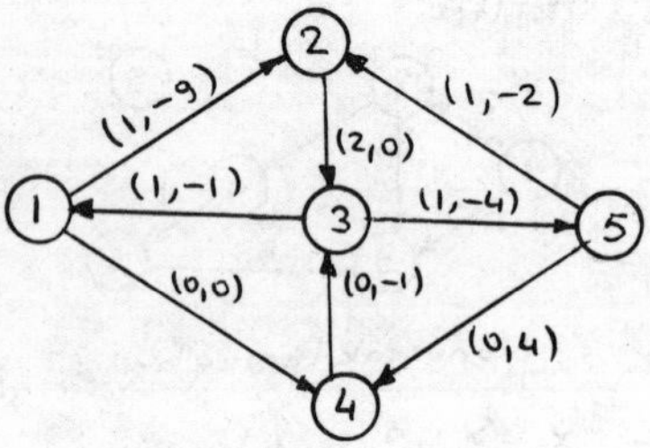

Arc (1,2) is out of kilter.

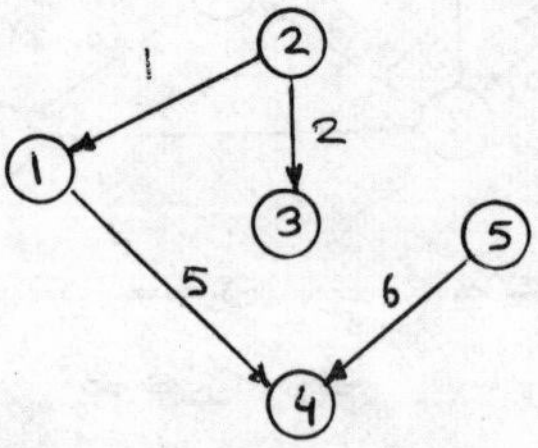

Nonbreakthrough.

$X = \{1, 4\}$

$\bar{X} = \{2, 3, 5\}$

$$\left.\begin{array}{l}\theta_1 = \min\{9, 1\} = 1 \\ \theta_2 = \min\{4\} = 4\end{array}\right\} \Rightarrow \theta = 1$$

Modify the dual variables. The new $z_{ij} - c_{ij}$'s are depicted below.

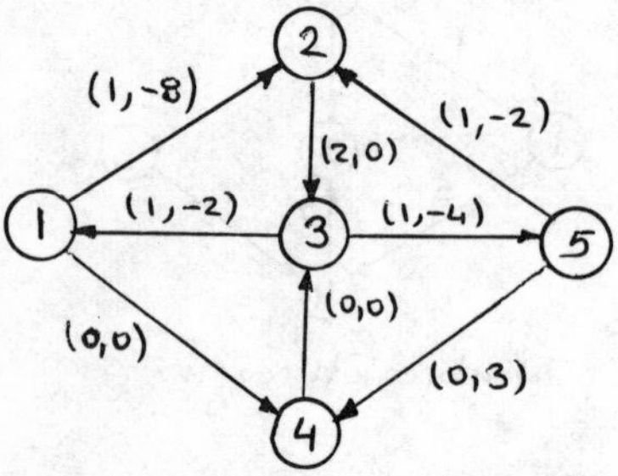

Arc (1,2) is out of kilter.

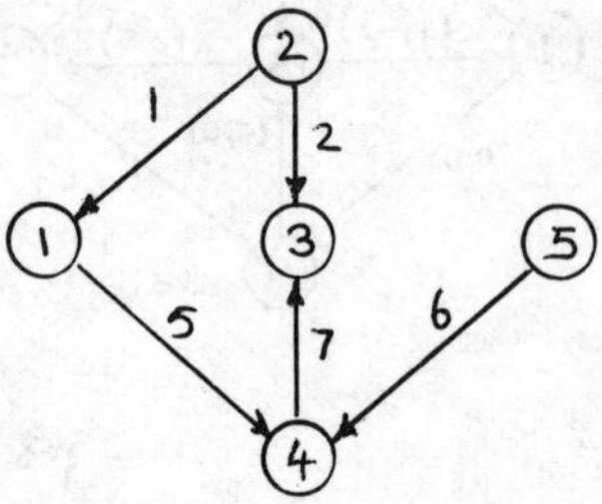

Nonbreakthrough.

PROBLEM 10.3 (Continued)

$X = \{1,4,3\}$, $\bar{X} = \{2,5\}$

$$\left.\begin{array}{l}\theta_1 = \min\{8,4\} = 4\\ \theta_2 = \min\{3\} = 3\end{array}\right\} \Longrightarrow \theta = 3$$

Modify the dual variabes.

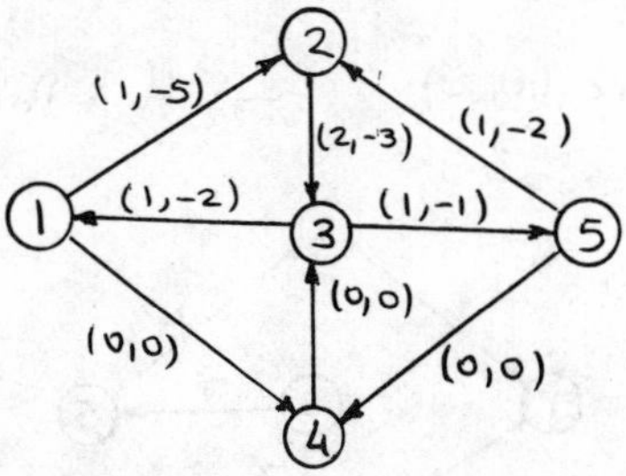

Arc (1,2) is out of kilter.

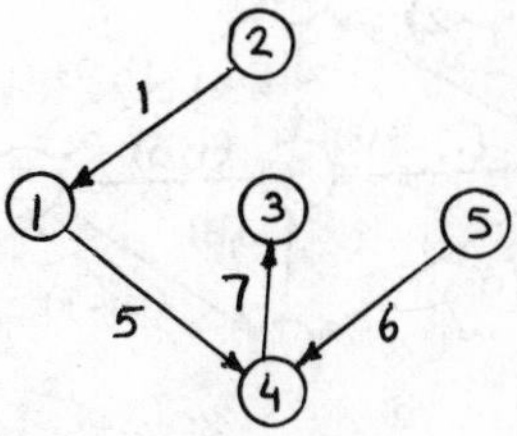

Nonbreakthrough.

$X = \{1,4,3\}$

$\bar{X} = \{2,5\}$

$$\left.\begin{array}{l}\theta_1 = \min\{5,1\} = 1\\ \theta_2 = \infty\end{array}\right\} \Longrightarrow \theta = 1$$

Modify the dual variables.

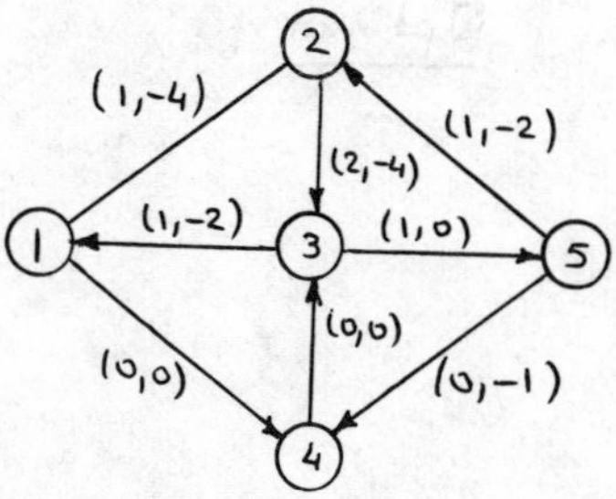

Arc (1,2) is out of kilter.

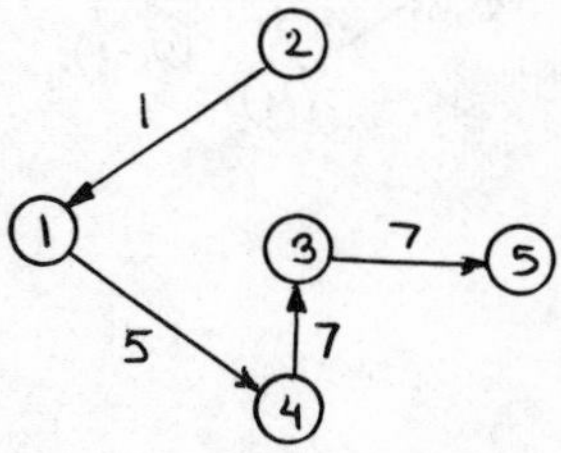

Nonbreakthrough.

PROBLEM 10.3 (Continued)

$X = \{1,4,3,5\}$, $\bar{X} = \{2\}$

$$\left.\begin{array}{l}\theta_1 = \min\{4,2\} = 2 \\ \theta_2 = \infty\end{array}\right\} \Rightarrow \theta = 2$$

Modify the dual variables.

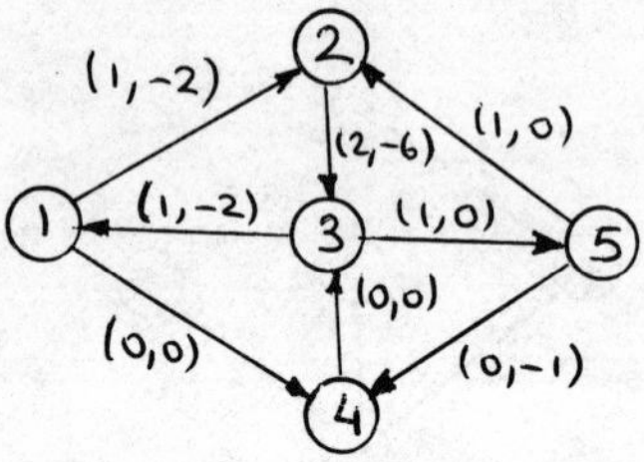

Arc (1,2) is out of kilter.

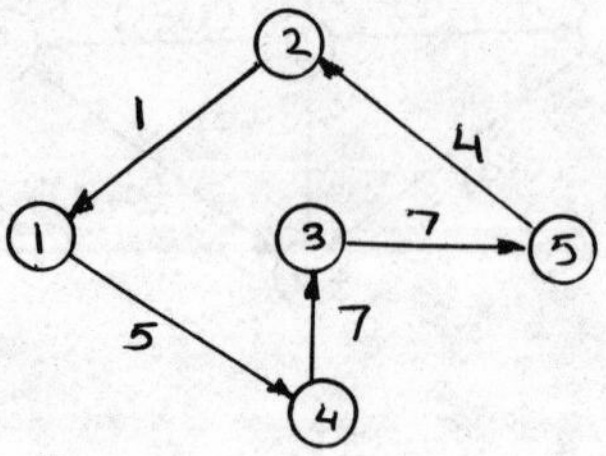

Breakthrough !

Change the flows around the cycle.

New Primal Solution:

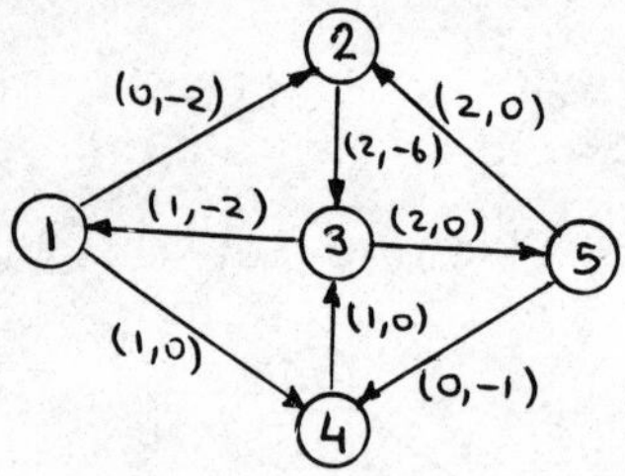

All arcs are in kilter.

Optimal !

PROBLEM 10.4

Obviously the problem has no feasible solution.

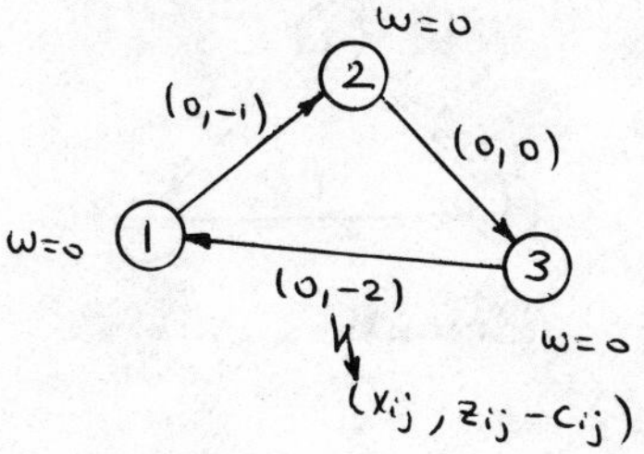

Arc (2,3) is out of kilter.

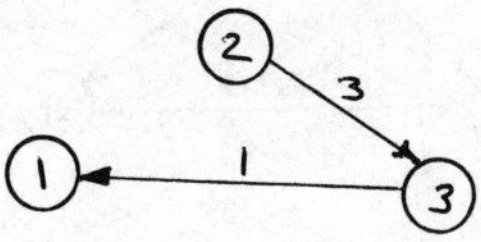

Nonbreakthrough.

$X = \{3,1\}$, $\bar{X} = \{2\}$

$\left.\begin{aligned}\theta_1 &= \min\{1\} = 1\\ \theta_2 &= \infty\end{aligned}\right\} \Rightarrow \theta = 1$

Modify the dual variables.

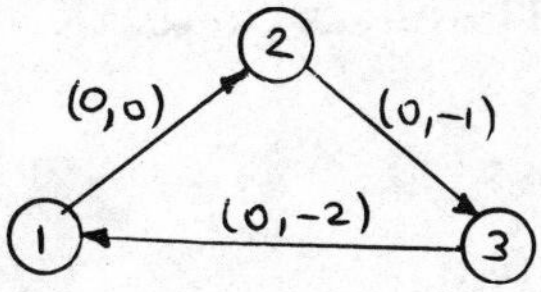

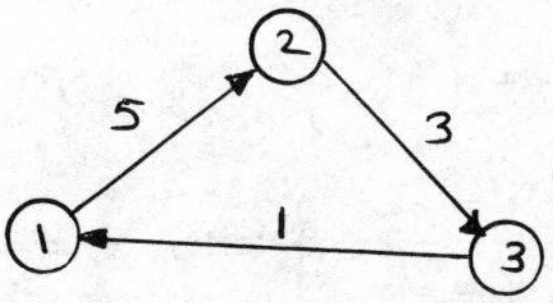

Breakthrough!

Change the flow around the cycle.

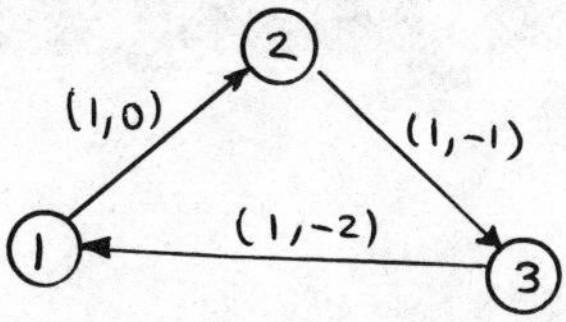

Arc (2,3) is out of kilter.

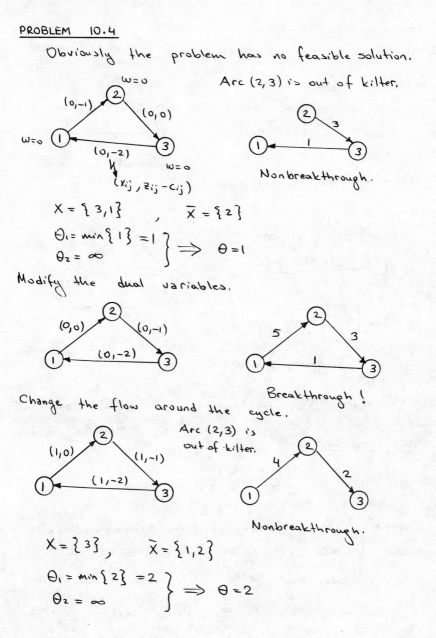

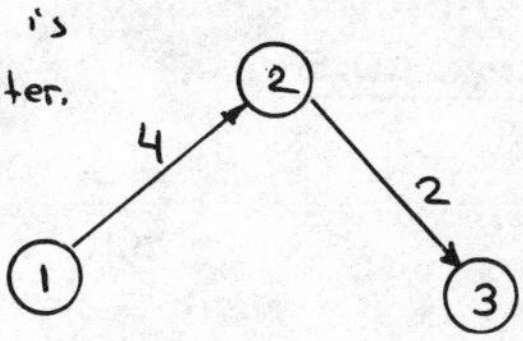

Nonbreakthrough.

$X = \{3\}$, $\bar{X} = \{1,2\}$

$\left.\begin{aligned}\theta_1 &= \min\{2\} = 2\\ \theta_2 &= \infty\end{aligned}\right\} \Rightarrow \theta = 2$

PROBLEM 10.4 (Continued)

Modify the dual variables. Arc (2,3) is out of kilter.

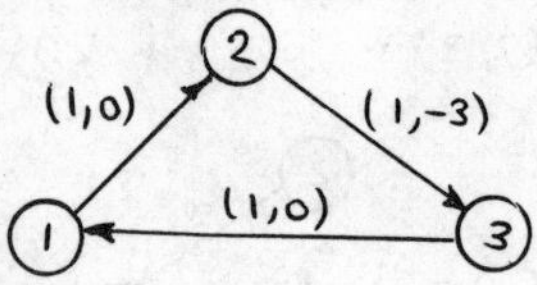

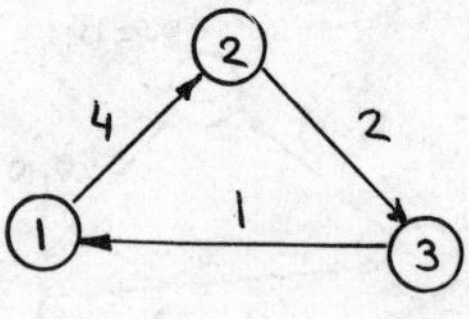

Breakthrough!

Change flow around the cycle.

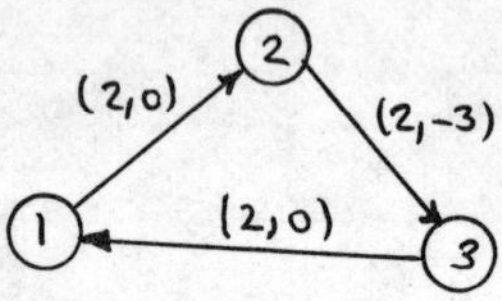

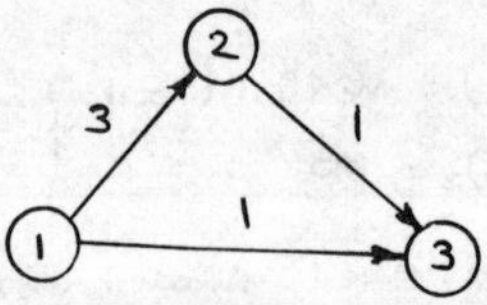

Nonbreakthrough.

$X = \{3\}, \quad \bar{X} = \{1,2\}$

$$\left.\begin{array}{l}\theta_1 = \infty \\ \theta_2 = \infty\end{array}\right\} \Rightarrow \theta = \infty$$

Therefore, the problem has no feasible solution.

PROBLEM 10.5

$$\begin{array}{ll} \min & cx \\ \text{s.t.} & Ax = b \\ & \ell \le x \le u \end{array}$$

where A is a node-arc incidence matrix and $\underline{1}b = 0$. If $b_i > 0$, define a variable $x_{m+1,i}$ such that $x_{m+1,i} = b_i$. In order to insure that $x_{m+1,i} = b_i$, we let $\ell_{m+1,i} = u_{m+1,i} = b_i$.

PROBLEM 10.5 (Continued)

Similarly, if $b_i < 0$, then we define a variable $x_{i,m+1}$ such that $x_{i,m+1} = -b_i$. In order to insure this we let $\ell_{i,m+1} = u_{i,m+1} = -b_i$.

Thus:

$$\sum_{j=1}^{m} x_{ij} - \sum_{j=1}^{m} x_{ji} = x_{m+1,i} \qquad \text{if } b_i > 0$$

and

$$\sum_{j=1}^{m} x_{ij} - \sum_{j=1}^{m} x_{ji} = -x_{i,m+1} \qquad \text{if } b_i < 0$$

Variables of the form $x_{i,m+1}$ or $x_{m+1,i}$ could be interpreted as flow from node i to a new node $m+1$ and flow from node $m+1$ to node i, respectively.

By transforming right hand side to the left hand side we get:

$$\sum_{j=1}^{m} x_{ij} - \sum_{j=1}^{m+1} x_{ji} = 0 \qquad \text{if } b_i > 0, \text{ and}$$

$$\sum_{j=1}^{m+1} x_{ij} - \sum_{j=1}^{m} x_{ji} = 0 \qquad \text{if } b_i < 0.$$

Adding all these equations we get:

$$\sum_{j=1}^{m} x_{m+1,j} - \sum_{j=1}^{m} x_{j,m+1} = 0$$

Thus we transformed the problem into a circulation form where the size of the nodes is increased by 1 and the number of arcs is increased by m.

PROBLEM 10.6

Alternative optimal solutions could be detected if, at optimality, as the network G' is formed, a cycle consisting of arcs with $z_{ij} - c_{ij} = 0$ could be found along which the flow could be increased.

PROBLEM 10.7

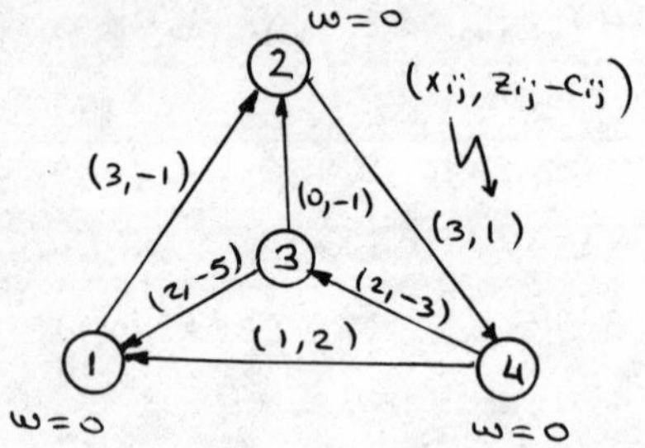

Arc (2,1) is out of kilter.

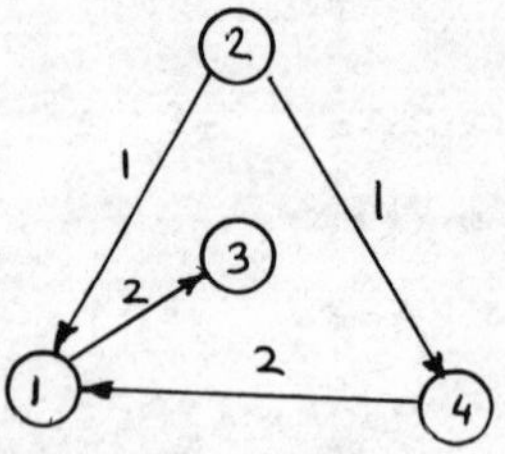

Nonbreakthrough.

$\bar{X} = \{4, 1, 3\}$, $\bar{\bar{X}} = \{2\}$

$$\left.\begin{array}{l} \theta_1 = \min\{1, 1\} = 1 \\ \theta_2 = \min\{1\} = 1 \end{array}\right\} \Rightarrow \theta = 1$$

Modify the dual variables, i.e., modify $z_{ij} - c_{ij}$.

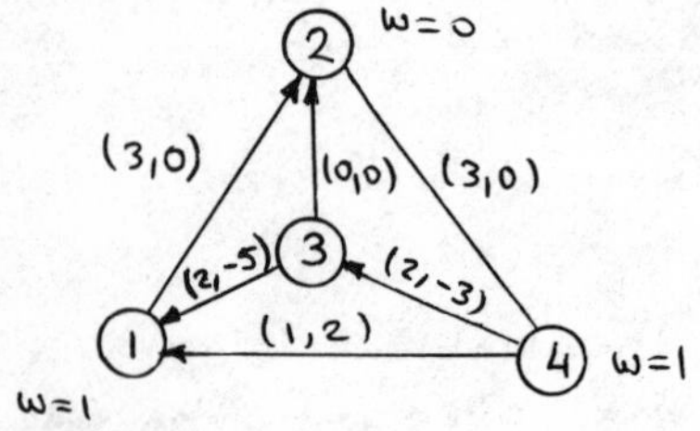

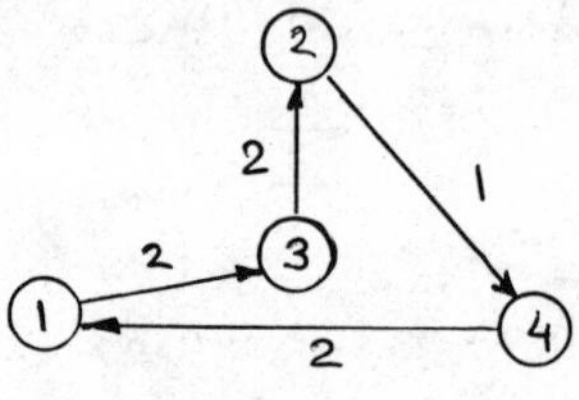

Breakthrough!

PROBLEM 10.7 (Continued)

Change flows around the cycle. Arc (3,1) is out of kilter.

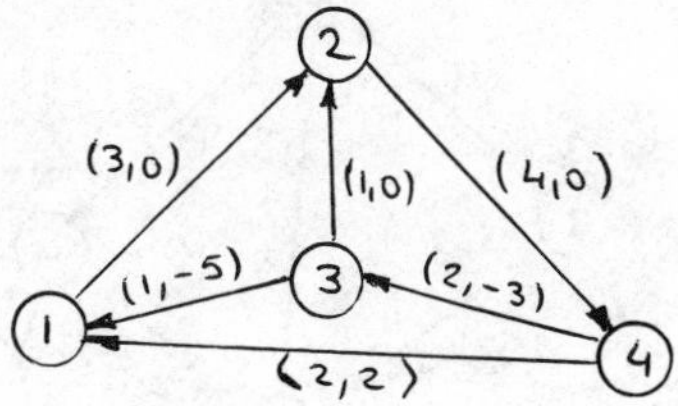

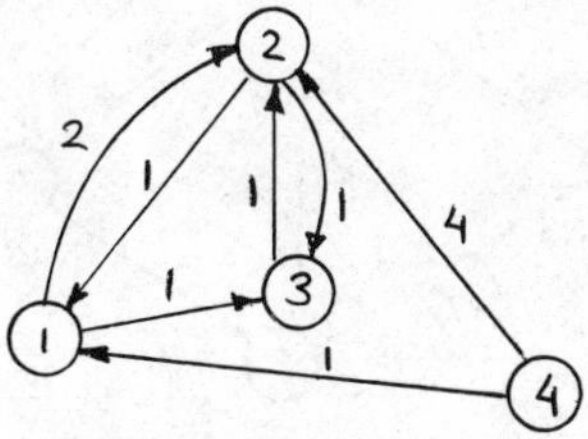

Breakthrough!

Change flows around the cycle.

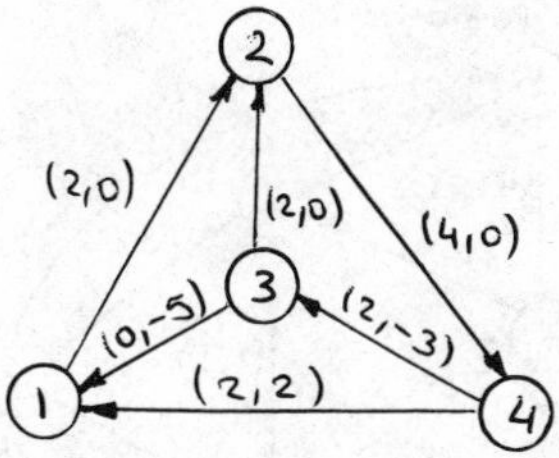

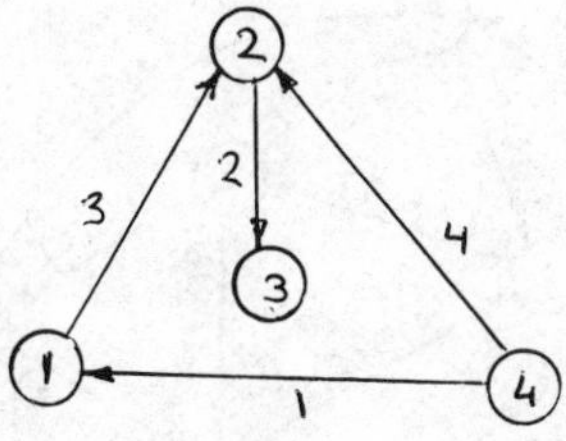

Nonbreakthrough.

$X = \{1, 2, 3\}$, $\bar{X} = \{4\}$

$$\left.\begin{array}{l} \theta_1 = \infty \\ \theta_2 = \min\{2\} = 2 \end{array}\right\} \Rightarrow \theta = 2$$

Modify $z_{ij} - c_{ij}$.

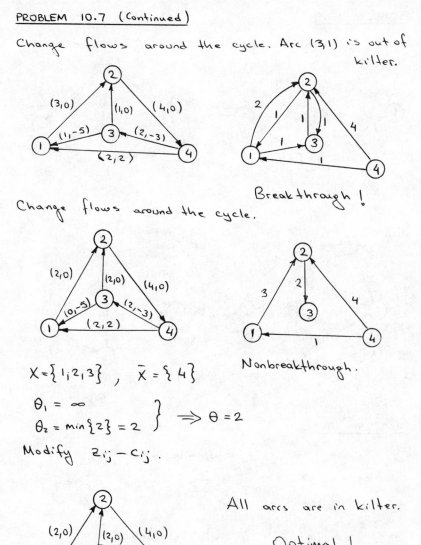

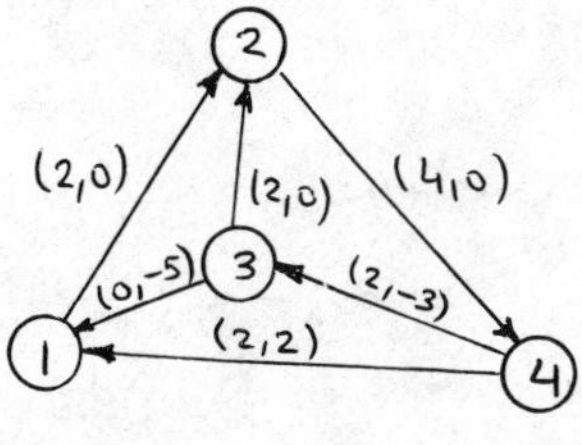

All arcs are in kilter.

Optimal!

PROBLEM 10.8

a)

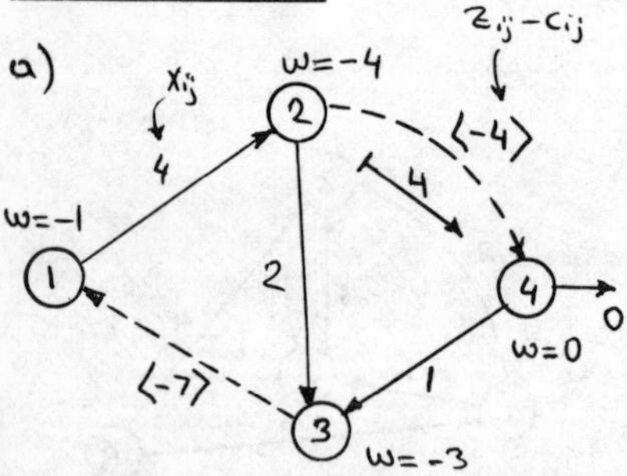

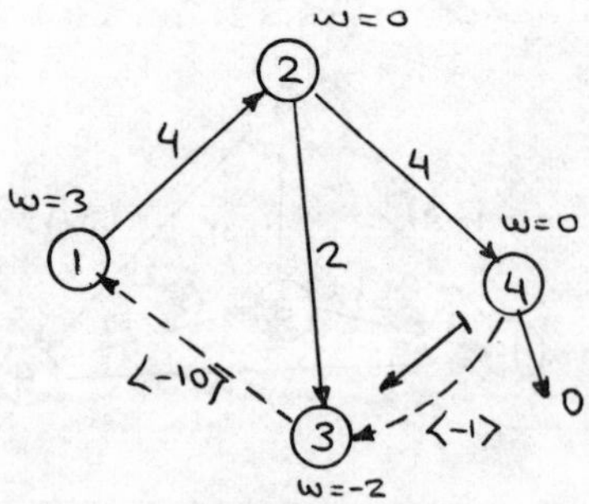

X_{24} enters.

Optimal !

b)

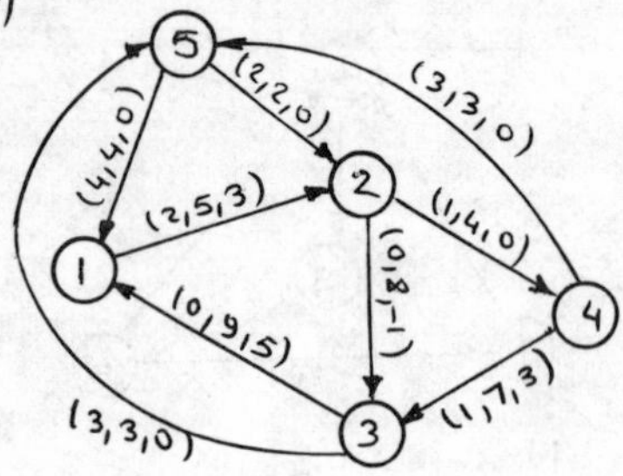

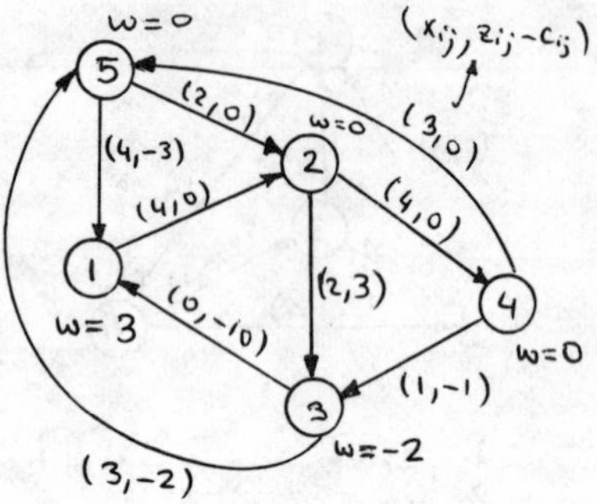

Optimal !

PROBLEM 10.9

Since $z_{ij}-c_{ij}=w_i-w_j-c_{ij}$, then if we replace w_i by w_i-w_k and w_j by w_j-w_k, then

$$(z_{ij}-c_{ij})'=(w_i-w_k)-(w_j-w_k)-c_{ij}$$

$$=w_i-w_j-c_{ij} = z_{ij}-c_{ij}.$$

Thus, the results are the same. Nothing else is affected by such change.

PROBLEM 10.10

Primal: Dual Var. **Dual**

$$\begin{array}{lll} \min & cx & \\ \text{s.t.} & Ax = 0 & \ldots w \\ & x \geq l & \ldots v \\ & -x \geq -u & \ldots h \end{array}
\qquad
\begin{array}{ll} \max & \sum_i \sum_j l_{ij} v_{ij} - \sum_i \sum_j u_{ij} h_{ij} \\ \text{s.t.} & w_i - w_j + v_{ij} - h_{ij} = c_{ij} \\ & h_{ij}, v_{ij} \geq 0 \\ & w_i \text{ unrestricted.} \end{array}$$

For given w_i,

$$v_{ij} = \max\{0, (c_{ij} - w_i + w_j)\}$$
$$h_{ij} = \max\{0, -(c_{ij} - w_i + w_j)\}$$

Suppose that the dual variables are changed. Then

$$w_i' = w_i + \theta \qquad i \in X$$
$$w_i' = w_i \qquad i \in \bar{X}$$

The new dual objective is:

$$\sum_{i \in X} \sum_{j \in X} (l_{ij} v_{ij}' - u_{ij} h_{ij}') + \sum_{i \in X} \sum_{j \in \bar{X}} (l_{ij} v_{ij}' - u_{ij} h_{ij}')$$

$$+ \sum_{i \in \bar{X}} \sum_{j \in X} (l_{ij} v_{ij}' - u_{ij} h_{ij}') + \sum_{i \in \bar{X}} \sum_{j \in \bar{X}} (l_{ij} v_{ij}' - u_{ij} h_{ij}')$$

$i \in X, \ j \in X \Rightarrow v_{ij}' = v_{ij}, \ h_{ij}' = h_{ij}$

$i \in \bar{X}, \ j \in \bar{X} \Rightarrow v_{ij}' = v_{ij}, \ h_{ij}' = h_{ij}$

$i \in X, \ j \in \bar{X} \Rightarrow v_{ij}' = \max(0, -(z_{ij} - c_{ij}) - \theta)$

$$h_{ij}' = \max(0, (z_{ij} - c_{ij}) + \theta)$$

If $z_{ij} - c_{ij} \geq 0$, then $h_{ij}' = z_{ij} - c_{ij} + \theta = h_{ij} + \theta$ and $u_{ij} h_{ij}' > u_{ij} h_{ij}$ and $l_{ij} v_{ij}' = l_{ij} v_{ij} = 0$.

PROBLEM 10.10 (Continued)

If, on the other hand, $z_{ij}-c_{ij}<0$ then (by definition of θ and assuming that $x_{ij}\le u_{ij}$) we must have $z_{ij}-c_{ij}+\theta\le 0$, thus $h'_{ij}=0$ and $v'_{ij}=-(z_{ij}-c_{ij})-\theta<v_{ij}$. Thus $\ell_{ij}v_{ij}>\ell_{ij}v'_{ij}$ and $u_{ij}h_{ij}=u_{ij}h'_{ij}=0$. Hence

$$\ell_{ij}v_{ij}-u_{ij}h_{ij}>\ell_{ij}v'_{ij}-u_{ij}h'_{ij}.$$

For $i\in\bar{X}$, $j\in X$,

$$\ell_{ij}v'_{ij}-u_{ij}h'_{ij}=\ell_{ij}\cdot\max\{0,-(w_i-w_j-c_{ij}-\theta)\}-u_{ij}\cdot\max\{0,(w_i-w_j-c_{ij}+\theta)\}$$

If $w_i-w_j-c_{ij}\le 0$, then $c_{ij}+w_i-w_j+\theta>0$ and $h'_{ij}=h_{ij}=0$ and $v'_{ij}=v_{ij}+\theta$. Thus

$$\ell_{ij}v'_{ij}-u_{ij}h'_{ij}=\ell_{ij}v_{ij}-u_{ij}h_{ij}+\ell_{ij}\theta>\ell_{ij}v_{ij}-u_{ij}h_{ij}.$$

If $w_i-w_j-c_{ij}>0$ (and $x_{ij}\ge\ell_{ij}$), then by definition of θ, $w_i-w_j-c_{ij}-\theta\ge 0$, thus $h'_{ij}=h_{ij}-\theta$ and $v'_{ij}=v_{ij}$. Hence

$$\ell_{ij}v'_{ij}-u_{ij}h'_{ij}=\ell_{ij}v_{ij}-u_{ij}h_{ij}+u_{ij}\theta>\ell_{ij}v_{ij}-u_{ij}h_{ij}.$$

We thus see that for $i\in X$, $j\in\bar{X}$ the dual term decreases but for $i\in\bar{X}$, $j\in X$ the dual term decreases. Therefore, we can not make general conclusion about the behavior of the dual objective.

PROBLEM 10.11

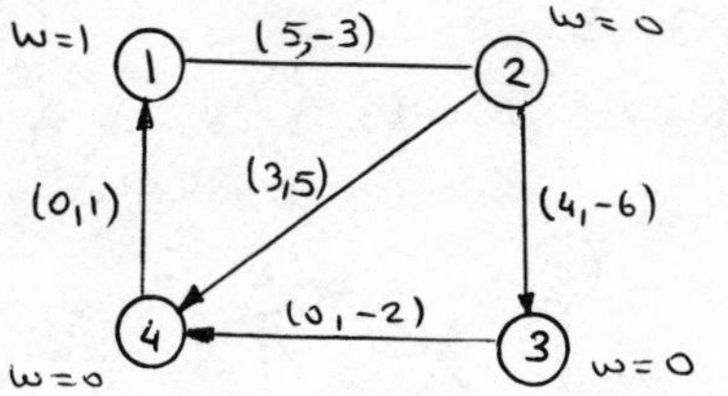

Arc (1,2) is out of kilter.

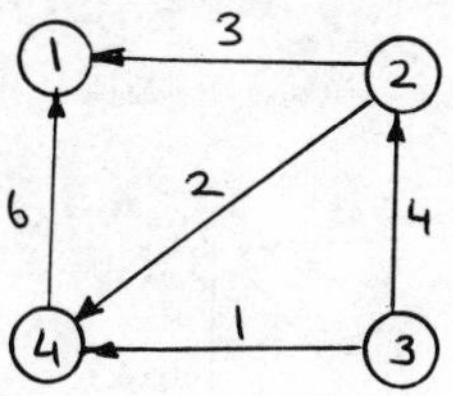

Nonbreakthrough.

$X = \{1\}$, $\bar{X} = \{2,3,4\}$

$\left.\begin{array}{l}\theta_1 = \min\{2\} = 2 \\ \theta_2 = \infty\end{array}\right\} \Longrightarrow \theta = 2$, modify $z_{ij} - c_{ij}$.

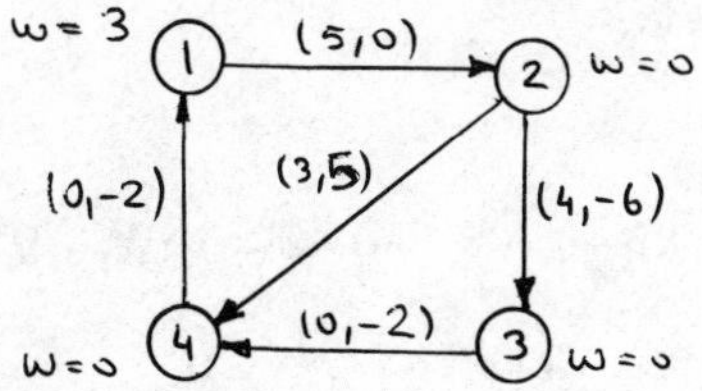

Arc (2,4) is out of kilter.

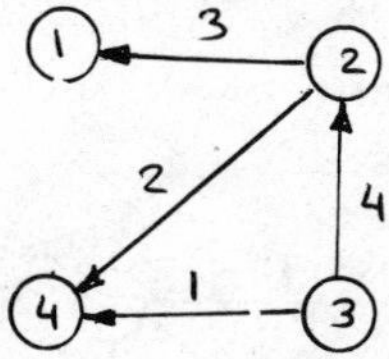

Nonbreakthrough.

$X = \{4\}$, $\bar{X} = \{2,3,1\}$

$\left.\begin{array}{l}\theta_1 = 2 \\ \theta_2 = 3\end{array}\right\} \Longrightarrow \theta = 2$, change $z_{ij} - c_{ij}$.

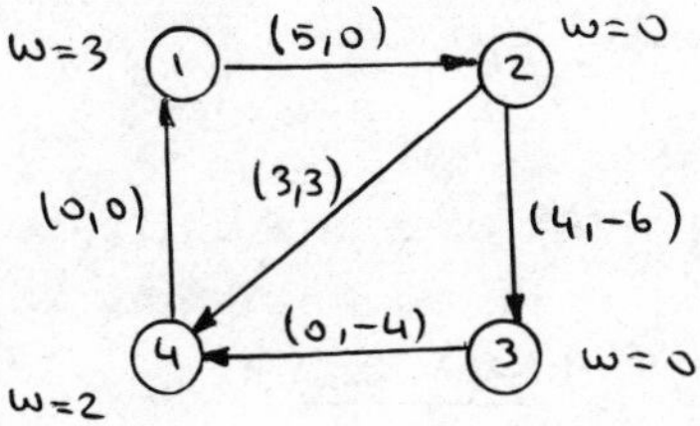

Arc (2,4) is out of kilter.

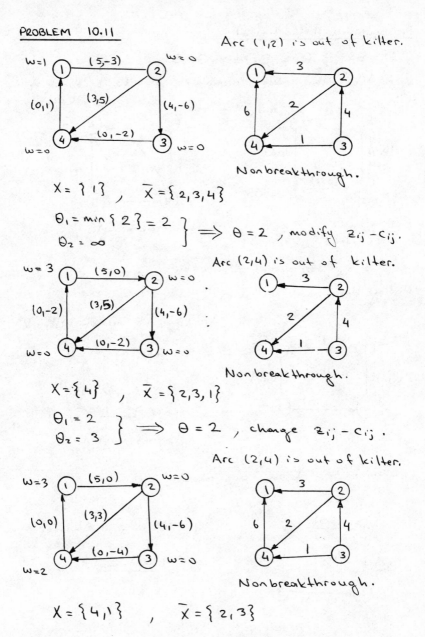

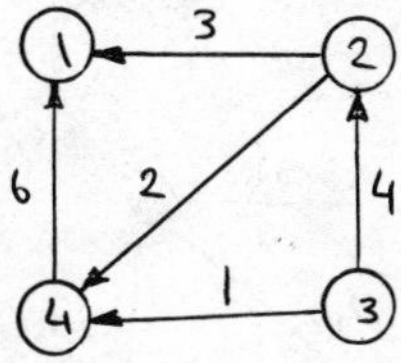

Nonbreakthrough.

$X = \{4,1\}$, $\bar{X} = \{2,3\}$

PROBLEM 10.11 (Continued)

$\theta_1 = \infty$, $\theta_2 = 3 \implies \theta = 3$

Modify the dual variables. Arc (3,4) is out of kilter.

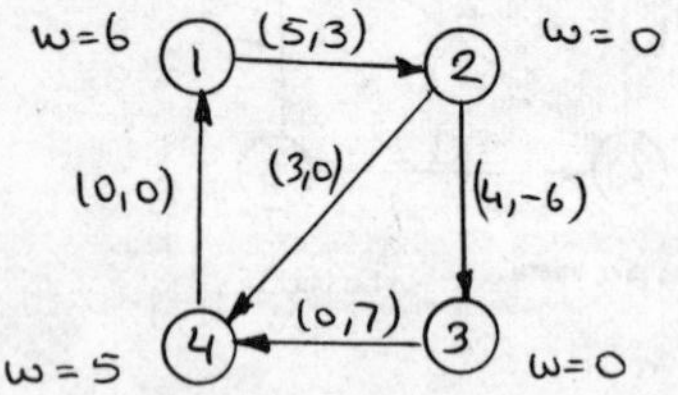

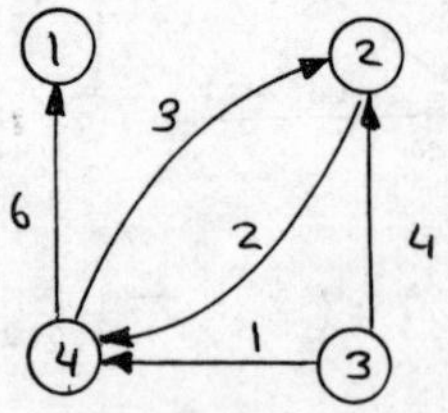

Nonbreakthrough.

$X = \{4,1,2\}$, $\bar{X} = \{3\}$

$\theta_1 = 6$, $\theta_2 = \infty \implies \theta = 6$

Modify the dual variables.

Arc (3,4) is out of kilter.

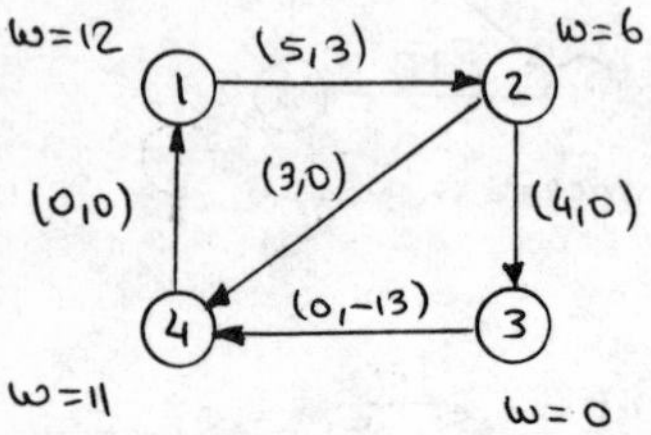

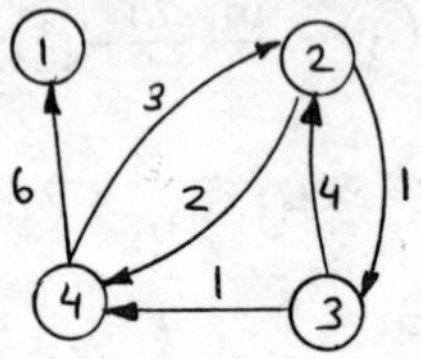

Breakthrough!

Change the flow around the circuit.

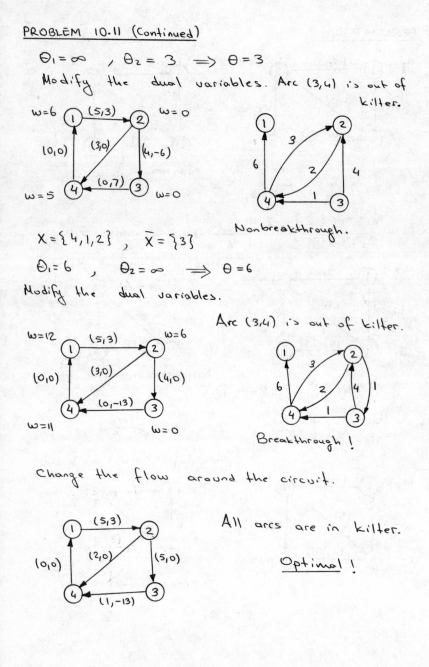

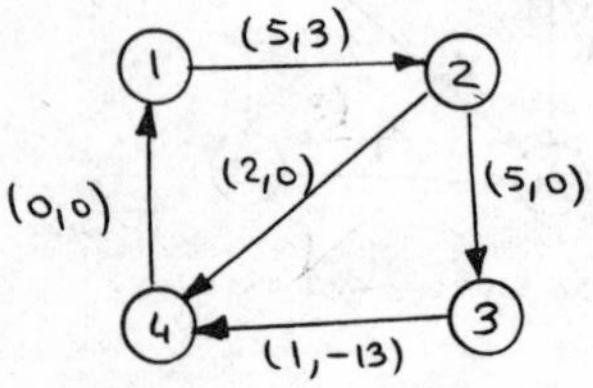

All arcs are in kilter.

Optimal!

PROBLEM 10.11 (Continued)

b)

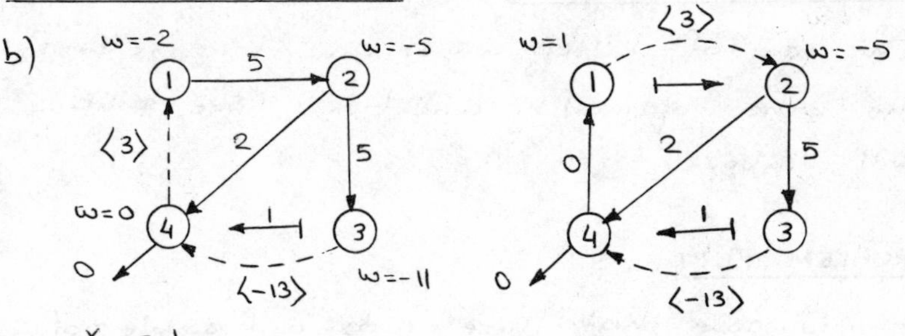

x_{41} enters.

Optimal!

c) Obviously, the solutions of (a) and (b) are the same. We can start the out-of-kilter algorithm even if the problem is not in circulation form, provided that the starting solution satisfies $\Sigma_j x_{ij} - \Sigma_j x_{ji} = b_i$

PROBLEM 10.12

If we start with a solution x satisfying $Ax=b$, without changing the problem into a circulation form, the out-of-kilter algorithm will stop in a finite number steps with an optimal solution, or with the conclusion that no feasible solution exists. Since we start with a flow satisfying the supplies and demands at each node and since the flow is modified along cycles, then the supplies and demand are always met.

PROBLEM 10.12 (Continued)

The out-of-kilter algorithm tries to satisfy the other optimality conditions. (See problem 10.11 above).

PROBLEM 10.14

Suppose that there exists a feasible solution x and let X and $\overline{X}$ be a decomposition of the node-set N. Then by feasibility we must have:

$$\sum_{j \in N} x_{ij} - \sum_{j \in N} x_{ji} = 0 \qquad \forall i .$$

Summing the above equation for $i \in X$, we get:

$$\left\{ \sum_{i \in X} \sum_{j \in X} \cancel{x_{ij}} + \sum_{i \in X} \sum_{j \in \overline{X}} x_{ij} \right\} -$$

$$\left\{ \sum_{i \in X} \sum_{j \in X} \cancel{x_{ji}} + \sum_{i \in X} \sum_{j \in \overline{X}} x_{ji} \right\} = 0$$

But $\displaystyle\sum_{i \in X} \sum_{j \in X} x_{ij} = \sum_{i \in X} \sum_{j \in X} x_{ji}$ and

$$\sum_{i \in X} \sum_{j \in \overline{X}} x_{ji} = \sum_{i \in \overline{X}} \sum_{j \in X} x_{ij} , \quad \text{therefore}$$

$$\sum_{i \in X, j \in \overline{X}} x_{ij} = \sum_{\substack{i \in \overline{X} \\ j \in X}} x_{ij} .$$

PROBLEM 10.14 (Continued)

But x is feasible so that $l_{ij} \leq x_{ij} \leq u_{ij}$ for every arc (i,j). Thus:

$$\sum_{\substack{i \in X \\ j \in \bar{X}}} l_{ij} \leq \sum_{\substack{i \in X \\ j \in \bar{X}}} x_{ij} = \sum_{\substack{i \in \bar{X} \\ j \in X}} x_{ij} \leq \sum_{\substack{i \in \bar{X} \\ j \in X}} u_{ij}$$

Conversely, suppose that for every X and $\bar{X} = N - X$ we have

$$\sum_{\substack{i \in X \\ j \in \bar{X}}} l_{ij} \leq \sum_{\substack{i \in \bar{X} \\ j \in X}} u_{ij} .$$

Construct the following network: Add the source node s and the sink node t. Add arcs from s to all the nodes of the original network N and arcs from each node in N to t. Furthermore, the lower bound on the flow on any arc iz zero and the upper bound $\bar{u}$ is given by:

$$\bar{u}(i,j) = u(i,j) - l(i,j) \qquad i,j \in N$$

$$\bar{u}(s,i) = l(N,i) = \sum_{j \in N} l(j,i) \qquad i \in N$$

$$u(i,t) = l(i,N) = \sum_{j \in N} l(i,j) \qquad i \in N$$

Obviously the original problem has a feasible solution if, and only if, the maximal flow from node s to node t in the network is:

PROBLEM 10.14 (Continued)

$\ell(N,N) = \sum_{\substack{i \in N \\ j \in N}} \ell(i,j)$. We will show this by proving the capacity of any cut seperating nodes s and t is greater than or equal to $\ell(N,N)$, and then utilizing the max-flow min-cut theorem (see Chapter 11). Let X and $\bar{X}$ be any decomposition of the node set N. Let $X^* = X \cup \{s\}$ and $\bar{X}^* = \bar{X} \cup \{t\}$. Then

$$\bar{u}(X^*,\bar{X}) = \bar{u}(X \cup \{s\}, \bar{X} \cup \{t\}) = \bar{u}(X,\bar{X}) + \bar{u}(s,\bar{X})$$

$$+ \bar{u}(X,t) = \bar{u}(X,\bar{X}) - \ell(X,\bar{X}) + \ell(N,\bar{X}) + \ell(X,N)$$

$$= u(X,\bar{X}) + \ell(\bar{X},\bar{X}) + \ell(X,N)$$

$$= u(X,\bar{X}) + \ell(\bar{X},\bar{X}) + \ell(\bar{X},X) - \ell(\bar{X},X) + \ell(X,N)$$

$$= u(X,\bar{X}) + \ell(\bar{X},N) + \ell(X,N) - \ell(\bar{X},X)$$

$$= u(X,\bar{X}) - \ell(\bar{X},X) + \ell(N,N)$$

If $u(X,\bar{X}) \geqslant \ell(\bar{X},X)$ (by assumption), then

$$\bar{u}(X^*,\bar{X}^*) = \ell(N,N)$$

Thus the capacity of any cut from s to t is greater than or equal to $\ell(N,N)$. But the capacity of the cut $X^* = \{s\}$ and $\bar{X}^* = N + \{t\} - \{s\}$ is precisely $\ell(N,N)$. Thus the capacity of the minimal cut is $\ell(N,N)$. Thus

PROBLEM 10.14 (Continued)

a feasible solution exists if, and only if,

$$u(X,\bar{X}) \geq \ell(\bar{X},X)$$

for any decomposition of N into X and $\bar{X}$.

PROBLEM 10.15

Make the change of variable $y_{ij} = x_{ij} - \ell_{ij}$. Then $0 \leq y_{ij} \leq u_{ij} - \ell_{ij}$. The balance equations are modified accordingly.

PROBLEM 10.16

No difficulties if for some arc (i,j) we have $\ell_{ij} = u_{ij}$. The arc is in kilter regardless of $z_{ij} - c_{ij}$.

PROBLEM 10.17

The problem of degeneracy does not arise in the out-of-kilter formulation.

PROBLEM 10.18

After a dual variable change, either the out-of-kilter arc is brought in kilter, or else it is still out of kilter. In the latter case the new values of $z_{ij} - c_{ij}$ are given by:

PROBLEM 10.18 (Continued)

$$(z_{ij}-c_{ij})' = (z_{ij}-c_{ij}) + \theta \qquad (i,j) \in (X,\bar{X})$$

$$(z_{ij}-c_{ij})' = (z_{ij}-c_{ij}) - \theta \qquad (i,j) \in (\bar{X},X)$$

Thus by construction of θ, at least one $z_{ij}-c_{ij}$ will be forced at zero level. Suppose that $(i,j) \in (X,\bar{X})$. Since we had a feasible solution and $i \in X$ and $j \in \bar{X}$, then $x_{ij} = \ell_{ij}$ (x_{ij} could not be less than ℓ_{ij} since x_{ij} is feasible by assumption). Now, since $z_{ij}-c_{ij}=0$, then the flow on arc (i,j) could be increased (if $u_{ij} > \ell_{ij}$) and node j is placed in X, i.e., the set X is enlarged. Similarly, a new node comes to X if the arc (i,j) whose $z_{ij}-c_{ij}$ becomes zero has $i \in \bar{X}$ and $j \in X$.

PROBLEM 10.19

For a given set of w_i's we need to choose v_{ij}'s and h_{ij}'s such that:

$$w_i - w_j + v_{ij} - h_{ij} = c_{ij}$$

$$v_{ij} \geq 0 \ , \ h_{ij} \geq 0 \quad \text{and}$$

$\ell_{ij} v_{ij} - u_{ij} h_{ij}$ is maximized. Then:

$$z_{ij} - c_{ij} = w_i - w_j - c_{ij} = h_{ij} - v_{ij}$$

PROBLEM 10.19 (Continued)

$$h_{ij} = v_{ij} + (z_{ij} - c_{ij})$$

$$\ell_{ij} v_{ij} - u_{ij} h_{ij} = \ell_{ij} v_{ij} - u_{ij}(v_{ij} + (z_{ij} - c_{ij}))$$

$$= (\ell_{ij} - u_{ij}) v_{ij} - u_{ij}(z_{ij} - c_{ij}).$$

To maximize this term and since $\ell_{ij} \leq u_{ij}$ we must choose v_{ij} as small as possible such that $v_{ij} \geq 0$, and $h_{ij} = v_{ij} + (z_{ij} - c_{ij}) \geq 0$. If $z_{ij} - c_{ij} < 0$, the smallest such v_{ij} is $|z_{ij} - c_{ij}|$. If $z_{ij} - c_{ij} \geq 0$, the smallest such v_{ij} is 0. Thus

$$v_{ij} = \max(0, -(z_{ij} - c_{ij})) \quad \text{and acurdingly}$$

$$h_{ij} = \max(0, z_{ij} - c_{ij}).$$

These are the rules of Section 10.2.

PROBLEM 10.20

Set some $w_i = 0$. Consider arcs of the form (i,j) and (j,i). Since $z_{ij} - c_{ij} = w_i - w_j - c_{ij}$ is known we could compute $w_j = w_i - (z_{ij} - c_{ij}) - c_{ij} = -(z_{ij} - c_{ij}) - c_{ij}$. Similarly, for arcs of the form (j,i) we compute w_j by $w_j - w_i - c_{ji} = z_{ji} - c_{ji}$ or $w_j = w_i + c_{ji} + (z_{ji} - c_{ji}) = c_{ji} + (z_{ji} - c_{ji})$. With w_j known we could compute w_k for arcs of the

PROBLEM 10.20 (Continued)

form (k, j) and (j, k). We proceed in this fashion until all w_i's are computed.

PROBLEM 10.21

If the variables with $l_{ij} < x_{ij} < u_{ij}$ do not form a cycle, then the out-of-kilter solution is basic. If the arcs with $l_{ij} < x_{ij} < u_{ij}$ form a single spanning tree, we obviously have a basic feasible solution. If, on the other hand, they form several unconnected trees, these trees could be connected with arcs having either $x_{ij} = l_{ij}$ or $x_{ij} = u_{ij}$ without forming a cycle thus giving a degenerate basic feasible solution.

Example:

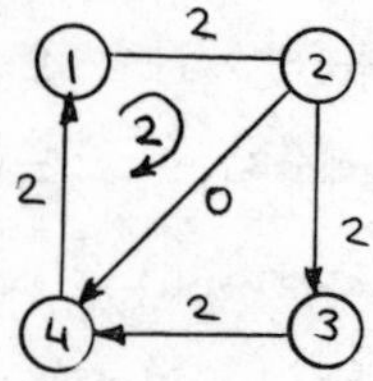

Send a flow of 2 around indicated cycle.

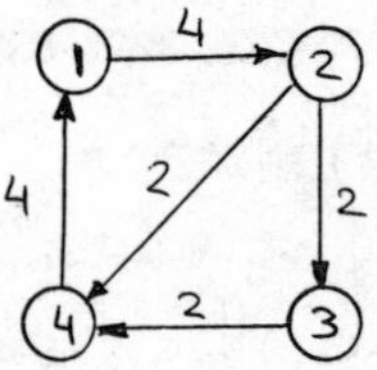

This solution is now basic (also feasible).

Basis

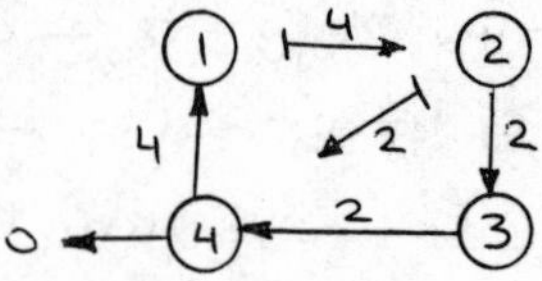

PROBLEM 10.23

One straight forward method to ensure finite convergence of the out-of-kilter algorithm in the presents of the noninteger values of c_{ij}, ℓ_{ij}, and u_{ij} is to maintain a basis throughout the procedure. This can be done by employing the method of Problem 10.22.

In this case all of the arguments again will follow through.

PROBLEM 10.26

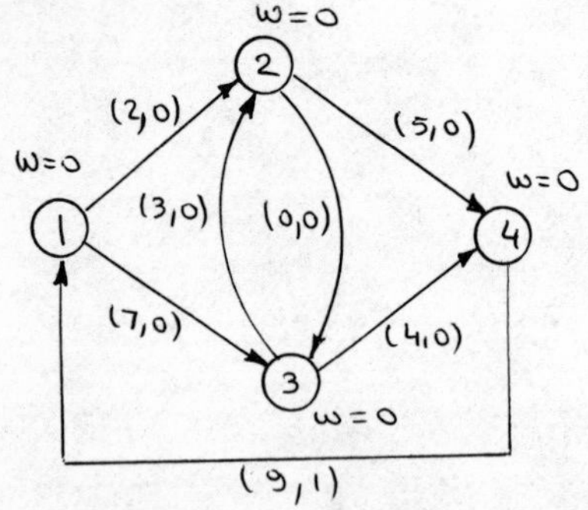

Arc (4,1) is out of kilter.

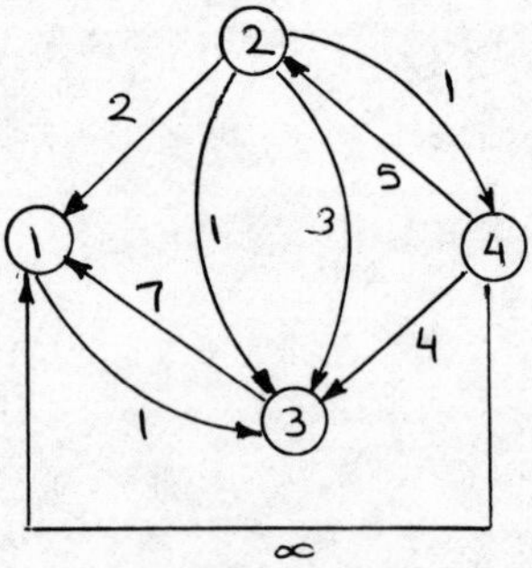

Nonbreakthrough.

$X = \{1, 3\}$, $\bar{X} = \{2, 4\}$

$\theta_1 = \infty$, $\theta_2 = 1 \Rightarrow \theta = 1$

Modify the dual variables.

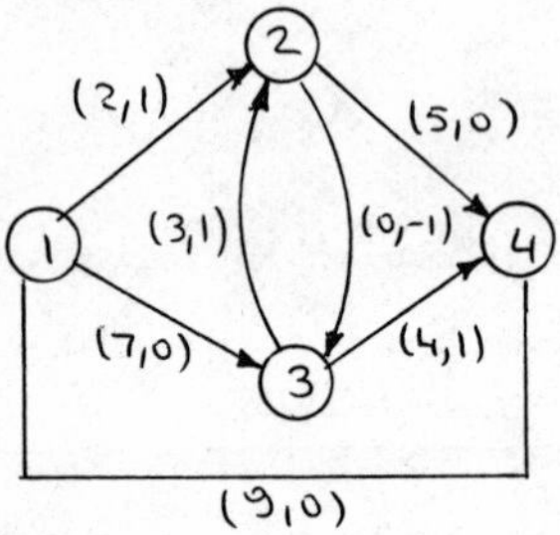

All arcs are in kilter.

Optimal !

PROBLEM 10.28

Suppose that we have a solution x such that $Ax = b$ (if not, introduce a new variable x_{n+1} with activity vector $-b$ and $\ell_{n+1} = u_{n+1} = 1$. Replace the right hand side vector by zero. Start with $(\underline{x}, x_{n+1}) = (\underline{0}, 0)$). Choose a vector w

PROBLEM 10.28 (Continued)

For each variable x_j compute $z_j - c_j = wa_j - c_j$.
If

$$z_j - c_j > 0 \Rightarrow x_j = u_j$$

$$z_j - c_j < 0 \Rightarrow x_j = \ell_j$$

$$z_j - c_j = 0 \Rightarrow \ell_j \le x_j \le u_j$$

stop; we have an optimal solution. Variables not satisfying the above conditions are out-of-kilter, while those satisfying these conditions are in kilter.

If $z_j - c_j > 0$, $x_j \neq u_j$, let $\Delta_j = |x_j - u_j|$. Place j in I. We have to decrease x_j if $x_j > u_j$ and increase x_j if $x_j < u_j$.

If $z_j - c_j < 0$, $x_j \neq \ell_j$, let $\Delta_j = |x_j - \ell_j|$. Place j in I. x_j has to be increased if $x_j < \ell_j$ and has to be decreased if $x_j > \ell_j$.

If $z_j - c_j = 0$ and $\ell_j \le x_j \le u_j$ place j in J.

Let $\Delta_j' = u_j - x_j$ and $\Delta_j'' = x_j - \ell_j$. If $z_j - c_j = 0$ and $x_j \notin [\ell_j, u_j]$, let $\Delta_j = x_j - u_j$ if $x_j > u_j$ and $\Delta_j = \ell_j - x_j$ if $x_j < \ell_j$. In the former case x_j must be decreased and in the latter case x_j must be increased. Place j in I.

Let x_k be any variable violating the above optimality conditions. Solve the following problem:

—

PROBLEM 10.28 (Continued)

PRIMAL PHASE

$$\max \quad \delta_k$$

$$\text{s.t.} \quad \sum_{j \in I} \pm a_j \delta_j + \sum_{j \in J} a_j \delta_j' - \sum_{j \in J} a_j \delta_j'' = 0$$

$$0 \le \delta_j \le \Delta_j \qquad j \in I$$

$$0 \le \delta_j' \le \Delta_j' \qquad j \in J$$

$$0 \le \delta_j'' \le \Delta_j'' \qquad j \in J$$

where (+) corresponds to an increase in x_j and (−) corresponds to a decrease in x_j. If $\delta_k > 0$ modify the x_j by adding or subtracting δ_j as appropriate. Repeat the process until $\delta_k = 0$. Switch to the dual phase.

DUAL PHASE

Let w^* be an optimal dual solution of the above problem. Note that:

1. $w^* a_j = 0 \qquad j \in J$
2. $\pm w^* a_j \geq 0 \qquad j \in I \quad j \neq k$
3. $\pm w^* a_k \geq 1$

From (3) $w^* \neq 0$. Consider modifying the dual vector according to $w - \theta w^*$ where $\theta > 0$ to be determined.

If $j \in J$ (in kilter), then

PROBLEM 10.28 (Continued)

$$(z_j - c_j)' = (w - \theta w^*)a_j - c_j = wa_j - c_j - \theta w^* a_j \quad (\theta w^* a_j \to 0)$$

$$= z_j - c_j = 0$$

In general,

$$(z_j - c_j)' = (z_j - c_j) - \theta w^* a_j$$

Let

$$S_1 = \{ j : z_j - c_j > 0,\ w^* a_j > 0,\ x_j \le u_j \}$$

$$S_2 = \{ j : z_j - c_j < 0,\ w^* a_j < 0,\ x_j \geq l_j \}$$

$$\theta_1 = \min_{j \in S_1} \frac{|z_j - c_j|}{|w^* a_j|}, \quad \theta_2 = \min_{j \in S_2} \frac{|z_j - c_j|}{|w^* a_j|}$$

Let $\theta = \min(\theta_1, \theta_2)$. Update the dual variables by $w' = w - \theta w^*$. Repeat the primal phase.

PROBLEM 10.29

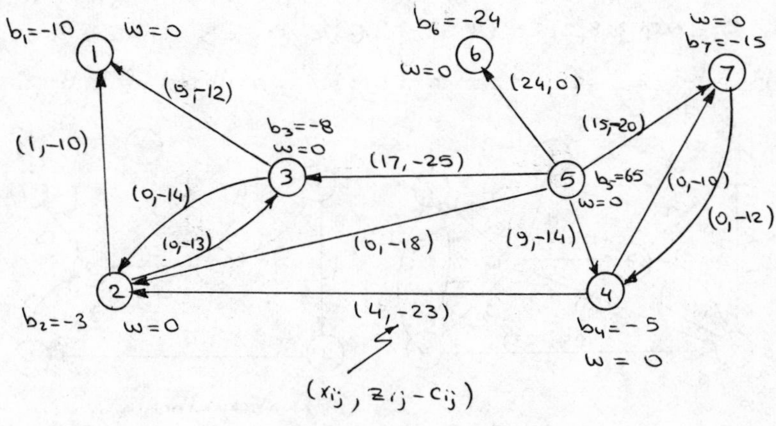

PROBLEM 10.29 (Continued)

Cost of arc (5,6) is zero. The above network shows a feasible solution (not in circulation form) in addition to $z_{ij}-c_{ij}$. Arc (3,1) is out of kilter.

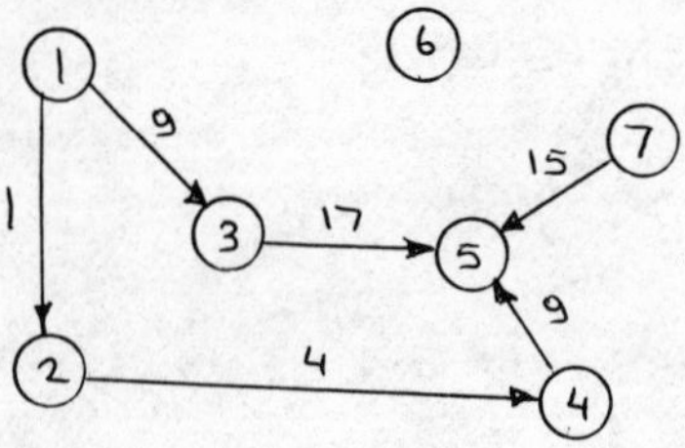

$X=\{3,5\}$, $\bar{X}=\{1,2,4,7\}$

$\theta_1=\min\{12,14,18,14,20\}=12$

$\theta_2=\infty$

$\theta=12$

Nonbreakthrough. Modify $z_{ij}-c_{ij}$'s. Arc (5,3) is out of kilter.

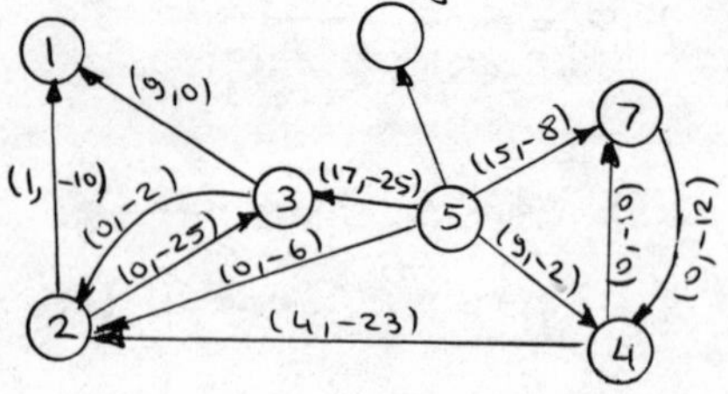

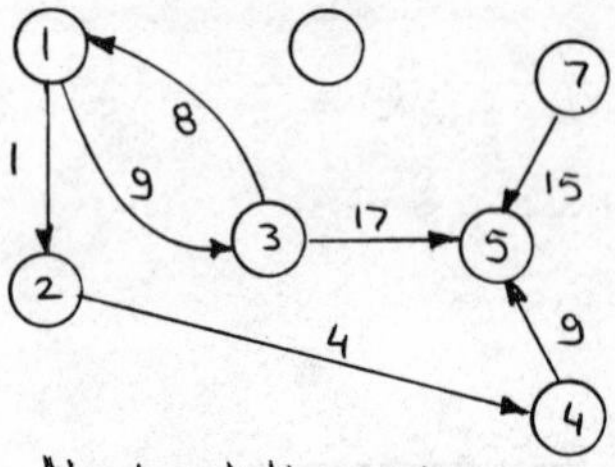

$X=\{5\}$, $\bar{X}=\{1,2,4,3,7\}$ Nonbreakthrough.

$\theta_1=\min\{8,2,25,6\}=2$, $\theta_2=\infty \Rightarrow \theta=2$.

Modify $z_{ij}-c_{ij}$'s. Arc (5,3) is still out of kilter.

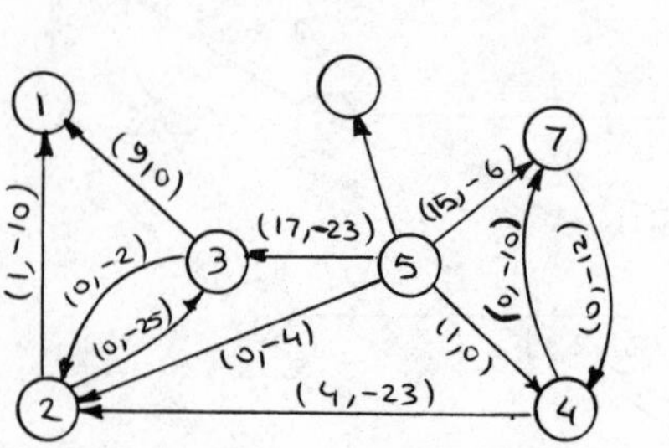

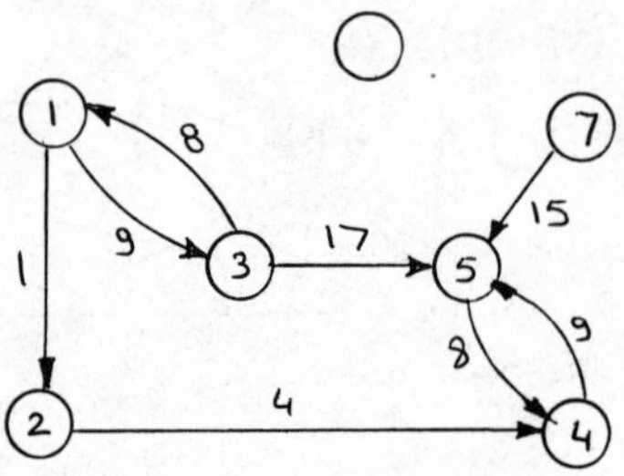

Nonbreakthrough.

PROBLEM 10.29 (Continued)

$X = \{5,4\}$, $\bar{X} = \{1,2,3,7\}$

$\theta_1 = \min\{4, 23, 8, 23, 10\} = 4$, $\theta_2 = \infty \Rightarrow \theta = 4$

Modify $z_{ij} - c_{ij}$'s. Arc (5,3) is still out of kilter.

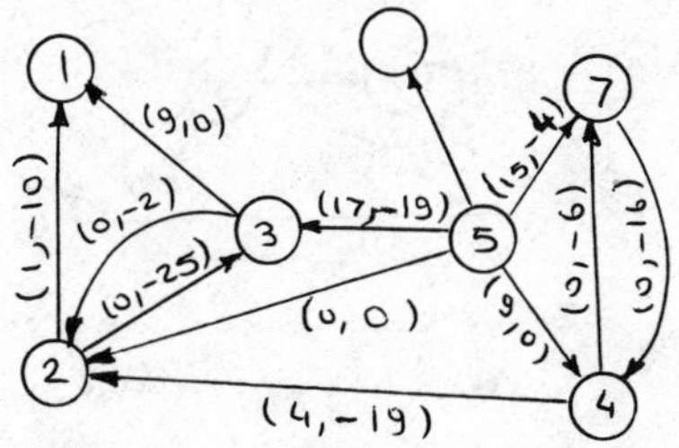

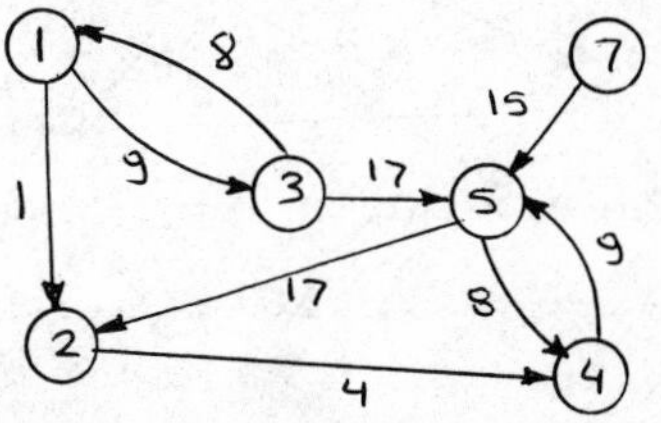

Nonbreakthrough.

$X = \{5,2,4\}$

$\bar{X} = \{1,3,7\}$

$\theta_1 = \min\{19, 4, 10, 25, 6\} = 4$

$\theta_2 = \infty$

$\theta = 4$

Modify $z_{ij} - c_{ij}$'s. Arc (5,3) is still out of kilter.

If we continue this process first we reach to a breakthrough and modify the flow but arc (5,3) still remains out of kilter. In the first modification of $z_{ij} - c_{ij}$'s arc (5,3) goes into kilter. Following is the step before the optimal:

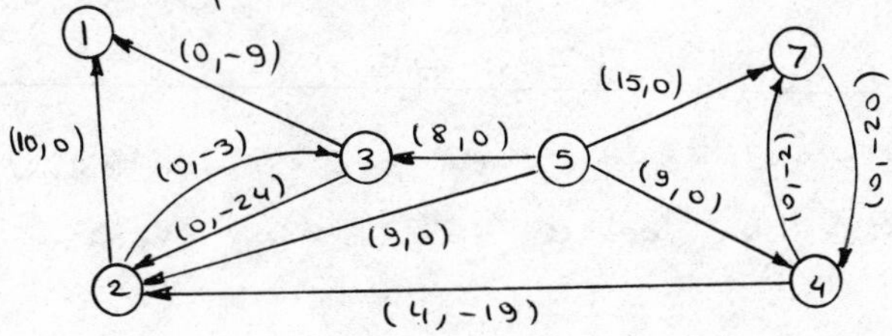

PROBLEM 10.29 (Continued)

Arc (4,2) is out of kilter.

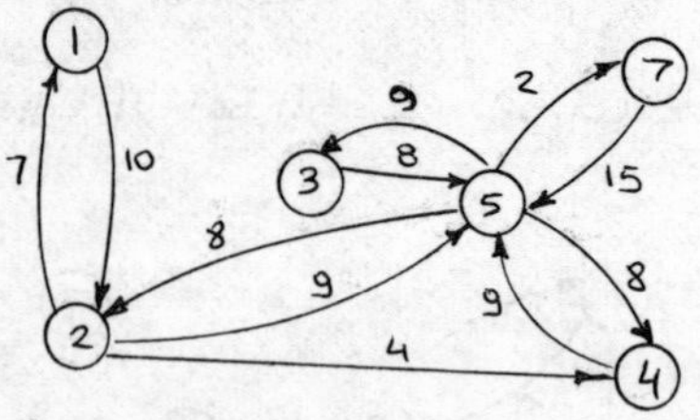

Breakthrough! Change the flow around the cycle.

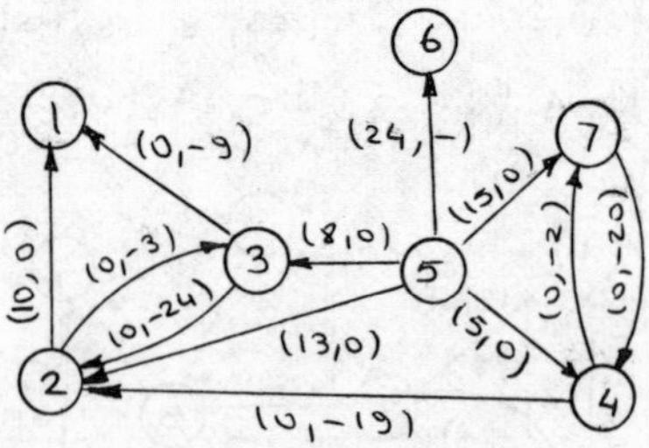

Since all arcs are in kilter this is the optimal solution.

PROBLEM 10.30

We can convert the problem into a circulation form as depicted below.

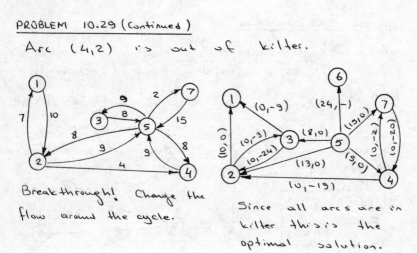

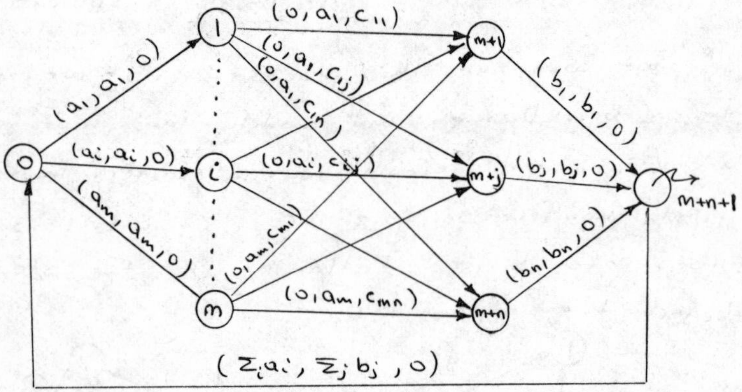

The figures on each arc indicates (l_{ij}, u_{ij}, c_{ij}). It would be better to find a starting solution

PROBLEM 10.30 (Continued)

of the transportation problem satisfying the supply and demand and work with the transportation array itself.

For the assignment problem the figure is the same as the transportation problem except $m=n$ and $a_i = b_j = 1$ for every i and j.

PROBLEM 10.31

a)

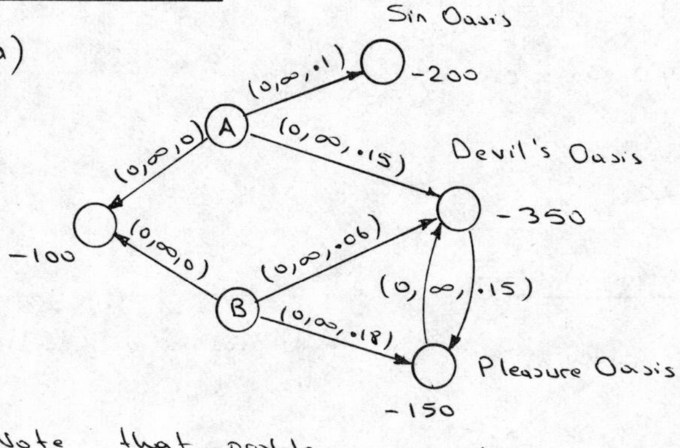

Note that problem is not in a circulation form. We can apply out-of-kilter algorithm directly on this network provided that we start with a feasible solution.

b) Following is the last two steps of the out-of-kilter Algorithm applied to the given network:

PROBLEM 10.31 (Continued)

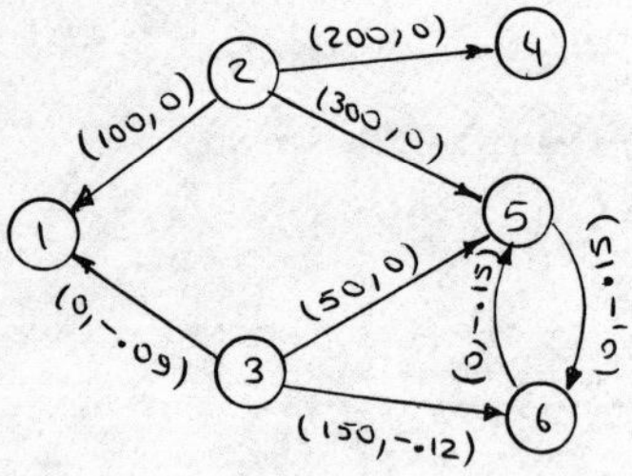

Arc (3,6) is out-of-kilter.

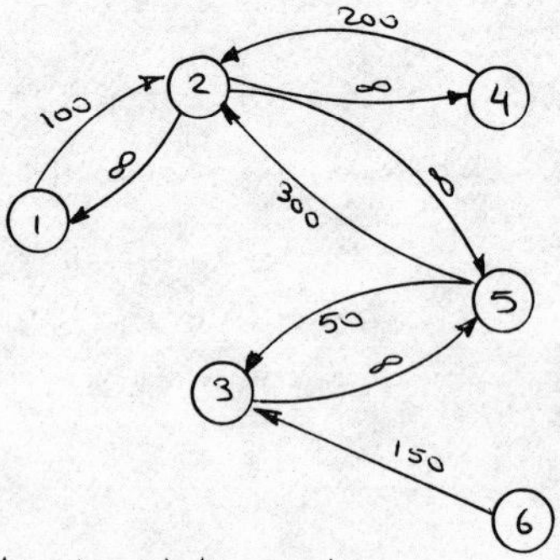

Nonbreakthrough.

$X = \{3,5,2,1,4\}$, $\bar{X} = \{6\}$

$$\left.\begin{array}{l}\theta_1 = \min\{0.12, 0.15\} = 0.12 \\ \theta_2 = \infty\end{array}\right\} \Rightarrow \theta = .12$$

Modify $z_{ij} - c_{ij}$'s.

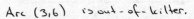

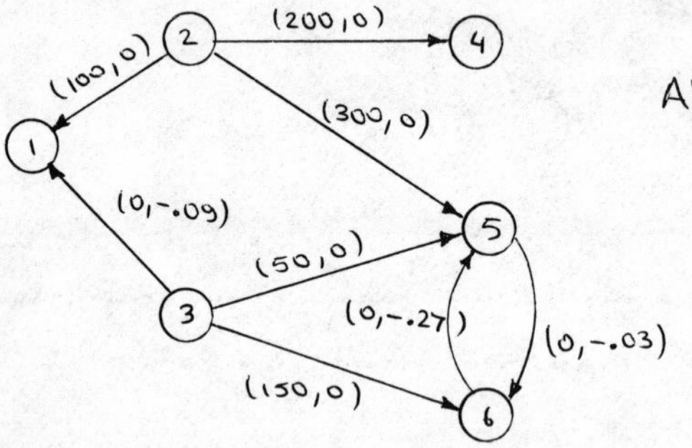

All arcs are in kilter.

Optimal!

c) First compute w_i's. Let $w_1 = 0$

$$w_2 - w_1 - 0 = 0 \Rightarrow w_2 = 0$$

$$w_3 - w_1 - 0 = -.09 \Rightarrow w_3 = -.09$$

$$w_2 - w_4 - .1 = 0 \Rightarrow w_4 = -.1$$

PROBLEM 10.31 (Continued)

$$w_2 - w_5 - .15 = 0 \Rightarrow w_5 = -.15$$

$$w_3 - w_6 - .18 = 0 \Rightarrow w_6 = -.27$$

Consider arc $(4,5)$. $x_{45} = 0$ and

$$z_{45} - c_{45} = w_4 - w_5 - c_{45} = -.1 + .15 - .1 = -.05$$

Consider arc $(5,4)$, $x_{54} = 0$ and

$$z_{54} - c_{54} = w_5 - w_4 - c_{54} = -.15 + .1 - .1 = -.15$$

Therefore the old solution is still optimal, since both $z_{45} - c_{45} < 0$ and $z_{54} - c_{54} < 0$ and x_{45} and x_{54} are at their lower bounds.

PROBLEM 10.32

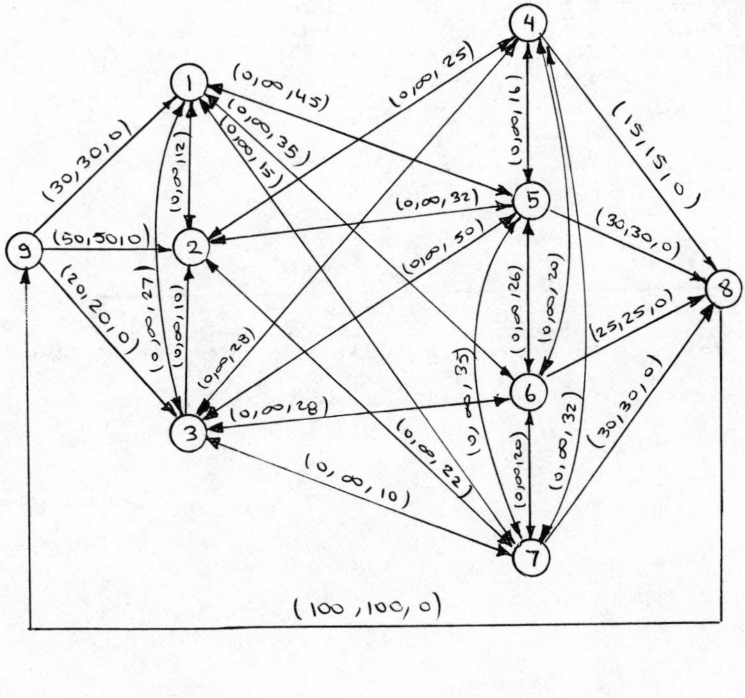

PROBLEM 10.32 (Continued)

Where every arc shows two directions. This means that we can ship in both directions with the same cost, except the arcs from node 8 to node 9, node 9 to nodes 1,2,3 and from node 4,5,6 and 7 to node 8.

Following is the optimal solution of the above problem. Arcs without a flow are eliminated.

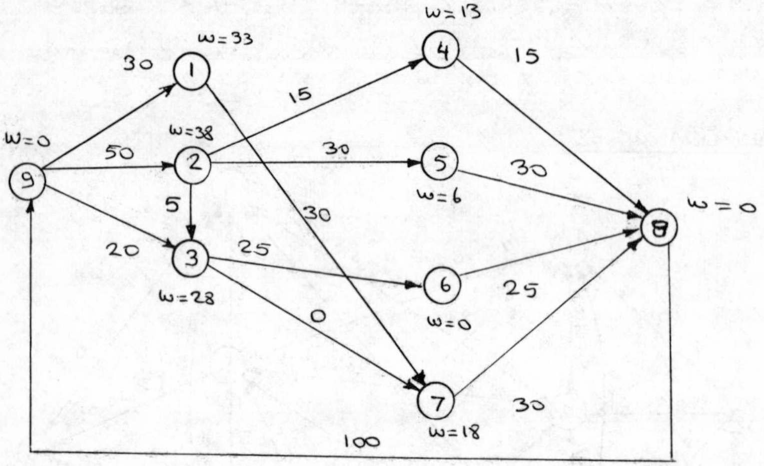

All arcs are in kilter in the above solution. Hence the given flow is optimal.

PROBLEM 10.33

We can represent the problem in circulation form as follows:

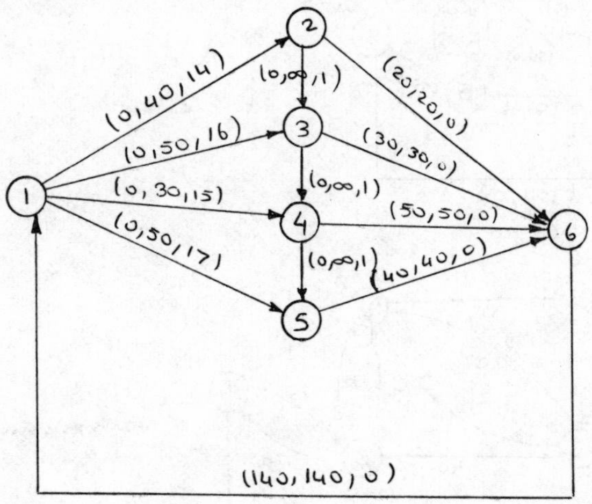

PROBLEM 10.34

a)

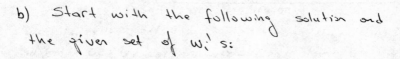

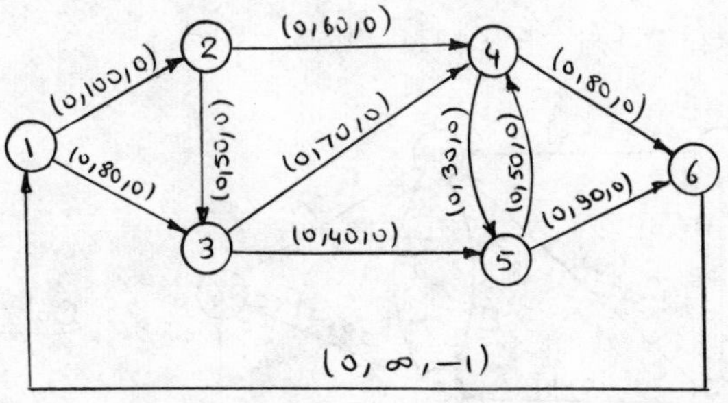

b) Start with the following solution and the given set of w_i's:

PROBLEM 10.34 (Continued)

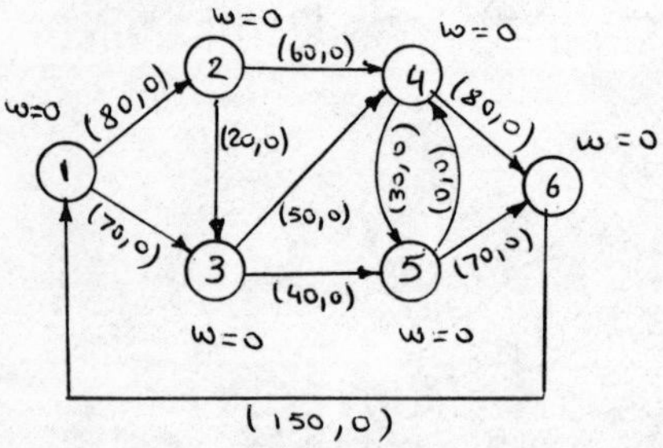

Arc (6,1) is out of kilter.

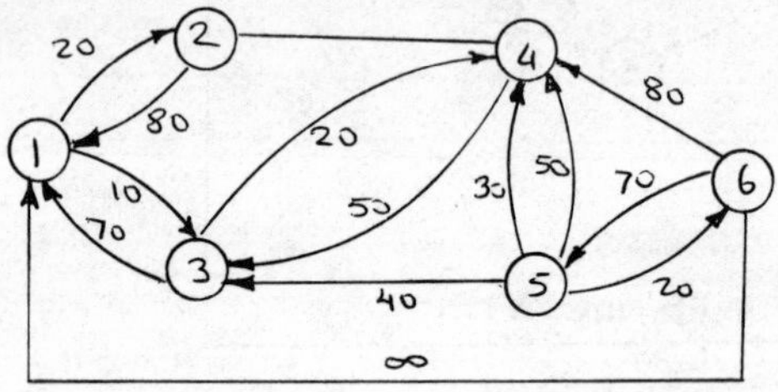

Nonbreakthrough!

$X = \{1,2,3,4\}$, $\bar{X} = \{6,5\}$

$\theta_1 = \min\{1\}$, $\theta_2 = \infty$ $\Rightarrow \theta = 1$

Modify $z_{ij} - c_{ij}$'s.

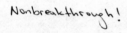

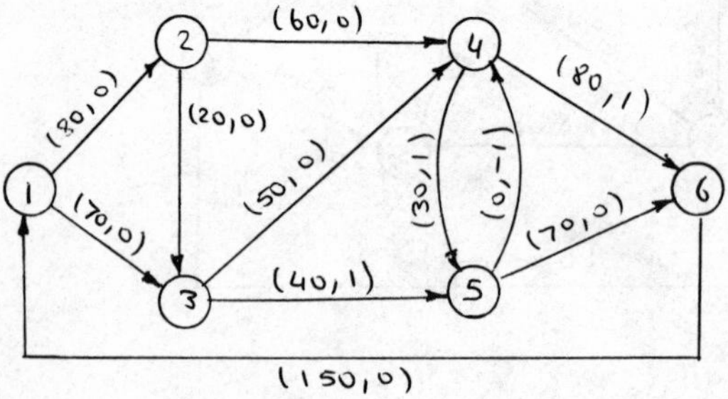

Optimal!

Since all arcs are in kilter, the solution is optimal. The maximum flow is 150 k-ton/hr.

PROBLEM 10.34 (Continued)

c) Increase the capacity of arc (4,6) from 80 to 90. This will cause the max-flow to increase from 150 to 160 by shipping 10 more units around the cycle 1-3-4-6-1.

PROBLEM 10.35

To find the shortest path in a network between node 1 and node m, add the arc (m,1) with lower bound 0 and upper bound 1, and cost of unit flow 0. Arc (i,j) receives $\ell_{ij} = 0$, $u_{ij} = 1$, and $c_{ij} = c_{ij}$.

To find the maximum distance between arcs 1 and m, add the arc (m,1) with lower bound 0 and upper bound 1, and cost of flow 0. Arc (i,j) receives $\ell_{ij} = 0$, $u_{ij} = 1$ and $c_{ij} = -c_{ij}$.

PROBLEM 10.36

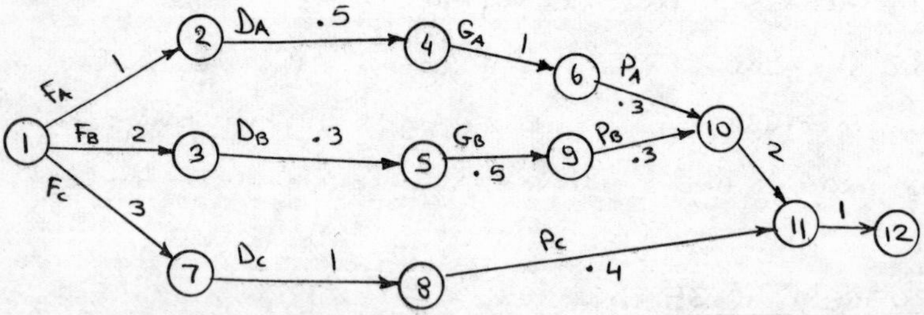

We wish to find the longest path from node 1 to node 12.

a) By inspection the longest path is $1 \to 3 \to 5 \to 9 \to 10 \to 11 \to 12$, with length (duration) 6.1 days.

e) During the first day parts A and B are processed on the forging machine while part C not. This causes the delay of starting on part C for one day. The path $1 \to 7 \to 8 \to 11 \to 12$ will have length 6.4 and will be the longest. Thus this restriction will cause a total delay of getting the assembly of 0.3 days.

CHAPTER 11 MAXIMAL FLOW, SHORTEST PATH, MULTICOMMODITY FLOW PROBLEMS

PROBLEM 11.1

Start $x_{ij} = 0$ for each arc (i,j)

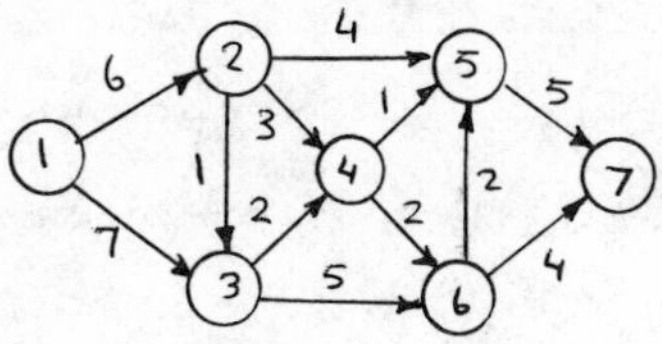

$P = \{1,2,5,7\}$

$\Delta = 4$

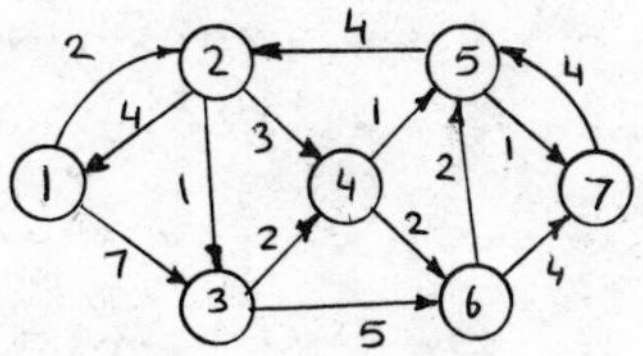

$P = \{1,3,6,7\}$

$\Delta = 4$

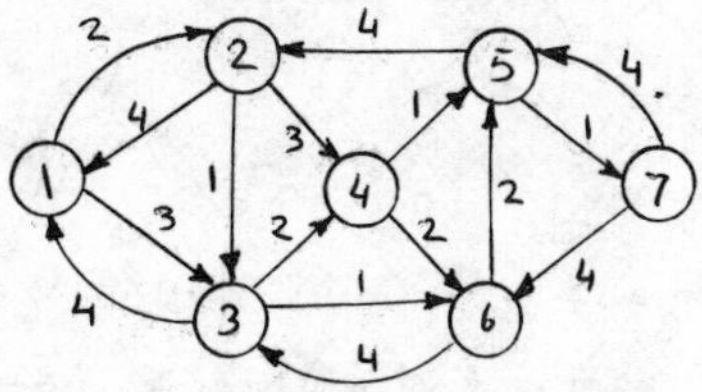

$P = \{1,3,4,5,7\}$

$\Delta = 1$

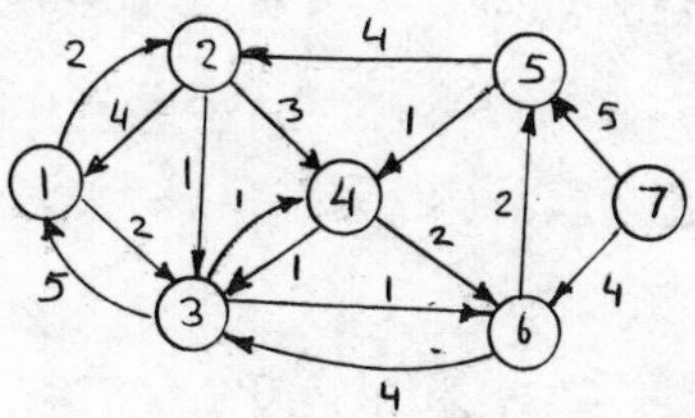

No path from node 1 to node 7. Optimal reached.

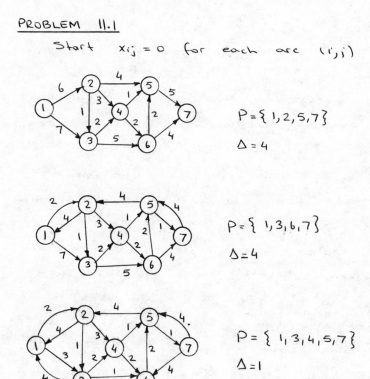

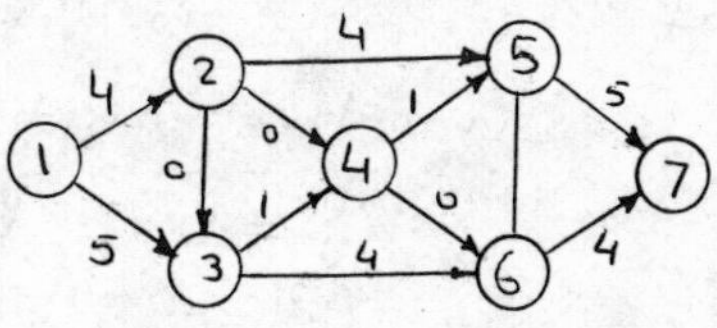

PROBLEM 11.2

Recall that at optimality

$$w_i^* = \frac{\partial z^*}{\partial b_i}.$$

Thus, w_i^* represents the expected increase in z^*, in this case f^*, with a unit increase in b_i. But b_i represents the amount of flow available at node i. Thus, $w_i^* = 0$ for $i \in X$ indicates that one more unit of flow available at any node in X wouldn't do any good. This is intuitive since the additional flow couldn't get across the already saturated cut-set $(X, \bar{X})$. On the other hand, $w_i^* = 1$ for $i \in \bar{X}$ indicates a "potential" for getting that flow to the sink node, thereby increasing the total flow in G. Again this is intuitive.

Also, $h_{ij}^* = 1$ for $(i,j) \in (X, \bar{X})$ is intuitive since $h_{ij}^* = \partial z^* / \partial u_{ij}$, and it would be desirable to increase the capacity of an arc in the cutset $(X, \bar{X})$. It is also intuitive that

$$h_{ij}^* = 0 \quad \text{for } (i,j) \notin (X, \bar{X}).$$

PROBLEM 11.3

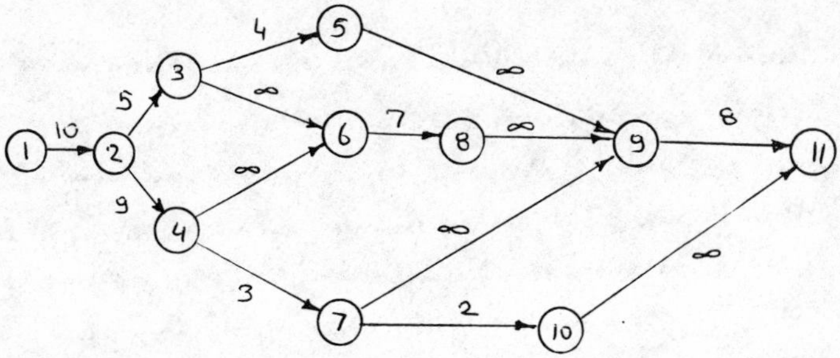

a) Maximum number of parts per hour = 10. Following paths carry the indicated flows on them:

$P = \{1, 2, 3, 5, 9, 11\} \Rightarrow$ Flow = 4

$P = \{1, 2, 4, 6, 8, 9, 11\} \Rightarrow$ Flow = 4

$P = \{1, 2, 4, 7, 10, 11\} \Rightarrow$ Flow = 2

b) Operation corresponding to arcs (1,2), (9,11) and (7,10) could be improved with a total increase in number of parts handled per hour.

PROBLEM 11.4

The problem of finding the maximal number of arc disjoint paths can be stated as follows:

$$\text{Max} \sum_{k=1}^{n} X_k$$

$$\text{S.T.} \quad \sum_{k=1}^{n} \delta_{ijk} X_k \leq 1 \qquad \text{for all } (i,j)$$

$$X_k \geq 0 \qquad k = 1, \ldots, n$$

PROBLEM 11.4 (Continued)

where

n = number of paths from node 1 to node m.

X_k = variable associated with path k. $X_k = 1$ means that path k is choosen among those arc disjoint paths and 0 otherwise. (Note that the constraint X_k is either 0 or 1 need not be enforced explicitly due to the structure of the other constraints).

δ_{ijk} = a known parameter. $\delta_{ijk} = 1$ if arc (i,j) belongs to path k and $\delta_{ijk} = 0$, otherwise.

Note that the above Linear Program is feasible (e.g., $X_k = 0$, $\forall k$) and has a finite optimal solution($\leq n$). Thus the dual problem has a finite optimal solution, whose objective is equal to that of the primal. Let the dual variable corresponding to arc (i,j) be w_{ij}. Thus the dual is:

$$\min \sum_{i,j} w_{ij}$$

$$\text{S.T.} \sum_{i,j} w_{ij}\,\delta_{ijk} \geq 1 \qquad \forall k$$

$$w_{ij} \geq 0 \qquad \forall (i,j)$$

PROBLEM 11.4 (Continued)

The dual problem could be interpreted as follows:

$$w_{ij} = \begin{cases} 1 & \text{if arc } (i,j) \text{ deleted} \\ 0 & \text{otherwise} \end{cases}$$

Then the dual problem is to minimize the number of arcs to be deleted from the network such that at least one arc is deleted from every path. Thus the dual is to find the minimal number of arcs needed to seperate nodes 1 and m. By duality, the minimum number of these arcs is equal to the maximal number of arc- disjoint paths.

PROBLEM 11.5

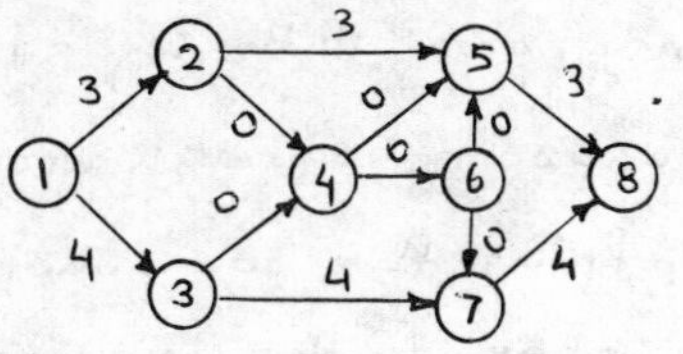

Maximal Flow = 7

PROBLEM 11.6

a) Minimize $\sum_i \sum_j u_{ij} w_{ij}$

S.T. $\sum_i \sum_j w_{ij} \delta_{ijk} \geq 1 \qquad k = 1, 2, \ldots, n$

$w_{ij} \geq 0 \qquad \forall (i,j)$

PROBLEM 11.6 (Continued)

where

$$\delta_{ijk} = \begin{cases} 1 & \text{if arc } (i,j) \text{ belongs to } k\text{th path from the commander node to the subordinate node} \\ 0 & \text{otherwise} \end{cases}$$

b) Suppose that only a subset of the paths 1,2, --, t have been generated. Solve the following problem:

$$\min \sum_i \sum_j u_{ij} w_{ij}$$

$$\text{s.t.} \quad \sum_i \sum_j w_{ij} \delta_{ijk} \geq 1 \qquad k = 1, --, t$$

$$w_{ij} \geq 0 \qquad \forall (i,j)$$

Given the optimal solution w, from the original network construct a new network where each arc of the original network with $w_{ij} = 0$ is deleted. Only arcs with $w_{ij} = 1$ are allowed. Let the capacity of each arc be 1. Maximize the flow from the commander node to the subordinate node in the new network. If the maximum flow is positive, then a new path $t+1$ is generated which violates the constraint $\sum_{i,j} w_{ij} \delta_{ijk} \geq 1$ for $k = t+1$ and the problem is resolved with t replaced by $t+1$. Otherwise, if the max-flow is zero, then no paths exists from the commander node to the subordinate node and the optimal solution is w.

PROBLEM 11.9

If there exists no cycles in the set $E = \{(i,j): 0 < x_{ij} < u_{ij}\}$ either these arcs form a spanning tree (in which case we have a basic feasible solution), or else they form several trees. An arc with $x_{ij} = u_{ij}$ or with $x_{ij} = 0$ could be added between each two disjoint trees leading to a basic feasible solution.

Placing the root of the spanning tree at node m, letting $c_{ij} = 0$ for all arcs except $c_{1j} = 1$, for all j (thus the cost function becomes that of maximizing the flow from node 1), we can compute the dual variables and thus $z_{ij} - c_{ij}$. The vectors y_{ij} could be computed for each nonbasic variable x_{ij} by tracing the cycle formed by adjoining the variable to the basis tree. This information leads to the construction of the simplex tableau.

PROBLEM 11.10

Find a basis B and a w such that:

1. $w_i - w_j - c_{ij} = 0$ for each basic variable
2. $w_i - w_j - c_{ij} \geq 0$ for nonbasic variables at their upper bounds and
   $w_i - w_j - \bar{c}_{ij} \leq 0$ for nonbasic variables at their lower bounds.

PROBLEM 11.10 (Continued)

3. Conservation of flow is satisfied at each node.

Since feasibility of the basis (i.e., $0 \le x_{ij} \le u_{ij}$ for basic variables), finding such a basis is trivial. Note that $c_{m1} = 1$ and all other c_{ij}'s equal to zero.

If $0 \le x_{ij} \le u_{ij}$ for basic variables, we are through. Otherwise, pick a basic variable x_{ij} such that either (a) or (b) below holds.

a) x_{ij} basic, $x_{ij} < 0$

Identify nonbasic variables with nonzero coefficients in the x_{ij} row. For lower bounded nonbasic variables identify those with -1 coefficient and for upper bounded identify those with $+1$ coefficient. Choose the nonbasic variable $x_{k\ell}$ with the smallest

$$\frac{w_k - w_\ell - c_{k\ell}}{y_{ij,k\ell}} \,.$$

This variable enters the basis and x_{ij} leaves the basis.

b) x_{ij} basic, $x_{ij} > u_{ij}$

Identify the lower bounded nonbasic variable with coefficient $+1$ and upper

PROBLEM 11.10 (Continued)

bounded nonbasic variables with coefficient −1 in row (i,j). Choose the nonbasic variable $x_{k\ell}$ with smallest

$$\left| \frac{w_k - w_\ell - c_{k\ell}}{y_{ij,k\ell}} \right|$$

$x_{k\ell}$ enters the basis and x_{ij} leaves at its upper bound.

PROBLEM 11.12

See the answer to Problem 9.22.

PROBLEM 11.13

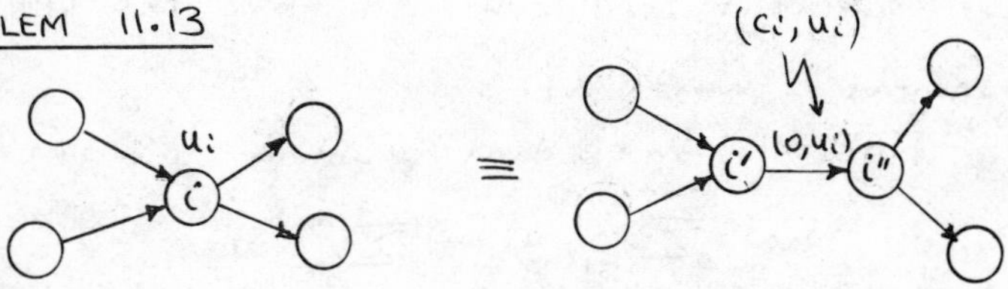

PROBLEM 11.14

Replace each arc by two directed arcs.

PROBLEM 11.15

Consider the following problem:

$$\max \sum_{(i,j)\in I} x_{ij}$$

$$\text{s.t.} \quad \sum_{(i,j)\in I} a_{ij} x_{ij} \le 1$$

$$x_{ij} \geq 0 \qquad (i,j) \in I$$

where

PROBLEM 11.15 (Continued)

$a_{ij} = e_i + e_{m+j}$

$I = \{(i,j): \hat{c}_{ij} = 0\}$, $\hat{c}_{ij}$ is the reduced cost coefficient in cell (i,j).

The problem could be interpreted as that of maximizing the number of zero cells such that at most one job is assigned to a man and at most one man is assigned to a job (these are the maximal number of independent zero cells in the reduced assignment matrix).

Taking the dual problem we get:

$$\min \sum_{i=1}^{m} u_i + \sum_{j=1}^{m} v_j$$

$$\text{S.T.} \quad u_i + v_j \geq 1 \quad (i,j) \in I$$

$$u_i \geq 0 \quad i = 1, \ldots, m$$

$$v_j \geq 0 \quad j = 1, \ldots, m$$

The above problem could be interpreted as minimizing the number of rows and columns which would cover all the zero cells.

Note that
$$u_i = \begin{cases} 1 & \text{if row } i \text{ is covered} \\ 0 & \text{otherwise} \end{cases}$$

$$v_j = \begin{cases} 1 & \text{if column } j \text{ is covered} \\ 0 & \text{otherwise} \end{cases}$$

PROBLEM 11.15 (Continued)

By duality, the minimum number of rows and columns to cover all the zeros of the reduced matrix is equal to the maximum number of independent zero cells in that matrix. The latter problem could be solved as a max-flow problem as follows. If entry (i,j) is zero in the reduced cost matrix draw an arc $(i, n+j)$ with upper capacity 1.

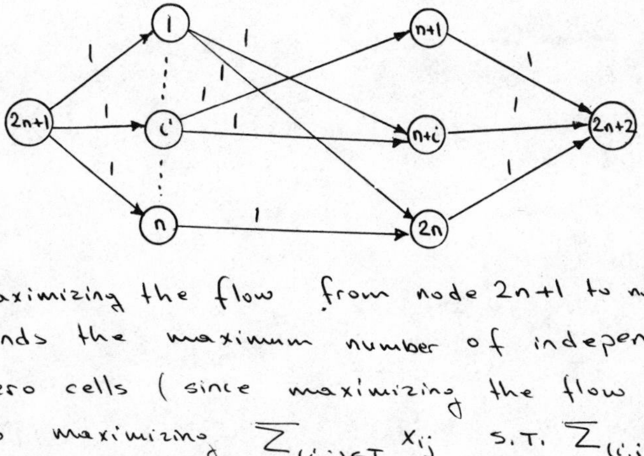

Maximizing the flow from node $2n+1$ to node $2n+2$ finds the maximum number of independent zero cells (since maximizing the flow is equal to maximizing $\sum_{(i,j)\in I} x_{ij}$ s.t. $\sum_{(i,j)\in I} a_{ij} x_{ij} \leq 1$, $x_{ij} \geq 0$). Thus the maximum flow gives the minimum number of rows to cover all the zero cells. To determine which rows and columns to cross-out examine the hint of the problem.

PROBLEM 11.16

The maximum flow is 3 given as shown. Hence, the minimum number of rows and columns to cover the zeroes is 3. They are: row # 1, row #4, and column # 4.

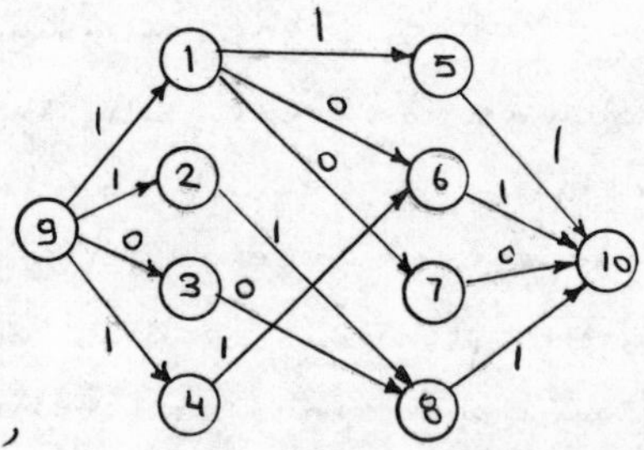

PROBLEM 11.17

a) The paths from node 1 to node 4 are:

$P_1 = \{1, 2, 4\}$

$P_2 = \{1, 3, 4\}$

$P_3 = \{1, 2, 3, 4\}$

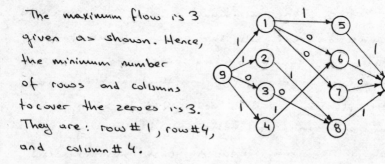

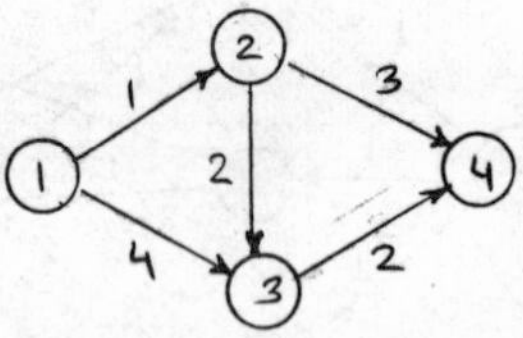

$$\max \quad x_1 + x_2 + x_3$$

S.T.	$x_1 + x_3 \le 1$	--- arc (1,2)
	$x_2 \le 4$	--- arc (1,3)
	$x_3 \le 2$	--- arc (2,3)
	$x_1 \le 3$	--- arc (2,4)
	$x_2 + x_3 \le 2$	--- arc (3,4)
	$x_1, x_2, x_3 \geq 0$	

b) Considering constraint 1, constraint 3 and 4 are redundant. Considering constraint 5, constraint 2 is redundant. Hence we have left with:

PROBLEM 11.17 (Continued)

$$\begin{aligned} \max \quad & x_1 + x_2 + x_3 \\ \text{S.T.} \quad & x_1 \quad + x_3 \le 1 \\ & \quad x_2 + x_3 \le 2 \\ & x_1, x_2, x_3 \geq 0 \end{aligned}$$

The optimal is $x_1 = 1$ and $x_2 = 2$, $x_3 = 0$. objective $= 3$.

PROBLEM 11.18

$$\max \sum_{j=1}^{t} x_j$$

$$\text{S.T.} \quad \sum_{j=1}^{t} p_{ij} x_j + s_j = u_i \qquad i = 1, \ldots, n$$

$$x_j \geq 0 \qquad j = 1, \ldots, t$$

$$s_j \geq 0 \qquad i = 1, \ldots, n$$

a)

i) Entry criterion for slack variables: $w_i < 0$.

ii) Entry criterion for path variables: $\sum_{i=1}^{n} w_i p_{ij} < 1$.

b) In order to check if there is a path j with $\sum_{i=1}^{m} w_i p_{ij} < 1$, we could solve the shortest path problem from node 1 to node m, the cost of arc i as w_i. If the shortest path has $\sum_{i=1}^{m} w_i p_{ij} \geq 1$, then no path variable is eligible to enter the basis. Otherwise, if $\sum_{i=1}^{m} w_i p_{ij} < 1$, then in the process we have generated a path which is eligible to enter the basis.

PROBLEM 11.18 (Continued)

c) If we insist on using slack variables first to enter the basis, then no slacks could enter the basis only if $w_i \geq 0$ for all i, in which case we could use the shortest path algorithm with nonnegative cost coefficients w_i's in order to determine if there is a path variable which is eligible to enter the basis.

d) Initialization:

Start the revised simplex method by:

z	0	0
s	I	u

where the vector $w = 0$, $z = 0$, the basis consists entirely of slack variables, and $B^{-1} = I$.

Main Step

1. Given w, if $w_i < 0$, then the corresponding slack variable s_i is eligible to enter the basis. $z_i - c_i = w_i$ and the column e_i is updated by premultiplying it by B^{-1}. Pivot to update the vectors w and the inverse basis, and repeat 1.
2. If $w \geq 0$, then solve a shortest path problem from node 1 to node m with

PROBLEM 1.18 (Continued)

the nonnegative cost of arc i as w_i. Let the shortest path be path j. If $\sum_{i=1}^{n} p_{ij} w_i \geq 1$, the current solution is optimal, otherwise path j is eligible to enter the basis. $z_j - c_j = \sum_{i=1}^{n} p_{ij} - w_i - 1$. The column p_j is updated by premultiplying it by B^{-1}. Pivoting updates the dual vector and the inverse basis. Repeat step 1.

e)

						RHS
z	0	0	0	0	0	0
s_1	1					1
s_2		1				4
s_3			1			2
s_4				1		3
s_5					1	2

$w = 0$.

Solve the shortest path problem from node 1 to node 4 with cost coefficients 0. The path 1-2-4 is an optimal solution.

$z_1 - c_1 = \sum_{i=1}^{5} w_i p_{ij} - 1 = -1.$

Mutiply (update) the vector $P_1 = (1, 0, 0, 1, 0)^T$ by B^{-1}. We have:

						RHS	x_1
z	0	0	0	0	0	0	-1
s_1	1					1	(1)
s_2		1				4	0
s_3			1			2	0
s_4				1		3	1
s_5					1	2	0

						RHS
z	1	0	0	0	0	1
x_1	1	0	0	0	0	1
s_2	0	1	0	0	0	4
s_3	0	0	1	0	0	2
s_4	-1	0	0	1	0	2
s_5	0	0	0	0	1	2

PROBLEM 11.18 (Continued)

Solve the shortest path problem with cost coefficients (1, 0, 0, 0, 0). An optimal path is 1-3-4 with cost = 0. Thus $z_2 - c_2 = \sum_{i=1}^{5} w_i p_{ij} - 1 = -1$. $P_2 = (0,1,0,0,1)$. $B^{-1}p = (0,1,0,0,1)$.

						RHS		y_2
z	1	0	0	0	0	1		-1
x_1	1					1		0
s_2	0	1				4		1
s_3	0		1			2		0
s_4	-1			1		2		0
s_5	0				1	2		(1)

						RHS
z	1	0	0	0	1	3
x_1	1				0	1
s_2	0	1			-1	2
s_3	0		1		0	2
s_4	-1			1	0	2
x_2	0				1	2

Solve the shortest path problem with the given cost coefficients. The path 1-2-4 is an optimal solution and $\sum_{i=1}^{5} w_i p_{ij} - 1 = 0$. Thus we already have the optimal solution, since we have no candidates to enter the basis.

$x_1 = 1$, $x_2 = 2$. The flows on the arcs thus:

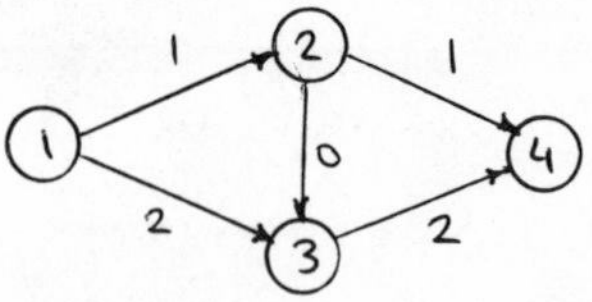

PROBLEM 11.19

a)

$$\text{Minimize } \sum_{i=1}^{n} u_i w_i$$

$$\text{s.t. } \sum_{i=1}^{n} w_i p_{ij} \geq 1 \qquad j = 1, \ldots, t$$

$$w_i \geq 0 \qquad i = 1, \ldots, n$$

PROBLEM 11.19 (Continued)

b) If the dual variables assume value zero or one, then the problem can be interpreted as follows:

$$w_i = \begin{cases} 1 & \text{if arc } i \text{ is deleted} \\ 0 & \text{otherwise} \end{cases}$$

The restriction $\sum_{i=1}^{m} w_i p_{ij} \geq 1$ stipulates that at least one arc of path j must be deleted so that node 1 and m are sepeiated. The capacity w_i can thus be interpreted as the effort expended to delete arc i. Thus the problem becomes: delete certain arcs of the network so that nodes 1 and m are seperated in such a way that the total effort is minimized.

c) The dual solution in Problem 11.18 above given by $w_1 = 1$, $w_2 = w_3 = w_4 = 0$, $w_5 = 1$ could be interpreted as follows: In order to seperate nodes 1 and 4 with the minimal possible effort, delete arcs 1 (i.e., arc (1,2)) and 5 (i,e., arc (3,4)).

PROBLEM 11.20

The constraint matrix for arc-path formulation is not necessarily totally unimodular.

PROBLEM 11.20 (Continued)

Counter Example

Consider the network below:

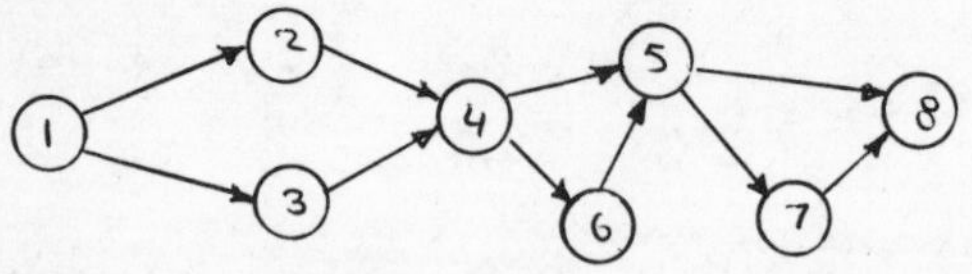

Consider only the following three paths from node 1 to node 8:

$P_1 = \{1, 2, 4, 5, 8\}$

$P_2 = \{1, 3, 4, 5, 7, 8\}$

$P_3 = \{1, 2, 4, 6, 5, 7, 8\}$

Consider the restriction of the vectors P_1, P_2 and P_3 to the arcs (2,4), (4,5), and (5,7).

	P_1	P_2	P_3
(2,4)	1	0	1
(4,5)	1	1	0
(5,7)	0	1	1

The determinant of the above matrix is 2. Thus the constraint matrix of the arc-path formulation of a maximal flow problem is not totally unimodular.

PROBLEM 11.21

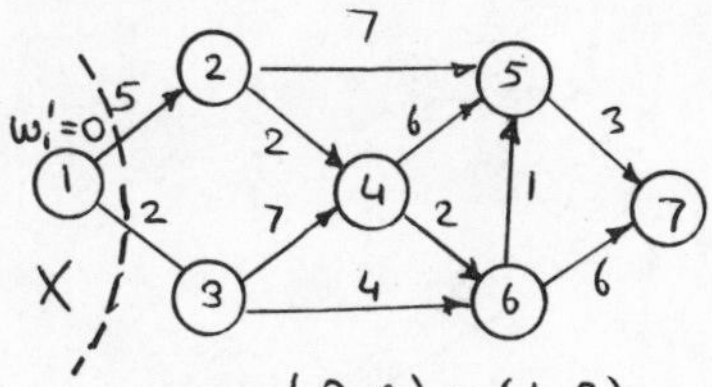

(p,q) = (1,3)
$w_3' = 2$

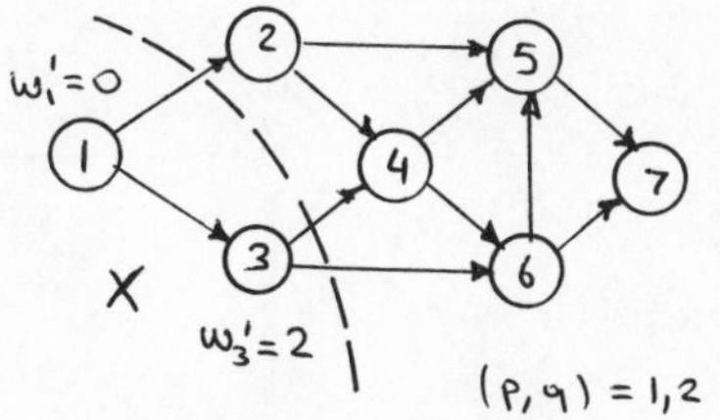

(p,q) = 1,2
$w_2' = 5$

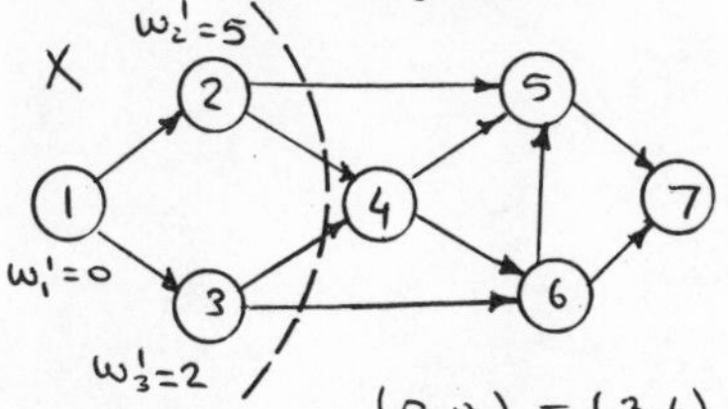

(p,q) = (3,6)
$w_6' = 6$

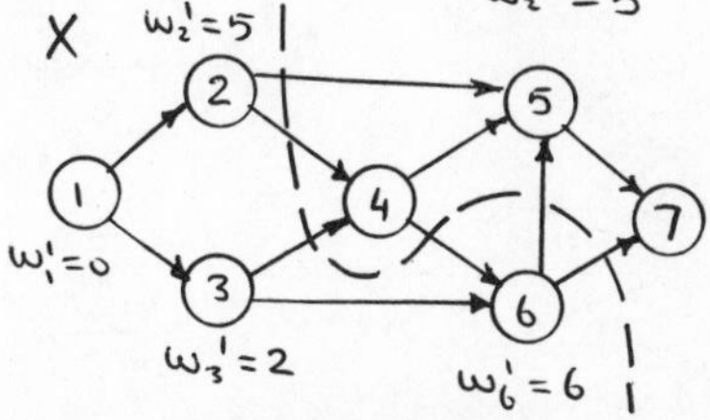

(p,q) = (2,4)
$w_4' = 7$

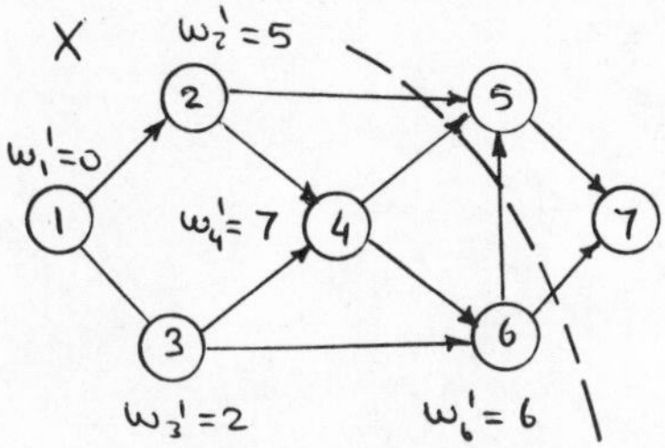

(p,q) = (6,5)
$w_5' = 7$

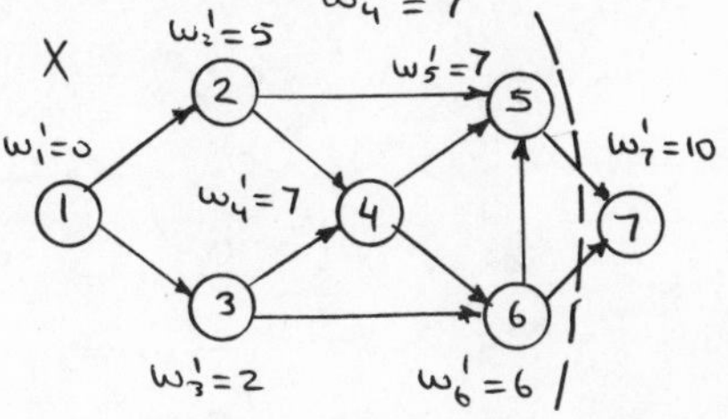

(p,q) = (5,7)
$w_7' = 10$

Shortest paths from nodes 1 to 2 : 1 → 2 cost = 5

1 to 3 : 1 → 3 c = 2

1 to 4 : 1 → 2 → 4 c = 7

1 to 5 : 1 → 3 → 6 → 5 c = 7

1 to 6 : 1 → 3 → 6 c = 6

1 to 7 : 1 → 3 → 6 → 5 → 7 c = 10

PROBLEM 11.22

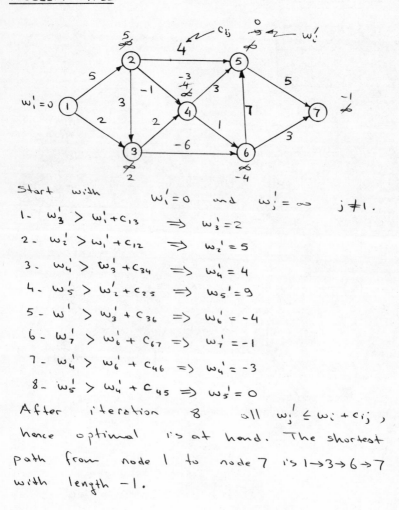

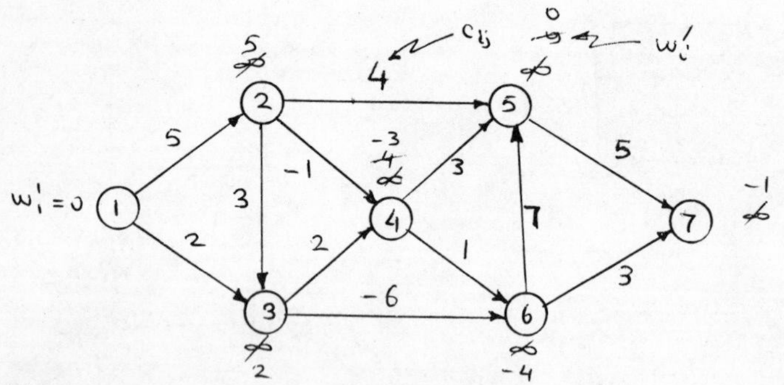

Start with $w_1' = 0$ and $w_j' = \infty$ $j \neq 1$.

1- $w_3' > w_1' + c_{13}$ $\Rightarrow$ $w_3' = 2$

2- $w_2' > w_1' + c_{12}$ $\Rightarrow$ $w_2' = 5$

3- $w_4' > w_3' + c_{34}$ $\Rightarrow$ $w_4' = 4$

4- $w_5' > w_2' + c_{25}$ $\Rightarrow$ $w_5' = 9$

5- $w' > w_3' + c_{36}$ $\Rightarrow$ $w_6' = -4$

6- $w_7' > w_6' + c_{67}$ $\Rightarrow$ $w_7' = -1$

7- $w_4' > w_6' + c_{46}$ $\Rightarrow$ $w_4' = -3$

8- $w_5' > w_4' + c_{45}$ $\Rightarrow$ $w_5' = 0$

After iteration 8 all $w_j' \leq w_i + c_{ij}$, hence optimal is at hand. The shortest path from node 1 to node 7 is $1 \to 3 \to 6 \to 7$ with length -1.

PROBLEM 11.23

a) Replace c_{ij} by $-c_{ij}$ for each arc (i, j)

PROBLEM 11.23 (Continued)

b) To find the longest path we must insist that the sum of the costs around any circuit is less than or equal to 0.

c) Start with $w_1' = 0$, $w_j' = \infty$ for $j \neq 1$.

If $w_j' < w_i' + c_{ij}$, replace w_j' by $w_i' + c_{ij}$. Repeat the process until $w_j' \geq w_i' + c_{ij}$ for each (i,j). w_j' gives the length of the longest path from node 1 to node j for each j.

PROBLEM 11.24

$w_i - w_m$ gives a lower bound on the cost of the shortest path from node i to node m. To verify this let $P = \{(i,j), (j,k), \ldots, (u,v), (v,m)\}$ be any path from node i to node m with cost $c_{ij} + c_{jk} + \cdots + c_{uv} + c_{vm}$. Noting the dual constraints we have:

$$w_i - w_j \leq c_{ij}$$

$$w_j - w_k \leq c_{jk}$$

$$\vdots$$

$$w_u - w_v \leq c_{uv}$$

$$w_v - w_m \leq c_{vm}$$

Adding these inequalities we get:

PROBLEM 11.24 (Continued)

$$w_i - w_m \leq c_{ij} + c_{jk} + \cdots + c_{uv} + c_{vm},$$

the length of the path. Note, also that $w_i - w_m$ is not necessarily the length of the shortest path. For example, by letting $i = 5$ and $m = 7$ in Problem 11.22, we see that $w_5 - w_7$ is not the length of the shortest path from node 5 to node 7.

PROBLEM 11.25

First suppose that $w_m' = \infty$ at termination. Suppose by contradiction that there is a path $\{(1,i),(i,j),\ldots,(u,v),(v,m)\}$ from node 1 to node m. Then by termination of the algorithm we must have:

$$w_i' - w_1' \leq c_{1i}$$
$$w_j' - w_i' \leq c_{ij}$$
$$\vdots$$
$$w_v' - w_u' \leq c_{uv}$$
$$w_m' - w_v' \leq c_{vm}$$

Adding we get:

$$w_m' \leq w_1' + (c_{1i} + c_{ij} + \cdots + c_{uv} + c_{vm})$$

$$= 0 + (c_{1i} + c_{ij} + \cdots + c_{uv} + c_{vm}),$$

contradicting the assumption that $w_m' = \infty$. Thus there exists no path from node 1

PROBLEM 11.25 (Continued)

to node m. Now, suppose that $w'_m < \infty$. Thus there exists a node v such that $w'_v < \infty$ and $w'_m - w'_v = c_{vm}$. Backtracking, there must exist a node u with $w'_u < \infty$ such that $w'_v - w'_u = c_{uv}$. Continue in this fashion until node 1 is reached. The arcs generated in the process form a path $\{1, i, j, \ldots, u, v, m\}$ from node 1 to node m. Furthermore:

$$w'_i - w'_1 = c_{1i}$$
$$w'_j - w'_i = c_{ij}$$
$$\vdots$$
$$w'_v - w'_u = c_{uv}$$
$$w'_m - w'_v = c_{vm}$$

Adding $w'_m - w'_1 = c_{1i} + c_{ij} + \cdots + c_{uv} + c_{vm}$, the length of the constructed path from node 1 to node m.

PROBLEM 11.26

$X = \{1\}$, $w'_1 = 0$, $(p, q) = (1, 2)$, $w'_2 = 2$

$X = \{1, 2\}$, $(p, q) = (1, 4)$ $w'_4 = 3$

$X = \{1, 2, 4\}$, $(p, q) = (4, 3)$, $w'_3 = 5$

$X = \{1, 2, 3, 4\}$, $(p, q) = (3, 5)$, $w'_5 = 8$

PROBLEM 11.26 (Continued)

$X = \{1,2,3,4,5\}$

$(p, q) = (5, 6)$

$w_6' = 9$

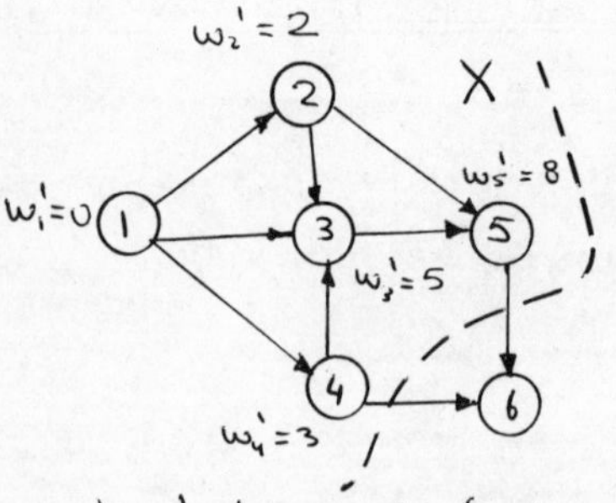

The shortest path from node 1 to node 6 is $1 \to 4 \to 3 \to 5 \to 6$ with the cost of 9.

b)

$w_2' < w_1' + c_{12}$

$w_2' = 2$

$w_3' < w_1' + c_{13}$

$w_3' = 6$

$w_4' < w_1' + c_{14}$

$w_4' = 3$

$w_5' < w_2' + c_{25}$

$w_5' = 10$

$w_6' < w_4' + c_{46}$

$w_6' = 12$

$w_3' < w_2' + c_{23}$

$w_3' = 7$

$w_j' \geq w_i' + c_{ij}$ for all (i,j),

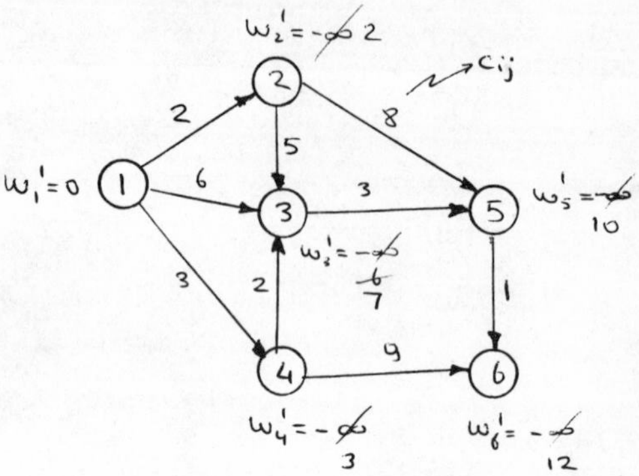

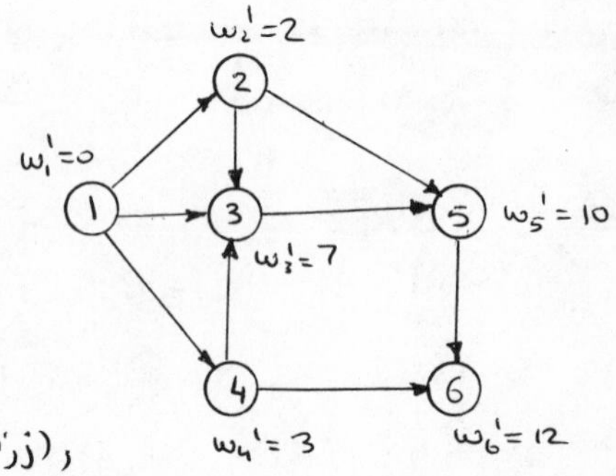

so the longest path from node 1 to node 6 is $1 \to 4 \to 6$ with length being equal to 12.

PROBLEM 11.27

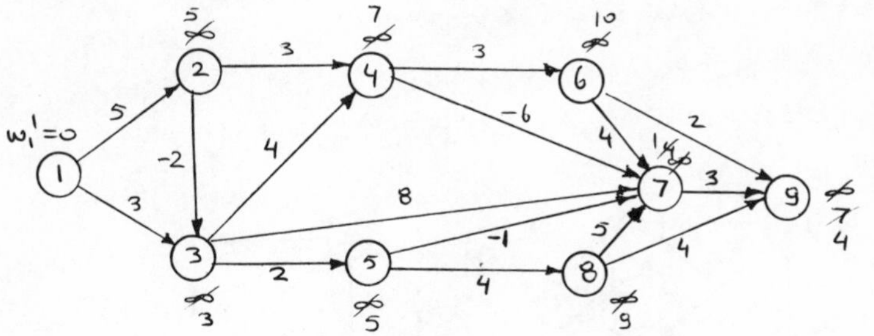

Start with $w_1' = 0$, $w_j = \infty$ for all $j \neq 1$.

$$w_2' > w_1' + c_{12} \Rightarrow w_2' = 5$$
$$w_3' > w_1' + c_{13} \Rightarrow w_3' = 3$$
$$w_4' > w_3' + c_{34} \Rightarrow w_4' = 7$$
$$w_5' > w_3' + c_{35} \Rightarrow w_5' = 5$$
$$w_7' > w_5' + c_{57} \Rightarrow w_7' = 4$$
$$w_6' > w_4' + c_{46} \Rightarrow w_6' = 10$$
$$w_8' > w_5' + c_{58} \Rightarrow w_8' = 9$$
$$w_9' > w_7' + c_{79} \Rightarrow w_9' = 7$$
$$w_7' > w_4' + c_{47} \Rightarrow w_7' = 1$$
$$w_9' > w_7' + c_{79} \Rightarrow w_9' = 4$$

Now $w_j' \leq w_i + c_{ij}$ for all (i,j). Thus the optimal solution is obtained.

Shortest path from 1 to 2 : $1 \to 2$, length = 5
Shortest path from 1 to 3 : $1 \to 3$, length = 3
Shortest path from 1 to 4 : $1 \to 3 \to 4$, length = 7
" " from 1 to 5 : $1 \to 3 \to 5$, length = 5
" " from 1 to 6 : $1 \to 3 \to 4 \to 6$, length = 10
" " from 1 to 7 : $1 \to 3 \to 4 \to 7$, length = 1
" " from 1 to 8 : $1 \to 3 \to 5 \to 8$, length = 9
" " from 1 to 9 : $1 \to 3 \to 4 \to 7 \to 9$, length = 4

PROBLEM 11.28

(p,q) is determined as follows:

$$c_{pq} + w_q' = \min\{c_{ij} + w_j' : (i,j) \in (\bar{X}, X)\}$$

place node p in X, $w_p' = w_q' + c_{pq}$.

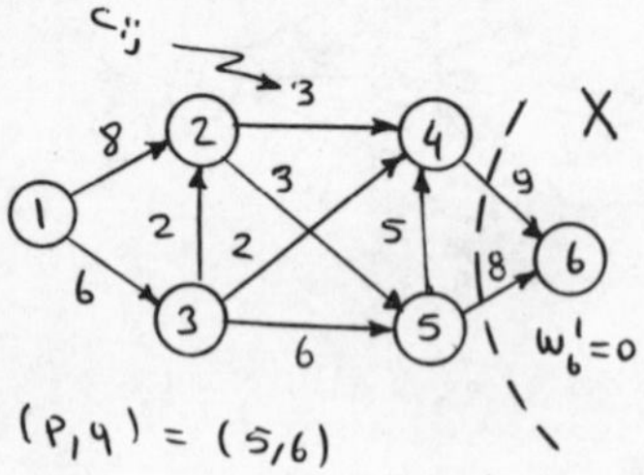

$(p,q) = (5,6)$

$w_5' = 8$

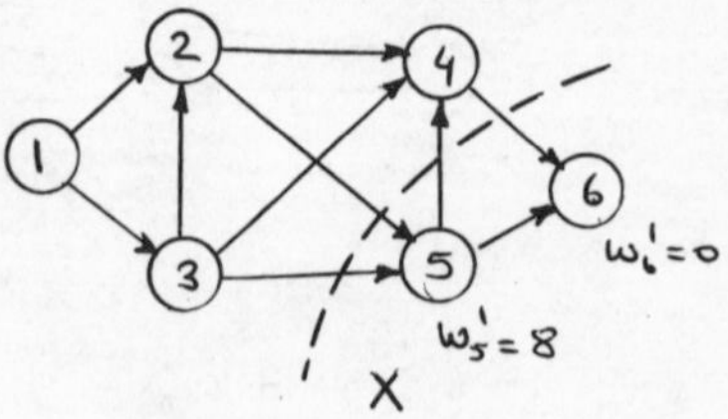

$(p,q) = (4,6)$

$w_4' = 9$

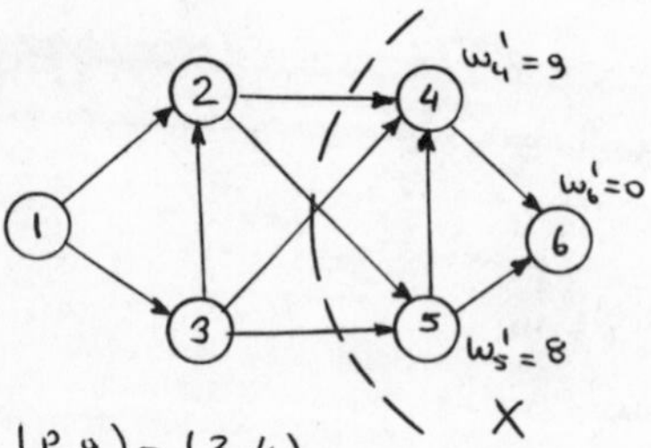

$(p,q) = (3,4)$

$w_3' = 11$

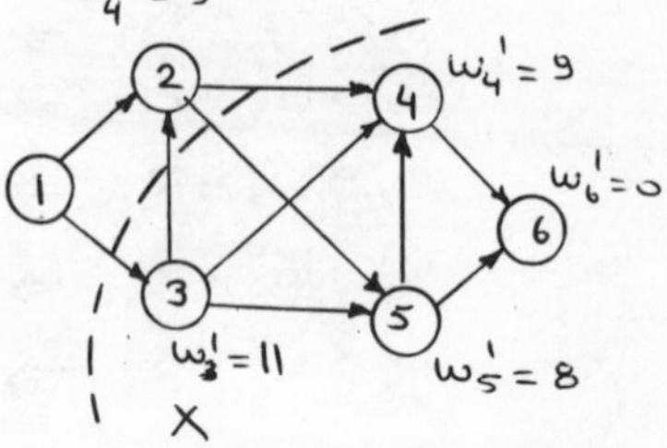

$(p,q) = (2,5)$

$w_2' = 11$

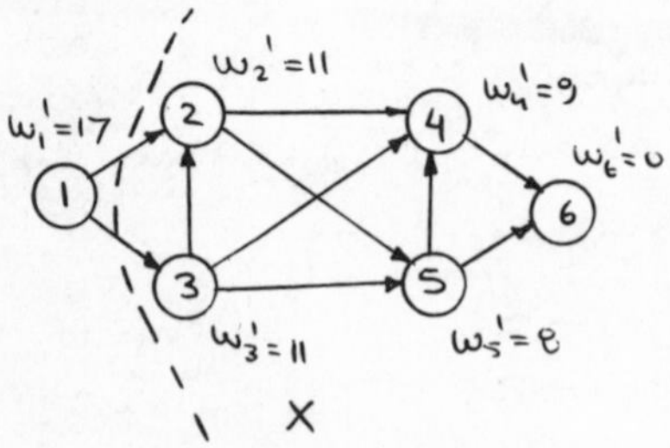

$(p,q) = (1,3)$

$w_1' = 17$

Shortest Path	Length
$1 \to 3 \to 4 \to 6$	17
$2 \to 5 \to 6$	11
$3 \to 4 \to 6$	11
$4 \to 6$	9
$5 \to 6$	8

PROBLEM 11.29

INITIALIZATION

Let $w_m = 0$, $w_j = \infty$ for $j \neq m$.

MAIN STEP

If $w_i > w_j + c_{ij}$ replace w_i by $w_j + c_{ij}$. Repeat the main step until $w_i - w_j \leq c_{ij}$ for all (i,j).

PROBLEM 11.30

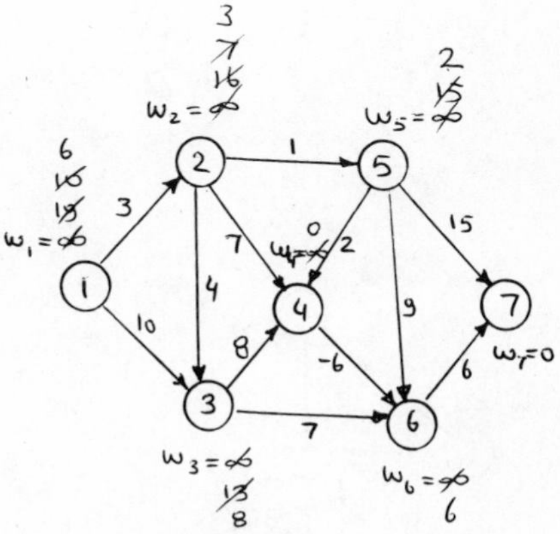

$w_5 > w_7 + c_{57} \Rightarrow w_5 = 15$

$w_6 > w_7 + c_{67} \Rightarrow w_6 = 6$

$w_2 > w_5 + c_{25} \Rightarrow w_2 = 16$

$w_3 > w_6 + c_{36} \Rightarrow w_3 = 13$

$w_4 > w_6 + c_{46} \Rightarrow w_4 = 0$

$w_1 > w_2 + c_{12} \Rightarrow w_1 = 19$

$w_2 > w_4 + c_{24} \Rightarrow w_2 = 7$

$w_1 > w_2 + c_{12} \Rightarrow w_1 = 10$

$w_3 > w_4 + c_{34} \Rightarrow w_3 = 8$

$w_5 > w_4 + c_{54} \Rightarrow w_5 = 2$

$w_2 > w_5 + c_{25} \Rightarrow w_2 = 3$

$w_1 > w_2 + c_{12} \Rightarrow w_1 = 6$

Since $w_i - w_j \leq c_{ij}$ for all (i,j) we have the optimal.

SHORTEST PATH	LENGTH
$1 \to 2 \to 5 \to 4 \to 6 \to 7$	6
$2 \to 5 \to 4 \to 6 \to 7$	3
$3 \to 4 \to 6 \to 7$	8
$4 \to 6 \to 7$	0
$5 \to 4 \to 6 \to 7$	2
$6 \to 7$	6

PROBLEM 11.31

a) Same as the directed case except that the sets $(X,\bar{X})$ is interpreted as the set of undirected arcs of the form (i,j) with $i \in X$, $j \in \bar{X}$.

b)

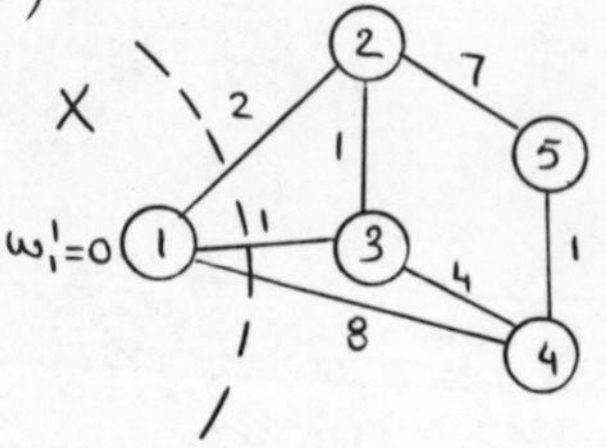

$(p,q) = (1,3)$, $w_3' = 1$

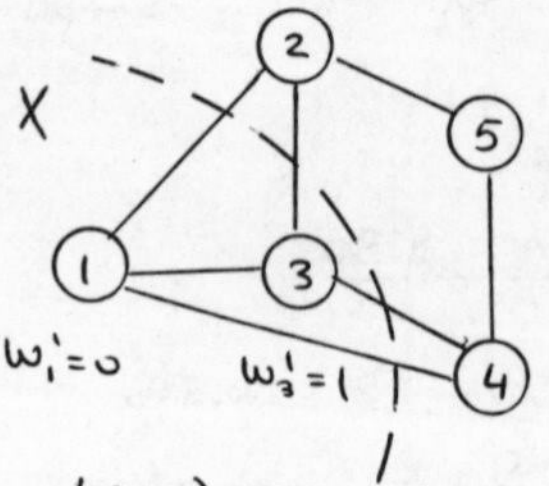

$(p,q) = (1,2)$, $w_2' = 2$

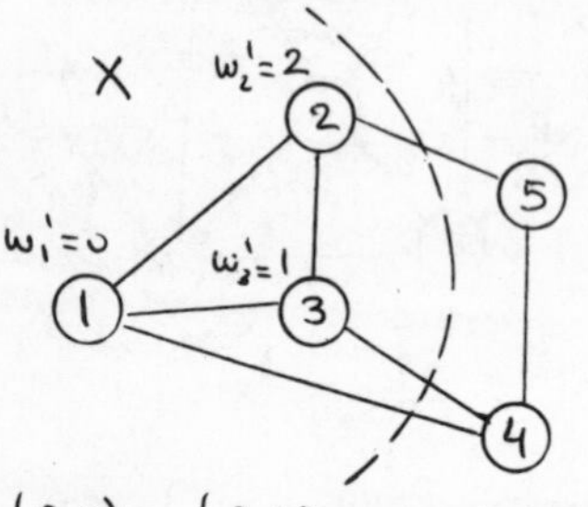

$(p,q) = (3,4)$, $w_4' = 5$

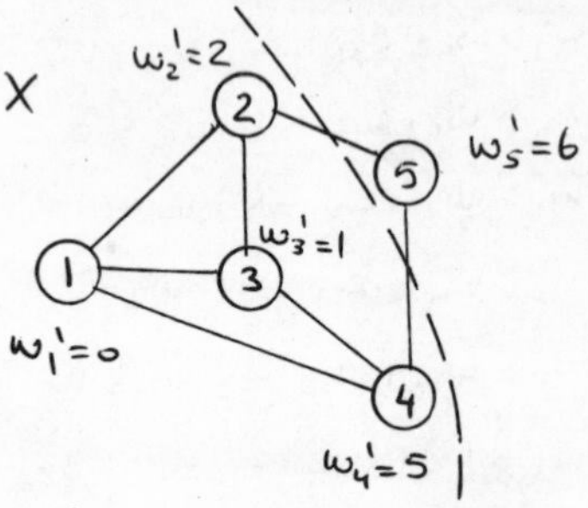

$(p,q) = (4,5)$, $w_5' = 6$

FROM	TO	SHORTEST PATH	LENGTH
1	2	1→2	2
1	3	1→3	1
1	4	1→3→4	5
1	5	1→3→4→5	6

PROBLEM 11.32

Let the arcs joining nodes i and j be undirected. Suppose that the undirected arc is replaced by two directed arcs.

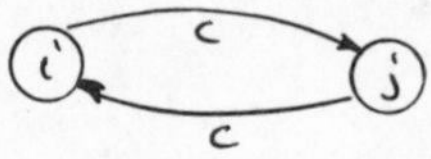

We see that a cycle is created whose cost is $2c < 0$ (note $c < 0$). Thus the application of the shortest path algorithm leads to the unboundedness conclusion. Also note that the dual constraints $w_i - w_j \le c$ and $w_j - w_i \le c$ are not compatible (adding the two constraints gives $0 \le c$ which violates that $c < 0$). Hence, the shortest path algorithm could not handle undirected arcs with negative costs.

PROBLEM 11.33

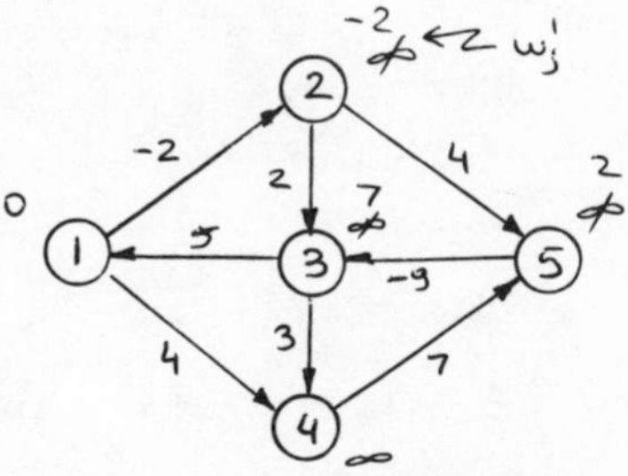

Set $w_1' = 0$, $w_j' = \infty$ for $j \neq 1$.

$w_2' > w_1' + c_{12} \Rightarrow w_2' = -2$

$w_5' > w_2' + c_{25} \Rightarrow w_5' = 2$

$w_3' > w_5' + c_{53} \Rightarrow w_3' = -7$

$w_1' > w_3' + c_{31} \Rightarrow w_1' = -2$

Going through the same sequence six times $w_2' = -12$, after which we stop, since the sum of the cost of negative arcs is -11.

PROBLEM 11.33 (Continued)

b) In part (a) we concluded the existance of a negative cycle [Note the cycle $1 \to 2 \to 5 \to 3 \to 1$ with the total cost of -2].

c)

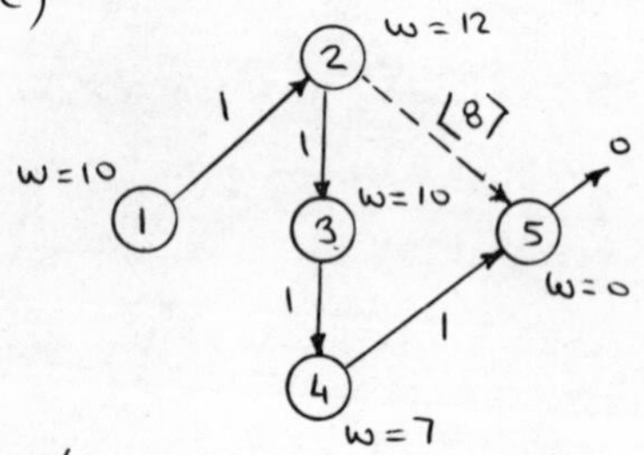

X_{25} enters, X_{23} leaves.

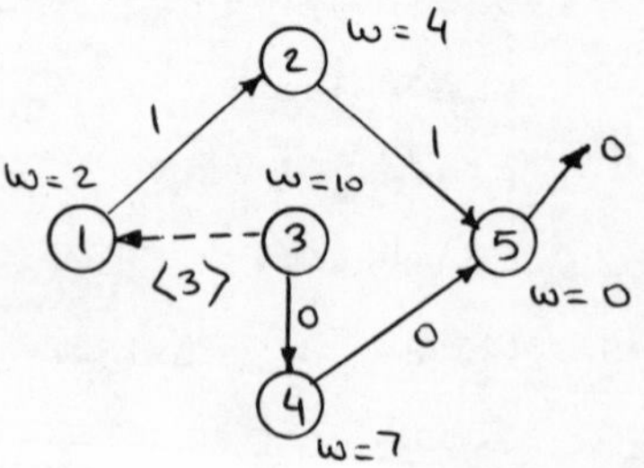

X_{31} enters.

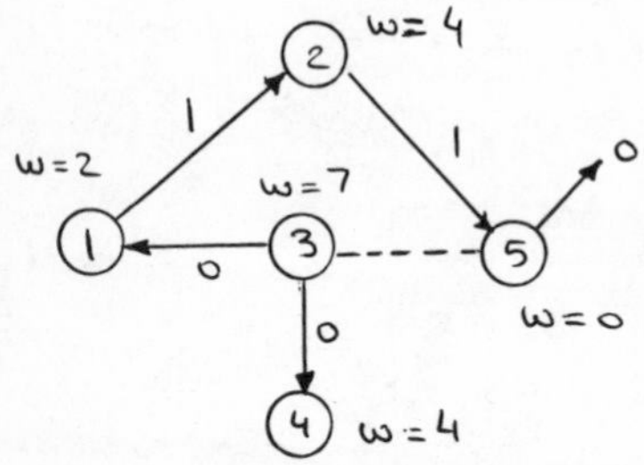

X_{53} enters.

As x_{53} enters (or increases) the basic variables x_{31}, x_{12}, x_{25} increase, as well. Thus, the problem has an unbounded solution.

Note that if we put an upper bound on each arc of 1 unit of flow, we could find the shortest path. In this case x_{53} enters and x_{12} leaves at its upper bound of 1, and all $z_{ij} - c_{ij} \le 0$ for lower bounded arcs and $z_{ij} - c_{ij} \geq 0$ for the upper bounded arcs. The shortest distance (with $u_{ij} = 1$) from node 1 to node 5 is $1 \to 2 \to 5$ with length being equal to 2.

PROBLEM 11.34

Find the shortest paths from each node in the network to node 10.

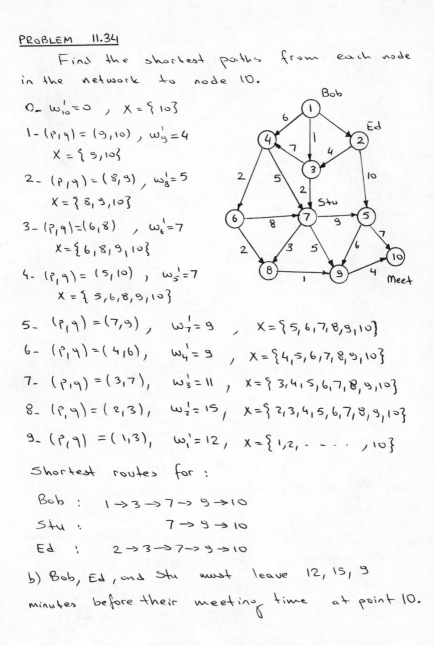

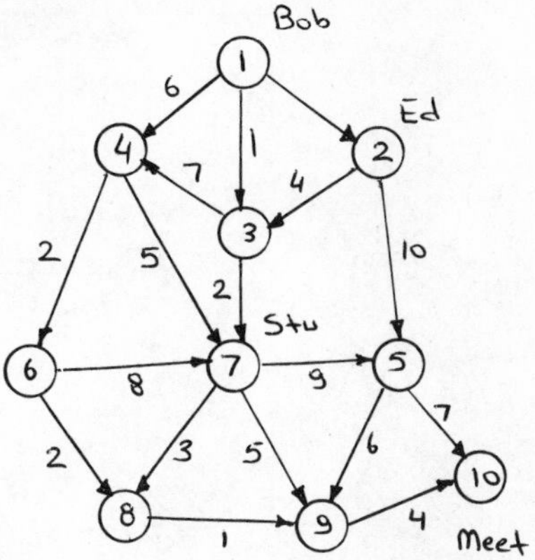

0- $w'_{10} = 0$, $X = \{10\}$

1- $(p,q) = (9,10)$, $w'_9 = 4$
$X = \{9,10\}$

2- $(p,q) = (8,9)$, $w'_8 = 5$
$X = \{8,9,10\}$

3- $(p,q) = (6,8)$, $w'_6 = 7$
$X = \{6,8,9,10\}$

4- $(p,q) = (5,10)$, $w'_5 = 7$
$X = \{5,6,8,9,10\}$

5- $(p,q) = (7,9)$, $w'_7 = 9$, $X = \{5,6,7,8,9,10\}$

6- $(p,q) = (4,6)$, $w'_4 = 9$, $X = \{4,5,6,7,8,9,10\}$

7- $(p,q) = (3,7)$, $w'_3 = 11$, $X = \{3,4,5,6,7,8,9,10\}$

8- $(p,q) = (2,3)$, $w'_2 = 15$, $X = \{2,3,4,5,6,7,8,9,10\}$

9- $(p,q) = (1,3)$, $w'_1 = 12$, $X = \{1,2,\ldots,10\}$

Shortest routes for:

Bob : $1 \to 3 \to 7 \to 9 \to 10$

Stu : $7 \to 9 \to 10$

Ed : $2 \to 3 \to 7 \to 9 \to 10$

b) Bob, Ed, and Stu must leave 12, 15, 9 minutes before their meeting time at point 10.

PROBLEM 11.35

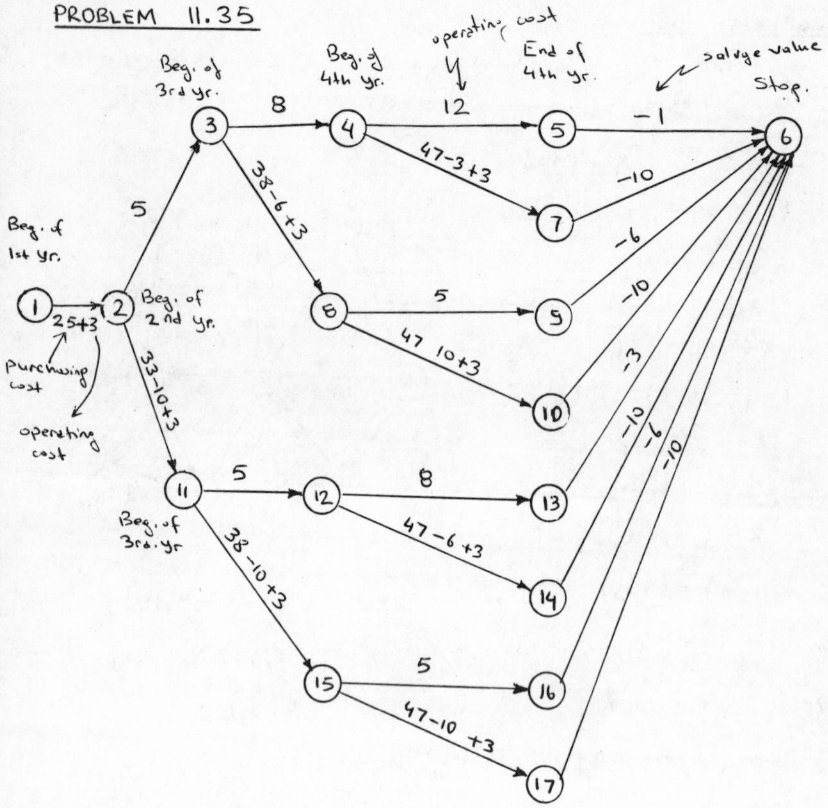

In order to find the optimal purchasing, operating, and selling policy, we must find the shortest path from node 1 to node 6.

The best policy states to keep the single machine until the end of the fourth year and then sell it. (i.e., the shortest path is $1 \to 2 \to 3 \to 4 \to 5 \to 6$ with minimum cost of 52)

PROBLEM 11.36

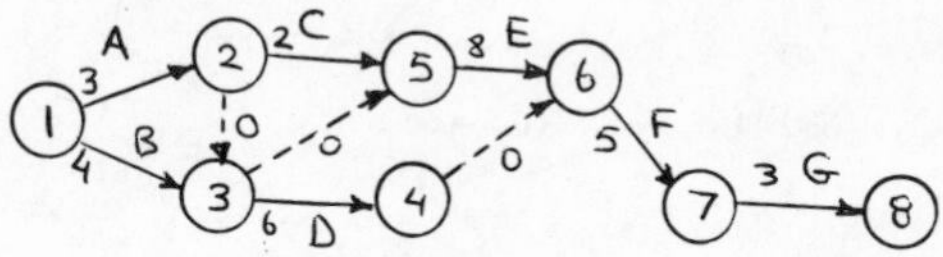

Find the longest path from node 1 to node 8. The longest path is $1 \to 2 \to 5 \to 6 \to 7 \to 8$. The duration of the project is 21 days. The critical activities are A, C, E, F and G.

PROBLEM 11.37

a) Suppose we found a shortest path from a source node to a sink node. In the process we generate a set of w_i's which satisfy $z_{ij} - c_{ij} = w_i - w_j - c_{ij} \le 0$ for all (i, j) with $z_{ij} - c_{ij} = 0$ for the arcs along the shortest path. This set of w_i's could be used as the initial dual variables. In addition we must find a set of x_{ij}'s such that

$$\Sigma_j \, x_{ij} - \Sigma_j \, x_{ji} = b_i \quad \text{for all } i.$$

b) The only possible advantage of starting with the above set of w_i's (as opposed to all w_i's at zero, say) lies in the case where most of the obtained x_{ij}'s are at their lower bound. In this case most of the arcs will be in kilter since $z_{ij} - c_{ij} \le 0$ and $x_{ij} = \ell_{ij}$ for most of the arcs.

PROBLEM 11.38

See Bazaraa and Langley [23].

PROBLEM 11.39

a) We wish to find the maximal flow from node 1 to node m with minimal cost. The flow is represented by x_{m1}. The minimal cost–maximal flow problem is thus formulated as follows:

$$\max \lambda x_{m1} - \sum_i \sum_j c_{ij} x_{ij}$$

$$\text{s.t.} \quad \sum_j x_{ij} - \sum_j x_{ji} = 0 \qquad i = 1, \ldots, m$$

$$0 \le x_{ij} \le u_{ij} \qquad \forall (i,j)$$

where λ is a large positive number.

Since we are trying to maximize the objective function and since λ is sufficiently large, we would first maximize x_{m1}. Among all maximal x_{m1}, we would choose the corresponding flow which minimizes the cost of flow.

b) The out-of-kilter could be used to solve the problem. The cost of arc (i,j) for $(i,j) \neq (m,1)$ is c_{ij} and the cost of arc $(m,1)$ is $-\lambda$.

c) Start with $x_{ij} = 0 \ \forall i,j$ and let $w_i = 0 \ \forall i$.

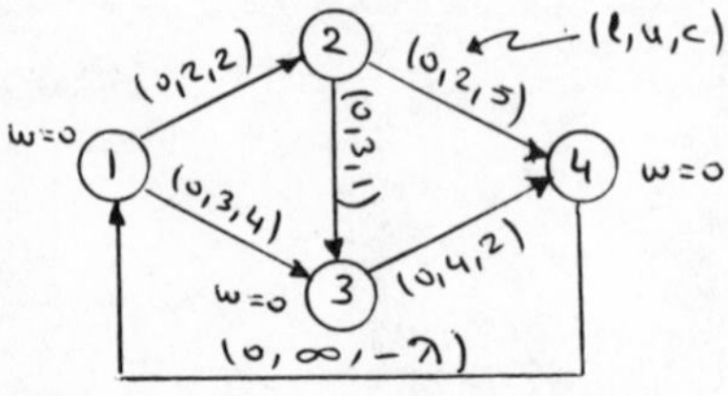

Starting solution all $x_{ij} = 0$; $w_i = 0$.

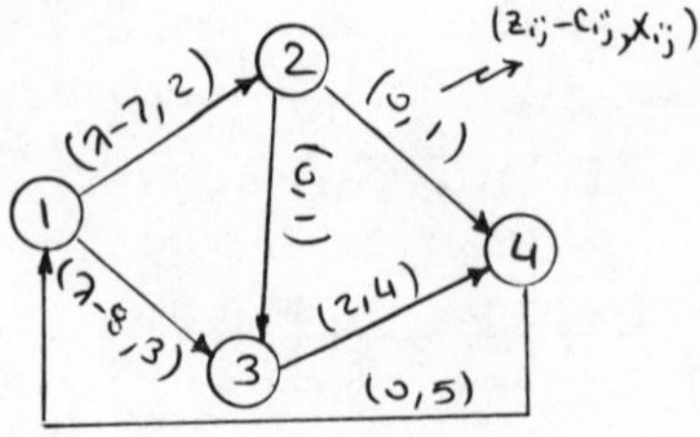

Optimal Solution.

PROBLEM 11.40

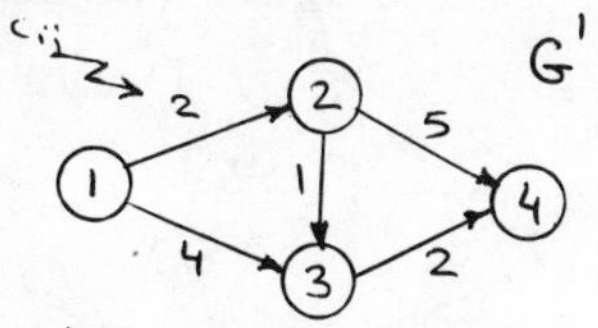

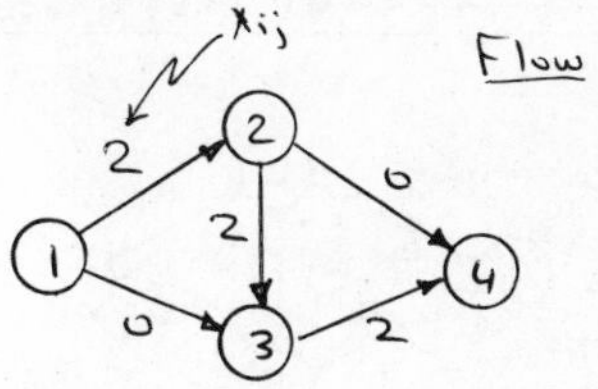

Shortest path 1→2→3→4
Δ=2.

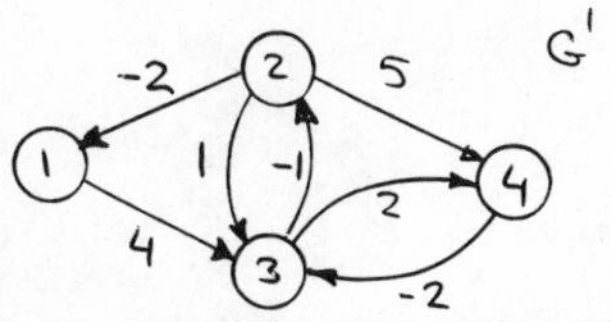

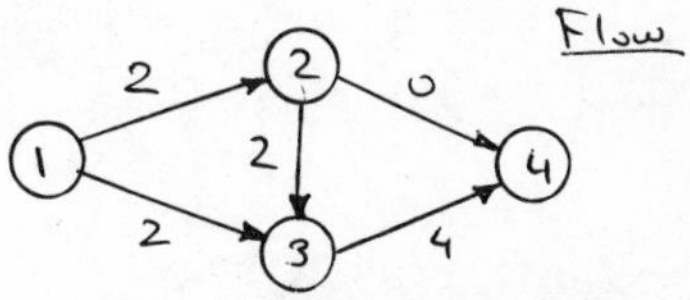

Shortest path 1→3→4 , Δ=2

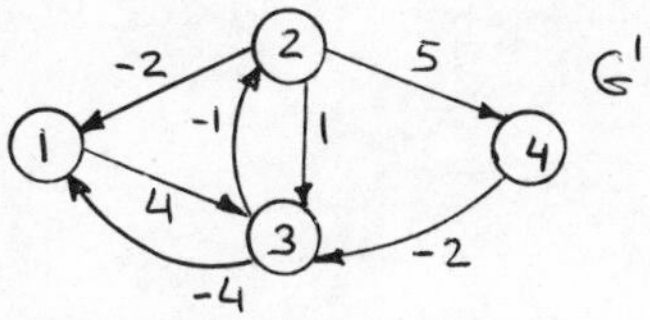

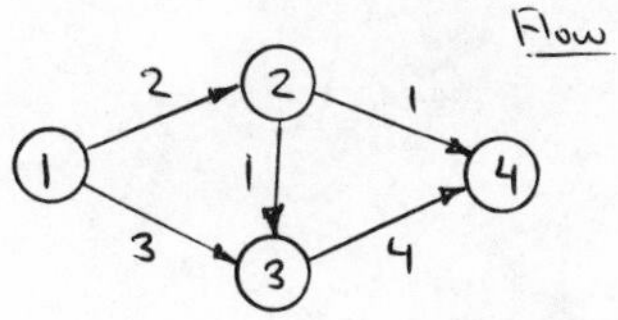

Shortest path 1→3→2→4, Δ=1

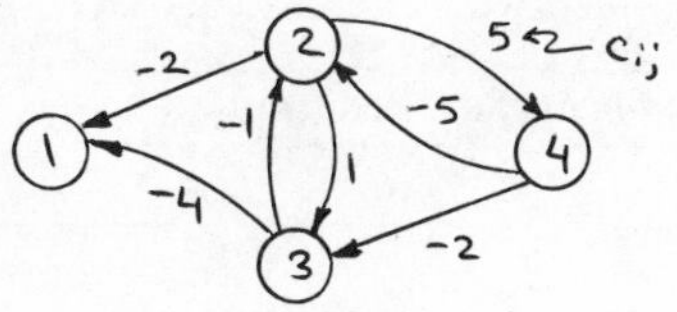

No path from node 1 to node 4. Optimal is achieved. Flow structure is equal to the flow structure obtained in the previous step.

PROBLEM 11.41

a) INITIALIZATION

The maximal flow is given in the network as shown.

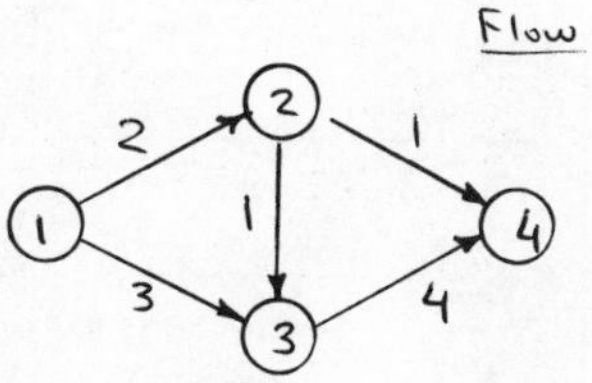

PROBLEM 11.41 (Continued)

G'

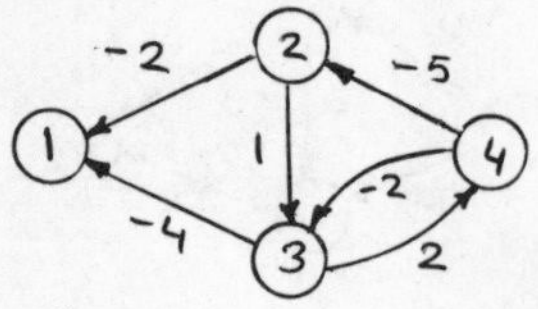

Flow

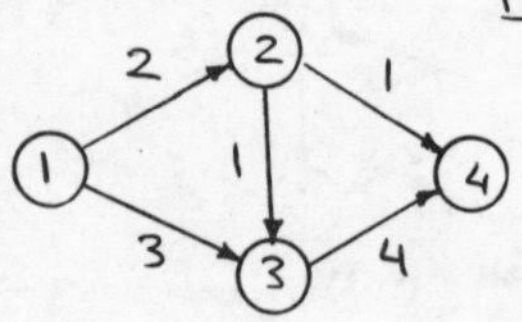

Negative circuit detected.

$2 \to 3 \to 4 \to 2$

Cost = -2 , $\Delta = 1$

G'

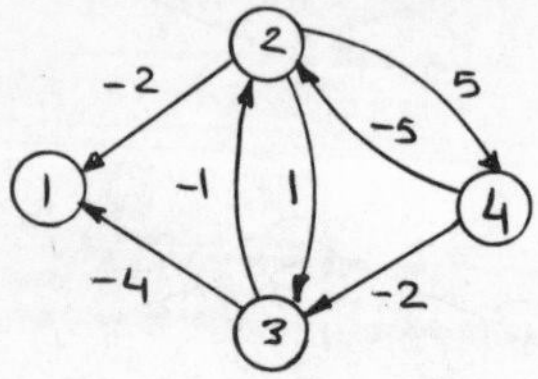

There exists no negative circuit. Hence the above solution is optimal.

PROBLEM 11.42

a)

Variables for Commodity 1 (x_{112} … x_{171}); Variables for commodity 2 (x_{212} … x_{267})

	x_{112}	x_{113}	x_{124}	x_{135}	x_{146}	x_{152}	x_{156}	x_{167}	x_{171}	x_{212}	x_{213}	x_{224}	x_{235}	x_{243}	x_{246}	x_{252}	x_{256}	x_{267}	
max									1					1					
S.T.	1	1							-1										= 0
	-1		1			-1													= 0
		-1		1															= 0
			-1		1														= 0
				-1		1	1												= 0
					-1		-1	1											= 0
								-1	1										= 0
										1	1								= 0
										-1		1				-1			= 0
											-1		1	-1					= 0
												-1		1	1				= 0
													-1			1	1		= 0
															-1		-1	1	= 0
																		-1	= 0

PROBLEM 11.42 (Continued)

$$x_{1ij} + x_{2ij} \leq 1 \qquad \forall (i,j)$$

$$x_{1ij},\ x_{2ij} \geq 0 \qquad \forall (i,j)$$

b) Suppose that we send λ units of commodity 2 via the only possible path $3 \to 5 \to 2 \to 4$. We can send $(1-\lambda)$ units of commodity 1 on each of the following two paths:

P_1: $1 \to 2 \to 4 \to 6 \to 7$

P_2: $1 \to 3 \to 5 \to 6 \to 7$

Note that arcs (2,4) and (3,5) will be saturated. Also the flow on arc (6,7) cannot exceed 1. Thus

$$2(1-\lambda) \leq 1 \qquad \text{or}$$

$$\lambda = \frac{1}{2}\ .$$

Hence the maximal flow is 3/2 as shown on the network below:

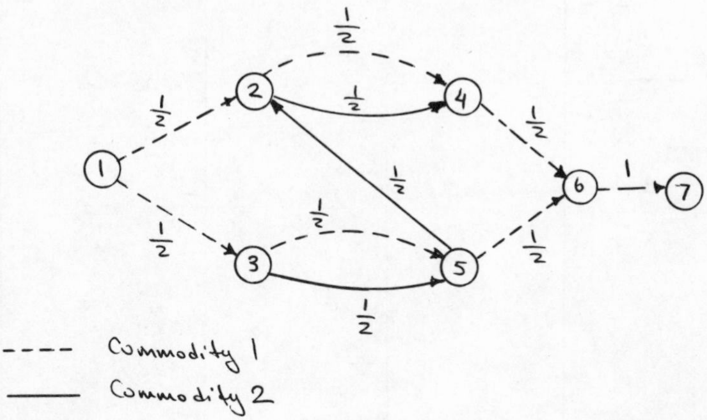

PROBLEM 11.43

The lower bounds can be handled similar to that of the single commodity case. Make the change of variable $y_{kij} = x_{kij} - \ell_{kij}$ and adjust the upper limits accordingly as well as the balance equations.

PROBLEM 11.44

Commodity 1						Commodity 2						Commodity 3						Slacks						
X_{112}	X_{123}	X_{134}	X_{141}	X_{145}	X_{153}	X_{212}	X_{223}	X_{234}	X_{241}	X_{245}	X_{253}	X_{312}	X_{323}	X_{334}	X_{341}	X_{345}	X_{353}	S_{12}	S_{23}	S_{34}	S_{41}	S_{45}	S_{53}	RHS
1						1						1						1						6
	1						1						1						1					6
		1						1						1						1				5
			1						1						1						1			4
				1						1						1						1		4
					1						1						1						1	5
1			-1																					3
-1	1																							-2
	-1	1			-1																			0
		-1	1	1																				-2
				-1	1																			1
						1				-1														1
						-1	1																	-1
							-1	1			-1													-3
								-1	1	1														1
										-1	1													2
												1			-1									1
												-1	1											0
													-1	1			-1							-2
														-1	1	1								0
																-1	1							1

PROBLEM 11.44 (Continued)

Commodity 1

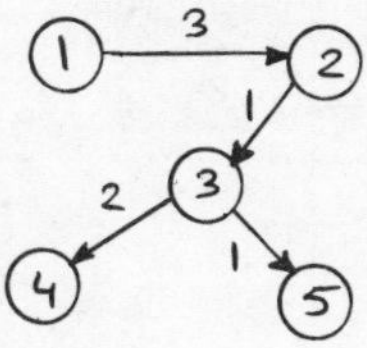

Commodity 2

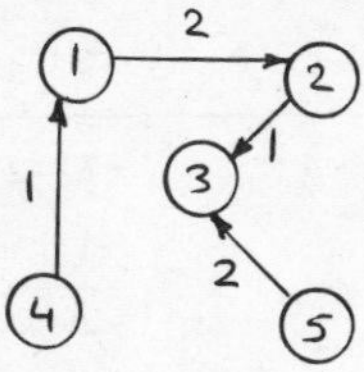

Commodity 3

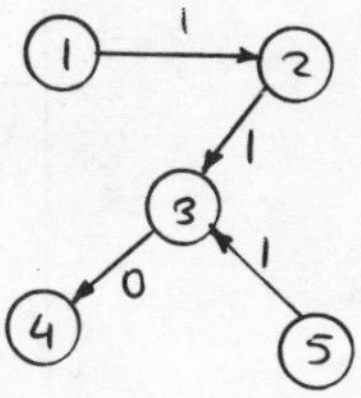

These flows given above are the starting solutions. The basis consists of s_{12}, s_{23}, s_{34}, s_{41}, s_{45}, s_{53}, λ_{11}, λ_{21}, λ_{31}, corresponding to the above three bases.

$B =$

s_{12}	s_{23}	s_{34}	s_{41}	s_{45}	s_{53}	λ_{11}	λ_{21}	λ_{31}
1						3	2	1
	1					1	1	1
		1				2	0	0
			1			0	1	0
				1		0	0	0
					1	1	2	1
						1	0	0
							1	0
								1

$c_1 x_{11} = 15$, $c_2 x_{21} = 3$, $c_3 x_{31} = 8$

$(w, \alpha) = (0, 0, 0, 0, 0, 0, 15, 3, 8)$, $\bar{z} = 15 + 3 + 8 = 26$

The tableau

$$\left[\begin{array}{c|c} w, \alpha & \bar{z} \\ \hline B^{-1} & \begin{array}{c} b \\ 1 \end{array} \end{array}\right]$$

is given below:

PROBLEM 11.44 (Continued)

	w_{12}	w_{23}	w_{34}	w_{41}	w_{45}	w_{53}	α_1	α_2	α_3	RHS
Z	0	0	0	0	0	0	15	3	8	26
S_{12}	1						-3	-2	-1	0
S_{23}		1					-1	-1	-1	3
S_{34}			1				-2	0	0	3
S_{41}				1			0	-1	0	3
S_{45}					1		0	0	0	4
S_{53}						1	-1	-2	-1	1
λ_{11}							1	0	0	1
λ_{21}								1	0	1
λ_{31}									1	1

ITERATION 1

Consider if a candidate variable from any of the subproblems is eligible to enter the basis.

SUBPROBLEM 1

$$\max\ (w - c_1)x_1 + \alpha_1$$
$$\text{s.t.} \quad Ax_1 = b_1$$
$$0 \le x_1 \le u_1$$

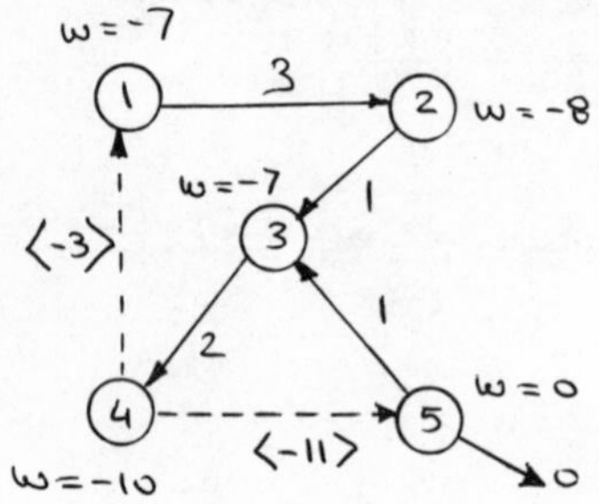

Optimal of Subproblem 1.

$$\max (w - c_1)x_1 + \alpha_1 = 0$$

No candidates from subproblem 1.

PROBLEM 11.44 (Continued)

SUBPROBLEM 2

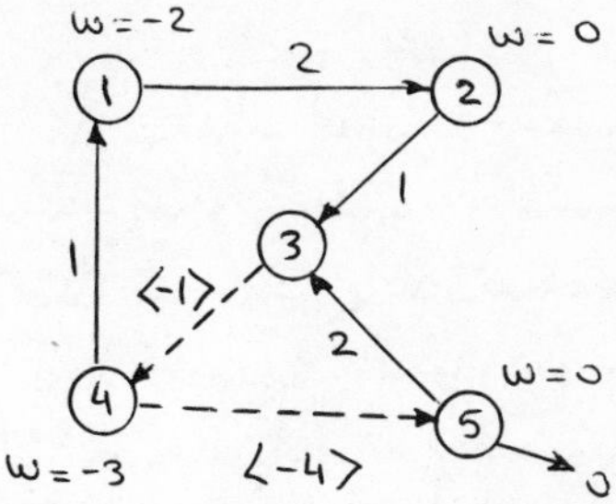

Optimal of subproblem 2

$\max(w - c_2)x_2 + \alpha_2 = 0.$

No candidate from subproblem 2.

SUBPROBLEM 3

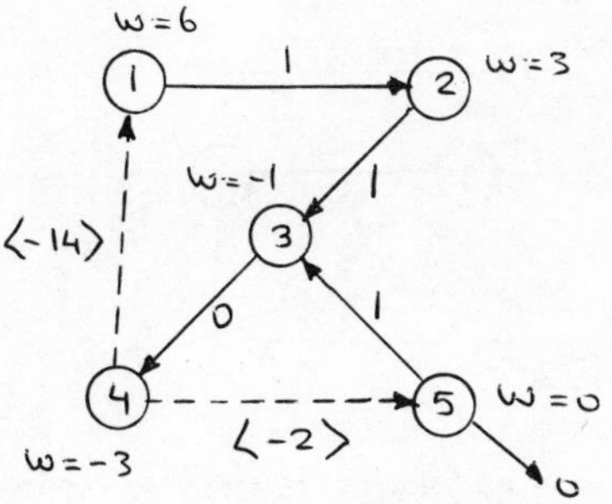

Optimal of subproblem 3.

$\max(w - c_2)x_2 + \alpha_2 = 0$

No candidate from subproblem 3.

Hence, the optimal solution is at hand.

$$\begin{bmatrix} x_{12} \\ x_{23} \\ x_{34} \\ x_{41} \\ x_{45} \\ x_{53} \end{bmatrix} = 1 \begin{bmatrix} 3 \\ 1 \\ 2 \\ 0 \\ 0 \\ 1 \end{bmatrix} + 1 \begin{bmatrix} 2 \\ 1 \\ 0 \\ 1 \\ 0 \\ 2 \end{bmatrix} + 1 \begin{bmatrix} 1 \\ 1 \\ 0 \\ 0 \\ 0 \\ 1 \end{bmatrix} = \begin{bmatrix} 6 \\ 3 \\ 2 \\ 1 \\ 0 \\ 4 \end{bmatrix}$$

with the total cost = 24.

PROBLEM 11.45

a) Let w be an optimal dual vector of the master constraints. As the kth subproblem is solved with the modified costs, the dual vector w_k gives the dual variables of the subproblem constraints $Ax_k = b_k$. The dual variables of the constraints $x_{kij} \le u_{kij}$ is $w_{ki} - w_{kj} - c_{kij}$.

b) Subproblem 1

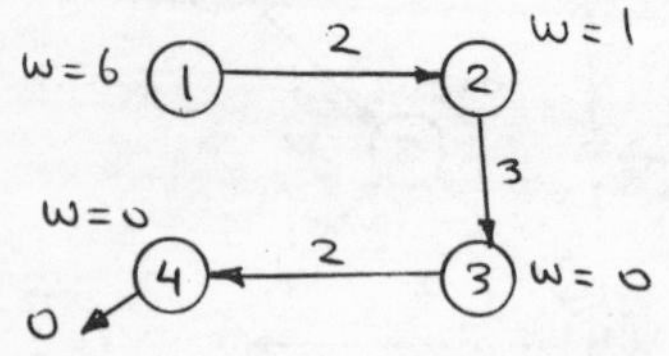

Dual variables of conservation equations are respectively 6,1,0,0.

Dual variables for $x_{ij} \le u_{ij}$ are 0,0,0,−7,−5 for arcs (1,2), (2,3), (3,4), (4,1) and (4,2) respectively.

Subproblem 2

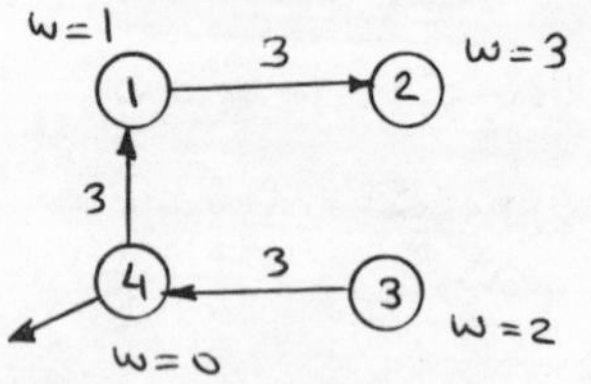

Dual variables of conservation equations are respectively 1, 3, 2, 0

Dual variables for $x_{ij} \le u_{ij}$ are 0,1,0,0,−9 for arcs (1,2), (2,3), (3,4), (4,1) and (4,2) respectively.

PROBLEM 11.47

As any of the subproblems is solved, the optimal solution of the subproblem may be unbounded (in this case, a nonbasic variable is increased, the associated cycle is such that

PROBLEM 11.47 (Continued)

the basic variables would increase indefinitely since their upper bound is $+\infty$). In such case a direction d is identified such that $(w - c)d > 0$. The vector $(d, 0)^T$ is premultiplied by B^{-1} and the updated column

$$\left[\begin{array}{c} (w-c)d \\ \hline B^{-1}\binom{d}{0} \end{array}\right]$$

is used for pivoting, thus updating the inverse basis, the values of the variables and (w, α).

PROBLEM 11.48

The decomposition procedure described in section 11.3 could be interpreted as a method that starts with minimal cost flows of the individual commodities provided that the initial dual vector used is equal to zero.

After the initial iteration, the method proceeds to adjust the flows where violating the coupling constraints is penalized by adjusting the cost

PROBLEM 11.48 (Continued)

coefficients by the dual vector.

Grigoriadis and White [215] give a procedure for solving the problem by generalizing the dual simplex method. This could be viewed as approaching the solution in an optimality sense.

PROBLEM 11.49

See Ford and Fulkerson [157].

PROBLEM 11.50

For subproblem k, the number of paths from the source to the sink are t_k. The flow on the jth path of subproblem k is denoted by x_{jk}. Let the arcs be enumerated by 1,2,..., n. If arc i belongs to the jth path of subproblem k, then $P_{ijk} = 1$, otherwise $P_{ijk} = 0$. Thus the arc-path formulation of the problem is:

$$\text{maximize} \sum_{k=1}^{t} \sum_{j=1}^{t_k} x_{jk}$$

$$\text{s.t.} \quad \sum_{k=1}^{t} \sum_{j=1}^{t_k} P_{ijk} x_{jk} \le u_i \qquad i = 1, \ldots, n$$

$$x_{jk} \ge 0 \qquad j = 1, \ldots, t_k$$
$$\qquad\qquad k = 1, \ldots, t$$

PROBLEM 11.51

Let x_{kij} be the flow of the kth commodity along arc (i,j) from i to j and x_{kji} be the flow of the kth commodity along arc (j,i). We must require that:

$$\ell_{ij} \le \sum_k x_{kij} + \sum_k x_{kji} \le u_{ij}$$

for the undirected arc (i,j), where ℓ_{ij} and u_{ij} are the lower and upper capacities of the undirected arc (i,j).

Basically, this doubles the number of master constraints in the LP formulation unless some bounded simplex method is used (see Jarvis J. J., [258]).

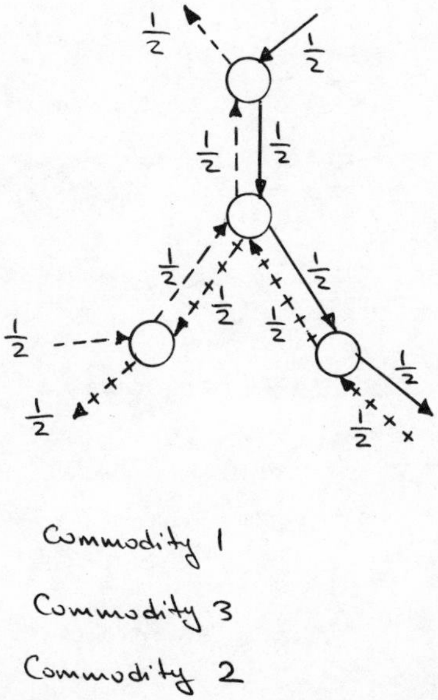

PROBLEM 11.52

a) Minimal disconnecting set is any of the following sets:

$\{(1,2),(2,3)\}$,

$\{(2,3),(3,1)\}$, or

$\{(3,1),(1,2)\}$.

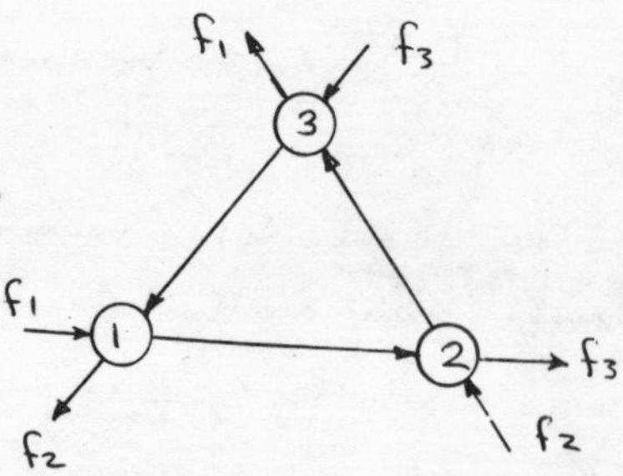

The capacity of the minimal disconnecting set is 2.

b) The maximal flow is equal to 3/2. Note that the capacity of the minimal disconnecting set is greater than the value of the maximal flow.

The multicommodity maximal flow problem can be stated as:

$$\max \sum_{k=1}^{t} \sum_{j=1}^{t_k} x_{jk}$$

$$\text{S.T.} \quad \sum_{k=1}^{t} \sum_{j=1}^{t_k} P_{ijk} x_{jk} \le u_i \qquad i=1,\ldots,n$$

$$x_{jk} \geq 0 \qquad \begin{array}{l} j=1,\ldots,t_k \\ k=1,\ldots,t \end{array}$$

where x_{jk} is the flow on path j of commodity k and u_i is the capacity of arc i.

$$P_{ijk} = \begin{cases} 1 & \text{if arc } i \text{ belongs to the } j\text{th path of commodity } k. \\ 0 & \text{otherwise} \end{cases}$$

PROBLEM 10.52 (Continued)

Take the dual of the problem:

$$\text{Minimize} \quad \sum_{i=1}^{n} w_i u_i$$

$$\text{S.T.} \quad \sum_{i=1}^{n} w_i P_{ijk} \geq 1 \quad \text{for all } j,k.$$

$$w_i \geq 0 \quad \text{for all } i.$$

Note that the primal problem is feasible and bounded and thus has a finite optimal solution. Thus by the main duality theorem the dual problem posesses a finite optimal solution and both objectives are equal at optimality.

Also note by examining the above dual problem that each $w_i \leq 1$ (if $w_i > 1$ and $P_{ijk} = 0$ or 1 then a cheaper feasible solution could be obtained by replacing w_i by 1). Thus the above problem is equivalent to

$$\text{Minimize} \quad \sum_{i=1}^{n} w_i u_i$$

$$\text{S.T.} \quad \sum_{i=1}^{n} w_i P_{ijk} \geq 1 \quad \text{for all } j,k$$

$$1 \geq w_i \leq 0 \quad i=1,..,n$$

If the constraints $1 \geq w_i \geq 0$ for $i=1,..,n$ are replaced by the constraints w_i either 0 or 1 for each i, we get:

PROBLEM 11.52 (Continued)

$$\min \sum_{i=1}^{n} w_i u_i \quad \underset{\text{by reducing feasible region}}{\geq} \quad \min \sum_{i=1}^{n} w_i u_i \quad = \max \sum_{j,k} x_{jk}$$

$$\text{s.t.} \sum_{i=1}^{n} w_i p_{ijk} \geq 1 \qquad \text{s.t.} \sum_{i=1}^{n} w_i p_{ijk} \geq 1 \qquad \text{s.t.} \sum_{j,k} p_{ijk} x_{jk} \leq u_i$$

$$w_i \ 0 \text{ or } 1 \qquad 0 \leq w_i \leq 1 \qquad x_{jk} \geq 0$$

Finally, the dual problem where w_i is restricted to 0 or 1 can be interpreted as finding the multicommodity minimal disconnecting set where

$$w_i = \begin{cases} 1 & \text{if arc } i \text{ is disconnected} \\ 0 & \text{otherwise} \end{cases}$$

The constraint $\sum_{i=1}^{n} w_i p_{ijk} \geq 1$ means that at least one arc along the jth path from the source to the sink of the kth commodity must be disconnected.

c) Minimal disconnected set of Figure 11.9 is given in part 1(a). For the network of Exercise 11.42

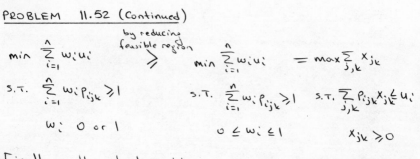

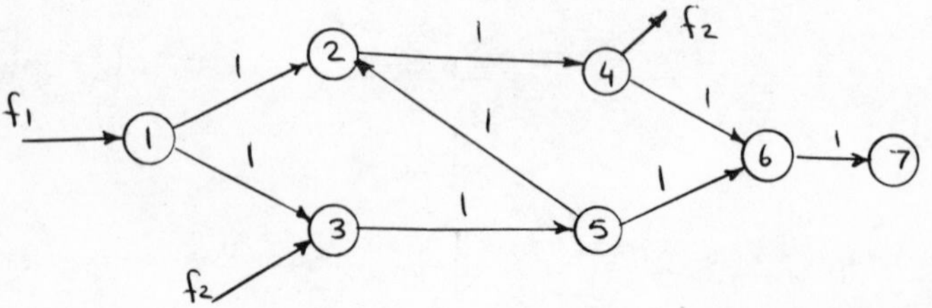

Minimal disconnecting set $\{(1,2),(3,5)\}$ with capacity 2. From the Exercise 11.42 the max-flow is 3/2.

PROBLEM 11.53

From the definition of multicommodity minimal disconnecting set, we know that the arcs in D_o blocks all the paths from source s_i to the sink t_i for each commodity i. Hence D_o is a cut set for each commodity i (and maybe additional arcs that can be ignored but the remaining arcs would still be a cut set for commodity i).

Hence, let the set of arcs $a_i, a_j, \ldots a_p, a_v$ be a cut set for commodity k, which belong to D_o (we can find such a set). Let $a_j, a_m, \ldots, a_s$ be the set of arcs, that form a cut set for commodity ℓ, which belong to D_o. This argument can be applied to each commodity individually. Hence

$$D_o = \{a_i, a_j, \ldots, a_p, a_v\} \cup \{a_j, a_m, \ldots, a_s\} \cup \cdots$$
$$\cdots \cup \{\ldots a_t \ldots\}$$

or
$$D_o = \bigcup_{i=1}^{k} D_i$$

where D_i is the cut set for the commodity i $(i = 1, \ldots, k)$. For details of the proof see [31], [376].

PROBLEM 11.53 (Continued)

The multicommodity minimal disconnecting set is not necessarily the union of the single commodity minimal cutsets. Following is a counter example:

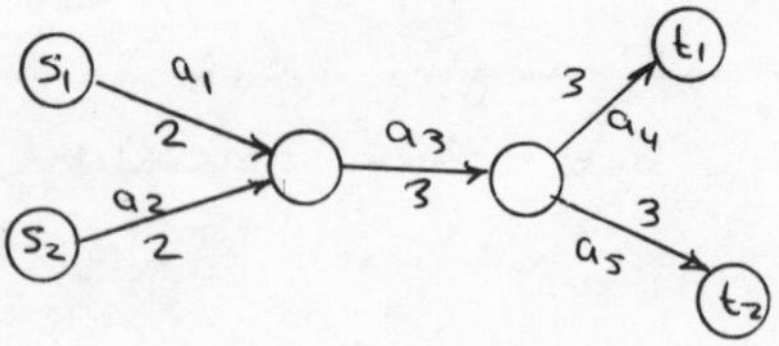

Here, $D_0 = \{a_3\}$ with $c(D_0) = 3$ while $D_1 = \{a_1\}$, $D_2 = \{a_2\}$, $c(D_1) + c(D_2) = 2 + 2 = 4$.

PROBLEM 11.54

Let each row represent a commodity in the given problem. The sum of each row gives the amount of commodity (number of people) to be shipped from district k to the others districts via some path. Let X_{ijk} be the number of people from district i using road (j,k) to reach their destination. The minimal time traffic assignment is as follows:

$X_{112} = 30$, $X_{125} = 8$, $X_{124} = 12$, $X_{132} = 0$, $X_{143} = 7$, $X_{151} = 0$

$X_{154} = 3$

$X_{212} = 0$, $X_{225} = 6$, $X_{224} = 7$, $X_{2232} = 0$, $X_{243} = 3$, $X_{251} = 2$

$X_{254} = 0$

PROBLEM 11.54 (Continued)

$x_{351}=6$, $x_{325}=11$, $x_{324}=1$, $x_{332}=14$, $x_{343}=x_{354}=x_{312}=0$

$x_{412}=x_{424}=x_{454}=0$, $x_{425}=7$, $x_{432}=11$, $x_{443}=18$, $x_{451}=2$

$x_{525}=x_{524}=x_{532}=0$, $x_{512}=1$, $x_{543}=3$, $x_{551}=1$, $x_{554}=7$

PROBLEM 11.55

See Hartman and Lasdon [233].

PROBLEM 11.56

The solution procedure follows exactly the same manner given on pages 497 and 498, 499, 500. But on page 500 when we solve the subproblem 2 we realize that a positive cycle (note that problem is a maximization problem) is created as depicted below:

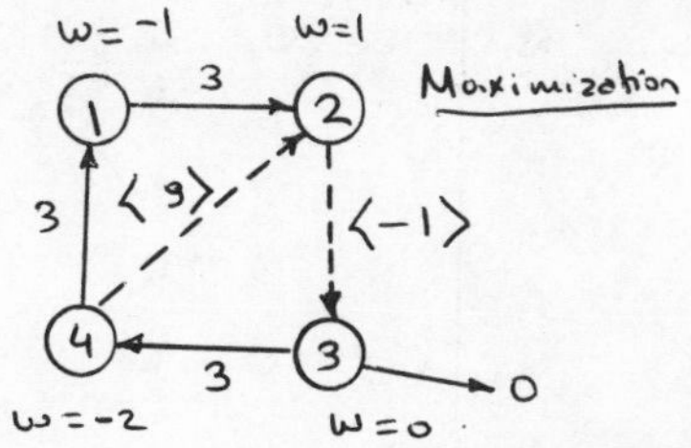

as we see $z_{23}-c_{23}=-1<0$ in this single commodity problem. (note it is a max cost problem). Hence x_{23} enters. As x_{23} increases, x_{34}, x_{41} and x_{12} increases as well.

x_{34}, x_{41}, x_{12} reach their upper bound, as $x_{23}=1$. We created a positive cycle around $1\to2\to3\to4\to1$. Following is the optimal solution for the above network:

PROBLEM 11.56 (Continued)

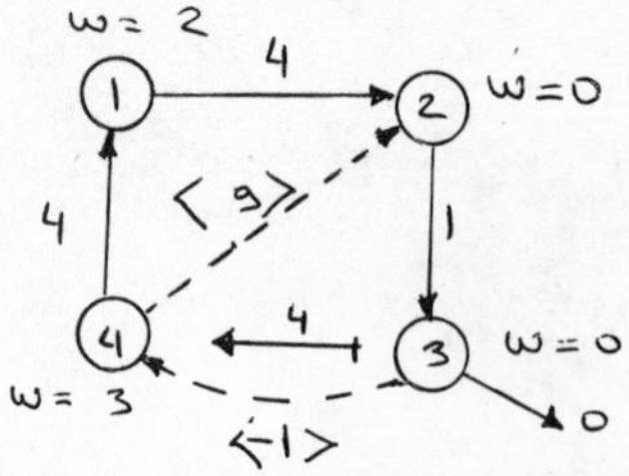

$z_{34} - c_{34} = -1 < 0$

and $x_{34} = u_{34}$

and $z_{42} - c_{42} = 9 > 0$

and $x_{42} = \ell_{42}$ (maximization problem), hence the solution is optimal, with

$\underline{x}_{22} = (4, 1, 4, 4, 0)$

$$(w - c_2)\underline{x}_{22} + \alpha_2 = 4 + 24 = 28$$

Thus λ_{22} is a candidate to enter the basis.

$$B^{-1}\begin{bmatrix} \underline{x}_{22} \\ 0 \\ 1 \end{bmatrix} = (4, 1, 1, 4, -3, 0, 1)^T$$

	w_{12}	w_{23}	w_{34}	w_{41}	w_{42}	α_1	α_2	RHS	
z	0	0	0	0	0	13	24	37	28
s_{12}	1	0	0	0	0	-2	0	2	4
s_{23}	0	1	0	0	0	-3	0	0	1
s_{34}	0	0	1	0	0	-2	-3	2	1
s_{41}	0	0	0	1	0	0	0	1	(4)
s_{42}	0	0	0	0	1	0	-3	2	-3
λ_{11}	0	0	0	0	0	1	0	1	0
λ_{21}	0	0	0	0	0	0	1	1	1

One can carry the solution further from here by normal revised simplex method. This situation is not common in practice.